P9-APZ-578

UNDERSTANDING HUMAN RESOURCES

Perspectives, People, and Policy

Eli Ginzberg

UNIVERSITY
PRESS OF
AMERICA

LANHAM • NEW YORK • LONDON

ABT
BOOKS

University Press of America,® Inc.

4720 Boston Way
Lanham, MD 20706

3 Henrietta Street
London WC2E 8LU England

Library of Congress Cataloging in Publication Data

Ginzberg, Eli, 1911-
  Understanding human resources.

  Bibliography: p.
  Includes index.
    1. Manpower policy—United States—Addresses, essays,
lectures.   2. Manpower planning—United States—Ad-
dresses, essays, lectures.   I. Title.
HD5713.G56   1985   331.11'0973   85-20384
ISBN 0-8191-4869-5 (alk. paper)

To
Elizabeth Tang and Sylvia Leef
in deep appreciation for their unique
support over many years

and to their predecessors

Helen Mayer   Jeanne Tomblen
Helen Albert   Chrys Lieberfreund
Rosella Litovchik   Mary Hagigeorgiou

Contents

Preface

PREPARING A COMPENDIUM of my research was an idea I had contemplated from time to time but did not act on until I was encouraged to do so by Clark Abt. He suggested that many younger scholars were unacquainted with my early field research, the results of which are no longer readily accessible. With his encouragement I decided to attempt to cull representative pieces from a half century of work focused on exploring the role of human resources in economic life.

Over the past two decades I had prepared and published three volumes of contemporaneous essays (see Bibliography, 24, 28, 39) as well as one collection drawn primarily from my early books (36). In the present comprehensive collection there is no overlap with these earlier publications. Moreover, the present effort has a much wider reach in both time and scope, since it includes a selection from my earliest book (79) and a Foreword and Afterword to this book, written in early 1984, a half century after I initiated my research.

With the single exception of the manpower problems of developing countries (31), the ten parts of this book provide selections from all the areas of human resources and manpower in which I have worked and which have engaged most of my research energies over the past half century. I have also omitted selections from two other research areas to which I have directed attention: the changing economic and social role of the Jews in the United States and in Israel, and medical economics (83, 84, 85, 87, 88–98).

A few points may assist the reader. There is a rough temporal sequencing to the ten parts: The early selections have been excerpted from my early books or from articles focused on these early investigations. With minor exceptions, each part also follows a temporal sequence.

To improve the prospect that the book would be read and not treated as a handbook, stringent criteria were followed to restrict and restrain its size. The first selection would have resulted in a volume of about 425,000 words! We therefore reduced the number of potential selections from over eighty to fifty, and further significant reductions were achieved by eliminating many pages from the chapters and articles that were selected — omissions that, as far as I can judge, result in no real loss and often considerable gain. Note is taken of such omissions by the use of ellipses (. . .) and, if the reader wishes, he or she can locate the uncut version through references in the Sources and Bibliography. The other principal change involved the elimination of the footnotes and bibliographies that were part of the original publications.

I took some liberties with some but not all of the titles of the selections, but the interested reader will be able to check on these alterations through recourse to the Sources and Bibliography. Many of the key selections in Part VI, Blacks, date from the 1950s through the mid-1960s, when the term *Negro* was accepted usage. After considering the matter, I decided that more confusion than clarity would result from bringing the old usage up to date.

I have followed the same practice of not altering the dollar values in the original texts. Clearly the reader would be misled by contemporary figures unless he or she could translate them into current values. To help in this effort, my colleague Dr. Dean Morse has been good enough to prepare a conversion table (see Appendix) that will enable the interested reader to obtain a quick appreciation of the relative dollar values over a time span of more than a half century during which dollar values underwent substantial change.

Although tempted to do so, I finally decided against eliminating such terms as *current* or adding the apposite year, on the ground that the reader knows the date when the selection was first published. I also avoided deleting statements reflecting initial anticipations that had been proved wrong by the passage of time. It would be fatuous for a social scientist to pretend that he always reads the future correctly.

Similarly, I withstood the offer of my wife to edit the entire manuscript and in the process eliminate many awkward and inelegant formulations. I have altered the original text only rarely, to eliminate an error or to add a connective required by a deletion.

I have had four active roles over the past half century, as researcher, research director, teacher, and consultant. There is no possible way I can disentangle the first two roles. Without exception, the pieces included in this book were written solely by me or reflect joint output where I was the senior author. But this comment should in no way be read as a claim to exclusive credit. The co-authors listed in the Sources and Bibliography were major contributors. They have been my teachers and collaborators, as well as my assistants, and I am deeply in their debt.

In the final preparation of the present manuscript I was aided by Shoshana Vasheetz, who assumed primary responsibility for reproducing the fifty chapters with the assistance of Patrick Muldowney. Anna Dutka and Penny Peace prepared the bibliography and the other back matter. To all, I express my sincere appreciation.

Foreword:
The Human Resources Frontier

THE GOAL OF THIS FOREWORD is to provide the interested reader with some understanding of the forces that led me, early in my academic career, to focus my research on human resources, before the term had become part of our vocabulary.

I grew up in the home of a great scholar and an activist mother. My father, by example, inoculated me against monistic theories of societal behavior; my mother, by word and deed, insisted that ideas that do not result in constructive action were unimportant.

The opportunity to spend my sophomore year in college at Heidelberg University provided me with a unique experience. I learned about the strength of tradition, the appeal of nationalism, the dangers of unemployment, the emotional and the irrational aspects of political life. Within three years of my return to the United States, Hitler was chancellor of the Third Reich.

My undergraduate and graduate studies at Columbia University (1929–1933) coincided with the onset and continuation of the most devastating depression in U.S. history; this increased my innate skepticism toward the beatitudes of the theories of the competitive market that held that all disturbances in the economy would create counterforces that would lead to a restoration of equilibrium. Two years of research on Adam Smith (my dissertation) and the emergence of economics as a discipline added to my skepticism.

Graduate training in economics at Columbia in my day was a mixed bag: The Department of Economics included Wesley Clair Mitchell and John Maurice Clark, which gave it first rank in the nation. But neither Mitchell nor Clark required a doctoral candidate to acquire and demonstrate competence in neoclassical economics. They were satisfied if he or she had some appreciation of the evolution of economic thought. A student was able to take many courses in other departments, and I took advantage of this opportunity to study with world-renowned scholars in anthropology, history, sociology, and philosophy. Three of my earliest publications (80; Notes: Foreword 1, 2) grew out of the challenges presented to us to understand the role and limitations of ideas in shaping and transforming reality. I was willing to recognize the importance of economic factors in human experience, but I balked at the extensive claims that both conservative and Marxist economists advanced for them. I was searching for a less deterministic approach.

A William Bayard Cutting Traveling Fellowship in 1933–1934 gave me an opportunity to visit many of the nation's leading corporations and to have extended conversations with members of senior management. These encounters confirmed for me the need for a more sophisticated framework, one that would have room, in addition to the dictates of the market, for organizational imperatives, the vagaries of human behavior, and the instabilities of politics.

I joined the staff of the School of Business at Columbia in 1935 and two years later had an opportunity to assist Professor Mitchell in a new seminar on "Economic Theory and Economic Change." The theme we selected was "Psychology and Economics." At the end of the year it was clear that, however inadequate the psychological assumptions of contemporary economic theory might be, little progress could be made by seeking to borrow directly from modern psychology. At that point, Mitchell urged me to initiate empirical research that might yield useful findings. With his assistance, in 1939 I received a research grant from the Columbia University Council for Research in the Social Sciences to undertake studies of the long-term unemployed in South Wales and in New York City.

My principal collaborator was Sol W. Ginsburg, a psychiatrist-psychoanalyst, and we were assisted by several psychiatric social workers. Milton Friedman helped us in the statistical design of the investigation of the long-term unemployed in New York City. In 1941 the Rockefeller Foundation provided funding so that we could expand our inquiries from unemployment to occupational choice and adjustment to work. The years 1938–1942 were crucial. We took the plunge into exploring the role of psychological factors in economic behavior through empirical research; we committed ourselves to an interdisciplinary team approach; and we took care to link our research to policy.

World War II, both directly and as a result of its aftermath, transformed the scale, scope, and nature of our work. During my four years in Washington (1942–1946), I held two positions in the War Department. As Consultant on Manpower and Personnel to the Commanding General, Army Services Forces (ASF), I learned a great deal about human resources management in a large organization. In one ninety-day period, I participated in removing 180,000 civilians from the ASF payroll and converting 60,000 soldiers from supply to combat functions (43).

During my second assignment as director, Resources Analysis Division, Surgeon General's Office, I had planning responsibility for all medical personnel and all patients worldwide, which at peak amounted to about 1.3 million, or roughly one-sixth of the total Army. This assignment brought me into close contact with Major General Howard Snyder, assistant inspector-general and long-term personal physician to General Eisenhower.

Through General Snyder I met and talked at length with General Eisenhower when he was still chief of staff (1947) and president-designate of Columbia University. At that time Eisenhower explored the possibility of the university's undertaking a large-scale investigation into the military manpower experience of World War II so that its lessons could be extracted for management and the nation. Shortly after assuming the presidency of Columbia, Eisenhower took the initiative to structure this effort and to assure its financing through corporate donations. My small interdisciplinary staff was substantially expanded and renamed The Conservation of Human Resources Project, which I have directed from that day to this.

In 1951, because the Conservation Project had been established at Columbia University, the Ford Foundation decided to establish there a National Manpower Council whose charter was to analyze and report on important national manpower issues. Over the next thirteen years, the NMC published ten major reports (73–79). The Conservation staff was an important contributor to the work of the Council in its formative years, when I served as director of research for the Council.

In 1962 Congress authorized the funding of an external research program for the Department of Labor, and the Conservation Project became one of the grantees of the Department's Office of Research and Development (ORD). This new source of major funding shifted the emphasis of our work in the direction of manpower utilization, with special attention to the problems encountered by hard-to-employ groups in their efforts to obtain and hold regular jobs.

Not until the mid- and late 1960s was the Conservation Project's assistance sought by the government of the City of New York, specifically the City Planning Commission. Partly as a response to requests from the Planning Commission and partly reflecting its growing awareness that manpower utilization always involves a spatial dimension, the Project broadened its approach and initiated studies in metropolitanism and suburbanization.

In the late 1970s, the Conservation staff, in collaboration with the Strategic Planning and Economics Department staffs of Citicorp, undertook a major inquiry into the transformations then under way in the United States and other advanced economies, which led to the growth of the service sector, particularly of producer services.

In the world of applied research, those who control the funding almost always determine the research program. It was the good fortune of the Conservation Project that the personal interest of General Eisenhower guaranteed ten years of corporate support and, further, that Dr. Howard Rosen (director, ORD, U.S. Department of Labor) allowed us wide discretion in designing our research into the labor force and labor markets. Moreover we were able to obtain critical funding from an array of foundations, including, in particular, Ford, Carnegie, Rockefeller Brothers Fund, Rockefeller, German Marshall Fund, and—most recently—Revson and Sloan, as we initiated studies into newcomers to the United States.

As noted earlier, the two anchors to our ongoing research efforts have been an interdisciplinary staff and an involvement with policy. In the late 1940s, after returning to Columbia University, and in the 1950s, I had a series of continuing consulting arrangements with the federal government, specifically with the departments of State, Defense, Labor, Commerce, and Health, Education and Welfare (HEW). With the passage of the Manpower Development and Training Act in 1962, I was appointed chairman of the National Manpower Advisory Committee (NMAC) and served in that capacity until the expiration of the act in 1973. The new Comprehensive Employment and Training Act (CETA) provided for a National Commission for Manpower Policy, later renamed the National Commission for Employment Policy (NCEP). I served as chairman of that commission from 1974 until the end of 1981—a nineteen-year tour of duty in all.

The NMAC and NCEP had oversight over the expenditure of about $100 billion for unemployment and training programs. As chairman, I had to interact frequently with the White House, the Executive Departments, and the Congress. This experience created a unique opportunity to link research and policy, so that each might contribute to the other.

From the mid-1960s until the mid-1970s, I spent between one and two months each year, on behalf of the Department of State, advising foreign governments on their manpower policies and programs; this took me to five continents and forty countries. Here was still another opportunity to explore and strengthen the interactions between research and theory. I also want to note that distance provides perspective; I was better able to recognize subtle aspects of the U.S. manpower scene from afar.

Although most of my consulting work was directly with the federal government, through periodic assignments I became acquainted with selected human resources problems of leading U.S. corporations, which helped to broaden and deepen my understanding of the critical interface between organizations and human resources utilization.

I have now commented briefly on three of my four roles: author, research director, and consultant. The fourth is that of teacher. The dedication page of *The House of Adam Smith Revisited* contains the following:

> To my colleagues, past and present, in the Graduate School of Business, Columbia University, who made room in 1935 for a young economist interested in economic theory and gave him the freedom to develop the field of human resources and manpower.
>
> In collegial appreciation and friendship

I want to add only that I learned much from the hundreds and thousands of my students who over the years have taken my course on "Human Resources and Economic Welfare."

I have attempted to convey to the reader how I came to the human-resources frontier and why I have spent my entire life in exploring it. I had the great good fortune to have had a great scholar as a father, Wesley Mitchell as a mentor, President Eisenhower as a sponsor, and a unique government bureaucrat as a grantor.

PART I

Ideas and Reality

EINSTEIN ONCE SAID that every great physicist has one opportunity to move beyond his teachers by transcending the established doctrine and opening a new path to a more correct and inclusive view of nature. He went on to note that when a physicist has made a breakthrough, he will not be able to make another—in part because he no longer has the energy, in part because his own thoughtways hold him prisoner.

The following pieces provide a contemporaneous account of my early attempts to break through the established doctrines of economics. My struggles with the conventional wisdom started while I was still in college and led to three publications not here reproduced (80, Notes; Foreword). In the first, *Studies in the Economics of the Bible,* I sought to understand whether the Sabbatical Laws and the Jubilee Laws, which instructed the Hebrews to let the land lie fallow in the seventh and fiftieth year, to manumit their slaves, to cancel all debts, and to return all acquired land to its original owners, could possibly have been enforced among a people who had to support themselves from the produce they raised. And if they were not enforced, how could the attention they received in the Canon be explained? I cut my research teeth on a problem that Max Weber had defined as "indigestible."

Two shorter pieces, "The Decline of Antiquity" and "The Economics of British Neutrality During the American Civil War," also grew out of my graduate studies, when I tried to loosen the hold of Karl Marx's monistic explanations of historical change while permitting economic forces to have wide play. The first article argued that economic surplus is a precondition for the emergence and flowering of a great culture and that the Athenian navy and the Roman legions were the instruments for those earlier accumulations on the basis of which elaborate social super-structures were erected, first in Greece, later in Rome. But in time the sources of these surpluses eroded, and neither Greece nor Rome was able successfully to shrink its superstructure, with the result that the entire edifices eventually collapsed.

Britain's presumed dependence on Northern wheat during the U.S. Civil War was said to balance its need for Southern cotton. This all-too-rational formulation piqued my skepticism. A detailed review of the data and the arguments disclosed that British leaders were not aware of this dependence; it did not really exist, and they surely did not weigh it in formulating their policies.

My first full-length book postulated that Adam Smith was a reformer who sought to gain adherents by sketching the gains of a competitive market over the extant mercantilistic restraints, which were adding only to the illegitimate wealth of princes, merchants, and manufacturers.

The Illusion of Economic Stability (1939) asks why business and politi-cal leaders during the New Era (1922–1929) so seriously misjudged the Great Depression of 1929–1933. The answer is simple: Expectations play a major role in economic decisions, and they are formed by experience. The United States had been free of a serious depression since the early 1890s. To expect business leaders to anticipate a major collapse in 1929, even discounting the speculative frenzy in the stock market, was unrealistic. The economists of today who advance the doctrine of "rational expecta-tions" could profit from a close reading of events in the 1920s and 1930s.

Grass on the Slag Heaps: The Story of the Welsh Miners (1942), my first empiric inquiry into human resources, sought to illuminate what large-scale and persistent unemployment does to people and their communities, and the delayed threats it poses to the future of a democracy. Many analysts have been perplexed by the economic troubles that have beset Great Britain since the end of World War II. As early as 1939 it was clear to me that Britain would eventually pay many times over for its long-term neglect of the unemployed Welsh miners and their wives and children.

Chapters 1 and 3 represent my second involvement with Adam Smith on the occasion of the bicentennial of *The Wealth of Nations* in 1976, when I delivered a series of lectures under different auspices. Since this was the only time I returned to the materials that had engaged me earlier, I found it a little disconcerting to realize how much of an author's message depends on the knowledge and experience of the reader.

Chapter 6 is from *The Human Economy*, which also was written in 1976 and which is the nearest I have come to elaborating my "system." I hope the reader will be able to find the links between my earliest efforts to break loose from the tradition to which I had been exposed in my youth and my more mature reformulations.

CHAPTER 1

What Kind of Man
Was Adam Smith?

WHEN I WROTE *The House of Adam Smith* in my early twenties, I could have provided a clear-cut answer to the question, What kind of man was Adam Smith? Today I am uncertain even about how to approach the question. Let me therefore select a few passages from *The Wealth of Nations*, add a few biographical details, and encourage the reader to draw his own portrait. No man ever truly sees another because his own personal qualities and foibles intrude.

Adam Smith appreciated the essence of scholarship, not its trappings. He was comfortable at the University of Glasgow, where many serious students and teachers worked, but he eschewed the social snobbery and lack of sincere intellectualism of Oxford, where he spent six years as a student.

The bicentennial celebrations being held on the North American continent would have pleased Smith by confirming his vision of the potential of the new colonies. If ever proof were needed of Smith's sensitivity to emerging developments, which were hidden at that time from the politician and the public alike, it can be found in several passages in *The Wealth of Nations* which contain his forecast of future events on this side of the Atlantic. To quote just one:

> Such has hitherto been the rapid progress of that country in wealth, population and improvement, that in the course of a little more than a century, perhaps, the produce of American might exceed that of British taxation. The seat of the empire would then naturally remove itself to that part of the empire which contributed most to the general defence and support of the whole. [*The Wealth of Nations,* p. 590][a]

It would also have pleased Adam Smith if he had known that two hundred years after the publication of his work, a haberdasher in North Adams, Michigan, would be doing a brisk trade by selling Adam Smith ties in several colors. Smith believed in entrepreneurship, and he would probably not have objected to being both the subject and the object of an ingenious approach to profit-making.

Let me outline the essential biographical facts about Adam Smith to help the reader develop his own picture of this extraordinary man, who was even more extraordinary because of the absence of real drama in his own life.

Adam Smith was born in Kirkcaldy, an east coast town about forty miles north of Edinburgh, in 1723. His father had died several months before his birth and consequently his ties to his mother were strong, but not so strong that they prevented his being separated from her at age fourteen when he was sent to Glasgow to start his serious education. Some three decades later, in 1766, after he had completed his Continental tour with the future Duke of Buccleugh, he again lived in his mother's house. From then until her death, which preceded his own by only a few months (1790), Smith and his mother lived together, first in Kirkcaldy and later in Edinburgh, except for the three years when he stayed in London to see *The Wealth of Nations* through publication.

During my "psychoanalytic period" early in my research career, I was once asked on a radio program whether I thought Smith's advocacy of laissez-faire was the sublimated response of a man who could not break his oedipal ties. This seemed to me at the time, and even more so now, to be psychoanalytic theorizing run riot.

Nevertheless, there is no evidence that Smith was ever romantically involved with a woman. In fact, I know of no reliable evidence of even a casual involvement with another woman. The reason for stressing this point is to contrast Smith's celibacy with the sensitivity and emotional balance which are among the outstanding characteristics of his work. Most men cannot survive, much less prosper, without the love and support of a woman. But Adam Smith was an exceptional man.

During the course of his life, which ended just short of three score and ten years, Adam Smith filled five occupational roles—student, professor, tutor, scholar, and civil servant. We know that he was a good student at Glasgow because he won the Snell exhibition to Balliol College at Oxford. We know that he was largely self-taught during his six years at Oxford. Note his caustic comments about the university in *The Wealth of Nations,* comments which were substantially confirmed by two other eighteenth-century greats, Gibbon and Bentham.

> In the university of Oxford, the greater part of the public professors have, for these many years, given up altogether even the pretence of teaching. (718)

That he demonstrated a strong independence of mind and character is suggested by his early admiration for and later close friendship with David Hume, a relationship which was resented by the Anglican establishment, which considered Hume dangerous, if not heretical. Moreover, he left Oxford before his fellowship had run its course, apparently because he tired of being among people with whom he was not able to develop close social or intellectual ties.

As a professor or, more correctly, as an academician, since his university career included a term as dean and vice provost, his record was outstanding. He started as a lecturer in literature at Edinburgh; after two years he was invited, at the age of twenty-eight, to fill the chair of logic at his old university, Glasgow; by the end of his first year he was appointed to succeed Francis Hutchinson as professor of moral philosophy. His lectures encompassed the entire domain of the moral and social disciplines, the frontiers of which he extended to make room for the new field, economics. He enjoyed the respect of his colleagues, who considered him a man of good sense who could get things done. During his years at Glasgow, he was charged with purchasing books for the library and representing the university in difficult financial negotiations with the authorities in Edinburgh; he performed successfully the functions of dean and vice provost. In addition, he found time to write *The Theory of Moral Sentiments,* which established him as a leading intellectual not only in the British Isles but on the Continent as well. This book eventually changed his career, when Lord Townshend, author of the infamous Townshend Acts, seeking a tutor for his stepson, explored the availability of the author of a work that had greatly impressed him.

When the offer was made, Smith stood in the first rank of British academicians. His friends, including David Hume, expected Smith to refuse the offer, which would require that he resign his professorship and travel on the Continent with the future duke. But to their surprise, he accepted.

I think I know why. In the first place, at the end of less than three years as a tutor, Smith would be financially independent for life, an attractive prospect for a man who knew what he wanted to do with his time. Next, he probably anticipated, since he had demonstrated a capacity to perform administrative duties well, that there was a danger that he would be caught up in this role indefinitely. Parenthetically, John Dewey told his young protege Irwin Edman, when the latter was first appointed to the Columbia faculty: "Be sure to fail in your first committee assignment; otherwise your academic career will be at an end." Third, Smith took seriously his duties as lecturer and advisor to students which, together with his growing administrative duties, left him too little time for writing. He knew that he had one more important book to write. Finally, while he enjoyed the companionship of the spirited businessmen of the growing seaport that was Glasgow, from whom he learned a great deal, there is scattered evidence that he found the town increasingly confining. The strict Presbyterians who set the tone of the town were unbending. It was a rigid community which frowned on music and drama, and we know from *The Wealth of Nations* that Smith considered the arts important:

> The second of those remedies is the frequency and gaiety of public diversions. The state, by encouraging, that is by giving entire liberty to all those who in their own interest would attempt ... to amuse and divert the people by painting, poetry, music, dancing; by all sorts of dramatic representations and exhibitions. . . . (748)

Even a man as self-possessed and disciplined as Smith would eventually balk at making Glasgow his permanent home. Moreover, Smith probably welcomed the opportunity to rejoin his mother's household, as in fact he did when he returned from the Continent.

In his introduction to his translation of the *Odyssey,* T. E. Lawrence said of Homer that he was a married man but not exclusively so. One could adapt this remark to Smith's university career—he was an academic, but not exclusively so. He had acquired the reputation of being the best educated man in Europe since Aristotle, an accolade not likely to be bestowed on a bookworm. Much of the empiricism and hard-headed analysis that characterize *The Wealth of Nations* are derived from Smith's long years of tavern discussions with the merchants of Glasgow.

During his two and a half years of travel on the Continent with his tutee, Smith picked a provincial town, Toulouse, as their headquarters, after he concluded that it would provide a conducive environment for study. But there was more to the Continental tour than the education of the young duke. Smith traveled to Geneva and to Paris, where he sought out Voltaire, Rousseau, and many of the Encyclopedists who played so large a role in hastening the French Revolution. In the British revulsion to the excesses of the revolution during the last years of the century, Dugald Stewart, the first professor of economics at Glasgow, was forced to resign; in the McCarthy-like backlash of the day, economics had become suspect because of Smith's earlier ties to the revolutionary cadre in France. During the six months or so that Smith spent in Paris, visiting the fashionable salons of the day, he was acclaimed by many distinguished men and attractive women who, we are told, looked forward to his return. He never did return, however, despite periodic promptings from his many admirers and would-be hosts.

Smith had suggested to Hume that they both settle in London, but nothing came of the plan, so Smith went back to his birthplace, Kirkcaldy, and took up residence in his mother's home. It was here, between 1767 and 1773, that he labored on *The Wealth of Nations*, elaborating, refining and systematizing the theories which he had first begun to fashion as a young faculty member in Glasgow. The intensity with which he worked on his chef d'oeuvre is indicated by the fact that he turned down repeated invitations from his friends in Edinburgh to visit them, pleading shortage of time. And Edinburgh was forty miles away!

When Smith went to London in 1773 to arrange for the publication of his book, he was exposed for the first time in eight years to the rush of new ideas and new events. During his seclusion in Kirkcaldy, he had been completely dependent on his excellent personal library for the materials he needed to develop his theories and policy recommendations. But after a very few weeks in London, Smith realized that his manuscript was not ready for the printer. He had to bring his analyses up to date, correct them, and add to them, especially those dealing with foreign trade and the colonies, developments he had been unable to follow closely while working in Kirkcaldy. Smith worked for another year and a half before he released the manuscript in 1775, and the book was not published until March 9, 1776. I cannot resist the temptation of asking how many of Smith's followers, especially those who call themselves economic theorists, would hold back what they considered to be a finished manuscript, one that had engaged their interests and energies for more than a quarter of a century and their best energies for six years — how many of them would return to their desks to ensure that their theories were congruent with the rapidly changing reality?

But remember, Smith was not worried about publishing or publishing quickly. His academic career was behind him. In his own words, *The Wealth of Nations* represented a broad-scale attack on the economy of Great Britain; consequently, he was utterly surprised to find that, when this attack was finally published, it went largely unnoticed. The publication of the book was followed by only a ripple among the conservative forces in the community that earlier had taken him severely to task for having written a few words in praise of his friend, David Hume.

Shortly after the publication of *The Wealth of Nations,* his former tutee, now the Duke of Buccleugh, full of admiration for his teacher and wanting to show his appreciation, arranged that Smith be appointed one of the commissioners of customs and salt duties at Edinburgh. For the last time in his life, Smith changed his residence and his work. For one short period during this last decade and a half, Smith returned to literary pursuits. He asked the indulgence of his fellow commissioners to reduce his work schedule to permit him to prepare a third edition of *The Wealth of Nations.* This resulted in the addition of considerable new materials, most of which extended and deepened his criticism of the mercantile system. If Smith's own statement left any question about the basic thrust of his magnum opus as an attack on the British economy of his day, the new materials in the third edition resolve it. It was mercantilism that Smith sought to exorcise.

The materials are now at hand to answer the question posed in the title "What Kind of Man Was Adam Smith?" Adam Smith was a Scot; he had not known his father; his principal companion in his mature years was his mother, whom he survived by less than a year. We know of no emotional ties to any other woman. He spent his youth as well as the years during which he wrote *The Wealth of Nations* in a sleepy east coast Scottish town, Kirkcaldy, far from the beaten track, whose inhabitants were knowledgeable in the art of smuggling and little else. He was, in turn, an academic, a gentleman scholar, a civil servant. His literary output consisted of two major works, the less important of which, *The Theory of Moral Sentiments,* was the more acclaimed. He was a man of independent mind and he enjoyed the company of thinkers and doers, but he was circumspect and sought to avoid controversy. He was not impressed with establishments, religious or other, and he worried about their capacity to oppress people and waste resources. He was a man of sympathy and evinced concern for the common man. He was an optimist who believed that people would work hard to better their condition. He was a scholar and a reformer but not a revolutionary.

With respect to each of the characteristics noted here, the record is clear. But we can sharpen the portrait of the man by taking note of some of the positions he developed in *The Wealth of Nations.* To paraphrase Feurbach: Smith is what he writes.

In *The Wealth of Nations,* Smith analyzed the human and political elements in the economy of his day. He reveals himself to be an environmentalist, ascribing the differences between a street porter and a philosopher to differences in their nurturing, education, and experiences. Smith urges the state to provide educational opportunities for all children, since education alone will enable them to develop their latent talents and provide them with the competences they will need to manage their lives effectively and perform their roles as citizens in a constructive fashion.

Smith states that if people know they will be able to enjoy the fruits of their labor and will not be exploited by those in power, they will work hard to improve their position and help their children get a better start in life.

In assessing the role of political factors in shaping the economy and in propelling it in the right directions, Smith recognizes the importance of public security for both person and property. In assessing the remarkable economic advance of the American colonies, he repeatedly stresses the contribution of the British Constitution with its guarantee that every person and his possessions be secure from injury and expropriation.

Unlike his famous successor, Karl Marx, Smith appreciates the force of nationalism even though he sees the potential gains from the growth of comity among nations. He modifies his basic theory about the noninterference of the state in the marketplace to make room for subsidies to the merchant marine and for retaliatory tariffs when a nation's exports are discriminated against. Here, as elsewhere, Smith is responsive to reality, not a prisoner of dogma.

With respect to monopoly, Smith considers large landowners to be ill-suited by temperament and deficient in knowhow to improve their land. Many prefer riotous living, a pattern of life that consumes, rather than adds to, capital. Smith stops short of recommending the breakup of the large landed estates—a proposition that John Stuart Mill later advanced in the case of crown lands.

With respect to manufacturing and trade, Smith is convinced that the bureaucracy in London cannot possibly be as knowledgeable, interested, and concerned about the efficient use of resources as the resident owner-entrepreneur. The elimination of monopoly profits and the improved use of resources can best be achieved, he feels, by a thorough disengagement of government in the detailed affairs of the economy. This was the hope and promise that undergirded Smith's advocacy of laissez-faire.

What kind of a man was Adam Smith? He was first and foremost an optimist who believed that people could add to their individual and collective well-being through restructuring their economy and society. He was a man of ideas who had faith in the role of reason to improve the lives of men and nations. Finally, he was a moral philosopher who recognized that man does not live by bread alone. Adam Smith was the world's first and foremost political economist.

At the beginning of its third century, the discipline of economics faces a simple alternative. It can continue to postulate that the market alone controls the behavior of men, or it can go back to the roots Smith planted and become the discipline of political economy.

NOTES

^aAll citations are to the Modern Library Edition (1937), Random House, edited by Edwin Cannan.

CHAPTER 2

The Realistic Reformer

BOOKS BEGET BOOKS; books beget actions. They can amuse and they can teach. Now their educative, reforming interest has not been of like intensity throughout the ages. It reached a high point in the eighteenth century. . . . Voltaire, the leader of the Enlightenment, was especially well liked by English liberals, and Adam Smith's regard for the famous critic was pronounced. The bonds of friendship between the product of Scottish Presbyterianism and Gallic Catholicism must never be overlooked in the interpretation of these two very different geniuses. For instance, Smith pointed out that in the past grave philosophers have written many tomes, but few have taken the trouble to read them. However, the writings of Voltaire, which have made the lives of fanatics miserable, are read by all; hence the world has benefited more from this one essayist than from all the other subtle metaphysicians. Smith had greater respect for Voltaire than for any other living man. During his European trip, he traveled to Geneva with the young Duke of Buccleugh in order to be in the company of the French author, who was then living on the shores of Lake Leman.

Adam Smith admired another man, a native of Geneva, who was in only a slightly lesser degree than Voltaire responsible for the Bourbons losing their throne. Though Smith at one time called Jean Jacques Rousseau a great rascal and a hypocritical pedant, he was not blind to Rousseau's contributions to the cause of reform. Smith once remarked that the *Social Contract* would one day avenge all the persecutions which its author had suffered.

Paris, prior to the revolution, though it could boast of but one Voltaire and one Rousseau, was nevertheless remarkably rich in talented people. The large circle of scientists, philosophers, and economists who frequented the salons formed one of the most important groups in contemporary French society. A foreigner like Hume was most impressed with these intellectuals, and they were also sufficiently cosmopolitan to appreciate the Scottish genius. Hume was ignored in his own country except by the clergy who attacked his atheism, but in France his praise was loudly sung. Adam Smith was also in close spiritual contact with this circle, for one of its members supervised the translation of his *Theory of Moral Sentiments*. Despite the differences between the cultures on opposite shores of the Channel, the friendship between French and English intellectuals was not difficult to understand. They had a common interest in reforming the societies in which they lived and, though their specific objectives differed, their methods were very similar. The Continental and Island liberals were both forced to use the pen as their principal weapon of attack; they were brothers in arms fighting for the same cause under different banners.

Smith at various times in his life illustrated his attitude and approach to problems of social reform. His predecessors at Glasgow had taught their pupils much logic and metaphysics, but he believed that it was preferable to direct the attention of young scholars to more interesting and practical disciplines. Furthermore, Smith, in his lectures on economics, pointed out the great advantages of using the art of persuasion in social struggles, which he believed could be most effectively developed by appealing to the self-love of one's fellow men. He advised all reformers not to neglect this valuable instrument. Obviously, there is nothing naive about Smith. He was amused by the pedantry of Gallic philosophers, and in fact criticized Turgot because that statesman had failed to discount the selfishness, the stupidity, and the prejudice that prevailed in the world. Dugald Stewart, Smith's first biographer, relates that the Scottish professor was wont to treat economic problems in terms of expediency rather than of justice; nor was he likely to underestimate the cupidity of mankind, for when he erred it was on the side of discounting the forces for good. During the 1750s, the Chair of Logic became vacant at Glasgow, and Smith writes that he would prefer David Hume to any other man for this position; the public, however, was not of like opinion, and he felt that popular prejudice must be respected. Any attempt to run counter to a widespread bias would end in dismal failure, illustrating nothing more than the infantile mind of the venturous individual.

The Wealth of Nations was written by one who might well be called a practical idealist, for Smith did believe that many improvements could be introduced into the social structure. But any reform, no matter how well intentioned, was certain to be stillborn if the advocate failed to consider the attitudes of the people with whom he dealt. Smith was too keen a student of human nature to believe that radical measures could be successful if they ran counter to the prevailing psychological outlook.

Mercantilistic England, or what remained of high mercantilism in the eighteenth century, was thoroughly disliked by Adam Smith. The privileges of the merchants and manufacturers had been unfairly obtained and were now being unfairly maintained. Of late the landlords had attempted to imitate the shrewd and crafty tradesmen in the hope of securing important benefits from the system, and even the laborers in certain corporations had secured the power to fleece the public for their private advantage. The exploitation of the population by special interests was most unfortunate, and any system which permitted, and in fact encouraged, such thievery was clearly unworthy of respect. Unfortunately, the corruption was not confined to the economic realm; political life had also become diseased. . . .

> At Toulouse, time hung heavily on Smith's hands, and he therefore commenced to write on economics; but it was not until twelve years later that *The Wealth of Nations* appeared. During this period he analyzed the materials which demonstrated the disadvantages of permitting the existing economic system to remain unaltered. He painted the society of the future in bright colors, for he well appreciated the problem which confronted him. Nothing could be gained by preaching of a new and better world in the abstract; nor would it be wise to rely upon the insight and understanding of the masses. . . .

Man is most concerned with his own fortunes and misfortunes, and therefore Adam Smith addressed himself to the instinct of self-love in his audience. There is no use in flying in the face of common truths and affirming that man has a highly developed sense of social responsibility. The constant reference to the individual in the economic analysis of *The Wealth of Nations* has pertinency only if one clearly appreciates the author's approach. Smith realizes that his program of reform has no chance of adoption unless it is skillfully maneuvered, and he therefore proceeds most circumspectly. His attack upon mercantilism is so directed as to impress the populace with the losses which it suffers from the existing system, and to illustrate the benefits which it would derive by reforming the existing economic organization. Smith appreciates the fact that he cannot appeal to the private interest of every individual, and he is quite willing to antagonize small minorities so long as he has the support of the majority. The removal of tariffs would lessen the profits of native manufacturers, but benefit all other classes; now Smith feels that if the landlords, the farmers, and the laborers were to act in concert, he need not fear the opposition of the disgruntled producers. . . .

The contention that the state must control the economic life of its citizens for their own sake is clearly a sham, because there is no reason that a population, if left to itself, would undermine the prosperity of a country. It has, however, not been unusual for a government to ruin a country in its desire to further the public welfare.

Adam Smith, like all social philosophers except anarchists, was more interested in the commonwealth than in the individual members of the commonwealth. He believed that increasing the individual's scope of action was the surest way of speeding the progress of the community. Unseen hands facilitated this transformation; the procedure was not, however, very mysterious; it depended only upon the establishment of perfect justice, perfect liberty, and perfect equality. Perfection is not within the realm of human attainment, and Smith realized that he was guilty of wishful thinking in advancing these desiderata. He doubtless hoped that a struggle for natural liberty would at least result in the death of unnatural restraint. . . .

Adam Smith did not preach the doctrine of economic freedom for its own sake; he was much too critical of fanatics to be guilty of any fanaticism himself. He believed that the state control of industry was inimical to the true interests of the public and therefore, as a reformer, he was confronted with but two possible lines of action. He could either suggest improvements in the techniques of regulation, or else advocate a more radical alteration of society which would make regulation unnecessary. Smith decided on the second approach.

He did not attack blindly, for he did not believe all state interference to be bad; consistency, in terms of an abstract principle, did not appeal to him. He did not hesitate for a moment to suggest that the commonwealth should be responsible for the upkeep of the highways, because it might be dangerous to permit private individuals to control them. The importance of inland trade routes need hardly be emphasized, although the fallacious mercantilistic doctrine maintained that the wealth of the country could be increased only by foreign trade. The more numerous and varied aspects of domestic commerce clearly prove its preeminent significance for the economy as a whole. The state, out of consideration for the public welfare, should therefore control the highways of the land, and ought not to trust private individuals with this vital business. . . .

Although Smith greatly disliked state interference with the investment of capital, he did suggest the retention of the statute which regulated the interest rate. He feared that if the law were repealed, spendthrifts and profligates would contract at inordinately high rates with the result that large amounts of capital would find their way into the hands of unproductive prospectors.

The Scottish economist hoped that his reforms, if introduced, would lead to a reduction in the price of goods and an enhancement in the quality of workmanship. He believed that these beneficial results could most easily be obtained by increasing competition in economic life. Despite this general approach, Smith did not object to the interference of the state with certain economic forces and, in the case of labor, argued strongly in favor of such action. In his opinion, the public interest could best be served by the education of the populace, and he proposed the use of public monies for this purpose.

Smith advocated one reform which must have appeared reactionary even to the people of his time. It concerned the judiciary. The economic relations between members of a society are in no small measure influenced by the prevailing code of law, for wherever there is great property, there is great inequality. The law alone permits the prince to live in peace among the paupers. The acquisition of valuable and extensive property would be impossible without the prior guarantee that its ownership and use will be protected by the civil authority.

The judiciary is therefore one of the most important of social institutions, and any inefficiency in the administration of the law is likely to have serious consequences. In very early times the sovereign dispensed justice with not unsatisfactory returns, for the adjudication of disputes netted him large sums of money. Corruption soon became prevalent. The rich plaintiffs who were usually on intimate terms with the king invariably won their suits. With the development of the modern state, the administration of justice was put upon an independent basis. Judges became civil servants.

Adam Smith did not view this development with favor; he therefore suggested that judges should be paid by the litigants. This proposal looked at first glance anomalous, but upon consideration it appeared more reasonable. Under the existing system, even though the state remunerated the interpreters of the law, the administration of justice was not free. The costs of counsel and the incidental court fees were high; now certain advantages might have resulted from adding the salaries of the judges to the general expenses of a lawsuit. The judiciary in England was not industrious; in fact, the diligence of the judges was very slight: one of the surest means to improve the work of the magistrates would have been to recompense them for their actual rather than for their supposed labor. This was the reason for Adam Smith's unusual proposal.

Smith believed political economy to have a twofold purpose: that of enriching the people and the sovereign. He found no difficulty, because of the broadness of his general approach, in including in his economic treatise lengthy discussions on education, government, and law. Social institutions could obviously exert a pronounced influence upon the economic scene. Though certain of his contemporaries considered Smith the best informed man since Aristotle, he was no devotee of learning for learning's sake. In his native country the cultivation of the humanities for the ennoblement of the individual would have been scorned as un-Christian and immoral. Hume's difficulties with the public resulted largely from his belief that the world was a stage upon which the actor had the right to perform for his own rather than for his audience's amusement. Smith, though he had genuine appreciation for Hume's intellectual powers, rather resented his friend's skepticism. The Scottish philosopher was intrigued by the thoughts of men; the Scottish economist was fascinated by the actions of men. When the latter published his treatise on economics, his earlier manifested predilection for the practical was more clearly accentuated. The complete title read: *An Inquiry into the Nature and Causes of the Wealth of Nations,* and might have continued with the subheading: *For the Purpose of Increasing the Same....*

Smith studied the nature and causes of wealth because he assumed that his researches would enable him more easily to attain his principal objective, that of increasing the prosperity of his own and other countries. Once the weak pivots in the existing social mechanism were discovered and repaired, the machine would function more smoothly. His treatise purports to outline the means to this end. But Smith was not interested solely in the creation of additional commodities. He realized that there would be little purpose in augmenting the products of industry unless more people could subsist in a better way. Education played an important role in the Smithian analysis because it offered one of the principal instrumentalities for reform; if the people knew how to read, they could learn to shun evil and seek virtue.

The keynote of Adam Smith's program was the extension of freedom in economic activities, but at no time did he become a worshiper of his own fetish. The benefits which were to accrue to the public through the introduction of the new techniques were always to be weighed against the disadvantages deriving from the new approach. This pragmatic attitude was at times obscured, because the master stylist occasionally wrote very floridly. The devil had to be painted in deep black in order to impress the ignorant with the true glory of God. Smith wrote in caressing terms about laissez faire because he was out to attack and if possible demolish the system of restraints which were choking English economic life. A few individuals had a stranglehold on the body corporate, and Smith demanded in the name of the public that they release their grip. Timid souls had become so used to oppression that they feared the freedom which they did not possess. To reassure these people, Smith drew a colorful picture of the future, though it is extremely doubtful whether he had much faith in his own art except as propaganda.

The nineteenth-century writers, however, did not bother to discount Smith's work, for they felt certain that he had developed a coherent laissez faire philosophy. Did he not suggest that churches should compete with one another; that judges ought to be paid only for the work they perform; and that a colonial empire which proves costly ought to be sacrificed? Clearly, these interpreters could quote page after page to substantiate their analysis. On the other hand, they must have been slightly bothered by Smith's advocacy of state interference with education, highways, interest rates, specific industries, and the like. The casual student, however, would have been justified in assuming that these formed minor deviations from a general thesis. The Scottish economist must have favored freedom, for it was the religion of the educated man of his day. One of his contemporaries even went so far as to remark that they were living in an "Age of Freedom." . . .

An attempt has also been made to explain Smith's work as a rationalization for the changes in eighteenth-century society. The merchants and the manufacturers in the new commercial and industrial centers of England and Scotland were anxious to put an end to the existing system of governmental restraints, which, they discovered, were costing them a pretty penny. Adam Smith supposedly obliged them by working out in a methodical fashion—he was a university professor—a defense for their attitude. The evidence to the contrary, however, is not easily dismissed. One of the leading men in Scotland wrote to Smith after the publication of *The Wealth of Nations* that his book had managed so far to "provoke the church, the universities, the merchants—and likewise the militia." An exponent of popular prejudices seldom antagonizes many classes and individuals. A careful reading of Smith's attacks upon the princes of trade would hardly leave one reason to believe that he was their attorney; nor does the least evidence exist that he ever committed himself to plead their case.

The spirit molds the flesh. Historical analysis must attempt to recapture the emotional characteristics of the subject under investigation; all else is secondary. The many pages devoted to the prices of wheat and silver in *The Wealth of Nations* are most unimportant, for they shed very little light upon the author; but the many paragraphs which extol the agricultural and the laboring classes do offer very significant clues. Adam Smith devoted his genius and his energies to enhancing the social and economic status of the community, and these two groups combined, represented by far the larger sector of the population. In his opinion a strong minority had successfully feathered its nest at the expense of farmers and laborers. Hence the nation at large had suffered. Laissez faire can be a powerful weapon in the class struggle; it can deprive the wealthy of their illegitimate gains. Smith's treatise is weighed down by much extraneous material; it is not easy fully to appreciate the focus of the attack. But fortunately we possess a lengthy dissertation by Smith on a noneconomic problem in which his laissez faire approach is clearly delineated. This time he was not writing for publication, and therefore his remarks are likely to be an even truer reflection of his intimate beliefs.

The Duke of Buccleugh, his old pupil, wrote to him requesting his views on a proposal then before Parliament to investigate the lax practices of Scottish universities in granting medical degrees. Smith introduces his reply by stating that he would favor an investigation if the matter appeared to be of great public concern; but, on the other hand, it would be foolish for the government to meddle in the affairs of a body corporate if the issues raised were of only slight interest to the community. One of the proposed reforms would prohibit any student from being admitted to final examinations for the degree unless he could prove attendance at the university for at least two years. Smith believes this to be a foolish regulation, and very oppressive upon private teachers. Assuredly, the students of Hunter and Hewson, who are taught privately, are as well trained as any university graduate. To enforce two years of academic training upon all future members of the medical profession would result in establishing a monopoly in favor of the colleges. Now monopolies are usually dangerous, and the service which they render is seldom of high quality because they are always assured of a market for their product. Smith is firmly convinced that the public would suffer through the establishment of this new regulation. . . .

Smith concludes his epistle with the remark that he will probably get his lug (ear) in his lufe (hand) for what he has written, but having been asked for his opinion he could do no less than give it. He is not overjoyed with his own conclusions, for clearly his advice against the visitation is tacit approval of the existing system of roguery and sham. It is exceedingly difficult for a former professor of Christian ethics to defend these depraved conditions, but Smith has the courage of his convictions. He prefers to flirt with the devil rather than to worship false gods. He is first and foremost concerned with the public welfare, and all his judgments on matters of social policy are determined with reference to this one criterion. Smith is fully aware that the public suffers distinct hurt from the prevailing immoral practice which enables students to buy their doctor's diplomas, but he is by no means convinced that governmental interference could remedy the situation. In fact, he is certain that if the state commenced to meddle it could succeed only in making bad worse.

Perhaps laissez faire will still make this a better world for all.

Founder of Human Resources

IF ADAM SMITH is more than a market economist, what is he? In this chapter we will seek to demonstrate that among his other accomplishments he is the founder of the discipline of *human resources*. In establishing Smith's claim, I want to recall the comment that Wesley Clair Mitchell made in his capacity as chairman of a doctoral committee at Columbia University in the late 1930s, when my first student offered "human resources" as a field for examination. Mitchell observed that he was pleased that economics, which had been rooted by Smith in human resources but had been deflected by his successors to a preoccupation with commodity trade, was now back on the main track.

Adam Smith did not use for the title of his great work an abstract term such as *economics, the market economy,* or *capital;* he chose the more descriptive phrase *An Inquiry into the Nature and Causes of the Wealth of Nations,* which emphasized his search for the sources of wealth which he located in the skill, dexterity, and judgment of the people who make up a society.

In explicating Adam Smith's views about the role of human resources, I wish to begin with his philosophical stance, which, influenced by the reformers on the Continent, saw man as the product of his environment.

In recent years, U.S. academia has been wracked by dissensions over claims advanced by the neo-Galtonians that blacks are intellectually and genetically inferior to whites. Here is Smith's clear-cut position on the relative roles of heredity and environment:

> The difference between the most dissimilar characters, between a philosopher and a common street porter, for example, seems to arise not so much from nature, as from habit, custom, and education. When they came into the world, and for the first six or eight years of their existence, they were perhaps, very much alike, and neither their parents nor playfellows could perceive any remarkable difference. About that age, or soon after, they come to be employed in very different occupations. The differences of talents comes then to be taken notice of, and widens by degrees, till at last the vanity of the philosopher is willing to acknowledge scarce any resemblance. (15–16)

Such an extreme environmentalistic view of human ability, which postulates an equality of potential among all people and ascribes differences in their later performance to their relative opportunities for having acquired skills and competences, goes far to explain why Smith urged state action with respect to education.

> The public can impose upon almost the whole body of the people the necessity of acquiring those most essential parts of education, by obliging every man to undergo an examination or probation in them before he can obtain the freedom in any corporation, or be allowed to set up any trade either in a village or town corporate. (738)

One should note in the present context that Smith the moral philosopher saw benefits to the public support of education beyond the gains in productivity that attracted the attention of Smith the economist.

> A man without the proper use of the intellectual faculties of a man is, if possible, more contemptible than even a coward, and seems to be mutilated and deformed in a still more essential part of the character of human nature. Though the State was to derive no advantage from the instruction of the inferior ranks of people, it would still deserve its attention that they should not be altogether uninstructed. The state, however, derives no inconsiderable advantage from their instruction. The more they are instructed, the less liable they are to the delusions of enthusiasm and superstition, which, among ignorant nations, frequently occasions the most dreadful disorders. An instructed and intelligent people, besides, are always more decent and orderly than an ignorant and stupid one. (740)

Having studied in Heidelberg, Germany, in the late 1920s, I cannot resist the temptation to point out that a relatively well educated people is not immune to the scourge of fanaticism; witness the Germans under Hitler. But in my view, this important exception does not vitiate the validity of Smith's insight about the relation of education to political stability.

Since Karl Marx's doctrine of class interest and class struggle has had such a potent influence on modern societies, it is interesting to consider how Adam Smith dealt with this subject.

> But though the interest of the labourer is strictly connected with that of the society, he is incapable either of comprehending that interest, or of understanding its connexion with his own. His condition leaves him no time to receive the necessary information, and his education and habits are commonly such as to render him unfit to judge even though he was fully informed. In the public deliberations therefore, his voice is little heard and less regarded. (249)

Let us now look more closely at Smith's views about workers and the work environment. These will go far to reinforce the claim that Smith was the founder of human resources.

To begin with the individual worker: Smith had no illusions about the fact that while people gain as a result of working, they also make sacrifices when they accept employment. "In his ordinary state of health, strength and spirits, in the ordinary degree of his skill and dexterity, he must always lay down the same portion of his ease, his liberty, and his happiness" (33). These are not unimportant or incidental sacrifices. When a worker accepts a job, he gives up control over his time, his energies, himself.

Smith was not sentimental. Unlike present-day consultants who seek to persuade managements that they can contribute to the morale and productivity of their work forces by rearrangements that will add to the prestige of work held in low esteem and reduce the unpleasantness of dirty and routine jobs, Smith saw little point in denying the obvious. He said: "In the inferior employments, the sweets of labour consist altogether in the recompence of labour" (122). On the basis of this insight, Smith argued in favor of reducing the time of apprenticeship, believing that it would help form young people to industry if they were able to earn wages sooner rather than later. Those among the more conservative contemporary American economists who are convinced that a high level of youth unemployment can be cured by reducing the wages of young people might well ponder this observation of Adam Smith, which in full reads:

> The institution of long apprenticeships has no tendency to form young people to industry. A journeyman who works by the piece is likely to be industrious, because he derives a benefit from every

exertion of his industry. An apprentice is likely to be idle, and almost always is so, because he has no immediate interest to be otherwise. In the inferior employments, the sweets of labour consist altogether in the recompence of labour. They who are soonest in a condition to enjoy the sweets of it, are likely soonest to conceive a relish for it, and to acquire the early habit of industry. A young man naturally conceives an aversion to labour, when for a long time he receives no benefit from it. The boys who are put out apprentices from public charities are generally bound for more than the usual number of years, and they generally turn out very idle and worthless. (122)

Little attention has been paid by economists, particularly those concerned with economic development, to another insight of Smith, who saw the prosperity of Great Britain in terms "of the security of enjoying the fruits of labor." This was his explication of this basic theorem:

The natural effort of every individual to better his own condition, when suffered to exert itself with freedom and security, is so powerful a principle, that it is alone, and without any assistance, not only capable of carrying on the society to wealth and prosperity, but of surmounting a hundred impertinent obstructions with which the folly of human laws too often incumbers its operations; though the effect of these obstructions is always more or less either to encroach upon its freedom, or to diminish its security. In Great Britain industry is perfectly secure; and though it is far from being perfectly free, it is as free or freer than in any other part of Europe. (508)

I would like to add personal testimony to this formulation. In my view the excessive German inflation of 1922–1923, which robbed hardworking men and women of their lifetime savings, prepared the ground for Hitler's ascent to power. In 1966, while I was on a study mission in Ethiopia, I discovered that, as soon as migrant workers on coffee plantations were paid, they spent their wages on orgies; they had learned that if they still had money when they returned home, they would be charged with trumped-up crimes and would be forced to hand over their savings to the authorities.

There are two more passages from *The Wealth of Nations* that bear on Smith's view of the worker. The first deals with wages; the second concerns application or, to use the word in vogue today, *motivation.*

The notation along the margin of Smith's opus puts the wage issue succinctly: "High wages encourage industry." The key sentences of this crucial paragraph follow:

The wages of labour are the encouragement of industry, which, like every other human quality, improves in proportion to the encouragement it receives. A plentiful subsistence increases the bodily strength of the labourer, and the comfortable hope of bettering his condition, and of ending his days perhaps in ease and plenty animates him to exert that strength to the utmost. Where wages are high, accordingly, we shall always find the workmen more active, diligent, and expeditious, than where they are low; in England, for example, than in Scotland; in the neighbourhood of great towns, than in remote country places. (81)

In the second part of this long paragraph, Smith speaks to the issue of whether workers are industrious or lazy. In consonance with his general approach that minimizes inborn traits and sees the environment as determining behavior, Smith adumbrates the principle that if men want to improve their condition they are more likely to overwork than opt for leisure:

Some workmen, indeed, when they can earn in four days what will maintain them through the week, will be idle the other three. This, however, is by no means the case with the greater part. Workmen, on the contrary, when they are liberally paid by the piece, are very apt to over-work themselves, and to ruin their health and constitution in a few years. A carpenter in London, and in some other places, is not supposed to last in his utmost vigour above eight years. Something of the same kind happens in many other trades, in which the workmen are paid by the piece; as they generally are in manufactures, and even in country labour, wherever wages are higher than ordinary. Almost every class of artificers is subject to some peculiar infirmity occasioned by excessive application to their peculiar species of work. . . . Excessive application during four days of the week, is frequently the real cause of the idleness of the other three, so much and so loudly complained of. (81–82)

Although Smith saw economic progress as dependent on employers' aggressively pursuing their search for profits, he warned them not to press their laborers too hard. "If masters would always listen to the dictates of reason and humanity, they have frequently occasion rather to moderate, than to animate the application of many of their workmen" (82).

The foregoing quotations underscore the importance that Adam Smith ascribed to the individual worker in shaping the performance of the economy and society. Smith appreciated what so many of his successors overlooked, namely, that the individual is never an isolated atom but is always an integral part of a complex social environment which both offers him opportunities and constrains the scope of his accomplishment. Let us look at certain additional passages where Smith assesses how different work environments affect those exposed to them. We will deal with four: the environment of the industrial worker, the farmer, the professor, and the manager.

By way of introduction to the industrial work environment, we must recall that Smith saw the division of labor as the principal mechanism responsible for increasing productivity and for the accumulation of wealth. Division of labor, Smith contended, is not an incidental process but is of paramount importance to the material progress of mankind. Despite the paramountcy of this principle, Smith was worried about the effects of excessive specialization on the worker. Once again there is an overview of Smith's position in the margin of his text: "Division of labour destroys intellectual, social, and martial virtues unless government takes pains to prevent it." The great advocate of laissez faire did not hesitate to give government a major role to play in preventing the destruction of both men and society!

The whole of his argument about the dysfunctional nature of the division of labor is important:

> In the progress of the division of labour, the employment of the far greater part of those who live by labour, that is, of the great body of the people, comes to be confined to a few very simple operations, frequently to one or two. But the understandings of the greater part of men are necessarily formed by their ordinary employments. The man whose whole life is spent in performing a few simple operations, of which the effects too are, perhaps, always the same, or very nearly the same, has no occasion to exert his understanding, or to exercise his invention in finding out expedients for removing difficulties which never occur. He naturally loses, therefore, the habit of such exertion, and generally becomes as stupid and ignorant as it is possible for a human creature to become. The torpor of his mind renders him, not only incapable of relishing or bearing a part in any rational conversation, but of conceiving any generous, noble, or tender sentiment, and consequently of forming any just judgment concerning many even of the ordinary duties of private life. Of the great and extensive interests of his country he is altogether incapable of judging; and unless very particular pains have been taken to render him otherwise, he is equally incapable of defending his country in war. The uniformity of his stationary life naturally corrupts the courage of his mind, and makes him regard with abhorrence the irregular, uncertain, and adventurous life of a soldier. It corrupts even the activity of his body, and renders him incapable of exerting his strength with vigour and perseverance, in any other employment than that to which he has been bred. His dexterity at his own particular trade seems, in this manner, to be acquired at the expense of his intellectual, social, and martial virtues. But in every improved

and civilized society this is the state into which the labouring poor, that is, the great body of the people, must necessarily fall, unless government takes some pains to prevent it. (734–735)

According to Smith, the consequences of further acceleration of the division of labor would lead to greater material accumulation, but at the same time it would speed the degradation of the laboring poor, the great body of the people. Contemporary social science has traced the doctrine of alienation and dehumanization to Karl Marx. Apparently present-day ideologists could not conceive that the father of modern capitalism, as they see Smith, could have been alert to dangers incident to the extreme division of labor and at the same time have warned of the need for governmental action to counter its deleterious effects.

What about the environment in which the farmer works? The following encapsulates Smith's views:

> Not only the art of the farmer, the general direction of the operations of husbandry, but many inferior branches of country labour, require much more skill and experience than the greater part of mechanic trades. The man who works upon brass and iron, works with instruments and upon materials of which the temper is always the same, or very nearly the same. But the man who ploughs the ground with a team of horses or oxen, works with instruments of which the health, strength, and temper, are very different upon different occasions. The condition of the materials which he works upon too is as variable as that of the instruments which he works with, and both require to be managed with much judgment and discretion. The common ploughman, though generally regarded as the pattern of stupidity and ignorance, is seldom defective in this judgment and discretion. He is less accustomed, indeed, to social intercourse than the mechanic who lives in a town. His voice and language are more uncouth and more difficult to be understood by those who are not used to them. His understanding, however, being accustomed to consider a greater variety of objects, is generally much superior to that of the other, whose whole attention from morning till night is commonly occupied in performing one or two very simple operations. How much the lower ranks of people in the country are really superior to those of the town, is well known to every man whom either business or curiosity has led to converse much with both. (127)

Almost without exception, those who compare the industrial laborer to the farmer see the former as the more sophisticated, the more competent. But not Smith. He looks beyond surface differences and finds that in terms of skill and competence the farmer is clearly superior. Equally iconoclastic is Smith's critique of professors, an occupation with which he was intimately acquainted.

He begins his analysis by differentiating those whose income depends in whole or part on fees from students (whom they must attract and hold) from those who receive a salary. In the latter instance, Smith sees little involvement and less output by faculty members. To quote him directly:

> His interest is, in this case, set as directly in opposition to his duty as it is possible to set it. It is the interest of every man to live as much at his ease as he can; and if his emoluments are to be precisely the same, whether he does, or does not perform some very laborious duty, it is certainly his interest, at least as interest is vulgarly understood, either to neglect it altogether, or, if he is subject to some authority which will not suffer him to do this, to perform it in as careless and slovenly a manner as that authority will permit. If he is naturally active and a lover of labour, it is his interest to employ that activity in any way, from which he can derive some advantage, rather than in the performance of his duty, from which he can derive none.
>
> If the authority to which he is subject resides in the body corporate, the college, or university, of which he himself is a member, and in which the greater part of the other members are, like himself, persons who either are, or ought to be, teachers; they are likely to make a common cause, to be all very indulgent to one another, and every man to consent that his neighbour may neglect his duty, provided he himself is allowed to neglect his own. (718)

In his analysis of the East Indian Company, Smith gives his views on managers. "All the members of the administration, besides, trade more or less upon their own account. . . . Nothing can be more completely foolish than to expect that the clerks of a great counting-house at ten thousand miles distance . . . should . . . abandon . . . all hopes of making a fortune . . . and content themselves with the moderate salaries which those masters allow them . . . " (603). Here is the prototype of Berle and Means's distinction in *The Modern Corporation and Private Property* (1932), between owners and management, though Smith referred to them as masters and clerks!

Another observation of Smith's about a characterological fault in managers warrants attention:

> The pride of man makes him love to domineer, and nothing mortifies him so much as to be obliged to condescend to persuade his inferiors. (365)

There are additional insights of Adam Smith about human resources, a few of which should be noted. At the time when Smith wrote, slavery was still ensconced in many parts of the globe—in Russia, Africa, and North and South America. But it was Smith's view that slavery was an inefficient way of organizing human work. He would have been suspicious of Fogel and Engerman's work, *Time on the Cross* (1974), on the ground that the productivity of recalcitrant workers would always be less, far less, than that of persons who are encouraged by liberal rewards to do their best.

> The wear and tear of a slave, it has been said, is at the expence of his master; but that of a free servant is at his own expence. The wear and tear of the latter, however, is, in reality, as much at the expence of his master as that of the former. The wages paid to journeymen and servants of every kind must be such as may enable them, one with another, to continue the race of journeyman and servants, according as the increasing, diminishing, or stationary demand of the society may happen to require. But though the wear and tear of a free servant be equally at the expence of his master, it generally costs him much less than that of a slave. The fund destined for replacing or repairing, if I may say so, the wear and tear of the slave, is commonly managed by a negligent master or careless overseer. That destined for performing the same office with regard to the free man, is managed by the free man himself. The disorders which generally prevail in the economy of the rich, naturally introduce themselves into the management of the former: The strict frugality and parsimonious attention of the poor as naturally establish themselves in that of the latter. Under such different management, the same purpose must require very different degrees of expence to execute it. It appears, accordingly, from the experience of all ages and nations, I believe, that the work done by free men comes cheaper in the end than that performed by slaves. It is found to do so even at Boston, New York, and Philadelphia, where the wages of common labour are so very high. (80–81)

With respect to the imbalance between the preparation of workers and the job opportunities open to them, Smith offers the following insight:

> The over-weening conceit which the greater part of men have of their own abilities, is an ancient evil remarked by the philosophers and moralists of all ages. Their absurd presumption in their own good fortune, has been less taken notice of. It is, however, if possible, still more universal. There is no man living who, when in tolerable health and spirits, has not some share of it. The chance of gain is by every man more or less over-valued, and the chance of loss is by most men under-valued, and by scarce any man, who is in tolerable health and spirits, valued more than it is worth. (107)

Smith elaborates on this universal tendency by pointing out:

> The contempt of risk and the presumptuous hope of success, are in no period of life more active than at the age at which young people

choose their professions. How little the fear of misfortune is then
capable of balancing the hope of good luck, appears still more evi-
dently in the readiness of the common people to enlist as soldiers, or
to go to sea, than in the eagerness of those of better fashion to enter
into what are called the liberal professions.

What a common soldier may lose in obvious enough. Without
regarding the danger, however, young volunteers never enlist so
readily as at the beginning of a new war; and though they have scarce
any chance of preferment, they figure to themselves, in their youthful fancies, a thousand occasions of acquiring honour and distinction
which never occur. These romantic hopes make the whole price of
their blood. Their pay is less than that of common labourers, and in
actual service their fatigues are much greater. (109)

If compulsion is a poor motivator, then the belief in one's own good
fortune is likewise an untrustworthy guide. Smith warns about the distortions that occur in the occupational choices that people make because
they overestimate their own abilities and prospects.

The distortion that Adam Smith noted growing out of what he called
conceit can be illustrated by reference to current survey data, which
reveal that although only 17 percent of the labor force are currently
employed in professional and managerial occupations, 44 percent of
young people recently queried are looking forward to entering these
fields.

In contrast to the work of two Nobel prizewinners in economics,
Milton Friedman and Simon Kuznets, who, in their early work on professional incomes, explained the higher earnings of physicians in terms of
monopoly power resulting from artificial restrictions of entry into medical school. Adam Smith offered this interpretation:

We trust our health to the physician; our fortune and sometimes
our life and reputation to the lawyer and attorney. Such confidence
could not safely be reposed in people of a very mean or low condition.
Their reward must be such, therefore, as may give them that rank in
the society which so important a trust requires. The long time and
the great expence which must be laid out in their education, when
combined with this circumstance, necessarily enhance still further
the price of their labour. (105).

There are many more passages in *The Wealth of Nations* that could be
drawn upon to reinforce the claim that Adam Smith is the founder of
human resources, but the evidence already presented, which covers so
many different facets of work and workers, should suffice.

CHAPTER 4

The Illusion of Economic Stability

NO PERIOD IN HISTORY can approximate, far less parallel, the rate of change in economic relations that followed the invention of Watt's steam engine. Most people viewed these changes approvingly; criticism was limited to an occasional romantic who hated the machine, or to an occasional materialist who hated its owners. . . .

The balance sheet of the United States after the onset of industrialization was conspicuously good. With the exception of the 1870s and the 1890s, prolonged depressions were unknown. During the two decades preceding our entrance into World War I, the economy had expanded rapidly but without serious interruption. The liquidation of 1920–1921 was severe—estimates placed the number of unemployed as high as 5 million—but the speedy recovery reduced the devastation to a minimum. The seven good years that followed 1922 made optimists of us all. Never was change more rapid and never were the results more beneficial. While economists analyzed the marvelous mechanism of economic balance, the population sang hymns of praise to the New Era.

The analyses were scarcely completed and the hymns were still echoing when the long period of economic expansion came to an abrupt halt. As the contraction gained momentum, the optimism engendered by the prosperity of the past was gradually obliterated. No longer could one blithely maintain that a competitive system held wastes to a minimum; no longer could one be certain that a renewed expansion was inevitable. As industry after industry was unable to earn a profit, and as the number of unemployed was augmented by millions, economic stability became a remembrance of things past.

Just as the remembrance was itself fading, the economy began to revive under the protection of President Roosevelt. With the passage of time, the recovery was accelerated and belief in economic stability was rehabilitated. But the expansion petered out, and a contraction of unparalleled rapidity set in. When hope of self-correction faded, President Roosevelt proposed new measures to ensure by legislation that which could not be secured by competition. The stabilization of the economy remained the *summum bonum* of the New Deal. . . .

When one recalls that between the Civil War and World War I the expansion of the economy was subjected to only two major interruptions, one can well appreciate why economists considered depressions a minor matter. Moreover, the period after 1914 reinforced the optimistic bias; except for the readjustment incidental to shifting from a war to a peace basis, the economy prospered. The belief in economic stability—the cornerstone of the New Era—appeared reasonable. The events after 1929 proved, however, that the belief was founded more on fancy than on fact. Despite its dénouement during the depression, the belief in economic stability survived. The New Deal was largely created in its image and the Recovery Message of April, 1938, was written under its spell. A belief so potent should not escape analysis.

Although economists have seen fit to ignore or minimize its importance, technology is the true master of the modern world. . . . From the end of the Civil War until the close of the century, the expansion of the railroad industry was of the greatest importance in determining the course of the economy. As many miles of track were laid in the five-year period from 1868 to 1873, as in the thirty years preceding the outbreak of the war. Moreover, the revival in railroad building contributed greatly to the recovery of the late 1870s and guided the fortunes of the economy until the depression of the 1890s. Between the turn of the century and the outbreak of World War I, the electrical industry forged to the front. The production of kilowatt hours increased in the decade from 1902 to 1912 no less than fourfold, and the total mileage of electric railways increased threefold.

Less obvious but perhaps of even greater importance was the doubling of the population between 1870 and 1900. From a base of 38 million in 1870, there occurred a regular decennial increase of approximately 12 million; at the turn of the century, the population totaled 76 million.

The gain between 1900 and 1910 was even greater, for this decade witnessed an increase of approximately 16 million. Not less than 40 percent of the total increase of 50 million between 1870 and 1910 could be accounted for by immigration. Although the detailed figures are unavailable, there can be no doubt whatever that this phenomenal increase in population must have been associated with phenomenal activity in residential, commercial, and industrial construction.

To concentrate upon the trio—population, construction, and railroads—in sketching the period between the Civil War and World War I doubtless leads to the neglect of important variables; but the basic pattern is probably correct. During the 1920s, the props of the economy were construction and the automobile.

Important for the student of economic stabilization is the incontrovertible fact that retardation in the rate of growth is typical of all industries. This observation gains in significance when one recalls that the articulation of the modern economy facilitates the transference of stimuli. Acceleration, retardation, and decline are never isolated; their influence always transcends the boundaries of a single industry.

For instance, at the beginning of the 1920s, a large building boom got under way, precipitated by shortages brought on by the low level of wartime construction and enhanced by additions to, and redistribution in, our population. Before many months had elapsed, the railroad, steel, lumber, cement, copper, and a host of other industries felt the stimulus. The mutual dependence of industrial expansion on rising incomes and of rising incomes on industrial expansion ensured a boom of considerable magnitude. Activity in residential construction was concentrated on providing dwellings for the lower and upper middle class: Small houses were sold or mortgaged to the former; apartment houses and hotels were erected for the latter. By 1928 the market appeared amply exploited. Since private capital has always shied clear of building for the poor—the risks are too great and the returns too small—residential construction began to peter out.

Automobiles tell a similar story. Although the industry was able to expand rapidly in the years immediately preceding and following World War I, the depression of 1920–1921 found it in serious straits. The wealthy were supplied with vehicles, and those in moderate circumstances were unable to purchase—above all, were unable to finance—such a sizable investment. Technological improvements reduced the costs of manufacturing, and installment credit proved a great marketing boon. The expansion was renewed and, in turn, it stimulated the rubber, petroleum, steel, glass, lumber, and many other industries. Between 1918 and 1922, registration figures increased from 6 to 12 million, and during the next four years they mounted to 22 million. Conspicuous consumption might prove a further stimulus, but clearly the rate of growth could not be maintained. Since the poor could purchase used cars at a price that new units could not hope to approximate, a marked retardation in the rate of expansion was inevitable.

Just as rapid advances in the construction and the automobile industries swelled the national income, the retardation in their rate of growth was certain to depress the economy. The automobile had been especially stimulating, for it conditioned the growth of suburbs, the radical alterations in distribution, and the diversification of recreation. Above all, the road system was vastly enlarged and improved. As the number of automobiles grew more slowly, repair work would in part take the place of new construction. In many sections of the economy, additional capacity would be less urgent; replacement of existing capacity would suffice.

Only the emergence of new industries, or the more rapid growth of old industries, could have prevented the decline in general economic activity that retardation in the rate of growth of construction and automobiles was certain to engender. The latter 1920s did witness a marked expansion in the radio and electrical-appliance industries, but these could not fill the gap. It must not be overlooked that the combined value of output of the construction and automobile industries in 1928 exceeded $10 billion, while radio was not even in the billion-dollar class.

The experience of the United States after the collapse of the New Era illustrates even more clearly than does the New Era itself the instabilities that result from marked variations in the growth of important industries. Residential construction totaled almost $3 billion in 1928, but in 1932 the figure was less than $300 million; commercial and factory construction declined at a parallel rate, from $1.4 billion in 1928 to $165 million in 1932. Automobile production likewise plummeted from a record of more than 5.5 million cars in 1929 to one of less than 1.5 million in 1932. These reductions were, of course, reflected in the production of allied industries. Early in 1933, the output of the iron and steel industry totaled but 24 percent, that of the cement industry but 18 percent, of their July 1929 production.

Allies during the New Era and the Depression, the automobile and construction industries parted ways shortly before the beginning of the New Deal. So strong was the replacement demand for automobiles that the industry was able to expand in midsummer of 1932, an expansion that became considerably broader after the inauguration of President Roosevelt. Although less than 1.5 million cars were produced in 1932, more than 4.5 million were turned out in 1936. Not until the latter part of 1937 was the progress of the automobile industry arrested. Construction, however, made only a modest comeback during the New Deal, and even this revival largely reflected governmental spending for public works.

The inability of the Roosevelt recovery to maintain itself can, in the first instance, be explained by the failure of construction to revive.

Another contribution of technology to the instability of modern economies results from the fact that the enlargement of the means of production is greatly affected by the acceleration in the demand for finished products. Although the output of manufactured consumption goods declined only 20 percent between 1929 and 1933, the production of the capital-goods industries dropped no less than 80 percent. During the 1920s, the equipment industries were rapidly expanded to enable the consumption-goods industries to meet the rising demand for their products. Since a reduction in the rate of increase for consumer goods would have cut the output of capital goods, a decrease of 20 percent could not fail to raise havoc. Unfortunately, "no magic of institutional formulae can make these two rates equal." . . .

If technology is at the root of modern economic instability, it receives yeoman assistance from psychology. Subject to constant change, economic data are difficult to interpret. Since all interpretations are influenced by the preconceptions of the interpreter, the genesis and growth of these preconceptions are crucial. Projection is the key mechanism, for past experience is the only guide to future action.

Despite the phenomenal alteration in the U.S. economy between the Civil War and World War I, the major outlines are clear. Although the depressions of the 1870s and the 1890s brought a halt to the expansional development, they were unable to deflect the trend for long. Nor could the minor reversals succeed where the major ones had failed. Based upon the most solid foundation of expansions in physical production and employment, a strong tradition of business optimism was generated, a tradition that became increasingly entrenched as the 1890s were left behind.

During the postwar liquidation of 1920–1921, the economy was rudely shaken. The collapse was severe, but the fact that it had been more or less expected—a readjustment from a war to a peace basis could not be painless—modified its evil consequences. . . . As increasing numbers of the business community viewed the future optimistically, the future had increasing possibility of justifying their optimism. Favorable evaluations led to new investments and new investments increased the stream of purchasing power, a development that justified the favorable evaluations. Demand was supply and supply was demand. Although the tables and graphs of statisticians could be appreciated only after study, the millions of new houses and the tens of millions of new automobiles were beyond dispute. If opportunities for investment exist—and the U.S. economy had an excellent record of such opportunities—expansion awaits upon a favorable evaluation of the future. In the 1920s, automobiles and con-

struction appeared promising; a strong optimism did the rest. The New
Era was no historical sport; it followed a conventional pattern.

Sentiments are infectious. Eras of religious frenzy share the stage
with eras of speculative frenzy. The 1920s were vulnerable to speculation:
Tradition favored optimism; the facts favored optimism; it is hardly
surprising that optimism came and conquered. Special interests left few
stones unturned to heighten the mood, a process that cheap printing and
cheap speaking greatly facilitated. The advantages of investing in stocks
and real estate were related to the blind by ear and to the deaf by eye; the
public at large was bombarded by brochure and broadcast. . . .

Throughout the New Era, the technological and psychological factors were mutually stimulating. So, too, on the decline. The severe
reduction in the prices of equities during the last months of 1929—a
reduction that cut the value of shares on the New York Stock Exchange
from approximately $100 to $65 billion—although a reflection of past
declines in business activity, could not fail to hasten future declines. New
investment was held in abeyance, and even new consumption was stayed
in its tracks. As many awakened to the fact that their wealth was not only
intangible but also ephemeral, the demand for country estates and expensive automobiles dropped swiftly.

The tradition of business optimism was, however, so firmly entrenched
that even the disastrous decline in stock-market prices was viewed calmly.
The reiteration of President Hoover that the economy was fundamentally stable, and his promise that the decline in business activity would
be short-lived, was more than political propaganda. This conviction was
not restricted to party lines but rather reflected general sentiment. In
view of the ingrained optimism, it is small wonder that every bend in the
statistical indicators was hailed as the turning point. Not until midsummer of 1931 was faith abandoned. Thereafter pessimism swept the land,
feeding on itself in much the same way as had the optimism of the New
Era. Though new capital issues totaled in excess of $10 billion in 1929,
they dropped to $3 billion in 1931, and in 1932 they did not exceed $1
billion.

Since the existing level of business activity left unutilized a large
percentage of available capacity, the disinclination to invest was well
founded. But the reluctance to expand also reflected a pessimistic attitude about the future level of activity, which itself depended in large
measure upon the rate of new investment. If optimism led to mania,
pessimism led to panic. Liquidity became the new fetish. The constant
decline in prevailing prices precipitated the turning of assets into cash, a
process that led to the further reduction of prices. As the banking crisis
of March 1933 so clearly illustrated, the mad scramble for liquidity
brought the economy very close to self-liquidation. . . .

Since the level of business activity is intimately dependent upon the expectations of the business community, and since the immediate future is so directly determined by these expectations, nobody can afford to disregard the mass. One must swim with the tide, and the exceptional man is he who knows when the tide is about to turn. Under pressure to estimate the future, the business community carefully evaluates the past, not the far-distant but the more recent past, for in a changing economy, the data of old blur rapidly and are subject to accelerated obsolescence. . . .

Truth and error are statistical concepts. In a world gone mad, insanity is no disease. During the 1920s an occasional banker might have doubted the wisdom of lending to South American countries, recognizing that the annihilation of political opponents was at best an uncertain investment. Yet as long as debtors were able to service their loans, and as long as a segment of the investment community was willing to take a chance, only the most powerful banker could withstand the pressure. Although expensive apartment houses were being erected at a very rapid rate toward the end of the New Era, entrepreneurs of still more and more expensive ones, whose plans indicated reasonable prospects of returns, could not be denied funds. One can afford to go against the trend only when the trend is about to turn. To assess the future of the economy, it is necessary to assess the attitudes of the business community, making due allowance for the fact that irrational attitudes frequently justify themselves.

Expectations can, however, be proved false. Failure to discount the weakening of expansionary stimuli is the most frequent cause of error. If approaching retardation in the rate of growth of the automobile industry had been appreciated toward the end of the New Era, reduced investments in expensive housing would have been advisable. Moreover, if retardation in the rate of growth of new construction had been perceived, new additions to automobile plant and equipment could have been kept at a more modest figure. . . .

In reviewing the New Era, one is impressed with the fact that its prosperity was enhanced—but not caused—by the expansion in the money supply. If bank deposits had not been enlarged, an expansion in general business might well have taken place, but it would probably have been considerably more moderate. If all new investment had been forced to depend upon real savings, the rate of capital accumulation would have been vastly slower. Moreover, additions to the money supply stimulated speculation in real estate and securities. While the prices of equities were on the rise, business sentiment became increasingly optimistic, a factor of no small importance in furthering the general expansion.

The gain was, of course, short-lived. Once business began to contract, the behavior of money proved as depressing as it had previously proved stimulating. With the collapse of the stock market, business expectations underwent a marked turn for the worse, which reduced the willingness of bankers to lend and of investors to borrow. As old loans were called and new loans were refused, bank deposits declined. This process led to accelerated declines in business activity. As the demand for men and materials weakened, prices fell and profits disappeared. By 1931 the cumulative process was well under way, and the half-hearted attempts of the government to expand the money supply were woefully inadequate.

By the end of 1932, total bank deposits had declined $15 billion, or more than 25 percent from their New Era high, and the banking crisis that welcomed President Roosevelt into office was not solved without liquidating an additional $2 billion of deposits. Although forces working toward the expansion of business were present at the beginning of 1933, the further weakening of an already weak banking structure could not fail to have bad results. The new administration, however, took drastic steps to counteract the contraction of deposits. Appropriations for direct relief were partially responsible for an increase in bank deposits, and other recovery measures stimulated further increases. December 1934 found deposits at a figure $7 billion greater than that of June 1933; and by December 1935 they had increased $11 billion, a total rise of 30 percent in less than three years. Large-scale spending, financed through the sale of government bonds to the banks, was almost solely responsible for the increases in deposits. Between June 1933 and December 1935, all member banks enlarged their holdings of direct and fully guaranteed governmental bonds by $5.4 billion dollars, while during this same period their loans decreased $700 million.

Total deposits continued to mount rapidly, until they reached a high of almost $54 billion in December 1936, an advance during the New Deal of $16 billion, or more than 40 percent. Although loans continued to increase thereafter, investments declined, in largest measure a reflection of reduced holdings of government bonds.

The New Deal bears striking similarity, yet stands in striking contrast, to the New Era. In both periods, bank deposits increased, though the acceleration was more marked in the latter. So much for the similarity; more important is the contrast. During the 1920s, increased loans and investments, a reflection of the increasing optimism of bankers about the future trend of business, were responsible for the expansion in the money supply. Bank portfolios contained an increasing number of loans and investments in real estate and securities. The rapid rise of bank deposits during the New Deal must be interpreted largely in terms of federal deficit financing through the banking system; increased investments in government bonds predominate.

The collapse of the New Era showed that price fluctuations in the assets of the private economy can be so intense as to precipitate declines in business activity and bank deposits. But one need be no Cassandra to view with concern, if not with alarm, the expansion of bank deposits backed by public assets. Clearly, increases based on governmental deficits cannot continue indefinitely; clearly, the values of government bonds may likewise fluctuate. . . .

The review of the postwar developments has disclosed frequent and large changes in the money supply. Controlled largely by the demands of entrepreneurs and the government, influenced greatly by the anticipations of bankers about the future trend of business activity, fluctuations in the money supply can themselves affect the activity and anticipations of business. . . .

Although the prewar economy established a presumption in favor of the belief in economic stability, a belief that the New Era surely strengthened, economic developments since 1929 have proved discomforting. Itself a testimonial to economic instability, the decade of the 1930s has afforded us an opportunity to revise our evaluation of the stable 1920s. Cumulative interactions of technological, psychological, and monetary forces have kept the postwar economy in constant turmoil. Differential rates of growth of important industries, and exaggerated reactions of the capital-goods industries to changes in the demand for consumer goods, have laid the foundation for substantial fluctuations. Since the business community usually estimates the future by projecting the present, prevailing trends are intensified. Finally, a banking system possessed of the power to increase and decrease the money supply by 30 or 40 percent within a three-year period cannot fail to stimulate fluctuations already under way, and can, upon occasion, actually generate such fluctuations. Only as these factors are brought under control can economic stability be transformed from a pious wish into a solid fact.

But further difficulties would have to be met. Since the adjustment among the myriad pieces of the economy depends upon the price mechanism, and since the price mechanism suffers from serious imperfections, the underutilization and the inefficient utilization of available resources would remain to mock.

In the past as in the present, the price mechanism has been manipulated. Individual or collective control over supply has been frequent, if not typical. Enlarged investments in plant and equipment have increased the incentives of industry to cooperate. Failure to place limits upon competitive behavior ensured that, under conditions of excess capacity, prices would be driven to a point so low that no firm could earn a profit. The history of the steel, cement, gasoline, and copper industries—to mention only outstanding examples—illustrates the efforts currently devoted to controlling price competition. Nor is this surprising, for "to insist that producers shall compete unchecked appears to amount to inviting competition, and private enterprise with it, to commit suicide." ...

The economic fluctuations of the last decades can largely be explained by the interaction of technological, psychological, and monetary factors, though the fluctuations were intensified by imperfections of the pricing mechanism. Unless these several factors are subject to control, economic stability must remain an illusion. Since complete control appears neither imminent nor potential, belief in economic stability must be scrapped. Yet cynicism need not replace faith. Partial controls can accomplish much. Technological progress and speculative investments will probably continue in the future, as they have in the past, to precipitate periods of substantial expansion. A more careful application of existing controls, and an enterprising search for new controls, can contribute greatly to moderating the advances and to checking the retreats. But this modest expectation may well be extreme.

Although much of life is spent working to eat and eating to work, man does not live only in the market or only for the market. In a world divided not only into those who have and those who have not, but also into those who believe and those who do not believe, warfare between men is firmly established. Soldiers drill, for tomorrow they march. Cannon must answer cannon. Increasingly the resources and labor of every country are conscripted for military purposes. Increasingly, dictatorships and democracies differ only in the means of conscription. Increasingly, all criteria of economic efficiency save one—military preparedness—are being scuttled. In many lands, naive youngsters approve enthusiastically; in others, mature men act with serious deliberation; in still others, the public is just beginning to comprehend. The race gains momentum; the costs begin to mount; opposition is limited to a sigh of regret. Fear is master; no one denies him tribute. Gold does not suffice; even dreams must be sacrificed. On the altar of political expediency, the illusion of economic stability is finally consumed.

CHAPTER 5

Morals for Democracies

CONFRONTED WITH NEW AND SERIOUS PROBLEMS during the post–World War I decades, the British public in appraising them was greatly conditioned by tastes and beliefs acquired in an earlier day. Although a visitor from Mars might have concluded without great hesitancy that when people are without work because of a decline in private industry, it is sane and sensible for the public authorities to put these people to work, the well-trained and disciplined body politic of Great Britain could not see things this way. For it knew that public expenditures must be balanced by public revenues, and it knew further that high taxes could throw more people out of work than large expenditures could put to work.

The visitor from Mars might also have concluded that if it were impossible to offer employment to large numbers of individuals in areas such as South Wales where they were living, and if good opportunities existed elsewhere, it would be reasonable to bribe or coerce them to move. But Englishmen knew that it was undemocratic to bribe minorities with public monies and that it was equally undemocratic to coerce them. When the visitor from Mars had been apprised of the fact that large numbers of people in South Wales refused to leave the valleys and that

industries refused to locate there of their own free will, he doubtless
would have concluded that the government should bribe or force industry to locate there. But Englishmen knew that their great industrial
development was largely the result of industry's freedom from political
shackles and that clearly little could be gained and much lost by bribing
or forcing industry to locate where it did not choose to go. Nor can there
be much doubt that, when the visitor from Mars became aware that the
unemployed would not leave the valleys and that little was being done to
bring industry to the valleys, he would have advocated bringing the facts
to the attention of the public, to warn it of the dangers of ignoring the
demoralization not only of the unemployed but, even worse, of the
children of the unemployed. The visitor from Mars would have expected
that once the facts had been brought to the public's attention there would
have been speedy action, for all sensible people realize that it is both
wicked and stupid to permit men to rot in idleness and breed children in
despair.

But the man from Mars might have overlooked the fact that the
wealthy were worried about taxes, that the trade unions were intent upon
guarding their monopolies, that churchmen were bogged down in doctri-
nal disputes, that army officers were preoccupied with tactics, that physicians discussed the relative importance of psychic and somatic factors,
and that ordinary people were just too busy with their own problems
and their own pleasures to concern themselves with the plight of men,
women, and children whom they had never seen and probably never
would. The man from Mars would have returned to his planet greatly
confused. . . .

Loss of income and loss of status for hundreds of thousands of coal
miners were bad enough, but emphasis must be placed on the direct and
indirect results of loss of work. As men were weaned from laboring they
no longer had the ability to submit themselves to discipline, to find joy
in a job well done, to plan for the morrow. These serious consequences
could have been avoided only if the government had followed a radically
different approach in dealing with the long-time unemployed. Unless
work had been made a condition for relief, not even the most liberal
allowances nor excellent administration could have prevented the deterioration of the unemployed. With the Labor party preoccupied in
establishing the right of the unemployed to relief without the performance of task work, with the Conservatives desirous of saving the Exchequer
any untoward strains, with experts devising new regulations that would
force men on relief to seek jobs in the private economy—with all this effort
concentrated on such important objectives, it is not surprising that little
was done to provide work for the unemployed. By actions that it took and
by actions that it failed to take, the government was directly responsible

for the demoralization of several hundred thousand excellent workers.

It is difficult to read without resentment that in the late 1930s the second-richest nation in the world prided itself on providing one-third of a pint of milk per day for the children of the unemployed in the valleys of South Wales, children who were suffering many insufficiencies. Poverty, even extreme poverty, has long plagued societies ancient and modern, but it must be remembered that these British victims had not been born to that state; they had been forced into it by industrial decline and governmental stupidity. Used to hard labor from his early teens, the miner frequently suffered such a long spell of unemployment that when he went back to work his hands bled like a stuck pig. Although men were growing soft, the leaders of Labor fought in South Wales against the acceptance of public amenities, especially parks and swimming baths, because these had been constructed by volunteer workers. And the Labor party devoted much attention in its propaganda to outlining the specific rights and privileges that the unemployed had under the law—to go half fed and remain in idleness.

That men forced to trade work for idleness, self-support for a pensioner's status, and adequate wages for paltry allowances would deteriorate physically and emotionally is not surprising. And the wives of such men could not escape deterioration. Most serious, however, was the influence of their unemployment upon their children. No one saw the problem more clearly than Sir Malcolm Stewart, who wrote, in his Third Report:

> I am alarmed when I think of the future of those unemployed youths, whose disastrous start in life is to be consigned to idleness, and who are consequently early enmeshed in its attendant evils. Many of these youths are brought up in homes where no member of the family has worked for many years, where the daily bread is not won, but provided by assistance from the State, a position often so long established that it comes to be looked upon as a normal feature of life. It is difficult for the best instincts to survive in such atmosphere; all sense of independence and enterprise is lost. An unhealthy outlook subtly grows at a period when character is most easily formed. Life drifts on without experience of work. Lack of inclination to work is followed by complete indifference either as to its procuration or its performance when secured. Practical experience shows that many such youths fail to hold their jobs. Rejected from industry, they again find themselves in the ranks of the unemployed, but with even worse prospects than before. Under these conditions future citizens are being created, who can but become a burden to themselves and to the State. These youths must be saved from the dread consequences of idleness, quickly and at all costs. Their circumstances are particularly intolerable in a prosperous state with high ideals as to the social

welfare of its citizens. However pressing other reforms may be, here
is one which brooks no delay and to which precedence should be
given.

That the government was aware of these dangers is proved by the
strenuous efforts it made to subsidize juvenile transference from the
depressed areas. But the fact remains that, despite Sir Malcolm Stewart's
insistence that the pauperization of the young must be prevented at all
costs, the government was unwilling to take adequate measures. Although
persuasion had failed to do the job, the government shied away from
using coercion, with the result that many thousands of youths were
thrown on the scrap heap of unemployment without ever having had the
opportunity of knowing what work really meant.

Tradition is largely responsible for bungling the problem of the
long-time unemployed. To proceed slowly in experimenting on the body
politic, to avoid the use of coercion, to follow rather than to lead public
opinion, were good traditions though their influence in this instance was
unfortunate. Yet, tradition aside, there were other reasons for this bungling performance. . . .

As spells of unemployment lengthened from weeks to months and
from months to years families discovered that it was possible to survive
on the relief allowances. When conditions reached a point where entire
communities and regions were in collapse adjustment became still easier,
for the remembrance of an earlier day dimmed and the contrast between
unemployment and work was no longer clear. The highly imperfect
system of unemployment allowances not only helped to stem migration
by cushioning the initial blow, but operated, in later years, against
transference out of the stricken areas by enabling people, without working,
to survive if not to flourish.

Many unemployed failed to leave the distressed areas, and some
students have contended that this immobility was the result of the existence and persistence of unemployment throughout the whole of Great
Britain. Since London, the Southeast, and the Midlands—the expanding
areas—were seldom completely free of unemployment in the postwar
years, and since sometimes the number of persons out of work in these
prosperous regions was substantial, there were few if any prospects for a
penniless migrant. But this is not the whole of the story, not by far, for
the fact remains that a person living in Birmingham, Oxford, or London
had much better chances of securing a job, despite a sizable number of
local unemployed, than if he had remained in a distressed area such as
South Wales. And the opportunity to become self-supporting was even
greater if he would emigrate overseas.

True, the jobs that the migrants might have obtained either in

England or overseas would have demanded much and offered little, but if the unemployed of South Wales had been without an alternative they could not have refused these jobs. They were not in this predicament, however, for their unemployment allowances covered their minimum needs, and they always weighed migration against this basic security. Since most men manage to get a living from their work and little else — and the people of South Wales were getting a living from the government — they saw little point in risking the uncertainties of migration and uncongenial work. Once the men of South Wales had been weaned from work — usually after one or two years of unemployment — few opportunities in other parts of the country appeared attractive. A coal miner could obtain only unskilled work at wages that were, even in the prosperous areas, barely sufficient for survival. But survive one could in South Wales on allowances from the Board. . . .

The communities of the Northern Outcrop first began to slip in the early 1920s, and the following years witnessed the closing of additional mines. So matters continued for a decade and more. In some years the closings were many, in others few, but the trend was unmistakable. At first the government concentrated on relief; later it became interested in the transfer of workers; but not until 1934 did it face the crying need of the region — namely, the revival of industry in the valleys of South Wales.

The reluctance of the government to act on this front and the picayune efforts that it finally made permits of explanation. In the early 1920s the number of people affected by the collapse of the coal-mining industry in the valleys of South Wales was relatively small, and in a world rich in misery the plight of a few is seldom noticed. The General Strike of 1926 was so overwhelming that it hid from view the more pervasive but the less dramatic decline of the coal industry. The strike finally came to an end, but many mines failed to reopen; and when these were added to the mines that had been shut down before the strike began, serious difficulties were at hand. No sooner had the public become aware in 1929 that all was not well in South Wales than this awareness was dulled by the problems presented by the severe depression that afflicted the entire country. It was not until the depression receded, in 1933, that South Wales as well as the other depressed areas came back into the public's consciousness.

The delay and half-heartedness with which Parliament legislated on behalf of the special areas might be explained by the force of tradition — the tradition against special legislation for special groups. But this is not a tenable explanation when one recalls that it was during the early 1930s that Parliament passed protective tariffs — clearly special legislation for special groups.

But the interests that pressed Parliament to pass tariffs were much more powerful than those that agitated for relief for the distressed areas. The protectionists had in their ranks leaders of British industry and finance, men adroit at getting what they wanted. The coal miners of South Wales, the shipwrights of Clydeside, and the miners and shipwrights of Northumberland were not skilled in the nuances of political lobbying and public propaganda, and what little skill they had they could not put to use, for they were bankrupt.

So great, however, was the plight of the Special Areas that Parliament was forced to act, since it could not silence its own guilt nor escape the indictments of responsible citizens. In 1934 funds were placed at the disposal of the Commissioners for the Special Areas—neither large funds, nor free funds, yet it was a beginning. The commissioners could not make grants for direct relief, nor could they subsidize private manufacturers who might consider locating in the depressed areas. They were even prohibited from making contributions for public works if other government departments had jurisdiction. They were hemmed in on every side and at best could contribute only to increasing the amenities so as to check the worst ravages of long-time unemployment.

After Sir Malcolm Stewart's Third Report as Commissioner for the Special Areas of England and Wales the government reluctantly added to the funds at the disposal of the commissioners and increased the commissioners' discretionary powers. They could now make grants to private industries and bribe them to locate in the Special Areas. But only a beginning was made; for the Conservative Party, which was really in control throughout the decade, disapproved of spending large sums to subsidize the location of industry in the stricken areas, without which subsidies industry would never locate there. But the Conservatives were not solely to blame.

It is difficult to help people who will not help themselves, and many of the tragedies that befell the Welsh during the postwar decades can be traced to their own shortcomings and to the shortcomings of their allies, the trade union movement and the Labor party. The failure of the Welsh to help themselves must in part be explained by their inability to do so. As early as 1934 Lord Portal called attention to the fact that the leaders of South Wales were noticeably inept, a result of the fact that the most virile and able people had migrated. This kindly interpretation of the ineptitude of Welsh leaders cannot, however, explain and surely cannot justify such stupid practices as sending trade union leaders to Parliament as a reward for faithful services to the federation. Nor does the theory of selective migration explain adequately the failure of the Labor party to go to the country with a reasonable program for the distressed areas.

Worse still were the rampant jealousies in South Wales that contributed to thwarting even those few efforts that were made to resuscitate the region. Nothing is more depressing than to read, in the annual reports of the National Industrial Development Council of Wales and Monmouthshire, of the great difficulties of securing even minimum cooperation from the several communities. Equally depressing is the inability of the council itself to formulate reasonable plans for action. One cannot suppress the feeling that the several members of the council enjoyed the opportunity of coming to Cardiff now and again at the expense of their Local Authority and that they viewed the trip as an outing—a harsh judgment, but supported by experts. For instance, Sir Malcolm Stewart bemoaned "the insufficient degree of wholehearted cooperation between the various classes of the community" and he was convinced that revival was "being partially hindered by this lack of co-operation." He and his successor, Gillett, repeatedly called attention to their inability to secure wholehearted support for the Severn Bridge, the erection of which would doubtless have gone far to stimulate industry and commerce in South Wales.

Nor was the South Wales Miners' Federation, despite its reputation for radicalism, able to face up to the issue. The federation's solution for the coal industry emphasized the elimination of cut-throat competition among the several districts of the country and pleaded for the erection of hydrogenation plants for the distillation of oil from coal—hardly an imaginative program for an area as severely stricken as South Wales. Bereft of intellectual and emotional leadership, Labor was unable to challenge the pennywise policy of the Conservatives, and even this pennywise policy was frequently hamstrung.

A government is run by officials, and officials like other folk do not like to be disturbed. Before Parliament began to legislate in behalf of the Special Areas, officialdom had developed routines which it considered adequate. When His Majesty's government was so unwise, in 1934, as to set sail on uncharted seas, Whitehall became greatly agitated. Appalled by the recklessness of Parliament, the bureaucrats at Whitehall did everything in their power to turn it back into known waters. Sir Malcolm Stewart's blistering indictment of the bureaucracy suggests that it had engaged in large-scale sabotage. If Sir Malcolm had been less of a gentleman and less of a stylist, his stinging rebuke would have made an excellent leader for the Communist press. Not all the ministries were equally obstructionist. The Treasury was the worst, for Parliament's legislation in behalf of the Special Areas was viewed as a frontal attack on the principles of sound finance.

With the Conservatives appropriating pittances, Labor bereft of ideas, and the bureaucracy antagonistic, there is small wonder that the efforts to bring industrial revival to South Wales and the other Special Areas proved unsuccessful. A few small factories were erected and a few thousand persons were placed in employment, but the basic outline remained unchanged. These were regions where industry was stagnant and men remained without work. The efforts of the government in dealing with unemployment, migration, and industrial location during the postwar decades must be adjudged a failure. Despite the expenditure of large sums several hundred thousand of the most skilled British workmen were permitted to deteriorate because of idleness, and a younger generation was permitted to grow up without working or hope of working. Despite elaborate schemes to further the transfer of surplus workers from areas where industry was declining to areas where industry was expanding, the end of the 1930s did not find the resolution of the paradox of noticeable surpluses of labor in close proximity to noticeable shortages. Despite the herculean efforts of the commissioners for the Special Areas and despite Parliament's belated attempts to cooperate with the commissioners in bringing industry to the stricken regions, little was accomplished. Total expenditures of the commissioners in all the Special Areas approximated £20 million, of which not more than a third went into the erection of plants and the purchase of equipment, a figure so small that it precluded important achievements.

South Wales presents an even gloomier picture, for its losses during the two decades probably exceeded those of any other region. Not only did South Wales rank first in the number of employment exchanges with high rates of unemployment, but family income probably declined more in South Wales than elsewhere. Transference of workers also bore particularly hard on the Welsh. Although few people enjoy leaving their birthplace, the coal miners of South Wales had particular reasons for resisting the forces that were driving them to the Midlands and to London. Theirs was a rich culture, and the miner who went east from South Wales left much more behind than did the miner who went south from Durham. Moreover, the Welsh had greater difficulties in adjusting to the English than did other migrants, for anti-Welsh prejudice ran high in England. Yet the migration from South Wales exceeded the migration from any other depressed area. Since South Wales was even more dependent upon a single industry than was Tyneside or Clydeside, the failure of the government on the industrial front bore particularly heavily on the Welsh.

The balance sheet for these two decades is indeed bad reading, but bad as it is it might have been worse. Confronted with striking increases in the number of the unemployed, British democracy was able during the postwar decades greatly to expand its care for these victims of industrial instability. And when it became clear in the later 1920s and the early 1930s that postwar readjustments were bringing in their wake an unbalance in the geographic distribution of the employed, and more particularly of the unemployed, British democracy evolved a series of new approaches aimed at compensating for these untoward trends. Such was the meaning of the Governmental Training Centers, the subsidizing of family removals, and the elaborate schemes of juvenile transfer. When it had become clear in the mid-1930s that, despite action already taken to relieve the unemployed and to facilitate their transference, there remained striking differences in regional prosperity, British democracy was able to break through crippling tradition and to venture, by persuasion and by bribery, to bring industry to the more stricken areas. Clearly British democracy was not impotent. Viewed in the light of its own past it was flexible and resourceful. Yet its flexibility and its resourcefulness were woefully inadequate, for after twenty years of effort the problems of the long-time unemployed, the maldistribution of the laboring population, and the industrial stagnation of the Special Areas remained unsolved.

The failure of British democracy to find tolerable solutions for these pressing problems is, however, easily understandable. England has been a victim of her own strength, a strength in tradition. Widespread and deepseated has been the conviction that experimentation on the body politic is dangerous and action should be taken only for the most weighty considerations.

Although the difficulty of the problem and the liability of tradition must be weighted heavily in the search for an explanation of the tragic errors in postwar policies, there is more to the story. Incisive and skillful action would not have prevented all these errors, although it might have prevented most. But British democracy was unwilling to pay the price for preventing them, and therein lies its failure. The Conservative party must bear much of the blame, but not all. To provide work for the unemployed and to bring industry to the stricken regions would have necessitated the expenditure of large sums, and the wealthy members of the Conservative party balked at such expenditures. But their resistance alone does not explain the failure, for the history of England is replete with examples of legislation that was fought, and bitterly fought, by the wealthy. Had the leaders of Labor risen to the occasion by correctly analyzing the problem, by formulating a bold program for action, and by propagandizing for its acceptance by the country, the wealthy might have been shamed or forced out of their niggardliness. But the leaders of Labor failed. Nor can the bureaucracy escape without censure. Although the integrity of the civil servants cannot be questioned, serious doubts must be entertained about their powers of imagination. There is much evidence to suggest that the bureaucracy's desire for peace and security worked against the welfare of the country. The miserliness of the wealthy, the incompetence of the reformers, and the stodginess of the bureaucrats go far to explain the victimization of South Wales. But the sacrifice has a deeper meaning.

The evil that rides supreme in Germany and the tragedies that have stricken all of Europe from Norway to the Bosporus, the wanton destruction of people and property in Great Britain, and the dangers that have started to undermine the strength of the United States—these tragic happenings have much in common. Hitler might never have come into power, the democracies of Western Europe might never have been conquered, Great Britain might never have been forced to engage in a struggle for her very life, and the United States might yet be enjoying the security that was hers in an earlier day, if men had recognized that in the world of today their lives and their fortunes—and, what is even more important, the lives and fortunes of their children and their children's children—are irrevocably linked with the lives and fortunes of neighbors near and far. Had Germany provided jobs for her unemployed, Hitler would have lost his major appeal. Had France realized that her safety depended on Spain in the south and Belgium in the north, her security might not have been whittled away. Had England perceived that Manchuria, Ethiopia, and Czechoslovakia were her concern, Londoners today might not be the victims of sudden death from the air. If the United States had appreciated earlier that her frontiers were even farther east than the Rhine and farther west than the Philippines, her vulnerability today would not be so great.

The tragedy of South Wales is the tragedy of the modern world, but if the moral of the tragedy is understood then the Welsh will not have suffered in vain, for then, as Churchill has said, "All will come right. Out of the depths of sorrow and sacrifice will be born again the glory of mankind."

CHAPTER 6

Values in Social Theory

THE HUMAN-RESOURCES APPROACH emphasizes the instability of the values and institutions that shape the goals and activities of nations, especially advanced nations. A reading of modern history, and particularly the history of this century, delineates the discontinuity and change which are the common elements of their experiences. Implicit in the human resources approach, therefore, is the search for a model that can accommodate this dominant dynamic of social existence.

A second element of social inquiry relates to the research agenda. The founding fathers of social science, especially the British and French leaders in the late eighteenth century and at the beginning of the nineteenth century, believed that they were engaged in an effort directed to contributing to the betterment of man. *The Wealth of Nations*, Adam Smith's opus, was written to guide the legislator and the statesman in the realm of political economy. Smith's followers, Bentham, Malthus, Ricardo, and James Mill, who put a firm foundation under classical economics, were directly concerned with the bearing of their work on the formation of public opinion and policy. They addressed the critical issues of the day—agricultural tariffs, welfare, population policy, noninterference with business, free trade, income distribution, emigration, and trade unionism. The work of their continental colleagues—Helvetius, Holbach, Rousseau, Diderot, and Voltaire—was given credit for hastening the French Revolution. In its formative years, social science was sensitive to the dynamics of societal change and sought new and improved knowledge in the expectation of directing that change to desirable goals.

The initial success of the founding fathers of social science led to later difficulties. This was particularly true with regard to economics, where Smith's model of the competitive market was used as a basis for policy prescriptions which did not necessarily fit the changing reality. *The Wealth of Nations* did not justify Parliament's slow response to the evils of industrialization. However, Smith's theory of laissez faire came to be invested with a transcendental value. The captains of industry and finance and their followers used the theory to ward off efforts at social intervention. Faced with a choice between directing their efforts to elaborating and refining the inherited corpus or coming to grips with the unanswered problems of a rapidly changing reality, more and more of the economics fraternity opted for the former. The primary explanation of this is to be found in the process of institutionalization; practitioners of economics and the other social sciences became the captives first of the higher educational establishment, later of government and of business.

The importance of this institutionalization can be seen in the contemporary role of the social sciences on the American scene, the leading center of large-scale research. A large number of social scientists are employed in a staff capacity in government, nonprofit institutions, and private enterprises, where they assist decision makers by assessing trends and pointing up alternative policies; but they function primarily as specialists who work on problems that others set for them. The decisions about which goals are to be pursued remain the prerogative of the politician or the executive, not the social scientist, who seldom challenges them. The analyst thus employed makes his technical skills available in exchange for a salary and career. There is little to distinguish the social scientist from the large number of other professionals and technically trained persons who, in an advanced economy, constitute an ever-larger segment of the hired work force. These professionals literally belong to the establishment.

What of the numbers who are based primarily at colleges, universities, and research centers, where they instruct the young and pursue research? First, it should be recalled that it took the universities the larger part of a century to capture the social sciences, but captive they now are and are likely to remain.

The dynamism of the modern university is shaped by the intellectual orientation of the natural sciences, which, with their emphasis on models, quantification, and prediction, early came to serve as prototypes for the social sciences. The success of experimental science was so impressive that social scientists opted for imitation.

This scientific ethos was reinforced when, shortly prior to World War I, Max Weber's advocacy of "value-free" social research won the day. According to Weber and his followers, the social scientist must leave *his* values, politics, and social preferences behind when *he* studies society. The value orientations of groups and nations are very much within the orbit of inquiry. But the investigator must not permit *his* personal values to intrude. The description, ordering, analysis, and evaluation of social institutions, it was believed, should proceed according to the rules of inquiry prevailing in the natural sciences, with their emphasis on hypothesis formulation and hypothesis testing, using empirical data wherever possible.

Even a cursory inspection of post–World War II developments in the social sciences attests to the continued dominance of this approach. Economics, sociology, political science, and social psychology are increasingly dominated by mathematical model building, sophisticated statistical methodology, and hypothesis testing. As social scientists became engrossed in problems of methodology, their concern with policy lessened. Their principal preoccupation has been to improve the models that engage their attention. For them, "relevance" has increasingly become the improvement of the scientific apparatus with which they work. Relevance in terms of social policy has receded into the background.

Although the Weberian prescription of value-free social science has been challenged by an occasional analyst, it has escaped serious attack since its most likely opponents, the Marxists, did not want to undermine their own claims that dialectical materialism was a "scientific" theory. But, as will soon be made clear, value-free social science is a contradiction in terms, since no social scientist can escape his or her own values.

People create institutions to help them accomplish their collective aims, but once created, institutions take on a life of their own, and in the process both the goals that people pursue and the means that they employ are modified. At each stage, the members of the body politic must consider whether the existing social structures are responsive to their current needs and aspirations. Judgments about the effectiveness, efficiency, and equity of existing structures differ according to the qualifications of each evaluator. But no evaluator can be neutral in making assessments. As Aristotle noted, man is by nature a political animal, which means that he cannot stand outside the society to which he belongs.

Since there is always a less-than-perfect fit between the institutions that men have created and the effectiveness with which these institutions function, social inquiry is value-laden, not value-free. The investigator must select one rather than another problem for inquiry; likewise, he must decide how much time and effort to devote to exploring the subject he has selected—for research itself is a scarce resource constrained by talent, money, and time. Finally, the skillful investigator cannot prevent his conclusions from impinging on policy; even if he fails to make the linkage, others will. In short, value considerations are present at every stage of social inquiry from start to finish.

How then can we square the scholar's preoccupations with methodology with this primacy of values in all social inquiry? The answer is simple. Those who are largely indifferent to the social import of the problems they explore, who do not feel compelled to consider the reasonableness of the assumptions they build into their models, and who have little interest in whether the answers they develop provide guides for policy reinforce the status quo by their disinterest and aloofness. By concentrating on improving their discipline, an intellectual undertaking which in their opinion needs no justification, they avoid applying their critical faculties to issues of substance. Occasionally, a scholar who is uneasy about his preoccupation with methodological issues may reassure himself that his concern with model building is worthwhile because improved tools may later yield improved solutions.

The institutionalization of social science inquiry, however, is not as benign as might at first appear. True, there is a simple trade-off when a society invests a limited amount of resources in the support of academic social science and provides opportunities for teachers and researchers to earn their salaries by instructing the young and pursuing their intellectual interests. But the academic community itself is a large and potent institution with its own structures, modes of operation, and criteria of evaluation. Those at the helm control the admission of students, the curriculum, the subjects for dissertations, the appointment of faculty members, and the articles accepted for publication. It is not an accident that market economists are not appointed to chairs of political economy in the USSR or that there are only a few Marxist or radical social scientists at leading American universities. When Thorstein Veblen wrote his incisive analysis of American universities in 1918, he argued that the conservative orientation of social science faculties reflected the dominant role played by bankers and industrialists among university trustees. Today the fulcrum of power resides with the tenured faculty, which is comfortable in the environment it has established, which facilitates their avoiding the conflict-laden arena of social critique.

The burden of these observations about the relation between social theory and values has been to point out that the present work stands apart from the dominant academic ideology. This book denies the parallelism between nature and society and therefore challenges the transfer of analytic models developed for the study of physical phenomena to the study of man. Further, it holds that controlled experimentation, that potent instrument of the natural sciences, cannot generally be used in the study of people and societies. This in turn suggests that the criteria employed in the natural sciences for assuring the quality of the research design and the testing of findings cannot be directly transferred to the social sciences. Finally, if institutions are subject to constant but largely uncontrolled change, the social scientist must pay close attention to issues of relevance at every stage of work—in the selection of a problem, in the research approach, and in the formulation of findings and recommendations. All relevant research must speak to problems of social change. An investigator can ignore this challenge, but he cannot deny it.

These strong positions are not presented as a denigration of the role of empirical verification. If social inquiry is to avoid deteriorating into subjectivism, systematic efforts to square theories with facts are essential. Still, verification cannot rely solely on a simulation of models. It requires the assessment of institutions and mechanisms that are in place, since men and societies have the capacity to learn from experience.

It behooves every social scientist to set forth as clearly as possible the values that inform his work. That is the task to which we now turn.

Every society must critically appraise the arrangements that exist for allocating and distributing its available assets—property, power, privilege, prestige, and participation—among individuals and groups, since these assets largely determine their well-being. No society can evolve a pattern of distribution which will meet the needs and expectations of all its members. The continuing changes in the availability of resources and the expectations of individuals and groups rule out the possibility of a permanent arrangement that is satisfactory to all. In some societies, the existing distributional arrangements are more or less acceptable to the majority; in others, a dominant minority precludes through force, at least for a time, any radical shift in the existing pattern.

In addition to the basic consideration of equity, every society must repeatedly reassess the arrangements governing the freedom of the individual, since certain limitations must always be placed on that freedom to assure communal security and survival. Here too, no one arrangement long commands agreement. Whether individuals or groups opt for more freedom or more security reflects the relative importance they attach to each, the objective circumstances in which they are, and their estimate of the future conditions to which they will have to adapt.

The complex considerations involved in the search for equity and freedom confront the theorist with a stark choice. He either includes these values in his analysis or accepts the fact that his work will be unable to talk to these critical issues. Since men live only in societies, since cooperation among them is critical for their survival and welfare, and since their willingness to cooperate depends in no small measure on their sense of equity, a meaningful social analysis cannot skirt the distributional problem.

The value position underlying the present analysis can now be formulated: A society must strive to reduce gross inequalities in the distribution of opportunities and rewards for distinct but related reasons. The first relates to the principle of stability. A society that values its survival must be able to contain its dissidents. If an ever-larger number of its members come to view the existing arrangements as inherently unjust, they will strive to topple the existing structure, and eventually they will succeed. Next, justice is a value in its own right. If we believe that all men are children of God, we must view as inhuman and immoral a situation where one man's life is shortened by lack of food while another's is prematurely ended by excessive self-indulgence. Third, a society concerned about its future must consider how changes in the distributional pattern can contribute to the fuller development of human potential through the broadening of opportunities.

Freedom presents a parallel challenge. Freedom has both a negative and a positive connotation. Freedom implies that a person's inalienable rights—to use the words of the Declaration of Independence—are not arbitrarily denied by those in authority. Positively, freedom implies that individuals have sufficient resources to enjoy broadened options.

Some theorists hold that as long as people do not transgress the rules which a society has established for its own protection, they are entitled to accumulate as much property and power as they can. But here, too, as in the case of justice, the stability principle, the common bond of humanity, and considerations of social efficiency and effectiveness come into play. To paraphrase Anatole France: To say that a poor man is as free as a rich man to attend the opera conveys very little. The enjoyment of broadened options, a cornerstone of freedom, involves control not only of one's time but also of resources without which people become bound to the unending task of surviving. A society must ask whether the restraints on personal freedom are so pervasive and oppressive that more and more persons will challenge the existing arrangements and seek to upset them. As the long struggle over slavery made clear, the right of every human being to control his own labor takes precedence over the property rights of the slave owner. Finally, the freedom of people to think, discuss, and publish what they believe should be broadly tolerated. This freedom should not be arbitrarily constrained by those who exercise political power; no society can prosper if new and different ideas are arbitrarily repressed.

If justice and freedom are the goals of the good society, and we stipulate that they are, then the search to realize them must be seen for what it is—a process in which intermediate goals and mediating mechanisms are not fixed but are subject to continuing change as the society seeks to learn from its experiences. The third premise on which this work is predicated is the role of critical thought in the process of goal clarification and the selection of means to accomplish the stipulated goals. The dominant view holds that the social sciences have nothing to contribute to the clarification of goals; the position held here is the diametric opposite. It postulates that the principal tasks of the social scientist are to evaluate both the immediate objectives the society is pursuing and the institutions it has established and is modifying to accomplish them and to assess whether these objectives and methods are congruent with the ideals of a just society of free people. The contributions of investigators who perform these tasks with insight and responsibility will themselves become part of the ongoing process of goal setting and institution building, which is, and must remain, open-ended as long as people use critical thought to help them pursue their goals.

The thrust of this position is that social inquiry can justify its role and function only if it contributes to illuminating the problems and solutions which will enable a society to expand both social justice and individual freedom. The basic propositions so far delineated can be briefly recapitulated:

All social inquiry is concerned with values, since the investigator relies on his own values to help him to select his problem, determine his approach, and place his findings in context.

The twin objectives of decreasing inequity in opportunity and income distribution and enlarging the scope for the individual to shape and lead his own life are the hallmarks of social development.

The institutional structures which enable a society to pursue these primary goals cannot be specified once and for all, but must be continually redefined and reformulated in light of each society's experiences.

Critical thought has a unique role to play in these clarifications and redefinitions, including the specification of intermediate goals and the mechanisms to achieve them. A social science which limits itself to tracing how existing institutions function is twice deficient. It fails to contribute to the clarification of goals and thereby helps to reinforce those in place. It further deprives the society of the criticism it needs to make the existing institutions more responsive to a changing reality and changing aspirations.

The human-resources approach emphasizes the time-conditioned nature of all social goals and institutions. No matter how well each has served the society, in a world in which change is endemic, critical thought must be brought into play to help redefine the goals and redesign the institutions so that they can become more responsive to changing circumstances and aspirations.

The processes of manpower development and utilization can be effectively analyzed only within a broad framework that includes four major systems—the value structure, the government, the economy, and the manpower development institutions. The concern of the present chapter is to explore the values that inform these major systems on which a society must rely in its efforts to expand justice and freedom.

We will consider each system in turn.

First, only a society that has reached a certain stage in its development will recognize the desirability of pursuing the ends of expanding justice and freedom. Unless it has reached such a stage of commitment, the ensuing analysis of the reinforcing values that can assist in implementing these objectives is irrelevant.

A second premise relates to the society's basic stance toward experimentation. Unless it looks upon change as more than a threat to its established ways and sees it also as an opportunity to narrow the gap between its goals and their realization, it will hesitate to alter its basic institutions.

Third, a society must be sufficiently sophisticated to appreciate that not every ill that it faces justifies its intervening, that interventions can fail, and that even if they prove successful the initial policies and programs will require modification as experience is accumulated.

Finally, the society must have reached a point in its development where it knows how to temper strong emotions with disciplined analyses in deciding among alternatives by weighing the evidence and seeking a balance between risks and returns.

These, in brief, are the basic conditions that must characterize a society if it is to have a reasonable chance of success in its pursuit of greater justice and freedom. Assuming that they are in place, we can proceed to explore the value orientations that must inform the three other major systems to assure a favorable outcome.

A first requirement of government is that it be capable of eliciting a consensus among its members without resort to violence and under conditions that assure tolerance for an opposition that abides by the rules. A people who live under a government which can arbitrarily deprive them of their lives, their freedom, or their property will plan accordingly and deploy much of their energies and substance to protecting themselves from untoward consequences. Individuals must enjoy reasonable security of person and property if they are not to be diminished in spirit and action.

Government is a precondition for social development. Only through government can men accomplish common objectives that require collective action. If they participate in the selection of those who govern them, they may broaden their freedom by expanding the tasks of government.

Unless they believe that enlarging the scope of government will result in a gain to themselves, they will hesitate to add to its powers. They may err and find that, having enlarged the powers of government, their opportunities have in fact been not broadened, but narrowed. But a citizenry that makes laws can also, on the basis of experience, change them. The critical issue is whether they are able to play an active role in the political process. A government that is chosen and controlled by the electorate is an extension of the individual citizen. Such a government does not stand in opposition to the individual, as a constraining influence on his freedom, but as a collaborator capable of enlarging his opportunities.

If all power were concentrated in the representatives elected by the voters and in the officialdom that operates the state apparatus, there would be reason to fear that those in control of the decision-making mechanisms might sooner or later succeed in pursuing primarily their own interests. The larger the scope of governmental decision making and the more technical the issues being decided, the greater is this danger; witness the difficulties of the legislature, even more those of the public, in attempting to assess alternatives in the arenas of defense, intelligence, scientific research, and nuclear technology. Since effective power depends on many elements—organization, knowledge, money, control of opportunity, and the distribution of rewards and punishments—a society concerned with the enhancement of justice and freedom must prevent the few from gaining control of the levers of power.

If the use of force to gain consensus is proscribed by tradition, the only alternative is persuasion based on freedom of discussion and dissemination of information. Therefore, a critical test of the integrity of government is its approach to communications. If those in power are able to put forward their views and deny this privilege to others, the decisions of the electorate will be uninformed. If men are prevented from hearing opposing opinions and arguments, they are not free to make a meaningful choice. They will be puppets whose opinions and votes are manipulated by those who control the flow of information. Reasonable access for all groups to the communications system is an essential precondition for the proper functioning of a good society.

There is one other foundation of effective government. Every society needs a feedback system which will enable it to alter or reverse earlier decisions. Since the outcomes of social intervention in the form of new laws, new regulations, and new procedures are always problematic, and since the conditions which evoke such intervention are subject to change, it is essential that a society have built-in mechanisms through which it can reappraise the results of earlier actions and decide to continue, modify, or rescind them.

Effective evaluation devices are difficult to institutionalize, since the fortunes of politicians depend on the electorate's approving their earlier actions. Although the circumstances which led those in power to act in a specific fashion may have changed, although too little time may have passed for the new interventions to become fully operative, and although the evidence is inconclusive, the opposition will not be constrained from seeking to persuade the electorate that a governmental program was faulty in conception, in execution, or both. Those in office who recognize their vulnerability will be more interested in keeping damaging data out of the hands of their opponents and the public than in encouraging an objective evaluation, since they know that the electorate will make a decision for or against them long before all the evidence is at hand and sifted. The importance of establishing and maintaining feedback mechanisms for the critical assessment of public policies and programs remains a major challenge to all democratic governments, particularly since officials may seek to rationalize the need for secrecy on the grounds of national security or some similar basis.

The foregoing discussion has directed attention to the powerful value premises that underlie our conception of the role of government in a progressive society. An effective government has the responsibility to:

- Achieve consensus in an environment that proscribes violence and that provides for the participation of all members of the society in different aspects of the decision-making process.
- Prevent concentration of excessive power in the hands of any group and keep access to economic opportunity as open as possible, which will, among other benefits, inhibit the coercion of political dissidents.
- Provide all political groups with reasonable access to the channels of communications to facilitate open and free discussion, the only true basis for meaningful citizen participation.
- Experiment to strengthen feedback mechanisms so that policy and programmatic changes can be made in light of experience.

The value premises by which the functioning of the economic system is to be judged involve no fewer than six distinct criteria spanning a broad range from adequate employment opportunities to a lessened inequality in the distribution of rewards.

A society whose economy fails to provide employment opportunities for all who are able and willing to work falls short of meeting a basic precondition for justice and freedom, since underemployed and unemployed persons often lack sufficient income for sustenance, without which no individual is truly free. Poverty, like racism, can restrict a person's freedom. The availability of work is a first requirement of a properly functioning economy, and as more women seek employment out of the home, a society must strive to make jobs available to all persons who need or desire to work.

Men cooperate in economic activities because they know that, through specialization and scale, they can enjoy more benefits with less effort. A primary challenge to every economy therefore is to develop organizations and mechanisms which will facilitate cooperation among individuals and groups and thus add to the effective use of human and physical resources. The more efficient production and distribution of goods and services remain a basic challenge to the economy.

Important as the criterion of efficiency is, however, it does not stand alone. To elicit the cooperation on which it depends, an economy must be responsive to the demand for equity. Otherwise, those who feel exploited will withhold part of their efforts and will be less productive than they might otherwise be. Analyses of equity are particularly complex in a society which values individual initiative and which approves personal accumulation, since there is no broad agreement about how best to apportion the profits which accrue from an enlarged output that results from the combined contributions of various groups, including workers, managers, and stockholders.

Although equity considerations are complex and do not permit a simple solution, the social scientist dare not ignore them. One of the limitations of economics is that issues of distribution have been neglected or treated in a banal manner. For instance, the dominant view is that every contributor to output is paid according to his marginal contribution, but proof of this generalization is adduced by arguing in a circle and inferring the value of the resource from the reward that it earns.

Another criterion is the ability of the economy to avoid wide fluctuations in activity, since such fluctuations result in the waste of human and physical resources. An important test of the performance of an economy is the size of the gap between its available resources and their effective use.

There are two additional demands which a well-functioning economy should meet. The first is to provide opportunities for the continued growth of the skills and competences of the work force. At forty-five, people should be able to perform more effectively than they did at twenty. The extent to which an economy enables the members of the work force to broaden and deepen their skills and to make effective use of them is a critical measure of its performance.

The final measure of an economy is its effect on the lives of those who spend so many hours on the factory floor or in the office. To neglect the interaction between the worker and the work is to overlook a major segment of a person's life. At the end of every working day, a person's physical, emotional, intellectual, and even moral energies have been consumed, conserved, replenished, or eroded. At the end of every day, a worker has either grown or been diminished. Whether the workday is good or bad should be a matter of concern to the social investigator; its importance cannot be minimized with the comment that, after all, men must work if they are to eat, and work is not to be confused with play. As men escape from living at a precarious margin of subsistence, the question of how they spend their time, particularly their time at work, becomes a critical determinant of the quality of life they lead. A related facet of this new concern extends beyond the workplace to the role that the larger society must play in ensuring that, in increasing current output, the environment is not permanently damaged, for this would place unconscionable costs on later generations.

We have found that the demands on the economy are many and complex. They include:

- The establishment of a sufficient number of jobs so that all who desire and are able to work, women as well as men, have the opportunity to do so.
- Arrangements under which men cooperate in the pursuit of their economic goals which are conducive to efficiency.
- The establishment of equitable rewards for the different contributors to output.
- Freedom from severe fluctuations in the level of economic activity.
- Work so structured that opportunities are available for people to add to their skills and competences.
- Conditions of the workplace that add to rather than detract from the quality of the worker's life.
- The structuring of production and distribution so that social benefits are increased and social costs reduced.

Since the principal aim of this work is to delineate the manpower development system and to explicate its operation, only brief attention will be directed at this point to summarizing the value premises which underlie it.

The family is the cornerstone of the manpower development institutions. Unless parents are able and willing to put forth the effort required to nurture their offspring, their children will not be properly prepared for life and work. If esoteric experiments such as the kibbutz in Israel are put to one side, there is no alternative to leaving the onus on the family as the responsible unit for rearing children. However, there are important differences among societies in the assistance which they provide to the family in its rearing task.

Because families differ in their abilities to meet their responsibilities by virtue of differences in educational background, emotional stability, and economic resources, the developmental opportunities available to their children vary. It has been observed that if a child chooses the right parents, his future will take care of itself. Even in affluent societies many families are unable on their own to rear their young properly. Because of a variety of lacks—competence, health, income, emotional stability—many families need help in raising their children.

Societies with surplus disposable income must use part of it to provide support to parents who need assistance and, on rare occasions, to arrange for the transfer of children to foster homes. Without such help, many children, by accident of birth, will be unable to obtain access to opportunities available to other young people whose parents are able to meet their responsibilities.

Affluent societies must also provide access to educational and training opportunities so that every young person will be able to acquire the general and specific knowledge which is essential to enable him to participate effectively as an adult—as a citizen, a worker, and a parent. Since young people differ markedly in their interest in and ability to master different types of knowledge and in their ability to extract value from different developmental experiences, a responsive society will seek to provide a range of learning opportunities to help meet the needs of each new generation. To try to force all young people into a single mold will ensure that many will not reach adulthood prepared to cope effectively with their responsibilities.

No society to date has succeeded in providing a desirable range of learning opportunities. Each has encountered difficulties on one or more fronts: the provision of adequate facilities, staff, curricula, planning, and experimentation aimed at adapting resources to the needs of different groups of pupils, or adequate articulation between school and employing institutions. To date, no society has met the test of fairness. Each child is entitled not to be arbitrarily cut off from access to opportunities, irrespective of the status and competence of his or her parents. In fact, children whose families are seriously deprived have a special claim for consideration.

Even if a society were to provide more support to disadvantaged families, many young people would complete their adolescence poorly prepared to assume their adult responsibilities. There are just too many places for slippage within the family, between family and school, between school and work, and between rebellious youngsters and the law enforcement authorities to enable all young people to make a smooth transition to adulthood. A responsive society must be concerned not only with the needs of adolescents but also with other groups in the process of transition from one sector to another, such as veterans, persons being released from prison, and patients discharged from long-term hospitals or other therapeutic environments such as drug rehabilitation centers. No society can eliminate failure, but a good society should attempt to provide a second chance for those who fail a first time.

Most people, with the help and guidance of family and friends, are able to negotiate the complex institutions that constitute a modern society. However, the effectiveness with which they do so is influenced by the presence or absence of facilitating mechanisms. Schools without competent guidance and counseling services, a labor market without an effective employment service, and a high-consumption economy without consumer protection agencies will fall short of performing at or close to their optimal levels. Consequently, a society which invests heavily in basic institutions aimed at the effective development and utilization of its human resources should be alert to the necessity of providing informational and related support services so that the public can make more effective use of these institutions. As a society becomes more specialized and the number of its special-purpose institutions increases, the role of informational services which can help link the individual to the ever larger complex of institutions becomes critical.

This summary consideration of the manpower development system stipulated the following:

- The family plays a critical role in rearing its children and in laying the foundations on which their performance in adulthood is based.
- The society must invest a significant part of its disposable income to provide special support for families which are unable, on their own, to assure their children a reasonable start in life.
- The society must underwrite a broadly diversified educational and training system so that it can engage the interests and develop the potential of all youngsters, thereby helping to ensure that they will acquire a range of skills and competences.
- The basic preparatory system must be supplemented by other institutions so that young persons as well as adults who have encountered difficulties have a "second chance."
- The society must collect and disseminate information about the operations of its principal developmental and employment structures, and it must provide counseling and related services so that individuals can better formulate and implement their plans.

Early in this chapter the proposition was advanced that the values which inform the approach of the social scientist determine the problems he or she selects, the methodology employed, and the conclusions for policy which are drawn from the findings. The purpose of this chapter has been to set forth one investigator's views of the values that should guide a dynamic democratic society which seeks to expand the freedom of its members while encouraging their fuller participation in its work and providing equitable rewards for their efforts.

Many social theorists hold values at variance with those just elaborated. Some deny the existence of a moral imperative or the collective competence of a society to enlarge the freedom of its members and to broaden the opportunities for those who are currently deprived. Others place a higher value on social stability or individual opportunity than on the redistribution of rewards and privilege. And many would deny that the social scientist should be concerned with advocacy and change.

However, differences in value premises are not the critical issue here. Rather the contention is advanced that every social investigator has an obligation to set forth his or her value premises so that his analytic structure and policy recommendations can be seen in context. This has been the aim here so that the reader will not have to ferret out for himself the assumptions that underlie this work.

To go one step further: The central concern of this analysis is the critical role of human resources in providing the motive power for the economy and the direction for the society. All institutional arrangements should be designed to further the well-being and welfare of the human beings who, living in association with each other, constitute the society. Of course, many societies, in fact most of them up to this point in time, have not been so oriented but have reflected instead the control of the many by the few. If, as has just been postulated, societies are to be measured by their contribution to improving the quality of life of their members, primary attention must be directed to how well their institutions serve the whole citizenry.

Accordingly, this analysis provides a framework for analyzing the alternative approaches that societies can follow in developing and utilizing the capacities and skills of their members. While human beings are the critical actors in the process of social development, it is their well-being and welfare which are the goals toward which all development is, or should be, directed.

A question that has been skirted until now should be at least briefly confronted. Does the value position put forward here hold only for the democratic–private enterprise economies of the West and Japan, or does it have applicability for nations with quite different social and economic systems? The simplest answer is that the principal criteria used here reflect primarily the experience of the Western world. While important differences attach to what they are seeking to achieve in the near and far term, most of the developing and developed nations alike confront comparable tasks of modifying and changing their governmental, economic, and manpower development systems in order to be better able to accomplish their priority goals. Therefore, the human resources approach has a wide reach. . . .

The final question bears on the potential of a theory of human resources to contribute to public policy. If the analytic framework does in fact provide a new understanding of how skill is developed and utilized, then it should prove useful for policy. All societies, poor as well as rich, expend a significant proportion of their national income on human resources development. Their actions are guided by theory, although in most instances the theory is implicit. This chapter has insisted that social inquiry and social action should be in tandem. Improved theory therefore should contribute to improved policy, although it is only one of the critical elements. To claim more would be naive; to claim less would be to misread the process of social change.

PART II

Career Choice
and Performance Potential

IT IS NOT EASY for a writer to discriminate among his books — to know which were more and which were less successful, and why. I face this tantalizing problem as I seek to place *Occupational Choice: An Approach to a General Theory* in the cycle of my work.

The book was published in 1951. With time it has come to be recognized as the first broad theoretic treatment of the subject. But my collaborators and I were outsiders: an economist, a psychiatrist, a sociologist, and a psychologist.

Inevitably, it created waves: We did not belong to the field; we were critical of the rampant empiricism that dominated this research arena; our skepticism about the role of guidance counselors as agents of social change was upsetting to the leadership. Many years later, when the Rockefeller Brothers Fund gave us a grant to study *Career Guidance*, our far-reaching criticisms about every aspect of the field worsened the earlier strained relationships. It has been our good and bad fortune to have had a major impact on a field, the leaders of which view us at best as interlopers, at worst as unsympathetic critics. We were pleased that we were able to help the field to strengthen its intellectual foundations; we provided a number of leads for subsequent researchers; we called attention to many soft areas in the domain of policy. We have been able to absorb the fact that those who profited most from our work have been generally restive about the book.

A word about the four selections. Chapter 7 is taken from *Occupational Choice*. Recently I was asked to provide a comprehensive autobiographical and critical assessment of our theory, and I have reprinted it here as Chapter 8. In the early 1960s, through funding from the Carnegie Corporation, we returned to the subject of career development among the talented; Chapter 9 is taken from that effort. Chapter 10 comes from *Career Guidance*.

CHAPTER 7

A Developmental Theory
of Occupational Choice

IF THE ACCIDENT THEORY of occupational choice were valid, it would be impossible to study how individuals select their careers. The only reliable investigations would be those based on a statistical analysis of the correlation between significant social and economic changes and the resultant occupational patterns. It would thereby be possible to trace the impact of broad changes in the economy on the choices of successive generations of workers. For instance, the intensification of industrialization and the concomitant mechanization of agriculture during the past decades are reflected in the relative shrinkage of the labor force in manufacturing and mining, and the increase in the service industries, such as transportation, the distribution of goods, and personal services.

Within the last few years, two major environmental changes exercised an important influence on the occupational distribution of the population. The exposure of many millions of young men to military service and the postwar expansion of the Armed Forces have resulted in a marked increase in the numbers following a military career. And the liberal allowances for further education made available to veterans have led many to reappraise their occupational objectives and to change them. The full impact of these environmental changes will be reflected in the occupational pattern of the next decade.

These examples, which could be multiplied, indicate that while a statistical approach to the study of occupational decision making may be important, it would illuminate only certain facets of the problem. It can contribute little, if anything, to an explanation of how a particular individual decides upon an occupation. It does not enable one to understand what work really means to the individual. Further, statistical analysis provides no basis for helping those who have not reached a satisfactory choice.

The advocates of the impulse theory, on the other hand, contend that there is little point in studying the problem with conventional research techniques, particularly through reliance on interviews, since the individual who is making the choice is not conscious of what is determining his behavior. They base this conclusion on their general theory of behavior—that the major determinants are unconscious and therefore unknown to the individual and, equally important, actually outside of his control.

However, although unconscious factors play a role in the behavior of every individual, many forces are in his realm of consciousness and are therefore known to him and subject to his control. One of the interesting findings that emerged from our interviews was that much of the material significant in decision making was never before brought to the surface and discussed. However, it was readily available to the individual, and a few general questions brought it into consciousness. Repeatedly, the persons we interviewed stated that they were amazed at how much they remembered about their occupational choice, especially since up to the time of the interview they had never had an opportunity to discuss the problem in a coherent manner. A first step in rational action is for the individual to outline his problem. A second step is to select the appropriate techniques to resolve it. The statements he makes concerning his problem cannot be dismissed as mere rationalizations unless one were to deny the existence of rational thought and action.

In view of the limitations of both the accident and the impulse theories of occupational choice, we set out to construct a more comprehensive and valid theory. Our basic assumption was that an individual never reaches the ultimate decision at a single moment in time, but through a series of decisions over a period of many years; the cumulative impact is the determining factor. It is important to note why this is so: The actions following a considerable number of decisions are made at great cost and are more or less irrevocable, and this indicates their importance for the future. A young adult goes to college only once; if he decides to major in engineering, it means that except in rare circumstances he cannot become a lawyer or a doctor. After he has devoted four or more years to specializing in one subject, it is expensive in terms of both dollars and emotions to turn his back on his prior decision and enter a new field.

The importance of viewing the choice of an occupation as a chain of decisions can be illustrated by considering the predicament of a man from another planet suddenly confronted with making an occupational choice on this earth. He would have no basis for a rational selection because he would not have the essential knowledge: He would be unable to judge what he would like or dislike about the different types of work available to people here; he would have no knowledge of the rewards or hazards of different types of work. A knowledge of one's own strengths and weaknesses, and of one's likes and dislikes, and a knowledge of the conditions and rewards which attach to various types of work is an outgrowth of living and learning. Hence only those who have been exposed to this world — and who have had an opportunity to live in it and to learn about it — can acquire the information requisite for making a rational choice of occupation.

The relevance of this example becomes clearer if we consider the difficulties actually encountered by those whose living and learning opportunities have been interfered with or who have to make adjustments to a new environment for which their prior training and experience offer little guidance. Immigrants are frequently hesitant and confused about the problem of work, especially if they come to an economy substantially new to them. Much the same confusion is felt by patients who have been hospitalized for long periods of time, as those suffering from tuberculosis. As a matter of fact, this same bewilderment existed for many veterans when they were first demobilized, although so many were affected that it appeared as if the difficulty arose from the readjustment of the economy from war to peace. As part of our larger investigation of "The Conservation of Human Resources," we undertook a preliminary study of the readjustment of one group of veterans — *An Investigation of the Determinants of Occupational Choice among Veterans Aided by the G.I. Bill of Rights*. The common factor in all the cases studied was the individual's difficulty in appraising himself or the alternatives in his environment; yet only on the basis of such appraisals could he make a satisfactory decision.

Convinced that the problem of occupational choice could be understood only as a developmental process in which past behavior exercises the major influence upon present and future decisions, we constructed a framework to facilitate the recognition and evaluation of the significant factors that determine the actions of the individual while he is deciding about his occupational choice. Although a child of six or ten will readily answer the question of what he wants to be when he grows up, obviously he cannot make a firm and definite decision at this age. Lazarsfeld's study of the Viennese working classes indicated that the thirteen-year-olds who were within six months or a year of entering the labor market had at best a very limited understanding of their options. They had little knowledge or understanding even of those vocations with which they came into direct contact: streetcar conductor, butcher, carriage driver, baker, shoe-maker. Lazarsfeld found that these youngsters approached the question by singling out one of the complex factors involved. They were unable to cope with more than one, or at the most two, important variables. They did not yet possess the degree of intellectual and emotional maturity necessary to deal with a multiplicity of factors.

The key to a study of occupational choice appears to lie in an appraisal of the way in which the individual, as he matures, reaches decisions with respect to his eventual occupation. This means that the analysis must follow the way in which he becomes increasingly aware of what he likes and what he dislikes; of what he does well and what he does poorly; the values which are meaningful to him and considerations which are unimportant.

As the individual matures, he becomes aware not only of the forces within himself, but also of the external environment; as he changes, he develops new ways of looking at and appraising those aspects which have a direct bearing on him. Moreover, as he becomes aware of his environment, he begins to exercise increasing control over it. Certainly, his occupa-tional choice is influenced both by the standards of his community and by the impulses deep within himself. Our approach proceeds on the assumption that it is desirable, at least initially, to concentrate on how he reacts to these forces which he seeks to manipulate for the purpose of reaching the most desirable decision.

In developing our framework, we were particularly concerned to devise a method that would take account of the multiple factors, both subjective and objective, involved in the occupational decision making of individuals. We have called attention to the limitations of prior investi-gations of narrow focus as, for instance, studies of the influence of the fathers' occupations on the occupational decision making of their sons, or the influence of interest patterns on occupational choices. Because we found it impossible to analyze the process when only two factors were selected, we took particular care to develop a framework broad enough to encompass all the forces at work, other than those deep in the unconscious. There is perhaps no better way of emphasizing the multiplicity of factors that are likely to be operative than to present a complete interview of a college freshman, aged nineteen, who, it should be noted, was somewhat more mature than his classmates. The interviewer's questions are in parentheses.

INTERVIEW OF ROBERT

(Why Columbia?)

I don't live too far away—Scarsdale—had contacts with Columbia; my father went here, and I realized what a fine school it was. It was always my ambition and desire to go. My father is in the Alumni Association—belongs to Columbia Club in New York. Quite a few friends are Columbia grads and I never considered going any place else. No, I didn't apply to another school. Sent a preliminary application to two others but didn't follow up after I found out I was accepted at Columbia. Lafayette, and I've forgotten the other school. Had a teacher in high school that went here—history teacher—that's my field of major interest. He thought Columbia was the finest possible school along those lines—it was the place to really come and learn about the subject. He spoke in glowing terms about it. I always admired his way of teaching and I'd like to learn a little of what he knows.

In my last year in high school I started doing something about getting in. I was a little anxious—was led to believe it was impossible to get in any place. They were all overemphasized reports. I indicated that I was possibly prelaw but revised that opinion after consideration and realized that I might as well make my major work along lines of major interest and not something I'm not even interested in. It's a correlation between burning desires and ambitions and how to make a living. Like to get into political science—very interested in it. I looked through a catalogue and did some wishful thinking in comparison to courses I'm taking now. That was in the faculty of political science—history, sociology, anthropology, psychology. I want a complete background—the beginning of a broad vista—not sure where it's going to lead me. History and government is my major. It's a firmly considered opinion now. Thought of it since I've been here.

Gave up law because I was never overly interested in it. Several of my friends just can't wait to get in. It's a long three years and I can't see going into it unless I can be like that. Selected it in the first place because my father is a lawyer and I worked in a law office several summers. My father didn't say he wanted me to be a lawyer but he would be pleased if I were and would go into his firm but I have discarded that idea.

I've been interested in history as far back as I can remember; back to my grammar school days. Did quite a bit of reading but never as much as I would like to. I do well in the social sciences—far better than in the natural sciences. Realized that in my early high school years. After graduation I'd like to take some graduate work and after that I don't know. Possibly teaching or going into the government in some way. Not quite defined in my mind. I have a friend graduating in June, a history and government major, and he is taking a job in Washington in administrative planning in foreign relations. That's just an example. But I don't really know enough about it.

I'm led on by things I'm adapted for and interested in and have a talent for. After I have a lot more experience with courses, I will probably know better. Going to discuss Monday my proposed program with my adviser—government and history courses—after a semester of that I will be a little surer of where I'm going and maybe I might not be until I'm almost getting out but I can adapt the training to something specific after. Pretty certain I'm going to graduate school.

My parents say that if I am sure, it's all right with them. Haven't talked it over extensively. They are pleased enough.

Mother doesn't do anything. Have a younger sister. Father likes his work very much. It's not something he puts on and puts off. He lives it when he's working, when he's home. He's content. It's work and a hobby both. Law and he have become one and I can't see that happening to me. That's one of the things I can't see happening to myself in law, but I can in history and government because it's always been that way for a fairly good number of years. It always remained a major interest.

(What do you want to get out of work?)

Satisfaction. Personal satisfaction. Not great financial return. Satisfaction that I am accomplishing something, doing a job. Feeling that I am creating something after there's been enough menial work put in. Creativity might mean that I had improved something or completely revised some theories, or put something into practice or got out something and made it more workable. That's the crying need today. Making certain ideas more practicable in government. Maybe I can do that after training and experience.

I get fun out of working only in some things. It's a distinct chore to do something I don't like, like German, geology, humanities. Get nothing out of it. It's the unfavorable conditions of the humanities course. The rush is fantastic. I'm licked before I start. If I didn't have things that I was really interested in waiting for me, I'd have no fun. Instead I'm reading humanities. I get fun out of Contemporary Civilization Course but lack of time causes me to read about two thirds of the assignments. But I do definitely enjoy the assignments and classes because I have a dynamic and wonderful instructor— Professor H. It's a wonderful thing to sit and listen to him when he gets going.

The time I spend studying varies from nothing to all. Typical week: about three hours every night and maybe one hour in the afternoon. Maybe that's a little overgenerous. Spend hours in discussions, important and unimportant, with my friends and in the last month or so have been spending some time with a girl friend whom I met down here living on campus. Go out usually once on week ends. If my work is up I go out the entire week end and am only in my room to change my clothes. Other times I work far into the night. If it's a choice between going out and studying, it depends on the circumstances. If it's something important, I go. Studying is waiting somewhere in the indefinite future. I expect to carry out my occupational choice without difficulty because when I do get into it, I have nothing that will be distracting. Everything will be of great interest and there won't be any blocks before I start. I hate that. In any procrastination a large part of it is subconscious. A hating to get started. That will be eliminated.

(What would make you change your occupation choice?)

A change of heart would be the main thing. If I found that I really wasn't as crazy about these things or as apt or that I couldn't get anywhere with these studies. A change of heart would be the most important thing. Don't think anything else could.

(Marriage?)

I think that the work is more important and we both realize that — the girl is interested in the same things that I am interested in. She goes to Barnard and majors in history and government herself. We have a great common ground. She would realize that the life-time thing is more important. I don't think that after waiting two years, we would be unable to wait more. We would have conditioned ourselves.

(Work you'd never do?)

Engineering, medicine, anything mathematical, and I would never be a professional soldier or bus driver or bartender. It's a strange array. Professional soldiering is such a limited life and boils down to nothingness. They are getting no place. They never arrive anywhere particularly in their life. Almost all of them that I have known are bound up in small and petty things and never see over protocol. Seemed like a very pointless existence. Of course, I hear that the Army is changing all that and becoming the "men of the future" but I don't know. Bartending just popped into my head as a joke. It might be a bit more attractive than other things, in fact, I might very well like to be a bartender — talk to all kinds of people.

(Your idea of success?)

That I was happy in my work. That I had made advancement in the effectiveness of my work. Made some concrete advancement in my position. Received promotion. Wouldn't get somewhere and stay that way all my life. Money — just enough. I'm not out for money. I'd never be interested in a lot of money. Just enough to live comfortably.

Wouldn't go back to live in Scarsdale. Too many empty people in that town just stuck on their means. Probably live in a city — New York, Detroit, Washington.

Starting out I'd be satisfied with a fairly small income and if it gradually expanded to small home, be able to own a car, able to take a three-week or month vacation in the summer, send my children to school, have a few dollars for entertainment, I'd consider having enough.

For a long time I had no set occupational choice. This is the first time in my life that I have said with any degree of emphasis what I want to do. When I was eight years old, I wanted to be a Packard motor-car salesman because the people across the street owned a yellow one that was very nice. If I were a salesman, maybe it would mean I would have Packards. When I was 10–11, I wanted to live in Maine and do something up there in a hotel connected with the tourist trade. Liked the peaceful life and the country. Then I was interested in politics and thought I would like to get into the swirl and tumult of politics but that would be going against a lot of things I believe in as principles, I realized. I'd hate to have to stoop down and throw a lot of mud. I never realized I wanted to make history my work but it was always a real interest and goes back to the fourth grade. The very successful teaching of a very charming woman who is still a very good friend of mine helped me. When I was taking ancient history about three years ago it crystallized. During my high school years I talked to this teacher, Mr. M., about it.

Actually I haven't decided until the past two weeks. I'm thinking of teaching. Can't say that I may teach — just don't know. When I get on further I'll have to see what kinds of grades I get. You have to be Phi Beta Kappa or near it to get a responsible position in college teaching. If I find I satisfy myself by not getting all A's I will discard teaching in college. High school teaching isn't broad enough. You teach the same thing over and over to group after group of kids. I suppose that proves I haven't a real interest in teaching. I'd like college teaching. It's hard to put myself in all these places. Can't put my ideas across yet. I'd be completely unnerved by forty eager and wolfish guys ready to tear me down. (Remarked that he feels conscious of slang because he's speaking for the record.)

Don't know about the conditions of work really so I hesitate to define my bent. I need the information and I'll ask people, certain professors who understand the situation here.

I've earned money in the summer working as a law clerk. Went to law courts, etc. The early part of law is very uncreative and much like drudgery, running around delivering briefs and serving summonses and looking up material in law books. Unless you're wrapped up in it, it's not very interesting. After you're successful, like trying a case or writing a brief, it's very interesting. It's taking a background and working all those things into a weapon for proving something or other. Some lawyers never try cases. My father is a trial lawyer and his partner is not. Even with my father, it's not a major part of his work; maybe one third of his time is spent trying cases or in courtrooms.

Two weeks ago I wouldn't have had this so crystallized. For one thing I have been undergoing a lot of emotional strain since February 1. I have been in a perpetual state of disruption. Every man has a fair amount of problems and I was very tired from the term just ending, and for one thing I became involved amorously, and—well—I know it's trite—but it "affects me as no one else has been affected." It's a great flood tide of emotions and it stirred everything up. Everything was moving and I suddenly felt that everything was well defined. Spent several weeks of torment, couldn't sleep, couldn't eat. Was stimulated from all sides. The people you live with here are wonderful, unusual people. It all came to fruition at once with the emotional side of it too, and I realized that it was what I was down here for. That interests everyone's mind when they look into the place. Finally, I realized there's one type of thing I am attracted to and capable of being successful in and want to be a part of. Of necessity, finally, I had the strength to realize what I want and what I can have. I think I'll be happy. It was there in the background but from February 1 until now I have thought about it. I am, firstly, unofficially engaged and, secondly, I know what I am going to concentrate on here. A lot of things are more ordered in my mind than I have expressed. The component parts have always been there.

A relatively few questions were needed to stimulate Robert to tell his story and to bring a great wealth of materials to the surface, not only about his present approach to his occupational choice, but about his past behavior and the possibility of changes in the future.

The questions were aimed to elicit information about each of the major areas of experience that were likely to have had a significant influence on occupational choice. Before we started to interview, we developed a category scheme to facilitate the analysis of the materials in terms of "the self," "reality," and "key persons."

Under *the self* we were concerned with materials which dealt first with the question of capacities. When does an individual first take cognizance of his strengths and weaknesses and to what extent does he make a choice on the basis of his capacities? Does he ever give up a tentative choice because he recognizes that he does not possess the required capacity?

Next was the problem of interests. To what extent does the individual predicate his choice on a strong interest? Have his interests changed in the past and does he contemplate that they might change again in the future? Is there a connection between his interests and his capacities?

Third, we were interested in goals and values, particularly those which are closely related to work and the rewards from work. Does the individual hope to make a lot of money? Is he concerned with finding a job which will enable him to use his capacities and interests and thereby yield him a heightened degree of work satisfaction? Is he insistent on following a particular path in life—such as farming—and is he willing to make the necessary adjustments to achieve his goal?

Finally, under this category we were concerned with the time perspective of the individual. At what point in the choice process does he become aware of such considerations as the length of the training process, the possibility that he will marry in the early twenties, the probability that his interests may still change? Thus, under the major category of "the self," we organized materials relating to capacities, interests, values and goals, and time perspective.

The next major category was *reality*. Under this heading we included first the influence of the family as a social and economic unit. Is the young person determined to earn as much money as his father? To what extent does he take it for granted that the family will cover all of his educational expenditures? Does he feel any special need to plan his life so as to discharge an important familial responsibility, such as, for instance, to aid his younger brothers and sisters to go to college? Education is an important reality consideration. To what extent does the individual relate his plans of a career to the choice of a college and, more particularly, to the choice of a major subject in college? Does he take account of specific educational hurdles, such as the difficulty of gaining admission to medical school? Perhaps most important of the reality considerations is an evaluation of the workaday world. What does a boy really know about the economy, the range of desirable jobs, and the advantages and disadvantages of each? Clearly, he could not proceed very far in planning realistically about his choice without reference to these factors. Although work is usually the central activity of adulthood, it can be greatly influenced by the type of "life plan" evolved. Among the important reality factors subsumed under the term "life plan" is the desire of the individual to marry early or late and to have a large or small family. These, then, were the principal subcategories under "reality"— family, education, world of work, and life plan.

The third major category was *key persons*. There was clear indication in our preliminary interviews that almost every individual is influenced in resolving various aspects of his choice by the help which he seeks from key persons or the pressures which key persons exert on him. Parents are frequently found to play a strategic part in the choice process. At other times it is a relative, teacher, or friend.

This category scheme served as a structure for the analysis of each one of our cases. It might be helpful to indicate its use by evaluating our interview with Robert. With reference to his capacities Robert commented that he "does well" in the social sciences, that he feels he has a talent for these subjects; however, he is not sure that he could obtain a responsible college teaching job, which he believes requires grades of a "Phi Beta Kappa level." He points out that he is a little at a loss to convey his ideas. Of one thing he is sure, however, and that is that he wants to work only in a field in which he has the capacity to do well.

In talking about his interests, he stated that he gave up the study of law because of a lack of interest and chose political science because of a strong interest. He believes that he will continue in this field because he expects his interest to be permanent, and adds that he would only change his occupational choice if he "had a change of heart." He knows there are certain fields that he would never enter because of a lack of interest; and he thinks that it is important for a person to be "all wrapped up" in his subject if he is really to enjoy it.

Robert knows that he does not want to do uncreative work, which to him would be pure drudgery; he would like to "accomplish something" and to move ahead. He feels that if he were successful in this he could get real satisfaction out of his work. He wants to earn a living but is not primarily concerned with making a lot of money. At one point he indicates that his principles would make it difficult for him to engage in politics because of the mud-slinging which would be involved. Such are his values and goals.

Robert indicates clearly the importance of time perspective for the occupational decision-making process. He points out that he reacted negatively to the law because of the need for three years of preparation in law school and because the early years as a law clerk seldom offer interesting assignments. For a long time Robert had no firm occupational plans, but during the last few weeks they became crystallized. He does not anticipate any real difficulties in carrying out his present plans.

There do not seem to be any powerful familial pressures on Robert. He recognizes that his father would prefer to have him join his firm, but apparently his negative decision did not create major tensions. As far as the educational influences are concerned, Robert plans to get some help from his professors in resolving particular problems connected with his occupational choice. He makes allowance in his planning for the possibility of additional training and experience, including the pursuit of graduate studies.

Robert has rather diversified reactions to the working environment as he knows it. He calls attention to one friend who has recently gone into governmental work. He thinks that the Army may no longer be as uninteresting an environment in which to work as it was in former days. Robert will not consider high school teaching because he feels that the challenge would not be broad enough for him. He is sufficiently acquainted with the law to know that some lawyers never try cases. As a casual comment, he indicates that he could even contemplate becoming a bartender because of the opportunity which this would afford him to talk with people, which he enjoys, but in this he is not really serious.

The interview with Robert took place a very short time after he had undergone a major emotional crisis which had culminated in his becoming engaged. He recognizes that this major decision about his future life has had much to do with crystallizing his occupational choice. He also appreciates that as far as the planning of his future is concerned, his fiancée is important and he underlines this by stating that she has agreed to postpone their marriage until after both have completed their education.

The strategic role played by key persons is well illustrated in Robert's recital of the way in which his occupational choice developed. He points out that his choice of a college was influenced by the fact that his father is an alumnus of Columbia. He talks with warm feeling about his high school teacher. He plans to consult with his professors about his proposed program. He is aware that his parents approve in general of the way in which he is handling his problem. And, as we have mentioned, he knows that his future will be influenced by the attitudes and reactions of his fiancée.

In this analysis of Robert's interview, no attempt has been made to explain every statement; rather, a selection was made of the major factors in his decision making. The example supports our contention that only a broad framework can do justice to the problem. We found it possible to work with three major factors—the self, reality, and key persons—and with eight subcategories: capacities, interests, values, and time perspective making up the self; family, environment, world of work, and life plan making up reality. This framework made it possible to order the rich materials. Establishing the interrelations among these several factors can provide a firm basis for a theory of occupational choice.

CHAPTER 8

Ginzberg's Theory:
A Retrospective View

ONE–THIRD OF A CENTURY has passed since my colleagues—Sol W. Ginsburg, M.D.; Sidney Axelrad; and John L. Herma—and I first presented the outlines of our theory of occupational choice to the annual meeting of the American Orthopsychiatric Association in 1949. Thirty-one years ago, our book, *Occupational Choice: An Approach to a General Theory*, was published by Columbia University Press. I regret to report that none of my collaborators—a psychiatrist-psychoanalyst, a sociologist, and a psychologist–lay analyst, respectively—is still alive; each died in his late fifties or early sixties.

I have devoted the last three decades to intensive research in human resources and medical economics, and my inability to check out this reconstruction with those who played critical roles in the formulation of what has come to be known as Ginzberg's theory must be kept in purview by the reader. Time may add perspective, but it surely blurs, if it does not completely erase, events of an earlier period. In preparing this chapter, I reread *Occupational Choice* and found many facts and formulations that I had forgotten and much else that I only vaguely remembered. But enough remains sharp and clear to justify this effort at reconstruction, particularly since I returned briefly to the subject in writing a note on life-styles, in reformulating our theory at the request of Van Hoose and Pietrofesa in 1970 and again in a more fundamental fashion at the request of the editor of the *Vocational Guidance Quarterly* in 1972,[1] and in publishing in 1979 some notes to supplement views advanced by Donald Super about the origins of our respective works.

Most students of occupational choice are psychologists. It is important, therefore, that I emphasize that my discipline is economics and that my interest in occupational choice derived directly from antecedent research into human resources—specifically, studies of the long-term unemployed in South Wales and New York City—which put into sharp relief the extent to which work exercised a compelling influence over the lives of individuals (especially men) and over their communities. In 1940 I sought and obtained funding from the Rockefeller Foundation to pursue inquiries into "the choice of and adjustment to work." The first product of this research was completed before World War II interrupted our work. By the time I returned to Columbia in the fall of 1946, the Rockefeller Foundation was no longer supporting individual research workers, and I began a complex process of negotiating support from the Columbia University Council for Research in the Social Sciences. One facet of this process warrants recounting.

Professor Paul Lazarsfeld had a negative response to the modest case study I had outlined. He sought to persuade me to undertake a large-scale statistical investigation and even obtained for me a feasibility grant from the council. Fortunately, Abraham Wald, one of the great contributors to modern statistics, and Robert Morrison MacIver, the distinguished Columbia sociologist to whom *Occupational Choice* is dedicated, encouraged me to hold fast to a simpler approach. The feasibility study revealed that a large-scale quantitative study would be excessively costly. My recollection is that the council eventually made a grant of $4,500 for *Occupational Choice*. Neither the psychiatrist nor I drew any salary, and our collaborators were paid only token amounts.

Nevertheless, there was a positive outcome to this drawn-out and not always pleasant negotiation. I had the opportunity to learn from Lazarsfeld about his earlier work in the field, in which he had shifted the strategic question from *why* young people pick an occupation to *how*.

Let me note that the Columbia research program in human resources, which got under way in 1939 and which I have directed from its beginning, was a second-best choice. My mentor, Professor Wesley Clair Mitchell, and I had selected as the theme for a graduate seminar on economic theory and economic change the modernizing of economics through the infusion of contemporary psychological thought. The effort failed. At that point, Mitchell persuaded me to start empirical research into the behavioral aspects of economics, and the willingness of Dr. Sol Ginsburg to join forces with me got us started. Mitchell's prestige was such that the psychologists on the council did not raise objections to interlopers from economics and psychiatry when we made our initial request for research assistance.

In an early effort to help us find our way, we asked my colleague at Teachers College, Donald Super, to undertake a critical review of the literature. Section IV of the Bibliography in *Occupational Choice* contains seventy titles he reviewed, but in fact we were still at sea after reading his appraisal. He had been unable to clarify the conceptual underpinnings that guided the investigations he reviewed, because most of the studies had no theoretical foundation.

We continued to flounder until Sidney Axelrad brought John Herma into our group. As I have recounted elsewhere,[2] Herma, a pupil of Karl and Charlotte Buehler and Jean Piaget, suggested that we adopt a modified genetic approach, long favored by the Vienna school, and that we study occupational choice as a developmental process. We began to experiment with Herma's suggestion and soon found that it provided us with the handle for which we had been searching.

In our preliminary efforts to uncover the strategic aspects of the process of occupational choice, we used several modest probes. The first was focused on the impact of a major change in the macroenvironment on the choice process. We reviewed the occupational adjustment of 1,000 Army selectees who had served their one-year terms and were released from military service in the fall of 1941. We felt the experience of a young man who had been uprooted from civilian life to serve twelve months in the military, and then was returned to civilian life, would often lead him to reopen his occupational choice. We found, however, that for many, particularly skilled workers, the temporary uprooting resulted in little occupational change.

Our second approach was to consider the relation of college education to the occupational adjustment of a group of graduates from one of the prestigious Seven Sister colleges. This investigation threw into high relief many inadequacies in the curriculum, counseling, and placement activities of this distinguished woman's college with a superior student population. Most of the women we studied entered gainful employment after graduation, though in low-level jobs, and many remained at work for only a short time.

Our third effort, aimed at advancing our understanding of the role of emotional factors in the choice process, involved tapping into the experiences of a group of psychoanalysts in an effort to learn what their analysands reported about the factors influencing occupational choices.

To our surprise, the analysts told us they heard very little that was of interest.

Our fourth and final approach involved young men who opted for the ministry, a career not fully congruent with the dominant values of our society. Although religious and value considerations turned out to loom large in their decisions, we also learned that for many, especially those entering Protestant or Jewish seminaries, subsidized education and the prospect of a reasonable livelihood and status were strong motivating factors. Placed in context, their choice of the ministry was not aberrant.

By the end of these probes we were reasonably sure of the following: Neither the accident nor the impulse theory had much intellectual validity; and, although we had learned from Super's survey that many vocational practitioners used some implicit theory, we were unable to specify the critical elements and, further, realized that no two practitioners necessarily used the same theory.

One more introductory observation: Ours was a truly interdisciplinary team with representatives from four disciplines—economics, psychiatry, sociology, and psychology. In a world of academic and professional specialization, it is not easy to get four researchers to downplay their own disciplines in favor of a larger integrated approach. I believe that my success in persuading not only these early collaborators but all who came later of the value of an integrated, policy orientation to research in human resources has been the key ingredient to our collective productivity. It is not easy to build good interdisciplinary research teams; but if the effort succeeds, the prospects of success are increased.

PRESENTATION OF THE THEORY

My collaborators and I were driven by a search for understanding. We were sure that, as Freud had observed, work is one of two foundation stones for a healthy life—love is the other. But we had learned from our exploratory efforts that we did not know how people make their occupational choices. This search for understanding was the beginning and the end of our efforts to develop a theory of occupational choice. Although our concern with policy implications was never far distant, analysis rather than policy was the driving force.

Our approach, once Herma joined us, clarified quickly. We decided to interview young men from an affluent subsection of the population (with optimal degrees of freedom to choose) and planned to compare their thinking and actions about their occupational choices at key points in their educational-maturational process from childhood through young adulthood. Through open-ended interviewing and careful analysis of what the respondents told us, we were able to distinguish three major periods in the choice process—fantasy, tentative, and realistic; and, further, to distinguish several stages within the tentative and realistic periods, which we designated as follows: in the tentative period, covering roughly the years from eleven to eighteen—years during which young people move through junior and senior high school—we identified four stages— interest, capacity, value, and transition. In the realistic period, there are three stages—exploration, crystallization and specification—covering the years when a young person is in college, in graduate school, or first beginning to work.

The following provides some further insights into the developmental nature of our theory by considering the several stages in the two critical periods, tentative and realistic. During the tentative period, we find the young person steadily broadening his consideration of the elements underlying his emerging choice. At first his *interests* serve as the major (often the sole) basis for his choice. But with the passage of time, new elements intervene: The young person becomes aware that his interests are changing, and new ones emerge; equally, if not more important, he begins to consider whether his *capacities* are congruent with his interests. He realizes that he must consider his capacities in arriving at a choice.

At fifteen or sixteen a new element comes to the fore: The young person first becomes aware that he must order the importance he attaches to his emerging *values,* such as autonomy in work, making money, having a lot of free time, being able to travel. As he sorts out which values are most important to him, he will slough off certain tentative choices and be driven toward others as he seeks a better fit.

For the college-bound, the last stage of the tentative period— transition—and the first stage of the realistic period—exploration—offer the young person a renewed opportunity to reopen the occupational choice process in light of his growing maturity and the opportunities that will become available to him during college and possibly graduate school. A tilting occurs during these *tentative-exploratory* stages from the highly subjective realm of interests, capacities, and values to a growing concern with the opportunities and limitations set by reality, such as the years of study required to qualify as a physician, the differences in earnings between a journalist and a business executive, the advantages and disadvantages of becoming a teacher or a government official.

The core decision making during the realistic period involves the stage of *crystallization,* when the individual is finally able to synthesize the many forces, internal and external, that are relevant to his or her decision about occupational choice. Time pressures, such as having to select a

major field, contribute to closure. Many find the challenge of crystallization onerous and, reluctant to make a premature commitment, seek to
delay it. Sooner or later, however, educational-employment pressures
force them into a decision.

The final stage of the realistic period was designated by the term
specification. The young engineer, chemist, economist, all of whom have
moved through the process of crystallizing their occupational choices,
now must decide whether they prefer to work in the private or public
sector, in research or in operations, for a small or a large employer.

This framework of periods and stages enabled us to inflict order and
extract meaning from our interviews. We postulated that when a youngster of five says he wants to be a fireman or a policeman he is responding
to some charged element in the adult role with which he identifies. We
grouped such early "choices" under the rubric *fantasy* because they clearly
did not reflect mature deliberations. A boy of five, the son of a banker or
physician, may be impressed by the policeman on the beat—but he is
unlikely to become a policeman.

The maturational principle is critical during the *tentative period,*
when young people become increasingly aware not only of their interests
and capacities but also, later, of their emerging values, all of which must
be weighed as they move toward some and away from other tentative
choices.

At the time they enter college—and our basic sample was composed
of young people who were definitely college-bound or in college—they
have an opportunity to reconsider their tentative choices and renew their
explorations. But sometime, usually by their junior or senior year and
often before, they are under increasing pressure because of age, curriculum choices, peers, parental concern, matured interests, and other forces
to move toward crystallization. At a later point, in professional school or
soon after they begin to work, they are likely to take a further step and
specify their choice by moving from medicine to surgery, from physics to
solid-state physics, from engineering to electrical engineering, from
economics to banking.

At the beginning of Chapter 13 of *Occupational Choice,* "The Basic
Elements of the Theory," the following summary formulation appears:

- The outstanding conclusion from our findings is that occupational choice is a developmental process—not a simple decision
  but a series of decisions made over a period of years. Each step
  in the process has a meaningful relation to those that precede
  and follow it.
- The process is largely irreversible, because each decision made
  during the process is dependent on the chronological age and

development of the individual. Time cannot be relived; basic
education and other exposures can be experienced only once.

- The process ends in a compromise. A series of factors, both internal and external, affect his decision. He must renounce to
  some degree the satisfactions he might derive if he based his
  choice exclusively on a strong interest, a marked capacity, or a
  realistic opportunity. He must find a balance among the major
  elements—hence the element of compromise in every occupational choice.

- The basic elements in our theory of occupational choice, then,
  are three: *it is a process; the process is largely irreversible; compromise
  is an essential aspect of every choice.*

As noted earlier, our basic sample was constructed exclusively from
among males from upper-income families, of Protestant or Catholic
backgrounds, to minimize the distortions of discrimination, which were
still prevalent shortly after the end of World War II. But we did not limit
ourselves to this one group. We supplemented our mainline analysis
with two additional groups, males of high school age from low-income
families and a small group of college women, in order to get some first
impressions about how parental income and gender influence the choice
process.

In brief, we found that the basic developmental stages held for both
groups, but we noted that among youths from low-income homes, the
decision-making process gave the appearance of being "passive and
stunted." After all, most entered the job market at eighteen, if not before,
and they did so with little prior planning and limited expectations of
being able to guide their own destinies. In the case of the college women,
the process was not markedly different from that of their male counterparts,
except that concerns about marriage became important in their planning
as they approached the end of their undergraduate studies. We thought
we could distinguish three subgroups: those who were marriage-oriented,
those who were work-oriented, and those who hoped to combine both.

These two ancillary investigations into the occupational choice process
of young men from low-income families and a small subgroup of college
women from upper-income homes were modest, and we did not draw
broad conclusions from these efforts. From the outset, our study of
occupational choice had been designed and carried out among a relatively small group in the total population—males born and brought up
in families with above-average incomes, whose fathers were often professionals and many of their mothers had graduated from college. The
young men we interviewed knew from their early years that they would
go to college, and before then many would have the opportunity to

attend superior private schools. Moreover, they were under little or no family or other pressures to make early decisions about what they would study and what they would eventually choose for a career. In short, we chose to study a subgroup in the population that had the broadest opportunity to make whatever choices they wanted with respect to their future careers.

We did not have the time, the resources, or even the inclination to broaden our investigation to include a great many other groups whose choice processes we suspected would be much more under the domination of reality constraints: Jews, who still suffered from considerable discrimination with respect to admission to elite colleges and to certain preferred occupations; blacks, who, weighed down by centuries of slavery, segregation, and discrimination, were hard pressed to find their way in a white society that hemmed them in at every turn; and, particularly, young men and women from families with modest or low incomes who would find it difficult to prolong their preparation for a career beyond high school. We knew that our design, whatever its heuristic value, did not permit us to generalize our findings to groups that did not share the advantages that characterized those included in our major sample.

In the decades following the publication of our theory my colleagues and I continued under the aegis of the Conservation of Human Resources Project, Columbia University, a broad program of research into human resources and manpower, many of which investigations broadened and deepened our understanding of occupational choice and work adjustment. The most important of these later investigations, all published by the Columbia University Press and of which I was the senior author, included:

- *The Uneducated*
- *The Negro Potential*
- *Patterns of Performance,* Volume III of *The Ineffective Soldier: Lessons for Management and the Nation*
- *Talent and Performance*
- *Life Styles of Educated Women*
- *The Middle-Class Negro in the White Man's World*

When I presented a broad restatement of our theory of occupational choice in the *Vocational Guidance Quarterly* in the early 1970s, I paid particular attention to the findings that had emerged from our research. We had learned a great deal in the intervening two decades, and the *Restatement* represented not a minor but a major reformulation.

The initial version of the theory had been constructed around the concepts of process, irreversibility, and compromise. My colleagues and I had assumed that the process of occupational choice came to closure in young adulthood, around the time a person enters his first regular job. Our reformulation no longer considers the process to be confined to a period from early adolescence to early adulthood, but rather as one that is coextensive with a person's working life. I identified three factors in this lifelong choice process: the feedback between the original choice and later work experience. If the original choice did not lead to the anticipated satisfactions, the individual was likely to reopen the choice process, which in turn would be conditioned and influenced by the degrees of freedom permitted by family circumstances and the economy. The contributions of other co-workers, Dale L. Hiestand's *Changing Careers after 35*[3], and two books by Dean Morse and others, *Early Retirement: Boon or Bane?*[4] and *Life after Early Retirement: The Experiences of Nonsupervisory Personnel*[5], provide documentation that the occupational choice process can be reopened not only in a person's mature years but, most interestingly, even after retirement from a long-term career.

I also found it necessary to modify the concept of irreversibility. Although the early decisions a young person makes usually delimit his options, they are not necessarily determining later on. What happens to a person before he reaches twenty will affect his career, but he retains considerable scope for later decision making. In fact, the major challenge young people face is to pursue a strategy in their late teens and early twenties that does not close off the choice process prematurely. Moreover, many who do not go on to college will end up in jobs and careers that have more to do with the opportunities they uncover in the employment arena than with the courses they took or the marks they received in school.

The third building block of our theory, the concept of *compromise*, also required revision in light of our later research. Although an element of compromise unquestionably is present in every person's occupational choice, an improved formulation replaces compromise by *optimization*. Men and women seek to find the best fit between their changing interests and goals and their changing circumstances. In short, emphasis is shifted from a one-time compromise to a lifelong dynamic.

Reformulated, this is how the restatement came out: *Occupational choice is a lifelong process of decision making in which the individual constantly seeks to find the optimal fit between career goals and the realities of the world of work.*

With the benefit of an additional decade's research, I would now make a further modification: *Occupational choice is a lifelong process of decision making for those who seek major satisfactions from their work. This leads them to reassess repeatedly how they can improve the fit between their changing career goals and the realities of the world of work.*

Taking into consideration the costs of shifting to new careers, these emendations, improvements, nay, corrections of our original theory, first developed in 1951, still conceive of occupational choice as a process, in which the early decisions an individual makes will restrict his later scope of action, and in which, as with all adult decisions, the individual will make a choice that will represent a balance among competing interests and values in which reality considerations are important.

I leave it to the reader to decide whether the previously published restatement and the one just formulated represent a major or a minor gloss on our 1951 theory. I like to believe the original theory illuminated much that had hitherto been clouded, but our research over the last three decades has led us to a greater understanding of the decision-making process. Although I followed in varying degrees the work of the other theorists reviewed in this book, my own research program was so demanding that I never acquired a critical mastery of their work, which, had I done so, might have led me to further modifications of our theory.

EMPIRICAL SUPPORT

The spine of our original study consisted of ninety-one interviews, exclusive of the additional number of children, young people, and adults whom we interviewed during our many months of exploring what questions to ask and seeking to determine the preferred ages at which to interview them. The question of how large a sample was needed to reach valid conclusions about the determinants of occupational choice was not easily resolved. Lazarsfeld, with his quantitative predilections, had pressed hard for a study that would contain many hundreds of subjects. He believed a smaller number would lead to misinterpretations because of the variability among the multiple elements that play a part in the decision making of different individuals.

It seemed to me at the time, and since, however, that there is a necessary sequencing in the design of research projects in which concept clarification must precede statistical testing. Unless we were able to bring preliminary order into the arena, there was little point in adding one more empirical study.

It is difficult for me to report on the studies stimulated by the publication of *Occupational Choice.* Donald Super and Albert Thompson of Teachers College, who were pursuing related investigations, sent me students, most of whom went on to write dissertations on the subject of occupational choice. I tried to be helpful, and I sat in on their examinations. But the relationship was not easy, since the Teachers College faculty insisted on tight experimental designs with statistical findings that could be achieved in most instances only at the cost of narrowing the questions to a point where I lost interest.

Nevertheless, some of my students reported that a steady stream of articles and studies were appearing that had been directly stimulated by our work—investigations aimed at checking, broadening, correcting, revising the theory we had formulated—but I made no attempt to keep abreast of these developments.

I have reviewed four articles in order that the reader be alerted to how selected researchers have dealt with our theory explicitly or how their findings corroborated or contradicted our major contributions.[6] In retrospect, we were overly venturesome to use as a subtitle "Approach to a General Theory" with fewer than 100 interviews as our basic sample. But we believed that what the field needed above all was a theoretical foundation. That we sought to provide with our three-period, seven-stage framework.

I was not surprised to find that the four contributions I reviewed uncovered shortcomings in our formulation. More surprising, and most gratifying, is the wide area within which later research was broadly supportive of our approach and conclusions.

The four articles focus on the following critical issues: the developmental nature of the occupational choice process; the validity of the period-stage analysis; the sequential broadening of the elements the adolescent and young adult consider in occupational decision making; and the role of compromise in the final choice. If I have read and interpreted the several contributions correctly, this is the verdict.

Without exception, each of the authors sees merit in the developmental approach to the study of occupational choice, although Tierney and Herman conclude that "accurate self-estimates is an individual skill that may not be uniformly or developmentally acquired." In his elicited comments on their article, however, Tiedeman pointed out that "Tierney and Herman elected to deal with discrepancies in domains and in high school grades when interests and work values had already been fairly well clarified."

In an earlier study by Tiedeman and O'Hara in which the authors sought to test our categories and conclusions, the result was positive. They concluded as follows: "These data in no way contradict the stages of development proposed by Ginzberg. Ginzberg identified his stages in the *talk* of boys who were asked to consider themselves in relation to school and work." However, the authors concluded that "*aptitude is relatively poorly perceived throughout grades 9 through 12 even by academically able boys.*"

Geoffrey Kelso, in his study of a large group of Australian students— "The Relation of School Grade to Ages and Stages in Vocational

Development"—concluded that "Ginzberg's (1951) detailed account of the gradual emergence of realism as a basis of vocational choice is largely supported here."

Linda S. Gottfredson, in her recent monograph "Circumscription and Compromise: A Developmental Theory of Occupational Aspirations," makes extensive use of our study of *Occupational Choice;* her theory and applications are generally supportive of our approach, although her emphasis on "sextype, prestige, and field of work" introduces specifications affecting the compromise process that extend beyond our original formulation.

Stepping back from the details, I was struck in reading the foregoing by the desirability in studying the development of occupational choice to give more weight to grade in school rather than to chronologic age and to the pressures introduced by decision points in the educational system. I balk, however, at the idea that early intervention by counselors will make much of a difference.

I am sure a more inclusive review of the literature would have revealed major criticisms of our theory that might have persuaded me to more radical reformulations. I was encouraged to find that these selected researchers who came after us found merit in the approach we had pioneered. Considering that a third of a century has intervened, that is comforting and reassuring.

PRACTICAL APPLICATIONS

The propelling factor that led us to study work, which in turn led us to study occupational choice, was our concern about "how to reduce the waste that is so widespread in both the individual and the social adjustment to work." In the concluding chapter of our book we set out a limited number of policy recommendations, addressed to parents, teachers, and vocational guidance counselors, that were grounded in the theory we had developed.

Specifically, we advised against parents' adopting a withholding or neutral attitude toward the occupational choice determination of their children. We noted that such parents would be unable to hide their own anxieties about their children's problems. Moreover, many children need to talk out their problems with their parents and, if they are deprived of this opportunity, are likely to find their decision-making task more difficult.

With regard to the educational system, we recognized that its primary task is not to help students clarify their occupational choices but to provide them with the instruction they require to achieve basic and advanced competences that will prepare them for work or professional training. In addition to this primary goal, we felt the schools could be more constructive in the area of occupational choice through making adaptations in their curricula that would enable them to hold the nonbookish student; by considering whether the preparatory period might be restructured for those who become restive in the classroom; by altering the grading system so that it is geared more to a student's progress than to his native ability; and, above all, to relate more closely what is transpiring in the classroom to what goes on in the world of work. We realized the foregoing was a tall order, but we felt justified in laying down such a broad challenge because of the dominant role the educational system plays in the process of occupational choice determination.

In the arena of counseling and guidance, we offered the following suggestions: a shift in guidance from those who were floundering in young adulthood to earlier interventions but not earlier than adolescence that might reduce the numbers who later were likely to encounter difficulties in making an occupational choice. We called this a redirection of effort toward prophylaxis. We expressed the opinion that counselors were relying excessively on tests of capacity and interests and questioned how much such tests could add beyond what could be learned from a review of the student's grades. The two principal challenges facing counselors and guidance personnel are to assist students who are procrastir.ating about dealing explicitly with this choice arena and to help them to adopt a strategem that would bring them closer to a resolution.

In rereading this chapter of advice to the advice-givers thirty years after it was written, I have a clearer perception of why I returned to this theme when the opportunity was offered in the late 1960s when the Rockefeller Brothers Fund asked me to undertake a critical review of the extant guidance and counseling structure. It was in that book that I dealt at length with the potentials and limitations of improving the ways in which different groups could cope with the problems engendered in making an occupational choice.

We had eight major recommendations to the advice-givers:

1. Educational and career guidance should be the primary commitment of the profession.
2. The primary responsibility of the guidance counselor should be to his or her client rather than to organizational goals as defined by the administrator.
3. Guidance can be effective in helping disadvantaged groups only if it couples its services with other inputs that can help change the clients' situation in reality.

4. The education of guidance personnel must include more training in the dynamics of the labor market. Moreover, supervised
   field work in appropriate settings should be an integral part of
   all professional training.
5. More services should be provided in high schools for non-
   college-bound youth, girls, and minority-group members; more
   attention should be devoted to the needs of college students
   for career guidance; services for mature men and women should
   be broadened; guidance in elementary schools should not be
   expanded.
6. The requirement of teaching experience for the certification of
   school counselors should be rescinded.
7. Improved counselor performance should be sought through more
   emphasis on group techniques; more reliance on nonguidance
   colleagues and other specialized manpower resources; greater
   use of support personnel; and improved supervision.
8. More rapid progress toward professionalization can be made
   through actions aimed at improving accountability, taking more
   steps to innovate, expanding research, and playing a more active
   role in formulating policies and programs aimed at meeting the
   needs of the public for improved services.

On certain critical issues, I adopted positions at variance with many
if not all of the professional leadership. To begin with, I balked at the
excessive claims that many of the leadership were advancing—claims
that suggested that if society provided for the training and employment
of more and better counselors and guidance specialists, many ills beset-
ting individuals and groups would recede, in fact evaporate. I could find
little if any support for such an optimistic view of the outcome of
advice-giving, no matter how many people had access to the advice and
no matter how skilled the advice-givers. This overselling of counseling
and guidance smacked of the false optimism that had accompanied the
popularity of psychoanalysis in its heyday.

Second, and closely related to the foregoing, was my conviction that
counseling and guidance had weakened themselves by moving away
from concerns with the world of work toward an emphasis on the total
personality. Specialists who had acquired a broad knowledge of the labor
market and its key institutions could unquestionably be of help to individuals who were uncertain about how to proceed with either their
preparation or their job search. Since a job and a career play so large a
role in determining the individual's status, income, and satisfaction,
specialists who could help their clients improve their adjustments to the
world of work were clearly performing a useful service that society

should support. But even an affluent society had reason to question whether it should underwrite psychotherapeutic sessions for all who requested them.

Considerations of cost and a focus on the area of work led to a third suggestion—namely, that the guidance fraternity consider the potentials of moving increasingly from a one-to-one relationship to a greater use of group sessions. In many instances, the information people need can be provided as effectively, if not more so, by specialists who deal with groups.

Finally, on the basis of several of the research investigations identified earlier, I felt strongly that although guidance has a continuing role to play in secondary schools and in colleges—though not in elementary schools, since our theory had demonstrated that effective career decision making is linked to the maturational process—it was essential that more guidance resources be redirected toward those most in need of assistance. These include many adults, especially women entering or returning to the work force; members of minority groups who often have had only a marginal attachment to the labor force; and many middle-aged and older persons who, because of changes in the labor market or in their own value systems, want to find new jobs and careers.

Up to now I have kept this explanation close to the written record, interpolating where I thought a brief commentary could help the reader understand better the continuity of our long-term research. In this concluding section, I will allow myself more freedom and set forth some considered views based on more than four decades of consulting with the federal government and with large corporations. I will not, however, attempt to link these views to my research or to the research of others; rather, I will present them as distillations informed by both. These are among the more important views I hold about work and careers in the winter of 1982–1983, in the third year of the administration of President Reagan.

- The most important preconditions for effective career development—defined as encouraging people to develop and use their potentials to the full—are reasonably open access to the educational-training system and a continuing strong demand by the economy for labor. In the 1950s the United States moved aggressively through state and later federal action (the National Defense Education Act) to lower the financial barriers that earlier had blocked access to higher education for many young people from low-income families. With minor interruptions, the United States has had since the end of World War II a continuing strong demand for labor, especially to fill the higher rungs of professional, managerial, and technical personnel. Although there have been periodic imbalances in the market for engineering manpower—and, in the 1970s, PhDs in the humanities moved into surplus and other disequilibria could be identified—on balance, the preconditions for career development have been favorable.

- Significant improvement occurred also as opportunities broadened for large groups that formerly had been severely discriminated against in both preparation and employment—women, blacks, members of ethnic and religious minorities. The fact that discrimination still exists must not blind us to the substantial gains that have been achieved and that, it is hoped, will be built on in the decades ahead.

- There have also been setbacks, the most serious of which stem from the inability of many public schools in the nation's large cities to provide effective instruction for the large numbers of their pupils who come from disadvantaged families and neighborhoods and who face the challenge of making their way in an increasingly science-oriented economy, where literacy and arithmetic skills are prerequisite for access to good jobs and attractive careers.

- Another important facilitation of improved career development opportunities has been the striking growth in government employment and in government contract employment (in aerospace and other fields) which have expanded the not-for-profit sector (government and nonprofit institutions) to a point where it accounts today for at least one out of every three jobs, including many good jobs at the middle and top of the occupational ladder.

- The years from 1950 to 1970 also saw the rapid growth and diversification of large U.S. corporations into multinational institutions; the transformation of many smaller companies into large national corporations; and the emergence, particularly in the computer sector, of a large number of new and highly successful R&D firms. An important concomitant of this period of rapid economic growth was the opening up in large organizations of what in the jargon of the day are called "fast tracks," where young people who prove themselves in jobs are moved within eighteen months or two years to a position of greater responsibility, salary, and prestige, from which they are advanced again if their record warrants, so that they can reach the threshold of top management by their late thirties or early forties. In such a growth environment the career development path is exciting for those on the fast track. It is well to remember, however, that no matter how fast the economy and the firm grow, most people will not be on the fast track. The question that arises and must be answered is: How do the majority fare?

- In my view, corporate America has made a deal with its junior and middle managers. It has offered them good working conditions, not too much work, interesting adjunct activities such as opportunities to participate in educational seminars, business meetings, travel, periodic raises, good fringe benefits. In turn, it has expected and generally obtained loyalty, respect, commitment to corporate goals and procedures. I do not believe, however, that the essential elements of the deal as just outlined have contributed much to the career development of most men — and even less to the larger proportion of the female work force once they reach their early thirties and find they are not on a fast track. At that point another bargain is struck. Most of those who realize they will not move very fast or very far begin to reorder their priorities, with work and career being downgraded in favor of family, sports and recreation, hobbies, or voluntary service. In a cynical moment I have commented that more executives are interested in their sailboats than in their work. The corporation needs a reliable group of middle managers; it recognizes that although the steam has gone out of many, possibly most, of them, nevertheless their accumulated knowledge and experience of how the corporation operates and their continuing sense of responsibility provide a reasonable trade-off for their lessened drive and productivity.

- The situation at the beginning of the 1980s is much less favorable. Our rate of growth has slowed, and most economists do not expect a quick return to the high growth of the 1950s and the 1960s. Most large corporations are staffed — in my view, overstaffed — and there is no prospect that they will have the same number and quality of openings that they had in the early post–World War II decades. To complicate matters further, many women and minority-group members are competing with white males, whose numbers have been swollen by the baby boom cohort at the very time that the number of attractive job and career opportunities has become constrained. There is not a great deal that even a well-structured career development system can do in these altered circumstances. My customary advice to corporate management includes recommendations to thin ranks, to make better use of the assignment-reassignment mechanism, to avoid lifetime commitments, and to identify and pay special attention to the few for whom work is the central value in their life.

- Unless I am misreading the data, other adjustment mechanisms are being developed that are likely to become more important in the years ahead. The first involves the growth of self-employment, where, after a prolonged decline, the figures have turned around. More and more young people, as well as workers who after one or more decades of experience have concluded that their prospects for promotion with their present employers are small or nil, have decided to strike out on their own. Others, more cautious, often with the help of a spouse, have started an enterprise on the side to which they devote most of their enthusiasm and energy while continuing to receive their regular paychecks. Still others accept an offer of early retirement because it will enable them to make a new start.

- We may be approaching a major turning point in the development of an advanced capitalist society in which more than one-quarter of the age group completes college or goes beyond. People who pursue such long periods of preparation, often at substantial economic and emotional costs to themselves and their families, are not likely to become and remain bureaucrats even if they work for a multibillion dollar corporation. Most middle managers, after all, no matter what their titles, are in fact bureaucrats, pushing papers so that the large enterprise can keep on an even keel. Most of the captains of industry with whom I am acquainted seem to be unaware that they may confront a major challenge in their attempts to attract and retain the quality of human resources they need to ensure the vitality and profitability of their enterprise.

- It is not outlandish to suggest that the difficulties of an increasing number of leading U.S. corporations in meeting the challenges of an intensified internationally competitive market result from shortcomings in the management of their human resources. If so, more trouble lies ahead, because the breadth of the problem has not yet been identified; it certainly has not been solved. It may turn out that the modern hierarchic corporation with its minions of bureaucrats is doomed; perhaps it will survive if it makes radical changes in its organization and operation so that it provides more opportunities for individuals with competence and energy to use their talents and be rewarded accordingly. It is unlikely that individuals will spend the first twenty-five years of their lives preparing themselves to work and then accept a working environment in which only a small percentage of their capacity is put to use.

In sum, the challenge of a more effective resolution of occupational choice and career development remains as critical to the well-being of the individual and to our society as it did when we first addressed the issue in the early 1940s — but certain parameters have shifted, and some for the better. All Americans have more opportunity to develop their potential. But the challenge of how they can use their talents and abilities to pursue meaningful careers remains elusive in a world of large organizations that are experiencing slow growth. Another decade may provide better answers if, indeed, we don't self-destruct before then.

CHAPTER 9

Performance Potential

THE POINT OF DEPARTURE of our study of the career development of a group of intellectually able young men was the search for factors that might help to explain their level of performance in the world of work. They had all demonstrated superior capabilities in graduate or professional school and had been awarded a fellowship. We wanted to uncover the factors that led some to be much more successful in their careers than others. This chapter will synthesize what we have learned. . . .

To begin with, original endowment is of course crucial for the level of accomplishment that an individual eventually reaches. Other factors, circumstances, and conditions may play a major role in determining whether the individual makes optimum use of his endowments, and will unquestionably determine the direction he follows, but mental prowess counts; and to judge from our data it counts a great deal.

Second, the quantity and quality of the education and other preparation that an individual undertakes before he starts to work are also clearly important in determining differential performance. On a canvas large enough to encompass the entire labor force, it can quickly be seen that without certain general and specialized types of educational preparation, individuals will be excluded from many preferred lines of work regardless of their basic endowment. While an occasional individual may overcome the handicap of limited schooling, the probability is that this will not happen. If handicapped by inadequate education, some will never be able to enter the race, and the question of their competitive performance will never be raised. But for those who prepare and train for professional or technical work, the opportunities and limitations that they encounter along their educational route will probably have an important influence.

Third is the ease or difficulty they experience in crystallizing their choices. If young people are unable to resolve this decision while in college, or if they experience difficulties in resolving it adequately, they will be without a rudder in steering their way through the complex and variegated educational opportunities which they encounter. They may flounder and consequently be retarded in getting launched on their careers. Some of those who flounder may later make up the lost time. Some who resolve their occupational choice early come to find after a few years at work that their solution was not the right one, and they are then back where they started. They must choose anew and prepare for a different career. This too sets them back, some permanently.

What people achieve in their work and career depends, fourth, in substantial measure on their motivation, attitudes, and values. Other things being equal, those who seek to achieve the most will in fact achieve more than those who are less inclined to invest as much in their work and in the pursuit of their careers.

Fifth, we have seen that the shaping of a career involves the individual in building bridges between the present and the future. He does this in part by constructing a system of expectations and by projecting himself into the future. This helps to direct and guide him as he moves from the present into the future. But men live not only with their ideas and ideals; they also must cope with the world of reality, which on occasion can prove that their expectations were either too high or too modest. Whenever a man's expectations are not fulfilled by reality, he must reassess them in order to bring them more in line with what he has come to learn about himself and the world in which he lives and works. Some men are more adept than others in profiting from their experiences and in adjusting their expectations when necessary. These men are more likely to be successful. Others may waste much of their substance running after illusions; still others may settle for too little.

Sixth, a man's wife and family can be a major source of support to him in his work or, on the other hand, can be the focal center for difficulties and disturbances that drain him of much of his enthusiasm, his energy, and his capacity. Many men are forced to invest so much of themselves in keeping conditions at home in tolerable balance that they have little left over for their work. Others, of course, can accomplish more at work because of the satisfactions and support that they realize at home. It can make a very great difference in a man's life, for instance, whether his wife has a modest income of her own and is willing to use it to further his career, or whether she refuses to move to another city where her husband can get an excellent job.

Finally, men live in a world that transcends the limits of their job. They encounter many opportunities to gain satisfactions from activities that lie outside the area of their work. How they respond to these opportunities, whether they seek major gratifications from activities and relationships in the nonwork area, will have much to do with what they are able to accomplish in the world of work. While some reasonable investment of time and energy in nonwork activities can prove constructive in relation to work, preoccupation with this sector of life can easily lead to lessened accomplishment or even an unsuccessful career.

These, then, are the principal factors that were significantly related to differential performance as evidenced by the preceding analysis. With these as background, we sought to construct profiles of respondents in the different achievement levels. Those in the higher achievement levels had the following characteristics:

1. Outstanding grades in graduate school.
2. Resolution of occupational choice by junior year in college.
3. Early completion of education, including early doctorate.
4. Quick start and progression in careers.
5. Successful assumption of adult responsibilities, including military service, marriage, and family formation.

Following is the profile of those who were least successful in their careers.

1. Good but not outstanding marks in graduate school.
2. Uncertainty and delay in formulating occupational choice.
3. Delay in the completion of formal education, including a delayed doctorate or no doctorate.
4. Considerable floundering in early career.
5. Difficulties in responding to the demands and opportunities of adulthood, including military service, marriage, and children.

While each of the foregoing differentiations appears to be independent of the others, there may be a hidden underlying factor that gives shape and direction to the careers and lives of these generally successful persons. It may be useful to think of the factor as something akin to Spearman's G-factor (G standing for general) in his theory of intelligence. This factor or constellation is difficult to describe or even outline, but it manifests itself in the individual's dealing successfully with all of the factors enumerated as determinants of occupational success. Hence, we propose to refer to it by the somewhat broad expression *performance potential.* This concept has in fact worked its way into conventional language and thought; for example, when we say, "he will go far," "he is slated for the top," or "he is presidential timber," we refer to certain qualities which are not readily definable or specifiable, but which are not simply equatable with endowment and which seem to appear in retrospect. Sometimes observers are surprised about an individual's actual performance because they had not recognized his performance potential in advance.

Superior performance potential favors, but does not insure, a high level of performance. Conversely a low performance potential does not preclude eventual high-level achievement. The reasons for these caveats were suggested earlier. Personality characteristics, among them the performance potential, represent only one set of determinants. A second set are embedded in the social reality that the individual encounters during the course of his adult work and life and against which his personality determinants are played out. And the ways in which they are played out constitute the third set of determinants.

Here are some of the major findings about the ways in which social reality influenced the level of achievement of the members of our group. We will summarize the findings by setting out the circumstances that had a negative influence on career achievement.

Men whose fathers were in the lower occupational levels were more likely to be in the lower achievement levels; this probably reflects their reduced opportunities to acquire a superior education.

Those who secured their doctorates relatively late were likewise overrepresented among the lower achievers; sometimes this indicated a career deflection as they were forced to take jobs to earn money to complete their studies.

Those who served in the military services and never rose above enlisted rank were likely to be in the lower achievement level. Apparently, failure to demonstrate leadership capacity in the military was indicative of some lack of initiative or force that also handicaps a man in civilian life.

Those who reported serious marital troubles were also more likely to be on the lower achievement level. Disturbances within the home apparently did not end there, but carried over into the work arena.

Numerous job shifts were also a negative indicator. Men who changed employers frequently were more likely to end up on the lower achievement level. Most men will not willingly leave jobs where they are relatively well paid and where the other conditions that they seek in work are satisfactory. Therefore, those with multiple job changes probably had more than the average difficulty in the labor market. But irrespective of the reasons for frequent job changes, when a man looks for a new job his prospective employer will usually study his work record. A record of frequent changes is often a deterrent to securing a good job.

One other situation deterrent to high-level achievement can be extracted from our earlier analysis. While our group contained a relatively small number of persons in the general category of creative artists — musicians, painters, authors — even this small number alerted us to the extent to which a poorly structured market for the services of these people exercises a negative influence on their career development. There are outstanding rewards for the exceptional, but only modest rewards for the merely talented. Facing an unresponsive market, it is not surprising that most of this group found themselves on the lowest achievement level.

The determinants anchored in reality cannot always be classified as clearly favoring or interfering with the development of a man's career. A generally negative constellation such as identified earlier may on occasion precipitate behavior that results eventually in the individual's performing at a high level. We encountered in our study many examples of men whose long period of military service afforded them an opportunity to reconsider their careers, their values, and their goals. As a result of this opportunity for reconsideration, they sharpened their perspectives and moved more purposefully to accomplish their new objectives. Serious illness forced one of our respondents to change his occupational choice. Required to remain sedentary, he developed a highly specialized skill that he could fully exploit.

In summarizing this second set of determinants, we must point out their essential duality: The situations that people encounter during the course of their career development may provide them with opportunities or may place limitations and hurdles in their path. The strong demand for physicists that developed in the 1950s was a special opportunity; the lack of interest of the American public in the work of poets is a deterrent to the development of young creative writers.

Reality situations can also operate to make demands on individuals to which they can respond positively or negatively. The requirement that young men serve in the Armed Forces is a demand, but to some it can prove to be a constructive experience. On the other hand, if a young man is forced to remain on active duty for a very long time, he may feel pressure to shift his career goals because of the many years during which his plans were in suspension.

Some situations can result in stimulation; others have more of the quality of a temptation. When a lawyer, acting as house counsel, learns

about the inside of a business, he may contemplate broadening his
horizon and eventually shifting into work that will be both more demanding and more rewarding. But other situations that hold forth large
immediate returns may present a temptation that the individual cannot
withstand. Many a promising scientist was lured away from the research
laboratory into a lucrative administrative position.

Finally, some situations provide support and encouragement to the
individual in the pursuit of his career goals; others are fraught with
danger and discouragement. There is the old adage that nothing succeeds like success. Some individuals find themselves in situations where
they have an opportunity to use their ability fully, others in situations
that lead to setbacks and failures. Several respondents indicated that they
had at one time worked under supervisors who were incompetent or
jealous and who had impeded their progress.

For analytical purposes, situational factors in career development
can be organized in terms of the following four dualities: opportunities
and limitations, demands and pressures, stimulation and temptation,
encouragement and discouragement. The significance of any particular
situation will often depend less on its objective aspects than on the way
the individual perceives and responds to it.

We have seen that people differ in their performance potential, but
these differences alone do not suffice to explain differences in career
development. People also confront a different social reality, but again
these differences alone do not explain the differences in performance.
How the reality is interpreted by the individual and how he responds to
it is a portion of his total personality. We can single out certain tenden-
cies in our group that we call response mechanisms, and which are
considered as a third set of determinants.

Just as objective situations assume highly subjective importance for
different individuals, so the responses that people make to these situations can vary widely. In our approach to this third set of determinants—
the responses people make to the situations which they encounter—we
face many of the same methodological difficulties we confronted in
trying to establish some order among the other sets of determinants of
performance. Once again we will have to be satisfied with a partial rather
than a comprehensive analysis. Our effort will be devoted to delineating
a limited number of response mechanisms that can be used to describe
the process of interaction in a more systematic manner.

We were able to discern in our group three response mechanisms,
and to them we applied the following descriptive terms: investment,
time perspective, and what we call the *stance,* whether it is active or
passive. A word about each. *Investment* refers to the time and effort
people are willing to put into their work. *Time perspective* is the short-

range or long-range point of view an individual takes toward his career. The third mechanism refers to the phenomenon that people can approach their careers by adopting and following either an active or passive stance. . . .

The following findings bear on the investment mechanism. Men in the top achievement level gave clear evidence that they were heavily committed to the pursuit of their work and career goals. They were deeply involved in their work and made substantial investments of time and energy. They tended to start very early to devote themselves to their studies, and then to perform well in the work arena. One caveat is that a high degree of investment need not necessarily manifest itself in superior achievement. . . .

There were also some relationships that can be suggested, if not demonstrated, between the time perspective and the differential performance of the members of the group. Those who had been able to determine their occupational choice early were more likely to be found in the top achievement level. This was also true of those who had been able to finish their educational preparation early and particularly those who earned their doctorate as expeditiously as possible. Those who fulfilled their military service requirement early were also in a stronger position to pursue their career goals. . . . Men who had difficulty in getting started or who got started in the wrong direction had to pay a big price because of the delay occasioned by changed goals or changed jobs.

Subsumed under the concept of time perspective are such considerations as the desirability of developing a proper sequencing of one's career decisions; the recurrent need to balance immediate against more distant satisfactions and goals; the testing of reality; and the capacity to project oneself into the future and to know what one wants to be, where one hopes to be, and when.

Successful career development also demands that one be able to develop realistic expectations and then to revise them upward or downward as reality requires. In our group, difficulties in effectively linking the present to the future were likely to be reflected in a lower level of achievement.

A few relationships can also be suggested between our earlier findings and the active-passive stance that people adopt in relation to work and careers. Among those who were in the top achievement level were many who gave clear evidence of following an active stance toward all matters affecting their work and career. They not only responded to pressures from the outside but also moved energetically to find and take advantage of opportunities that would enable them to further their career goals.

In contrast, among those on the lower achievement level were many who were passive with respect to their career development. They conveyed the impression of being in a particular groove and then being unable or unwilling to do anything other than continue in it, even though they might have improved their situation with some effort.

The more striking examples of an active stance were found among those who had reached the top achievement level. Some were men who had made a wrong start, but, as soon as they recognized their error, quickly set about to remedy it and succeeded in doing so.

Those who had served as officers in the Armed Forces were more likely to be in the top achievement level. A reasonable assumption is that the same active stance that helped these men advance in the military service also played a part in their success in civilian careers. . . .

The behavior of men with respect to their activities off the job also appears to be related to this active-passive stance. Those who were more likely to seek out and find work-related activities in their free time were more likely to be among those in the top achievement level.

Care must be taken not to confuse mere activity with an active stance; those who took an active stance were not necessarily those who engaged in the greatest amount of activity. Our data revealed that those in the top achievement level were much more likely to have had only one or two employers. Apparently, those with a truly active stance toward work and career were able to appreciate that frequent changes in jobs might hinder rather than advance career prospects. Even a move to a job paying a higher salary or a shift into a position offering more prestige could prove in the long run to have a negative effect on one's career. Careful deliberation about whether to accept what appears to be a better job and a decision not to do so may be an indication of an active stance.

There are some additional conclusions of a more general nature suggested by the foregoing discussion of response mechanisms in career development. Closely associated with heavy investment appears to be a deepseated interest in a particular field or function. This interest contributes to the establishment of a need that can be fulfilled through certain types of work. Generally this need is likely to be satisfied through intrinsic aspects of work. Often, however, a high order of investment is made because the individual's goals are concerned with such externals as making money or achieving higher status. The intensity of the need is what counts. Unless the individual has such a need, he is likely to seek more immediate satisfactions more readily available outside the area of his work.

The time-perspective mechanism helps the individual to structure and order the choices he must make. It helps him relate what has gone before to the alternatives he confronts and the goals he hopes to achieve in the future. Without these linkages, his actions would be without aim or purpose.

A related but distinct aspect of time perspective is the way it operates to give the individual an opportunity to test out, not once but repeatedly, his ability to realize the intermediate and long-range goals he has set for himself. Successful career planning requires that the individual obtain confirmation from the environment in which he works that he is on the right track, right at least to the extent that he can overcome the obstacles in his path.

But time perspective is not merely an ordering mechanism. It also contains the element of imagination, a key quality in shaping a career. Imagination makes it possible for the individual to see in dim outline what he might become or accomplish in the future. And the pull of these future goals can help him organize and mobilize himself more effectively.

Time perspective also facilitates the individual's exercising control over the demands for short-run gratifications. These are always present and frequently very powerful. The individual needs support to be able to postpone or forego the gratification of current needs and desires. Time perspective also makes it possible for the individual to make sacrifices in favor of a distant goal. Unless the distant goal can assume a present value, the individual will not make sacrifices on its behalf; time perspective helps the individual to raise his tolerances to current frustrations.

The time-perspective mechanism encourages action, including the assumption of risks, directed toward achieving distant goals. To assume considerable risk today is reasonable and possible only if one can count on substantial rewards tomorrow.

The last mechanism, the active stance, implies that the individual realizes that through his actions he can materially affect the shape of his career and his level of achievement. It is the antithesis of the position that what happens to one is solely a matter of luck. While no sensible person can ignore the fact that he must find the solution to his career problems in a real world—and that a real world establishes boundaries in the form of both opportunities and limitations—the key characteristic of the active stance is that the individual sees himself as capable of working on the situations he confronts and altering them at least in part in his favor.

In contrast, those who have a passive stance are much more likely to respond to external influences, whether they are events or people, and to act only in response to a strong external influence. They do not attempt to create situations that they can manipulate to accomplish their objectives more readily.

Now two simplifying generalizations can be ventured. The first calls attention to the role of continuity in career plans and achievement. What happened in the past always exercises a strong and frequently a compelling influence on the present and the future. This helps to explain why careers often appear to be characterized by either a benign or a vicious cycle. We talk of lucky and unlucky people. Those who get off to a good start are likely to keep on in the same direction. For those who falter along the way, the outlook may not be favorable. The explanation of this tendency toward cumulation lies in the mutual reinforcement of the objective and the subjective. A favorable objective situation makes it easier for an individual to realize his more ambitious goals; and, as he begins to realize them, he finds himself in a better objective position to continue to do so. The success he has experienced adds to his confidence and conviction that he is heading in the right direction. The world has helped him confirm his concept of the self he has projected into the future, and this in turn makes it easier for him to realize it. The continuity-cumulation tendency gives new meaning to the adage—nothing succeeds like success.

The same cumulative sequencing can occur when shortcomings and failures begin to follow one after the other. If the individual fails and fails again, he will soon lose his nerve, and this in turn makes it more difficult if not impossible for him to pursue his career goals.

The second generalization refers to the way motivation (or the subjective factors generally) and environment can be considered functional equivalents in the structuring of a person's behavior with respect to his career. We all know of the exceptional person who, when confronted by what appear to be insurmountable obstacles, can overcome them by an act of will—by determination, drive, and work. But we also know that a high proportion of the people who reach the top come from backgrounds that were relatively supporting and encouraging. These two conventional pieces of wisdom can be understood more readily within the context of the generalization that sees motivation and environment as functional equivalents. The individual with substantial drive can overcome a greater number and more severe environmental hardships. The person with less drive may reach the top if he receives strong support. Motivation and environment, while discrete phenomena, can act at times as rough equivalents in the realization of long-range career goals.

The sketch of a comprehensive framework for the study of career development just outlined provides the basis for developing answers to three crucial issues in the field of career development: why individuals with equally good endowment frequently perform at quite different levels; why talented persons facing the same objective situations respond differently with consequent different impact on their later careers; and why men with quite different personality characteristics are able to perform at the same high levels.

To find adequate answers to these and other important career questions requires an elaboration of the foregoing matrix. There is need for further research along several axes. The first involves a deepening of the approaches for delineating and evaluating personality elements. New methods are required to probe reality situations, particularly the way they operate to open opportunities or set limitations. There is also a need for the systematic study of response mechanisms through which people establish the sequences and continuities—and sometimes the shifts—out of which their careers are shaped and their level of performance achieved. The final challenge is to explore more thoroughly the concept of the performance potential. More systematic analysis could make more concrete this elusive but suggestive concept, which appears to provide one important key to the understanding of personality factors in performance.

CHAPTER 10

Advice for Guidance Counselors

GUIDANCE makes many claims and counterclaims. Its enthusiastic protagonists believe the field is making a major contribution to the welfare of individuals and to the progress of society. They argue that if more funds were invested to train guidance counselors, to establish new guidance programs, and to improve existing ones, the contribution would be even greater. When the leadership is challenged about a deficit in accomplishment, the answer is a simple one: Counselors have an excessive caseload.

But during the last decades there has been a substantial increase in available resources, and caseloads have dropped to the desired level in some locations.... Yet the promised results are still not forthcoming. Observations, impressions, and systematic investigations of guidance programs generally do not confirm claims that guidance plays a decisive role in the career plans and outcomes of its clients.

School counselors appear to spend the bulk of their time in approving courses of study, assisting with college applications, dealing with rule infractions, and administering tests. Few spend a significant amount of time in activities specifically designed to lead to improved decision making and long-range planning, the expressed goals of guidance.

Furthermore, while most of the leadership and practitioners proclaim that guidance has the responsibility of serving the entire adolescent group, there is considerable evidence that middle-class students preparing for college predominate among its clients and that far less attention is paid to the educational and vocational problems of the large numbers who are not college-bound.

Employment counselors tend to provide routinized services to their clientele and have demonstrated inadequacies in dealing with the problems of the hard-to-employ. Despite the developmental approach espoused by the profession, the adult population receives relatively little attention.

Rehabilitation counseling, by its selective focus, has been able to achieve more success than other forms of guidance. But the specialized character of its clientele and the wide range of the services on which it can draw prevent its becoming a model for guidance services for the general population.

The gap between unlimited aspirations and mundane achievements has many causes. Predominant among them is the lack of congruence between ends and means. Counselors say they help their clients realize their full potentialities, but it is difficult to trace the consequences of their actions. It is hard to think of other services in which intervention alone is equated with results.

In light of these ambiguities and confusions, what can be said about the present and potential value of guidance? Some analysts believe its potentialities are so modest that it is not worthwhile to invest additional resources in an effort to change and strengthen the field. These skeptics do not believe guidance can significantly affect people's lives in the face of the powerful institutions that shape career outcomes—the family, the school, the labor market.

To buttress their skepticism toward the potentialities of guidance and counseling, these observers call attention to the following "facts of life," which they believe justify a withholding attitude:

- Since many young people see guidance personnel as authoritarian adults who try to control and regulate their lives, few are likely to benefit from their services.
- Differential aptitudes and interests are developed early in life and are subject to change only with great difficulty.
- Guidance cannot affect the type of jobs employers have to offer, or add to a worker's skills.
- Guidance for education and work makes little more sense than guidance for marriage. People may act irrationally, but they often are able to change if they are dissatisfied with the choices they have made.

- Without the help of guidance, young people come to recognize that adults fare better or worse in the labor market as a result of their preparation and skill and the position of their family.
- Those who are intent on careers seldom need prodding or support.

These strictures, reservations, doubts cannot be blithely ignored. Each makes a relevant point. Together they are a challenge to the advocates of more and better guidance services. Yet each argument can be countered.

- The response of most youths to adult aid can be affirmative if the adults are sensitive and perceptive and if they encourage free interaction among peers without authoritarian intervention.
- Differences among individuals have little to do with the validity of guidance. Every person has some options, regardless of his aptitude or interests, and it is desirable to encourage and assist him to make an informed choice.
- Guidance does not claim to be able to influence the demand for labor. But it can convey labor-market information to the job seeker so that he can make a knowledgeable occupational decision. Moreover, while guidance cannot provide a worker with additional skills, it can encourage him to enroll for and complete skill training.
- Guidance cannot guarantee successful career choices, but decisions will be more satisfactory if they are made with deliberation and if the critical factors are weighed.
- To be informed about job requirements is not the same as to meet them. To fulfill vocational aspirations, one must know how to proceed to meet specific requirements.
- Differences among the career aspirations of people are not necessarily related to their need for guidance. Whether a person aims for a career in the traditional sense or for a secure job, a gap exists between his aspiration and its realization. Guidance along the path can often assist the individual to reach his desired goal.

We believe there is a rationale for guidance services that derives from more modest aspirations than the practitioners in the field have enunciated. Guidance, like education, has been caught up in its own rhetoric for so long that it balks at anything less than remaking man and society. We prefer to present a limited set of challenges to guidance, which, if effectively met, would justify not only the present level of social investment but a larger one. These are our premises:

- Everybody is confronted repeatedly with the need to make decisions with respect to education and work. These decisions can be

facilitated if people have relevant information about the shorter
and longer consequences of alternative choices.

• Better decision making with respect to career development also
requires the clarification of goals, the development of plans, and
their implementation.

• People need help in learning to negotiate complex and changing
institutions—the educational system, the Armed Forces, the labor
market.

• While informal advisers such as one's peers and especially one's
family help young people define their goals and initiate them in
the ways of the institutions of our society, they frequently do not
have important information or objectivity.

The case for career guidance is embedded in the foregoing propositions. It does not follow that without career guidance, many young
people and adults would make faulty educational and occupational
decisions. Many would not or, if they did, they could correct their
mistakes without serious loss. But many others would make better decisions if they had clearer goals, improved information about alternatives,
and assistance in implementing their choices.

The rest of this chapter is devoted to the actions the guidance and
counseling profession might take to realize its potentialities more effectively.
In formulating our recommendations, we have been acutely aware of the
margins that restrict the profession. To assume it can reverse course,
deny its history, or operate without reference to manpower, money, and
other constraints would be as foolish as to assume that the status quo
cannot be altered.

In seeking a framework within which to place our advice to the
advice-givers, we have identified *within* the guidance movement the
following centers of power, authority, leadership:

• The counselor educators.
• The counselor supervisors.
• The guidance researchers.
• The guidance counselors.
• The professional organizations.

We have pretested each of our recommendations to be sure that one or
more of the foregoing groups is in a position to act on them, although
individually and even collectively they may not be able to implement
them. The guidance field may require support and action from outside
forces, and to these we direct our attention in the following chapter. . . .

Guidance has an expressed goal—"the full use of the human potential."
We are pleading for a refinement and specification of this overambitious

goal. Since public funds are tight, guidance must present a strong case to obtain the resources it needs. Our *first* and overriding recommendation is that educational and occupational guidance be made the primary commitment of the profession. This recommendation seeks to bring guidance back to its origins. It postulates that education and work are critical dimensions of human life and experience and that improved decision making through guidance intervention can make a difference for a considerable proportion of the total population.

The priority claim for career guidance implies a shift in focus and resources away from certain objectives that have won adherents in years past. In the first instance, it means that school counselors can be concerned but cannot alone deal with all the developmental problems young people are likely to encounter, from conflicts with parents to experimentation with drugs. This is not to deny that such problems are pervasive, that they frequently swamp more mundane matters of educational and occupational decision making; nor does it argue that they should go unattended. But if guidance counselors are to develop competence, they cannot at one and the same time be informed sources of career information and assistance and continue to serve as psychotherapists or administrators. They must rely more on referrals to psychologists and social workers. The burden of this recommendation is that guidance counselors should no longer devote most of their time to such tangential activities.

However, our recommendation does not imply that guidance counselors or, for that matter, any group of advice-givers, can afford to operate except on a basis of an understanding of the stages and varieties of human development. The greater their understanding the better. But regardless of their psychological sophistication, this knowledge alone does not suffice. Guidance personnel must become more informed about work and careers and about the pathways into them. This is, or should be, their unique role. In the other areas where they are active, there are other professionals, usually with more training and expertise.

Our *second* recommendation is that the guidance leadership seek to inform employers of counselors and instruct future counselors that their role is that of specialists who help clients with respect to their career development; their role is not to serve in a line capacity to accomplish organizational goals. This is particularly apposite with respect to guidance personnel in school settings, where so many young people correctly see the guidance specialist as part of the administration, whose advice is often more responsive to the aims of the school than to student needs. . . .

One of the reasons school counselors identify with the administration is that for many the only possible career advancement is to move from guidance into administration. . . . The inevitability of the movement of many school counselors, as well as employment and rehabilitation counselors, into administrative or training positions if they are to keep their career options open is not necessarily all loss. As administrators, former counselors should have more understanding and support of their guidance staffs and what they are seeking to accomplish. As educators they should be able to sensitize their students to the impact of work realities.

Our *third* recommendation relates to the need for linking guidance to other services. Sophisticated observers of the current scene know that in guiding and counseling the underprivileged, the critical factor is whether the counselor can intervene in some direct way to better the life conditions and circumstances of his client. If he can get him into a training program or if he can get him a job, he may be able to counsel him later and to help clarify his position and future prospects. But unless the guidance counselor can deliver concrete help, he might as well forego the counseling effort. Clients who are outside the mainstream need a sign that counseling is not one more attempt at whitewash. . . .

Our *fourth* recommendation flows directly from the preceding ones. If career guidance is to be the critical intervention and if guidance counselors are to become staff specialists, then it follows that the education of counselors must be responsive to these facts. The major reforms of the educational and training program must be along the following lines:

- More emphasis on the world of work and on the pathways into it.
- Greater stress on training the guidance counselor to mobilize and utilize informational and other resources existing within his setting and on the outside.
- Supervised field work in a relevant setting to improve the trainee's ability to listen to and interact with his clients and to observe how people change their attitudes and behavior. . . .

If young people are to be encouraged seriously to consider guidance and counseling as a career rather than as a derivative or residual choice, and if they are to use their time in college to move in this direction, the almost universal state regulation that only teachers can become certified school counselors should be rescinded. This is our *fifth* recommendation. The leadership should speak out clearly on this issue. If it does, it is likely that one state after another may favorably consider a change in the licensing requirements.

In any case, a major effort must be launched soon, since guidance cannot move toward professional status if it continues to insist that a teaching license and classroom experience are essential for the proper discharge of the functions of career guidance specialists in a school setting. This is a false hypothesis. The fears of the rank-and-file guidance counselor that he will lose prestige and bargaining power if the requirement is eliminated should be thoroughly aired and assessed. If these fears are groundless, the leadership should reassure the membership. If these fears have validity, it is the task of the leadership to find alternative ways of protecting the rights of school counselors while gaining support for the removal of this anachronism. Guidance counselors should no more be compelled to have teaching experience than are school social workers or school psychologists. . . .

Our *sixth* recommendation is to expand guidance resources for youth, in and out of school, as well as for adults, and to retard the slow but steady trend toward bringing guidance services into the elementary school. Many secondary schools still have a high ratio of students per counselor, and various subgroups of high school students receive little or no guidance services. We will address both these issues after clarifying our broad position.

Our recommendation that services for young and mature adults be expanded is predicated on the following: the limited amount of such services currently available, except for particular groups such as veterans and those in rehabilitation programs; the inevitable tendency for young people to delay their occupational decisions as a concomitant of the elongation of their education and training; the tendency of young adults to reopen their tentative decisions as a result of early experiences in the military or in the civilian labor market; the increasing number of mature women who wish to enter or return to the world of work; and the large number of middle-aged adults who seek to make job and career shifts. All these groups need guidance; few of them have access to it.

The only significant financing of guidance to date has been derivative—that is, in connection with major programs focused on education, vocational rehabilitation, or employment. Consequently, the recent strategy of the guidance profession has sought to profit from the mounting public concern over education of the young by appealing for the incorporation of guidance services into programs to strengthen early education. . . .

To suggest that neither more guidance nor more testing is the answer to the malperformance of the elementary school is not an endorsement of the status quo. Clearly, when a child fails to acquire basic skills in his first years in school—as so many do—the rest of his years in school are likely to be of marginal value. Many reforms are required, which involve staff, curriculum, and community relations.

We do not argue that if elementary schools hire guidance personnel there will be no work for them. We are merely stipulating that properly trained guidance counselors primarily concerned with career development have little to contribute to the elementary school. . . .

In contrast, we do urge the leadership to recognize the need and press for the expansion of guidance services for young adults and for the mature population. We urge them to shift available guidance resources in high schools from the privileged to those groups who need extra help in career planning, such as those requiring special assistance in order to attend college; to the non-college-bound who need help in making a transition into training, work, or the Armed Forces; and to young women and members of minority groups for whom many options are opening up for the first time.

We realize that all who are bound for college need help in filling out the necessary applications, but we question whether this requires most of the time of a skilled guidance staff. We believe that the guidance staff might limit its efforts to broad group indoctrination sessions about college admissions for middle-class students and their parents. There is considerable evidence that indicates the preference of educated parents to be operative with respect to their children's choice of a college. School counselors should be available to those who seek them out but they should not preempt this area. In any case, they must do more for the non-college-bound. Otherwise they discriminate, which is no less reprehensible because they may do so unwittingly and without deliberate design.

Our recommendation that special attention should be devoted to females and members of minority groups flows directly from the theory and practice of career guidance. These are the two groups that are most likely to be misinformed about their options; they lack adequate models; their informal informational systems are likely to be deficient. These shortcomings reflect a sudden and substantial change in the paths that have opened up and the opportunities that lie at the end. An important social role for guidance and counseling is to cut the time lag between the new reality and the awareness and response to it, particularly among the young generation which is making its plans for the future.

We know that many young people who drop out of high school or who even acquire a diploma flounder in the labor market for several years while they consider or reconsider their job and career objectives; a significant minority become interested in returning to school or in entering formal training programs in order to add to their competences and thus broaden their opportunities. While they pick up a lot of information from employers, co-workers, and friends, much of it is misinformation, and they often could profit from an opportunity to explore in more depth the range of opportunities open to them. This would require that they have access to a competent guidance service which has a broad overview of the whole gamut of educational, training, and employment paths and institutions. . . .

The Employment Service has an unfortunate record in terms of attracting young and mature adults with career problems and helping them. Even with respect to its primary function of placement, its record leaves a great deal to be desired. Nevertheless, we believe that it is more sensible to build on the only major labor-market institution which has offices throughout the country and to try to strengthen it so that it will become more responsive to the needs of youth than to try to duplicate it, with almost certain failure, by expanding the functions of the high school counseling staff.

In view of the nature of the labor market, the counseling and guidance services of the Employment Service should be expanded and strengthened not only for youth but also for adult men and women who want to explore a job or career change or who are returning to work and need assistance. The large and growing numbers of "loosely attached" workers underscore the desirability of expansion and improvement of guidance services. Once again we stress that an effective service would have to offer advice with respect to the gamut of education, training, employment, and even retirement.

In addition to the Employment Service, we believe that expansion of services should also be centered in post–high school training and educational institutions and in nonprofit and even profit-seeking guidance agencies.

The supporting arguments are ready at hand. The elongation of the educational-training cycle implies that more and more young people will delay considering their occupational choices until they are out of high school. The large and growing proportion of young people who are going to community colleges need advice about occupational programs and about transfer possibilities. Too many of them drop out or complete their studies without clear ideas of the next steps to take and they could profit from career guidance. This is one locus for priority expansion.

With regard to four-year colleges and universities, we believe that while there has been considerable improvement in the provision of psychological counseling, especially in large institutions, too little attention has been directed to career guidance, although many students need help with respect to their career development.

This then is a summary of our *sixth* recommendation, which is concerned with priorities among clientele groups:

- A moratorium on the expansion of guidance into the elementary school until its functions have been more clearly delineated and alternative solutions explored.
- A redirecting of guidance services in high school toward non-college-bound males, toward girls, and toward minority-group members.

- A high priority for the expansion and improvement of guidance services in the Employment Service for youth and adults.
- A high priority for the expansion of guidance services in community colleges.
- An expansion of career services in senior colleges.

Our *seventh* recommendation relates to the several actions that would improve the effectiveness of the guidance profession through new patterns of work and manpower utilization. The first and simplest action is to shift wherever possible away from the one-to-one relationship between counselee and guidance specialist that has been the dominant pattern since the inception of the movement. In the absence of unequivocal evidence that this is the only relationship that is appropriate, the guidance leadership should explore systematically what functions can be equally well and perhaps even better performed on a group basis.

Many aspects of course selection and college admissions—the two functions on which high school counselors spend so much time—can be handled on a group basis. Moreover, as we have noted, group counseling appears to be the preferred technique in dealing with young people who are loosely attached to the labor force. They trust each other and are able to learn from listening to each other, and they apparently are reassured when they learn of common problems. If, as we suggest, more emphasis be placed on group techniques, counselor educators should include them in the required curriculum and practicum.

A second action involves intensified efforts by guidance counselors to obtain assistance from their colleagues.... From the viewpoint of guidance, teachers represent a force of 2 million paraprofessionals. While teachers may resent counselors' coming into their domain with ideas about restructuring the curriculum and about other adaptations in school procedures and practices, they are likely to agree if they are asked to assist in the guidance task. With justification, teachers believe that they are often in a preferred position to make recommendations to students about course selection. Similarly, they might be willing, especially in connection with instruction in English and social studies, to give more attention in the classroom to the world of work and the paths leading into it. In addition, they are often better able than the counselor to identify the underachiever or the student with unusual strengths. Indeed, unless school counselors can work with and through the teaching staff, they have little prospect of making more than a marginal contribution to the student body.

Similarly, the employment counselor should develop closer working relations with other members of the Employment Service staff, in particular the job developer and the placement officer. The rehabilitation counselor faces the challenge of improved coordination with his colleagues.

A third action is to create more effective liaison between the institutions that contribute to career decision making and the encouragement of guidance personnel both in their basic training and subsequently to use lateral coordination involving contacts outside their own setting. Closer liaison is important between school counselors and employment counselors; between guidance counselors in every setting and professionals who are qualified to handle clients who need specialized help; between employment counselors and the staffs of health and welfare agencies in order to resolve problems that interfere with the realization of career objectives; between guidance specialists at different levels of the education-training-employment structure as well as between them and admissions, training, and employment staffs who make critical decisions.

Another desirable action is to encourage guidance personnel, particularly those in secondary school, junior college, and college, to learn to make greater use of the specialized resources available in the community in order to help them explicate and concretize many of the realities of the world of higher education, of work, and of the Armed Forces, and to let informed outsiders answer many of the questions that concern their clients. . . .

The profession has insisted that it does not have and is not likely to have in the near future the trained manpower it needs to meet the priority claims for service even for those population groups that society has singled out as entitled to service. The logical response of the profession would be to seek to attract a large number of less trained persons at lower salary levels and to restructure the way in which the total workload is performed and thus increase the total output of services. But . . . the guidance profession is unwilling to endorse a rapid increase in the number of support personnel.

We believe that this is an error and that if career guidance is ever to make a serious attempt to meet the potential need and demand for its services, it has no alternative but to experiment with making greater use of support personnel. We have suggested many alternative ways in which career guidance might be strengthened through new work patterns, so that we do not need to spell out again the ways in which support personnel can be most effectively absorbed and used. But the principles are clear. The first is to designate those functions that require less training time and assign them to the support group.

As we have seen, the leadership is convinced that a reallocation of some of its functions might jeopardize the improvements in professional education and training for which they have striven for so long. But at present there is little if any momentum in the direction of the two-year training program. Graduates of the present one-year part-time training program are concerned that the distinctions between them and the baccalaureate holders who undergo short training on or off the job will be obliterated with corresponding loss of prestige and income for those with master's degrees. This is not an irrational fear, but there are factors that should be added to the equation in order to allay it.

It is not necessary that support personnel be recruited from among college graduates; in fact, there are reasons that they should not. They would be overeducated for the functions allocated to them, and their salary levels would tend to be higher than those of others with less education who could cope with the work. It would be better to recruit personnel from among high school and junior college graduates. In this case, the distance between the present certified or otherwise recognized "professional" counselor and the support personnel would be widened. However, it would be necessary to provide for career progression for support personnel in which both experience and additional education would play a part. . . .

We believe that all elements of the guidance profession should recognize the need for and desirability of attracting more support personnel as part of the larger objective of redesigning the way in which they carry out their work so as to broaden services at a cost that the American people can and will support. The major challenges we see in this connection are for more controlled experimentation in the use of support personnel, the adjustment of the education and training structure of professional counselors to reflect such a trend, and improved supervision.

We have referred earlier to the fact that the counselor educators are fully aware that the most serious weakness in the present education and training is inadequate field training. Even when there is field training, the quality of the supervision is often inadequate; it tells counselors what they should do but does not alert them to what they can do within a particular setting, and it fails to monitor their counseling. A second weakness is that often newly trained counselors are thrown into work with no instruction, guidance, or support. With rare exceptions, such as the Veterans Administration and well-run community agencies, there is conspicuously little supervision of the day-to-day work of the counseling staff. Each counselor is permitted to act as if he were a private practitioner who must meet the vagaries of competition and attract and hold his clients on the basis of demonstrated competence. But most clients are assigned; they seldom have any recourse if they do not like their counselor; and there is little or no check on outcomes. There is much to be said for introducing more "choice" in the selection of a counselor by a client as well as more follow-up of his response, subjective and objective, to the services he received.

Counselors should be informed while in training that as part of their professional development they will be subject to continuing supervision by senior guidance staff, not only to help them to acquire greater competence but also to protect the client. No profession can progress if each practitioner makes his own rules and works alone, without active supervision or structured exchange of information with his colleagues.

An expanded and improved system of supervision of and by guidance personnel is a sine qua non for any additional investment of the American people in a service which, while having the potential for improving the career development of many individuals, can be harmful in inexpert hands. Improved supervision is urgent if, as has been strongly recommended, the field plans to attract and use large numbers of support personnel. Without supervision there can be no responsibility, and without responsibility there is no accountability. Without supervision, there can be no professional growth.

Our *seventh* recommendation, therefore, involves the reorganization of the work patterns of career guidance. In summary, it includes the following:

- Greater use of group techniques.
- More interaction between counselors in their own and other settings, and with specialized community resources.
- The attraction and effective use of large numbers of support personnel to enable counselors to broaden their services and yet keep within manpower and money constraints.
- Stronger supervision to insure quality control and systematic progress of counselors. Improved supervision will be more urgent if changing work patterns accompany the employment of large numbers of support personnel.

Our *eighth* and last recommendation to the profession is that the leadership encourage accountability and innovation. . . . It is not possible at present and it may never be possible to develop a scientific approach for appraising the effectiveness of guidance and counseling, but it does not follow that the leadership and the profession as a whole do not have to strive continually to improve effectiveness.

There is today little meaningful data about counselor interventions and client outcomes. A first responsibility of every guidance supervisor is to insist on the collection of operational data, especially follow-up information, and to provide for its analysis. Such data might not provide unequivocal evidence about the utility of guidance in effecting critical behavioral outcomes, but systematic information could be highly illuminating in assessing actions taken after guidance intervention. Perhaps the most important gain from the collection and assessment of operational data would be the opportunity it would offer supervisors and administrators to use the results for planning, programming, and on-the-job training. Practitioners would have to look at their performance. The discipline of self-criticism is essential if a professional ethos is to prevail.

The several recommendations advanced for the increased use of support personnel and alterations in work patterns to include broader use of group techniques will lend themselves to experimental designs. It is important that the leadership carry through an experiment on a sufficiently large scale that greater reliability will attach to it than to a single effort where idiosyncratic factors might prevail. While cooperative research is never easy to plan and carry out in applied fields, including guidance, it is essential if progress is to be made. The group of regional educational laboratories financed by HEW and the multiple units in which guidance services are provided in the Employment Service and in vocational rehabilitation agencies provide a favorable background for cooperative research. The missing link is a research orientation with strong leadership both within and outside of the individual guidance systems. Research is the cutting edge of every profession; unless interest can be awakened and resources commanded for research, the discipline cannot grow into professional status.

The guidance movement is only sixty years old; and much of its growth, at least in numbers of practitioners, has occurred recently. It has spent much of its organizing and structuring efforts on seeking to define a unique role for itself, particularly in relation to closely allied fields such as teaching and psychology. This has made its outlook and orientation parochial. The leadership and the rank and file appear to be preoccupied with intraorganizational and professional nuances.

The hallmark of a profession is that it assumes a leadership role in seeking to improve the quality, broaden the range, and otherwise enlarge its contribution to the public weal. Guidance has not yet risen to this challenge. It has continued to neglect the needs of large groups. Moreover, until recently it had not joined with other professional and political groups to point out the necessary reforms in basic institutions, particularly the schools and the labor market, or the need for new transitional mechanisms from one to the other if the promise of career options for every American is to be a reality. The guidance profession has been in a preferred position to learn about the shortcomings of education, particularly in high schools. But its leaders have not been in the forefront of those recommending reforms so that high schools can better serve the many students who today are being more abused than educated. As it seeks to grow into full professional status, guidance must be more concerned with matters of public policy; it must use its special insights and strengths to contribute to the formulation of better policies.

It is not enough for a group to want to become a profession or to keep repeating that it is one. A group becomes a profession by earning the public's confidence. It must be sensitive to the needs of the public for its services, take the leadership in seeking to meet them, be willing to account to itself and to the public about the quality of its services, seek to improve them through research and demonstration, and join with other concerned groups to help bring about changes in the underlying institutional structures that are desirable in their own right and essential if the profession is to fulfill its social obligations.

There is only one way to read the record to date. Guidance has been ingrown and introspective. Its best chance to gain full professional status is to act like other professional groups. . . .

The Unsuccessful

PART III INCLUDES ONE SELECTION (Chapter 11) from our study of the long-term unemployed in New York City in the late 1930s, but it is composed primarily of chapters from *The Uneducated* and the three-volume work on *The Ineffective Soldier: Lessons for Management and the Nation*, the two principal investigations that contain most of the findings from the Eisenhower-initiated and -sponsored studies of the human resources experience of World War II. Together with the chapter on "The Negro Soldier" in *The Negro Potential* and a short monograph on *Psychiatry and Military Manpower Policy in World War II*, these four volumes — *The Uneducated, The Lost Divisions, Breakdown and Recovery,* and *Patterns of Performance* — contain most of what we learned about those who were rejected for military service as well as those who were selected but later discharged because of ineffectiveness.

In contrast to the conventional wisdom, then and now, we demonstrated that a major cause of ineffectiveness in the military was embedded not in the shortcomings of the individual — although many were inept and poorly prepared to answer the call to arms — but in the faulty policies and procedures that the Army, Navy, and Air Corps pursued in their handling of men under stress.

A second critical finding emerged from our stitching together of the premilitary, military, and postmilitary experiences of men who broke down while in the service and were later discharged. These lifetime patterns of performance revealed the erroneous nature of highly deterministic theories of human behavior. It is simply not true that all those who were ineffective in the military had demonstrated serious defects in their earlier ability to adjust to civilian life. Moreover, most of those who suffered breakdowns while in uniform recovered when they returned to a less stressful environment. Some remained broken, but most men were able to cope with the more moderate demands of the civilian environment.

These studies, focused on a life-cycle perspective, led us to the concept of *adjustment potential*. We defined this concept in commonsense terms, free of the psychological baggage of various schools—psychoanalytic, developmental, behavioral. Adjustment potential, we feel, is best assessed in terms of the following four criteria: the ability of a man to get and hold a job; to support his dependents, if any; to avoid trouble with the criminal justice system; and to be able, if called, to serve in the Armed Forces. These are modest standards; but it appeared to us at the time, and even now with the benefit of hindsight, that they have more validity than approaches that resort to such subtle variables as anxiety, self-esteem, satisfaction, happiness. A wise neurologist once remarked that it is fortunate that societies are so ordered that most of the time people interact with each other only at arm's length. If the relationship were more intimate, no society could avoid being ripped asunder.

CHAPTER 11

The Unemployed:
The Corey Family

Status   Home Relief   *Religion*   Catholic
    Man   born 1904 Ireland to U.S.A. 1927 Citizen No
    Wife   born 1909 Ireland to U.S.A. 1929 Citizen No
Education
    Man   Graduate, Catholic High School — Ireland
    Wife   Elementary school — Ireland.
Medical Status
    Man   Negative.
    Wife   Very thin, looks undernourished.
Woman's Work History   Domestic from age of 14 in Ireland.
    In U.S.A., department store packer, factory worker until marriage.
Married   June, 1930, N.Y.C.
Number of Children in the Home   Seven   *Ages* — 5 months to 8 years.
Basic Occupation Before Relief   Billposter.
Average Income before Relief $35 to $40.
Private Employment Terminated   March, 1937.
First Accepted for Relief   May, 1937.

SUMMARY

Home Relief   From May, 1937, *to date.*

ABSTRACT OF HOME RELIEF RECORD

OCT., 1933

First Application: (Social Service Exchange—No record.) Man is a billposter, employed by an outdoor advertising company since 1928. Since September, 1932, he has had only two or three days work a week at $5 a day and, during the past three months, only a few days all told. Last week he worked only one day, and the week before only six hours. Friends have helped with food. The couple and their two children live in two furnished rooms at $6 a week. They have moved four times in the last year. The children were described as robust and healthy and, according to the investigator, "home very untidy and ill-kept. Furniture old and battered. Evidence of poverty but no suffering."

Case Rejected because part-time earnings exceeded the deficit that would have permitted Home Relief supplementation.

MAY 12, 1937

Reapplied. Billposters have been on strike for the past six weeks and the family has had no income during that time. They are destitute. The woman is pregnant. The family saved $60 for confinement expenses but were forced to use it for food. The investigator described the Coreys as pleasant and willing to co-operate. Their rental at this time was $30. The investigator communicated with the advertising company and learned that Mr. Corey had an excellent record. So far as the company is concerned, they did not recognize the strike and stated that in their opinion Mr. Corey had quit his job and their responsibility was at an end. They said that there was no strike, that the places of those who left had been filled by other employees. The man to whom the investigator spoke made no prediction about re-employment.

The family had bought furniture on the installment plan and now the company was threatening to repossess it. Investigator wrote the furniture company, asking them to wait.

MAY 19, 1937

Case Accepted.

JULY, 1937

Investigator "explored re-employment possibilities." The local to which Mr. Corey belongs appears to have split with the international union and the international now refuses to do anything about reinstating members of the local.

AUG., 1937

Josephine born at home. Berwind Clinic physician and Henry Street Settlement visiting nurse in attendance.

SEPT., 1937

Man going to employment agencies, looking for work. He asked for WPA employment, but this was denied because he is an alien.

OCT., 1937

Investigator helped the family reach an agreement with the furniture company permitting them to pay $2 or $3 a month out of their Home Relief budget instead of the required $5 a week.

JAN., 1938

Family received court summons about the furniture. Investigator wrote the company asking for leniency.

FEB., 1938

Employees of the furniture company arrived with a marshal's notice and removed all the furniture, with the exception of two mattresses. Mr. Corey was told by a representative of the furniture company that he was unjustified in leaving a $40 a week job to go out on strike. Investigator referred the family to the St. Vincent de Paul Society for furniture.
Investigator called St. Vincent de Paul and asked that the family be given furniture.
Investigator called the Department of Public Welfare housing unit about the possibility of a furnished apartment for the family.
Family moved to a ground-floor apartment, five rooms, rental $30.

APRIL, 1938

Budget revised to deduct Unemployment Insurance Benefits at $15 a week, but the man did not receive them and much hardship resulted while this matter was investigated. The Unemployment

Insurance Benefits were to have been received automatically, ten days after the "notice of rights," but this did not happen.

MAY, 1938

Full food allowance was granted, but no rent was given until the matter of Unemployment Insurance Benefits could be clarified.

JUNE, 1938

Man reported that he is receiving Unemployment Insurance Benefits, $15 each check. It was decided that since the family had been deprived of their Home Relief income during recent weeks, the first four checks were not to be deducted from the budget, but were to be used for the rent arrears of $60. The man is to make further application for the four additional checks to which he is entitled.

JAN., 1939

Investigator discovered a new floor lamp in the apartment and questioned the family about it. Investigator knew that such floor lamps were being sold in a "bargain package" by Edison Company. This "bargain package" included a radio, an electric iron, a toaster and a floor lamp, all for $24.50. The family denied this until the investigator confronted them with proof. She had checked with the Edison Company and learned that Mrs. Corey had made the purchase. Finally Mrs. Corey admitted that she had bought this package, but had sold the radio to a friend for $10. She used $2.50 of this $10 to make the necessary deposit and planned to use the rest of it for the monthly payments of $2 each until the amount is exhausted, after which she will take the payments out of her food budget. Investigator also visited the woman who was said to have bought the radio to check on this statement and found it to be true.

APRIL, 1939

Man goes out daily looking for work. He goes to markets, etc., any place which might need someone who is strong and able to do manual labor. He stated that he is willing to do anything. He reports at the New York State Employment Service office regularly.

MAY, 1939

Family took $5 from their food budget to buy a communion outfit for their daughter. Investigator questioned the family closely about the possibility of outside income.

JUNE, 1939

Last Entry: Woman five months pregnant. She hadn't told investigator about it earlier because she "didn't think it was important enough."

The social worker who had abstracted the Home Relief record talked with the investigator and unit supervisor. In the investigator's opinion—he feels he knows the family quite well—the Coreys are a good, simple couple, who worry about their large family but continue to have children because they are deeply religious and feel that they must obey all the dictates of the church. He thinks that there is an excellent marital relationship. He knows that Mr. Corey helps his wife with all the work in the home and that he is more than willing to do anything in the way of a job. He is without skills, other than billposting, and there is little chance of his getting back into this work because the local of which he was a member has been ousted by another local which now has a strong contract with the advertising company. Investigator believes that there will have to be a really widespread upswing in business before an unskilled person such as Mr. Corey could be placed. He knows that there is real need in this family, believes that they are deserving people, and helps them as much as he can with clothing allowances whenever he has them to give. (This investigator is not the one who made an issue of the purchase of the floor lamp—he considered that episode unfortunate and needlessly painful.) The investigator thinks that it would be good for Mr. Corey to be given a WPA job because the man needs work in order to maintain his self-respect. He thinks that Mr. Corey should be helped to achieve citizenship since this would make him eligible for WPA. In his opinion and that of the supervisor, private agencies should help these people become citizens. In this instance they think that the Catholic Charities should assume that responsibility.

HOME INTERVIEW

Mr. Corey, who was busy washing the floor in the kitchen, said that his wife was at the clinic with the baby. He had all the chairs up on the washtubs and table and was in the midst of his work. When worker explained who she was, he said that he remembered the letter and was sure that his wife would be glad to talk with her. He agreed to worker's suggestion that she come back the next day.

Mr. Corey was again alone and had apparently just finished washing the floor again. The children were in and out of the house during the visit. Mr. Corey said that he was sorry worker had failed to find Mrs. Corey in today after making a special trip to see her and explained that someone had given her the gift of a permanent wave and that she had been gone several hours. He said that she worked very hard and was somewhat run down and he thought it would do her good to get her hair fixed up. He did not know how long it might take and when worker said that it might be several hours before Mrs. Corey returned, he replied that he was surprised that anything should take so long. He was friendly and might have talked freely, but the children were milling about and worker suggested that he seemed busy and that she would come back another time. Mr. Corey agreed to this quite readily, saying that Mrs. Corey was usually in mornings. On the next visit Mrs. Corey and the children were at home.

Home—Five rooms on the ground floor, rear, of an old tenement building in the southernmost part of the lower East Bronx. These blocks south of 138th Street and east of Southern Boulevard are comprised almost entirely of wide streets with factories, garages, etc., and a small number of old buildings. The Coreys live in one of the few tenements in this section. Most of the other dwellings are small frame houses. The Coreys have lived in this apartment for four years. With the exception of the kitchen, which is enormous, the rooms are small and at the time of visit were crowded and somewhat littered, though the floors were clean and the general effect was that of lack of space rather than untidiness. The chairs were again up on the tubs and table in the kitchen and when worker asked had the floor been scrubbed again, saying that Mr. Corey had been in the midst of such an operation on both previous visits, Mrs. Corey explained that they try to keep the chairs off the floor as much as possible because of Josephine, who is very active and climbs about so recklessly that she might harm herself if the chairs were not out of the way. The furniture was simple and rather shabby. Several of the chairs were unsteady.

There are two rooms between the living room and the kitchen. In one of these rooms three girls sleep in one bed and in the other two boys occupy another bed. The twins have a large crib in the parents' bedroom. The twins sleep at opposite ends of this crib, with their feet toward the middle. The apartment, though clean, had a peculiar odor, which, Mrs. Corey explained, comes from the cellar. The floor was warped and seemed damp and Mrs. Corey said that this was the result of the dampness of the cellar, which is flooded every winter. The furnace is on the other side of the building and they get none of its warmth underfoot. Mrs. Corey said that she believes the dampness of the floor is responsible for Mary's illness (the child has rheumatic fever). The family plans to move

from this apartment before next winter because they are afraid that the
other children might become ill.

Background

Man

Born in Ireland, October 1904. He was the second of eight children,
with four brothers and three sisters. Mr. Corey attended the Christian
Brothers' High School in Ireland and was graduated from that institution.
His wife talked about his education with some pride, saying that he went
as high as one could go in Ireland and that his relatives and friends
consider him an unusually well educated man. Mr. Corey worked in the
stone quarries but was dissatisfied with the work. He saved some money
and came to the United States in 1927 to join his older brother, who had
emigrated in 1926.

Mr. Corey's father and mother are living in Ireland; his father
makes a meager living as a shoemaker. His older brother is the only
member of his family in the United States. He was also a billposter and a
member of the same union. He was formerly on Home Relief and is now
on WPA. He is married and has one child. They have three brothers in
Ireland and three sisters in London. Mr. Corey was rather vague about
whether or not his siblings were married and about their financial
circumstances.

Woman

Born in Ireland, April 1909. She was the second of four children; she
had three brothers.

Mrs. Corey says that she had a very hard life as a child in Ireland
and bemoans the fact that she had so little education. She completed the
equivalent of the seventh grade in parochial school. She stated that she
had known her husband as a child because they both lived in the same
community. But her father died when she was eleven years old and she
and her younger brother were sent to live with an aunt in the country.
She did not see Mr. Corey again until she met him in New York. At the
age of fourteen, Mrs. Corey went into service in Ireland as a houseworker.
She remembers vividly her experiences as a kitchenmaid at the age of
fifteen, when she lived in a large house in the country and had to get up
every morning at 5:30 in order to get the fires going for the baths. She
repeated—"seven days a week at 5:30 in the morning." Gradually she
worked up to the position of cook, but her clearest memory of the entire
experience is that of very hard work.

Mrs. Corey said that she would not go back to Ireland no matter how hard life might become here. There is much more chance for education and a future for the children in this country than in Ireland. She feels that perhaps she made a mistake in coming to the United States, instead of going to England with her brothers; but at any rate, now that she is here, this is her home. She came to the United States and got a job as a wrapper in a large department store at $14 a week. Later she worked in a paper box factory at $16 a week. She also tried doing domestic work but did not like it and gave it up almost immediately. The Coreys were married in June 1930.

Mrs. Corey's father and mother are both dead. Her mother died in 1919 and her father in 1920. She has no relatives in this country. One brother is dead. The two remaining brothers live in London. Her older brother is married and works as a private chauffeur, earning a small but steady wage. Her younger brother works in an airplane factory and was married recently. He is twenty-three years old.

Before Relief

Upon his arrival in the United States, in 1927, Mr. Corey got employment as a delivery boy in a local branch store of a large grocery chain and remained there until 1928, earning $18 a week. In 1928, through his brother, he got a job with an outdoor advertising company, as a billposter and remained with that company until 1937, when his local union called a strike. He earned $40 a week and the union was striking for a $42 weekly wage. In the course of the strike, a rival local, #2, acted as strikebreakers and took the jobs which Mr. Corey's local, #112, had held. Both these locals were members of the same International Bill-Posters Union, but local #2 was out of favor with the international. There was a court fight and the court finally ruled in the favor of the original local, but the company refused to consider taking the men back. According to Mrs. Corey, her husband always worked hard and this is corroborated by the statement of the personnel manager of the company, who had told the Home Relief investigator that Mr. Corey had had an excellent record. Mrs. Corey said that her husband was always a very willing worker and that the men used to tell her that the employer would call Mr. Corey for any of the hard jobs that nobody else wanted to do. According to Mrs. Corey, the family didn't have much money but got along quite well on what they had. She said that she and her husband were very happy together and that they planned for the future and for their children. She told about buying new furniture and how proud they had been of it. She said that Mr. Corey was always a good man, that he never stopped to drink on Friday nights like other men. Sometimes he brought something home to drink, but he was entitled to it because he worked so hard.

First Reactions to Unemployment

Mr. Corey went "everywhere" looking for work. He tried all the big plants, the railroad companies, the American Express, any place where they might need a good, strong, healthy man. He said—and Mrs. Corey repeated it when he left the room—that he used to get up at five in the morning to go to work in the old days and that he got up at the same time to go looking for work after he lost his job. He kept going, tried hard not to become discouraged, but when he was unable to find anything to do, the family was forced to ask for Home Relief. At that time they felt that it was only a question of waiting for the strike to be settled. When they applied for Home Relief their debts totaled about $350: grocer—$50; furniture company—$285. Their friends had helped with food. They were paying $2.15 a week for insurance policies, which had not been allowed to lapse.

Present Situation

Man

A tall, well-built, powerful-looking man, dressed in old, patched trousers and clean, faded blue shirt. His appearance is typically Irish; he has black hair, blue eyes, good color, and fine features. Mr. Corey is a pleasant person, with a ready smile and a mild, quiet manner. He talked with a rich brogue. He seemed rather embarrassed to be talking alone with worker and, while he answered questions readily, volunteered little. He said that he is worried about the fact that he is getting soft and losing his ability to work, that it is very disturbing to find nothing at all to do when he is so willing to do anything.

Woman

A short, very thin, tired-looking young woman, who must once have been quite pretty. Her hair, with its new permanent wave, was disheveled and seemed very much in need of attention. She was wearing an old housedress and a torn sweater, old shoes, no stockings. She greeted worker in a friendly manner, saying that she was sorry not to have been home when the worker called before. She said that a friend, who lived in the house, and for whose little boy her husband had given a transfusion, had presented her with money for a permanent wave and she had been at the beauty parlor on the occasion of the worker's second visit to the home. The permanent wave had cost $1.98 and she was obviously quite proud of it. Worker told her that Mr. Corey had been pleased that she was having a permanent, that he thought her great responsibilities in the home prevented her from getting enough rest or paying enough attention to herself and her appearance. Mrs. Corey smiled and replied that her husband is a very good man and that he worries about her and helps her a great deal.

Mrs. Corey talked freely and seemed to enjoy doing so, but it was difficult to keep the conversation going since the children were in and out of the house throughout the interview distracting their mother's attention by their questions and requests.

Present Adjustment

When seen alone, Mr. Corey said of his wife that she is a very good woman who has a hard life. He said that together they try to get along as well as they can, they help each other and never quarrel. She knows that it is not his fault that they are having so much trouble. He said that so long as he is unemployed, he spends a great deal of his time making it as easy for her as he can and that he helps her with all the housework. He thinks that all this quarreling and drinking which he knows goes on among the poor people in the neighborhood is bad because it helps no one and just makes life harder for the people themselves. When seen alone, Mrs. Corey said of her husband that he is a wonderful man. He is good to her and to the children. He does all the heavy work in the home, helps with the care of the children and she added that, while she wants nothing more than for him to get a steady job, she doesn't know what she would have done with the twins without his help. Not only does he share all the housework, but he does most of the shopping because the shopping center is quite a distance from their home and, since the bundles are usually quite heavy, they are more than she can manage. He also goes to the surplus commodities depot, which is an even greater distance from their home.

Mrs. Corey also talked about those people who, despite the fact that they are either on Home Relief or employed at very low wages, drink to excess. This is apparently a very real problem in their neighborhood, since there are a number of such families in the apartment building in which the Coreys live. Mrs. Corey thinks it a terrible thing for a man or woman to use for drink the money which would have bought food for their children. It is like taking food from the children's mouths. Mrs. Corey said that she and her husband never quarrel, because they know that each is devoted to the other. She knows that their present trouble is not his fault; he could not have gone against his local and refused to strike since he would probably have been beaten up as a strikebreaker. She knows that there is no one more willing to work than her husband. He still goes job hunting almost daily, and she knows that he is registered in almost every place of business in the neighborhood. She thinks it is getting even harder for him to find work now because his clothing is shabby and there is less chance of his making a good impression on a prospective employer. According to Mrs. Corey, her clothing and that of her husband is shabby because the children need so many things that everything the family can spare from household expenses must be used for them. She added that even by making sacrifices they have been unable to give the children all that they need.

Children

Margaret

Born December 1931, is a pretty, red-haired child who is rather thin. Her color is poor. She is in the third grade at school.

Mary

Born February 1933, is a thin, pale, obviously delicate child who is suffering from rheumatic fever. She has been out of school for several weeks, and the Home Relief doctor has been visiting regularly. She has swollen ankle joints and seems to be in considerable pain. Despite this, it is rather difficult to keep her in bed because she becomes restless and has almost no toys to keep her amused. According to Mrs. Corey, the Home Relief doctor has been kind to the entire family. Whenever he visits he brings the children lollypops and plays with them in so friendly a manner that Michael, who has always been very much afraid of doctors, has begun to like him and look forward to his coming. Mrs. Corey said that the Henry Street nurse has also been kind to the family and is trying to arrange to send Mary to a convalescent home.

Michael

Born November 1934, is small, also rather pale. He seems to be a quiet, shy child.

John

Born June 1936, has red hair and freckles and is an attractive, rather impish child. He was friendly and talkative.

Josephine

Born August 1937, a small, dark-haired, blue-eyed child, is the most troublesome of the lot. She is aggressive, talkative, and seems quite disobedient. Both parents agree that she gives them more trouble than any one of the others or all of them put together. She climbs about on the furniture and it is because of her that the chairs have to be kept off the floor. They had to put a latch on the door, almost at the top of the doorjamb so that she would not be able to reach it by means of chairs and table. She gets at knives, falls off things, and upsets the household generally.

Twins, Patrick and Cathleen

Born October 1939, are plump, attractive babies, who appear to be thriving. They were unusually large at birth—Patrick weighed seven pounds and Cathleen seven pounds, eight ounces—and have been doing well ever since. Someone gave the family a twin carriage; and, on the occasion of the last visit, the twins were out in this carriage in the sun on the other side of the street. The other youngsters run across the street from time to time to keep an eye on the babies. There is almost no traffic on this block, and it seems quite safe.

All but the first two children were born at home with Berwind Clinic physicians and Henry Street nurses in attendance. Mrs. Corey said that it was better that way because, while her husband did not need her to do the work, he did need her there to advise him as to what to do for the children. She got little rest and said that she would have preferred to be delivered in a hospital because that would have meant complete rest in bed for nine whole days with no responsibility. She admitted, however, that she probably would have worried so much about the children that she would not actually have rested. The Henry Street nurse, who assisted at the delivery, has been very good to them. She has obviously taken a personal interest in the family, and Mrs. Corey is grateful. Mrs. Corey showed worker a picture of the nurse bathing one of the twins with the mother looking on; this had been taken for New York Fund publicity purposes.

Mrs. Corey said that the Berwind Clinic doctor told her that her heart is weak and she must have no more children unless she wants to die young. He was so emphatic about it that she is afraid he really meant it and she has therefore "practically" made up her mind to have no more children. The Henry Street Settlement nurse referred her to the birth control clinic, but she has not gone as yet. The Coreys have abstained from sexual intercourse since the birth of the twins. As soon as she is stronger she will go to the birth control clinic. Mrs. Corey said that she went through a trying time before the twins were born because, in desperation at the thought of having another child, she took something which the druggist recommended. This was a bitter medicine (probably ergot) which had been ineffectual. It made her very sick but did not bring about miscarriage. Throughout her pregnancy she worried all the time about the possibility of having injured the baby by this medication, and was very happy to find that the twins were in perfect health at birth. Mrs. Corey said that she was so glad no harm had been done by the medicine and so relieved after feeling guilty for eight months, that she was even happy to find that she had twins instead of a single newborn child.

According to Mrs. Corey, tired and weak as she is, she enjoys the children very much, and from her manner worker was inclined to believe her. The children trooped in and out, ringing the doorbell each time, asking for things, coaxing and teasing, but throughout this her manner remained mild and calm. She answered all their requests as best she could, there was no scolding, she patted them affectionately whenever they came near her to ask for something, and at no time was there any evidence of annoyance with them.

Use of Time

Mr. Corey usually goes job hunting early in the morning. He still goes to the large factories asking for laboring work, to the markets, to the American Express or the railroads, and then comes home and helps his wife with the housework. As stated earlier, he does all the heavy work, helps with the care of the children, goes shopping, goes for surplus commodities, takes the children out when his wife wants to rest. He generally keeps busy.

Religion

Both Mr. and Mrs. Corey are Catholics, were given religious training in childhood and now attend church regularly. Mrs. Corey says that she does not know whether the priest will accept the doctor's orders about her having no more children because she understands that, even when it is a matter of life or death for the mother, the church still believes that birth control is the same as murder. In discussing what might happen if she should tell the priest in confession that she had practiced birth control, she laughed, blushed and said, "Well, I've done my share already. Seven of them. He can't kick." Her husband is deeply religious but he wants her to do anything that will safeguard her health.

Newspapers

They read the *Daily News* which is given them by one of their neighbors. They are also given books and magazines from time to time. Mrs. Corey says that her husband reads "anything he can get his hands on." He sometimes goes to the public library, but that's a long walk and he seldom has time.

Political Affiliations

Both Mr. and Mrs. Corey are aliens. If they were able to vote, Mrs. Corey said that they would probably vote for Roosevelt, because they believe he is a good man and they don't know why the others want to get rid of him.

Management

The Home Relief allowance is $42.55 semimonthly. Rental is $27 a month, and Home Relief grants the entire amount in the budget. According to Mrs. Corey, their funds are usually exhausted before the next check arrives and they are forced to borrow a little from one of their friends or neighbors. They would rather do this than buy on credit because running up a bill in the store is much too expensive, since the grocer usually adds on more than the fixed price. Mrs. Corey says that she tries to see that the children get plenty of vegetables. She buys seven quarts of milk a day and thinks that the children are fairly well fed though they have none of the extras that are tempting and interesting. She talked with much feeling about the difficult time they had with the company when their furniture was repossessed. She said she was out one day and came back to find only two mattresses left in the whole apartment. They were forced to sleep on the floor on these two mattresses for five nights. Finally they got some furniture from the St. Vincent de Paul Society. She gets discarded clothing from friends and neighbors and makes it over for the children. She says that this is easy because she sews fairly well.

Attitudes

Toward Relief

Mrs. Corey says that they are grateful for help because otherwise they would have starved. It is very hard to manage; they have not had a clothing allowance in a long time, but Mrs. Corey supposes that the Home Relief funds are low. The investigator understands their trouble, tries to do what he can for them, but he, of course, is limited by rules and regulations and shortage of Home Relief money. She does not believe WPA is any real help when a man has a large family, since it means that the Home Relief Bureau must supplement the WPA wage. Her husband, however, feels that he would like very much to be on WPA because then he would be working and might not get so restless and discouraged. She thinks he's busy enough now; Home Relief would have had to send in a WPA housekeeper after the birth of the twins if her husband had been working on a WPA job.

Toward the Future

Unquestionably Mr. Corey will continue to look for work and his wife added, "who knows—maybe he'll find it." True, he is getting disgusted and discouraged, but he will never stop trying to find a job. At the moment, he has some hope of getting work with a cement company which is opening a branch up at Huntspoint. He tries every place he hears about; most of the firms in the Bronx know him and keep promising him that when things pick up he'll be called. One happy thought, in all this difficulty, is the fact that here in America the children will, at least, get an education and perhaps be fitted for something that will enable them to make a living later on.

Toward Us

Mrs. Corey, as well as her husband, was friendly; she welcomed worker and talked freely. She said that she would be happy to see worker again because she enjoyed talking with her. When worker asked whether she might bring a book or something to keep Mary amused while she must lie in bed, mother said that this would be a great help and Mary, when asked, said that she would like a Mickey Mouse book.

OFFICE INTERVIEW

Impression

Mr. Corey is a large, dark-haired, good-looking Irishman, who looks younger than his thirty-six years. He appears to be in excellent health. His clothes were in poor condition and he did not have a hat. He speaks with a pronounced brogue, so thick that it is difficult to understand him. (He was forced to wait quite a while before the interview began, and he made every effort to be unobtrusive during this waiting period.)

Employment History

Mr. Corey was a gardener in Ireland, but he also did other kinds of laboring work. When he arrived in this country, he did unskilled work and then secured a job as a billposter at which he worked steadily for twelve years, earning approximately $40 to $50 a week. Because of intraunion trouble, he lost this job.

Relief

Mr. Corey says that he gets just enough from Relief to make a go of it. The surplus commodities are a real help, and the major deficiency is lack of clothing. On the whole he feels that Relief workers are nice people. He said that while on Relief his children have been able to have good medical attention, especially the one child who has rheumatic fever. Since he is not a citizen, Mr. Corey cannot get on WPA, although he says that he would much prefer to do so. He fears that he is getting soft and this will make it even harder to get back into a good, hard, laboring job.

Family

Mr. Corey says that his wife has her hands full caring for their seven children. One of the older children has rheumatic fever, and one of the younger ones has just come down with scarlet fever. His brother, who worked for the same firm and lost his job for the same reason as did Mr. Corey, is now on WPA. The rest of his family is in England, and this is true also of his wife's family. To the best of his knowledge they are doing well.

Time

Mr. Corey tramps all over town in search of employment, seeking out those spots where he thinks there might be need for a strong, healthy man who is anxious and willing to work. He tries to aid his wife as much as possible in order to make things easier for her.

Politics

Mr. Corey feels very bitter about unions because he holds them responsible for his loss of employment; also because he feels that they have stood in the way of his being reemployed. He emphasized that his old employer was perfectly willing to take back the men who were thrown out during the union trouble, but was unable to do so because of the union. Mr. Corey said that most of the men who lost their jobs at the time of the trouble—there were approximately seventy-five—are still unemployed.

Future

Mr. Corey believes that his best chance for work will come if business improves sufficiently so that all union men secure employment, and then employers will be able to take on nonunion men like himself. He said that until recently he had not been very worried, but as his period of unemployment lengthens and all of his efforts are of no avail, he is getting worried.

CHAPTER 12

The Uneducated

... IT IS DIFFICULT to study and evaluate any group, large or small, simple or complex, without relying on averages. But statistics can never present the full picture. In reducing individuals to numbers and behavior to categories, much is gained but much is also lost. The purpose of this chapter is to provide summaries of the life histories and army experiences of individuals representative of the various categories.

THE NONCHARGEABLE

Some of the men who were sent to the Army's Special Training Units, including some who graduated, were found to possess serious disqualifications for military service that were present at the time of induction but were not picked up by the examining physician.

W.E.B., a twenty-nine-year-old white soldier from Kentucky, was one of these. He was inducted in September 1943, and, after spending about ten weeks in the Special Training Unit at Camp Atterbury, Indiana, was assigned for basic training to the Anti-Aircraft Replacement Training

Center at Fort Eustis, Virginia. After completing his basic training, he was sent to Camp Stewart, Georgia, late in May, where he was assigned to an antiaircraft unit for further training. Starting in December 1943, with a visit to the dispensary at Fort Eustis because of a "pain in chest," Private B. reported on sick call twenty-seven times between December 1943 and September 1944. In addition, he had three stays in the hospital: at the end of January because of nasopharyngitis, acute, catarrhal; at the end of June because of pleural adhesions; and again in the middle of July for the same reason. In May the medical authorities at Fort Eustis noted that Private B. had "permanent bronchial asthma" and therefore did not meet induction standards. No action was taken at this point, however, to separate him from the service. After his second hospitalization for pleural adhesions, the Medical Officer at Camp Stewart found him "unfit for overseas assignment." As early as February 1944, however, a special form had already been filled out disqualifying him for overseas duty. At that time his basic training had been discontinued. Late in April the Medical Officer recommended that he "avoid physical overexertion," but stated that the soldier was qualified for overseas assignment. The first notation that he should go before a board for possible discharge appeared in his record at the end of July, but it was not until the end of September that he was in fact discharged.

Prior to coming into the service, Private B. had married. His last job had been as a "spreader of cloth" in the cutting room of a garment factory, for which he had been paid $17 weekly. Earlier he had worked on a 150-acre farm, where he had raised corn and tobacco, tended cattle, and driven a team of horses. Although he had completed six years of school, his score on the Army General Classification Test at the time of induction was only 57; it was because of this that he was sent to a Special Training Unit. Had the Army been able to assign this soldier to light work, in a reasonably dry environment, it might have succeeded in getting some service out of him. But the evidence accumulated rather early — as indicated by the soldier's frequent appearance at sick call — that he would be unable to live the life of a field soldier, even if excused from most strenuous duties. From the Army's viewpoint, the major error was the delay in reaching a decision to discharge him. It is rather amusing to note that he was awarded the Good Conduct Medal while awaiting separation.

W.W.S., a young white soldier inducted at Fort Oglethorpe, Georgia, in August 1943, likewise represents a screening error. Because he made a score of only 64 on the Army General Classification Test, he was sent to the Special Training Unit at Camp Shelby, Mississippi, where he spent almost four months. After being judged literate, he was assigned to an

Infantry Training Battalion at Camp Wolters, Texas, where he remained until June, when it became necessary to separate him on medical grounds. His hospital record shows that, while at Shelby, he entered the hospital with a diagnosis of "tuberculosis, pulmonary, minimal, inactive, upper lobe." After three weeks he was returned to duty. Shortly thereafter he was in the hospital again, this time with a diagnosis of "psychoneurosis, anxiety state, mild." Shortly after his arrival at Wolters, he was again in the hospital, this time with a diagnosis of "mental deficient, borderline condition." He was tested and found to have an intelligence quotient of 89, which was high enough to justify returning him to duty. A fortnight later he was back in the hospital again, this time with the original diagnosis of tuberculosis. The outpatient record shows that he was sent into the hospital because he was "spitting up blood."

Prior to his induction Private S. had been employed as a pipe layer for a short period, and before that as a hoist operator. He had earned about $40 a week, but he did not have any record of extended employment in these fields. While in the service he was absent without leave over the Christmas holidays for a period of ten days, and he was subsequently sentenced by a summary court-martial "to be restricted to company area for one month and to forfeit $33 of his pay." The report of a special physical examination made while he was still at Shelby contained the following notations: "He says that his health was good until 1939, when he got measles and pneumonia. He says that since then he has had trouble with his head, chest, and stomach. . . . At the time he got sick he had been working on odd jobs (construction since), changing jobs frequently because of his health, laying off a considerable part of the time." Here again, the record suggests that the Army was slow in reaching a decision that a chronically sick recruit would fail to make the grade. . . .

These cases seem to give support to the Army belief that the poorly educated man was a real military hazard when he also suffered from other defects. Many officers believed that, even though no one of the defects of such a man was clearly disqualifying, all of his handicaps taken together would probably prevent him from performing effectively. But before accepting this theory, logical as it sounds, one must be sure that there were not many other men who, despite other handicaps in addition to their lack of schooling, were able to perform effectively. As always, when dealing with Army records, certain mysteries remain unexplained. It is surely not clear how W.W.S. was diagnosed as mentally deficient one day and given an I.Q. of 89 the next. Nor is it much easier to understand why he should have been hospitalized repeatedly for tuberculosis within a very short period.

THE NOT ACCEPTABLE

From many points of view the individuals whose performance we judged as not acceptable are more important than any other group. Unacceptable performance is always costly to an organization, as well as to the individual, but it becomes a major danger in time of war when a military organization must gain maximum strength in the shortest possible time. There is good reason to study these cases carefully, for there would be a great gain if it were possible to identify the particular qualities of these individuals which contributed to their failure. Such knowledge would then provide one with a sounder basis for developing a future program. It must be recognized, however, that the factors responsible for the behavior of such individuals may not stand out clearly before they are inducted and given a trial.

K.L., a native of North Carolina, was living in Tennessee when he was inducted in the fall of 1943. He had been employed in a furniture factory, smoothing rough surfaces, and was earning about $34 weekly. At the time of induction it was not disclosed that he had been married three times and had "served time in jails for fighting, drinking, and bastardy charges." He had completed three years of school. He was sent to the Special Training Unit at Camp Shelby, Mississippi, where he spent about a month. Although he was adjudged literate at that time and sent on to the Armored Replacement Training Center at Fort Knox, Kentucky, his record indicates that less than thirty days after he left the Special Training Unit, he was found "unable to read at fourth-grade level." Both the outpatient and hospitalization records show the diagnosis of "alcoholism, acute" on several different occasions. Toward the end of May the soldier went absent without leave for about eight days. The psychiatrist's examination after he was apprehended led to the following report:

> This is a 37 year old, well developed soldier, who went AWOL 8 days after finishing his basic training. He was worried about the fact that he could not get an allotment to his child by the first wife, because his 3rd wife, whom he describes as a tramp and who married him under the influence of liquor, is trying to get the allotments. He wants to divorce the woman. The soldier got drunk to drown his sorrows and went AWOL. The EM had a 3rd grade education at 11 years. He has an IQ of 63 and mental age of 10 years. He worked as a logger, farmer and furniture worker.
>
> Recommendations:
>
> 1. Average punishment.
> 2. Suspend sentence.

This soldier was given not one but three chances; but, as was brought out in the testimony before the board which held hearings on whether to separate him, "Anytime he got hold of liquor, he lost all sense." The Army tried to salvage him: "We had to be very careful what kind of a job we picked for him because he does not get along, does not like to take orders from noncommissioned officers. So we gave him an outside job where he does not have noncommissioned officers around." The sergeant directly responsible was "fed up" with him:

> This soldier was a very poor soldier. His morals are bad for the men he works for. He is a chronic alcoholic, cannot stay away from it. He causes a lot of commotion. When he gets ahold of some drinks he gets out of his head. He will do this often if left alone. He is a very bad actor and does not have respect for anyone. When we put him on a job he had to be watched or he would leave and show up in the evening intoxicated. He is not trustworthy at all. On any job he is just no good as far as our company is concerned. To me a man like him would be better off away from the Army than in it.

After additional witnesses were called and various exhibits were introduced, the board concluded that this soldier should be separated from the service because of "habits or traits of character which render retention in the service undesirable." The Commanding General approved the recommendation and the soldier was separated early in December with a "blue discharge," which is a discharge "other than honorable." The applicant appealed, but the Secretary of War's Discharge Review Board concluded that there was no additional evidence of sufficient weight and credibility to warrant reversal of the previous action of the War Department. Here was the prototype of the soldier that the old Army officer referred to when he said that the illiterate or semiliterate was frequently an "expensive soldier."

A twenty-three-year-old Negro soldier from Ohio, L.H., after spending one month at the Special Training Unit at Camp Atterbury, Indiana, late in 1943, was assigned to the 613th Training Group at the Army Air Base at Lincoln, Nebraska. Within a month he was sent into the hospital with a diagnosis of "mental deficiency, borderline." He spent thirty days in the hospital and was then sent back to duty. Within a fortnight, he was returned to the hospital with the same diagnosis. During his first hospitalization the Commanding Officer of the hospital requested the Commanding Officer of the Lincoln Army Air Field to institute proceedings so that the man might be discharged on the grounds of ineptness. At the time of the hearing, the psychiatrist testified that "this man is a mental defective with an IQ of 75 and a mental age of ten years and two months.

He is below the minimum standards of Mobilization Regulation 1–9 and is a risk if retained in the Army. It is impossible to get any useful service out of him, and he should be discharged under Section VIII proceedings on the basis of ineptness and lack of adaptability."

Private H. testified that he was thirty-three; was born in Akron, Ohio; and was married. He continued:

> I can write to my wife—and read, write a little. I only went to the third grade in school. I was waiting tables in a hotel; I was getting $12.50 a week, and $3.00 a week tips, and I got my food and uniform.
>
> I have been in the army since the 18th day of October, 1943. I have never been punished by company punishment and have had no trouble with the M.P.'s. In civilian life didn't have nothing but trouble with drinking.
>
> I been drillin' and marchin' and doin' everything I was told to do since I am in the army. I have taken some basic at Camp Atterbury in Indiana. I went to school to learn to read and write there; graduated from there, and they sent me here for basic. I went as far as I could go—up to the rifle range. They had cut out the obstacle course before we got that far. Drillin' was all right if they didn't do too much walkin'. My sides started to hurtin' me. I had trouble before I came in the army. I was in the hospital for it. I was drinkin' and picked up one end of a piano and lifted it up and something popped in my back. I was strapped in bed because I wouldn't stay in bed. . . . I got scared.
>
> I get along very fine with the other fellows. Have no trouble with noncoms. I never been scolded by the lieutenants. My only trouble is that back. I don't know what kind of job I could do; anytime I start sweeping my side starts to bother me. Even carrying coal gets me down. If I get out of the army, I'll get medical treatment and try to fix myself up so I can work. I can't do anything but wait tables; I was turned down in a defense plant because of my back.

The record goes on to note that Private H. admitted that "I drink quite a bit, just when I can get it. I don't throw any out. I get nervous, and that's the only thing that settles me." With limited mentality, a tendency to alcoholism, and a physical disability, it is not surprising that his company commander acted to have him discharged as quickly as possible. Because of the fact that he had not gotten into serious trouble because of drinking, the board was willing to give him an honorable discharge on the ground that he was inept.

J.H.B., a nineteen-year-old Negro soldier, was born and grew up in rural North Carolina, and was inducted into the Army at Fort Bragg, North Carolina, in October 1944. After spending two months at a Special

Training Unit at Fort Benning, Georgia, he was assigned to a quartermaster unit at Camp Lee, Virginia, where he remained from January until the end of August 1945, at which time he was given an honorable discharge because of ineptness and lack of ability for military service. The following quotation, entitled "Gist of Testimony," is found in his records:

> Private B. testified that his head and chest hurt him all the time during civilian life and after his induction. Private B. completed two years of grammar school. According to the testimony of the witnesses, Pvt. B. has never caused any trouble and does all he is told to do but is not very intelligent. The witnesses stated the Army could not reeducate or rehabilitate him to the point where he could do a useful day's work. He is able to do only light jobs around the company area and even at that requires close supervision. It is the opinion of the Board that Pvt. B. should be discharged from the Army due to inaptness and lack of adaptability for military service which render his retention in the Service undesirable.

A white coal miner who had been earning about $30 a week was inducted from his home state, Kentucky, late in 1943. After spending about one month in a Special Training Unit at Camp Atterbury, Indiana, he was declared literate and was sent for basic infantry training to Camp Croft, South Carolina. Three months later, he was ordered to appear before a board of officers who were holding hearings on whether he should be separated from the service. The record shows that he did not know what is meant by "the Axis countries"; that he did not know President Roosevelt's first name; that he thought there were ten nickels in a dollar; that he had heard of Pearl Harbor but did not know what or where it is. He thought that Roosevelt was the Governor of Kentucky, his own state. When asked how many would be left if a boy has fifteen newspapers and sells eleven of them, he claimed there would be five left, and he did this computation on his fingers. His platoon leader testified that "he didn't seem any too interested in his training; he just seemed to stare off into space. He never seemed to pay much attention. His inspections were not any too good. I feel that he is dull mentally. I do not believe he can be trained to be a satisfactory soldier." The board agreed with this evaluation and gave Private C. an honorable discharge because the board members considered him inept and unsuited for military service. This soldier had been absent without leave twice during his short army career and had received two summary courts-martial. There may be some question of whether this soldier was in fact as dull as he appeared or whether he simulated stupidity in order to avoid discipline and to escape from service.

The four soldiers described so far whose service was adjudged not acceptable were discharged early in their army careers. Several others were classified as not acceptable even though they remained in the Army for a considerable period of time, and even though they received honorable discharges.

S.C.H. was inducted in September 1943 and was not separated until May 3, 1946. Despite this long period of service, we concluded that his service was in fact not acceptable, that he was more trouble than he was worth to the Army. He was absent without leave for the first time in the spring of 1944 for a total of fifteen days, and again from November 5, 1944, to February 14, 1945, a total of ninety-seven days. He was sentenced to confinement at hard labor for six months, but on April 17 the balance of his sentence was suspended. His record shows one major hospitalization, which occurred after he went overseas. He developed "new syphilis" and was hospitalized for thirty days. In his first major assignment after completing basic training in 1944, his efficiency rating was "unsatisfactory" for a period of seven months. Since his period of service coincided with the end of the war, a time of frequent reassignments from one unit to another, Private H. was seldom in a unit long enough for the commanding officer to assess his performance. However, since he lost 142 days by being absent without leave and by confinement after apprehension, and an additional thirty days because of "new syphilis," and since there were no strong counterindications, this soldier's performance was evaluated as not acceptable. He was separated during the demobilization period in the spring of 1946. The following year he was confined to a state reformatory "for a period of two to fourteen years for the crime of conspiracy to commit a felony. . . .

We have presented the records of five soldiers whom we placed in the not-acceptable category. . . . They were the men on whom the Army took a chance and lost. In war the investment of limited resources in men who fail to perform is dangerous. It is not possible for us to analyze in detail the factors contributing to the ineffective performance of this group. . . . Even on the basis of these few cases, however, several comments can be made about the Army's manner of handling the men who failed to perform effectively. Although supposedly a strict disciplinary organization, the Army actually gave a man not only one chance but several chances before punishing him severely or removing him from the service. Several men who were kept in the Army until demobilization really failed to give any worthwhile service but were never severely disciplined. Like most large organizations, the Army apparently was able to carry a considerable amount of "dead wood." It may well be that this considerate approach, though not necessarily adhered to in every case, was sufficiently prevalent to be noticed by m ny soldiers. Instead of contributing to efficiency, it may actually have militated against it. There were probably a considerable number of men who would have tried harder to succeed if they had been sure that swift and certain punishment would follow their unacceptable performance. The extent to which the Army was unduly relaxed is also indicated by the fact that it was willing to grant honorable discharges to men as long as they had not become serious troublemakers during their period of service.

THE ACCEPTABLE

Although there were a considerable number of graduates from Special Training Units who were not acceptable, there were many more who served in an acceptable or superior manner. The acceptable group was really composed of two different types of men. One was the soldier who was more or less average; he met the demands which were made on him without performing in a distinguished manner, but likewise without causing the Army any special trouble. Then there was the man whose acceptable performance was really a composite of good performance counterbalanced on occasion by unacceptable performance, so that his acceptable rating was an average of the two.

W.G., a nineteen-year-old Negro soldier from South Carolina, was inducted in November 1944, and sent immediately to the Special Training Unit at Fort Benning, Georgia, where he spent a month. Prior to his entrance into the service, he had been employed in general farm work. His record shows that he had completed seven years of school, which probably explains why he was able to finish his special training in less than four weeks. After completing his basic training at the Infantry Replacement Training Center at Fort McClellan, Alabama, he was sent overseas to the Pacific Theater. He served there for about fifteen months as a member of a quartermaster service company. His efficiency rating was excellent. He was returned to the United States for separation in September 1946. At the time of his discharge, he was a cook. He had won two Bronze Service Stars for the Philippine and Luzon Campaigns. He had lost no time for disciplinary reasons; had never been in a hospital; had been on sick call only twice, once for a cold and a second time for gonorrhea. In October 1945 he was promoted to private first class. Clearly, here was a soldier whose service was acceptable.

E.M., a thirty-year-old Negro born in Georgia, had migrated north and was working as a laborer at a weekly wage of $24 when he was inducted at Fort Benjamin Harrison, Indiana, in October 1943. He had completed only four years of school, and so was sent to the Special Training Unit at Camp Atterbury, Indiana. He was assigned upon the completion of this training to a quartermaster service company at Fort Devens, Massachusetts. After six months of training, the company was sent to the European theater, initially to a general depot in England. He remained with this company until it was returned to the United States a year later. Except for a few weeks prior to separation in November 1945, his entire service was with this company. For such periods as efficiency ratings were available, Private M. was rated excellent. He was admitted to the hospital only once, for an acute nasopharyngitis. Immediately after induction, he was confined to quarters because of a urethritis, which was stated to be nonvenereal. These illnesses kept him from duty for fifteen days, but he lost no other time. He had no disciplinary troubles and was awarded three Bronze Service Stars for the campaigns of Northern France, Central Europe, and the Rhineland.

R.L.C., white, was born in rural Mississippi and was inducted from there in October 1943, at the age of nineteen. In civilian life he had been a farmer. He had completed six years of school. Shortly after induction he was assigned to the Special Training Unit at Camp Shelby, Mississippi, and remained there for more than three months. During this time he was hospitalized for a fortnight with German measles. He was sent to the Field Artillery Replacement Training Center at Fort Sill, Oklahoma, and, after a number of reassignments, found himself en route to the European theater at the end of November 1944, as a member of the 254th Infantry Regiment. In the middle of January 1945, while cleaning his carbine, he wounded himself and was hospitalized for a period of about a month, after which he was sent back to duty with the notation "limited assignment." For the rest of the war and until he was returned to the United States late in 1945, he was assigned to an aviation engineer battalion. He was separated from the Army in March of 1946 during the general demobilization. His record shows that he qualified as a sharpshooter, with both the carbine and the rifle. He had been awarded two Bronze Service Stars for the Campaigns of Northern France and for the Rhineland. His record was free of disciplinary infractions, and he had been on sick call but once because of a cough which hung on for three weeks, during which he lost ten pounds. All of his efficiency ratings were excellent, though in many cases the comment was "unknown." This was to be expected in light of the frequent changes in his assignments. . . .

These cases speak for themselves. Certainly these men gave the

Army acceptable service. The only point one might raise is whether some, if not all, of them should not have been placed in a category higher than acceptable. They were men who did their job competently, who did not lose time for medical reasons, and who did not get into disciplinary trouble.

Two further points are worth mentioning. We might speculate about how these men would have performed had the Army made greater demands on them by presenting them with greater challenges and greater opportunities for distinguished performance. It was a general impression of many well-informed observers of and participants in military life that the average soldier was always willing to do what was required of him but seldom strained to do more. Hence to a considerable extent his performance level was determined by the situation that confronted him rather than by his own personality constellation. The other point that should be mentioned is that these acceptable soldiers did not try to get away with anything, particularly by seeking respite from their obligations and duties through medical channels.

GOOD SOLDIERS

Whatever questions the skeptic still may have retained at this point about the success of the program of inducting and training illiterates should be dispelled by the reading of the following cases, which demonstrate very clearly that considerable numbers of the poorly educated group turned out to be good soldiers—not merely acceptable, but clearly good men. In reading these cases it is important to keep in mind the extent to which education was required to enable a man to meet certain performance standards.

H.L.B. was thirty-one when he was inducted from Chattanooga, Tennessee, where he was born. He was a finisher for a furniture manufacturer, and was earning $20 weekly. He had been a general painter for almost fifteen years, earning, when employed, up to $40 a week. He had been married and divorced, and had remarried. Before starting work he had completed six years of school. Inducted at Fort Oglethorpe, Georgia, he was sent to the Special Training Unit at Camp Shelby, Mississippi, to which he was assigned for only five weeks. He was then sent to the Armored Replacement Training Center at Fort Knox, Kentucky, where he received his basic training, at the end of which he was classified as a "light tank crewman." His efficiency during basic training was assessed as excellent. He had a short assignment, about ten weeks, with the Headquarters Company of the 20th Armored Division at Camp Campbell, Kentucky, and then spent seven months with the 8th Armored Infantry Battalion at the same camp, during which he received a new duty assignment, rifleman. In all these assignments his efficiency was rated as excellent. During this period he also qualified as a sharpshooter with the rifle. Early in February he shipped out for Europe as a member of the 20th Armored Division. This division arrived late and was in combat for a relatively short time, although at one point, just before the German capitulation, it ran into fanatical opposition in the Munich area. H.L.B. was awarded the Combat Infantryman Badge, which made him automatically eligible for the Bronze Star Medal. Throughout his service overseas, he continued to receive excellent ratings. While still at Camp Campbell, he had been promoted to private first class. At the time of induction his physical defects record noted "syphilis, latent; defective hearing." However, throughout his entire tour of duty—he was separated just prior to the end of 1945—he was in the hospital only twice: once for pneumonia and a second time for only two days for observation because of pains in the abdomen. Moreover, he was on sick call but twice. He never lost any time because of disciplinary action.

E.F. was a twenty-five-year-old Negro from rural Mississippi at the time of his induction in August 1943. He was single. For the two years preceding his induction, he had been working in a civilian capacity as a mess-hall hand, cook, and dishwasher at Camp Shelby for $20 a week. Before that he had been a farmer. He had completed five years of school. Shortly after his induction he was assigned to the Special Training Unit at Camp Shelby, Mississippi, in which he spent two months. Directly thereafter, he was sent to a quartermaster service company at Fort Devens, Massachusetts, with a military occupational specialty of laborer. He spent six months with this company, receiving an efficiency rating of excellent, and then went with it to the European theater. He stayed with this same company throughout his entire tour of duty, his efficiency rating remaining excellent. Shortly after returning to the United States in August 1945, he became a member of the detachment at the Veterans Administration Facility, Fort Howard, Maryland, with which he remained until he was separated from the Army toward the end of January 1946. All his ratings were excellent. He received three Bronze Service Stars for the campaigns of Northern France, the Rhineland, and Central Europe. Moreover, in February his unit was cited and received the Meritorious Unit Award. In June 1944 E.F. was promoted to private first class. He had but one hospitalization, for acute appendicitis. His outpatient record shows occasional visits for chest colds and coughs and once for gonorrhea. E.F. had no disciplinary trouble and lost no time.

F.N.J. was only eighteen when he was inducted late in November 1944. He was a Negro from rural Georgia, and his record suggests that he had spent all of his life close to his birthplace. Prior to entering the service, he had earned $20 a week dressing chickens. Earlier he had been a farmer and had received wages in kind. He had been married but was separated from his wife. Inducted at Fort Benning, Georgia, he was immediately assigned to the Special Training Unit at that post, but remained there for only three weeks. His record indicates that he had completed five years of schooling. He was sent to the Army Service Forces Training Center at Fort Warren, Wyoming, where he remained during the first half of 1945. In June he was en route to the Pacific theater as a member of a quartermaster truck company. He spent thirteen months overseas, and for this service he received a rating of excellent. He was returned to the United States at the end of September 1946 and was separated shortly thereafter. He was promoted to technician fifth grade in October 1945 but lost the rating because of a summary court-martial for speeding in violation of traffic regulations. Two other summary courts-martial convictions were also for traffic infractions, but he was never sentenced to confinement, only to loss of pay. Apparently these were considered minor violations, for they did not stand in the way of F.N.J.'s being promoted to corporal in May 1946. Aside from a fortnight's hospitalization as a result of mumps, he lost no time for medical reasons. His outpatient record shows that he had contracted gonorrhea on four occasions. At the time of separation there was a notation on his record, "recommended for further military training," which indicates that the Army considered him a good soldier. . . .

It is worth noting that these good soldiers came from very limited backgrounds, many from isolated rural areas, but that nonetheless they were able to make the difficult transition to the big impersonal organization that the Army was and to do so without loss of balance or personal direction. It is true that these particular individuals were subjected to relatively little combat action, but there is little reason to question that they would have been able to perform well had they been so challenged.

VERY GOOD SOLDIERS

Although the Army had more than 8 million men at its peak strength, it was not a mass army in the sense that the Russian and the Chinese armies were. Hence the efficiency of the U.S. Army depended to a greater extent on the performance of each individual, and more particularly on the performance of those individuals who had the ability and the motivation to do better than the average. It is very important, therefore, to appraise any manpower program in terms not only of the numbers who fail but also of the numbers the program makes available who do an outstanding job. It may well be that, in our critical appraisals of manpower programs, we are much too conscious of those who fail and pay too little attention to those who are outstanding successes. This gives special importance, therefore, to those few men who turned out to be very good soldiers.

J.S.H. was just over eighteen when inducted into the Army from Cleveland, Ohio, late in 1944. He was white, single, and had completed eight years of schooling. He was born in West Virginia but had been living for some time in northern Ohio. He had been working, immediately prior to induction, as a semiskilled aircraft assembler earning $32 weekly. Before that he had been a general assistant and laborer in an aircraft plant. In light of his eight years of schooling, he did very poorly at induction on the Army General Classification Test, for he scored only 56. For this reason he was assigned to the Special Training Unit at Camp Atterbury, Indiana, but shortly thereafter he was retested and made a score of 75, which, if not distinguished, was satisfactory. He was therefore determined capable of absorbing military training, and early in the new year was sent for basic training to the Infantry Replacement Training Center at Camp Wolters, Texas. He spent five months there and received an excellent efficiency rating. Shortly thereafter he was sent to Hawaii and assigned to the Headquarters Company of the Personnel Center of the Central Pacific Base Command. After three months service, he was promoted to sergeant. During the year he spent overseas, all in Hawaii, he had several different assignments; but in every instance his efficiency rating was superior. When separated from the Army in August 1946, he was a platoon sergeant. He lost no time in the hospital throughout his Army career. His preinduction examination noted that he had "occupation dermatitis," and during his tour of duty he visited the outpatient clinic five times because of skin eruption. He had lost no time for any disciplinary cause. Although Sergeant H. was inducted too late in the war to participate in combat, he must be adjudged a very good soldier because of the grade he achieved and because of the consistency with which his work was evaluated as being superior. It is well known that the rating of excellent was handed out too easily, but there is little doubt that a superior rating was reserved for soldiers of relatively high efficiency. Sergeant H., moreover, received a superior rating from five different organizations during his year in Hawaii.

E.S.S., a white married man of twenty-seven, was inducted at the end of October 1943 at Camp Atterbury, Indiana. He, too, had had eight years of schooling but was found to be illiterate at induction. Just prior to his induction, he had been working as a riveter and assembler in a farm machinery plant, and before that he had spent eleven years as a machine operator, earning, at the end, about $45 weekly. He had been born in central Indiana and, as far as one can judge, had spent his entire life in the town of his birth. Shortly after induction, he was assigned to a Special Training Unit, where he spent a month, at the end of which he received a score of 66 on the Army General Classification Test, quite disappointing considering his school record and his special training. He was sent for further training to an engineer company at Camp Gordon Johnston, Florida, where he remained for five months and was trained as an ammunition handler. During this period, he was rated as excellent. In May he was shipped with his company to the Pacific, where he remained with the same company until early in 1946, when he was returned to the United States. During the period of his overseas service, his specialty was changed from ammunition handler to semiskilled construction foreman. In every instance his work was graded excellent. Before going overseas, he qualified in the use of the carbine and the 30 and 50 caliber machine guns. E.S.S. earned four Bronze Stars, for the Philippine Liberation, New Guinea, Northern Solomons, and Luzon campaigns. He also earned the Bronze Arrowhead Award for participating in the amphibious operation at Morotai. In February 1945 he was promoted to private first class, later that year to technician fourth grade, and then in December to staff sergeant. Just after getting overseas in August 1944, E.S.S. received a summary court-martial because "he struck a non-commissioned officer in the face with his fist." Apparently there were some extenuating circumstances because his only punishment was to forfeit $20 of his pay for one month. Since he later received a Good Conduct Medal and was promoted to staff sergeant, we have disregarded this incident. He lost no time for any disciplinary action, was in the hospital but once for less than a week, and was on sick call only once.

J.B., a thirty-two-year-old married Negro, was inducted at Camp Blanding, Florida, in October 1943. He had never been to school. However, he stated at induction that his hobbies were "hunting, horseback riding, and rifle shooting." His civilian labor record showed that he was a semiskilled laborer and prior to that had been a section hand on a railroad. His earnings were between $25 and $30 per week. Shortly after induction, he was assigned to the Special Training Unit at Camp Shelby, Mississippi, where he spent three months. At the end of this period, he received a score of 61 on the Army General Classification Test.

His record suggests that even after spending three months in a

Special Training Unit, he had scarcely acquired a minimum level of literacy. However, such men did not have to be discharged if they seemed to possess the overall capacity that would make it likely that they could complete training and serve successfully. J.B. was one of the men who was retained in the service on the ground that despite his limited literacy, he could probably make the grade. He was sent to Camp Claiborne, Louisiana, for training as a member of an engineer general service unit, where he was assigned an occupational specialty of "bridge builder." After eleven months of training, during which he was rated as excellent, the unit sailed for the European theater. Shortly after the end of the war in Europe, the unit was sent to the Pacific. Throughout this period, J.B. was rated excellent. While in Europe, he earned one Bronze Service Star for the Rhineland campaign. While in training he qualified as a rifle sharpshooter. Late in 1944 he was promoted to private first class, and in January 1945 he was promoted to technician fifth grade. His record shows no evidence that he was ever in the hospital or that he ever appeared at sick call. When he was profiled at Camp Claiborne, he received a perfect mark on each item—general physical condition, upper and lower extremities, hearing, eyesight, mental and emotional stability. He had no disciplinary difficulties throughout his Army career, and at the time of separation from the service in the spring of 1946 he joined the Enlisted Reserve Corps in an inactive status. . . .

E.H., a white soldier, born and still living in rural Kentucky when inducted, represents perhaps the clearest case of a man who should be classified as a very good soldier. He was inducted at the age of nineteen in the summer of 1943. While being examined for registration a year previously, he fainted and fell and suffered a simple fracture and a lacerated wound, for which he was hospitalized at the local Air Force Station Hospital. Shortly after induction, he was sent to the Special Training Unit at Camp Atterbury, Indiana, where he spent two months. He had attended school for four years. The date is not given; but when E.H. took the Army General Classification Test, probably prior to his assignment to the Special Training Unit, he received the very low score of 42. After completing the special training, he was sent to the Infantry Replacement Training Center at Camp Blanding, Florida. Although many men received ratings of excellent for character and efficiency during basic training, E.H. was graded very good in character and only satisfactory in efficiency. He was trained as a rifleman. Immediately after D–Day he was en route to the European theater as a member of the 8th Infantry Division. He received the Combat Infantry Badge, which made him automatically eligible for the Bronze Star Medal. Moreover, he earned three Bronze Service Stars for the campaigns of Northern France,

and Rhineland, and Central Europe. But his most important achievement was the award of the Silver Star for gallantry in action, which
carried the following citation:

> Sgt. H., a squad leader, exposed himself to enemy small arms,
> mortar and artillery fire to work his way to within 25 yards of an
> enemy machine gun position which was holding up their advance.
> He threw 2 hand grenades and then overran the positions, killing
> one of the enemy and wounding two others. Later, during the attack,
> his squad accounted for more than 30 Germans. Sgt. H.'s great
> courage, coolness under fire and devotion to duty were an inspira-
> tion to his men.

H. was promoted to private first class in October 1944, to sergeant
early in March, and to staff sergeant in October 1945. During his army
career he was in the hospital but once for a slight injury. His outpatient
log shows two entries, once for a mild acute gastritis and a second time
during basic training for painful right foot.

There is clearly no single pattern discernible with respect to the
backgrounds of these very good soldiers. Although two of them had
considerably more education than the average for the group, it is worth
noting that one man had never been to school, failed to pass the examination in the Specialized Training Unit, and was retained in the Army only
by administrative discretion. It is also worth noting that one man's
record was marred by a civilian conviction for manslaughter, and that
the winner of the Silver Star had hardly an auspicious beginning in the
Army, either at induction or during basic training. This is simply further evidence of the extreme caution that must be exercised in singling
out any one factor from which to predict a man's later behavior. . . .

We believe that our categories are most reliable at the extremes—
those classified as not-acceptable soldiers and those whose performance
was adjudged to have been good or very good. We place less importance
on the intermediate gradations, particularly the subtle differences between
acceptable and good, and between good and very good. But whatever the
limitation of the classification system may be, we are convinced that more
than four out of every five Special Training Unit graduates gave satisfactory performance, and more than one out of three were good or very
good soldiers.

CHAPTER 13

Soldiers Who Failed

THE ARMY dominated the life of everybody in uniform. No man, day or night, weekday or weekend, could get free of it. The aim of this chapter is to illustrate how various organizational policies and procedures affected the performance of the individual soldier. . . .

No organization can benefit from the advantages of specialization without strict adherence to established principles and procedures. The larger the organization, the greater is the need for basic policies to guide those in subordinate positions. It has been said that the great virtue of this approach for the Army is that it enables a sergeant to carry on even if all his officers become casualties.

The fact that the Army expanded more than thirtyfold in less than four years precipitated problems for which satisfactory answers could not always be readily found. This chapter will call attention to some of the policies that had an adverse effect on the performance of particular groups of soldiers. We are not seeking to reach a judgment about these policies and procedures. The Army and the other armed services did succeed in defeating the Germans and the Japanese. Our sole interest is to illustrate how organizational factors can have an adverse effect on the performance of particular individuals.

Four facets of military organization—investment, planning, discipline, and assignment—have been singled out for specific consideration. The Army could never have expanded so rapidly had it not devoted major resources to the task of converting civilians into soldiers. In addition to investing in their training, the Army had to devote considerable resources to supportive activities. For instance, all Americans insisted that the Army supply excellent medical service for the soldiers who became ill or injured. The investments the Army made in its men had a considerable influence on their effectiveness as soldiers. Pressed for time, the Army could not make an optimal investment in each man to bring him to his highest level of performance. It had to be satisfied with making a reasonable investment.

The Army's lack of experience in screening and training very large numbers obscured some of the steps it might have taken to reduce unnecessary losses. The Army's only direct experience with large-scale mobilization was in World War I. Time dimmed some of these lessons, while changes in resources and requirements made others obsolescent. Planning lagged behind these changes. It was not until the third and fourth year of mobilization that the Army developed mental hygiene clinics and special training units to help handicapped soldiers. Entering the conflict with incomplete and inadequate plans, the Army had to fight and learn at the same time. Inevitably it paid a price for improvisation.

No organization, large or small, can exist without basic discipline: The members must have a clear understanding of what is required of them and realize that failure will lead to punishment. The Army had an elaborate system of discipline. But no system is better than the men who operate it. The Army had to rely primarily on recently commissioned officers who had no experience with its traditions, who knew little about the men for whom they were responsible, and who frequently had never before held a leadership position. As a result, gross inequities often developed in the administration of military justice. Soldiers guilty of the identical offense might initially receive sentences varying from three to thirty years in prison.

But not all the difficulties, or even most of them, arose because of excessive severity. Often it was failure to enforce discipline that led to the ineffective performance of many soldiers. Officers found it easier to get rid of a troublemaker by reassigning or discharging him than to prepare formal charges and hold him for trial by court-martial.

The Army's disciplinary problems were compounded by the fact that the American public insisted and the Army agreed that a soldier whose ineffectiveness grew out of emotional illness should not be disciplined. Since the sick were entitled to the best medical attention, everything possible was done to restore a soldier to health. And it was not until late in the war that the Army came to recognize that the discrepancy between conditions in combat—where injury or death might come at any moment—and those prevailing in rear hospitals was so great that many soldiers sought to escape from the front lines by becoming or remaining invalided. Most of them were not malingerers; they were more the victims of their own unconscious fears and anxieties. The war was over before the Army was able to resolve the dilemma between its desires to provide the best hospital treatment for those in need of it and to prevent soldiers who feared to return to duty from holding on to or exaggerating their symptoms.

Among the most important personnel decisions the Army made was the duty to which it assigned a soldier. If a man was assigned to work beyond his capacities—either physical, intellectual, or emotional—it was only a matter of time before the strain made it impossible for him to serve effectively.

It was often just as difficult for men who were given work far below their capacity. Although most soldiers could accept such assignments, a minority could not tolerate work that made a mockery of their capacity, training, and aspirations. Among the many who were underassigned, some developed such deep frustrations that they broke down.

INVESTMENT

We have noted earlier that no man could become a soldier unless the Army made an investment in converting and training him, and that in the midst of a major war the Army was under great pressure to invest only in those who were most likely to prove effective. It could not afford to devote too much time or too many resources to conversion and training; but neither could it afford to skimp, for in that case large numbers would be inadequately prepared to perform effectively.

Optimal investment for the Army was a function of four variables: the size and quality of the nation's manpower resources; the time schedule that the enemy was forcing on the Army to get trained divisions into the field; the risk the Army was willing to assume with respect to men who might fail if they were forced through an accelerated program; and, finally, the number of trained instructors the Army could allocate to the training task. The following cases indicate some of the consequences for the performance of individual soldiers that resulted from the Army's attempts to balance these complex variables.

Little is known of C.B.E.'s early life, other than the fact that he was born in a rural area of the South and was brought up on a farm. He did complete three years of schooling. Later he worked as a farm laborer until drafted for military service at the age of thirty-three.

After leaving the reception center, he was shipped across the country to the West Coast and joined a newly formed infantry division. His group arrived shortly after basic training had started, and, because of further delays in processing, they missed over a week of the thirteen-week training period. Private E. found the work very difficult from the beginning. Because of his limited intelligence, he could not absorb new material as rapidly as many other soldiers. Military drill was particularly difficult. Nevertheless, he was healthy and in good physical condition from his work on the farm. He had no difficulty keeping up with the others on hikes in spite of the fact that he was somewhat older. Furthermore, he liked the Army and felt strongly that it was his duty to serve. He was generally well liked and was considered a man who tried hard to be a good soldier.

Ten weeks of training, however, proved rather conclusively that Private E. would not make the grade without some special instruction and assistance. He had learned some things but was still far behind the majority of his group. Accordingly, he and five other soldiers were removed from regular training for special classes, in accordance with a recent directive from division headquarters. Over a two-week period they received twenty-eight hours of instruction in basic military subjects from one of the company officers. The rest of their duty hours were spent in performing various work details around the company area. On the latter Private E.'s performance was quite satisfactory as long as he was told exactly what to do and was guided until he understood clearly what the work entailed. It took a long time to instruct him, but once he had learned what was expected, he worked hard. In the special classes, however, it was a different story. Twenty-eight hours were quite insufficient, and he failed a test given at the end of the two-week period. Possibly with the twelve to sixteen weeks of special training that the Army later introduced for such individuals, he could have become a soldier; but two weeks were certainly not enough.

At that time, in early 1943, it was official Army policy to discharge any soldier who, after a reasonable trial at duty, was considered so lacking in the necessary intelligence that, even with intensive training, he might not be able to meet minimum requirements. In other words, the Army, already faced with a tremendous training burden, did not want to increase this burden by investing in intensive instruction of soldiers who might have to be separated from the service anyway. In the division of which Private E. was a member, this policy was interpreted to mean that any soldier who could not satisfactorily complete the special two-week course should be evaluated with a view to discharge. A board of officers was established for this purpose.

After failing the test of basic military subject matter, Private E. was immediately sent for psychological testing. He was found to have the intelligence of a child of eight and one-half years old. His I.Q. of 60 was sufficiently low to bring into question the advisability of further military training. It was possible that he might eventually be able to learn the necessary material, but how long that would take remained in doubt. There was no certainty that he could ever absorb enough to be a competent soldier. The board of officers felt that the Army should not make the investment in further training, and accordingly he was discharged with just over four months of service.

As a civilian C.B.E. has made a quite satisfactory adjustment at a level consistent with his limited intellectual capabilities. He has been employed primarily as a farm laborer, but he has done some highway construction work. In 1950 he married a woman who had recently been widowed and shortly thereafter started farm management training under the Veterans Administration. He continued for sixteen months, performing quite satisfactorily. At present he is sharecropping his own farm....

M.E.O. completed the eighth grade in school at the age of seventeen, having failed several grades because of irregular attendance. For the next three years he worked in a sawmill. After that he drifted from one job to another, working usually as a welder or mechanic. Although he traveled a good deal, he always remained in the deep South. Except for one hospitalization, during which he was treated for syphilis, his health was good. In 1941 he married, and a child was born shortly thereafter. He and his wife lived near an Army base, where he worked.

In the summer of 1942 he began to feel weak and began to think that he was "rotting away." His family physician referred him to a mental hospital, where he was found to be suffering from an acute psychosis. He remained in the hospital for two weeks, during which time he was given electric shock therapy. Although considerably improved, he did not get a job after returning home, and this, combined with many family problems, led to frequent fights with his wife. Finally they separated. Shortly afterward an induction order arrived, and M.E.O. entered the Army. At that time his mental condition appeared to be quite normal, and he did not inform anyone that he had been discharged from the hospital only four months previously.

Although his performance in basic training was satisfactory, Private O. reported on sick call several times during the first month complaining of what appeared to be mild convulsions. The doctor at the dispensary, suspecting epilepsy, sent him to the hospital for a more complete study.

There he appeared cheerful, mixed well with the other patients, and did not exhibit any signs of epilepsy or other illness. He seemed quite normal. For the first time, however, he discussed his prior hospitalization for psychosis.

Army policy at that time barred the induction of all individuals who were known to have been hospitalized for a psychotic condition. This policy had been adopted because such men tended to become psychotic again, thus frequently making any training investment valueless; moreover, once these men broke down again, an extensive investment in treatment was required to rehabilitate them, an investment that in many cases did not yield satisfactory results. The Army's objectives were military, not medical, and it was policy to avoid extensive medical treatment of soldiers who probably could not be returned to full duty.

Accordingly, Private O. was given a medical discharge, even though he was not psychotic at the time, because the Army did not want to take the risk of investing in training a man likely to break down in the future. He was, in fact, returned to duty, although not to training status, and served for over a month while awaiting his release. At no time did he exhibit any psychotic symptoms.

In civilian life M.E.O. maintained a relatively good adjustment, although he did not go back to live with his wife and they later were divorced. His work pattern was similar to that of his pre-Army period, although possibly more irregular. He held jobs in many different parts of the country. Employment was easy to obtain and, having worked as a welder and mechanic, he was paid well even though he rarely stayed on a job for more than three months. He died in 1946 as a result of an accident that occurred while he was repairing farm machinery.

These cases illustrate some of the difficult problems the Army had to resolve in determining whether to train a man and how much of an investment to make in him in the hope of securing an effective soldier. In the case of C.B.E., it was willing only to give him two weeks of remedial instruction. Later in the war, when manpower became tighter, the Army was willing to make a much greater effort to bring the uneducated up to minimum standards. . . . As far as M.E.O. was concerned, the Army had a firm policy that men who had suffered from a psychosis would not be accepted for military service; and, if they slipped through the screening, they would, upon identification, be discharged. The likelihood of their future ineffectiveness was too high to justify holding them or investing in their training.

PLANNING AND IMPROVISATION

In establishing standards of performance, the Army was hampered by the absence of reliable experimental data that would have enabled it to judge the advantages and limitations of various criteria. The prewar Army had operated on such a small scale with such different personnel that its experience could not safely be used as a guide for wartime decisions.

Moreover, during the early years of the war there was relatively little understanding of, or sympathy for, operational or any other type of research that might have provided a more solid foundation for the decisions of the General Staff. Most senior officers believed that they had accumulated sufficient knowledge over their years of service to reach sound judgments about manpower policy. Therefore, instead of being based on careful planning, manpower policy in World War II was largely one long effort at improvisation. How lack of planning could adversely affect the performance of individual soldiers can be seen in the following cases. . . .

G.G.T. had been a rather timid child who tended to avoid other people. At the age of nine he was in bed for a year with tuberculosis, but he recovered and has since been in good physical health. As he grew up he concentrated on his school work and did not participate in athletics or social events. He entered a southern state university, which was located near his home, and did quite well his first year. As a sophomore, however, he lost interest in his studies and became quite disturbed over the thought that he was a homosexual, in spite of the fact that his homosexual activity had been confined to several minor episodes many years before. He was able partially to overcome these disturbing thoughts and continue his education, majoring in mathematics.

At the time of his induction into the Army in the middle of his senior year in college, G.G.T. was a rather emotionally unstable individual. Nevertheless, he scored very high on the intelligence test and, with his background in mathematics, seemed to be a person the Army could well use. Certainly his emotional problems were not of sufficient magnitude to justify his rejection.

He was immediately sent to the West Coast for training in the use of antiaircraft weapons. The physical work was extremely difficult for him. He had always withdrawn from physical activity and people to his schoolbooks, and now that this was impossible he began to experience shortness of breath, a rapid pounding of his heart, and high blood pressure. With the other soldiers talking about girls all the time, he became extremely conscious of his own lack of interest in the opposite sex, and his former fears of homosexuality were revived. After about ten days his company commander noticed the difficulty he was having with drill and marching, as well as his tendency to withdraw from the other soldiers. He was sent to the Neuropsychiatric Clinic, where an extensive examination was carried out. The conclusions of the psychiatrist were as follows:

> Were it not for the fact that this man's civilian training, namely, mathematics, might be utilized in our school, I would recommend that he immediately be given a C.D.D. However, the soldier himself states that he would like very much to remain in the Army in order to be "able to do something." I do not believe that his latent homosexuality will in itself be a problem with this boy. For the present, therefore, I would recommend that he be reclassified Limited Service on the assumption that he can be assigned to the school for teaching mathematics. If this recommendation is accepted I will want to see this man in the Neuropsychiatric Clinic approximately once a week for follow-up interviews.

In spite of this recommendation and the very real need for men with his training, Private T. was discharged approximately one month later. The examining psychiatrist was overruled by higher authorities who were unwilling to make available the type of assignment and the outpatient treatment that were necessary. Although outpatient facilities later became a regular part of the Army medical establishment, there was no regular provision for them in early 1943. Thus a soldier who, although suffering from a neurosis, could have been maintained on duty in a critical specialty was discharged because of a lack of appropriate procedures for his retention.

In civilian life G.G.T. has become a teacher of mathematics. After three years of graduate study he worked for two years in a research institute, and for the last five years has been employed as a university teacher, first as an instructor and later with the rank of assistant professor. His mental health seemingly remained good, and he received no psychiatric treatment until 1953. At that time he became quite disturbed and spent six months in a state mental hospital. His recovery has apparently been quite satisfactory. He is still unmarried. . . .

Likewise, many competent men such as G.G.T. could have been salvaged had they been able to receive some psychiatric support to ease them over the rough spots. The Army eventually acted, but not before many had been discharged. Some large corporations have learned this lesson and have come increasingly to recognize the importance of easing the adjustment of new workers.

DISCIPLINE AND OVERPERMISSIVENESS

As we noted, the Army was not an excessively disciplined organization. This can be primarily explained by the moderating influence of civilian attitudes and values, which made themselves felt through Congress, the press, the senior officials of the War and Navy Departments, and above all the prior conditioning of the officer personnel—the vast majority of whom were civilians in uniform.

It is well known that during the war Negro soldiers were not generally held to the same strict account as were white troops, which helps to explain at least in part the extreme case of J.Y. discussed later. Moreover, as has also been pointed out earlier, soldiers who were hospitalized were granted many special privileges. But the greatest privilege for the patient was his relative safety. It was not until the latter part of the war that the Army took steps to insure that in its efforts to provide good medical care it did not undermine the fighting morale of the troops by offering them a respectable escape route.

Psychiatrists, especially those serving with combat units, came to recognize that they had to temper their humanitarian approach to the individual patient with a concern for the impact of their professional decisions on the morale and efficiency of the group. Frequently they kept men in the line whom they would have preferred to send to a rear hospital because they did not want to encourage other soldiers to seek relief in the same manner. . . .

T.J.M. was born of immigrant parents in a large midwestern city. His childhood was a happy one, and his family was quite close. At the age of sixteen—after two years in a trade school, where he studied a variety of subjects including machine shop, typing, and baking—he went to work as a truck driver. A good worker, he enjoyed his job and spent the ensuing twelve years at it. Then he was drafted. T.J.M., although quite willing to serve his country, was loath to leave what had been a very pleasant life. He knew that he would miss not only his parents, his fiancée, and his job, but also the participation in athletics—boating, horseback riding, baseball—that he enjoyed so much.

Nevertheless, he was a good soldier. Although the training was especially difficult because of an extremely severe winter, he rapidly developed into a very competent infantryman and was assigned to duty as a jeep driver in a heavy weapons company. Except for a month when he was hospitalized for a tumor operation, he was in good health. After almost two years of training, his division was sent to England and shortly thereafter to France. In early September 1944, T.J.M. entered combat.

However, it was not until the first of the year that he was exposed to very heavy fighting. During January and February his division participated in some of the heaviest fighting in Europe as they approached the Siegfried Line.

In late February, while attacking across a river, Private M.'s outfit was reduced from a strength of eighty men to nine. As he was pulling up the bank on the far side, two shells landed very close to him; and, while in the act of jumping out of his jeep, he was hit by a third. He lost consciousness and awoke in the basement of a house with the medics attending him. Within seven hours he was on the operating table. His body had been badly cut by shell fragments; he suffered a large wound on his hip, another on his ankle, and a broken finger on his left hand. None proved to be serious. In two days he had been transferred through Paris to a hospital in England. Suddenly the front seemed much closer to England than he had ever realized. Two and a half months later he was flown to Scotland and from there to the United States. He still had the feeling that it was only a matter of a day's trip back into the terror of combat. Perhaps this feeling was reinforced by the realization that his wounds had healed completely and that he might be sent back into combat again.

Quite suddenly he developed a nervous tremor and rather severe back pains. It was almost as if he had decided he wanted to stay in the hospital longer rather than return to duty. And yet his symptoms were completely real. Subsequent experience with patients of this type has led the military to adopt a policy of returning those who have recovered from wounds to duty as quickly as possible. In T.J.M.'s case, however, the long period of hospitalization had already contributed to the development of psychological symptoms. His life in the hospital as contrasted with combat was pleasant; he was taken care of and, most important, as long as he stayed there, he would not have to fight again. It was not that he did not want to return to combat; he just felt that he was sick and could not return.

The medical authorities, rather than assuring T.J.M. that he had no physical disorder and returning him to duty in the hope that his symptoms would disappear, further reinforced his conviction that he had received a back injury when wounded that had only later manifested itself. He was fitted with a brace and then transferred to another hospital without appropriate neurological studies.

Finally, after two months in the States he was referred to a psychiatrist because there seemed to be no physical basis for his backaches and tremor. By that time, after almost five months in various hospitals, after being returned to this country because of his wounds, and after wearing a brace for a month, it was impossible to convince him that he was not suffering from a serious injury. T.J.M. was discharged for psychoneurosis.

Within a month the veteran was back at his old job as a truck driver. For a while his back pains continued. He lost about a day a week from work, and once in a while he went to see a doctor. His conviction of the physical nature of his complaints was once again reinforced when he received a pension from the Veterans Administration for anxiety neurosis and spinal sprain. His pension was eliminated, however, at a later date after an extensive physical examination. By late 1948 T.J.M. was no longer losing any time from work. Although he still suffered occasionally from pains in his back, his condition was greatly improved.

Frequently men perform effectively, especially in difficult situations, only if they clearly perceive the consequences that will follow upon malperformance. . . . In T.J.M.'s case the hospital environment was so pleasant, in contrast to the dangers of combat, that it sapped his will to continue to perform effectively as a soldier. The military has special need to avoid such situations; for, unlike civilian life, where a man wants a job and tries to hold on to one when he gets it, there are obvious gains for a soldier when he is judged to be medically unable to perform his work effectively.

Assignment

It was inevitable that in classifying and assigning millions of men under great pressure, the Army would make many serious errors. Sometimes it was able to catch and correct these errors, but often soldiers who were overassigned or underassigned came to the attention of the authorities only after they broke down.

The most serious cases were the overassigned. Since a higher assignment gave a soldier more rank, money, and privileges, it was likely that he would struggle to perform adequately, and many undoubtedly outdid themselves. But strong motivation is not enough. No matter how hard a man tries, lack of skill or intelligence can lead to failure. Among the underassigned who broke were some who, disturbed on other counts, found an excuse in the way the Army treated them to justify their failure. They could not tolerate frustration and took the view that since the Army had broken faith with them, they were under no obligation to do their best for the Army.

P.W.A. was a member of a socially prominent family residing in an

Eastern city. His father was a successful lawyer, and both sons studied for the bar. P.W.A. attended local schools and graduated from a college near his home. Although not an outstanding student, he did well and was active in social affairs; he was a member of the golf team as well as a frequent speaker at student gatherings. After completing college in 1942, he entered law school while working part time in his father's office. During this period, as before, he was frequently in conflict with his father. The latter was prone to occasional alcoholic bouts, and on several occasions the son had to go out and round up his father. Other than this, the family life seems to have been normal, and P.W.A. gave no evidence of emotional disturbance.

In the summer of 1942, however, he had a disturbing experience in connection with some Civil Aeronautics Authority pilot training. Prior to graduation from college he became interested in flying and attempted to enlist in the Naval Air Corps. Rejected for physical defects, he was later accepted as a member of the Army Air Corps Reserve with the provision that he would be called to active duty for pilot training as soon as needed. Wishing to get some prior experience, he entered the Civilian Aeronautics Authority Training Program during the summer. From the beginning of the course he was a complete failure as an aviator; he lacked coordination, but this was attributed to the fact that he was frightened all the time he was in the air. After about eighteen hours of flying it was quite apparent that he would "wash out." Before this happened, however, he himself decided he would never make a flyer and resigned from the program. At this time he was emotionally disturbed, realizing he was terribly afraid of flying but at the same time not wishing to admit his failure.

Several months later he became an Air Cadet. Wishing to try once more to overcome his fear and thus convince himself and others that he was not a "sissy," he did not mention his prior failure. Air Corps selection procedures at that time did not include techniques that would reveal a fear of flying. He found even the initial instruction difficult and was rather relieved when after three weeks he entered the hospital with pneumonia. During the next two weeks he improved rapidly and was apparently emotionally normal, although he talked almost incessantly about an affair with a girl at home. A convalescent furlough followed during which he became increasingly nervous. His parents were especially concerned because his apathy and listlessness were in marked contrast to his earlier ways. As the time for his return to flight training approached, he worried almost continually. Driving back to camp with his parents, he became upset every time he heard a plane fly overhead. His behavior in the squadron orderly room when he checked in was so peculiar that he was sent back to the hospital.

For the next five months P.W.A. remained in the hospital suffering from an acute psychosis. He talked to himself, wandered about aimlessly, smiled inappropriately, and was careless about his appearance. He also wrote on the walls. At times he rolled his eyes up in his head and leaned back against the wall while staring at the ceiling. Later he explained that he had been listening to voices. At other times he would sit quietly and write the names of the states over and over again. His speech was disorganized: "Well, I think President Roosevelt was about right. I suppose you might say I was yellow. I can't figure just how I landed here. There are better men than I dying around here now." Again, for no apparent reason at all, "I would not want to disturb an old barracks roommate of mine on his career in aviation." The feeling of antagonism toward his father was especially evident in his discussions of "homopatricide." Once he seemed to think he had killed his father, but later denied it. When brought before a medical board for discharge, he was obviously psychotic, and a transfer to a civilian mental hospital was recommended. However, his parents finally obtained permission to take him home.

For a little over a year he remained at home doing very little. Gradually his thoughts of flying and glory and crashes and death began to recede. By mid-1944 the world of aviation had become a thing of the distant past, and he was able to take up his career again. Entering law school he worked hard and within two years had passed the bar examinations. Later he worked as a law clerk and by 1954 was an assistant district attorney of his county. He married in 1949, but to date he has had no children. He is now doing very well and has an income exceeding $10,000 a year. . . .

The early life of W.S.N. was one of almost constant turmoil. His father, an alcoholic, was frequently away from home on drinking bouts, and his return always brought on periods of quarreling between the parents. A brother was seriously injured in an automobile accident and has since been mentally deficient. W.S.N. was often beaten by his father. As he grew up he was forbidden to go out with girls, and most of his social life had to be hidden from his family. In spite of being forced to live in this far from healthy environment, he never suffered any severe emotional upsets, although he was prone to occasional temper tantrums and headaches. In school he did very well and, on graduating from high school, would have liked to go to college. However, because of his father's irresponsibility and intermittent employment, he had to give up his dream of further education. For a year he worked in several low-paying jobs as a laborer and mail clerk. Then he obtained a good position as a clerk with an automobile manufacturing company. One year later he was drafted.

After four weeks of basic training in a Field Artillery battalion, Private N. was shifted to a position as battery clerk because of difficulty with his feet, which made field duty impractical. Soon he was promoted to technician fifth grade. In the spring of 1943 he learned of the Army Specialized Training Program, under which soldiers were sent for college courses at various universities. His application was accepted, but with the proviso that he would have to accept a reduction in grade to private. This was the stipulation for all ASTP graduates. It was expected that they would be made either commissioned or noncommissioned officers on completion of their course. W.S.N. was happy to give up his rank in order to obtain college training, and he was soon engrossed in studying engineering.

By early 1944, with the increasing need for ground troops, especially infantrymen, produced by the buildup for the invasion of Europe, it became apparent that the ASTP program would have to be abandoned. There was a sizable shortage of manpower, especially at the higher intelligence levels, and the ASTP students were the best source immediately available. Private N. was bitter, not only because he had been led to believe he would get at least two years of college, but because he had expected either a commission or high enlisted rank. Nevertheless, the Army needed these men badly, and prior commitments had to be revoked because the war situation itself had changed. Combat losses had been higher than estimated, and the invasion date had been advanced. Moreover, most units had filled all their noncommissioned officer positions. Thus there was no alternative but to return many ASTP trainees to regular duty in ranks below those they previously held.

Private N., disappointed at having to leave college after only ten months, applied for air cadet training in the hope of still obtaining a commission. Although he was accepted, the training facilities were full at that time, and he was sent to an infantry division in training to await call. Several weeks later pilot training was all but eliminated for the same reasons as those that closed down the ASTP program, and many cadets were shipped to the Infantry. Deprived of his rating, a good job, a college education, and a commission by events he did not entirely understand, Private N. was angry and frustrated. Moreover, all he had to look forward to now was infantry training, pain from his feet, combat, and maybe death.

After less than three months of infantry training, the division was put to work packing equipment for movement overseas. By October 1944 they were in combat. Already bitter and upset by what he considered completely unjustifiable treatment at the hands of the Army, Private N. began to have severe headaches. Sometimes he became nauseated and vomited when emotionally upset.

As his division entered more severe fighting in early 1945, he had periods when he sobbed uncontrollably and became quite confused. He was angry at the Army for exposing him to physical hardships, suffering, and death when it had promised him so much. He felt cheated, and yet he was ashamed of himself. The other men kept going; they did not sulk and cry. He had to fight with himself to live up to their expectations of him. But always when the fighting was severe, he would think again that he should not be suffering so, that it was not fair, and that he would be justified in quitting. Once when ordered to crawl back from an advanced position, he was so confused that he stood up straight and ran back a hundred yards through machine gun fire. It was a miracle he was not hit. Finally, after four months of fighting and while his company was off the line for a short rest, the soldier gave up and begged to be sent to the hospital. There he was very depressed, stuttered when he talked, and suffered from vivid dreams of battle, which would awaken him out of a sound sleep, sweating profusely. He was returned to the States and discharged.

As a civilian, W.S.N. has gradually improved. He returned to his old job at the automobile company and stayed for almost two years. He left to look for a job in Florida but later returned to his home in the Midwest. He has since worked steadily, first as a cemetery salesman and more recently as an automobile salesman, a job he enjoys very much. In 1951 he was going steady with a girl but did not feel financially able to get married, although he was making $4,000 a year. He still suffered from occasional headaches and nightmares and still stuttered a little.

These soldiers were given assignments that added greatly to their difficulties in performing effectively. However, there was not much the Army could have done to save P.W.A. from himself. . . . Most men were able to tolerate the Army's breaking its promise once or twice, but W.S.N. was the unfortunate soldier with whom the Army broke faith repeatedly. That he was able to perform effectively for a considerable time before he broke down reflects the effort he made to swallow his disappointments and keep going. Only when the full impact of his bad luck became clear to him in combat did he finally collapse.

CHAPTER 14

Patterns of Performance

DURING THE WAR many speculations were advanced as to why so many young men were failing as soldiers. It was contended that men who were failing in the Army had also been ineffective prior to their military service—they were ineffective persons and that was that. The Army could do little about them but process and discharge them just as quickly as they could be identified. The same type of explanation was advanced to explain why certain men failed to readjust satisfactorily after their return to civilian life. It was maintained that the men who found it difficult or impossible to get and hold a job and to marry and settle down were the same individuals who had been poor performers before they entered the Army and who had performed unsatisfactorily while in the service.

The Army's manpower planners had based important personnel policies on this belief in continuity in performance. They sought to reject for military service any man who had ever been admitted to a mental or penal institution. They also sought to reject all who had a defect that might later cause them to perform ineffectively in the Army. Likewise, when soldiers who had been inducted began to give evidence of ineffective performance, the Army's policy at certain periods of the war was to encourage their speedy separation.

In connection with the analysis of the military performance of the ineffective soldiers prior to breakdown and the civilian performance of these men after their return to civilian life, we accumulated considerable information through which we could explore more thoroughly their life performance patterns. In addition to information about their performance, both in the Army and after their return to civilian life, we also have knowledge of their performance prior to their coming onto active duty. We are therefore in a position to explore whether significant patterns of performance could be delineated up to the end of our contact with them in 1953, at which time many of them were in their thirties and a considerable proportion in their forties.

Our data have inherent limitations. In the first place, they reflect the performance of a specially selected group of men—that is, men who proved ineffective in the Army in World War II, at least in the sense of having been prematurely separated from the service. Second, while we were able to follow most of them for almost a decade after their discharge from the Army, we have no way of knowing how they will perform during the many years that still lie ahead of them. Finally, the materials we have assembled about the quality of their performance, military and civilian, enable us to make only a rough estimate of the effectiveness with which they have been able to cope with life's problems. A refined analysis would require much more detail. Yet we do have a basis for undertaking a longitudinal analysis of the performance of this sizable group of men, which, despite various limitations, should enable us to determine whether, and to what extent, significantly different patterns can be established to describe the consistency and quality with which these men performed.

Military administration helped to strengthen the belief in continuity of performance. When a soldier who had been properly screened and accepted for military service later broke down, those who were charged with the responsibility for processing his discharge sought to explain his failure. Inevitably they searched his background for signs of weakness that had previously escaped detection. There are few indeed, even among the fortunate who have grown up in a reasonably good environment, whose personality on careful scrutiny would not reveal some defects that might appear to lead to later ineffectiveness. If the members of the disposition board were able to ascertain that the ineffective soldier came from a home that had been broken by death or divorce, or that his family had been buffeted badly by his father's prolonged unemployment, or that he had been exposed to other forms of economic or social deprivation, they frequently assumed that they had determined the roots of his ineffectiveness.

Belief in the theory of continuity in men's performance was further reinforced by the realization that intelligence—which includes the ability to learn—is to a marked degree determined by heredity, and its development can be influenced by environmental opportunities, or the lack of them, only early in life. This means that a man will tend to continue to perform within limits set by his intelligence. Additional reinforcement came from the recognition that the basic personality of an adult was shaped by the experiences of his infancy and childhood. The ineffectiveness demonstrated by soldiers in World War II could be traced back in many cases to serious emotional problems within the home, which had affected the soldier's childhood.

If intelligence and emotional stability are basic elements in determining the level of a man's performance and if, further, limitations and defects in each are present at birth or develop within the first few years of life, it is easy to understand why there is a widespread belief in the continuity of life performance patterns. But despite these reasons, theoretical and practical, for assuming basic continuity in life performance patterns, we have already presented in the earlier chapters a number of findings that suggest that we must consider discontinuity as well as continuity in the study of life performance patterns.

First of all, the vast majority of the men who were accepted for military service did not present any significant indications at the time of their induction examination that would have justified the Army's rejecting them. In point of fact, the composite evaluation of their premilitary performance that we undertook on the basis of the extensive information in their personnel files enabled us to conclude that the vast majority had been performing in an acceptable manner prior to their induction. Thus their breakdown in the Army was at variance with the expectations based on their prior performance. Despite the fact that the order of demands they faced in the Army was frequently much greater than what they had had to contend with at home, a careful evaluation of how they performed after they came on active duty revealed that once again the majority had a satisfactory performance record up to the point of their breaking down.

Moreover, in studying what happened to the soldiers who had broken down in the Army, we found that a substantial majority were able to readjust after their return to civilian life—some quickly, some only after a delay. However, approximately half of even those who failed to readjust had had a good or acceptable military performance rating up to the time of their breakdown.

These findings suggest that we must examine more carefully, and in quantitative terms, the group that shows continuity of performance— at an acceptable or poor level—and the group that does not. To do so we must enlarge the framework of our analysis to include the man's premilitary

performance record and to distinguish temporary from prolonged failure to perform effectively.

The question may be raised whether such an evaluation of performance patterns may not be vitiated by the fact that we have readings about
how men performed in two sharply contrasting environments—the civilian and the military. Military service during a major war presents new
and unusual demands to men who have had no prior experience with
fighting. Two such disparate environments as a civilian job in peace and
duty in an Army at war cannot be equated. But there is no need to equate
them; it is only necessary to recognize that the two have been tied
together by life itself. Men are called on to fight in war just as they are
required to earn their livelihood in peace, and stress and crises are
seldom completely absent from the lives of most civilians. Moreover,
various organizational groups—the Army, the Veterans Administration,
employers—must make judgments about how men are likely to perform
based on an evaluation of how they have previously performed, irrespective of the contrast in the environments.

As we have seen, many men who had performed successfully in
civilian life were not able to cope with the special stresses of war. Some
were not able to adjust to the Army at all, while others faltered along the
way. To make allowance for the special pressures of the military environment in the study of life performance patterns, we have disregarded the
fact that all the men in the cohort group were ineffective in the sense of
being prematurely discharged. We have included in our evaluations of
their military service only the quality of their performance in the Army
prior to their breakdown. The only way in which it is possible to study
continuity and discontinuity in performance in a world of rapid and
continuing change is to recognize that most individuals will at some time
in their lives be forced to cope with special orders of stress, and how they
respond to such situations must be considered a significant aspect of
their life performance pattern.

Our first step was to combine the multiple performance ratings
about each man in the cohort group into a meaningful composite—that
is, a life performance pattern. We had information about three periods in
each man's life: before he entered the Army, during his military service,
and after his return to civilian life . . . We were able to develop four basic
patterns—adjusted, vulnerable, broken, and poor—the components of
which are set out in Table 14.1.

Before briefly describing each of the four life patterns, we must
remind the reader again that, in assessing a man's performance in the
Army, we disregarded the fact that he had been prematurely discharged
and used as a basis of our evaluation his performance record up to the
time he broke down. No soldier would have been rated as good or

Table 14.1
LIFE PERFORMANCE PATTERNS:
COMPONENT RATINGS IN EVALUATION PERIODS

PERFORMANCE PATTERN	EVALUATION PERIOD		
	Premilitary	Military	Postmilitary
Adjusted	Acceptable or poor	Good or acceptable	Good or acceptable
Vulnerable	Acceptable or poor	Poor or not rated	Good or acceptable
Broken	Acceptable	Good or acceptable	Poor
Poor	Acceptable or poor	Poor or not rated	Poor
	Poor	Acceptable	Poor

acceptable, not even one who served in combat with distinction, had we used premature discharge as a criterion of military performance.

We designated as *adjusted* the life patterns of men whose ratings in both the military and postmilitary periods were either good or acceptable. While most of this group also had an acceptable rating of performance before the war, it included some with a poor prewar record on the assumption that they were still in the throes of finding themselves.

The second pattern, *vulnerable,* included men whose performance before and after their military service was good or acceptable but whose performance in the Army was poor or of such short duration that it could not be rated. They were vulnerable to the stresses of military life but were able to adjust to civilian life. A few whose performance prior to entering the Army was poor were included for the same reason that men with similar prewar performance records were included in the adjusted pattern.

The third pattern, *broken,* includes men whose performance had been acceptable prior to their entering the Army, and good or acceptable while they were on active duty up to the point of breakdown, but who failed after their discharge to readjust to civilian life.

The fourth pattern, *poor,* includes primarily men whose perform- ance in the military and in both civilian periods of their life was unsatisfactory, plus a few whose civilian records were poor but who per- formed acceptably in military service up to their breakdown and a few others whose premilitary performance had been acceptable but whose later performance had consistently been poor.

Table 14.2 summarizes the number and percentage of the cohort of ineffectives who fell within each of these four life performance patterns. . . .

. . . Our earlier analysis also gives us reason to believe that there are probably significant clusterings of factors that help to differentiate the men who fall in these several life patterns. We had repeated occasion to note that men with little or no schooling found it very difficult to perform effectively in either military or civilian life. And we further noted that men who developed a psychosis in the Army not only were of

Table 14.2

Life Performance Pattern	Weighted Number	Percentage
Adjusted	38,880	53.5
Vulnerable	13,914	19.1
Broken	7,371	10.1
Poor	12,535	17.3
Cohort	72,700	100.0

no further use to the military but had no prospect of adjusting satisfactorily to civilian life unless their illness receded.

In order to illustrate the extent of the differences among men in the four life patterns, the following case histories have been selected from among white soldiers, all of whom except for the vulnerable example had overseas service, and all of whom were discharged from the Army because of psychoneurosis.

ADJUSTED

S.T. was born and brought up on a Southern farm. He had graduated from high school with average grades and had been elected vice-president of his senior class. After a brief period of employment as a general mechanic with a metal manufacturing and repair company, he had entered college a few months before he was drafted.

After induction in November 1942, he was assigned to the Air Corps. Upon completion of basic training he volunteered for air crew gunnery training, which he completed satisfactorily in spite of the fact that he "was in misery all the time" and when he finished he "felt doomed." Assigned to the European theater of operations, he flew thirty combat missions as a B-17 waist gunner, and earned the Distinguished Flying Cross and the Air Medal with three Oak Leaf Clusters. Promoted to staff sergeant, he returned to the United States on rotation late in 1944. On a routine examination to determine his physical fitness for further aircrew duty, the medical officers noted that he was tense and anxious and complained of fatigue and insomnia. Hospitalized for several months at an AAF Convalescent Hospital, S.T. was found to be quite disturbed. He cried easily, had feelings of guilt and inferiority, tended to be seclusive and depressed. He was given a medical discharge in March 1945, after an attempt to return him to duty resulted in a psychological collapse during which he described himself as having a "sense of feeling utterly futile, helpless."

Returning home, S.T. rested and did a little work around the family farm for about a year. He reentered college in January 1946. He started in the School of Agriculture at a neighboring university, but soon switched to the School of Business, where he completed all requirements and was awarded his bachelor's degree in the spring of 1949. He then secured a job with a state commission and some time later became a field representative with increased responsibilities and a higher salary. Two years after discharge he married and at last account had one child. He claims to be in good health and considers his military experience to have been beneficial— "an experience comparable in some ways to a college education."

VULNERABLE

T.U. was raised on a midwestern farm. He completed high school in 1935, two years after he should have graduated, because his family had needed him to work on the farm. When economic conditions improved, he had returned to school and, although "always kinda scared of school," he made fairly good grades. As a youth he was closely attached to his parents, was somewhat shy, and did not make friends easily. In the late 1930s, shortly after he married, his father set him up in a business of his own—a small hardware store in his home town—but he sold it after a few years and returned to farming.

Drafted in December 1942, he shortly thereafter went to the dispensary at the Reception Center because he was unable to eat or sleep. Since he was quite upset, he was sent to the hospital for further evaluation. During a month in the hospital it became clear to the authorities that he was "so scared of Army life that he really couldn't stand it." He was depressed, confused, cried extensively during routine interviews, and had many somatic complaints as well. He was diagnosed as having a psychoneurosis, hypochondriasis, and given a medical discharge.

Returning home, he rested for a few months and then went back to farming. He now owns and operates his own farm. He claims his health is good but states that he has been afraid to have children since his wife's family has a long history of tuberculosis. His military service was too brief to qualify him for veterans' benefits under the G.I. Bill.

BROKEN

The youngest of five children, U.V. left his parents' midwestern farm shortly after completing two years of high school and secured employment as a carpenter's helper in a nearby town. Married in 1937, he continued working at this trade until inducted late in 1942. Assigned to an antiaircraft unit, he participated in the Normandy invasion and in the campaign across northern France. He was in good health, and his character and efficiency ratings were "excellent."

After about two months of combat he was knocked unconscious by the blast of an aerial bomb. Because he complained of headaches, dizziness, and a "roaring in the ears," the aid station transferred him to the evacuation hospital, where his condition was at first described as "mild." However, his headaches grew worse, and his dizziness was accompanied by spells of nausea and vomiting. U.V. developed increasing nervous tension, had battle dreams, and jumped at any loud noise. Five months of hospitalization in England failed to reveal any organic basis for his persistent headaches, but he showed no improvement. He was evacuated to the United States, where his hospitalization continued for another seven months in general and convalescent hospitals. Finally, shortly before V–J Day, he was given a medical discharge with a diagnosis of psychoneurosis, acute, severe, anxiety state.

U.V. went back to the family farm and tried to return to the carpentry trade but could not make it. He could not tolerate the noises nor could he climb ladders. Unable to work, he puttered around the farm, and received as his only cash income the 70 percent disability compensation the Veterans Administration had awarded him. Successive examinations failed to reveal any improvement in his emotional state. He started a liberal arts course at a junior college but soon dropped out. He was not considered suitable for training under Public Law 16 until he improved.

Over the next few years he worked occasionally at odd jobs, but never for long. He had difficulties in securing jobs because he detailed his symptoms and his disabilities to any prospective employer. At times he was able to work reasonably well, but either he quit or his temporary work had ended. One employer reported (in 1950) that the veteran was "an excellent painter and carpenter but that he doesn't seem able to work. He frequently blew up on a job and went to pieces." His wife had left him and later divorced him.

He is still rated as 50 percent disabled by the Veterans Administration, and the last information (1953) indicates that for the past several years he had been earning some money by working as a part-time contact man for the local post of a veterans' service organization. But his supervisor reports that he could never qualify for a service representative since he appears to be incapable of assuming responsibility. Even with close supervision he had not been doing very well, since he made more promises to veterans seeking help than he could possibly fulfill. In communal activities, he would start out on a new project with great enthusiasm but soon tired and moved on to something else.

POOR

A Southern farm hand before the war, V.W. started to drink steadily and heavily when he was fifteen years of age. He had a difficult time in school, attending intermittently for only three or four years, and finally left school at thirteen. He made only a marginal adjustment thereafter, working when he had to on his older brothers' or neighbors' farms. His drinking got him into numerous difficulties with the law, and his record shows many arrests for drunkenness. In spite of this pattern of life he was drafted at the age of thirty-five.

In the Army he was assigned to an infantry unit and trained as a rifleman. During his first eight months of military service he stayed out of trouble but then his pattern of irresponsible behavior reemerged. Before going overseas he had been AWOL three times, for which he was court-martialed, as well as for being drunk in uniform in a public place. In combat in North Africa and later in Italy he performed well for a time. Following the fall of Rome, he became bothered by shortness of breath, chest pains, and lack of stamina. He was hospitalized briefly for neurocirculatory asthenia and returned to duty, this time to noncombat duty as a basic soldier with an ambulance company. For several months he performed satisfactorily; but he began to drink again, even on duty, and was again court-martialed.

A short while later he was hospitalized with a diagnosis of anxiety, tension state, chronic and moderate; he was irritable, nervous, tired, and had headaches and occasional backaches. He had difficulty sleeping, and when he did he was disturbed by battle dreams. While in the hospital he obtained some alcohol and had to be confined for acute alcoholism. At one point he was diagnosed as schizophrenic because of seclusiveness, lack of normal responses, dullness, and auditory hallucinations. When he was evacuated to the States, the diagnosis of psychosis was not confirmed. For a time the authorities considered giving him a Section VIII discharge for alcoholism, but because of his clear-cut anxiety symptoms he was finally given a medical discharge.

V.W. initially was rated as 50 percent disabled because of his anxiety reaction, but in early 1947 this rating was eliminated. For several years following his discharge, the veteran worked only infrequently on farms near his home. He continued to drink and was arrested and jailed many times for drunkenness. It was reported that after his compensation was cut off, his mother gave him a small amount of spending money. In 1950 he entered an institutional on-the-farm training program on a rented farm, but quit within three months because he could not get along with his landlord. At last report this veteran was living with his mother and an older brother and had no gainful employment beyond an occasional odd job on a farm or at the neighboring sawmill.

The four cases presented here in summary form suggest that men with varying life patterns of performance differed from each other in personal characteristics and had to face different situational pressures in civilian and military life. In the following chapter we will seek to determine the internal or external factors that might explain, either singly or in combination, why these men revealed such different life patterns of performance. At this point it may be useful, however, to review briefly only one overriding question — the degree of continuity or change reflected in each of the four major patterns of performance.

First of all, it is worth noting that nearly 39,000 men, or 54 percent, of the 72,700 men represented by the cohort sample were found to have an adjusted life performance pattern. This means that their performance before they entered the Army, on active duty up to the time they broke down, and after their return to civilian life was acceptable or good. A relatively small number of those included in this pattern had a poor record before the war; but this fact did not weigh too heavily since, as these young men matured, they became capable of meeting the demands made on them. With minor reservations, however, the basic pattern of the adjusted group is one of continuity — by and large, these men were able to cope satisfactorily with the demands made on them in civilian and military life.

Those with a vulnerable life pattern of performance show distinctly less continuity. For the most part, the almost 14,000 in this pattern, or 19 percent of the total sample, performed satisfactorily in civilian life but failed in the Army. A relatively few were in the Army for such a short period of time that they could not even be rated, but their early discharge is indicative of poor performance. Since the 1930s were characterized by severe unemployment, and since many adolescents encounter great difficulty in settling down under any circumstances, the major test of adjustment to civilian life should be whether a man performed satisfactorily after his discharge from the Army. This group did. In terms of continuity and change, the performance of those in the vulnerable pattern was characterized, as the name implies, by discontinuity: They could not cope with military life but they were able to adjust to civilian life.

About 7,400 men, 1 out of 10 in the entire group, were found to have a broken pattern of performance. This meant that while they had performed satisfactorily prior to coming on to active duty and had continued to perform satisfactorily up to the point of breakdown, they were unable to readjust in civilian life. They represent clear-cut discontinuity.

The fourth pattern comprised men whose life performance was characterized as poor. The majority of the approximately 12,500, or 17 percent of the entire group, had a poor performance record both in the Army and after their return to civilian life. A minority had an acceptable record either prior to induction or during military service; but the predominant trend in their performance was poor, and they were therefore classified as having a poor life performance pattern.

By and large, men with adjusted or poor life patterns of performance, who together accounted for 7 out of 10 in the entire group, show a high order of continuity in performance from one period of their life to another. This high percentage would drop if we subtracted from the number in the adjusted pattern those whose records before the war were poor and from the number classified as poor those who had either an acceptable prewar or military record. Together they comprised 10,230 men, and, if they were eliminated, the percentage of men in the entire group with marked continuity in their life performance patterns drops to 6 out of 10.

Over 21,000 men, almost 30 percent of the total cohort, had life performance patterns that were either vulnerable or broken. This is the minimum number whose life performance patterns are characterized by some order of discontinuity, minor or major. At a maximum we must add the two special groups of adjusted and poor whose performance patterns contained a significant element of discontinuity. If this is done, the total with discontinuous patterns of performance amount to 31,515, or 43.3 percent.

This preliminary analysis of the life performance patterns of the cohort sample provides considerable support for the prevailing view that the performance of men is characterized by a basic continuity growing out of their fundamental strengths or weaknesses. At a minimum such continuity was found among about 6 out of every 10 men in the sample of ineffective soldiers. Among the other men who served and who were demobilized or separated for other reasons, the majority also would undoubtedly show a basic continuity in performance over time.

On the other hand, many of the men who served in the Armed Forces, and probably even higher proportions among those who were rejected for service particularly for mental or emotional reasons, would show some discontinuity in their performance. But the analysis of the ineffective soldiers alone represents a challenge to those who hold too firmly to the belief in continuity. At a minimum about 3 out of 10, and at a maximum more than 4 out of 10, show conspicuous discontinuity in their performance patterns. . . .

PART **IV**

Women

MY CONCERN with the role of women in the world of work goes back to the beginning of my teaching career at Columbia University in the mid-1930s, when I had a sprinkling of well-educated Vassar graduates in my classes who were trying to find an opening into the New York labor market other than by pursuing a secretarial course at Katherine Gibbs. Even after they had acquired a master's degree from our School of Business, most of them still faced hurdles.

The first three selections, Chapters 15, 16, and 17, are drawn from our study of educated American women, which was supported by the Rockefeller Brothers Fund in the early 1960s and which followed our earlier study of talented men.

When a reporter from *The New York Times* caught up with me by telephone on the West Coast and asked me to summarize in one sentence the findings of *Life Styles of Educated Women*, I said we had learned that American business prefers dumb men to smart women. On the basis of a special study of the mobility of women and blacks into the higher levels of management that my associate, Anna Dutka, and I undertook at the behest of Pepsico in 1982, the same conclusion could still be drawn, although during the intervening years the barriers blocking both women and blacks from the executive suite had been lowered.

The two selections on "Returnees" and "Reentry" (Chapters 19 and 20) are the outgrowth of a project undertaken by the Conservation Project under the aegis of the German Marshall Fund, which, in accordance with its charter, stimulates cross-national studies, particularly involving Germany and other OECD countries. The changing relations of women to employment invited inquiry and assessment. We arranged for parallel studies in five countries guided by a common research design: Germany, France, the United Kingdom, Sweden, and the United States. The long chapter on "Returnees" is the Foreword that I wrote for the book prepared by my long-term associate, Alice Yohalem, *Women Returning to Work* (1980). The shorter piece on "Reentry" represents the summary of a conference that I chaired, sponsored jointly by the German Marshall Fund and the assistant secretary of labor for women's employment of the Government of France, which was held in Paris in November 1979. Representatives of fifteen countries and a wide array of international organizations attended the three-day conference, which saw lively discussions, pointed to selected constructive actions that were under way, but highlighted difficulties that continued to face all women who were seeking to reenter the labor force.

Chapter 18 was my keynote address to a conference on "Women and the Work Force," under the joint sponsorship of AT&T and the *Ladies Home Journal,* which was held at the beginning of 1980.

CHAPTER 15

A World in Change

THE LIVES THAT WOMEN and, for that matter, men, lead reflect two sets of major forces. The first is composed of the external environment with its complex of opportunities and constraints. The second reflects the values and goals of the individual, who, always with some margins for discretion, must determine what he most wants and the price he is willing to pay for it.

The extent of transformation that takes place in the role of women is an important index of the rate of social change. The more rigid the society, the more fixed is the pattern of life that women must follow. In the United States, major changes have occurred in the structure and functioning of society during the present century, and these have led to fundamental transformations in the patterning of women's lives.

Changes in the lives of educated women in the post–World War II decades can be appreciated only against a background of the more important changes that took place during the preceding generations in the world of work on the one hand and in the home on the other.

By the turn of this century the United States was well on the way to becoming an industrialized urban society. The majority of the population lived in urban centers. The factory system was well established. The tertiary stage of economic development—the expansion of the service sector—was proceeding rapidly, while the number engaged in agriculture was nearing its peak and manufacturing was still experiencing a rapid growth.

As our society became more urbanized and as the service sector of the economy grew, the restricted life pattern followed by most women began to give way. Six factors can be singled out that have cumulatively changed the basic structure of woman's relationship to the world of work.

The first and possibly the most important factor has been the development of a great number of jobs that are particularly well suited to women. These have sprouted in many different sectors of the economy. In manufacturing, there has been a marked shift from heavy to light work, which means that women are able to meet physical demands, sometimes even better than men. Expansion of retail trade and of the communications industry also has increased opportunities for women workers. In addition, the beginning of this century saw the rapid growth of the educational and health industries, for which women have been considered well suited.

A second factor has been the expansion of secondary school and college education. Unlike European girls, girls in the United States have long shared with boys access to education. As free educational opportunities have been expanded, girls as well as boys have had access to them, surely through high school. As a matter of fact, for many decades, more girls than boys have graduated from high school. While the proportion of female graduates is reversed in college, young women have long made up a significant minority of the college population. The increased educational achievement of women has given a double stimulus to the employment of women. Many young women are undoubtedly stimulated to find an outlet in work for the knowledge and skills they have acquired, and in turn their education and training make them a potentially attractive manpower resource.

The ways people behave are changed by new ideas that come to dominate a society. Prior to World War I it was generally believed and accepted that the place of a married woman was at home. But wars have a way of uprooting hallowed traditions; with the manpower scarcities of World War I, some of the prejudice against married women working out of the home dissolved. The postwar era witnessed the removal of additional constraints that had previously shackled women. But the real breakthrough came when the manpower needs of World War II propelled many married women out of their homes and into factories and offices.

A further factor in removing these constraints has been the diffusion of the knowledge of birth control techniques throughout much of the population, with a corresponding decline in the average size of families. This has also made it possible for women to determine when to have children. No longer must a woman devote three or more decades to child rearing. She can collapse the span of years previously devoted to maternal responsibilities. And many have done just that.

Closely related to the foregoing has been the lightening of the burdens of homemaking as a result of the steady and substantial rise in the standard of living and steady advances in the technology of housekeeping, previously so time-consuming and physically exhausting. While women, if they wish, can continue to fill their days by taking care of their homes, electrical appliances and packaged foods permit them to economize markedly on the time and energy they previously devoted to domestic duties. And many have taken advantage of the opportunities thus presented to reallocate their time and get jobs outside the home.

The sixth change that has contributed to accelerating the entry or reentry of married women into the world of work has been the shift in the attitudes of men. In the past many husbands objected to their wives' working because, among other reasons, they thought it reflected on their ability to support their families. This is no longer true. Some men still discourage it; but, since so many married women now work—about 13 million have some kind of job during the course of a year—and since society at large tolerates, even approves of, the new trend, we may assume that few men actually oppose their wives' working. Among educated men, the number who now encourage their wives to take jobs is probably greater than the number opposed to their working, since they are more likely to recognize the need for fulfillment outside the home.

These then are the principal forces that have been operating since the beginning of this century to change the larger environment that shapes the lives and work of all women. Such radical transformations in the environment have had a most important effect on the way women today set their sights and order their lives.

However, these broad changes in the environment at large merely set the limits within which plans and adaptations are carried out. A second set of forces, individual values and goals, is of equal importance in influencing a woman's style of life. The specific life patterns a woman develops depend on three strategic variables: the shaping of her personality, the immediate circumstances of her adult life, and the way she responds to these circumstances.

Although a woman's genetic endowment is, of course, crucial to the character of her personality, the environment in which she grows up determines in considerable measure the type of goals and values she develops. The most significant influence is the family into which she is born and reared. Her parents play a large role in the determination of the amount and type of education she acquires, and this in turn affects her interests and outlook. Her parents' values influence her definition of her future role. They can encourage the development of a goal that stresses a career, or marriage, or a balance between a career and marriage. They can provide a home that stimulates the development of ideas, interests, and capacities, or one that furnishes limited opportunities for self-realization.

Other persons, adults and peers, also play important roles in personality development. So, too, do such institutions as schools, churches, and recreational groups, whose programs may affect the shape of a young girl's aspirations. Eventually, from all the influences to which she has been exposed, each woman develops a set of values and goals that contributes to the pattern and direction of her life.

No matter what plan a young woman develops for her life and work, her ability to realize her goals will be influenced by the circumstances of her adult life. If she remains single, she usually has no choice but to support herself by engaging in full-time work. If she marries while she is in school, her husband's income may help to determine the extent of her education, since she may have to interrupt her own studies to help him to complete his. After she has her children, her husband's earnings will largely determine whether she can afford household help, which in turn will affect her ability to hold a job.

Her husband's career may impose limitations on her own work. If he is transferred frequently, it may be difficult even for a well-prepared woman to pursue her career systematically because of limited opportunities in many communities. A woman often marries a man in the same or an allied field, and she may find that many institutions, especially colleges and universities, will not hire more than one member of a family.

The husband himself can also exercise a determining influence on the patterning of his wife's work and life. If he holds a negative attitude about a woman's working, he may interpose so many objections that his wife will forego a career in order to save the marriage. Another husband may take a diametrically opposite stance; he may push his wife into further education and work even though she prefers to remain at home with her children.

Another significant set of circumstances results from the presence of children. Depending on the number and, particularly, the ages of her children, a woman is under more or less pressure to adjust the pattern of her life to their needs and demands. Although, as we have noted, a woman can regulate the number and spacing of her children, she cannot always predict the constraints and pressures that a growing family may exert on her plans for a career.

We see, then, that her husband's income, his job, his attitudes, and the needs of her children all go far to determine the character of a woman's activities. In addition, there are restrictions due to the fact that many employers are reluctant to hire women.

The third determining factor is the response a woman makes to the particular circumstances she encounters. There are many different ways in which women can cope with the same objective circumstances. For instance, one woman may decide to work only if taking a job will yield the family a net increment in income. Another may decide to work as long as taking a job costs her nothing. In a family with some margins, a woman may work even if her salary does not cover the expenses incurred by her employment.

Some women are willing to leave their children to the care of a maid; others will work only if a close relative cares for the children; still others insist on bringing up their children themselves.

Some women who want to combine home and work will put forth a great amount of physical and emotional effort in order to meet their responsibilities in each sphere. Others will not or cannot expend so much energy and time; they either cut down their obligations at work or cut corners in their homemaking or make adjustments in both. Some mothers wish to spend their free time in paid employment; others choose to utilize their skills and pursue their interests by engaging in volunteer work or in creative leisure activities; still others think of homemaking and child rearing as full-time activities.

These are some of the many different ways in which women respond to given sets of circumstances. Their responses are determined by a type of balance sheet of sacrifices and rewards. This reflects, first, the importance each woman attaches to realizing specific values and accomplishing specific goals in the various areas of her life. In addition, the entries reflect the costs she ascribes to the different actions she must take to realize her values and goals.

Before the turn of the century alternative patterns of life were determined to a great extent by a more or less rigid environment. A woman who had completed higher education could generally pursue a career only at the cost of foregoing marriage and a family. If she married, she had to withdraw from work and devote her abilities and energies to raising her children and participating in voluntary activities. Her alternatives were a career *or* marriage.

Because of the revolutionary changes that have taken place in the environment, these limited alternatives have been significantly broadened. A woman is now able to work while she is studying, before her marriage, after she marries, while her children are very young, after they enter school, or after they have grown up. Or she may decide not to work.

Moreover, even if she decides to follow one pattern, she can shift to another. For example, if she finds that her decision to work while her children are very young is unsatisfactory, she may resign from her job. Or the reverse may happen. She may stop working at the birth of her first child anticipating that she will remain out of the labor market until her youngest child enters grade school, only to find that she cannot tolerate a life of total domesticity.

The highly educated women in our study were graduate students at Columbia University at some time during the six years following World War II. They include fellows, scholarship winners, and other students with high academic standing. . . . From our study of the women in this group, we were able to identify four major patterns of life. The patterns were revealed through our examination of the women's anticipations as they were clarified with time, of the actions they took as their lives progressed, and of the relationship between their goals and the realities they confronted. Each pattern is distinctive, but within each there is a great variety of goals and values, of life circumstances, and of responses. . . .

CHAPTER 16

Life-Styles of Educated Women

THE TYPES OF LIVES people lead and the lessons they transmit to a younger generation are determined by certain basic attitudes and values. This chapter will describe and analyze these attitudes and their effect on the behavior of the women in our group of graduate fellowship winners. It will also set forth their attitudes toward the role of adult women in contemporary U.S. society. . . .

Since the term *value* is used in many different ways, in both the general and the scientific literature, we will indicate what we mean by it. We see an individual's values as the reflection of his basic inclinations and generalized orientations. They are the elements that shape the preference systems he develops to guide him in the formulation of goals and in the exercise of choice. The sequential decisions that an individual makes are not random but are meaningfully related to each other, since his preference system rests on a limited number of distinct values that give meaning and direction to his life and influence his choices among the alternatives he confronts.

We have identified a variety of life-styles followed by the women in our group, which rest upon distinctions among basic values. By *life-style* we refer to that orientation to self, others, and society that each individual develops and follows—that is, her value orientation.

This approach confronted the staff with a twofold challenge. First was the identification of different life-styles. Second was the evaluation of each individual to determine into which category she was to be placed. The first problem was simplified by our earlier efforts to develop such a category scheme for educated men (see 22), which we modified and elaborated in light of our knowledge of the lives of these women.

The second problem was also met simply. In order to determine the appropriate category for every respondent, we looked in each question-naire for the dominant approach underlying the responses to the various questions. In most instances we were able to identify such an approach, although in a few cases the predominant style could be discerned only after probing and reflection. We were able to classify all the women as belonging to one or another type. It should be noted that our categories were arrived at empirically and do not reflect any preconceived social or psychological theory.

The first of the four types of life-style we identified describes those women whose underlying attitudes and preferences indicate a striving after autonomy—that is, women who want to direct themselves rather than direct others or be directed by them. Because of this emphasis on self-direction and self-determination, we have identified these women as the *individualistic* type.

M.P. is an example of the individualistic type. She is currently an associate professor of French at a leading eastern university. "I could never have been merely a wife and mother without making everyone around me nervous and unhappy," she wrote. "Fortunately, I have always wanted to be left alone to devote myself to work, reading, and daydreaming. My present career is perfect for this combination." Her basic orientation derives from a desire for freedom, to do what *she* wants to do, to be free of obligations growing out of her relations to others. Her own words, "to be left alone," are the key to her personality and life stance.

Another woman, a statistician for the government, said: "My mother wanted me to be independent financially ... she firmly believed I'd have a happier life. I now believe she is right." Although married with five children, she has worked continuously, and in a few years she and her husband expect to be financially independent and to "retire" to become "our own bosses." With regard to her working she said: "I would not be content to be just a housewife. . . . I must work to express myself—children or no children. The alternative is that I would be a frustrated woman in which case I would be no good to anyone—including myself." Her desire for independence and self-expression is evident throughout her questionnaire.

The second major type describes those women whose major drive is to influence people and events. They may want to dominate others, but not necessarily. But they do want to make an impact and have their ideas and values influence others. They have strong drives and motivation. We have designated this group as the *influential* type.

P.Y. is a representative of the influential type. She took her master's degree in student personnel administration with the aim of becoming a dean of women. "There was a dean of women that was a bit of a witch in my college. I think that rather influenced me to be one—different!" From the time she was in college, P.Y. attempted to attain positions in which she could influence and direct others. She has been, consecutively, service club director, regional executive director of a girls' organization, dean of women in a junior college. She knew before her marriage that she wanted to combine a career and marriage, "but the career was definitely to take precedence. I went with two boys (for four years and three years) but did not marry either because of career conflicts and attitudinal differences." Of her husband's career, she said: "Until now it has been largely determined by my career." Her husband was in the Army when they married, and he has since started his higher education with her support.

E.P. is another example of the influential type. She made substantial sacrifices to rise to a position where she would be in authority—able to influence and guide, and perhaps control, others. Her greatest pleasure, as she remarked, was to influence young people through ideas. She worked for many years as a teacher to support herself while she pursued her collegiate and graduate studies. She now holds the position of professor of education and coordinator of student teaching. She does outside speaking and writing, and she makes $15,000 a year. She identified as the most gratifying aspects of her work: "putting my ideas into operation. Opportunities I have to get to other sections of the country to speak. Most of all, the excitement of the teachers as they find themselves growing."

There are many women whose lives are geared to helping and supporting others. Some find expression for these needs and desires inside their homes, others outside, in their work and volunteer activities. We have designated this type of woman, whose basic orientation is to help and be of service to others, as the *supportive* type.

Such a person is A.T. She initially studied literature but was persuaded by her husband, whom she married in her sophomore year, to shift to a "more scientific career," which she did by majoring in psychology. She had completed one year's graduate work toward her doctorate when she left school because her physicist husband had to move to another city. "I had to decide whether being a full-time mother was more important than my work goals and I decided that nursing each baby for a year plus staying home with the young ones was more important. . . . If a woman wants to create a good marriage it is the labor of many years and much adaptation and rarely can her husband reach pinnacles of erudite or intellectual fulfillment and productivity if she is busy shoving onward and upward too, at the same time." In her lyrical formulation, she saw the most gratifying aspect of homemaking as creating "a safe, warm, free place in a senseless world of poised atomic threat. Here is the Garden of Eden where even serpents have a right to dwell — joy, sorrow, laughter, quarrels, yells — but still deep affectional bonds and a natural sense of belonging to each other and to our little world of garden, friends, children — home."

A.T. has found her satisfaction in making a home for her husband and children. She apparently has felt no deep urge either to put her graduate training to use, as an individualistic type would, nor did she seek a position of power or prestige as an influential type would. She was fully satisfied to find her fulfillment at home.

Others who have a supportive life-style are involved in the world of work. Trained as a social worker, M.C. worked for several years until her children required her presence at home. But she looks forward to returning to work as soon as the children are old enough that they will not require her constant supervision. She described the meaning of being of service to others: "The satisfaction of doing valuable and constructive work which makes a difference in the lives of people, directly and indirectly."

The fourth and last category includes women who direct their time and energy toward improving some part of the community. These women subordinate personal goals to larger aims and goals and devote their talent, their energy, and their means to the cause which they have espoused. Their commitment frequently is to a religious, ideological, or political system. We have called these women the *communal* type.

E.R. was born in Europe and emigrated with her family to the United States in the late 1930s. After completing her graduate work, she taught for several years and then accepted a position with the Catholic Interracial Council in a large eastern city "because of the great need of work in this field." In 1957 she became a nun. Her order lives among less privileged and minority groups, sharing the lives of their neighbors. They engage in the same kind of work as do those among whom they live, and they themselves live in small family-size groups. Sister E. works in a voluntary nondenominational hospital. "At the same time, we try to live a life of prayer, and simply to be friends to those around us, those with whom we work, and all those with whom we come in contact."

Sister E.'s story indicates that her entire life is communally oriented.

She lives as a member of a religious group, her work and life are devoted to living according to her faith, and she has turned her back on the accumulation of worldly goods. She is a dedicated person who acts in accordance with her beliefs.

Another example of a communal type is a woman with a strong commitment to political affairs. She is a journalist who switched from newswriting to become a full-time, paid party worker. "From interest in public affairs per se I have shifted to interest in their political implications and their conversion into votes, motivated by my belief in the philosophy of the Democratic Party." She spends at least sixty hours a week in her present job which she considers her "best opportunity to serve the Party." She says, "My interest in politics has converted me from a 9-to-5 employee to a 9-to-midnight devotee."

The foregoing examples illustrate both the strength and weakness of our simplified typology. We did place each of these women in one of our four categories, but even their abbreviated biographies indicate that there was overlapping in their orientation. Nevertheless, we believe that we succeeded in identifying the dominant life-style in each case, and the fourfold schema enabled us to make some significant differentations.

Table 16.1 shows the percentage distribution of the 311 women according to their principal value orientation. It is noteworthy that slightly over half of the entire group were characterized as individualistic, women who place a high value on self-determination and the exercise of autonomy. Only 10 percent were primarily concerned with directing and influencing other people. Even among this small group there were only a few who were primarily power-oriented and wanted to propel themselves into positions of leadership so that they could control others. Many of those in this group also showed the same qualities of self-determination and desire for autonomy that characterize the individualistic group. The last two groups, which account for almost 2 out of 5, were composed of individuals who wanted to meet the needs and demands of others— members of their immediate family or groups in the community. The supportive type, the conventional prototype of a woman, accounted for less than 1 out of 3!

Table 16.1

Value Orientation	Percentage
Individualistic	52
Influential	10
Supportive	29
Communal	9
Total	100

It should be noted that although the women were classified purely according to their attitudes and values and independent of their behavior, their attitudes naturally influenced their actions. We can now review the extent to which these several life-styles are related to various behavioral aspects of the lives of these women. Table 16.2 shows the relationship between life-style and present role.

Table 16.2

Role	Value Orientation (percent)			
	Individualistic	Influential	Supportive	Communal
Worker	70	90	37	64
Combination	11	0	20	14
Homemaker	19	10	43	22
Total	100	100	100	100

We see that those with either an individualistic or an influential life-style are much more likely to work full time than those with a supportive or communal life-style. But it is also noteworthy that women with the same life-style are pursuing different roles.

Table 16.3 sets forth the relationship between life-styles and the satisfactions the respondents derive from their work in terms of their responses. As one would expect, the dominant values that underlie an individual's life-style are related to the gratifications she finds in her work. We see that those with an individualistic life-style are most likely to find their principal gratifications from the intrinsic nature of their work. Those with an influential life-style reported gratifications from personal relations and from self-realization. Those with a supportive life-style singled out, to some degree, the social significance of their work, and those with a communal life-style, the interpersonal aspects of their work. The one surprising fact is that a greater proportion of those with a communal life-style did not report the social significance of their work as its most gratifying aspect.

Table 16.3

Source of Gratification	Value Orientation (percent)			
	Individualistic	Influential	Supportive	Communal
Self-realization	29	13	21	15
Personal relations	22	28	20	15
Social significance	24	30	23	39
Conditions of work	15	18	26	24
Nature of the activity	10	11	10	7
Total	100	100	100	100

Another aspect of the dominant values held by our group is provided by their opinions and attitudes about the proper role of the educated woman in the contemporary world.

With regard to higher education for women, there was almost unanimity that it is personally and socially desirable for girls, as well as boys, to pursue their education as far as they want and as long as they can profit from it. Moreover, there was substantial agreement that higher education for young women should not be different from that available to young men. Only a very small minority advocated radical changes in college curricula for young women in the direction of home economics and other courses directly related to homemaking and child rearing. A somewhat larger number saw some advantages to shifting the time when women attend college and graduate school. Some thought it would be wise if women would devote the early years of adulthood to raising their children and then undertake their higher education.

The following excerpts reveal the strong feelings of our group toward optimal educational opportunities for all able women. An educator wrote: "Education—as an enterprise—was designed by man for women. It is basically patterned to their career expectations. Through the years society has imposed different career expectations upon men and upon women even though the I.Q. of each sex runs the gamut from ignorance to genius. The current demand for educated 'manpower' can be satisfied to some extent at least by educated womanpower. . . . If a woman directs her potential into the raising of a family, the potential is still there and can be recalled and updated when she is ready to return to a career."

A librarian who has three children said: "I do not feel that undergraduate education should be postponed until after one's children are grown. . . . I think my children will be far better and more responsible citizens as a result of the educational opportunities I have had. I only hope they get a chance to grow up and become educated themselves."

An historian argued: "In a society which had long since ceased to provide a woman, whether married or single, any secure position within the family there can be no possibility of excluding women from higher education. . . . From the standpoint of the individual, I think higher education is 'wasted' only if a woman fails to achieve a balance between the activities involved in marriage and the demands of a career."

Another historian argued for women's education on the score that "educated men require educated wives although sometimes they don't realize it soon enough. . . . Women should certainly *not* drop out of college to put a husband through graduate school—the gulf between them may turn out to be all but unbridgeable." Another woman saw a different danger—when "husbands of young women of a certain type . . . expect their wives to go straight on to a Ph.D. *while* having children and keeping up the home front.... The effect is to put pressure on the graduate school to relax requirements ... for the Ph.D., which the husband seems to regard in a sense as a part of her dowry."

A research chemist with a Ph.D. and two children does not even see another side of the argument: "Educated women make better housewives, better volunteers and social workers, and are better able to educate their children. Many men do not perform the jobs for which they were educated either. Many women will eventually use a good measure of their higher education."

Their replies about higher education for women reflected their own convictions that they had profited from the opportunities they had had; they saw little point in educating women differently from men, and they were not disturbed by the fact that for some periods of time women do not use their education in a strictly vocational sense. They recognized that even when they are at home, husband and children and the community at large would profit from their being educated.

Their positive stance toward higher education for women did not blind them to the need for certain reforms. Looking back at her own experiences, one respondent discussed the changes that are needed at graduate school level: "At least when I was at graduate school, the professors were not all encouraging to the female students who planned to marry. Apparently they considered these students a 'lost cause.' I think it is time for professors and employers to re-think their attitudes and to realize that women *can* combine marriage and employment, and that they should not be rejected just because they will not work a forty-hour week. Some ways must be found to arrange more part-time employment for educated women. Otherwise, this country will lose much in the line of intellectual resources."

Many advocated major adjustments in the timing of a course of graduate studies. "It seems to me that there will always be and should be different kinds of women. Those who are not likely to make marriage their principal careers should be allowed to go straight on in graduate work if they are fitted for it. Those who marry early should have a chance to come back later and bring their general education up to date or go on to specialized study if they have the desire and aptitude for it. There is too much work in the world to be done by men alone."

Another wrote: "I think the real issue is when higher education should take place. If women were mature enough after high school perhaps to choose a mate and raise their children, I feel it would be wise for them to do so then. After raising their children to school age they would then pursue their college and graduate training so there is not the long hiatus between obtaining their training and their using this training in the job market."

Others also saw advantages to breaking the educational track between college and graduate school. "I am wondering if it is wise for a woman to go directly from college to graduate work. I think perhaps a few years of work would be wise. If her direction in life is homemaking the woman would likely discover this during the first years after college. If her direction is a career, general experience in the field would be helpful, as would her added maturity. Bearing in mind the fact that many women interrupt careers during childbearing years, it would seem sensible to wait to develop specialized careers until after this interruption, because during the homemaking period it is hard to keep knowledge and skills at a high level."

Another supported the same proposal: "It is difficult in our society for a woman in her early twenties to think single-mindedly about a career. For too many, perhaps, graduate education is a stop-gap until marriage and the raising of a family. Given the already existing strain on graduate faculties in the good graduate and professional schools, the common reluctance of such faculties to take women students seriously is understandable. Even if a woman completes her graduate training, it is likely that this training will have become obsolete or that her interests will have changed before she is in a position to pursue a career. One alternative is for women to think of postponing graduate training until serious concentration on such training is possible. Going back to school is difficult, though if such a course were to be institutionalized in our academic system, it could perhaps be made more feasible for more women."

A clear-sighted respondent linked reforms in education to changes in the world of work. One without the other would not solve the issue, she said. "I think some of the solution lies, first, in continuing to educate women in advanced studies and then, second, awakening the imagination of both universities and employers to the possible applications of their potential. Specifically, universities should expand their adult education programs and permit easy access to courses within their regular graduate and undergraduate faculties on a part-time basis; transfers of credits from one institution to another should be as flexible as possible to suit individual needs; easy access to university libraries, research laboratories, and equipment on a part-time basis at, perhaps, odd hours would be much appreciated by many women whose home schedules do not permit regular outside schedules; a new class of positions known as 'teaching assistants' could be established—the function of such assistants would be to take over some of the professor's teaching load, or even to teach one whole course in the subject matter of her specialty without being connected with the university on a full-time, fully salaried basis. . . . It's hard to estimate how much valuable work, now being left undone, could be accomplished by the available numbers of such women."

The interlacing of the educational issue with the other aspects of a woman's life is revealed in the following comment. According to this respondent, significant educational reforms would require simultaneous reforms over a wide front. "We need a new attitude towards women. The able ones who can contribute to our society should be enabled to do so. This means well-run day-care centers; equal pay for equal work; making available training through vocational schools for housekeepers who can function well as mother substitutes; dignifying the job of running a home so that those with the skill and temperament to do so can do so with pleasure or can take jobs as housekeepers. We need decent wages for men so that women are not forced to work from economic necessity, leaving their children without proper care. We need to teach our young men that marriage is a partnership and if they marry a career gal they both must cope with domestic responsibilities. Being a wife and mother is wonderful — but it is not enough if one is trained and able.... We need to set up special hours of work for professional women — four- to six-hour days, the four-day week, the nine-month year ... are feasible in many job situations."

With regard to the desirability of higher education for women, our group spoke with one voice. Even on the issue of whether marriage and work should be combined, about which there was considerable difference of opinion, there were substantial areas of agreement. There was unanimity regarding the need and desirability of work for single women and married women without children. It was generally agreed also that it should be made easier for married women who are under pressure to support themselves and their dependents to work. Similarly, there were no real objections to women working once their children were grown. Differences and disagreements were limited to whether married women with young children should work.

Table 16.4 sets forth the relationship between the women's present roles and their attitudes toward the combination of family and work for women in general. The findings are significant. As we might expect, those who work full time feel that mothers can work without conflict or that it is a matter for each individual to decide, whereas those who are homemakers are more likely to believe that mothers with young children should not work. Naturally enough, their opinions reflected the resolutions they had worked out for themselves.

Here are a series of viewpoints that cover the range of the opinions expressed about working mothers. One respondent said: "If a woman has prepared for a career and feels inadequate, unfulfilled, and restless because she no longer pursues it, then by all means let her follow and continue in that career." Another commented: "To pursue a career effectively one has to be free of any severe conflict in regard to family and

Table 16.4

	Role (percent)		
Attitude	Worker	Combination	Homemaker
Deny conflict	63	38	39
Think mothers should limit work	22	38	26
Think young children preclude work	15	24	35
Total	100	100	100

a job; in short, what is most comfortable for a particular woman should guide her, not a particular point of view of what a woman should or should not do." A single woman said: "Of my women friends who are married and have children, those who have the most satisfactory marriages and seem most satisfied with themselves also work. These particular women do not work out of financial necessity. . . . Their husbands do not object, because their wives are better as wives." Another respondent remarked: "For women with a number of children a full-time job means a hard life with serious sacrifices. . . . I have considered this question often and am unsure whether it is or isn't just a 'stunt'."

One wrote: "Although I personally have hesitated, I strongly approve of married women working if their individual circumstances point to it as the right thing to do." Another woman with strong opinions put her views thus: "I undoubtedly would not be working if I had children and feel mothers should not work until children are grown." A single woman presented one of the most extreme positions: "No woman should work while her children are still unmarried and at home unless compelled to do so for the necessities of life (not the luxuries)." But a mother of two wrote: "So much depends on the woman, the job, the husband. If a woman feels a vocation she is only fooling herself if she thinks she can submerge it to diapers and dishwashing."

A married correspondent wrote: "I think that women should realize that there are some years when the children are young during which their career must take second place. But with understanding on the part of all concerned I see absolutely no need to place the issue of career and family on an either/or basis." Finally, a mother of three said: "As to whether married women should work or not—let each make up her own mind. But it would be nice if they would refrain from turning their own personal decision into a categorical imperative."

These different views about the balance between family and work reflected not only the roles which these women pursued, but, even more broadly, their life-styles (see Table 16.5).

Those women with either individualistic or influential life-styles feel strongly that it is up to a mother to decide for herself whether or not to work full time even though she had children at home. On the other hand, about 2 out of 3 of those with a supportive or communal life-style believe that married women with children should stay home or at least adjust their hours of work.

Table 16.5

Attitude	Value Orientation (percent)			
	Individualistic	Influential	Supportive	Communal
Deny conflict	60	79	37	36
Think mother should limit work	26	7	26	41
Think young children preclude work	14	14	37	23
Total	100	100	100	100

The attitudes and values of the women in our group toward this central issue of family and work are revealed by the range of advice that these women offer the younger generation. One respondent summed up her advice to her daughter: "If possible don't meet the right man until you have packed in plenty of school and travel and men and jobs and living. The most important thing you must do is to meet enough men to find the right one and not settle for anything less along the way. . . . Don't rush to marry for if you marry too young, you will always wonder what you missed." So wrote a social worker, mother of two, married to a physician. A Ph.D. scientist wrote: "I intend to encourage my four daughters to obtain as much education as they can in directions they themselves choose, preferably before marriage." A mathematical statistician said: "I would repeat what my mother did—persuade my daughters to develop their intellectual capacities to the fullest and to be financially independent of anyone." A historian: "If . . . I have intelligent daughters I should, probably uselessly, encourage them to study as long as possible, to have some professional or career training, to return to it ultimately if not continue it along the way. Having only sons, I feel that they will in the long run be happier married to such women."

Many also hold general views about the role of women which carry overtones for guidance of the new generation. A mother of four with a master's degree in English said: "I do not feel that a woman must work professionally or earn money to justify her higher education. She is a better wife, mother, and person, and citizen as a result of her education and this is justification enough." An economist, mother of two, had a clear view about herself and a tolerant view about others: "While I personally enjoy my work and feel it an asset, rather than a burden, I am not a 'great emancipator' and I do not want to be considered the *equal* of a man in all regards. In other words, I am a woman first and foremost and I work outside the home because it makes me a more complete person and I am fortunate in being able to arrange my time accordingly. Nor do I advocate careers for all women."

A Ph.D. social scientist, mother of three, said: "Some women . . . feel there is some disgrace in 'working' when their husbands are able to support them. All women, or almost all women, work, of course. The only question is what kind of work shall they do. At any particular time a woman's (as well as a man's) direction will be affected by her own talents, her opportunities for developing and expressing these within her society and her priorities of responsibility. . . . She should avoid overemphasizing her own importance and thus incidentally save herself from envy of men. She should try to make her best contribution under her own circumstances, not worrying about the things she might have done if only."

A sociologist with diversified work experience wrote: "Women now go to college in droves, many have careers, numbers work after marriage. The significance and meaning of these activities in their lives will be very much influenced by the men they marry, the degree to which the career can be combined with marriage. I can't imagine myself as never having gone to college nor to work—nor would I recommend such an existence for my daughter, but I certainly don't believe higher education is a cure-all for unhappiness or the way to prevent neurosis."

A journalist said: "I frankly feel that too much is currently being made of the alleged 'dissatisfaction' among women with their lot in life. I see it merely as an outgrowth of our relatively overprivileged society— that we have come to feel we are entitled to be happy all of the time. . . . Even a man engaged in the most rewarding, fulfilling type of work would not be able to score 100 percent on this kind of happiness test."

And a geneticist offered the following: "Since I believe that the world would run most equitably (though not perhaps most harmoniously) were each person given the opportunity for development of individual talents, I think women as people should be educated, have careers, have husbands and children, climb mountains, do embroidery, etc., according to interest and/or ability. . . . It seems unlikely that the half of her genes a daughter receives from her father (and the half of hers she passes on to her sons) will be transferred by residence in her body into the accepted female stereotypes."

The women in our group had different viewpoints about the role of the educated woman today. But we must not overlook the wide area of agreement that underlies their expressed differences in attitudes and values. It should be noted that very few of the group held either that a woman should never work or that she should always work.

There was no real disagreement with the traditional stance that a married woman with young children has a primary obligation to her family. Differences arose as to the alternative ways in which mothers might discharge these responsibilities. Some believe that if mothers have adequate help at home they might work full time or surely part time, while others believe that it is best under most conditions for a mother to remain at home as long as her children are young. There was further disagreement as to the age at which children no longer need full-time supervision from their mothers.

But these differences fade when we recall that these women do not see a conflict between home and work. Most of the group do not find any basic incompatibility between a family and a career, although most of them realized that many women find it difficult to combine the two. They are generally relaxed about this problem since they know that if a woman finds herself unable to cope with the demands of both home and job, she will give her primary allegiance to her home and particularly to her children.

The conclusion from this review of their life-styles and values is remarkably clear and distinct. Our women are highly self-determined. They want to lead the types of lives they have discovered best suit their needs, desires, and the pressures under which they live. Expecting a high order of freedom and self-determination for themselves, they adopt the same attitudes and values toward other women.

Society offered our women the opportunity to become well educated. They availed themselves of this opportunity. Next, society offered many of them the further opportunity to marry and to have children and at the same time to continue to work and to pursue a career. Our women welcomed these broadened options, and most of them found it possible to derive high orders of satisfaction from both home and work.

CHAPTER 17

Four Types of Educated Women

THE PLANNER

WE HAVE USED THE TERM *planners* to describe women who follow a pattern that is directed toward the realization of particular goals and who remain steadfast in their dedication to these aims. It is their purposefulness and direction that suggest this term. These are women who know where they are going.

Women in this group do not necessarily anticipate in detail at an early age the kind of lives they hope to pursue, and they do not consciously and rationally weigh each decision in light of their goals. A few proceed in a deliberate manner, but most do not. Nevertheless, we can classify all of them as planners because the actions they take and their reactions to their experiences reveal an unfolding quality in their lives. They have established more or less definite goals, and they direct their efforts toward their chosen destinations. What they do and what they fail to do is directly related to the ends they seek.

Planning is not a one-time act. It is a process that may continue throughout a lifetime. A woman may have her sights set on a specific long-range goal, such as success in the career of her choice. At the opposite extreme, her goals may be less precise, such as an intention to leave her job at the birth of her child. Such a limited goal may make no provision for plans for later periods of her life; new plans will have to be formulated in the future.

One of the most important features of the planfulness of these women is their care to take only those actions that are consonant with their general goals and values and to avoid any involvement or commitment that might limit their freedom of action. A planner who is intent on acquiring a maximum of education and in pursuing a career may turn aside attractive proposals of marriage that might deflect her from her goal. On the other hand, a woman who is bent on acquiring a husband and children may abandon career opportunities in order to take up homemaking responsibilities. The age at which a woman is ready to consider marriage, and the size of her family, may be integral parts of a broader design. The source of this planfulness is a clearly structured system of values, which allows these women to order their goals and their lives in accordance with what is more important and what is less important to them.

It is not the content of her decisions that determines whether a woman is a planner. One woman may seek early marriage and children as basic to her happiness, while another avoids personal ties as possible interferences with her career plans. One may wish to work after marriage while another prefers to devote her time to her home and family. It is the clarity of her goals and her deliberateness in seeking to realize them that determines whether a woman is a planner. . . .

Planners can be differentiated as follows: those whose lives are organized around their preparation for and pursuit of a career; those whose goals are family-oriented and who hope to realize themselves primarily through their husbands and children; and those who wish to combine work and family. . . .

With the increasing growth of opportunities for education and careers for women that has characterized the twentieth-century United States, it is not surprising that many women prefer to seek their primary fulfillment in the world of work. As we have noted earlier, during the last several decades there has been a social revolution in attitudes toward women who work. In addition, since World War II society has begun to manifest increased tolerance and approval of the working mother. The obverse of this changing climate of opinion is the noticeable relaxation that has come to characterize women's planning with respect to marriage and motherhood.

A woman is no longer dependent on marriage for her status. Some women deliberately choose to remain single, and others can contemplate without undue tension and stress the fact that concentration on educational and career goals may mean they will never marry. Many have come to realize that they can have an emotionally satisfying life without the bonds of matrimony. Others who do marry prefer to remain childless rather than risk interference with their career aspirations, and still others are willing to postpone marriage despite the fact that delay may result in childlessness. Finally, there are those women who do marry and have children, but whose major efforts are directed toward their career activities.

Social revolutions always have antecedents, and sometimes the prelude is a long one. Families who had positive views toward their daughter's preparing for a career were in the vanguard of the much larger group who today encourage their daughters in this direction.

Parental opposition, on the other hand, does not necessarily result in the frustration of a girl's career goals. Often she is able to overcome family criticism, but sometimes she must estrange herself from her family if she is not to submit to the restrictions they impose. She is able to do this because the pursuit of an education or career is no longer considered deviant; there is, consequently, social support, if not family backing, for her endeavors.

A significant fact about all of these career-oriented women is that their pattern is the one that most closely resembles that of men. As with most men, their careers are central to their planning. And, as with most men, other sectors of their lives, although important, tend to assume subsidiary positions.

NANCY GRAVES

My family background is not altogether unique. There are many American families in which the women have always been expected to cultivate their talents and play a necessary role outside the usual one of housewife. My grandmothers and great-grandmothers ran plantations while the men were off fighting wars or sitting in legislature; they were in charge of the grist mill or the general store, while the men ran the farm or ranch; they were the local animal doctors before there were veterinarians; one was a botanist and specialist of some repute in medicinal herbs; as teachers or ministers' wives in western missions, they played important roles; one was left a widow, ran a large cattle and sheep ranch, and reared ten of her own children, four of her sister's children, and three tramping boys who came in the depression of '93. I don't believe it has ever occurred to anyone on either side of the family that a woman could be or ought to be "a mere housewife," and hardly a man in the family would be likely to choose a wife who saw herself in that single role. It is a family in which every woman is supposed to be *somebody.*

I was born in 1915 and raised in a small midwestern town where my father was a high-school principal. Both my parents were college graduates and my father had attended graduate school as well. My mother was a musician and, primarily out of personal interest, worked part time as a church organist until I was about twelve, when an arthritic condition prevented her from continuing. She always encouraged my interest in working, and it was taken for granted that I would have a career; I believe she has received much vicarious satisfaction from my career. I can never recall my parents expressing any expectations for me other than that I should get as much education as I wanted, find interesting work, and have a happy marriage. I have satisfied all but the last of these, which is a fair batting average. They never seemed overly concerned about marriage or the prospects of marriage for me, come to think of it.

I entered the State University in 1933, where I pursued a general education program in an integrated liberal arts setup, one of the earliest of its kind. While I found the program most rewarding and helpful in my career development, it was difficult to focus my career plans readily, both because there was little compulsion to do so in the program itself, and because my background always fell short of some of the expectations of employers interested in people with a highly specialized professional education. . . .

My family had a difficult time during the Depression. I helped somewhat through part-time work as a student assistant during my freshman year. This led to my present interests, since the professors under whom I worked encouraged study and experience in educational research. After I graduated, I entered Columbia in order to work for my M.A. I had decided to enter social group work, and graduate education was required. Anyway, I had always expected to get a graduate degree. I was interested in religious activities in college, and in New York I worked part time at a local YWCA as a group work assistant. After I received my master's degree, I went to work as a Girl Reserve secretary in a New England YWCA. This was a good entry into my desired occupation, and I liked the salary ($1,600) and the location. I left during the war because of my mother's illness, but I served in a similar capacity in a YWCA near the family home. I found this position to be a dead end geographically and professionally; there was poor supervision, a lack of adequate program resources, and lack of freedom for development.

I decided to enter college and university work and became a university YWCA director and assistant counselor for women. Here I had excellent supervision and an opportunity to do teaching, experimentation, and research. From this position I went to the national staff of the YWCA.

This meant a substantial advancement and salary increase, and I particularly enjoyed the opportunity to write. But my university experience made me want to undertake further training so that I would qualify for a college position.

I applied for fellowship aid to continue my graduate education and received a grant for further study at Columbia. I found an interdisciplinary program in philosophy and education, which suited my interest in relations among academic disciplines. Thus I was able to study subjects offered by both Teachers College and the Columbia Graduate Faculties. . . .

I had thought of teaching philosophy or philosophy of education, but was urged to enter college administration because of the shortage of personnel and my previous experience and interest. I found a university position in student personnel, in which I could also teach and, more important, participate in experimental administration. Two years later I became dean of students at a small liberal arts college, where I also taught counseling and engaged in a study of referral techniques. . . .

I left when there was a change of administration, and since then I have been in student personnel at a new branch of a state university. This position meant an advance in salary, an opportunity to build a new program on new principles in a new university from the very beginning, and association with outstanding professional people and close friends. I am in charge of residence, vocational guidance, and financial aid. My deepest satisfactions from work are in contributing to the development of students, developing research and teaching programs, and earning money. It is gratifying to watch a new institution develop, being free to experiment without having to consider what was done last year. However, we are still short of budget and manpower, which occasionally requires giving up major blocks of the program.

A problem for me accentuated by my breadth of interest has been a tendency to overinvest in work and take on too much on the job. This has occasioned health problems, and so I have had to learn to control this tendency. However, control has been easier because of the wealth of alternative activities available and because I have benefited from my academic work in physiology and psychology. This improved control has made my work more effective and enjoyable.

Professionally, my status and income exceed my expectations and, personally, my activities and interests have appreciably broadened to include such things as painting and politics, which did not particularly interest me earlier. Within my work, I find that my expectations have been exceeded in that I have been able to use my experience in general education and instruction to work toward a closer relation between personnel administration and teaching, and to apply psychological theory and philosophy to student personnel programs. . . .

I am presently well satisfied with my position. However, I might leave if there were a change in administrative policies or practices, if I were unable to carry out my responsibilities adequately, or if I were offered a higher-paying or top-level administrative position. I thought of doing straight research in education but rejected the idea when I was given the opportunity to combine research and teaching with administration and found my salary and associations with colleagues I admired most satisfactory. My articles and publications have helped me get several jobs I wanted, and research has sharpened my interest in my profession and opened up new professional contacts and activities.

I believe I am working at a level that is commensurate with my abilities. Factors contributing to my achievement have been the breadth of my educational background, the support of interested and influential friends, and a high degree of flexibility and geographic mobility. I believe that my major handicaps have included lack of customary specialization, lack of aggressiveness and consistent drive, and my emotional and financial involvement with my parents. . . .

I have my own home and enjoy cooking, gardening, and entertaining when I am able, but I deplore the lack of time to relax and enjoy my home. During my college years, I was sure I wanted to marry and I wanted to choose someone who could share my interests and whose interests I could share. I felt that I could not give up a career in order to marry. I was equally certain that I did not wish to engage in career rivalry, nor to dominate the career of a husband, any more than I wished to be dominated. I have not married, but I feel my personal relationships with men in the profession have been facilitated by some of these expectations and anticipated problems.

I would have been a very unhappy woman without a higher education and a career because I have scholarly ability and have wanted to develop it as far as I could. I cannot say whether I would be happier if I were also married—the hypothesis is untestable, since one cannot be at once married and unmarried! I enjoy being a woman; I enjoy working with both men and women; I believe I enjoy my professional relationships with men partly because I am a woman and "vive la difference"!

The discussion of the problem of women's roles seems rather fruitless to me. We are past the age when our culture can afford sex differentiation in roles, if, indeed, this country ever fully supported it. Men play multiple roles; so do women. . . .

I feel, too, that an important social gain might be made by giving some attention to ways in which relationships between men and women can be used to improve efficiency and enjoyment in work. There may be sex-related "styles" of work which could be used to reinforce the effectiveness of both men and women on the job. The affectional aspects of on-the-job relationships, for example, may be an important factor in motivation and reward for both men and women. . . . The institutional patterns within which employees operate might thus be based on more nearly accurate knowledge of the varying life-styles and work styles of both men and women. Women may stand to gain more from more varied and flexible work patterns, but men might also gain from such findings. . . .

It is interesting and gratifying to review a rather checkered career and see that it does make sense and show a pattern and direction. My education was made to order, both for the profession of college administration and for my personal enjoyment. I have employed in some way everything I ever studied. I believe that I found in graduate work, in particular, a sense of values that has been indispensable in the stresses and strains of administrative work: a feeling for scholarship as a vocation in its own right; for independence in research, experimentation, and thinking; and for intrinsic satisfactions in study and research regardless of success or failure, approbation or condemnation, in the outcome. When prospects looked most bleak, this sense of the value of the intellectual enterprise and my own confidence in its value made it possible for me to trust my own commitment to it and to keep on trying to find and make a place where I could participate happily in it. On the whole, I have found these over and over again in a variety of places and positions, in all of which I have been happy and in all of which I have learned something from both successes and failures. Like Saint Teresa, I am grateful to know that there is useful work for me to do, and if it does not find me, I have only to go out and look for it. . . .

THE RECASTER

The *recasters* are women who make a major change in the patterning of their lives. They are planners who do not carry out their original plans, either because they have lost interest or because they have encountered serious obstacles or attractive new opportunities along the way which they can neither surmount nor ignore.

Some women become recasters because their original values and goals lose their attraction and pull. Suddenly or slowly they find themselves responding to a different set of values and goals. Others become recasters because of an environmental situation. They find that they are unable to realize their original ends. No reasonable amount of effort on their part will dissolve the barriers they encounter, and they are unable to find a way around them.

Although these women redesign the patterns of their lives out of

desire or necessity, they do so in a manner that retains, rather than destroys, the continuity between the past and the present. When they find that
their original solutions for combining the strategic variables in their lives
have failed them, they seek to find new and more satisfactory solutions.

Recasting refers to the process more than to the elements that make it up.
In some instances it appears as if entirely new elements were introduced, as
when a woman who originally chooses an occupation in the humanities
shifts to medicine. But typically the shift is less radical, as when a woman
with early interest in the law studies graduate economics only to return
to law later on.

The striking point is that many women who change their goals because
of new occupational interests have made earlier decisions about a career.
These do not last, however. A forewarning that this might happen can be
deduced from the fact that some women have difficulty in committing
themselves to their first career choice. They make their initial decision
slowly, usually not in college nor even early in graduate school, but later.

Others make occupational choices that they like; they want to stay
with them, but this turns out to be impractical. They become recasters
because their original plans have foundered on the hard rock of reality.
Some women, for instance, discover that their original choice of field is
incompatible with the careers of the men they marry.

There are others who also knew what they wanted and had every
reason to expect that they could realize their plans, but fate treated them
harshly. Some looked forward to having families but found themselves
childless. Others looked forward to a long married life only to find
themselves widowed early.

The key to the necessity to recast for many of these women was found
in their marriages. Marriage presented many women with new opportunities, just as it presented others with new pressures and limitations.
Those who confronted opportunities in marriage that they had not
originally anticipated were often quick to take advantage of them. This
meant that they had to give up their early plans and design new ones.
Others became recasters because of the unanticipated pressures they
encountered in their marriages.

The impact of marriage was even more pervasive. In general, educated women tend to have small families, and within a relatively few
years the home no longer is filled with young children. A potent force
encouraging women to recast the pattern of their lives and work is the
inevitable change that time brings about in homemaking and child
rearing. Some women had allowed for the inevitable changes in their
original planning, but many others did not. For them, the only way out
was to recast their lives. . . .

When a woman marries, the terms of her life change, frequently drastically. But the nature of the changes is difficult to foretell. Therefore, many women find that marriage has produced conditions that have no place in their early plans, and they often recast their goals in light of these new circumstances.

Sometimes a marriage provides supportive circumstances, such as a husband who encourages a woman to pursue a new career. Some families' finances may be such that a woman who had anticipated leaving her job to raise her children finds that she can afford to hire domestic help and to continue working. And sometimes a woman with initially strong career goals finds that she prefers to remain at home with her children and is able to do so.

On the other hand, marriage may present obstacles to the fulfillment of early goals and lead to recasting of these plans. A woman may find her career goals thwarted by her husband's inability to cover the expenses of her working outside the home. Or her husband may prefer that she give up her work in order to take care of her home. Another woman may discover that if the marriage is to flourish she must not compete in the work arena with her husband. Another influential antecedent to the process of recasting is divorce or widowhood, either of which may compel a woman to give up her preference for homemaking in favor of work.

For some single women there is what might be called a negative family influence. These are women who expected to marry and raise families and did not. In this unanticipated position they reappraise their goals and are able to commit themselves to their work without too much regret. They have been forced to recast their plans, but they derive considerable satisfaction from their new goals.

Thus we see that for some women family influences present opportunities far beyond their early anticipation. Others are impelled to lead more restricted lives than they had anticipated. Nevertheless, none of these women is so disquieted by the change in her plans that she is unable to function adequately in her new role.

FRANCES HAZEN

My parents felt a woman's place was in the *home* and thought a woman should definitely *not* be gainfully employed. They did, however, feel a woman should be educated and were able to and did provide me with a college education. Both of them were born in Poland and emigrated to the United States as adults. My father, a rabbi, was a graduate of a rabbinical seminary. My mother had no formal education and no work experience, but she was literate. I was born in San Francisco in 1923 and lived there until I entered Stanford University when I was sixteen. I have two older sisters, one a housewife. The other is a business woman, and our parents' attitudes with respect to women working did not deter either of us.

At college I majored in political science and planned to go on to law school. However, my parents objected to a law career for a woman and so I applied to Columbia for a scholarship for graduate work. I wished to leave home and was attracted by New York. I was awarded a sizable grant and enrolled in the Department of Public Law and Government in 1944, since a continuation of my undergraduate major seemed most sensible. I considered social work but was deterred by the time and money involved in such a change.

I received my master's degree in 1945 and worked as a research associate at Stanford for six months to see if I would like the academic world. My primary objection to completing the Ph.D. was that I felt it would be a serious disadvantage in reference to marriage; I felt it would hinder my getting married. However, when I did marry in 1946, my husband, a rabbi with an M.A. and a rabbinical degree, urged me to complete the doctorate, and I returned to Columbia and made some mild attempts to do so. But I found graduate school government courses a repetition of undergraduate ones, and my work experience at Stanford convinced me that an academic life was not for me. Academic political science impressed me as much talk, and the obvious made complicated. It had very little permanent attraction.

From 1947 until 1953 I stayed home, gave birth to two children, and engaged in some volunteer work largely concerned with various women's groups, such as the League of Women Voters, religious organizations, political clubs, and human relations agencies. I enjoy meeting people and doing what I can for those things and causes in which I believe. It is good to aid the cause to which I subscribe and to help to see it through to fruition, despite the petty details involved in committee meetings. As a wife and mother, my deepest gratifications are in the companionship of my husband and the great pleasure and responsibility of rearing children and participating in their development and growth.

I resisted any prospects of working during the early years of my marriage, when my children were young. But the years passed, and my husband insisted that I go to law school and develop a career for myself, rather than spend my entire life in domestic chores. Therefore, in 1953 I entered Gonzaga University Law School in Spokane, Washington, where we were living. Law was what I had always wanted, and although I felt guilty about leaving my children while attending law school, as they grow older I am delighted that I made the decision. Having my husband's full and complete cooperation was the most important factor in my return to school.

After receiving my LL.B. in 1956, I established my own private law practice in Spokane. I am still at it and I love it. I spend about forty hours a week working at my practice and about four to five hours in volunteer work, which, in addition to some of my earlier interests, now includes professional associations and membership and occasional leadership of a study group. I continue my education through bar courses to keep abreast of the constant changes in the law and legal procedures.

Self-employment determines everything I do. I enjoy working with people, solving their problems, furthering the great system of law and jurisprudence under which we live—and making money ($9,000 to $10,000 a year). The only things I don't like are the petty complications, the burdensome paper work, and the red tape still required in many legal procedures. The only change that could possibly occur in my career would be a judicial appointment or a decision to run for political office. Self-employment enables me to arrange for time with my children when necessary or desirable. Household help is always a problem, but we manage. Taxes have no effect on my decisions whatsoever. My husband's income is between $15,000 and $20,000 a year.

Women in the practice of law have a disadvantage in the attitudes both of male attorneys, who consider them interlopers, and of clients, who evidence some lack of confidence in a female, particularly in areas of business and corporate law. However, we can always win confidence and respect by proving our ability and doing a better job without any chips on the shoulder. Being a woman is in itself sufficient compensation for any losses. . . .

I do feel that every person should have interests in life, whether that person be male or female. Some women can find satisfaction by being home-makers and clubwomen. Others need more. Many who are now home-makers apparently would be far happier if they had some other outside interests and for this reason are resentful and jealous of those women who do. On the other hand, a woman in a career encounters some resentments from men who feel she is competing and insulting their manly prerogatives. Only an insecure male, however, suffers from such great fears of being displaced. To those who are mature, both male and female, it is possible for a woman to have a career, combine it with an entirely satisfactory marriage and home life, and be a better person and mother as a result.

While I personally enjoy my work and find that it is an asset rather than a burden, I am not a "great emancipator" and I do not want to be considered the *equal* of a man in all respects. In other words, I am a woman first and foremost; I work outside the home because it makes me a more complete person and I am fortunate in being able to arrange my time accordingly. I do not wish, however, to abdicate my feminine role, nor to assume the full responsibility of breadwinner our society casts upon the male. . . . I think a woman who really wants and expects *full equality* in employment is headed for emotional problems, because that might mean full equality between male and female in all areas of life; it might damage the woman's psyche if she were to achieve the exact opposite of what she really wants. . . .

THE ADAPTER

The recasters demonstrate flexibility in adjusting their plans when they are faced with new circumstances or conditions. The adapters make a way of life out of this quality. From the start of their planning they adopt open strategies in order to cope with the many possible conditions and circumstances that they expect to encounter. They have sufficient prevision to realize that the pattern of their adult existence may be subject to repeated and important alterations. Thus, unlike many of the recasters, they often avoid committing themselves to any particular goal too early or too firmly.

Yet the adapters are not fatalists. They are realists. When they encounter the necessity to alter their plans and actions, their approach to life allows them to make rather small changes, in contrast to the more radical shifts characteristically made by the recasters. The adapters, having less ambitious and less firmly fixed objectives, find it easier to compromise. It is relatively easy for them to reduce or to modify their aspirations.

A question that remains open is whether their avoidance of firm occupational and life commitments is primarily a reflection of their weaker involvement in interests and values or whether it reflects a deliberate strategy. Many adapters seem deliberately to have decided that, since life is fraught with uncertainty and contingencies, it is wise to avoid too early or too firm a commitment to any single track or approach.

Many of the adapters pursue their education to the point of achieving the doctorate, but this does not commit them irrevocably to a particular career or life plan as it seems to for many planners and, at first, for many recasters. The adapters convey the impression of being more relaxed individuals who are less dedicated to accomplishing specific occupational and life goals. Therefore, they are not unduly disturbed if their original direction has to be altered because of new circumstances, usually marriage and a family.

There is one further quality to their lives that warrants attention. The shifts, adjustments in aspirations, and compromises they make are easier for them because they seem to know from the outset that life is made up of a galaxy of pluses and minuses. Although many regret that they are unable to carry through their initial plans, they feel they have lost little from altering them. In fact, some even gain from a shift. While they might, for instance, forego some of the satisfactions that they antici-pated receiving from working full or part time, they recognize that these might be more than compensated for by the satisfaction derived from devoting themselves exclusively to their husbands and children. The adapters do not find their way of life burdensome.

Although adapters are generally prepared to make adjustments in all areas of their lives, most find that modifications are necessary in only certain spheres. The women in this group tend to follow a pattern of adaptations in one of three ways. Some may modify their work commit-ments either in response to the needs of their families or because of employment restrictions. Some may withdraw from work entirely for long periods, if not permanently, in order to attend to their children and their homes. And some make adjustments in their family responsibilities in order to pursue their careers. However, in none of these instances are their actions as radical as those of the recasters. The adapters do not usually change their goals; they change their methods of achieving them. Most of the recasters suddenly discover that it is a woman's prerogative to change her mind. The adapters knew it all the time. . . .

While many adapters look forward to working and some contem-plate pursuing careers, when they find that marriage interferes with their original occupational intentions, they are prepared to modify their work goals accordingly.

For some adapters, a husband and children means they spend less time at work than they originally contemplated in order to devote more hours to their family's needs. For some women this means occasional rather than continuous work. It may also mean a reduction in weekly hours of work or a change from full-time employment to free-lancing.

Other women may make modifications in their work because em-ployers will not hire two members of the same family. Sometimes this means a change in the type of work they do or in the employer for whom they work. For example, an anthropologist may change from university research to museum work; a college teacher may undertake independent research.

Some women modify their occupational patterns because of the mobility necessitated by their husband's work. Since they must move frequently, these women find that they do not remain in one location long enough to pursue a career systematically.

There is another group who decides that, on balance, it is better to modify their working plans quite substantially in order to devote their free time and energies directly to helping their husbands in their careers. Although they might like to continue with their own work, they are not so determined in their own goals that they cannot put their personal plans aside. Some husbands need assistance; others welcome it even if they could do without it.

Still another type of work modification is made by women who, because of responsibilities at home, find it difficult or impossible to work at a level that uses their full skills—for example, teaching at college level—but who are able to keep their footing in the world of work by taking a position lower in the job hierarchy, one that requires less preparation and time, such as that of a high school teacher.

These women know they are dealing with total life situations in which compromise is their best answer to irreconcilable challenges. . . .

THEODORA EICHLER

Both of my parents were born and educated in Austria. My father was an industrial designer who had the educational equivalent of about two years at a technical school, and my mother was a graduate of a gymnasium. They were married after they immigrated to the United States, and my mother worked as a secretary and translator until I was born. Thus working after graduation from school seemed the normal course of things to me.

My parents respected education and "learning," though my mother originally felt college was unnecessary for a girl. When I showed aptitude, however, she went along with my desire for higher education; and my parents, though not well off, willingly paid for it. They showed pride in my scholastic achievements and advised me to finish my Ph.D. and work for a few years before marriage, partly to gain experience in the world outside, partly so that my education would not be "wasted." They regarded marriage, once made, as "for keeps" and as a full-time career. The influence of these attitudes is subtle and difficult to evaluate, but without my parents' support, I would have found it difficult to acquire higher education no matter how determined I was.

I was born in Philadelphia and entered Bryn Mawr College in 1942, when I was 16 years old. I was very interested in biology and chemistry and decided as a freshman to work in some field that would combine these interests. I eventually majored in chemistry and, by the time I graduated, I had decided to plan for a career in biochemistry. . . .

I worked each summer during my undergraduate years at various jobs including playground direction, laboratory assistance, and tutoring. These helped finance my studies and gave me work experience in my field. My family's poor finances would have hindered the pursuit of graduate studies without my fellowships and part-time work in my department.

I was married to a fellow student after one year of graduate study and continued for another year, receiving my M.A. in 1948, at which time I had completed all my course requirements for the Ph.D. I could not complete my doctorate because when my husband completed his Ph.D., he found a job in another city and I was obliged to take over the care of his four-year-old child by a previous marriage.

Since that time I have been serving solely as a housewife and mother. My husband's career has necessitated frequent changes of residence, both intra- and intercity, making it very difficult for me to establish a niche in any one location, or, if it had been established, to pursue it. Except for contributing a chapter to a textbook written by my husband, I have been prevented, so far, from pursuing my career. At present we live in Missouri. My husband travels and is absent for weeks at a time as an executive in a chemical firm. This increases my home responsibilities. He is not against outside work for me, but he has not actively encouraged it. . . .

I now have four children ranging in age from one to eighteen years. Their needs are the dominant influence in my life; they require my presence at home almost continually when infants, the greater proportion of the time during preschool years, at least after school during school years, and again almost continually during the summer. . . . This also has prevented further work toward the completion of my thesis. Obsolescence of knowledge during the years spent at home multiplies the difficulty.

Though my husband now earns about $20,000 a year (before taxes), I have household help only once a week and have become expert at all manner of trades, including cooking, accounting, plumbing, serving, carpentry, gardening, painting, cleaning, hostessing, wallpapering, and personnel management. In fact, I have little doubt that I could probably out-Spock Spock, out-report *Consumers Reports,* and out-handyman *Better Homes and Gardens' Handyman!* Three of my children take serious music lessons, and the cost of these and of keeping the family well supplied with books and records, plus all the familiar costs which make up living expenses — housing, taxes, maintenance, furniture, clothing, car, husband's professional society dues, food, and savings in the form of investments and insurance — leave me no choice but to meet most of the labor demands myself.

I have taken university courses in Russian for the enjoyment of the intellectual challenge, in consideration of the possibility of part-time employment in translation, and because of the desirability of knowing Russian in light of the present-day world political situation. . . .

Homemaking has many satisfactory aspects for me. There are the creative ones, such as designing an aesthetically pleasing environment in which to live, and, above all, creating a new life, nurturing it, watching it grow and develop under one's guidance and care. There are also the emotional aspects involved in the shared experiences with others, the deep intimacy of the relationship with a small infant, the feeling of rediscovering the world through the eyes of each child, the awareness of the constant renewal of life which amounts to a rejuvenation....

The major flaws in my homemaking role include the endless repetition of monotonous chores and of exhortations to the older children; the sense of isolation; the lack of appreciation, recognition, and respect for one's efforts; the fragmentation of time, preventing concentration of effort on any matter of interest; and the obvious low esteem in which homemaking is generally held.

I have often engaged in various types of volunteer activity.... It should be borne in mind that many women develop new interests in volunteer and community work over the years and do not choose to start over again in their previous professions. Such work can be a most satisfactory outlet for creative impulses and the urge for self-expression and, at the same time, fill a much needed social function—after all, where would our symphony orchestras be without the backing and dedicated efforts of such women in fund-raising, serving on boards of directors, and, more subtly, providing the social setting in which such community enterprises flourish?...

I have begun to think of the future and the past. The past, though it seems like yesterday, is ten years ago. Advances in my profession have left me hopelessly behind; employers do not hire and begin to train married women in their middle or late thirties, with no experience, for positions commensurate with their abilities. There are few part-time jobs available with any sort of responsibility, certainly none in biochemistry, and there are few refresher courses available except in large university areas.... So I drift, too often into a deadly routine of what has been called "circular puttering"—volunteer work of the most menial type, committees that, when disinterestedly dissected, reveal themselves as dedicated to producing nothing more than more unnecessary work under the guise of bettering community life. There is only one occupation open—teaching—and not everyone is suited to that....

Certainly my experiences are quite different from what I expected when in school, which has made adjustment quite difficult and frequently accompanied by disillusionment and disenchantment. On the other hand, I did not expect the deep sense of fulfillment that accompanies childbearing and nurturing. This provides the supreme creative outlet for a woman and is the most important function of her life....

Since housewifery and motherhood is the full-time occupation of nearly half the adult labor force, and many of these women, like myself, have been highly educated and trained in some special field of study and are not using their abilities in any professional way, I think it is important to consider why such valuable material and training is so often apparently wasted.... Whoever said, "Educate a man, and you educate a man; educate a woman, and you educate a family," had a valid point. However, this does not answer the question of why, in these so-called emancipated days, most women are still unable to utilize their talents and training *directly* within their specialities, if only in a small way.

In the first place, when a woman marries, she usually expects and intends to have children, and this means that her interests and career must immediately become secondary to those of her husband, on whom the main burden of supporting the family will fall. The family will therefore be located in a community where career opportunity is greatest for him, not for her. In fact it may be nonexistent for her, particularly if she has married immediately upon leaving school and has never had a chance to work at her specialty before becoming involved in the responsibility of home and new babies in a new and unfamiliar environment. She is, then, completely dependent on her husband's income, which will be none too large since he, too, is just starting out.... The analogy of the drowning man clinging to a straw is a good one; living becomes a matter of trying to cope with each day as it comes, and there is no time even for thoughts of either the future or the past.

Suddenly, five years have gone by, then six, eight, ten. By this time some of the children are in school and the family may have moved several times. The husband's income has risen, as have the cost of living and the demands of his job, his status, and his outside activities in professional societies, which increase his prestige and thereby further his career. This, of course, is good for the family. The wife can now probably afford household help at least once a week, possibly more, but the higher cost of living and of educating children in her own image and her own scale of values prevent the wife from hiring this help. For example, when a choice must be made between music lessons for her children and a gardener who probably charges much more than the music teacher, the wife does the gardening herself; when a choice must be made by her husband between going to a professional meeting and painting the bathroom, she paints the bathroom; professional painters charge prohibitive prices and the money will buy a desk for Johnny, etc. In a sense, it is the housewife who pays the price for everyone else's high standard of living....

I think some of the solution lies, first, in continuing to educate women in advanced studies and, second, in awakening the imagination of both universities and employers to the possible applications of their potential. Above all, what is needed is a bit of encouragement and an extended welcoming hand. . . . It's hard to estimate how much valuable work, now being left undone, could be accomplished by the available numbers of such women.

There is one other way of attacking the problem, and that is not to let it arise in its acute form in the first place. This can be done by means of a minor social change, namely, providing well-run day nurseries on an extended scale and at nominal cost, administered possibly by the departments of education. This, of course, is the system that enables Russia to utilize the educated talent of its women; its absence here is responsible for much loss of valuable talent which could be conserved by freeing the mother's mind and hands two or three days a week for work that furthers her own professional career. . . .

I favor a change of attitude, first, on the part of educators, women themselves, and society in general, restoring homemaking as a career to the position of dignity it once had, and, second, on the part of employers, in recognizing the assets of the mature, responsible, intelligent married woman. An awareness is needed on the part of all concerned of the importance of the educated homemaker to society because of the enormous influence she has on the next generation. . . . Surely most employers must be conscious of the assets (as well as the liabilities) of the married career woman—her stability, resourcefulness, flexibility, willingness to make an effort—and surely, after years of experience in managing a household and family, she is something of an expert at coordination of effort and in human relations!

THE UNSETTLED

The women who are classified as members of the group we have called the *unsettled* originally belonged to the planners, the recasters, or the adapters. But somewhere along the way their patterns of life have become clouded, and the steps they were taking to fulfill their goals have faltered. They are uncertain and dissatisfied because their original plans have gone awry and because they have not yet found satisfactory ways of rearranging their lives.

A woman's expectations and plans are rarely fulfilled in every respect. Sometimes it is in one's aspiration concerning the world of work that one is disappointed; sometimes it is in an aspect of interpersonal relations. But most people, especially those who have had the opportunity to pursue higher education and to make decisions slowly, are able to design approaches that they can follow more or less satisfactorily. Some may have to make radical shifts to realize their goals, some may have to lower their expectations; but they are still able to find acceptable ways of life. This is not true of the unsettled. Here we find women who have encountered barriers along the way and have not yet found new paths to their goals, or new goals.

Thus the unsettled represent a group apart. Unlike the women in the other three groups, each of whom has found a *modus vivendi*, the unsettled are still in the throes of searching, of trying to fit themselves into the larger world. Some have suffered a great deal of disappointment, and they know that they can look forward to contentment only if they can find better solutions to important problems in their lives.

These women so far have not been able to resolve satisfactorily their conflicting goals and circumstances. This is not to say that they did not develop life goals. Most of them did, but they have found part or all of them unsatisfactory or impossible to realize and they have been unable to develop more gratifying alternatives. Their dissatisfaction centers either about their careers, or their personal lives, or both.

We will present self-portraits of three types of unsettled women. The first two consist of women whose problems are restricted either to the area of work or to personal lives. That is to say, concerns in one of these areas have not significantly affected other areas of their lives. The third type has problems that were precipitated by difficulties either in their careers or in their personal lives, but these have affected the totality of their lives. . . .

Women who have spent at least seventeen years in formal study are understandably interested in making constructive use of their education, more likely than not in paid work. Despite the long preparation of our group, however, there were some who had been thwarted in achieving their career goals. A few women were close to acquiring their degrees when marriage or the necessity to earn a livelihood deflected them. When they left the university, they found that their career goals could not be realized. For this group, failure to complete their education has proved to be a serious roadblock.

Another group that is caught up in unresolved career problems is composed of women who regret that, because of personal or market considerations, they have been unable to make full use of their education and skills. Either family commitments have forced them to withdraw from work; or they have had to take jobs which do not utilize their competence; or they have encountered one or another type of discrimination in the marketplace, which has had the same result.

Others run into career troubles on more subtle grounds. A few women who made very large investments in preparing for and pursuing particular careers have developed, somewhere along the line, serious doubts about their chosen fields. But because of their heavy investments, they are loath to shift directions. They do not derive adequate satisfactions from their chosen fields, but they are not yet able to forsake them and to seek more satisfying outlets. They are still the prisoners of their first choices.

Still others discover that having children has had unforeseen effects on their careers. Some have had so many children, or their children are still so young, that they have not been able to free any significant portion of their time and energy for the pursuit of their careers, regardless of their desire to return to work.

All these women, and others with different sources of dissatisfaction with their work, attach importance to careers. They are not exclusively concerned with their traditional roles as wives and mothers, with which they may be satisfied. Satisfaction with homemaking is not a sufficient criterion of success for them; these women find that gratification outside the home is also a necessary ingredient of their lives, and it is this that they find lacking.

CLAIRE LAMBERT

My parents were anxious that I have a college education, and both worked to that end. My father did not care especially about what I did with my education, as long as I led a satisfied and happy life. My mother saw my intellectual competence, my academic honors, as a spear with which to shaft other women whose daughters were less bright and less well educated. I was always a means to her ends, not a person in myself.

My father lost an electrical company in the 1929 stock market crash; drifted to New York from Louisiana, where I had been born in 1927; did odd jobs in the NRA, WPA, and FHA until 1936, when he landed a job as a salesman for a large chemical firm and we moved to St. Louis. He had had one year of college, and my mother was a college graduate who had left elementary school teaching when she married. After my father's death in 1948, she went to work as a librarian and remained in the field for the following twelve years.

My father was a Roosevelt New Dealer, ebullient, loud, mercurial, and weak. My mother is conservative, prudish, unimaginative, cruel and cutting, strong and dominating. We have never gotten along. We never will. My parents' marriage was a violent and unhappy one. As a child I read to escape. Very early in life I became interested in Oriental civilizations, for what reason I cannot honestly say. When I entered college in 1944, I thought I would take one course in Chinese for the hell of it—I loved it and stayed on.

We moved around a lot during my youth and I went to high school in three different localities, finally graduating from one in Stamford, Connecticut. I then entered Smith, where I majored in foreign area studies, with special emphasis on the history and civilization of China. My major field encompassed history, philosophy, languages, and the economics of western Europe, the United States, the Middle East, and Latin America. With the exception of mathematics and music I took courses in almost every department at college. I was graduated magna cum laude in 1948, a member of Phi Beta Kappa, and a recipient of a fellowship for graduate study. I worked each summer during college, as a waitress, as a clerk, as a coat model, and as a companion to an elderly woman who did not like my cooking, my politics, or me.

My first and only career goal was to do diplomatic work in the Far East. When I was in college I believed (an opinion later confirmed by almost five years' residence and travel there) that world power is shifting back toward the Orient, specifically to China. The United States government needs personnel educated and keyed to the cultures of the Pacific. I attended graduate school to learn more in my field and to further my chances for employment in that area. My education in Chinese language and history at Columbia from first to last was magnificent — its excellence helped me to obtain and lose more than one good job.

I became a State Department employee after completing course credits for a M.A. in 1949, and I obtained the degree in 1950. Departmental requirements stipulated some experience in the Far East before continuing for the Ph.D. But I chose the diplomatic field at the wrong time in history. It was a deep disappointment to see people older and of greater education floundering, beaten, and broken, under a political persecution (McCarthy, Cohn, and Schine) no different from that experienced elsewhere in the world under dictatorships. Can you imagine the effect on me as a twenty-two-year-old girl of seeing a great teacher and good friend reduced professionally and personally to ashes on charges known to me to be outright lies! I defended this teacher personally before a State Department panel; this, together with my advocacy of recognition of the Communist government in China, resulted in my being allowed to resign from the State Department's hothouse atmosphere after six tumultuous weeks. I have never regretted the separation!

I then undertook work in the documentary division of a foreign military mission (NATO) and embassy, which entailed providing information to the U.S. government for aid and personnel exchange purposes. Two years later I became an English-language teacher at a Far Eastern university. I taught courses at the university level and to trainees at the National Police Academy. This was my finest work experience. I also taught English six hours a week in a local Chinese school system which was heavily financed by the "red" government in China. During the two years I worked there I was permitted to teach what I wished as I wished. No suggestions were made as to my personal or ideological behavior. The Chinese embassy officials were aware of the anomalous position I enjoyed as an American national and went out of their way to provide me with the materials and books I needed, to respond to each request courteously and quickly. My relations with my Chinese pupils and their parents were far superior to those with my other Asian students.

I also volunteered to be a group leader for thirty-five orphans who lived at a Buddhist temple and nunnery. I took them to festivals, picnics, outings, and such diverse and gaudy entertainment as the Chinese community provides these little ragamuffins. I enjoyed the color, confusion, and general bombast with which the old nuns did everything. In the process, I met and came to know Asians of every social stripe and political conviction, learning to work with them in the context of their civilization (and often to see the world as they saw it, which was frightening for a white woman when you consider what they really think of the white man at the very core of their being; and sad—because we deserve it).

On the other hand, my duties involved long hours of work and unsanitary conditions. Once, for four months, I lacked books, pencils, and paper; slept on a roach-infested mat (I got to like the roaches except when they crawled into my hair); had no medical facilities; and hence got malaria, dengue fever, and round-worm. Yet I would go back to it tomorrow. I like the Orient, and I loved teaching the little ones; physical discomfort cannot dispel the satisfaction of seeing the human mind open and flower.

I applied for the teaching job in Asia by writing to the dean of the faculty of letters at the local university. He was also coordinator and secretary of a division of the country's Communist party (made known to me six weeks after my arrival). For almost three years, I handled his English language correspondence, professional, personal, and political. It was a rare and valuable insight into the "Communist" mind. The Communist party, which was for many citizens their last hope, became a last chance for many Europeans and Americans as well. I cannot remember the number of missionaries, businessmen, students, tourists, and drifters who made their way to the university and party headquarters for help. These were people whom the official diplomatic community either would not or could not help. The Communist party paid transportation expenses, clothed, housed, fed these hardship cases, and got them out of the country. I handled the processing for most of these people, the majority of whom were Americans (I still receive Christmas cards from a few of them—after ten years). For no extra salary and with Communist money and passes, I did what American officials were highly paid to do, but did not. It was a very cold war in a very hot country.

When I returned to the United States in 1956, at the end of my contract, I became an executive trainee and then an assistant buyer at a department store in Los Angeles because I could not find employment in my field. I left after a year to get married and, the following year, became a researcher and writer with a state educational association. I left six months later just before my son was born and stayed at home with him for the first nine months. Since 1960 I have been employed as a market researcher for an advertising firm. It bores me to death, but we need the money ($100 a week) since my husband failed in business the year I began. All my changes in jobs and in intellectual and social pursuits have been dictated by financial pressures. Many do not reflect my basic interests.

I spend forty hours a week at work, many hours assisting in my husband's work, and every other waking hour in housework, reading, child rearing, and theater and opera attending. My husband is an antique dealer with some college credits and architectural training. He is an absolutely kind, sensitive person. His business difficulties since 1960 have been greatly aggravated by his awareness that I am not doing what I would like to be doing, by his struggle to provide a good and above-average standard of living, and by my mother's constantly reminding him that he is a bum and a bastard because he failed in business. Last year he developed severe angina pectoris because of these continued pressures.

My mother is considerably embittered now that I have not set the world on fire and has transferred her ambitions to my son, who must succeed where I have failed. His health and education are very important to my husband and me. We have put him in the kindergarten of a French–English (bilingual) school here where he is doing very well, and, barring death or other misfortune, we will keep him in this school. I have a maid who comes in one day a week, who is neither expensive nor satisfactory, leaving me with the really heavy physical household work to do. My husband and I have been able to pay off the large debts that could not be taken into his bankruptcy, accumulate two pieces of property, including the house we live in, place our son in a private school, and keep sunny-side-up financially by extremely hard work.

I enjoy cooking—and being with my child. I really did enjoy the months I was home with him. I shall always feel a personal loss at not having been home with him during his preschool years. I dislike plain, old-fashioned household cleaning, dusting, and the like. I am a meticulous housekeeper and resent the psychological compulsion to keep things clean and tidy at the expense of intellectual and educational pursuits. I have a child, a husband, and a home, and they cannot be neglected. My situation is not unique; to me it is the single greatest problem faced by the educated woman (and the woman longing for more education).

At present, my only volunteer activity involves membership in a symphony society. I support it financially and go to soirees to shake the conductor's hand. The drinks are great, music marvelous, and people terrible, but it's a break from home and office despite being pure dribble and social climbing. I do a great deal of reading of newspapers and periodicals in the course of my work, but I am now years behind on books. Reading gives me the entrée to foreign lands, art, politics, the whole changing world which I would not otherwise have. When I am too tired to read as much as I would like, I am just that much less informed, that much farther behind. It is not enough to age, we must also grow!

I had no formal education after obtaining my master's degree. I did have to learn an Asian language well enough to teach in it at an elementary level. This was done in a haphazard manner, largely a personal undertaking with little outside help. My education has greatly conditioned my political, religious, and cultural life; but it would be difficult for me to say where the formal education ended and the practical one began. I am as interested today in Far Eastern affairs as I was thirteen years ago. Like it or not, the United States is being drawn square around to face the reality of China as a world power. Sinology as a field of study will regain its luster — if only by sheer necessity! It is still my hope to reenter this field, to get a Ph.D., and to do something with my education for my own people. When my husband's business activities are such that I can leave my job and go back to school, I will have to rebegin my education with a thorough review of the Chinese language, emphasizing the spoken, before I can go on for a doctorate in this field. . . .

I would like to propose an educational program for women like myself, who need to earn a livelihood but desire more education. My proposal is, namely, that the U.S. government (or some private group if such there be) subsidize the student through his or her advanced education, allowing him enough money to support his family and live decently — a G.I. bill for civilians and especially for women. In return, the student must work for the government or the private group concerned for a certain number of years. This is hardly a novel idea, and its cost would be but a fraction of the millions spent yearly on shoring up dictatorships throughout the world.

My comments on the American attitude toward the educated woman echo those of many educated women. There is a lack of interest in the kind, quality, and extent of a woman's education when it is unrelated to commercial skills. Women are automatically barred from *consideration* for executive positions because they are women. They are paid *very* much less than men for identically the same job. They are hired last and fired first. They are expected to have more and better qualifications for jobs men may fill with fewer and inferior credentials. They are subject to moral criticism and even dismissal for behavior that, in a man, would be dismissed with a simple "boys will be boys" attitude.

Intellectual ability, professional skills, and ambition in women are treated with envy, distrust, scorn, and outright hatred by many men. These attitudes are breaking down, but it will be a long time before we utilize the training of women to the extent that our Communist adversaries do. In the United States, women's talents are too often wasted, neglected, and denigrated. We are engaged in a struggle for world domination with an intelligent, organized, and determined antagonist. He may be doing poorly on the farm, but he is doing better than well in the classroom. He is using women's skills to the hilt. If, as some predict, this war will be won in the classroom, then, in respect to the utilization of the educated women, he has already taken a giant step toward victory.

CHAPTER 18

Women in the Work Force

THE BEST I CAN DO is to tell you the ground I have been over relative to women and work, point out where we are, and suggest the directions we ought to go.

By way of introduction, let me mention that I used to be the chairman of the National Commission for Manpower Policy, but by act of Congress we are now designated as the National Commission for Employment Policy, an acknowledgment of the sensitivity of those who depend on votes toward the feelings of the female part of the electorate. Let me add, changes in language, in my view, are important.

My exposure to today's theme goes back to 1937 when, two years into my teaching at the Graduate School of Business at Columbia University, I became intrigued why Vassar graduates, among others, had to attend the Katharine Gibbs School in New York City to learn to type before getting a job!

In World War II, on my first assignment in the Executive Office of the President, where I reported five days after Pearl Harbor, I tried to sell the Committee on Scientific and Specialized Personnel the idea of looking closely at our womanpower resources. They thought I was mad, since the country still had millions of unemployed men. But

I calculated—and for once correctly—that these men would be absorbed quickly as, in fact, they were. But the committee members did not share this view, at least not at that time.

I have long believed that Hitler helped to lose the war that he was winning by failing to mobilize Germany's women.

A third World War II observation: I was amazed to discover in connection with my work for the surgeon-general of the Army that nurses over forty could not be sent overseas, although we had a great shortage of first-line medical personnel. Inquiry disclosed that Army regulations prohibited all female personnel over forty from service overseas on the ground that with the menopause women became emotionally unstable. It is worth observing in passing that women between the ages of forty to fifty soon became the age cohort with the highest proportion in the civilian labor force. In the early post–World War II period I had about one woman MBA student to every 50 or 100 males; today over one-third of the class is composed of women.

So much by way of background. Where are we?

I would say that there are some people—myself not included—who believe that the recent reductions in fertility since 1957 are likely to be reversed. Therefore, the trends that we have seen may not continue. I don't happen to believe that. But Professor Richard Easterlin at the University of Pennsylvania, who is a careful student of fertility, believes just that. I expect that we will continue to experience very low fertility. Since women, like men, need a role and don't like to be unengaged at home, and not at work, I expect them to be tied more closely to the workplace.

Second, of every five marriages that are now being consummated, two will eventually break up. It would be unthoughtful for women not to be concerned about their future, since we know that even if they could get alimony, it would not be much of an answer. But most divorcees don't get it; if they do it's very little and it does not come for very long. Just in self-defense, women have little option but to be concerned with work, if two out of every five marriages will end in divorce.

Third, as Mr. Charles Brown, chairman of the American Telephone and Telegraph Company, earlier emphasized, expectations are important. The women may be wrong, but they have a perception that men have more fun because men have both a home life and a work life, and can balance between these two. Now, women may be wrong to think that work is so exciting. It may not be, but nevertheless they want to find that out for themselves. They are surely entitled to have the opportunity to combine a life on the job and at home as men have been doing for a long time.

The next point relates to the growth of the service sector, where, according to my rough calculations, over seven out of ten jobs are now located. I believe there has been a very powerful interaction between the availability of women as a labor source and the ability of the United States to expand its jobs at a rapid rate. Mr. Brown alluded to this, but I am making it quite explicit. I do not believe that we could have had an economy that created 12 million new jobs since the first quarter of 1975 unless the female labor supply had been available.

The availability of women has been a major factor in the transformation and forward movement of the U.S. economy, and it goes beyond job creation. Consider the income distribution of families. The only reason the country is not up in arms about inflation is the earning power of wives. In households with two earners, inflation has had less of an impact, but there are lots of women heads of households who would like to have husbands who are earners. In terms of averages, however, we have a situation where the American consumer has not yet lost out badly because of two earners in many families.

Finally, it is quite clear that the drive toward equity in the Western world since World War II, which has in this country a racial component as well as a gender component, is not likely to stop. That means that since women have suffered a great number of inequities across a great number of fields, the momentum Mr. Brown talked about will continue. In a democracy in which people vote, they are going to keep on voting in favor of equity. It's inevitable.

I want to say a few things now to each of the discussion sections about the themes I believe worthwhile for them to worry about as they go into their sessions. And I will muddy the waters a bit because I don't think they ought to settle on simple formulations.

Let's take the first one, occupational segregation. It is very important to remember in discussing segregation which subgroup of women one is discussing, for there are great differences among women as among men. One must distinguish whether one is talking about professionals with three or four years of postgraduate training, or whether one is talking about high school dropouts. Let me make this point clear. In 1969 I wrote a book, *Men, Money and Medicine.* Today I couldn't even use that title. I had included a chapter, be it said in my own defense, on "The Female Physician." At that time only 8 percent of the physicians in the United States were women. Today 26 percent of the first-year class in medical school are women. The figures for law show the same order of magnitude increase, only greater. Earlier I gave you the figures for the Graduate School of Business at Columbia, which apply also to other business schools. The problem of occupational segregation is not primarily a problem of the professions, although science and engineering are a special case.

I think one ought to make distinctions between professionals, technicians, and craft workers and lower-level personnel in analyzing occupational segregation.

On the subject of accommodations in two-worker families, I would again say that I don't think it is useful to talk about accommodations for women in general. Two students graduating from the Columbia Law School this year—good students who are employed by leading downtown law firms—have a combined opening income, if they marry or if they decide to live together, of around $64,000. The hiring salary for a good student is $32,000. So I am not much interested in the accommodations of such two-worker families. They'll be able to work out their own accommodations. They'll start on Park Avenue and then, if they have a child, they may have to move into a side street!

On the other hand, if you're talking about people at the low end of the scale, saleswomen and telephone operators, then one has a wholly different question of accommodations. Admittedly gender is important at work and in the home, but one must try to distinguish and differentiate the subgroups of female workers or potential workers that one seeks to help.

That leads me into the next subject—the female head of household. Here one faces a serious unresolved social problem. A high percentage of all female heads of households are at poverty level somewhere between one-third and two-fifths and going still higher. They are bringing up a large proportion of all youngsters, particularly minority youngsters, and they are doing so with an income at the poverty level and with no husbands to help them. It is critically important that all leadership groups pay more attention to this critical and vulnerable subgroup.

Finally, what about the opportunities for upward mobility in the 1980s? It has been sixteen years since the Civil Rights Act was passed. I would say to Mr. Brown and to other corporate executives that one of these days the EEOC (Equal Employment Opportunity Commission) is likely to look at their payroll distributions, and if it finds that there is no more than a token woman in the top ranks, it is likely to conclude on the basis of that statistical finding that the company is discriminating. After sixteen years, more progress should have been made. I suspect that the next big push on equal employment opportunity will be to look at patterns. The chair of EEOC, Eleanor Holmes Norton, has indicated that her commission is moving in this direction. The burden of proof will be on the employer.

The 1980s will also probably see the emergence of equal pay for comparable work quality. Not equal pay for equal work—that's easy—but for comparable work, and that's tough. The job classification system must be defended and much more. Although the initial court decisions have upheld current practices, I think one of these days a case will wend its way to the Supreme Court, where, as we know, anything may happen. It is none too soon, in my opinion, to start researching this issue in depth and seeing what adjustments might be made over time.

I have long thought that people like myself who have the best jobs ought to be paid the least because of the psychic satisfaction they derive — more fun and less money would be fairer. Admittedly that's not the way the U.S. system operates. I could even conceive of a society in which one would have to pay money for the privilege of getting one of the best jobs. But all this is fine theory.

My concluding observations go as follows. If you increase options for one-half of personkind, you will inevitably help to improve the world. If you can improve not only the work and pay of women, but also their options, they will be better off. True, some may decide after working for a while that they prefer to stay home. I don't pretend to know how everything will work out in the end. All I know is that during the next stage women are going to demand the right to exercise broadened options.

Second, let us remember that we are not dealing with a zero-sum game. It does not follow that because an organization or a society helps women, it necessarily must take things away from men. That's an error. If we can improve the productivity of the female part of the population, which is half the population, the total pie ought to get bigger, and then men as well as women will be better off.

Third, I would suspect that since life on the job and life off the job are very much interconnected, if you can't earn a decent wage you are not going to have a great life off the job. On the other hand, if you have nothing to do at home and you want a more interesting life, you really do need a job. So the two are closely related. I would like to believe that restructuring may make it possible for both men and women to enjoy more options and a better life.

Let me conclude by pointing out that in my extensive travels overseas, usually on study missions, I have come to believe that one of the simplest and best criteria for judging a society is how it treats its women.

CHAPTER 19

Returnees: Cross-National Research

TO RESOLVE ANALOGOUS PROBLEMS, cross-national social research can facilitate the analysis of approaches followed by selected countries. Its principal aim is to provide information that will enable nations that currently or potentially face similar problems to judge the applicability of alternative resolutions to the challenges they face. The problem on which this study is focused has arisen as the result of the increasing propensity of adult women to reenter or belatedly enter the labor force, a phenomenon common to the countries under scrutiny—the Federal Republic of Germany, France, Sweden, the United Kingdom, the United States—as well as to virtually all other advanced industrial nations. This alteration in female behavior has added a new component to the employment problems of these nations, and the difficulties encountered by adult women in obtaining jobs after periods of nonwork activity have provoked demands for policies and programs to aid and abet their reentry. The ways in which each of these countries has responded to pressures for assistance to reentrants is the central theme of this inquiry.

The entry of long-time homemakers into the labor force has been the major element in the transformation of the labor forces of industrialized countries since World War II. Modifications in women's expectations that deemphasize the centrality of their family role point to profound and probably irreversible changes in social structures and in the functional assignments of men and women.

In the past, female labor force participation generally peaked at ages twenty to twenty-four years, followed by a progressive decline as marriage and childbirth depleted the ranks of women workers. In recent years, however, the pattern of participation in most developed countries has assumed a new shape as increasing numbers of older married women have entered or reentered the labor force. In most countries, instead of a one-time peak following school completion, there is a second, lower peak at ages thirty-five to forty or thereabouts. In Sweden, the female participation rate at ages thirty-five to forty-four is even higher than their twenty- to twenty-four–year level; and in the United States, the characteristic M-shaped curve has flattened as a result of reduced withdrawal in the twenties and a plateau in work participation among women between the ages of twenty-five and forty-four.

At the same time that women's work activity has been rising, that of men has been steadily decreasing as a result of declining participation of the young, because of lengthened schooling, and of the older group, because of early retirement. Hence the traditional gap between male and female labor force participation rates has been narrowing in many developed countries.

Although the proportion of older married women in paid employment varies considerably in developed countries, the trend toward higher participation is sufficiently pervasive to reflect underlying influences that transcend national boundaries. In each of the countries in this survey, efforts have been made to respond to the changed work aspirations of adult women, although more recently some of these efforts have been directed toward slowing their entrance into the labor force. The several approaches reviewed in these reports illuminate the pressures and conflicts that have arisen in the wake of the attempts of mature women to develop a new role for themselves in the world of work and the impediments they are likely to encounter in realizing this goal.

INFLUENCES ON REENTRY

The recent change in the role of work in the life cycle of women has multiple roots. The most common explanation is financial need—a powerful but not inclusive theory, for it fails to account for the fact that numbers of adult women have always needed additional income but were unable to satisfy this need through gainful employment. The preconditions for expanded reentry are to be found in changes in the labor market, in the larger society, and in women's own lives. Apart from idiosyncratic factors, the following elements have stimulated reentry to a greater or lesser degree in each of the countries included in this study. Shortages of young female entrants during the first two postwar decades created job opportunities for middle-aged married women that had not previously existed. The accelerated growth of the service sector resulted in an expansion of public and private jobs in such traditional female occupations as clerical work, retail sales, personal services, education, and health care. Early marriage and early family formation reduced the pool of single women, the conventional source of supply for female jobs, and opened opportunities for middle-aged women. Only in Germany did the rise in adult female work rates fail to match the sharp decline of teenage female workers, because employment in the service sector has grown relatively slowly, about 17 percentage points below that of the United States, which has the highest rate of service employment (66 percent) among these five countries.

The shrinkage of the agricultural sector accompanied by a growth of urban agglomerations placed more women within reach of newly expanding employment opportunities. The United Kingdom and the United States have the lowest proportion of employment in agriculture (under 4 percent), but all five countries have experienced marked declines in the proportion of farm workers.

A substantial proportion of new opportunities for women consist of part-time jobs developed in part to attract married women into the labor market while allowing them time to meet their homemaking responsibilities. The increased availability of labor-saving appliances in the household lightened their housekeeping burdens. Moreover, fewer children, born in the early years of marriage, shortened the years mothers allocated to child care and facilitated women's early reentry to the labor market.

Because of increased marital disruptions and births out of wedlock, more women became heads of household and, as a consequence, had to assume the primary burden of family support. Recently, inflationary trends have led more and more wives to seek employment in order to supplement their husbands' earnings and thus help to maintain their families' standard of living. While married women tend to slow their labor force entry during recessions because of decreased job opportunities, a longer period of economic slackness intensifies pressures on wives to obtain employment.

The lengthening of the years of women's schooling and their increased acquisition of specialized training have increased their potential earnings, thereby encouraging them to maximize their time in the labor force.

Furthermore, the elongation of education has reduced the participation of young females in the labor force, thus expanding the demand for older women.

Such factors as increased societal sensitivity to sex discrimination in employment and changing attitudes toward women's roles have also contributed to the greater participation of women in paid employment, but the stimulus has been mutual. Increased educational attainment probably has been the key factor, since it has raised the career expectations of women, particularly those best able to articulate and publicize grievances about barriers and inequalities that continue to confront them.

In certain countries, expanded work activity among mature women can be traced to the greatly accelerated demand for workers during World War II. In other nations, the sharp postwar declines in the agricultural sector, a concomitant of expanding industrial development, initially acted to depress adult women's employment by precipitating the exit of many from unpaid family work without opening new opportunities because of their lack of qualifications or their distance from the expanding job centers. In these situations, reentry did not make much headway until further urbanization, relocation, and rising living standards began to reshape women's aspirations, competencies, and opportunities.

The checkered history of reentry in different nations suggests that structural alterations in each nation's economy were the root cause of women's changed work patterns. Although altered personal circumstances undoubtedly encouraged women's affirmative response to increased job opportunities, absent demand, the number of mature reentrants would not have reached its current dimensions. Beyond poverty, a person's *need* to work is subjective, strongly influenced by living standards and personal qualifications; over the last generation, women's felt need to work has grown as a result of their increased desire for consumption goods and their higher level of education and skill. The rapid growth of the service sector was fortuitous, inasmuch as it offered many of them the opportunity to realize their expectations.

The receptivity of the labor market to adult women was the magnet for reentry, and they were attracted despite the mediocre nature of available jobs in terms of wages and benefits. At first, pressures for assistance in reentry were minimal because most women had no particular difficulty in finding a job, if not suitable employment. As time went on, however, it became clear that many reentrants were encountering problems that either discouraged them from job search or blocked their access to satisfactory jobs.

REENTRY PROBLEMS

Most middle-aged women who had worked briefly, if at all, before exiting from the labor force withdrew voluntarily at the time of their marriage or some time prior to the birth of their first child. That was the established pattern. Few women who were financially able to leave their jobs did so reluctantly. More relaxed attitudes, which do not censure young mothers from continuing to work, have developed in the wake of the feminist revolution, but they are too recent to have had much effect on the older generation. Reluctance to interrupt one's work and career for any length of time, however, is probably a major cause of decreased family size, since most women suspect that pursuing a career is not compatible with raising large families.

The persistence of financial disincentives and inadequate support systems for married women workers reflects the almost universal attitude toward culturally appropriate behavior, which views child raising as a mother's first duty. Tax provisions often penalize families with working wives; child care facilities give preference to women in financial distress; and family allowances seek to tilt the incentive structure in favor of child rearing. At this time, the foregoing conventional biases are in subtle and often overt conflict with the new aspirations and desires of married women to remain in or return to work in their twenties or early thirties.

Governments have been slow to recognize this heightened interest of many women in returning to work early, and even slower to revise their policies to facilitate this goal. This is not due as much to a lack of recognition of the change as to a reluctance to acknowledge it (because of the soft economy), reinforced by the strength of tradition. Except in Sweden, there is no national consensus about the desirability of assisting women to enjoy broadened options with respect to work. Consequently, tax, social security, and child care measures that would facilitate women's reentry have not been substantially adjusted. Equal employment opportunity laws, by themselves, are not directly responsive to this problem. Equal treatment in the labor market is not enough; equal access is the key.

In each of the five countries, the majority of women who enter or reenter the labor force after a period devoted to child rearing are able to do so without formal assistance. This has enabled policymakers to underestimate the realities of the situation facing many potential reentrants. Women who are able to make their own way into the labor market comprise two groups: those whose skills, even if somewhat dulled, are in demand; and those who take low-paying jobs because they need the money and cannot afford an extended search. The first group, if they make a connection, are likely to do fairly well, but many of them could profit from a period of retraining and informed job search. Those forced to accept what is immediately available are likely to be caught in a situation where their potential is underutilized. The situation of the second group of reentrants is more serious, since these women tend to be among the least skilled and most needy returnees. The opportunity for subsidized training and other support services in place of immediate placement holds promise of providing many of them with eventual access to better jobs, of increasing their productivity, and of improving the possibility of a permanent attachment to work.

Part-time jobs, held out of necessity, not desire, represent one form of underemployment. In Sweden, for example, female participation is so high that the current focus is on improving the relatively inferior status of women who are in the market by expediting their transition from part- to full-time work. In all countries, part-time jobs rarely provide the income, fringe benefits, and nonpecuniary advantages of full-time employment.

The availability of part-time jobs, however, is often crucial to the reentry decision and to maintaining continuity in work experience. The growth of part-time job opportunities has been a major factor in the parallel growth of the female labor force in all these countries except France, where the relative sparsity of part-time work has served to deter reentry. For women who do not have to provide sole or substantial family support, part-time work can be a satisfactory resolution to the dilemma of combining home and work responsibilities.

But such a solution runs afoul of the promotion of equal employment opportunities because part-time jobs, disproportionately filled by women, perpetuate the myth that women's labor force participation is peripheral and spurs occupational segregation. Yet efforts to limit part-time jobs are bound to increase women's exits from the labor force and prolong their period of nonwork. A solution posed in the German report is to promote the introduction of more part-time jobs and/or an overall shortening of the work week to enable both men and women better to meet their family and work commitments. In the long run, greater flexibility in work time might not only provide additional occupational choices for women, but also contribute to ensuring tautness in future labor supplies. Since women do not appear to be responding to incentives to increase family size, their acceptance as a stable component of the regular labor force can simultaneously contribute to equal opportunity and to an adequate labor supply.

Nevertheless, as long as the better jobs are full-time jobs, many reentrants will view part-time employment as a temporary expedient. Thus, the better prepared they are at the time of initial reentry, the easier it will be for them to make an eventual transition to full-time work.

Regardless of the apparent ease with which most reentrants have been able to reattach themselves to the labor force, there is evidence that this group may represent the tip of the iceberg. Every country can point not only to unemployed reentrants but to sizable pools of women who are out of the labor force because they have been unable to find jobs or because they do not believe that their job search will be successful. Sweden's aggressive full-employment policies are designed to minimize the number of discouraged workers; but in the other countries where unemployment has been rising steeply, any activation of the female reserve has been resisted because of the further disequilibrium it would cause in the labor market. Since helping women who want and need assistance in order to prepare for a resumption or late entry into employment would stimulate their inflow, policymakers faced with rising unemployment have shown preference for other groups, such as regularly attached males. For example, the requirement of a period of unemployment prior to admission to training programs effectively debars potential reentrants who, by definition, are out of the labor force. Furthermore, constraints on public expenditures have restricted the number of persons accepted into employment programs, so that only a portion of those eligible are actually served. In many cases, only those reentrants who are heads of households are assisted.

In Sweden this limitation does not apply, since this nation's employment policies have been designed to eliminate the concept of the secondary worker. In that country, disincentives to work are principally confined to single mothers and wives in low-income families whose prospective earnings may not compensate them for lost benefits, day care costs, and time that they could put to alternative use. Conversely, in some countries, such as the United States, public policy is directed to "forcing" women on welfare to enter or reenter the labor force.

The availability of adequate support systems and the elimination of financial deterrents to work are of equal concern to the young woman who is attempting to maintain her ties to work, and to the older woman who is planning to return to work or belatedly to enter the labor market. Most problems that set reentrants and delayed entrants apart from women with continuous work histories stem from their absence from the labor force. When the considerations that originally motivated women to opt for homemaking rather than gainful employment change—that is, their children grow older—many may encounter special difficulties upon seeking to enter or reenter the work force.

The difficulties involve evaluating their job readiness, orientation to the work world, preparation for employment, and job placement. Although most prospective entrants to the labor force require information, skill evaluation, and job search assistance, extended absence from the labor force and prolonged disuse of job-connected skills place many reentrants in particularly disadvantaged positions. Additionally, they are often psychologically unprepared to assume a work role because of uncertainty about their reception in the work force, unfamiliarity with the workplace, and anxiety about being able to combine work and family responsibilities. Hence their principal need is for specialized counseling to provide them with an accurate evaluation of their job potential, psychological support for their work decision, and assistance in negotiating the training structure and the labor market.

Because of universal inadequacies of data collection, it has not been possible to arrive at authoritative estimates of the numbers of women who reenter the labor force after a lengthy separation, nor of the proportion who have been assisted in making the transition from home to market. While large numbers of reentrants, as noted earlier, have made the shift without the intervention of third parties, this does not necessarily argue for a do-it-yourself approach. Some are too timid to try; others try and fail; still others settle for work below their capacity and potential.

THE CLIMATE FOR INTERVENTION

The attitudes and behavior of such key groups as employers, trade unions, government, and social welfare organizations in facilitating adult women's entry or reentry to the labor force are affected by their preconceptions about which groups should receive priority assistance and by the general conditions of the labor market.

In advanced industrial countries, the prime work force consists of adult males between the ages of twenty and fifty-five. When the labor market weakens and members of this group work on reduced schedules, are placed on furlough, or are provided with relief work or income transfers, employers, trade unions, and government authorities focus their efforts on returning these men as quickly as possible to full-time employment. Also singled out for priority assistance are youth, primarily males, who have reached working age. Young persons customarily have higher rates of unemployment than adult workers, and all the countries in the study have recently experienced a rise in teenage unemployment. In the United States and increasingly in the United Kingdom, minority youth are a major problem; on the Continent, all unemployed youth are viewed as a threat to social stability.

The recent acceleration of inflationary pressures has led to budgetary stringencies that have set rigid limits on new public expenditures for job training, job creation, and related social services (such as the expansion of child care facilities). Males generally have preference for available training and retraining opportunities, and ceilings or reductions have been placed on social welfare expenditures that might facilitate the reentry of women. Hence the environment at the beginning of the 1980s is no longer as receptive to encouraging a large-scale inflow of mature women into the labor force as was that of the 1960s.

In some countries there has been a growing concern about sharp declines in birth rates. Accordingly, governments are experimenting with neonatal policies that, if successful, would be a deterrent to women's resumption of work. It would be naive to underestimate the extent to which the machinery of the labor market and new concerns about a declining population have had an adverse effect on the movement to enlarge the scope of women's rights and options. Conservatives may have stilled their misgivings in the face of unmet requirements for female labor and the desire of families for more income and a higher standard of living, but now that the advanced economies are experiencing difficulties in providing regular employment for male heads of household and for young men entering the work force, opposition to equal employment opportunity has intensified.

Nevertheless, it is difficult to see how the cumulative changes that have occurred in the role of women in modern societies can be reversed. While one or another factor that helped to transform the conventional role of women and to expand their options may temporarily be weakened, such a development will have, at most, a limited effect. Barring a drastic reorientation of social values, the changes that paved the way for women's increased work activity should quicken as younger generations of females, less bound by tradition, assert their claims. Even in the face of recent adverse economic trends and a retardation in public expenditures, adult women are continuing to reenter the work force, although at a rate that differs from one nation to the next.

These differing rates are the ultimate manifestations of national perceptions and actions toward the reentry process. Although each of the five countries surveyed has initiated social policies with the explicit goal of fostering equality in the workplace, with one exception, programmatic response and administrative enforcement has rarely been as vigorous as statutory pronouncements. Only in the case of Sweden has a national commitment to equality been effectively translated into reforms that govern the range of social relationships between men and women at home and in the labor market. Uniquely, the Swedish contribution to this report describes government policy as designed to "induce" women to enter the labor force.

Although Sweden has encountered obstacles in realizing this commitment, due to the persistence of traditional social attitudes and modes of behavior and to the high costs of providing auxiliary services to foster women's employment, the high rate of labor force participation of females of all ages is due in large measure to special incentives to women to retain or quickly resume their ties to the work force. It may take decades before the requisite infrastructure for true equality between the sexes is in place, but it appears that an irreversible decision to move in this direction has been made.

In the other countries, the stance toward reentrants appears to range from neutrality to discouragement. Instead of governments' taking the lead, reentry has been a more or less spontaneous and autonomous decision, often without benefit of public support or patronage. Under such circumstances, to paraphrase Dr. Johnson, reentry may not be done well, but one is surprised to find it done at all!

A simple explanation for the differences between Sweden and the four other countries would direct attention above all to the former's relatively small and homogeneous population and a political consensus that for a long time has been generally supportive of social reform. Moreover, government, labor, and employers often collaborate as partners, so that the initiation and execution of social policy is more coherent than in larger countries.

Despite significant differences in attitudes and behavior toward the return of mature women to work, France, Germany, and the United Kingdom demonstrate several elements in common. Each of these countries gives priority in practice to programs for unemployed and unskilled youth and adult males and to persons seeking upgrading in skills in high demand. Such programs usually offer benefits that include compensation for earnings loss, social insurance coverage, travel expenses, and household maintenance. Facilitating the reentry of adult women is not deemed worthy of special assistance. Despite increases in the work activity of adult women in these nations, they are still regarded as a peripheral labor supply that can be adjusted to fluctuations in demand. Together with policies aimed at opening and closing the spigot controlling the flow of guest workers, women remain the major balance wheel.

The pattern of female labor force participation in the United States resembles that of Sweden, insofar as there has been a sharp rise in women's work activity followed by a decline of exits from the work force during the childbearing years. The job market, which has been expanding rapidly since 1975, has seen a continuing disproportionate increase of women among the additions to the work force.

Since 1977, when President Carter entered the White House, the United States has expanded rapidly its expenditures for manpower training and public service employment. Although women have participated broadly in both these programs, they have tended to be underrepresented in terms of their ratio among the unemployed and underemployed, and Congress has become increasingly restive about the assistance being offered those who need to become self-supporting.

Although the United States has established a series of measures to promote equal employment opportunity, they are not the equivalent of the national commitment to equality in all social relationships that underlies the Swedish model. Hence, while American women are not being actively discouraged from entering the labor force, they continue to be burdened with sex-linked inequities that prevent them from fully realizing their work aspirations.

NATIONAL INTERVENTIONS

Each of the reports provides the particulars of national labor market policies in response to the reentry or delayed entry process. Although these responses reflect national choices that are themselves reflections of a country's values, political pressures, economic circumstances, resources, and demographic developments, certain common threads can be identified.

The reports indicate that facilitating reentry has three facets. The first involves the preconditions for employment, such as the establishment of more child care facilities and the removal of tax disincentives; the second relates to the provision of employment-related assistance such as guidance, training, and placement; and the third pertains to measures affecting the level and allocation of labor market opportunities.

Preconditions for Reentry

Inadequate and costly day care arrangements, income tax penalties, and loss of entitlements are widespread inhibitors of women working. It would be incorrect, however, to assume that there would be a massive flow toward work in the absence of such deterrents, because many mothers would prefer to bring up their children themselves and, in the absence of financial need, delay reentry until their children no longer require continuing supervision.

Sweden's introduction of extended parental leave plus the option of working less than full time until a child's eighth birthday takes such preferences into consideration, although it also represents an accommodation to the inadequate number of child care places. It is instructive that France, with the most comprehensive publicly supported child care

system, has a lower female labor force participation rate than the United
States, where child care consists of fragmented ad hoc arrangements. One
explanation for this difference lies in differential opportunity structures.
No matter how favorable the preconditions for work may be, the lack of a
strong demand for women workers in what they consider suitable jobs, in
terms of both quality and scheduling, restricts reentry.

Ambivalence about exclusive attention to homemaking and child
rearing creates enormous conflicts. Mothers are rewarded by family
allowances or preferential tax treatment when they attend to wifely and
maternal duties but are often penalized when they return to work.
Moreover, the effective option of focusing on family-centered activities
or on work is usually reserved for middle- and upper-class women, who,
freed of heavy needs for income, can weigh what they prefer to do.

In Sweden, Germany, and France, increasing attention is being paid
to providing young working women with job protection during their
childbearing period; but children are still quite young when the parent
must return to work. Although longer leaves may not be feasible in view
of employers' staffing requirements, there is no evidence that a significant number of employers maintain contact with women who have left
their employ to raise children in order to encourage their eventual
return.

Reentry Assistance

The factors that lead to the decision to enter the market are of a
different order than those that directly facilitate reentry. The major
problems in the latter instance are twofold: limited access to opportunities
for training or retraining, and insufficient attention to the orientation
and support required to permit reentrants to evaluate their job readiness,
learn about training and career opportunities, proceed confidently on
job search, overcome anxieties, and deal with numerous job- and family-
related concerns. Despite lip service to equal employment opportunity,
it is obvious that adult women continue to be regarded as an elastic labor
supply that will automatically respond to the vagaries of demand. The
lag between this perception and the development of new female attitudes
and aspirations may turn out to be temporary, as more and more younger
women seek to maintain close links to work. In the latter event, they will
force a consideration of policies to help them realize their goal.

In the meantime, as long as the determination of recipients of
government employment assistance remains family-based insofar as it
favors household heads, wives are at a disadvantage in asserting a claim
to reentry assistance. The Depression-inspired goal of spreading work

has really never lost its hold on policymaking; and, in most countries, women are not acknowledged as having the same claim to employment aid as their husbands, even when the latter are unemployed or underemployed and the woman's earnings could compensate in whole or in part for lost income.

Where public training programs are available to reentrants, they are rarely designed to serve this constituency alone. While some programs are focused on women, hardly any are limited to reentrants. Displaced homemakers in the United States are one exception, but women who have been deprived of income because of the loss of spousal support after many years of homemaking represent a singular group since they lack social security protection available to wives.

Reentrants with access to training find that most programs, like the labor market itself, are largely segregated by sex, and this practice perpetuates occupational segregation. Recently attention has focused on providing nontraditional training to women, but expansion has been slow because of the limited job openings; that which is available goes mostly to young women. Adult women generally have eschewed nontraditional training because they have been inculcated with conventional notions about the "proper" sex division of labor, both in and out of the work force.

Shortcomings in guidance were widely noted. These center around insufficient sensitivity to reentrants' special needs by employment service personnel, which has inhibited women from seeking assistance at the very place that should be their first point of renewed contact with the labor market. Where public policy is deficient, however, other mechanisms have often been developed in the private (voluntary and profit) sector that substitute for or complement public programs and, in certain instances, have become supported wholly or partially by public funds.

While employers have been willing to hire reentrants, relatively few have established special programs to assist this group, although reentrants are sometimes eligible to participate in programs available to all new female hires.

In most countries, trade unions are bastions of male supremacy, and only when government has taken the initiative with respect to equal opportunity have unions followed. Reentrants are in a particularly weak position because their relatively advanced years would add costs to employers who qualify them for deferred benefits.

Yet, despite the aforementioned barriers and limitations, a range of innovative programs has surfaced that warrants consideration:

- Preorientation programs that bring women up-to-date on labor market developments; provide them with occupational information on which to base their decisions about how to proceed; offer them opportunities to test their job readiness; and assist them in job search. In some countries, the absence of such government-sponsored programs has been ameliorated in part by services offered by voluntary providers, who often receive considerable public financial support, as in the case of associations in France where, in addition, "Retravailler" centers located throughout the country provide occupational information, guidance, and orientation exclusively for women returnees. In the United States, similar organizations have emerged in the form of women's centers, which primarily offer counseling and referral for training and placement.

- Work experience and job orientation opportunities, usually subsidized, for women with practical skills who need to readjust to the workplace.
- On-the-job training for women without skills or those whose skills are not in demand.
- Expansion of apprenticeship opportunities for older women, particularly those with several decades of potential work life.
- Counseling that not only pays attention to direct work-related problems but also deals with peripheral concerns that affect women's ability to deal with a renewed work role. These include financial problems, particularly with respect to tax obligations or benefits; alimony and child support; housing; and social security.
- Attempts to motivate adult women to enter nontraditional occupations because of their superior earnings potential.
- The provision of special programs for hard-to-employ reentrants to provide close supervision and support while the trainees work on projects specifically designed to develop saleable skills, positive work attitudes, and eventual permanent placement.
- In countries where nonworking women engage in volunteer work, attempts to capitalize on this experience by orienting volunteer-developed skills toward comparable market requirements.
- Experimentation with job sharing and part-time career opportunities as transitional experiences during child-rearing years, with the eventual option of continuing on a full-time basis.
- An increasing commitment toward insuring the right to continuing training and education over a lifetime, especially in countries with relatively short periods of compulsory general education. Where the normal educational span is longer, as in the United States, there has been an expansion of opportunities for middle-aged homemakers to attend colleges and universities, including training in the liberal professions.

• Attempts to translate homemaking skills into their labor market equivalents for use as job qualifications.

Manipulation of Demand

Job creation especially designed for the reentry population is a rarity. Sweden has taken some special initiatives to open opportunities for women, and these are often reentrants. American displaced-homemaker programs have given attention to developing jobs that aim to utilize competencies developed in the home. These, like so many reentry jobs, have little present attraction and few future gains.

A policy of job creation for women through special subsidies and through plant location inducements is exclusively a Swedish phenomenon, except where on-the-job training subsidies are given for the hard-to-employ, who may include some—but not many—reentrants. There is no question that in all countries, employers of large numbers of women may deliberately locate where a female labor force is available. Textile, apparel, and electronics manufacturing are examples. But such jobs frequently are low-wage. In Sweden, locational subsidies are sometimes limited to employers' agreeing to open opportunities for women in nontraditional occupations.

Legislative commitments to equal opportunity have often been vitiated by the strength of the traditional ethos. Where progress has been made, young women and those already in the work force are the more likely beneficiaries, not middle-aged homemakers. Adult women, because of early social conditioning, often defer to the prior claims of other groups, a sentiment that makes them ill prepared to take action on their own behalf when they perceive the need for employment-related assistance.

RECOMMENDATIONS

... Since homemaking and child rearing confer social benefits and contribute to the gross national product, consideration should be given to certain forms of reward to mothers to facilitate reentry. One example is participation in the social security system (as is done in some countries) and/or in the unemployment insurance system during absences from work. In the latter case, benefits might be paid at the inception of job search. In addition, receipt of unemployment benefits would create eligibility for training programs that are now available only to the unemployed. A homemaker preference similar to veteran's preference might be worth studying and would counter women's criticisms of the latter as sex-biased.

Governments should consider foregoing inducements to increase fertility. Such inducements are unlikely to work unless women's access to education has been restricted, a policy that no one is likely to propose. The more reasonable assumption is that women will continue to have work aspirations, and accordingly the labor market should be restructured so that women are viewed as a normal component of labor supply.

Like any other large group, reentrants are diverse and require different types of assistance. Flexibility in programming is therefore essential.

Reentrants and delayed entrants who are most in need of assistance are the youthful hard-to-employ grown old. Women who have adequate educational qualifications and some work experience require training only if they seek to change occupations or to upgrade themselves. Updating may also be a factor, but, at present, most reentrants have had work experience in female fields that have been shown to be easily resumed without further training.

Further training and continuing education is of value primarily to women with low qualifications (or none at all) or to professionals who wish to refurbish their skills. They appear to be of lesser value to other women who are job-ready. Sweden's utilization of relief work as a countercyclical device can provide reentrants who are unable to find jobs with skill upgrading and work experience, which can improve their placement potential when the economy again moves ahead.

The principal form of assistance that argues for separate consideration of reentrants and delayed entrants to the work force is guidance and counseling, since relatively advanced age, remoteness from schooling and early work experience, and family responsibilities combine to present them with a series of problems unlike those confronting other job aspirants.

Child care systems are generally inadequate and, in any event, do not appeal to all mothers. It is possible that the establishment of high-quality centers with both a nurturing and an educational component might encourage more mothers to use them. Although such centers would be extremely expensive to operate, some of the costs might be balanced by the additional job opportunities generated—including jobs for reentrants.

Employers should explore the extent to which they could provide preferential employment opportunities for women who had previously been members of their work force but who had left to have and raise a child or for other family reasons. Such an approach might be mutually beneficial.

Whereas women are exhibiting greater interest in paid work, men are tending to retire earlier. Of course, many women with interrupted work lives cannot afford to retire early and may also be less jaded about work. But if the trend of males toward early retirement continues and low fertility persists, female reentrants may become a more attractive supply than at present, especially in occupations and industries where they have not heretofore been welcome.

Finally, it is important to recognize that improvements in reentry assistance do not of themselves enhance women's job opportunities. As the economies of industrial countries become increasingly open to both men and women workers, greater job competition between them is inevitable. Nontraditional training for women will be a frustrating exercise unless the job market is taut. Men will not surrender their hold on preferred occupations easily. If more men enter the service sectors dominated by women, the position of women workers could deteriorate by reducing their opportunities to obtain the preferred jobs. Reformulated, this means that broadened opportunities for women workers can never be dissassociated from improvements in the overall operations of the labor market. Only to the extent that the economy runs close to full employment and the proportion of good to poor jobs increases will opportunities for women workers, including reentrants, be improved.

CHAPTER 20

Reentry of Women to the Labor Force: A Fifteen-Country Perspective

IN THE FALL OF 1979 the German Marshall Fund, in collaboration with the assistant secretary of labor for women's employment, France, jointly sponsored a conference in Paris with attendees from fifteen countries and many international bodies, governmental and nongovernmental, to review the implications of the cross-national study on "Returnees" (see Chapter 19) with an aim of formulating policy recommendations. I served as chairman of the conference, out of which the following five major themes emerged.

1. THE SCALE AND SCOPE OF THE ISSUES

- There must be recognition of the number of diverse barriers affecting all women who want to work, from the structure of the family to the specificities of labor market requirements.

- A substantial number of women under severe economic pressure to work are particularly disadvantaged by these multiple barriers.
- Many women who never planned to work after marriage later find they either must or want to do so.
- Despite the existence of obstacles, there has been a large increase in the participation of married women in the labor force.
- The labor market is occupationally segregated, with women concentrated in a limited number of occupations, which tend to be the lowest paying and provide the least benefits and prospects for advancement.
- In most advanced countries, younger married women are becoming more regularly attached to the world of work and, if they do leave, do so for a shorter time than in the past.
- In many countries, because of home responsibilities, reentrants still settle for part-time jobs despite the absence of benefits, rather than full-time work.
- Women are more spatially constrained than men, with the industry structure to which they have local access generally determining the quality of their jobs.
- Historically, and in every country, women have underinvested in their preparation for the labor market because they did not anticipate a long-term commitment to work that would yield a return on large human capital investments.
- The labor markets of the advanced industrial countries have seldom been tight for long enough to force changes in occupational desegregation on a scale approaching equality for both sexes.
- Since World War II, the shift of employment to the tertiary or service sector has resulted in a high demand for female labor.

2. Needs and Responses

- For women in the middle and higher occupational ranges, a continuing relationship with the employing firm can be maintained, sometimes through the device of work at home. This has taken place in the United States in the last fifteen years, and this retainer system is now being tried on a limited basis by some British banks.
- Women with young children face the special problems of child care and shared responsibility in the home. The public child care system is seriously inadequate in all countries, even in France, which has the most comprehensive system in place. More

countries, however, are extending maternity leave, increasing financial support during such leave, and providing job security for increasing periods of time.

- With the exception of France, there has been a proliferation of part-time work. For many women, the absence of adequate child care arrangements means part-time work or none at all. Sweden is building part-time work into the structure of the regular labor market and also permitting shorter work hours for parents with preschool children.
- Reentrants, particularly those in the older age groups who have considerable uncertainty about the labor market, may require a range of services to negotiate reentry. If they are not to be relegated to the least desirable jobs, these must include guidance, counseling, training, and placement. Many need current income as well to make the transition; this must be supplied by training allowances, welfare benefits, or other forms of public subsidies.
- No country is totally unresponsive to the needs of reentrants, but none gives these women priority in the provision of employment-related services.

3. UNMET NEEDS

- No society is in agreement as to how girls should be guided by their parents or trained by the schools, a fact that leads to the perpetuation of conventional attitudes and work preparation and a lack of orientation toward new career directions.
- There is a reluctance on the part of older women to take up nontraditional work, where the rewards—but also the risks—are higher.
- In most advanced countries, high-level jobs in management, government, and the professions require lengthy preparation, a fact that delays the possibility of childbearing for women who desire such jobs.
- For promotion to good jobs, employees must be available for advanced training and multiple job opportunities, both of which may require long hours and extensive travel, conditions that women with children may not choose to meet.
- The absence of high-quality public day care has led to the use of informal arrangements, particularly in the United States. Although women with high earnings can often afford to make private arrangements, these are not possible for poor women.
- Most wives seriously interested in both career and family require

substantial accommodation by their husbands. For younger people, there has been a shift from the goal of maximizing the husband's career to optimizing the careers of both the wife and husband as a family unit. Changes in the attitudes and behavior of men are a condition antecedent to the achievement of full equality of opportunity for both sexes in the labor market.

- Three sets of schedules must be dovetailed — those of the father, the mother, and the children — both within the workplace and in the home. These involve the children's school time, vacation time, and sick time. In the case of the last, Sweden allows special leave for either parent without penalty.
- Low-income women may worsen their situation when they return to work if their anticipated wages do not compensate for the loss of publicly provided benefits. For such women, a reasonable incentive to work requires an adjustment of the wage-benefit relationship.

4. Constraints on Effective Responses

- When dealing with millenium-long discriminations deeply embedded in institutions and attitudes, rapid change is difficult to achieve, particularly in times of rising unemployment.
- Since the number of good jobs is limited for both men and women, the problem for women is inequality of opportunity rather than of results.
- Reentrants' problems are intensified by occupational segregation, which is related to quasi-segregation in education and development experiences.
- Major support systems, including comprehensive child care, are costly and quickly run into budgetary constraints.

5. Potentials for Effective Responses

- Demographic trends are generally favorable to reentry. Smaller family size is expected to continue, and fewer youthful competitors will be in the labor market in coming decades.
- The shift of advanced economies to the services provides job opportunities for women. The computer revolution and policies toward guest workers are intervening variables here.
- Full employment, a necessary if not sufficient condition for increas-

ing women's employment, is a serious social objective in all countries. Periods of decreasing growth must not deflect attempts to increase equality for women in the labor market. In fact, with the introduction of work sharing, the quality of family life may be improved.

- Antidiscrimination legislation can change behavior and, eventually, attitudes.
- Women are at present better organized politically and, by joining with other groups that are the targets of discrimination, may increase their political effectiveness.
- Some programs intended for disadvantaged youth and the adult unemployed have been extended to reentrants. Further pressures from women out of the labor force who wish to return may extend the reach of other programs.

In conclusion, although the women's revolution is one of the outstanding phenomena of our century, no country, not even Sweden, has yet neutralized the question of gender in the world of work. On the other hand, while a residue of convention, law, and social attitudes toward sex roles maintains the economic dependency of women, the pressure to increase the freedom and options of all human beings, including the option of work, is still strong in the Western world.

PART V

Older Persons

THE FIRST SELECTION (Chapter 21) dates from the mid-1950s. I prepared this paper for the Fourth International Gerontological Congress in response to a request from my friend Dr. Seymour Wolfbein, then a senior official in the U.S. Department of Labor. Wolfbein had assumed the responsibility to elicit contributions from the U.S. scholarly community. Although I did not attend the conference, which was held in Milan, and although the problems of the elderly were not then high on my research agenda, most of my present orientation toward the elderly is spelled out in these early summary notes.

In 1950 the administrator of the Social Security System, Oscar Ewing, held a major conference in Washington on chronic diseases in which I participated. After listening for several days to many of the nation's medical leaders promise the near-term eradication of chronic diseases, in light of the prior conquest of infectious diseases, I requested the floor to make one simple point: If chronic disease is closely linked to the process of aging, it is unlikely that the conquest of these diseases would be speedy, since we would first have to understand more about the mechanisms of senescence, which in turn would require more understanding of biological growth and maturity. Although progress on the biogenetic front has been rapid recently, only a confirmed optimist would believe we are close to understanding the causes of cancer, much less to being able to eradicate them. Much the same judgment holds with respect to arteriosclerotic and renal diseases, which, together with cancer, account for most premature deaths from disease.

The question I often faced in choosing selections for this book about the rationale for reproducing a piece that has been overtaken by history had special piquancy in my long piece on "The Social Security System." The Greenspan commission reported in January 1983 and Congress enacted into legislation shortly thereafter almost all of the commission's recommendations. Without any claim of having influenced the commission—surely not directly and possibly not even indirectly—a great many of its critical recommendations were foreshadowed in my article in *Scientific American*. The great accomplishment of the commission was to reach consensus and to persuade Congress to act.

My cautionary stance toward efforts in many less-developed countries to legislate benefits for the elderly stems from my knowledge of the fiscal problems of the Social Security System in the United States and comparable problems in the pension systems of other developed countries. It was a conclusion that the arrangers of the World Assembly on Aging (1982) did not find agreeable, but there is no reason that a researcher should succumb to the optimism and enthusiasm of politicians, especially those who address international gatherings.

The other two selections are closer to my center of interest. They present the role of work and retirement on the adjustment of older persons. There is a growing dilemma in most developed nations: men and women are retiring from work in their early sixties, often earlier, and they are living into the late seventies or eighties. Even if they have sufficient income, what are these *older* but not *old* persons to do with their time, their energy, and their need for a role and purpose in the many years still vouchsafed them?

CHAPTER 21

Strategic Factors in the Adjustment of Older Persons

SOCIAL RESEARCH is always confronted by a major dilemma. There is no limit to the problems about which new information would help to deepen understanding and to facilitate the formulation of public policy. But research is not a free good, and the cost of investment in it in relation to the value of return is relevant. Even if a deliberate effort is made to eschew problems of minor importance, success is not always assured by concentrating on significant issues. Unless the resources required for a comprehensive appraisal of a major social issue are available, significant results cannot be achieved.

A further difficulty besets the social investigator whether he or she selects a narrow or a broad subject. The rapid and continuing change which characterizes the social environment presages that his findings are subject to a high rate of obsolescence. Results cannot usually be cumulated.

In undertakings such as this one, when an effort is being made by experts from different countries to plan a coordinated, and possibly an integrated, study of old age, these difficulties are further compounded.

Here there is not a single problem, but as many problems as there are nations represented. Similar facets of the problem exist in many countries, but the differences among countries are likely to equal or exceed the parallels.

One escape from these many limitations is to search for the *strategic* factors involved in the adjustment of older persons. Of course, the constellation of factors will differ from country to country depending on the specifics of the national environment. Although such specifics are crucial in formulating sound public policy, they may be disregarded in this effort, which is aimed at developing a framework for identifying major problems for research.

STRATEGIC FACTORS

A basic principle underlies this analysis. Life, individual or social, is always a balance between continuity and discontinuity—between the projection of the old and the emergence of the new. In considering the strategic factors that determine the adjustment of older people—health, work, economic resources, family structure, and personality—each will be reviewed in turn from this double point of view, that of continuity and that of discontinuity.

Much that transpires in the lives of older people can be understood only in terms of developments that occurred earlier. But it is also true that the later years of life are very much influenced by factors embedded in the aging process itself. The adjustment people make in their later years is a result of the interaction of these two sets of factors.

1. *Health.* There are at least two universals: Age brings a decline in vitality and well-being, and death comes to us all. It may be suggestive to point out that although there has been an increase in the life expectancy of men and women today compared with the expectancy of those who reached adulthood at the turn of the century, this has not been nearly as spectacular as the gains in the quality of life. Improvements in standards of living and in medical care have contributed substantially to the fullness of the later years. Important as this gain has been, however, it represents only a modest postponement of the time when a person's faculties begin to fail and death overtakes him.

A person's health in the later years can be dominated either by conditions of long standing or by new developments. Many people who are endowed with good health take care of themselves throughout their adult years and are likely to enjoy physical well-being during most of their later years. Sooner or later even these fortunate individuals suffer marked losses in vitality and functioning, but this may not occur until a person enters the eighties.

The circumstances are different for a person who from childhood or young adulthood has been in mediocre health. Such a person is marked for serious difficulties in the later years since the disintegrative process starts at a lower level. It is likely that such a person will be forced to devote an increasing proportion of his dwindling energies to keeping barely functioning in his later years.

In each of these two situations the element of continuity predominates. But there are a great number of people who, having enjoyed good health throughout their lives, are suddenly stricken with a major disease. In many instances death comes quickly, but for others a long period of illness and disability may intervene. At present our knowledge does not permit us to foretell who will be stricken and who will not, nor how long a person will be ill before succumbing. But in developing a framework for the study of adjustment of older people, provision must be made for this important discontinuity.

There is a related phenomenon to which attention should be invited. The older people become, the more likely they are to suffer from cerebral arteriosclerosis or from senile psychosis. Probably much can be done to delay the onset of these conditions and to mitigate their ravages, but in the absence of new knowledge we must anticipate a steady increase in the numbers who will suffer from these two conditions. They represent a serious threat to good health.

2. *Work.* It has long been recognized that there is a very close relation between the work a man does and the life he leads. The old Talmudists had a saying: When a man stops working, he dies. In recent decades there has been a steady increase in the number of years between the end of a man's working life and the end of his natural life. Apparently, many have found it possible to live on without working. But we also know that many seek to delay the date of their retirement and that others, after retiring, find new work for themselves.

A high proportion of the labor force in an industrial society is attached to a single employer or group of employers within the same industry for most of their lives. In general, their skill consists of an intimate knowledge of particular machines or processes within a specialized working environment. They have little skill that is easily transferable to work in other sectors of the economy. Hence, when they leave their jobs, they are cut off from most other employment unless they are willing to perform unskilled tasks.

The situation is different for those who carry their skills largely within themselves—the professional person, the skilled machinist, the cook. These individuals are frequently able to taper off—to reduce their work as their strength begins to fail but still to remain as active as they desire. This is possible for the physician who takes on a young assistant; the professor who becomes emeritus but who continues to lecture; the carpenter who helps out his contractor when the latter has a rush job to do; the cook who has left her old job but can work two or three days per week.

We see, then, that for many old age brings no major break in the continuity of work, whereas for others old age destroys their life pattern. To the extent that a person has found work a positive force in his life, the ability to continue working in later years must be a major satisfaction; to the same extent, an inability to continue working must be a source of great deprivation.

But this is not the whole story. Many people who find little satisfaction in their work develop interests apart from their jobs. For them, retirement is not a deprivation but a boon, since it frees them from activity in which they had little interest for one which is very rewarding. Their middle and later years have a continuity based not on work but on other activities.

3. *Economic Resources.* In a money economy people can maintain their economic independence only if they are able to earn enough to meet their needs; or have saved enough out of their previous earnings to cover their current expenses; or have an income supplied by the government, their former employer, or members of their family. As the number of years between retirement and death increases, the financial needs of older people become greater. Social insurance programs have been developed in many countries in recognition of the fact that unless a man is encouraged to save during the years when he is regularly employed, he will not have adequate resources in his old age. But in a world characterized by inflation, no social insurance program has yet been able to provide adequate retirement benefits.

The economic circumstances of older people has been greatly affected by the amounts they have been able to save in addition to their contributions to compulsory social insurance. Once again the factor of continuity is important. If a person saves throughout forty or fifty years of his working life, there is a strong probability that he will be economically independent when he stops working. This probability will be heightened if he has had the good fortune to work in a company that has developed a pension system supplemental to the governmental system.

Whether old people will in fact be able to make ends meet depends on more than their own prior actions. If their expenses in old age remain modest, their prior planning may prove successful. But in the event that either spouse is stricken with a serious illness of long duration, they will see their savings rapidly dissipated. The likelihood of long-term illness underscores the need for medical insurance or appropriate alternatives so that older people will not be impoverished by excessive medical expenses.

4. *Family Structure.* Man does not live by bread alone. Important as are work and income for the adjustment of older people, family and friendship are equally important ties. One of the major tragedies of old age is the dissolution of marriage through the death of a spouse, usually the husband. After decades of life together, death breaks the pattern. Although a small number of widows and widowers remarry, the vast majority do not. The years of the surviving spouse must be passed without the major support on which he or she had for so long relied.

Some are fortunate enough to find new support in more intimate relationships with other members of their family and with their friends. But here, too, the element of continuity looms large. If the bonds between parents and their children have been loosened over the years, it is unlikely that the intensified need of the surviving parent can result in a sudden strengthening of these bonds. The same holds true for friendship patterns. Unless one has made and kept good friends throughout one's life, it will be difficult to turn to them for help and support in old age.

It is pathetic to see large numbers of older people living out their days in institutions or communities where they have few ties to their past. In these environments the only event of significance is the death of one of the group. Some older people can find new friends among other such displaced people, but it is difficult for intimacy to grow among people who do not share a common past. The loneliness of old age is perhaps its most severe burden.

5. *Personality.* Centuries ago observers sought to differentiate among people in terms of those who were of a choleric disposition and those who had a euphoric attitude towards life. In modern language we would talk about pessimists and optimists, introverts and extroverts. But those of us who are acquainted with modern psychology would be quick to add that such simple dualities are not valid.

As far as the problem of adjusting to old age is concerned, it is sufficient to note that some people have much greater difficulties than others in accepting their disabilities; just as some people are more anxious than others when they contemplate their approaching demise. Still another difference among people is the extent to which they mourn their lost youth. The large number of men who insist on becoming weekend athletes in their fifties and sixties are frequently seeking to prove to themselves that they are still young. The result is well known: As Professor Carlson of Chicago University was fond of remarking, more Americans die from exercise than from lack of it.

The psychological differences can be illuminated through a consideration of serenity. There are those who find the day sufficient unto itself, while others either regret their lost youth or are unsettled by fears of death. Since people lives as members of a community, the attitudes and behavior toward the aged prevalent in their culture will affect their own responses and reactions to the passing of the years. Both the dissolution of what sociologists call the "large family" and the weakening of religious belief in Western societies have contributed significantly to undermining the foundations of serenity. The emphasis on speed and change—an outstanding characteristic of American life—has further operated to hasten the social disenfranchisement of the aged. Beauty and competence are much preferred to maturity and wisdom. What the old have, the young do not want.

A Dynamic Approach

Continuities in Life.

The foregoing outline has called attention to the extent to which an individual's adjustment in old age is determined by his earlier years. The life a man leads in his thirties, forties, and fifties will largely determine the quality of his life in his sixties and seventies. Whether he will be well or sick, employed or idle, comfortable or impecunious, befriended or lonely, serene or morose—in short, whether he will enjoy his later years or find them a burden—can in large measure be foretold.

There is little need to belabor the obvious—that a man who abused his health by excessive drinking and dissipation is not likely to find security and serenity in his later years. This is also likely to be true of a man who found no satisfaction in his work, or who spent all that he made, or who was unable to maintain warm relations with his family. Consider in contrast a judge who has spent most of his adult years on the bench, following a balanced regimen of work and play, deeply interested in his work, with liberal pension rights, fortunate in his marriage and children, and possessed of a temperament that takes the good with the bad. Clearly, such a man is likely to find old age, if not exciting, at least serene.

The Misfortunes of Old Age

We have seen how important the pattern of youth and the middle years is for the later years, but we must not ignore the frequency with which developments occurring late in life can make a mockery of even the best laid plans for old age. The puritan as well as the bounder is subject to cancer. The conscientious employee who looked forward to retiring at sixty-eight may, through the dissolution of his employer's business, be forced to look for work at fifty-eight and fail to find it. A lifetime of saving can be destroyed by the failure of a bank. And if death should take first one's spouse and shortly thereafter one's only child, the family that yesterday gave meaning and direction to life no longer exists. Should misfortune follow misfortune, even the most equable and serene will lose their composure and sink into despondency.

Unless a person lives and plans with at least an occasional thought to old age, he or she is likely to find it cold and dreary. But no degree of caution and conservatism can insure that a person's last years will be full and happy. The Lord's ways are inscrutable, and the good man frequently suffers while the sinner escapes.

The Cumulative Process

The approach followed in this chapter can be pointed up by illustrating how any one of the strategic factors can exercise a determining influence on adjustment in old age by setting off a cumulative process. If a man's health fails suddenly, he may be forced to give up his job, which in turn may leave him with insufficient economic resources. If his illness requires a great amount of care, his family is subjected to additional strains. The loss of his job, plus financial difficulties and the strained environment, pyramided on top of his illness, will undoubtedly be reflected in the emotional unsettlement of the individual himself.

Suppose a man suddenly loses his job in his late fifties and is unable to find another. His financial circumstances become increasingly strained. His family is forced to contribute to his support, and this is likely to precipitate new problems. Worried and anxious about his inability to find work through which to support his wife and himself, his health and disposition are likely to suffer markedly. If this happens, his chances of ever again becoming self-supporting are still further reduced.

Again, insufficient income in old age may lead to the neglect of a condition that, were it attended to in time, would be minor. Neglect, however, might lead to a permanent disability that makes it impossible for a man to continue working. With small savings, no work, and a permanent disability, the stress within the family situation and on the individual are vastly increased.

Death of a spouse can be so upsetting that a man can no longer meet the demands of the work situation and therefore loses his job and his income. As a result of these many calamities his health may break.

Many people become emotionally disoriented in old age as a result of the physical changes incident to the aging process itself. Frequently their disturbance is so severe that they lose their job and with it their income.

As the foregoing points up, any one of the strategic factors, in the absence of reserves, may precipitate consequences that can make for a desolate old age.

IMPLICATIONS

The following tentative formulations emerge from this analysis of strategic factors in the adjustment of older people:

1. The quality of adjustment in old age is often predetermined by the quality of adjustment that prevailed during the earlier years of a person's life. Just as there is an important continuity between childhood and adolescence and adulthood, so, too, there is an important continuity between the middle and later years of a person's life.

2. Adjustment in old age is frequently complicated by events that are completely outside the control of the individual. Among the most important of these is serious illness or the death of a spouse, which permanently destroys the family structure.

3. Although medical progress will undoubtedly bring some of the major diseases of later life under control, there is no reason to anticipate that it will be able to free people of all serious disabilities. Death will still confront man. Hence old age will remain a period of life beset with dangers and difficulties, which individual and group action can reduce and alleviate but not eliminate.

4. Since the problems of old age are to a considerable extent inherent in life itself, each individual will handle them according to his or her own temperament and his own philosophy—his approach to adversity and his attitude toward life and death.

5. Although the individual himself largely determines his own level of adjustment, voluntary groups and government can play a significant role in establishing and maintaining a more agreeable environment for older people. Their actions should be directed in the first instance to reducing the number of people who are forced to retire against their will; to ensuring reasonable

minimum pensions for those who are retired; and to providing essential health services and facilitating their use.

6. The child can grow up happy only as a member of a family. The old person can adjust tolerably only if his or her family ties remain firm. Public policy can ignore this fact only at the peril of frustration and failure. A wise government will seek to aid older persons by helping their children and grandchildren to care for them. But, wherever possible, it will assiduously avoid taking over the full responsibility for their care.

CONCLUDING OBSERVATIONS

Enthusiasm is an essential ingredient of social progress. The past decade has witnessed a gratifying concern in many quarters with the problems of old age and with the urgent necessity to cope with them more effectively than in the past. But this very enthusiasm is fraught with danger: It can substitute a foolish optimism for a studied neglect. There is a further danger to unbridled enthusiasm. The complexity of the problems of old age can be ignored in favor of a few simple generalizations that are considered valuable as levers for social action. To consider old age as a singular phenomenon would be a disservice to both research and policy. There are tremendous variations in the characteristics of older people and in their social and economic circumstances. The real challenge to the student as well as to the politician is to identify the strategic factors that can assist men and women to reach old age with as much strength as possible; and to determine what lines of action are available to a society to help those who are in need. Finally, both the student and the politician must recognize the limits of social action—for the proper adjustment to old age requires a man to recognize that when asked how he is, he finds comfort in replying, "Fortunately, not much worse than yesterday."

CHAPTER 22

Life Without Work:
Does It Make Sense?*

THIS CHAPTER deals sequentially with four themes: cullings from a half century of work and research on work about the role of older persons in the work force; some analytic distinctions about the nature of work; placing work within the larger context of life's experiences; and a few modest suggestions as to policy with respect to older workers.

SOME OBSERVATIONS ON AGING AND WORK

When I entered Columbia College in 1927, Nicholas Murray Butler, the president, had been at the helm of the institution for two decades, during which time he had transformed it from a mediocre into a top-rated university. But Butler remained at the helm for another seventeen years, during which he declined in health and energy, and in the process the university was greatly weakened.

For those concerned with the rise and fall of institutions, none offers

more detail than the Catholic Church, which has survived for close to
two millennia. I was impressed when the pope acted some years ago to
establish a new policy replacing cardinals who could no longer perform
their duties because of their advanced age.

Second, I was struck by the different ways in which my parents
aged. My father was always in mediocre health and in his later years
(he died at eighty) was performing at a much reduced level of output.
My mother, on the other hand, slowed up only in her ninety-fourth
year.

The next point has to do with health. I spend most of my time
currently in research in health economics. There are many arguments as
to whether modern medicine pays off. We know that medicine has relatively little to do with longevity. It would be wrong to say that it has
nothing to do with longevity, but its major contribution lies elsewhere, in
its adding to the quality of life, particularly the quality of life of older
people. Only a few years ago, for example, if you broke your hip you
would probably be confined to bed for the rest of your days. There was
nothing that could be done in the days before new surgical techniques
were perfected. The question is not solely or primarily one of longevity,
but rather the improved quality of a person's later years. This is critical
for some of the issues to be addressed at this conference, for many older
persons now entering their later years in good health are capable of and
interested in remaining at work.

Another important trend points to the way in which the work and
life patterns of women are getting closer and closer to those of men. As
more women enter and remain in the work force, there has been a
parallel devaluation of voluntary activity. In the past, voluntary service
had much to do with the way in which older persons related to the world.
While many older persons are still concerned about their church or
hospital, the role of the volunteer has been devalued, which in turn has
affected the role and status of many older persons.

Next, career-oriented persons with strong ambitions who enter corporate enterprise will know by the time they are thirty-five years old or
so whether their rate of progress will enable them to achieve or approximate their career goals. By thirty-five, a person will have feedback from
his organization as to whether he is on the fast track or the slow track.
Many people in large organizations have plateaued by their mid-thirties.
If one's career plateaus in the mid-thirties and one keeps on doing the
same type of work year in and year out, early retirement may not seem
such a bad idea after all.

A correlative of the foregoing is that for the few who continue to
compete for the top jobs, their only chance of winning is for the old-
timers who are up at the top to get out of the way. Since there are only a

few jobs up at the top, those who hold these jobs must keep moving out with some regularity if others who are qualified are to have their chance. Professionals who are self-employed or who are members of a partnership or a small corporate group have an easier time of adjusting their workday and work week as they reach their sixties or seventies. They can shift from full- to part-time activity, and most do just that.

When it comes to the rank-and-file worker, I have been impressed with how many, as they near the end of their working life, look forward to spending more time on avocational or leisure activities such as moving out of the city to their "cabin in the Catskills." They no longer will have to limit themselves to a two- or three-week stay. They can, when they retire, spend all or most of their time there.

The last observation relates to the more affluent, those who look forward to dividing their golden years between pitching horseshoes in Florida and traveling to Europe. This is a typical American, not a European, approach to the later years. Many Americans put a high value on being able to escape from work permanently and to start doing new and different things. If one has never been out of the country, the first trip abroad is usually exciting. But the pleasure diminishes with the fifth or surely the tenth trip. This observation is a useful reminder that attitudes and behavior toward work and retirement must always be assessed within both economic and cultural contexts, which in turn are not stable.

THE MULTIFACETED NATURE OF WORK

My second theme takes off from the premise that work is a multidimensional phenomenon. In a recent article that I wrote on Social Security, which appeared in the *Scientific American* (January 1982), I presented a table showing that the group that was best off with respect to income in old age were those who were still working. For this group, work accounted for about 55 percent of their total income. Most people, if they want to be comfortable in the later years, need income from work. Only the rich can afford not to keep on working.

Second, in the United States we have always tended to place a person—first men but now also women—by asking "What do you do?" If we learn about the work a person performs, we can rank the individual. The work-status relationship is critical.

In analyzing the satisfaction people derive from work, it is well to distinguish among intrinsic satisfactions, extrinsic satisfactions, and concomitant satisfactions (see my *Occupational Choice*, 1951). For some, surely a minority, intrinsic satisfactions from work are critical. However, one of the consequences of aging is the diminution of one's mental and physical powers, which affect work performance. A lawyer friend is one of the nation's great litigators. But now that he is in his early eighties he does not accept certain cases because he can no longer remember all the details in a trial that might run ninety days or even longer. Similarly, a surgeon may still be a very good diagnostician as he gets into his seventies, but few of us would want to be operated on by him. In the case of many appellate judges, age does not seem to matter very much. Irrespective of age, they continue to write good or bad opinions. Great musical instrumentalists and conductors are a group apart. Many are able to perform at high levels into their seventies and even into their eighties.

Work has great importance for many persons because of its concomitant social satisfactions, the companionship it provides. This was first brought home to me in our studies of the long-term unemployed in New York City in the late 1930s (*The Unemployed*, 1943). What the men missed most was the daily interaction with their fellow workers on the job and sharing a beer after work. The loss of these social ties took a heavy toll. The vice president of AT&T recently made an interesting point at a Columbia University seminar. He reported that they found there were still some women in their middle seventies working the night shift in the Bell Telephone System in New York City who had to use the subways to get to their jobs. They won't stop because of the pleasure they get from meeting and interacting with their friends at work.

Work also provides a structure for the use of time. If one spends eight hours a day at work, what to do with the rest of one's time represents less of a burden. But to make effective use of twenty-four hours in a day, day after day, without the routine of work can prove burdensome.

THE SEVERAL CONTEXTS OF WORK

These then are the five dimensions of work: income, status, personal achievement, social relations, and the structure of time. A complementary approach is to consider briefly the different parties who may be involved in the structuring of work. The first point of reference is the individual. Whether an individual needs income, whether he has a drive for intrinsic work satisfaction, whether he is concerned about social interactions on the job — in all these respects the individual is the center.

Most of us continue to live in family structures — hence the importance of relating work to the family. We are in the midst of a major revolution, in which the majority of families now have two wage earners. Moreover, an increasing number of mothers of even very young children are in the labor force, and many fathers are caught up in a career that allows them to spend very little time with their children. In short, the interface of work and family is a critical dimension.

We know that a disproportionately large sector of our families living in poverty consist of families with only one wage earner. There are very few families in the United States trapped in poverty where both husband and wife are more or less regularly employed. The reports from Europe suggest that a strong force that is contributing to the expansion of flextime comes from the desires of married people who work to spend more time together and with their child or children.

The employing organization offers still another context in which to consider work. Among the more dynamic factors operating in a market economy are the decisions that firms make as to where to locate, expand, and relocate, the basis for which is often rooted in estimations of the competence and pliability of the work force. When a long-established plant is closed down, especially in a one-industry town, the toll of human suffering is often very great.

The community offers still another vantage point from which to assess the role of work. Consider the differences in the socialization in northern cities of the earlier immigrants and the more recent black migrants. Most Americans have failed to appreciate the differences in the infrastructure available to the two groups. The Italians and the Irish who came to New York had the Catholic Church and Tammany Hall to assist them. The Jews had support from their co-religionists who had come earlier and had put into place an elaborate system of social institutions, from schools to hospitals. In contrast, blacks as they moved North have not had the advantage of such self-help structures. I submit that the lack of such infrastructure explains many of the difficulties blacks have encountered in their efforts to secure a place in urban society.

The final vantage is societal. Does our society need the work that older persons are able to contribute; will it create the opportunities they need to continue to work; and if not, will it provide them adequate income if they do not work? This provides the bridge to a few observations about policy.

SOME POLICY QUESTIONS

The first observation relates to the changing perspectives from a life that is spent working to not working. Currently a college graduate starts to work in his early twenties and ends in his early sixties, a work life of approximately forty years. But the average additional duration of life for a man who reaches sixty-two is sixteen years; for a woman it is twenty-one. This points up the fact that at present a person will spend only half his life at work. The question that must be asked and answered is whether even an affluent society can afford to provide income for half of the population that at any time is not working. I doubt it.

But even if we could afford it, the question must be raised anew: Does it make sense? Again, I doubt it. In the penultimate chapter of *The Human Economy* (1976) I postulated that the overriding criterion for measuring societal progress was the broadening of options. Using that criterion, I would argue that many persons in their sixties and seventies and even a few in their eighties would prefer to keep on working and that a society that enabled them to do so would be better off. I am not arguing that they should work, only that they have the option to work if they so desire. But there is another side to the coin. Some workers become enfeebled or disabled in their late fifties and lose their jobs. I see considerable merit in a transition program, such as the French have put into place, that would carry such persons over until they qualify for Social Security. Moreover, I would consider broadening such a program to include persons who, although in good health, are the victims of plant closures and whose prospects for reemployment are minimal in years when the unemployment rate hangs high.

I see merit in slowly raising the retirement age from sixty-five to sixty-eight; in taxing one-half of the Social Security benefit; in correcting the indexing for inflation and introducing still other modifications to shore up the financial foundations of the system. In the absence of such reforms, a conflict between the generations, with all its ugliness, is likely.

There is no point of pushing the elderly to the wall, and faulty policies that result in such pressure could have serious repercussions. We saw a counterculture of the young in the 1960s that had little to commend it. I submit that inciting the elderly to take to the political ramparts could prove more destructive. There is nothing outrageous or impossible in the demands their leadership has advanced: a protection of the benefits that have been written into the law and an opportunity for the elderly, if they so desire, to work past seventy. The elderly understand that the value of their benefits is linked to the fiscal integrity of the federal government. They do not stand adamant against all modifications. But they will fight hard to protect the systems that are in place, and so they should. I have long believed that the quality of a people is to be measured by how it deals with children, women, and the elderly. On that criterion the United States gets a passing mark. Our aim should be to improve, not lower it.

NOTES

*I wish to acknowledge the assistance of Dean Morse in helping me transform my oral remarks into written form.

CHAPTER 23

Early Retirement: Boon or Bane?

RETIREMENT IS A RELATIVELY NEW SOCIAL PHENOMENON. Pensions were unknown in the past except perhaps to a favored few who, like Dr. Johnson, drew a pension from the crown but never stopped working. Today we have mandatory retirement, which forces some workers out of the labor market sooner than they would like. On the other hand, we have a relatively new twist to the retirement picture, in that some workers now want to retire early. This chapter, through the use of a survey of early retirees, explores some of the whys and wherefores of early retirement and what this trend implies for current and future policies at both the corporate and public levels.

THE NEED TO INVESTIGATE THE ISSUES OF EARLY RETIREMENT

A generation ago, the norm for retirement was age sixty-five. The Social Security Act gave powerful sanction to this retirement age, and the large numbers of private pension plans that developed since then usually accepted age sixty-five as a norm. In addition, many large corporations began to set sixty-five as the age of mandatory retirement, even if exceptions were often made. In spite of these powerful institutional rules, a steady erosion of that norm has taken place. The labor force participation rates of older age groups have shown a steady, and recently quite rapid, decline since the 1950s. In some well-publicized instances, prominent corporations have developed plans to induce the early retirement of certain segments of their labor force, particularly engineers. In other instances, less publicized and more indirect (even covert) pressures have been exerted to induce selected individuals to retire early.

Because of the nature of the managerial pyramid and the possible obsolescence of professional and technical skills, early retirement of middle-level managerial and professional/technical personnel has, in some cases, seemed to offer a solution to such troubling problems as career plateaus, blockage of promotions, and technological lags.

From the point of view of the employee, early retirement has become more tempting. Generous pension offers, very large accumulations of assets, and long tenure with a company (so that an individual can say to himself, "I have worked long enough, paid my dues"), combined with the new phenomenon of the two-worker family, have fueled the trend toward early retirement.

The following questions related to actual or potential policy issues of corporations or the public at large provide, in part, the framework and purpose for our investigation into early retirement.

1. If early retirement has become more common, what will be its effects on the manpower planning of large corporations, on pension plans, and on other employee benefit plans?
2. What will be the effect of changes in the law raising the legal age for mandatory retirement to seventy?
3. What will be the potential effects of the Age Discrimination in Employment Act?
4. Do managerial employees who have often spent many decades of loyal and productive service with a large corporation elect early retirement because the grass is really greener outside, or because the corporation has allowed its own pastures to seem (or be) very brown for many middle-level managers and professional/technical employees?
5. Do highly educated, experienced, productive individuals who retire when they are still vigorous represent an important underutilized resource that neither the nation nor they themselves can really afford to waste?
6. Have plans to retire early been frustrated by unanticipated inflation?

7. Have some early retirees found ways to reenter the private sector or found significant and satisfying roles in the public sector or in nonprofit services?
8. What lessons can be distilled from the experiences of early retirees that might help others understand the opportunities and challenges of early retirement?

WHO WAS SURVEYED?

A total of 1,045 persons filled out the retirement questionnaire. The participating companies drew a structured sample, which was developed by the investigators, to ensure a reasonable distribution among persons who had left employment within the last ten years. Persons were included in the sample if, on the basis of 1978 dollars, they earned not less than $20,000 on retirement and not more than $50,000. The following list provides a profile of the respondents:

1. Most retired before their sixty-third birthday, after an average of thirty-six years with their employer.
2. Over half worked thirty-six years or more with their company; only one in ten for less than twenty-five years.
3. Most were males, and most were married at the time of their response.
4. Over half did not have a college degree.
5. Most served in a managerial position before retirement.
6. Most who continued working did so in a professional or technical capacity.

THE RETIREMENT DECISION

The decision to make a life-style change as dramatic as retirement can't be an easy one. It affects a person's social life and personal life, and especially one's financial situation.

Unelected Retirement

Not all the respondents in the survey had the option to continue working, however. About 30 percent had been forced out of their job in some manner, or encouraged to leave. Changes in management, reductions in personnel, or interpersonal conflicts with superiors made early retirement the most comfortable option in an untenable work situation. One respondent in such a position wrote: "I had not planned early retirement, as my job was exciting, challenging, and management at that point in time was excellent. However—a complete change in management occurred in 1975." An additional 25 percent of the respondents reached mandatory age (something less than sixty-five years old) for their level in the company and had no choice but to retire.

Elected Retirement

The rest of the respondents initiated their own early retirement for several other reasons, the most common being monetary. Either they had accumulated enough assets, were attracted by the pension, or had calculated that after taxes the financial incentive to continue working was no longer sufficiently high when compared to the pension. Sixty-five percent of the retirees in the sample indicated that financial reasons influenced their decision to retire. By eliminating the number of persons who had reached mandatory retirement age, this percentage increases to 88 percent.

Respondents often checked more than one reason for deciding to retire early (see Table 23.1). For example, health factors and the stresses and physical demands of their jobs were cited by 58 percent of the respondents. Even so, about one-fourth of these people subsequently began working again; a relatively high proportion went into consulting work or became self-employed, where, perhaps, the stresses and strains of work were reduced from their preretirement level.

In addition to monetary and health reasons, respondents mentioned other negative feelings about continuing to work in general, or specifically, about their jobs. Thirty-one percent of early retirees said they no longer liked their work, and the same percentage said they felt they had worked long enough.

Among the possible reasons for an individual's initiating a request for retirement is, of course, an offer of employment by another company. It is interesting to note, however, that practically none of those respondents who initiated a retirement request did so because another company had offered them employment. In some cases, it is true, individuals had made arrangements for postretirement salaried employment before they retired, but these plans seem to have been made much more on their own initiative.

Table 23.1
Reasons Given for Early Retirement

Reason	Percentage
Finances	65
Health/job tension	58
Had risen as far as they could	33
No longer liked the job	31
Felt they had worked long enough	31
Layoff/change in management	30
Reached mandatory age	25

Note: Respondents could choose more than one reason.

Retirement Counseling

Retirement counseling offered by the retiree's company is one potential vehicle for reducing strains, both financial and otherwise, that result from poor retirement planning. However, for our sample, this resource does not appear to have fulfilled its potential, as 60 percent of the respondents did not use company-provided counseling to do their planning. About half of those were unaware that the counseling services were even available. Of the others who knew that their company provided counseling, 25 percent did not think it would be useful, and another 19 percent indicated that they did not wish to discuss their personal situation with retirement counselors provided by the company.

AFTER RETIREMENT: WORK?

One-half of the respondents were interested enough in employment after retirement either to take active steps to secure work or to think about it in a planning sense. Those retirees who had taken steps to secure employment were more likely to be employed and working for pay than those who did not. Some retirees who had not planned on working after retirement found they were forced to work for various reasons. About *two-fifths* of the respondents had some kind of work experience during their retirement years, even though the majority admitted they could get along quite well without work.

Type of Work Sought

Many retirees sought consulting jobs or self-employed positions, which they viewed as an escape from the rigid work schedules, conformity to organizational imperatives, and unwelcome stress and conflict associated with their former employment. Some retirees viewed new work not as an escape but as an adventure, as did this respondent: "I believe everyone owes himself a second career. They should retire early (60–65) and launch a new career utilizing their talents in a somewhat different direction or profession in order to enjoy life at its fullest."

The following list illustrates the wide variety of work activity that opened up to the respondents after retirement:

1. Male nurse (says he's in much demand).
2. Stockbroker.
3. Manager of a miniature golf course (having a wonderful time).
4. Economist.
5. Rancher.
6. Teacher ("my raison d'être").
7. Fisherman.
8. Psychologist.
9. Artist.
10. Dance teacher (having a wonderful time).
11. Priest.
12. Hotel manager (always wanted to be one).

Two-thirds of the respondents were managers before retirement, while three-quarters of the respondents who were employed at the time of the survey were engaged in professional or technical work. Of those retirees currently in salaried positions, only one in ten said their postretirement job was similar to their preretirement position. A change in work environment and work role was for some a welcome part of their postretirement work experience. In the words of one respondent, "My biggest problem after retirement was being available around the house for trivial chores I didn't want to do. The work I am doing now provides an escape from this."

Reasons for Seeking Postretirement Work

Many retirees responded that their work before retirement had ceased to provide sufficient challenge and that postretirement work had been a revitalizing experience because it offered new challenges and rich rewards (either financially, physically, or both). For some of the respondents who had accepted relatively undemanding salaried employment after retirement, the very fact that their work was unpressured and their schedule relatively flexible and relaxed was one of the major satisfactions of their postretirement work experience. The following list provides a profile of the postretirement work experience of the respondents:

1. For retirees who had worked forty to fifty hours per week before retirement, modal hours of work were around twenty after retirement.
2. Two out of five retirees worked. Those respondents with more education and higher incomes were more likely to work after retirement.
3. Most retirees who worked got their jobs prior to or shortly after retiring, mostly with smaller firms.
4. Retirees worked because they liked to or for the additional income.
5. Most retirees found their present work to be more satisfying than their preretirement work.
6. Most retirees who were not working did not want to work.

Income also plays a large role in the postretirement work experience. One respondent went from working fifty hours a week before retirement to sixty hours a week at his own business after retirement. But he has no regrets; his work is not only more satisfying but also much more rewarding economically.

Attitudes concerning what constitutes a sufficient postretirement income varied, in that they did not seem to be related to present total family income or to the standard of living the retiree was used to before retirement. No relationship existed between expected postretirement income and the person's annual salary in the year before retirement. The following list summarizes the relationship between preretirement and postretirement incomes of the respondents:

1. Mean preretirement annual earned income in 1978 dollars amounted to $28,800 and total family income to $34,500. The $5,700 difference represented an admixture of spouses' earnings and investment income. Mean family income in the twelve months preceding the survey totaled $19,500.
2. In seven out of ten cases, respondents' preretirement earnings accounted for all of the family's earned income; in the postretirement period only two out of five respondents accounted for all of the family's earned income.
3. In eight out of ten cases, income from investments accounted for 25 percent or less of preretirement total family income.

Postretirement investment income accounted for more than 50 percent of total family income in about the same proportion of families.

4. In one out of three families, pensions and Social Security benefits accounted for 75 percent or more of total postretirement income.

AFTER RETIREMENT: LEISURE?

While many people seek a new work experience upon retirement, others seek more leisurely activities. Several of the respondents in our survey devoted their newly acquired free time to volunteer work, home maintenance, and hobbies.

Volunteer Work

Slightly over half of all respondents participated in voluntary activities before and after retirement, the majority with religious organizations. During the preretirement period, about nine out of ten of these respondents devoted from one to five hours a week to voluntary activities. As one might expect, their involvement in volunteer work increased in the postretirement period. One respondent put it this way: "As for me, I wonder how I would ever find time to go to work [paid], as I'm so busy working for nursing home committees, health organization board of directors, trustee for a hospital, treasurer of church, state church board of directors, and so forth."

Home and Hobbies

In their preretirement years, three out of four respondents spent under five hours a week on home maintenance; after retirement over one out of four retirees spent ten or more hours a week on home maintenance. A comparable shift occurred with respect to domestic chores.

An even more radical shift occurred with respect to time devoted to hobbies. After retirement three out of five respondents reported spending ten hours or more a week on such activities. One respondent wrote:

> I worked for forty years and enjoyed my work. I retired because there were so many things I had never been able to do because there was no time. Now I can play bridge, raise flowers (I always did), cook and entertain; take a trip when it's not a weekend; belong to church

altar guild and daytime church groups; take regular college courses instead of at night—I'm not interested in a degree, but there is a college in my neighborhood and I enroll for subjects that interest me.

Table 23.2 shows the change in frequency of participation in recreational activities from preretirement to postretirement. With the exception of technical and business-related reading, all the activities show a significant increase in participation, especially sports, household repair, gardening, and travel. Sports participants were likely to be younger and more satisfied with retirement. They were also more likely to claim that both their health and their social life had improved since retirement.

Table 23.2
Change in Frequency of Participation in Recreational Activities

Activity	Percentage
General household repair	+32
Travel	+24
Active sports	+23
Gardening	+19
TV	+14
Reading newspapers	+12
Reading current fiction	+10
Woodworking	+ 9
Reading nonfiction, card games, arts and crafts	+ 7
Music, theater	+ 4
Photography	+ 3
Sports events	+ 2
Painting, adult education	+ 1
Technical/business reading	−20

Note: The figures represent the percentage of respondents who said they engaged in an activity frequently in the past twelve months of retirement, minus the percentage who engaged in the same activity frequently before retirement.

THE EFFECT OF INFLATION AND ADVERSE HEALTH ON RETIREMENT

Most respondents were not overly surprised by their retirement experiences, with 84 percent saying their experiences were at least fairly

similar to what they expected. Surprises tended to be in the areas of
inflation and poor health.

The severity of current inflation, however, was one factor that many
respondents had not planned on. Interestingly, those who had underestimated the inflation rate were also those not planning on postretirement work, feeling their financial position was secure. Over a third
of the respondents admitted that at the time of retirement they had not
given much thought to the average rate of inflation during the rest of
their lifetime. Of those respondents who had thought about inflation,
48 percent had seriously underestimated its rate—most had predicted
the average rate would be under 5 percent. When revenues were unex-
pectedly affected adversely, the retiree was more likely to return to work.
One respondent spoke for many retirees when he described his own
circumstances:

> The savings and security plan had delivered to me a very sub-
> stantial and comforting financial buffer. I used part of it to liquidate
> all open accounts, to purchase a new car, and to pay off the small
> unpaid balance of my home mortgage. My wife and I continued to
> live comfortably by drawing from our "buffer" to augment my pen-
> sion payments.
>
> The best laid plans of mice and men oft go astray. During the
> past two or three years, that old devil "inflation" and unheard of
> increases in local property taxes have drained the balance of our
> once substantial buffer. We cannot afford to live in our home any
> longer—in the home that we worked so hard and so long for. We must
> sell it this year and move, using the sale price to establish another
> financial buffer, which, hopefully, will carry us through the balance
> of our lives.

Adverse health also dampened the retirement experience. Only 48
percent of those respondents who had experienced increasingly poor
health since retirement said they were satisfied, compared with a satisfied response from 75 percent of those whose postretirement health had
improved. Still, in keeping with an overall expectation of worsening
health accompanying increasing age, half of the respondents still found
retirement satisfactory in spite of poorer health.

POLICY IMPLICATIONS OF EARLY RETIREMENT

Policy issues dealing with retired employees, the companies from which
they have retired, and governmental policy actions all share a common
problem—an overriding concern about the effects of high levels of infla-

tion on our existing patterns of retirement and the economic and social institutions that have grown up around the retirement process. Our respondents clearly state that this issue dominates their retirement experience. Although many retirees have continued to work in their retirement years because they want to work, others have begun to work because of inflation. Many respondents also indicated that they may have to work in the future. Although most of the respondents still feel they retired at about the right time, some admit that inflation is the main reason they are now beginning to feel that they retired too soon.

We have seen that an important concern of many retirees is whether to work. The quality and quantity of that postretirement work is very much an issue. Our respondents generally prefer short, flexible working schedules. Although they are often willing to change their occupation drastically, they resent being forced to do demeaning and low-paid work. In fact, more recent retirees favor professional and technical activities, especially those respondents whose educational attainments were relatively high and whose preretirement and postretirement incomes were relatively large.

Corporate Policy Issues

The policy issues relating to early retirement that face the firm subsume most of those facing the individual, but are often inverted. The firm necessarily directs most of its energies in human resources to the intake of new members into its labor force—their training, retention, and promotion. Traditionally, the firm has spent much less time on the effective utilization of employees during the years immediately preceding their retirement. Human-capital theory may seem to give the firm a powerful argument for the relative neglect of the older members of its labor force. Furthermore, the costs of fringe benefits, particularly defined benefit pension systems, fuel another argument against retaining or hiring older workers.

Age Distribution

The age distribution of a firm's labor force, however, and particularly the age distribution of its managerial and professional/technical staffs, is not something a firm can set arbitrarily. This age distribution is not only the product of the historical evolution of the firm but also the product of the labor market within which the firm operates. Probably most important, age distribution reflects the technological and organizational imperatives that circumscribe the firm's freedom of action.

Even so, the large corporation may believe that either its existing or its predicted age distribution is an actual or potential problem. How to reconcile the firm's perception of the desired age distributions of its managerial and professional/technical staffs with their actual distribution is bound to raise some difficult policy issues, the most important one being whether the firm should even have a policy with respect to the age distribution of these staffs. Another one is whether the normal course of events and the operation of the labor market can be relied on to solve what seem to be potential problems. Here the firm's sense of the potentialities of its labor force, its surrounding labor market, and the capacities of its existing staff to meet whatever stresses and strains may be imposed by the bunching of age distributions by occupation is of critical importance.

Since the firm, even if it might wish to, cannot just dismiss its middle-aged and older managerial personnel—and will be less able to do so in the future—another issue facing the firm is how to make best use of a group of managers and professional/technical personnel, some of whom are facing physical and mental problems associated with increasing age. It is one thing to cite instances of extraordinary energy, innovativeness, and managerial capacity that can be mustered at very advanced ages; it is another thing to say that all members of older age groups suffer no disabilities. This simply flies in the face of common observation. As they grow older, some people do have less physical and intellectual energy, less flexibility, and less combativeness and competitiveness. But even with these kinds of age deficits, such individuals, because of their experience and their accumulated wisdom, may still be able to make invaluable contributions if an institution knows how to utilize them properly.

Pension Systems

A particularly thorny set of policy issues is related to the incentive and disincentive effects of pension systems. Employees generally favor a defined benefit pension system because it allows them to know what sums they can expect during their retirement years. They particularly favor a plan whose benefit formula heavily weights the salaries of their last few years of employment. Some plans may also be designed so that early retirement does not lead to actuarially neutral reductions in benefits, a feature that favors employees contemplating early retirement and that provides an incentive to elect early retirement.

The conflict between older workers who want to continue to work and those who want to elect early retirement arises because the defined-benefit pension plan provides an incentive—often quite strong—for the firm to substitute younger workers for older workers. The more the pension benefit formula weights salaries in the last years of employment, the greater this incentive is.

What Corporations Can Do

Corporations, for their part, are concerned about the number of managerial and professional/technical personnel who may elect *not to retire early* in the near future. They are also interested in making use of the skills and experience of some of those employees who have in the past elected early retirement. It is our view that if large corporations would be more flexible in their use of retired personnel (their own and those of other corporations), the pool of early retirees willing to accept a new relationship to their former employers or new employers would maintain itself or possibly grow. Of course, the corporation would have to show initiative and use its preretirement contacts and the stage of the retirement decision itself to let those individuals who are contemplating early retirement know of the corporation's interest in their future work ambitions.

In the face of continuing inflation, which is likely to yield only very slowly (if at all), what can companies do to mitigate the high—and probably still higher—discontent that will arise from the erosion of pension benefits? Some of the stronger companies may be able to provide a cost-of-living adjustment for some minimum amount of a variable pension. Opportunity should be offered to employees to make voluntary contributions during their years of employment, especially when the needs for current income diminish. By building up a greater equity in their pension, employees will have a partial hedge against erosion from inflation. The last decade has demonstrated that more and more Americans are owners of homes and that such ownership has proved to be a major bulwark against the loss of asset value from inflation. In future corporate approaches to fringe benefit arrangements, the importance of home ownership as an appreciating asset to retirees should be taken into consideration.

Public Policy Issues

Private pension systems with defined benefits are not age-neutral in their effects on the supply of and the demand for labor and usually create incentives on the part of the employee to retire and on the part of the employer to dismiss or not hire older workers. Similarly, Social Security policy also has important disincentive effects on older workers in the preretirement stage. The provision of Social Security benefits being drawn at age sixty-two has had an immediate and pronounced effect on the labor force participation rates of employees reaching that age. Even if the reduction in benefits associated with electing age sixty-two rather than age sixty-five were actuarially neutral (which is not the case), the mere fact of being eligible for benefits at age sixty-two has probably had a strong disincentive effect on further work.

In other words, if early retirement were the desired goal of public and private policy, the system we now have would be efficacious, even if it were age-neutral. Those individuals on the margin of electing early retirement would be encouraged to do so, and those older employees desiring to keep their jobs would find it harder to do so and would encounter more severe difficulties when they sought reemployment than if they had been dismissed. But early retirement is not necessarily a desired goal. If a productive person retires to continue working in a new field, then it can be beneficial overall; but encouraging complete retirement at an early age reduces the overall size of the labor pool which then, in turn, decreases the potential for further output growth.

Over the recent past, and probably for some time in the future, increases in the amount of Social Security benefits and changes in the benefit formulas will occur. Without reducing any present benefits, Congress could allocate the increase in future benefit levels in ways that will over time substantially alter the incentive effects of the Social Security system. Raising, or eliminating entirely, the ceiling on earned income before reduction in benefits takes place is one obvious step in this direction. Lowering the formula for benefit reduction when the earned income ceiling is reached is another step. Both policies were strongly advocated by many of our respondents. Another change that would decrease, or remove entirely, the disincentive effects of Social Security would be an increase in the size of benefits for every additional year an employee worked after age 65. Sufficiently large increases would make it possible to achieve some of the objectives that people who advocated increasing the formal retirement age for full benefits from age sixty-five to sixty-eight have in mind. Changing the incentive structures of private and public pension systems will not be costless. However, what should be kept firmly in the minds of policymakers is the alternative of doing nothing. The trend toward early retirement has been one of the more massive social developments of the last few decades—a trend that has already cost the nation significant amounts of money in the form of the benefits paid to those early retirees and a significant decrease in the national output that their nonparticipation in the labor force has occasioned.

CHAPTER 24

The Social Security System

ON THE THIRD DAY OF EACH MONTH some 35 million green U.S. government checks are delivered to homes or deposited directly in banks across the nation. The checks, which averaged just under $300 each in 1979, represent the monthly installment in the country's largest system of transfer payments: the Social Security system. The total benefits paid out in 1979 to 22 million retired or disabled workers and 13 million dependents and survivors came to more than $104 billion. Unlike a funded pension system, in which contributions to the system are invested to pay future beneficiaries, Social Security is founded on a pay-as-you-go approach. This means that the taxes employees and employers pay into the system provide the funds to cover current payments to beneficiaries. These payments amount to more than 6 percent of the total disposable income of individuals in the United States.

Transfers of income through the Social Security system fulfill an implicit contract between younger people currently in the active work force and people no longer working. This intergenerational compact has been in effect since 1940, when the first person to qualify for Social Security benefits retired. Now the financial soundness of the contract is in question. Indeed, for much of last year the country was given to believe the Social Security system faced imminent bankruptcy. It did not, but in the absence of remedial actions taken by Congress in the fall it would have developed a serious cash flow problem in the next year or so. Nevertheless, the cash flow problem was a manifestation of an underlying imbalance between revenues and expenditures. The success of the remedy for the immediate difficulty should not divert attention from the root causes of the imbalance and the long-term need for a thorough reform of the system.

The sources of the difficulties can readily be identified. Since Social Security is a pay-as-you-go system, the taxes paid by employees and employers in, say, 1950 provided the cash for 1950s disbursements to beneficiaries, and this year's tax receipts will pay this year's benefits. Such a system is at the mercy of economic and demographic forces. For a long time those forces worked to the advantage of the system. As the U.S. economy expanded, employment increased and wages at least kept up with inflation; a high birth rate (which peaked during the baby boom of the 1950s) and a rise in women's employment brought into the labor force many more new workers than were lost through retirement. As a result income from payroll taxes exceeded benefit payments.

Now all of that is changing. Wages (which, together with the level of employment and the tax rate, determine payroll-tax receipts) have been lagging behind inflation while benefits (which are price-indexed) are protected, even overprotected. What is more important in the long run, lower fertility and greater longevity are changing the age structure of the U.S. population, increasing the number of potential beneficiaries faster than the number of workers who will be asked to support them. An eighteen-year-old who enters covered employment today is not scheduled to retire until the decade of the 2020s; the system may have to provide benefits for him and his survivors until the 2040s. As one analyst put it, 85 percent of those who will receive benefits in the next 75 years are alive today; 96 percent of all Social Security benefits to be paid during the next 75 years will go to people who are alive today; 99 percent of the payroll taxes to be paid in the next 25 years and 81 percent of the taxes to be paid in the next 50 years will be paid by people alive today.

Congress has no option but to consider how it is going to cover the liabilities it is assuming today. Before the year 2010 the baby boom cohorts will begin to retire. We therefore have some thirty years in which to restructure the Social Security system.

The United States came late to the idea that people should look to the central government to protect an individual against the loss of income as a result of age or disability and to provide for his dependents in the event of his death. Germany had established a government-sponsored pension program in 1889, the United Kingdom in 1908, and France in 1910. The Social Security Act was passed in 1935, in the heyday of the New Deal. President Roosevelt decided (over the objections of some advisers) to limit coverage at first to workers in industry and commerce and to limit their benefits to cash payments after they stopped working at the age of sixty-five, a retirement age chosen with less than full deliberation. It was generally understood, however, that the system would subsequently be broadened. Even before the first benefit checks were issued Congress amended the law to provide benefits for the aged wife and the children of a retired worker and to the widow and young children of a covered worker on his death.

Two major programs were grafted onto the original system. In 1956 disability insurance was added for covered workers who become unable to work because of sickness or injury. In 1965 Medicare was added. It has two components: hospital insurance and supplementary medical insurance, which help patients to cover physicians' charges. The original nucleus of the Social Security system is formally called Old Age and Survivors' Insurance (OASI). When disability insurance is included, the program is designated OASDI, and with hospital insurance OASDHI. All these programs are financed by payroll taxes. Supplementary medical insurance is funded separately. It is an optional program, although most Medicare beneficaries elect to participate in it; premiums paid by the beneficiaries now cover 30 percent of the cost and the remainder is paid from the general revenues of the federal government.

About 90 percent of all currently employed people are covered by the system. They are subject to a payroll tax (now 6.7 percent of their wages up to $32,400), which is matched by a tax paid by employers. A large proportion of the more than 8 million self-employed people are covered; they pay 75 percent of the combined employee-employer rate. The largest category of people not covered by Social Security are government employees, for whom there are sixty-eight federal retirement plans and thousands of other plans for employees of state and local governments. Workers in some nonprofit institutions are also not covered.

From its inception the Social Security system was designed to meet two conflicting objectives. The basic intention was to establish a compulsory system of mandated contributions that would provide income after retirement. In keeping with a national predilection for "paying one's own way" and to gain broad public support, the benefits were to be related to the amount of "contributions." The more tax money that was paid by a worker, the higher his benefits would be at retirement.

Another intention, however, was to ensure that even people who had earned low wages would have enough income in old age to meet their basic needs. That could not be accomplished if benefits were directly proportional to tax payments; the benefit-to-tax ratio had to be skewed in favor of low-wage earners. Today the average unmarried male worker who retired in 1979 after having earned wages at the maximum taxable level will have received by the time of his death 4.97 times as much in benefits as he paid in taxes; the ratio of total benefits to total taxes for an unmarried low earner is 7.07 for men and 8.82 for women. For a retired person with a dependent spouse the benefit-to-tax ratio rises to 9.19 for a maximum earner and 13.06 for a minimum earner. What has made such high ratios possible, of course, is the pay-as-you-go scheme, combined with the economic and demographic forces I mentioned earlier. (It is often pointed out, incidentally, that the Social Security tax is regressive: Not only is the tax rate the same at all income levels but also the fraction of the income on which the tax is paid is larger for a low earner than it is for a high earner. On the benefit side, however, the system is clearly progressive: it favors low earners.)

A retiring worker's benefit is based on his earnings in jobs subject to the payroll tax, except that for years when the earnings were higher than the maximum amount taxed, only that maximum is included. To calculate the benefit the earnings are first adjusted for the increase in wage levels since the money was earned. After a certain number of lowest-pay years are excluded, the wage-indexed annual earnings up to age sixty-two for retiring workers are divided by 12 and averaged. Then a benefit formula is applied to the average indexed monthly earnings to determine the "primary insurance amount" (PIA). The formula is complex, but in essence what it does is convert successively higher increments of earnings into the PIA at successively lower percentages. Thus the benefit for a low-wage worker is a larger percentage of his average wage than the benefit for a high-income worker is. That overall percentage is called the replacement rate. It ranges from almost 70 percent for the lowest-wage earners to about 33 percent for someone who has earned the maximum taxable wage each year; the average replacement rate is 40 to 50 percent. The PIA is the benefit for a retired sixty-five-year-old worker without dependents. It is adjusted if he retires before or after sixty-five or if he has a spouse or dependent children.

To the extent that Social Security is considered a social insurance plan, people who contribute to it are entitled to draw benefits. The concept of entitlement has protected Social Security from political attack (as President Roosevelt foresaw it would); it has also discouraged any reduction in benefits once they are granted. (It seems to me, however, that the high ratio of benefits to tax payments argues against the idea that any reduction in benefits would constitute a breach of faith with those who have been paying the tax, particularly if the adjustment is made after due warning.)

The concept of the system as contributory insurance has been reinforced by the decision to rely exclusively on the payroll tax as the source of revenue to pay OASDHI benefits. Most of the planners of the system assumed that in time there would be partial recourse to general revenues. They had in mind an eventual three-way division, characteristic of most European pension systems, in which employees, employers, and the central government each contribute a third of the necessary funds. The direct linkage between taxes and benefits has helped Congress resist pressure to raise benefits without consideration of how they would be financed.

Social Security cannot be discussed without attention to other measures intended to provide income maintenance. The same motives that led the federal government to pass the Social Security Act led to the establishment of various programs providing cash or other benefits for people whose income is too low to meet their basic needs. Whereas Social Security benefits are paid regardless of need to all qualified workers whose earnings have been taxed, most other public programs are means-tested: Benefits go only to those who have a demonstrated need.

The means-tested programs began modestly in the 1930s, when the federal government joined with the states to give aid to families with dependent children (AFDC), which still accounts for the bulk of what is referred to as welfare payments. Assistance was also provided for the blind and later for disabled and needy old people excluded from or not adequately supported by Social Security; in the early 1970s the federal government assumed responsibility for these groups with the Supplemental Security Income program. In 1965 the joint federal-state Medicaid program was established for people on welfare and for others defined by each state as medically needy. Other in-kind programs aim to provide adequate nutrition (food stamps and other assistance) and housing (rent subsidies) for low-income people. In 1979 the total federal outlay for means-tested programs was $35 billion, compared with the total outlay for OASDI of $104 billion.

In spite of the country's commitment to rely on social insurance to cover the basic needs of those unable to work because of age or disability, more than two million OASDI recipients in 1979 needed supplemental income. When all income from all sources, including Social Security and means-tested programs, cash as well as in-kind, are taken into account, no more than 3 or 4 percent of the elderly fall below the poverty line. About a third of the elderly, however, are not much above that line. Of course, Social Security benefits were never meant to be the sole source of income for older people. Most aged families with a satisfactory standard of living receive less than half of their income from OASDI benefits; they rely also, in different proportions at different income levels, on continued earnings by family members, on savings and on private pensions.

Private pension systems antedated the establishment of Social Security, although they became a significant factor only during and after World War II. Between 1950 and 1975 the number of workers covered by private plans grew from 9.8 to 30.3 million, the number of monthly beneficiaries from 450,000 to more than seven million and annual benefit payments from $370 million to $14.8 billion. In 1979 almost two-thirds of all male workers and half of all female workers were covered by private plans. Nevertheless, in 1980 such plans accounted for only 14 percent of all retirement, disability and survivors' benefits; 78 percent came from Social Security and other federal retirement systems, and 8 percent came from state and local systems.

The fundamental importance of the Social Security system is clear. It has often been stated (and it is probably true) that the system is the government's most successful social program. It is all the more imperative, then, that the system be kept financially sound.

The cash-flow crisis that was imminent last fall affected only one part of the OASDHI system. Under current law benefits for each Social Security program can be paid only from the specific trust fund for that program. It is the OASI fund that is in trouble. At the beginning of 1960 the money in that fund amounted to 195 percent of the total outlay for 1960; last October 1 (at the beginning of the 1982 fiscal year) the balance was down to 14 percent of the estimated expenditure for 1982. The Congressional Budget Office has a rule of thumb: the starting balance each year must be at least 9 percent of the year's expected outlay in order to cover benefits paid early in the fiscal year, before current payroll-tax money is collected. In the absence of congressional action the OASI balance would have fallen to less than 5 percent by next October.

The primary cause of the decline in the trust-fund balances in the 1970s was a series of three large increases in benefits: 15 percent in 1970, 10 percent in 1971 and 20 percent in 1972. In addition in 1972 the escalation of benefits was institutionalized: Congress decided that benefits should routinely be raised to match any increase of more than 3 percent per year in the Consumer Price Index. As a result, benefits have been raised every year since 1975. The increases were to be financed by raising the taxable wage base as current average wages rose. Prices outstripped wages, however; indexed benefits rose faster than the indexed wage base.

Faced with the combined effects of benefit increases, high unemployment and slow economic growth, Congress (having no inclination to alter reliance on the payroll tax and being loath to reduce benefits) enacted a series of increases in the total OASDHI tax rate in 1977. In conjunction with the rising tax base the rate increases were expected to ensure the financial stability of the system for the remainder of the century. It was not enough. Less than three years later Congress had to transfer some tax receipts from the disability-insurance fund to OASI. Then last fall it had to take emergency action again, diverting some future tax receipts from the disability and hospital-insurance funds to OASI and also allowing for the possibility of interfund borrowing. According to projections made by the Congressional Budget Office, however, neither interfund borrowing nor even a complete merger of the trust funds will sustain the system for long. By the beginning of fiscal year 1985, the combined balance for all three funds will fall below 9 percent of expected expenditures.

What then? Last February the Congressional Budget Office identified a number of alternatives that in various combinations could carry the system through the 1980s. For example, many economists now think cost-of-living increases tend to overcompensate for inflation and that they could be modified. The minimum benefit, which increases the payment that would otherwise be received by certain very low earners, could be eliminated. Congress has already eliminated the lump sum death benefit and special benefits for dependent students.

The Budget Office has also suggested a number of ways to increase revenue, such as allowing the system to borrow from the U.S. Treasury, accelerating scheduled tax increases, raising the tax base to include all earnings, and raising the self-employment tax. Hospital benefits might be paid in full or in part with money from specifically earmarked income tax receipts so that the hospital-care payroll tax could be allocated to OASDI. Congress could consider foregoing some future income-tax cuts and instead allocating some portion of any proposed cut to the Social Security trust funds. Others have suggested that half of each benefit payment should be subject to the income tax: the half financed by employers' contributions, on which no tax was ever paid. Although beneficiaries with low incomes would not pay the tax, the yield would still be about $4.5 billion per year.

Given all these options, it seems most unlikely that the system will fail to meet its obligations in the next few years. Combined with the action already taken by Congress, adding only 0.5 percent to the total payroll tax rate would right the balance between revenues and expenditures unless the economy goes into a long decline.

The real challenge to Social Security lies in the future. The proportion of the U.S. population sixty-five years old and older has been growing (from 9.2 percent in 1960 to 11.2 percent last year) and will continue to grow (to an estimated 12.2 percent in the year 2000). Retired people and their spouses are living longer: in 1950 the average life expectancy at sixty-five was another thirteen years for men and fifteen years for women, whereas in 1980 it reached fifteen years for men and twenty years for women. The key factor in determining the financial integrity of the Social Security system is the relation between the number of workers paying taxes and the number of retired workers, dependents and survivors entitled to benefits. In 1945 there were fifty workers paying taxes to support current payments to each beneficiary; now each beneficiary is supported by about three workers, and in 2035 the ratio may be less than two taxpayers per beneficiary.

The long-term outlook has been appraised by the secretaries of Health and Human Services, Labor, and the Treasury, who serve as the trustees of the Social Security system. In their 1980 report they estimated the average annual balance of revenue and expenditures for the next seventy-five years, assuming that there will be no change in the currently prescribed tax base and tax rate increases. The estimates were made under three sets of assumptions: optimistic, intermediate, and pessimistic. Between 1980 and 2004, the trustees reported, the system as a whole should have an annual surplus of revenue over expenditures. In the next twenty-five-year period the intermediate projection puts the annual deficit at about $12 billion. Between 2030 and 2054 the intermediate projection puts the deficit at about $46 billion per year.

The most obvious cure for a deficit is an increase in taxes. Last March the National Commission on Social Security estimated the increase in tax revenues that would be needed to keep the system in balance, assuming that some modest benefit changes recommended by the commission are enacted by Congress. The total tax (the employee's share plus the employer's) is already scheduled to rise from 13.4 percent this year to 15.3 percent in 1990. Additional increases would be necessary, raising the total to 15.7 percent between 2005 and 2009, to 20 percent between 2020 and 2024 and to 23.8 percent between 2035 and 2039. The commission saw two dangers in allowing the payroll tax to rise to these levels: the tax bite might be too big for young workers and other workers earning low wages, and the employers' share of the tax might discourage hiring. The commission therefore recommended that the payroll tax be limited to 18 percent, with the difference between that amount and the recommended tax level being covered from general revenues.

Is a rise of nearly 80 percent in the Social Security tax burden out of the question? Clearly the commission did not think so. The social security systems in some countries of Western Europe have a payroll tax rate (employee plus employer) of between 18 and 28 percent. In return for higher taxes they supply more comprehensive benefits. Contributions for other public and private social programs can push the total levy in those countries up to 50 percent of a worker's earnings.

Before considering further the financing of the Social Security system, it should be asked whether the benefits now provided by the system are adequate. I would submit that there is room for improvement in the system, and the improvements would add to future costs. Among the conspicuous problems are the inadequacy of the present minimum benefit, inequities for women, and the ineffective response of Medicare to the health care needs of the elderly.

Every retired worker eligible for any benefits receives at least $122 per month. Those who get this minimum benefit are mainly women who worked for very low wages. In 1979 the Advisory Council on Social Security Financing and Benefits held that "single people who have worked full time at the Federal minimum wage do not now receive a benefit sufficient to keep them out of poverty." The advisory council recommended corrective action. President Reagan went in the opposite direction: He recommended eliminating the minimum benefit on the ground that it is a windfall for people who have retired on other federal pensions but who also barely qualify for Social Security. Congress went along with the president in the first round of budget cutting but restored the minimum payment last fall. It remains inadequate.

When the Social Security system was established, it dealt with women primarily as dependents or survivors. That has changed with the entry of large numbers of women into the work force. By 1978 two in every five female beneficiaries were receiving benefits by reason of their own work, not as a consequence of their marriage; the proportion is likely to increase to 80 percent for women who reach sixty-five in 2000. Women workers pay the same payroll tax as men, but many women receive higher benefits as dependents than as retired workers because the replacement rate is skewed to their disadvantage. One perverse result is that a sixty-five-year-old couple get 17 percent more in benefits if only one of them was a wage earner than they do if both earned equal amounts. If a woman is divorced before the tenth year of a marriage, she receives no benefits when her former husband retires; if the marriage lasts for ten years, she receives the full spouse's benefit.

One proposal that might lead to fairer treatment of women is an earnings-sharing plan. Benefits would be based on the combined earnings of the couple, whether or not both had worked and regardless of how much each had earned and therefore paid in Social Security taxes. In effect all earnings would be vested equally in the husband and the wife. The advisory council favors moving toward such a plan but suggests that more study is needed to be sure dependents' and survivors' benefits now accruing to many women are not jeopardized. For now the council has recommended two steps. It would allow a surviving spouse to have benefits based on the couple's combined earnings, and it would adopt a limited form of earnings sharing for divorced couples.

Medicare now covers only about 40 percent of the medical costs of the elderly. It largely covers acute hospital care and, for those who elect to buy supplementary medical insurance, physicians' services. Each year a considerable number of older people have very large medical expenses (more than $2,500 or $3,000) that they must pay from their own funds. Much of the care required for chronic conditions is simply not covered. Medicare makes no contribution toward helping a patient remain in his own home with home nursing or attendants when he is chronically sick or feeble, and it makes no significant contribution toward paying the cost of his staying in a nursing home. In failing to support care in the patient's home or in a nursing home, Medicare encourages unnecessary hospital stays and thus runs up the country's total health care bill. In spite of these serious shortcomings, the hospital insurance tax rate will increase sharply beginning in the 1990s.

The demographic imperatives and the need for improvements in Social Security benefits provoke a series of questions. The first is: Can payroll tax increases sustain the system into the middle of the next century? A moderate increase in the tax rate is certainly feasible, and the tax could be imposed on all earnings. Because the rate is the same for both low earners and high earners, however, the tax bite would soon become too deep for some employees. As for the employer's share, there is no doubt that too high a payroll tax can inhibit employment, creating serious problems for the economy and the society; this may already have happened in some countries of Western Europe. The tax rate, then, cannot be raised indefinitely without such adverse consequences as depressing workers' wages, enlarging the off-the-record economy and decreasing the total tax revenues collected.

Is there some other way to enlarge Social Security revenues? One good opportunity, which should be pursued aggressively, is to bring into the system as many as possible of the workers in government and in nonprofit institutions who are not now included. Uncovered groups make up about 10 percent of the work force. Perhaps workers currently covered by state and local plans could not be compelled to join the system, but Congress could certainly extend coverage to all federal employees. Complex adjustments would be needed to protect the interests of such employees; the difficulties are formidable but not insurmountable. Many experts on the Social Security system advocate starting such a program of consolidation soon, arguing that no other system affords workers and their dependents as broad a range of basic benefits. The National Commission on Social Security has calculated that universal coverage would add an average of $5 billion per year to the revenues of the system over the next 75 years. Of course, it would also increase liabilities.

As for expenditures, is there any equitable way the system's future obligations might be significantly reduced? There is. A growing consensus among those who have studied the system in recent years holds that the standard age of retirement should be increased from sixty-five to sixty-eight. The change would be doubly effective in that it would augment the population of taxpayers while reducing the population of beneficiaries. It should be done only after adequate warning and gradually, perhaps at the rate of only a few months per year. The National Commission estimates that the change would save about $11 billion per year from 1980 to 2055.

The system now tends to promote early retirement. A worker can retire at sixty-two and get only 20 percent less per year than he would have received at sixty-five. As a result about three in four workers retire before they reach sixty-five. President Reagan proposed changing the early-retirement reduction to 45 percent but withdrew the plan when it met vigorous public opposition.

The increase in early retirement is paralleled by increasing unwillingness of most people to work beyond age sixty-five. Whereas one man in three and one woman in ten worked after the statutory retirement age in 1960, only one man in five and one woman in twelve does so now. This decline in labor-force participation, combined with increases in longevity, generates pressure on the system. In 1940 only 583 men per 1,000 and 687 women per 1,000 lived to be sixty-five; today the proportions have risen respectively to 711 and 839 per 1,000. Of all people sixty-five or over, fewer than a third were over 75 in 1974; by the end of the century the fraction will be close to a half.

As I indicated earlier, any increase in the retirement age would have to be phased in gradually. Rita R. Campbell of the Hoover Institution at Stanford University has suggested that allowances might be made for workers who have been employed continuously for as long as forty-five years; many private pension plans, she points out, consider the number of years worked as well as age in determining the time of retirement. Furthermore, many people have health problems that make it inadvisable for them to keep working beyond their early sixties, particularly if the job is physically demanding; the definition of disability might be modified to cover such cases.

One alternative to raising the retirement age (or perhaps a companion measure) would be to adopt a recent Swedish approach called phased retirement. Older people can choose a shortened or gradually declining work week instead of going from full-time employment to full retirement in one day.

Might it be possible to limit the increase in the obligations of the Social Security system by shifting some of the burden to alternative sources of income for retired people? The President's Commission on Pension Policy recommended that a compulsory system of private pensions be established. Employers would pay an amount equal to 3 percent of their payroll; changes in tax policy would ease the burden on small businesses. The commission also urged that the tax structure be modified in ways calculated to encourage personal saving.

There is little likelihood that a compulsory private pension plan will be approved by Congress. For one thing, there is continuing mistrust of existing private plans; although Congress attempted in 1974 to regularize such plans and expand their coverage, many workers are still left either without a pension or with a very small one. Private pension plans already cost the United States about $15 billion per year in lost tax revenues. Owners of small businesses, many of whom operate close to the margin of profitability, would oppose a compulsory plan bitterly. Effective social control over the reserves of large private pension funds is already a problem; a new program would exacerbate it. Moreover, what is the point of a new compulsory system if the present compulsory system — Social Security — can be made to work?

Many economists contend that the level of personal saving in the United States is too low and that this accounts in large part for a deficiency in capital that will have to be remedied if the country is to modernize its plant and equipment. (Martin S. Feldstein of Harvard University undertook some years ago to demonstrate that the Social Security system is directly responsible for the low level of savings, but many economists think he is wrong.) Whether or not additional saving is needed to provide adequate capital for industry (and some economists, including Thomas Juster of the University of Michigan, contest that assumption), Congress has already provided tax advantages for individuals who save for their retirement; the Keogh Plan and the individual retirement account (IRA) are two examples.

Additional tax incentives to encourage more people to save for retirement will probably be forthcoming, but only upper-income people can take full advantage of such opportunities. Any serious attempt to get middle- and low-income groups to divert more of their earnings into savings might require government subvention and protection against inflation for small savers, as is done in Germany. In any case, except for the very poor, private pensions and personal savings already contribute between a fourth and a third of the income of older people. That fraction is unlikely to be raised by more than a few percentage points. There is no alternative, then, to ensuring the financial integrity of the Social Security system so that it can provide basic income for older people.

To accomplish that, it seems to me, the following actions are needed. The Social Security system should be expanded as quickly as possible in order to provide universal coverage, which would add significantly to revenues and also broaden the range of benefits for people now outside the system. An early decision should be made to raise the retirement age gradually, probably to sixty-eight. The half of benefits that was based on income and that was never taxed should be made subject to the income tax, but only for those older people whose total income is high enough to make them liable to the tax. It must be determined what changes in Medicare would enable it to provide an acceptable level of medical care for the elderly and to do so more efficiently. The unconscionable inequities imposed on women as workers and as wives should start to be redressed. The benefits for long-service, low-wage workers, which have been adjusted in the recent past, need further adjustment to bring them above the poverty line.

The Social Security system can provide basic support for all older Americans, but only if it is not overloaded. That is why the key reform is to encourage people to work longer, thereby ensuring a comfortable income when they stop working. That is a sensible national goal, and not only for economic reasons. As the Talmud puts it: When you stop working, you are dead.

CHAPTER 25

The Elderly:
An International Perspective

AS A CONTRIBUTION TO THE WORLD ASSEMBLY ON Aging (Vienna, July 26 to August 6, 1982) the Sandoz Institute for Health and Socio-Economic Studies undertook a sixteen-nation survey on the problems of the elderly (defined as persons aged sixty and over) in consultation with the United Nations Center for Social Development and Humanitarian Affairs. The participating advanced industrial countries were Australia, the Federal Republic of Germany, France, Italy, Japan, Sweden, the United Kingdom, and the United States; the less industrialized countries included Brazil, Egypt, India, Israel, Kenya, Nigeria, the Philippines, and Poland.

Questionnaire responses were provided for each country by a small working group of three experts representing the broad areas of health, sociology, and social policy. There were two rounds of questions, the first focused on a ranking of the following problem areas—health, housing, health services and social services, family, community activities, income, work and employment, and retirement. The second round focused on the diversity of the elderly, employment, research, and political factors in policymaking.

I was invited by the Sandoz Institute to prepare an economic commentary, but it was not published initially, presumably because it was judged not congruent with the aims of the assembly. It later appeared in the *Milbank Quarterly.*

Many of the returns from the sixteen nations were downbeat because of the anticipated rapid rise in the number of the elderly during the next twenty years, the anticipated high levels of unemployment, and the presumption of slow economic growth in the future.

Although economics in its formative years had earned the sobriquet of "the dismal science" because one of its founding fathers, the Reverend Thomas Malthus, saw famine, disease, and war as the great equilibrators when population expands faster than the food supply, the gerontologists and the sociologists who answered the questionnaire appeared to be unduly pessimistic. In my view, they were extrapolating from the unsatisfactory present for too many years into the future. A moderation of inflation together with renewed economic growth and an improved employment outlook, at least in the economies of the advanced industrial nations, is surely possible, even likely, before the end of this century.

In developing my commentary, my approach was to review critically the assumptions and conclusions of the experts who contributed to the survey, to delineate realistic parameters within which future policies for older persons should be designed, and finally to make a limited number of concrete suggestions for constructive action in the public and private domains that hold promise of contributing to the well-being of older persons. Each of the respondent nations is unique, but this analysis will proceed with a simplified typology in which the developed nations are distinguished from the faster and slower growing less-developed countries (LDCs).

THE PRESENT UNFAVORABLE ECONOMIC ENVIRONMENT

The respondents from the developed countries noted the following trends that threaten the viability of existing economic supports for the elderly and that will impede efforts to improve their circumstances in the future. The combination of slow economic growth, high inflation, and high unemployment represents a triple threat. Slow economic growth means there will be only a small surplus available for improving the well-being of the total population, including the elderly, and in some years there will be no surplus. Under such strained circumstances, one cannot expect a society to use its small surplus solely to improve the well-being of the elderly to the exclusion of competing groups such as children, minorities, families with low incomes, and especially the working population who are producing the surplus and require incentives to increase it.

Continuing inflation is the second serious threat. On the one hand, inflation increases the difficulties national pension schemes face in their efforts to remain solvent, by distorting the rates of savings, interest, and investments. On the other hand, inflation erodes the value of private pensions. If employers act to index these private plans, the costs to them through raising wage and benefit payments can result in the loss of future markets and jobs. If the costs of indexing private plans are absorbed in the national budget, taxes will increase, the nation's competitive position will be weakened, and income and employment are likely to decline. High inflation also leads to the erosion of personal savings that individuals accumulate during their working years to help them through their later years when they are no longer employed.

The respondents were also pessimistic about the future trends in employment. The combination of slow growth and high inflation are almost certain precursors of a low level of new job creation. Slow growth of new jobs at a time when more young people and women are entering the labor force points to continuing high unemployment. Moreover, automation is likely to result in displacing considerable numbers who currently hold jobs and further job losses will follow as additional manufacturing jobs are lost as a result of plant relocations from developed to less-developed nations. Since an inadequate number of jobs will be available for persons of prime working age, older workers will face increasing pressures to retire early.

A second set of adverse economic developments identified by the respondents included: the increasing costs of health care; the growing determination of governments to bring and to keep their budgets under control; and the difficulties of finding sources of funding in the private sector to provide improved services for the elderly as well as for other priority groups who need assistance.

The respondents from the developing nations cited many of these same factors: the difficulties of assuring the financial viability of embryonic pension schemes in periods of high-level inflation; the growing imbalance between a rapidly increasing work force and a slower growth of employment opportunities; the intensified pressures to keep government expenditures under control. The developing nations called attention to additional problems to which they were particularly vulnerable, such as the large-scale inflow of the rural population into crowded urban centers; the erosion of the extended family, which had formerly provided for its elderly members; the acute competition for limited resources between economic development goals; and the maintenance needs of many groups, including the elderly.

A More Optimistic Economic Scenario

No economist will minimize the dangers of a prolonged period of high inflation such as has characterized most of the developed and developing nations since the early 1970s. Governments are now increasing efforts to contain and reduce such inflationary pressures. With a reasonable admixture of continuing fiscal restraint and the absence of renewed oil or other raw material shortages, inflation could by 1990 represent a considerably reduced threat.

The assumption of continued slow economic growth can also be challenged. Included in the sixteen nations surveyed are several that have been able to sustain high or satisfactory levels of growth in recent years even though most nations have experienced a slowing in their previous rates of growth. For the developed nations, the 1950s and 1960s represented an epoch of above-average growth because of the rapid rebuilding of capital plant and equipment after many years of war and economic stagnation. For many LDCs these decades saw rapid growth aided and abetted by much enlarged international lending, following their achievement of national independence. After two decades of rapid expansion, some slowdown was to be anticipated. However, the attraction of low-cost labor that has proved its ability to cope with modern technology points to an eventual quickening of investment in LDCs once the world's economy again begins to expand.

Attention must also be called to a subtle factor embedded in the ways in which growth is measured. Some economists believe that the actual growth in both developed and developing economies may be considerably higher than the official statistics suggest. In developed economies we have seen a rapid growth in tax evasion, illicit and illegal activities, as well as an expansion in noncash transfers as when dentists and accountants exchange professional services. In developing countries the shifting boundaries between the money and the nonmoney economies also create doubts about how well the statistical reporting systems provide a true reflection of real growth in employment and income.

There are also good reasons to question the forecasts of respondents from the developed nations about continuing weaknesses in the job market resulting from the continued rapid growth of the labor force. The odds favor increasing pressure from the side of adult women who are currently not working. More and more of them are likely to seek paid employment and to increase their years in active employment. But the situation is different with respect to young persons. In some developed nations the surge in the numbers of youth has already crested and in other countries the crest will occur shortly. Manpower planners in Germany are presently designing policies that will help compensate for the substantial decline in the absolute number of young people who will be entering the labor force some years hence. In the United States the number of young people reaching the working age of sixteen to twenty-four will decline by 15 percent in the 1980s.

Technological advances usually cut both ways. Along with the benefits come dislocations; some workers lose their jobs, and others find their skills obsolescent. But over the long pull, technological advances—a substitute term for automation—are likely to expand the total number of jobs and raise the skill levels of the labor force. That is the only reasonable deduction to be extracted from the record of the last two centuries.

The developed regions of the world do face a challenge from the loss of jobs incident to the relocation of manufacturing plants to the less-developed nations. But these job losses in manufacturing are the beginning, not the end, of this important transition. The evidence favors Adam Smith's insight that a broadening of the market results in expansion, not contraction, of both income and employment for all who trade.

Two developments—the expansion of the service sector and increased bilateral and multilateral trade—have, in the past, helped to cushion the relative decline in manufacturing employment that has been occurring in most developed nations, and there is every reason to assume that these trends will continue.

In the more rapidly growing developing countries—such as Brazil, Israel, and Nigeria—continuing inflation, some slowing in economic growth, and a surplus of job seekers represent threats to large-scale improvements in the standard of living, including better prospects for the elderly. But these potential threats are not to be equated with certain evils of stagnation and high unemployment and reduced funding for the elderly. If developed nations experience an easing of inflationary pressures, the same forces will contribute to moderating inflation in the developing world. Many of the developing countries should be able to continue to make good progress because of, among other reasons, the expansion of manufacturing incident to the transfer of plants from the developed nations. However, even if several LDCs are able to achieve a continuing satisfactory rate of growth, they will not be able to provide regular jobs for all of the new entrants into their labor forces, because of the larger numbers of young people who will reach working age; the many rural migrants who are relocating to the cities to find jobs; and the increased numbers of urban women who want to work outside their homes. If past is prelude, however, these countries will also face selective shortages of skilled workers even while they are encountering difficulty in absorbing the large numbers of unskilled workers.

The prospect is definitely bleaker for the LDCs at the lower levels of income because even a much reduced inflation rate, a satisfactory economic growth rate, and reasonable gains in total employment will fall far short of providing adequate jobs and income for their rapidly increasing populations.

It may be that the survey respondents will be proved right by events and their bleak forecasts confirmed. But I, for one, see little basis in history or in theory to accept their pessimistic forecasts. The human and material bases for continuing gains in productivity, particularly if assisted by reductions in the rates of population growth, remain strong.

At the beginning of the 1970s, a group of futurologists, who came to be known as the Club of Rome, put forward a number of highly pessimistic forecasts about the interaction of population, raw material, and economic trends, which suggested that the world would soon start becoming poorer, not richer. They and their forecasts have been discredited. Only a major collapse of the international financial system and a long-term shrinkage in world trade would restore their credibility.

KEY ELEMENTS IN IMPROVING THE POSITION OF THE ELDERLY

The survey focused on obtaining critical information on a selected number of key elements including income, work, medical services, and social services, which I will address seriatim, primarily with respect to the advanced industrial countries with occasional specification for the developing countries as well.

Income

If older persons want to enjoy a standard of living in retirement approaching the level they enjoyed in the years preceding retirement, they must continue to work past the age of sixty, and the economies of which they are a part must be restructured to make room for them. No national pension plan will be able to transfer from the working population the income required to keep retirees at a desirable standard of living for twenty or more years. Once the different age groups within a population are no longer growing or declining, active workers would have to pay over a third of their annual income solely to cover this one societal obligation. The financial pressures that currently afflict most national pension plans are a warning of worse trouble ahead, when the ratio of contributors to beneficiaries will decline as the longevity of the beneficiaries continues to increase and the proportion of active workers diminishes.

The pension enthusiasts will question this alarmist conclusion and point to the prospects of encouraging more personal savings (easier to do in a noninflationary period) and more private pensions (costly to fund and even more costly to index for inflation) to relieve some of the pressures on the public treasury. I see relatively limited scope for either or both of these alternatives to provide significant amounts of income to retirees without squeezing the working population. The simple fact is that income for retirees can only come out of current production. Only the cost of housing can be covered from earlier production and this disregards the costs of maintenance, heating, and taxes. While a higher rate of savings on the part of employed workers can broaden and deepen the nation's capital stock above what it would otherwise have been, and thereby increase its future GNP, the claims of workers when they retire can be covered only from current output.

Work

The only prospect for large numbers of older persons to enjoy a satisfactory level of income is to remain at work as long as possible and thereby reduce the years when they are dependent on pensions. But the survey respondents are pessimistic about jobs, full-time or part-time, that will be available to older workers if by choice or necessity they want to work until their late sixties or even into their seventies. True, if the current high levels of unemployment were to continue over many years, the prospects of older persons to continue to work would not be bright. But if the unemployment rate were to decline, the prospect for older workers could improve quickly and dramatically. Their employability would be assisted by their improved health, the lowered demand for physical labor as the economy shifts from manufacturing to service industries, and the gains that will accrue to employers from retaining experienced workers knowledgeable about the ways in which their organizations operate.

Since lack of skill, experience, and knowhow are among the constraints that impede the rate at which the modern sectors of developing countries are able to grow, one can stipulate that they too should encourage the productive members among their older workers to remain at their jobs as long as possible. Since larger employers using modern machines in developing nations are less constrained by government regulations and trade union agreements, they should face fewer difficulties in retaining such older workers.

Medical Care

The steadily growing sophistication of modern medicine expands the possibility for new useful interventions, many of which, such as open-heart surgery, carry a steep price and often an uncertain outcome. When it comes to the provision of medical care for the elderly, developed countries confront difficult decisions. For example, because of economic stringency the United Kingdom has found it necessary to deny access to the elderly to various costly procedures and other, more affluent countries are under increasing financial pressure to place limits on medical interventions on behalf of persons whose prospects of regaining functionality are problematic.

Broad access to improved medical care is clearly one of the ways in which developed nations can continue to contribute to the well-being of the elderly in the decades ahead. But an open-ended commitment to use all possible curative interventions on all older patients, without reference to their prospects of regaining functionality for self-care and work should be reassessed in the best interests of both society and the elderly.

Developing nations should profit from the experience of the more affluent countries and proceed cautiously in developing sophisticated hospitals and staff and in committing themselves prematurely to broad entitlement programs for costly inpatient care not only for the elderly but for all their citizens. Improved health care has a significant role to play in economic growth and development but the investment should be focused primarily on classic preventive health measures, targeted in the first instance on children and young adults, including improved water supplies, the suppression of malaria and other scourges, immunization, family planning, and improved nutrition. To the extent that these interventions succeed, future cohorts of elderly persons will be better off.

Social Services

The fourth parameter is shorthand for a wide range of supports that older persons require or can utilize. These involve assistance in the maintenance of family ties, living in one's own home, participating in social and community affairs, admission when necessary to a nursing home, and much more. The guiding principle should be caution on the part of governments in designing programs that speed the shifting of responsibility from the family to the state, both because of the burdens that such shifts place on the public treasury and the further difficulty for the bureaucracy in delivering human services of high quality. The introduction of social service programs for the elderly has been limited to the more affluent of the developed nations. The developing nations, with small resources, cannot afford to follow in the footsteps of the affluent. Their governments must move circumspectly in taking on responsibilities that have long been carried by family and community. When conventional family ties are cut, as when migrants move from the countryside to the city, some modest new public services for the elderly may well be needed.

IN SEARCH OF POLICY

What policy directions for enhancing the well-being of older persons in both developed and developing nations can be extracted from the foregoing analysis? The earlier analysis suggested that the present difficulties facing the world economy—reflected in slowed growth, continuing inflation, and excessive unemployment—are likely to be reversed, and that many current economic difficulties will be eased. Even if this optimistic forecast proves to be more accurate than the pessimistic extrapolations that now dominate the thinking of most academicians and politicians, it does not mean that it will be easy to improve the status of the elderly. The most that can be claimed is that the environment in which future solutions are developed will be more propitious.

Before considering the specific recommendations that the leaders of developed and developing countries should weigh in designing new and improved policies to improve the welfare of older persons, I will review briefly a series of propositions that have wide currency.

- *Additional income at the command of retired persons will help to stimulate the economy and create jobs.* It is true that additional disposable income at the command of the elderly has created new demands and, therefore, new jobs, ranging from the development of retirement communities to the manufacture of prepared foods. The critical question is whether the additional income of the elderly comes from transfers from younger workers in a stagnant economy, in which case the latter will have less to spend, or from an expanding economy in which both workers and the retired are better off. The best case of all would be that in which the economy expands to a point where the heretofore unused labor of the elderly would be in demand and their increased income would stem from additional wages and salaries, not from income transfers.

- *Additional jobs for the elderly can be specified and governments can create them.* It is clear that as the elderly have more income they spend it on high priority goods and services, from nursing home care to recreation. It does not follow, however, that if governments decide to increase their outlays for improved housing, health, and other services for the elderly, this would be beneficial to the economy. Money spent on the elderly must be raised by taxes that reduce the disposable income of other groups, so that jobs created to serve the elderly will, in large measure, be at the expense of jobs that would have been created to provide goods and services for children or young adults.

- *It is necessary and desirable to look to international arrangements and agreements among nations to "balance out" benefit levels for the elderly.* International trade has been expanding for the last two centuries to the advantage of both high- and low-wage countries. Because fringe benefits amount to between 35 and 50 percent of the basic wage, some developed nations are finding it increasingly difficult to compete with low-wage countries. But we must remember that consumers in high-wage countries are able to buy imported goods at lower prices. Large differentials in the labor supplies and cost structures of nation states will increase the mobility of both firms and workers, but it is doubtful that recourse to government interventions will lead to gains in efficiency or equity. With regard to benefits for the elderly, it is unlikely that they will reach a level where, on their own, they will have a seriously distorting influence on the international competitiveness of high-income, high-wage nations.

- *Lessons can be drawn from the experience of developed countries with the highest proportions of elderly persons.* In several west European countries—such as the United Kingdom, France, Italy, the Federal Republic of Germany, and Sweden—about 1 in 5 of the population is sixty or older. Moreover, estimates by the United Nations point to substantial gains in the over-sixty population by the year 2000. The optimists point to the success that the aforementioned countries have had in supporting so many elderly persons, but the pessimists point to the vulnerable financial condition of their social security and health care systems. Policymakers should refrain from attempting to improve benefits for the elderly on the ground that enlarged expenditures will stimulate their economies, that international agreements will protect their countries from loss of competitiveness, or that their experience up to the present in supporting the elderly provides assurance of the long-term future solvency of their social security systems.

A more cautious approach would aim to increase the employment opportunities for the elderly, to constrain high-cost medical interventions that offer little promise of adding to the individual's functionality, and to provide more and better social services via family and community.

For more developed nations, the following agenda requires early assessment and action:

- Hard-nosed appraisals of the financial positions of the national pension plans well into the twenty-first century under at least two sets of assumptions — optimistic and pessimistic — which take into account such matters as future rates of inflation, unemployment, demographic trends, and labor force participation. If these prospective assessments reveal a growing gap between current commitments and potential resources of the pension system, politicians must explore alternative ways of closing the gap and initiate early corrective action.

- In several developed countries the marginal tax rate is already so high as to be dysfunctional. In others, there may be some room for selective new taxes from which part of the revenues might be used to raise benefits for the elderly, if analysis demonstrated that they were seriously in need. But the preferred approach, as indicated later, would be to reduce the pressures on the pension systems by encouraging or requiring older persons, if they are capable, of continuing to work longer.

- In many countries, the national pension plans have accumulated additional obligations, some of which violate the principles of social insurance. As part of the process of shoring up the financial viability of national pension plans, such additions should not be grafted onto insurance plans.

- Many west European countries that are faced with rising unemployment have resorted to special measures aimed at reducing the retirement age to sixty or even earlier in the hope and expectation that this action will open additional opportunities for young persons to find jobs. These policies should be reappraised in light of the following: Young workers frequently cannot substitute for older skilled workers, surely not on a one-for-one basis; since more and more jobs are in the service sector, most men and women entering their sixties will not find continuing to work a strain on their health or capabilities; since longer periods are spent in skill acquisition both prior to initial employ-

ment and during an active career, the payout period should be
lengthened; when expectations of early retirement become entrenched, they are difficult to change; the costs of maintaining
people twenty or more years in retirement status are prohibitive.

- The United States recently revised its Social Security System to
raise the future age of retirement from sixty-five to sixty-seven,
and to increase the monetary incentives for people to remain at
work beyond sixty-five.

- Reductions in the age of retirement will not bring the labor
markets of countries with 8 to 13 percent unemployment into
balance. Such approaches are doomed to failure and involve
high, long-term costs. In an expanding economy, which alone
can provide new jobs for the excessive number of unemployed
persons and new entrants into the labor force, further gradual
reductions in hours per week and per year hold some promise of
contributing to long-term equilibrium. So too does paid time off
for continuing education and training, which should result in
higher productivity over an increased number of years. Another
adjustment device that can contribute to a more balanced labor
market is an increase in the number of less than full-time jobs.
When both spouses work, many couples prefer to have one or
both work less than full time.

- Employers should reassess policies and programs that currently
contribute to forcing older workers out of jobs rather than encouraging them to remain.

- The Swedish approach, whereby workers have an opportunity to
continue working part time while drawing a part of their pensions is one of a number of innovations that commend themselves to study and replication. Employers in the United States
are calling back retired employees to help out at peak seasons,
but the heavy "penalties" (recently reduced) for earning more
than the maximum allowed under the Social Security system
currently limit this approach.

- There are many private and public policies that require modification if older persons are to be encouraged to remain at work.
These policies involve such matters as group insurance rates,
taxes, and future benefits from public and private pension plans
for workers who stay on their jobs.

- Persons approach retirement in different health status, with different occupational skills, energy levels, income, prospects for
employment. The fact that some may no longer be capable of
working in their long-term occupations—coal miner, steelworker,
lumberjack, and other physically demanding assignments—should

not be used as an excuse to retain the current early retirement systems. Rather, national pension plans should be modified so that spent workers can retire without encouraging all others to stop working prematurely.

- We need an early dialogue among political leaders, the medical profession and other providers of health care, and the public about the range and depth of medical interventions for the elderly that the public treasury is expected to underwrite. A developed nation can surely afford to pay for basic ambulatory, inpatient, and home care for its older citizens, even though it may decide to draw the line at costly therapeutic interventions of questionable efficacy. A major frontier, where sizable economies and little loss of welfare (possibly even some gains) may be found, is in restricting major medical interventions among terminal patients.

- In most developed countries the feeble aged are institutionalized largely at public expense or continue to be cared for by relatives and friends at home or in the community where they have long lived. The United Kingdom probably has the most to teach other countries about caring for the feeble aged in their own homes and using public funds to supplement family resources by paying for a housekeeper when the family needs relief.

- More effort should be directed to developing programs whereby the functioning elderly can be employed part time or full time in assisting the home-bound. The costs of this kind of assistance are likely to be far below the costs of institutionalization. In the United States, large and small for-profit organizations are rapidly expanding personal services to the aged, most of whom prefer to remain in their own homes. The fact that more and more women are working and that increasing numbers of older persons live alone makes it necessary to look more to paid workers to provide essential services for the feeble elderly. There is also a continuing role for volunteers to help care for friends and neighbors.

Surprisingly, the principles underlying these suggestions require only slight modification to fit the agendas of developing nations. In brief:

- Developing nations should delay establishing national pension systems until they are well along on the path of economic development. Otherwise, deflection of limited tax revenues to improve the condition of the elderly can result in making everybody poorer.

- If and when they establish national pension schemes, LDCs should attempt to keep them actuarially sound and avoid encumbering them with desirable but costly benefits that should be dealt with outside the insurance framework, by government programs that are means-tested.

- LDCs should encourage public and private policies that aim at keeping older workers in their jobs as long as they are capable of performing effectively.
- LDCs should avoid sweeping commitments to provide sophisticated therapeutic care for all the population, including the elderly. Rather, they should use their limited health care budgets primarily to improve the health of the present and future working populations.
- LDCs should encourage the family, religious orders, and the local community to continue to provide services that they have traditionally made available to the elderly. When they are able to direct some public funds to the support of the elderly, they should provide them through these established instrumentalities.

One concluding observation: The developed countries have commitments to the elderly which, even under our optimistic forecasts, are not likely to be fulfilled, surely not in their entirety. But the proposed shift in policy and tactics from income maintenance to work may be less disturbing than most experts suspect. The well-being of the elderly does not rest on a prolonged period of check-collecting and check-cashing, but on active engagement in a world where work remains the principal arena of social involvement. Those who can work should be encouraged to do so. They will be better off, and society will be better off. If those who can work do so, the developed nations will be able to support those who cannot. The governments of the developing nations have little option but to leave most of the responsibility for the elderly with their families until such time that their annual economic surplus permits some transfer of responsibility to the state. As more and more of the developing nations increase their national and per capita income, they will surely want to devote some of their surplus to making life better for their elderly citizens, who will have only a relatively short time to enjoy the economic and social gains these nations are achieving.

PART VI

Blacks

THE FOUR SELECTIONS SPAN ALMOST A THIRD OF A CEN-
TURY, from the early 1950s, when I first became interested in the
experiences of blacks in the Armed Services, to the investigations I
undertook recently with two black graduate students to get a firsthand
picture of what young black students thought of their schools in Harlem
in New York City.

It should be no surprise that a group that has been discriminated
against for as long and as severely as blacks is likely to reflect the
consequences of this by poor performance when measured against others
who have had more opportunity. That is surely demonstrated in the
chapter on "The Negro Soldier" in *The Negro Potential*. It was, however,
my knowledge of these deficits that led me to look more broadly at the
waste of blacks' potential. Chapter 26 is the final chapter in *The Negro
Potential*, which was published in 1956.

The reasons that U.S. democracy has been unable and unwilling to
assimilate blacks in the same fashion that it had succeeded in assimilating
all other groups except American Indians, was a subject that engaged
and held my intellectual curiosity for many years. Finally, in the early
1960s, I was able to find sufficient time to pursue this issue and, with the

help of my colleague Alfred Eichner, to publish *The Troublesome Presence: American Democracy and the Negro* in 1964. Chapter 27 is based on what we learned and reported on in our full-length volume.

One of the most devastating consequences of uncontrolled prejudice is that all members of a group are seen in stereotypical fashion. By the mid-1960s, in fact much earlier, it was clear that not all blacks were poor, poorly educated, holding poor jobs. A significant and growing proportion had joined or were joining the middle class. To explore this facet of the changing role of blacks in the United States, we studied the career goals of middle-class black males (Chapter 28). Brief reference should be made to two related studies that are not included here: One, sponsored by the U.S. Commission on Civil Rights, was entitled "Mobility in the Negro Community" (1969); the second, undertaken in collaboration with the U.S. Air Force, was entitled *Desegregation and Career Goals: Children of Air Force Families.*

I consider Chapter 29 one of the most important and richest in this book. It makes readily available important case materials and raises a number of critically important policy issues about ghetto schools.

CHAPTER 26

The Negro Potential

IT IS NEVER SENSIBLE OR RIGHT for a nation to waste valuable human resources through failure to develop or utilize them. The consequences of such waste are a lower level of national strength and individual well-being.

In a time of international tension, such as now confronts the United States and is likely to continue for a long period, wastage of national resources can only result in a more vulnerable security position. Moreover, the frustration and stunting of individuals who cannot develop or utilize their full capacity involves costs to the nation which transcend military strength. The outcome of the struggle between the Free World and the USSR for the minds and hearts of millions of people who are not yet committed will depend on actions, not speeches. The hungry and the downtrodden will not be taken in by propaganda barrages. Their decision will be based on what actually happens to the men, women, and children who live under the different systems. In a period of such challenge, every nation must declare for what it believes and be counted for how it acts.

Strategy For Developing Potential

A study of the more effective utilization of 15 million Negroes, roughly 10 percent of the nation's population, has significance not only within the preceding context but also because it may contribute to the shaping of a strategy for developing latent manpower potential wherever it exists. The first and perhaps most significant finding emerging from this study is that improvements in the position of the Negro occurred primarily as the direct outgrowth and consequence of forces unleashed in the market place. They were not primarily a result of alterations in our social and political thinking and behavior. It is fashionable for critics of contemporary U.S. life to point with disdain to our national preoccupation with the material aspects of life—the production of ever greater quantities of goods and the desire of so many to secure an ever larger amount of these goods. But this precise state of affairs has led to marked improvements in the position of U.S. Negroes. Their higher standard of living since 1940 has been in large part a direct outgrowth of the growing demand for labor in U.S. towns and cities. Except for this quickening of the economic pace, which has resulted in fifteen years of uninterrupted economic expansion, it is questionable indeed whether the Negro would have been able to reach his present place on the economic scale. Poverty cripples while prosperity heals. Vestiges of the suffering endured during slavery and the hardships wrought by segregation cannot be eradicated by money alone. Nevertheless, the best hope for the Negro's speedy and complete integration into U.S. society lies in the continuation of a strong and virile economy in which his labor is needed and his skills and capabilities rewarded.

Although the review of the educational preparation of the Negro pointed out significant gains during recent decades, the same figures highlighted the extent to which the education of the Negro still lags behind that of the white man. Not only does the Negro continue to remain in school for fewer years; but, even more important, the quality of his schooling is still far below that of the white child. If the Negro is to participate fully in the economy at every level instead of only at the bottom rung, his education must still undergo substantial improvements. Increasingly, a high school diploma, or a college or advanced degree, is required of those who seek one of the better positions in the economy.

The study of the Negro soldier illuminated the impact of segregation on the utilization of Negro manpower in World War II. The review of the integration that took place during the Korean hostilities pointed up the gains that followed when opportunities were broadened. Perhaps the most important lesson of the integration experience is that the manner of the change was largely responsible for its success. Only the top civilian and military leaders could assume responsibility for eliminating segregation. Once they did, many of the fears, anxieties, and uncertainties that had been diffused throughout the organization, from the non-commissioned officer to the senior theater commander, disappeared. It was no longer necessary for the individual to determine for himself the wisdom of the move or his willingness to participate in it. From the viewpoint of mobilizing support for speedy action, hierarchical systems such as the armed services are at a great advantage. Clearly, however, the new policy would never have been embarked on nor would it have succeeded unless there was already some support for it throughout the organization and in the society at large.

Negro leaders must play a vital role in preparing the Negro to take full advantage of the new opportunities opening up in U.S. military and civilian life. They must first be interested in, and appreciative of, the significant changes that are taking place. They must develop appropriate methods for making those changes known to the Negro population. And, most important, they must develop appropriate means of helping parents and youngsters prepare for broadened opportunities. The intellectual and moral challenge is severe. Many favorite projects and beliefs must be discarded or significantly altered. Much imagination will be required to fashion appropriate new instruments for more effective interpretation and guidance.

But the Negro leadership cannot do the entire job by itself. White leaders must do their part in making it possible for the Negro to become a fully integrated citizen. This means they will have to help the Negro become part of the community from his birth, and not have him wait until he enters military service. The Negro needs the opportunity to grow up, go to school, play, and work together with the white population.

FUTURE TRENDS: THE ECONOMY

Although it is difficult enough to unravel the skein of the Negro's history during the past half century, it is far more difficult to estimate what is likely to occur during the decade or two ahead. Some of the following estimates of the future will be proved incorrect, but the chance of error may be reduced by using as a guide the principal lines along which past developments have taken place. On the basis of the analyses presented in the preceding chapters, four such lines of development may be discerned: trends in the economy; in public education; in the federal government, including the armed services; and in the community at large.

Although during the past fifteen years the economy has not experienced any significant decline in levels of output or employment, it cannot be concluded that the economy is now immune from such declines or that the future will bring uninterrupted growth. On the contrary, the study of long-run trends suggests that at some time within the next few years there is likely to be a period of reduced business activity which will probably be much more moderate than the great depression of 1929–1933. Although there is no certainty that a major economic disorganization cannot again occur, there are many reasons for contending that future business declines will be moderate. As the passage of the Full Employment Act of 1946 so clearly indicated, both major parties are now committed to the principle that the federal government should use its full power to help the economy regain its health whenever necessary.

Trends in the level of economic activity have direct and striking pertinence for the Negro: The longer the period of prosperity, the more secure he can make his position in the economy and the less he has to fear from a period of decline. With the passage of every year, the Negro acquires greater seniority in those areas of the economy where he has recently been able to obtain employment for the first time. Although job security is greater for those who are members of unions that have stringent seniority provisions in their contracts, even those who are not protected by collective bargaining agreements become increasingly secure the longer they hold their jobs. Over the past decade or two, many nonunion employers have established personnel policies that consider seniority when men are released as well as when they are promoted. Although it is hard to predict the impact of a serious depression on these policies, it is unlikely that the Negro would be singled out for differential treatment where such policies are in force, especially where they are written into contracts with unions.

The revolution in southern agriculture will undoubtedly continue, with the result that there will be much less demand for unskilled Negro labor in the future. It is reasonable to postulate, therefore, a continuing migration of Negroes from the rural areas of the South. Those who remain will be particularly handicapped because they will be older and less well educated, on the average, than those who leave. Yet there are some reasons for hope. The president is committed to the development of a constructive program to help the depressed economic areas of the country, and the Congress has also demonstrated an interest in this problem. A recent report of the Joint Committee on the Economic Report stressed the need for several kinds of actions to help low-income farmers. These included increased credit, intensive technical assistance, and the development of individual plans to improve family farms. The report emphasized the individual farmer's needs for encouragement and guidance as he seeks to fulfill his plan. In addition, the committee suggested three further lines of action: "(1) Encouragement of off-farm employment by development of new industrial location within the area; (2) assistance of farm families willing to migrate to other areas and who possess definite job opportunities in the new location; (3) provision for greater opportunity for rural people to obtain training for nonfarm occupations." If these and similar constructive actions are taken, the most handicapped Negroes—those born and brought up in the depressed agricultural areas of the Southeast—can look forward to an improved opportunity to secure a better living from the land, or to make a successful transition to urban industry.

There is no reason to doubt the continuation of the rapid industrialization of the South. This industrialization has helped the Negro to improve his economic position, even though he has rarely been able to gain a firm footing in the manufacturing labor force. Whether he will be able to do so in the years ahead is difficult to foretell. Breakthroughs that have already occurred on the periphery of the South and occasionally in the Deep South provide some ground for optimism. In these instances Negroes have been hired as production workers and have had an opportunity to move up the ladder as they acquired skill on the job.

The time is near when the South will have to make a major decision. Negroes represent approximately one fourth of the population of the South. It is indeed questionable whether the South will be able to keep pace with the rest of the country if it continues to lose its most competent and best-trained Negroes. At present, a young Negro who has acquired skills in the armed services and comes back even to such a metropolitan center as Atlanta finds it difficult to obtain a job that uses his skills. Before long his availability is made known to employment exchanges north of the Mason-Dixon line, and he is likely to be on his way, lost to the South forever. Other costs are also implicit in the maintenance and operation of a segregated system of employment. Such a system inevitably results in excessive overhead and faulty utilization practices since men must be assigned primarily according to their color rather than the needs of the plant. The South will have to give up the luxury of maintaining segregation in the work place and begin to make progressive moves to abandon it, if it is to strengthen its position in the never-ceasing competition for new plants.

Since the long-run trend of economic activity is definitely upward, the Negro can anticipate greater opportunities for employment, particularly outside of the South. It will be easier for him to get a job, and it will be easier for him to be promoted on the basis of merit. There are strong indications that U.S. industry will be able to absorb all the skilled workers who are trained. The unskilled Negro, however, will be vulnerable.

During the next decade improvements in machinery, including advances in automation, may well lessen the demand for such labor. Improved opportunities for the Negro in U.S. industry will depend in no small measure, therefore, on his ability to meet the demands of employers for men with a high level of education and skill.

It is difficult to predict the extent to which Negro women will be able to improve their economic position by gaining access to new occupations and by rising in them as they gain knowledge and experience. Since 1940 few Negro women in the South have been able to obtain manufacturing, clerical, or sales work. In the North, too, their opportunities are still severely limited. One important area of employment may present greatly increased opportunities for Negro women in both the North and the South over the next decade—the field of health services. Today many hospitals in the North could not operate without the help of Negro nurses and auxiliaries. There is also scattered evidence in the South that exceptions to segregation are being made in the health fields for properly qualified Negro women. An expanding economy with rising personal incomes will bring increasing demands for social and health services. On the other hand, a rapid integration of students in southern school systems would undoubtedly reduce the opportunities of Negro girls to obtain teaching positions, at least temporarily.

In sum, if the general upward trend of the economy continues, the position of the Negro should also continue to improve. There are, however, certain danger points: In a depression, all Negroes would be more vulnerable; with advances in automation, the unskilled Negro will be in a weakened position; the jobs of Negro women who are teachers in the South could be jeopardized by quick integration of school systems. On balance, however, an expanding economy foreshadows favorable developments for both Negro men and women.

FUTURE TRENDS: THE SCHOOLS

The second major line of development is education. Public interest in and concern with the quantity and quality of educational resources has quickened noticeably during the past few years. The American people are becoming aware that they should not permit the abilities of their children to be wasted, for the sake of the nation as well as for the sake of the children. To maintain the pace of its economic expansion and fulfill its commitments as a leader of the free world, the nation needs more well-trained men and women. It is difficult to see how this general stance of the U.S. public could fail to help the Negro. The increase in the number of well-trained Negroes could be very great indeed. The single most underdeveloped human resource in the country is the Negro. If the nation is to fulfill its promise as a democracy, it will have to do much more to develop the potential of its Negroes.

The U.S. public's mounting concern with the adequacy of its educational effort was reflected in the president's recent message to the Congress on a bill to aid education. Among the principles the president advocated was that of making funds available to the states according to their need. Two-thirds of the total Negro population live in the southern states, which would receive a more than average share of federal help under such a plan.

It is too early to foretell, for the immediate future, the full consequences of the Supreme Court's decision on segregation in education. In some localities in the border states, compliance with the new regulation has already taken place, and Negro children are now attending schools that are better equipped and better staffed. These Negro children will not grow up, as their parents did, cut off from normal relations with their white neighbors. In other localities, however, the Supreme Court's decision may result in at least a temporary deterioration in the schooling for both whites and Negroes. There is disturbing evidence that in several states certain white leaders are gaining support for plans that can only weaken the entire community and hamper the schooling of both white and Negro children.

The improvement of school buildings and teaching staffs and the integration of Southern schools are essential if Negroes are to have access to good educational preparation for life. But the extent to which Negroes benefit from future gains in these respects will depend in very large measure on the extent to which Negro leaders and parents succeed in convincing the younger generation of the importance of working hard in school. To accomplish this, many Negro families will have to reorder their lives and values. The schools can also help in this task, but only if they develop stronger teaching staffs and stronger guidance and counseling services. Rapid changes in the economic position of the Negro make it even more difficult for Negro than for white parents to provide guidance for their children about how best to prepare for life and work.

Leaders of the Negro community must guard against an uncritical imitation of past approaches as more resources become available to improve the education of Negroes. For a long time, for example, Negro leaders in the South have justifiably complained about the limited amount and poor quality of vocational education available to Negroes. On the other hand, there is increasing evidence that sound knowledge of fundamental subjects is the best preparation for becoming a skilled worker. If a high school student has control over such basic subjects as mathematics,

English, and science, industry finds it relatively easy to instruct him in specific skills. Moreover, these are the fundamentals required for admission to college. Although Negro leaders are right in pressing for broader and better vocational education both in the North and, particularly, in the South, it would be an error for them to place primary emphasis on this one aspect of secondary education.

The cost of a higher education is a major obstacle for most Negroes. In recent years there have been sizable increases in scholarship aid, because of both state action and the activities of industry and other voluntary groups. To the extent that increases in scholarship aid take place, it will be easier for a larger number of Negroes to attend college in the future than in the past.

Among the difficult problems confronting the Negro community is the future of many segregated colleges in the South. The weaknesses of many of these institutions show up very sharply when they are compared with the average college. As the Negro becomes more completely integrated into U.S. industry and society, he needs more than ever before schooling equal to that of the white population. Among the recommendations that have been advanced is that many Negro colleges in the South should be transformed into technical institutes providing a strong two-year course of study. The technician occupations may well prove to be one of the most important areas of expanding employment opportunities in coming years. On the other hand, if some Negro colleges in the South are transformed into technical institutes, young Negroes in the South will be confronted with additional difficulties in securing a college degree because of the higher cost of going to an institution away from home.

In spite of many uncertainties, the general outlines of several important educational developments of the near future are relatively clear. The American people will invest more in education. To a considerable extent this larger investment will do no more than meet the increased costs of educating a rapidly growing student population. But some increase in educational expenditures per child will probably occur as the public comes to understand more fully the wastage now resulting from insufficient resources for developing the potential of many children, especially those of poor parents. Particular efforts will probably be made to develop a much larger part of the Negro potential. It is also probable that transformations within the Negro community will result in young Negroes being more strongly motivated to take advantage of the resources that are made available.

FUTURE TRENDS: THE FEDERAL GOVERNMENT

The third line of development relates to the federal government, including the armed services. The effective integration of the Negro soldier during the last few years was summarized by the Department of Defense at the beginning of 1955 in a report that declared:

> The Negro citizen in the Armed Forces is now utilized on the basis of individual merit and proficiency in meeting the needs of the Services.
>
> Throughout the Army, Navy, Air Force, and Marine Corps, fully integrated units have replaced the all-Negro units which, until recent years, formed the only channel of military service for Negro enlistees and draftees since Colonial times.
>
> Thorough evaluation of the battle-tested results to date indicates a marked increase in overall combat effectiveness through integration.
>
> Economies in manpower, materiel, and money have resulted from the elimination of racially duplicated facilities and operations.
>
> The program has advanced more rapidly than had been considered possible in some quarters, and there have been no untoward incidents.

This is a remarkable story. But important problems remain. Integration is not yet fully accomplished in the Reserve Officers' Training Corps or in the National Guard. Since the purpose of these civilian components is to offer maximum support to the armed forces in an emergency, it is essential that they be organized and trained along the lines of the armed forces' structure. This will be difficult to accomplish in the South since the National Guard units are instrumentalities of state governments as well as of the federal government. Another problem in the military sphere is that opportunities for Negroes to obtain satisfactory civilian positions in the Department of Defense are still very limited. Although a few Negroes are employed in high-level positions, the typical Negro civilian employee is a file clerk, clerk-typist, messenger boy, or cleaning woman.

The Department of Defense report also points out that integration in the armed forces extends far beyond the utilization of men in military assignments: "The Armed Forces, within their own sphere, have developed notable examples of racial coordination and integration in housing, transportation, religious worship, schooling, recreation, and other aspects of community life for service personnel and their families." While several southern states are defying the Supreme Court's school decision, the armed forces have integrated all schools on military installations. There is one exception, where the problem is now being worked out in accordance with basic policy. Although it is easier to integrate a small number of Negro children in a post school than it is to integrate the public schools in a county where Negroes are a majority of the population, the success of the armed forces' challenge to tradition should help convince many who are undecided that change is possible and advantageous to Negro and white alike.

Since the United States will continue to require sizable standing forces, a high proportion of the young men of the nation will continue to serve on active duty for two, three, or four years. This means that a large number of southern whites and Negroes will have direct experience in living and working together as equals during a formative period of their lives. The armed services will continue to represent a pilot experiment in integration, which will show that there is a practical alternative to segregation. Military service will provide a major dynamic force for remodeling race relations throughout the nation, particularly in the South.

In addition to its tremendous impact through the armed services, the federal government will continue to exercise an important influence on the future position of the Negro. Consider the last fifteen years. Since the early days of World War II the federal government has helped to overcome discriminatory employment practices. Recently the government has taken energetic action to eliminate segregation in the nation's capital. In addition, the government has eliminated segregation of civilian personnel in its installations throughout the South. The Interstate Commerce Commission has ordered the abandonment of separate seating and other discriminatory practices by common carriers in interstate transportation. Particular mention must be made of the Supreme Court, whose decisions are moving in the direction of declaring unconstitutional all discriminatory practices based solely on race in all circumstances where the federal courts have jurisdiction.

For some time the federal government has been seeking to insure that employers with government contracts observe antidiscriminatory policies. Many contractors in the South are caught between federal regulations and deepseated local antagonisms toward the Negro, frequently buttressed by trade union practices and local ordinances. The federal government has been disinclined to resort to cancellation or nonrenewal of contracts but is actively seeking the cooperation of industry. President Eisenhower has stated:

> This problem and its solution are the job of all of us. Government can help and must help. But the final answer is up to you and me and must be achieved in the communities where we live. Every American who opposes inequality, every American who helps, in

even the smallest way, to make equality of opportunity a living fact, is doing the business of America. He is strength, against its enemies, in the cause of freedom.

An increasing number of Americans outside the South are willing to see the federal government act energetically to remove the barriers of discrimination as quickly as possible. In the years immediately ahead this attitude will exercise a growing influence on congressional action. This means that any new federal legislation, such as the important aid-for-education bill, must be consistent with this approach. Congress will find it difficult, if not impossible, to pass new legislation that overtly or even tacitly reinforces existing segregation practices. Southern members of Congress may be able to defeat legislation favored by the majority of people, including even those living in the South, not on the virtues of specific proposals, but solely on grounds of their impact on segregation. Such action can lead to no more than useless conflict and delay. The trend of national policy has been clearly set.

The president of the United States is not only the head of the executive branch of the federal government but also the highest elected official in the country. As such he is the leader of the American people. President Eisenhower, as well as his two predecessors, Presidents Roosevelt and Truman, each made significant contributions to mobilizing public opinion against discriminatory barriers in the path of the Negro. There is every likelihood that future presidents of the United States will act in the same manner, out of both inner conviction and heightened awareness of the dangers to the international policy of the United States that unfair treatment of the Negro represents.

FUTURE TRENDS: THE COMMUNITY

The final major line of development relates to the role played by voluntary groups, particularly at the local level. Segregation cannot long survive unless it is supported by many individuals. Nor can it be abolished unless many individuals change their attitudes, feelings, and behavior. At the very least they must change their behavior. For generations the churches were a major bulwark of segregation in the South. The doctrines of Christianity were often used not to challenge the white population to behave more justly and equitably towards Negroes but to justify segregation and discrimination. Recently, however, the Catholic Church and some of the Protestant groups have taken aggressive action against segregation.

In recent years, the trade unions also have taken important measures against discrimination. At the national and international level, union constitutions have been amended by removing discriminatory clauses. Labor leaders have spoken out strongly against unfair treatment of the Negro. But segregation is often firmly entrenched at the local level. Even in unions in which the national leadership has unequivocally declared for racial equality, many locals have been able to maintain discriminatory practices. Gains have been made, but, in general, and particularly in the South, the gains to date have been small. The Negro cannot enjoy a much greater degree of economic opportunity in the South in the years immediately ahead unless local unions change their practices. Such changes are most likely to occur if other groups — government, industry, the church — set an example. In such a situation it is difficult to conceive of trade unions' remaining far behind. Outside the South, it can be anticipated that the increasingly strong commitment of the leaders of the unified U.S. labor movement to the eradication of racial discrimination will prove an important lever in breaking down discriminatory practices where they still exist.

Only community action can bring about desegregation in housing. Southerners have frequently pointed out that the North, too, practices segregation. Although northern communities do not regulate relations between the races by law, segregation is firmly established in fact, as evidenced by all-Negro neighborhoods and the resulting segregated schools, segregated churches, segregated stores, and segregated recreational areas.

It would be foolish to minimize the difficulties of establishing integrated housing, but it is not necessary to exaggerate them. There are communities in the South where the housing of whites and Negroes has been less sharply segregated than in other areas of the country. In a few of the larger urban centers of the North, integrated housing has been initiated in government-financed projects. Although at first only a few white people may be willing to enter integrated projects, experience in some of them suggests the problem can be resolved. Although it will be a long time before this major stronghold of segregation falls, more government and even private funds will probably become available for interracial housing projects in the near future.

The major trends along each of the four lines of development that have been discussed all lead to the same general conclusion: The momentum established during the last decade and a half will result in accelerated improvement in the position of the Negro in the years immediately ahead. But there is one cloud on the horizon. The pressure exerted on the South by the Supreme Court to integrate its schools has sparked a countermovement dedicated to shoring up the entire system of segregation.

It is difficult to estimate the strength of this countermovement. It is more than likely, however, that the forces that will continue to be exerted against discrimination from every side—government, the armed forces, industry, labor, science, religion—will induce the South to steer away from a self-destructive recalcitrance. Only if the South fails to see the inevitable outcome, only if it fails to add up the total cost of a doomed struggle, only then might it be so profligate as to waste its resources in fighting integration instead of using them constructively to solve the problem of relations between the races.

The greatest danger is that the enlightened moderate leadership of the South may permit extremists to take control. If the constructive forces in the South assume responsibility for directing the inevitable process of desegregation, they will cut the ground from under extremists in both North and South, and will provide a firm foundation for the development of the full potential of white and Negro alike.

LESSONS FOR MANPOWER POLICY

What lessons for manpower policy can be extracted from this review of the major factors that will determine how fully and how fast the Negro population will be able to develop its potential? The first lesson is a negative one. Until society places a higher value on the individual than it has done in the past, it will fail to take the constructive actions required to emancipate disadvantaged groups. Until a society recognizes the value of human potential, it will do little to develop it.

For several thousand years the religious tradition of the West has stressed the importance of the individual, but religion alone has often been unable to improve the social and economic status of individuals. Judaism and Christianity have helped in raising the level of social conscience, but religious conviction alone has seldom led men to relinquish special privilege voluntarily. Major gains have come when societies have recognized that the brawn and brains of all their citizens are required for the accomplishment of important goals. Dominant groups have been willing to give up their special privileges when they have seen the value of people as an economic or military resource.

Discrimination against one group by another is seldom based on a single consideration. The maintenance of a system of segregation is reinforced by the specific returns the dominant group derives from the practice. Some of these are easy to recognize. Less apparent are the substantial costs the dominant group pays for maintaining segregation. Those who take advantage of their fellowmen pay a high price.

The elaboration of a system of rules to govern the relations between the dominant and the disadvantaged groups results in engulfing not only the minds but the emotions of all concerned. To challenge such a system is therefore difficult and frequently dangerous. A successful challenge hinges on four prior conditions: the development of effective leaders within the disadvantaged group; constructive leadership within the dominant group; a conducive environment, which will help to cushion whatever changes are introduced; and time to learn about the new situation and adjust to it.

In order to abolish a system of discrimination, the disadvantaged group must have reached a level of self-development and of organization that permits its leadership to crystallize its legitimate demands. Unless these demands are put forward, the dominant group will let well enough alone. Significant alterations in established relations always involve serious stresses and strains. Some members of the dominant group are likely to lose income and power. Unless the proponents of change exert strong and persistent pressure, no significant changes are likely to take place.

But competent leadership in the disadvantaged group is not enough to bring about the desired results, especially if the group is a minority. Help from outstanding individuals in the dominant group is also necessary. When such persons declare themselves, they act as a magnet and draw to the support of change others in the dominant group who are inclined to help. Moreover, their willingness to take a position helps to divide the opposition. Many individuals will favor the maintenance of the status quo only so long as they do not have to justify their position. Once they are challenged, they are likely to become neutrals if not actually protagonists of change. This leaves in outright opposition only those who insist on their accustomed privileges without regard for the legitimate claims of other members of the society. To maintain the existing situation, recalcitrants must be willing to argue against the ethical and democratic principles accepted by the majority in the society. When the tide is turning fast, only a few are willing to stand against it.

Without men of ability and good will in both the disadvantaged and dominant groups, no significant changes are likely to take place. But successful introduction of change also depends in no small measure on the environment. If the rights and privileges of the disadvantaged group can be increased without direct economic cost to members of the dominant group, acceptance of change will be eased. The history of the United States is testimony to the absorptive capacity of a nation that has been expanding most of the time. Tens of millions of European immigrants were quickly and successfully assimilated only because the economy offered a job to every man. A similarly conducive economic environment over the past fifteen years has given the Negro his opportunity.

To appreciate the importance of the economic factor, all that is required is to review the findings of Gunnar Myrdal's classic study of the American Negro, *An American Dilemma,* based on conditions prevailing in the 1930s. His deep concern about the marginal status of the Negro in U.S. society grew in large part out of his conclusion that the Negro had failed to gain a secure foothold in the industrial economy while his position in southern agriculture was becoming weaker. The contrast between the conclusions emerging from Myrdal's study and those of this appraisal are one indication of how far the Negro has come within the last fifteen years.

The most important element in effecting change is the element of time. The past cannot be expunged by a change of heart, for the evil men do to each other leaves deep marks. It is an ironic tragedy that considerable time must pass before a disadvantaged group can make full use of new opportunities that have been made available to it. How much time depends on how deeply its ways of thinking, of feeling, of responding, have been affected by the disabilities it has suffered. The delay can be shortened both by help from its own leadership in adjusting to new conditions, and by continuing help from the leadership of the dominant group. But it behooves us all to remember that equality can never be bestowed—it can only be earned.

For hundreds of years the private conscience and the public morality of the United States have been weakened by the guilt we have carried over our treatment of the Negro. Ninety years ago we expended a great treasure to expiate this guilt, but with victory in our hands we let it out of our grasp. The North rushed into money-making and the South was busy binding up its wounds. The Negro was denied the new freedom that had been given him by the Constitution.

For generations we have continued to live with this guilt, doing a little from time to time to assuage our consciences. When called on to help to free men from the forces of oppression in 1917, in 1941, and again in 1950, we did not falter. The greater challenge that now faces us as a leader of the Free World has at last forced us to recall and to act on Lincoln's warning: "Those who deny freedom to others deserve it not for themselves, and, under a just God, cannot long retain it."

CHAPTER 27

American Democracy
and the Negro

THIS CHAPTER WILL ATTEMPT TO ANSWER THREE QUES-
TIONS: How did we get to where we are? Where are we now? And what
alternatives do we face?

The answer to the first question has relevance for the second and
third. How did we get here? My own examination of this question goes
back to 1956, when I wrote a little book, *The Negro Potential*. At that time I
developed a few answers and then put the problem to one side. I stayed
interested, however, in what was happening with the nation's human resources as a whole and with minority problems in particular, and I continued to be disturbed throughout that period by an underlying awareness
that I did not understand how we had arrived at our present position.

One conspicuous strength of U.S. democracy has been its ability to
take all kinds of people, put them through similar experiences, and
absorb the end products with little difficulty. But Negroes, who arrived
in America in 1619 and therefore have been here longer than the Pilgrims,
have not been absorbed by our democracy. Their experience has been
different from that of all other groups.

This fact, inexplicable on the surface, proved to be so disturbing that about three years ago, I began to work on it. I started at the beginning of our history in order to see this piece of history in perspective. With a young and very able collaborator, Alfred Eichner, I sought to capture the reasons for this differential experience. The result of our study is a book, *The Troublesome Presence,* which carries the subtitle *American Democracy and the Negro.* The title comes from Lincoln's eulogy of his idol, Henry Clay, and refers to the presence of the *free* Negro in America. The book, with its emphasis on the broad historical picture and on some economic and political facets of the subject, provides a useful frame for a discussion of our first question—how did we get here? It suggests, further, that the answer to the question is threefold: by accident, by intent, and by neglect.

Let me illustrate each in turn. The Negro came to the United States initially by accident. He arrived in Colonial America through no deliberate plan but because a Dutch man-of-war carrying Negroes who had been bought in the West Indies happened to land in Jamestown. At that time the British had had little or no experience or contact with Africans. Unlike the Spanish and the Portuguese, who had lived in the Mediterranean world, they knew nothing about Negroes.

The British colonists in Virginia confronted persons such as they had never seen, strange, black people who spoke no European tongue and had no customs or religion in common with Englishmen or other Europeans. The Negroes had been demoralized by the brutal trek from inland Africa to the coast and were further demoralized by the journey across the Atlantic. They seemed not to belong to the human species, at least not to any segment familiar to the British. No question about it, these Negroes scared the colonists.

The first case on record involving a Negro appears in the Jamestown annals of 1630, where it is recorded that a white man was punished by the assembly in Jamestown for sleeping with a Negro woman. The decision indicates that the community was appalled by the notion that there could be close relationships between white and black. From the very start, then, the colonists had no intention of integrating the Negro into their community. The British colonists, who came from a culture that had had no experience with slavery, instituted slavery for Negroes and basically only for Negroes. They tried it for a short while with Indians, but it didn't work, and before very long, enslavement of Indians was prohibited.

Because they could not conceive of living cheek by jowl with free Negroes, the British community sought to develop some method of social control over these strangers in their midst. Englishmen had come to America to build a new society, and slavery was introduced to protect that nascent society. It evolved as a method of enabling the colonists to live with Negroes, not originally as a system of economic exploitation.

But before long, the expansion of southern agriculture made neces-sary the recruitment of large numbers of laborers. White farm laborers were available, but they were not reliable hired help; they wanted to farm land of their own. For a capitalistic successful plantation system, therefore, Negro labor became not only useful but essential. In fact, from around 1700, Negro labor alone made possible the expansion of southern plantations. Large-scale recruiting of white indentured servants—about 80 percent of all Britishers who emigrated came under some kind of labor contract—was expensive. White immigrants required better clothing, better food, and even wages! The colonists could entice more and more white people to come only if they were willing to provide attractive wages and working conditions.

With Negro slaves, however, they did not have to provide more than a minimum. The entire procedure operated differently. Negroes "immi-grated" after having been captured and traded. Therefore, there was no need to lighten the conditions of their servitude. They became a minor-ity that was soon completely under the control of the white majority. This was the first step in regularizing the relations between American democracy and the Negro. And as often happens, the first step had important consequences.

The second answer to our first question, how did we get here, relates to intent. The first significant attempt to study the relationship between Negro and white Americans was made in the early 1940s when the Swedish economist Gunnar Myrdal published his famous study, *An American Dilemma*. The Carnegie Corporation had asked a Swedish econo-mist to study the problem because it believed that any American student would be prejudiced. Myrdal, a distinguished social scientist from a country with no minorities and no colonial possessions, was their choice, and his study became the first comprehensive socioeconomic-political analysis of the Negro minority in the United States, cast largely in terms of developments since World War I. Myrdal's imaginative conclusion from his large-scale study was that there had been a continuing conflict between our conscience and our behavior—that is, the Declaration of Independence had proclaimed that all men are created equal, but we had been treating the Negro as if he were *not* equal.

In my opinion, Myrdal was wrong. No basic conflict ever existed between our conscience and our behavior because we did not include the Negro in our original commitment. "All men" meant "all white men." The Negro was excluded. Chief Justice Taney was legally correct, although he may have been politically unwise, when he said in the Dred Scott decision that at the time of the Revolution the law did not bestow citizenship on the Negro American. A state might grant citizenship to a

Negro, he held, but the Founding Fathers had not included him within the polity, and surely not as a full-fledged member.

We know that Jefferson considered assimilation impossible. He wanted to send 500,000 Negroes back to Africa and in their place import an equal number of white persons. There was, in his opinion, no resolution of the Negro problem except by an exchange of populations. This was the only solution recommended by the man who drafted the Declaration of Independence.

From George Washington to William Howard Taft, no president of the United States, not even Lincoln, had any answer for the Negro in the United States other than colonization or some variant thereof. George Washington once promised General Lafayette personally to help underwrite an experimental colonization scheme for American Negroes in the West Indies. Shortly after his election to the presidency, William Howard Taft, who considered himself free of any kind of color prejudice, told a Negro college audience in North Carolina that they had no future in this country, that they should go back to Africa. If they stayed here, he said, they would remain peasants. And Taft was the president who devoted a good part of his inaugural address to an assessment of the Negro problem in the United States.

In the middle of the Civil War Lincoln went to the Congress and obtained funds for the colonization of slaves who had recently been freed. He attempted first to develop a colony in Panama and when that failed, he supported a scheme in Haiti. Six weeks before Lincoln died he asked Major General Butler, chief of logistics for the Union Army, to explore the rate at which Negroes could be sent abroad if use were made of all naval and civilian shipping. Butler reported back to the effect that not much could be accomplished because Negroes were being born at a rate faster than the numbers that could be shipped out.

These excerpts from our history indicate that the colonization movement was not started or supported by rabid southerners with extreme positions. The plan had the support of the great leaders of American democracy, Washington, Jefferson, and Lincoln.

This does not imply that all Americans have always been insensitive to or pessimistic about finding a constructive solution to the Negro problem. The Quakers early attacked slavery. But the clearest and most unequivocal indication about the mood of the new nation is reflected in the Constitution, the basic law of the land. Three, and only three, propositions in the Constitution dealt with the Negro. One stipulated that the Congress of the United States could not interfere with the importation of slaves for twenty years. Not that importation had to stop at the end of twenty years, but Congress could not interfere until then. The second proposition provided that the federal government could use its power to return escaped slaves to their masters. In this the Constitution treated slaves as property.

The third proposition related to the counting of the population to determine the allocation of seats in the House of Representatives. For this purpose, the Negro was to be counted as three-fifths of a man. As one reads the debates in the Constitutional Convention, it becomes clear that the Negro issue per se was unimportant. Some of the Northern delegates would have preferred different action and different wording, but few would have gone beyond abolishing the slave trade. Delegates from some of the middle states—Maryland, Delaware, and Virginia—were more incensed about the failure to act on the slave trade than were New Englanders and New Yorkers. In short, at the time of the Constitutional Convention, white America—not just the Southern states, but white America—had no interest in and saw no possibility of bringing the panoply of American democracy over the Negro.

To shift focus, one year after the Civil War was under way, Lincoln told Horace Greeley that if the union could be reestablished without freeing a single slave, he would aim to do it. Certainly Lincoln believed that slavery was an evil, but he decided that, since ours was a constitutional government, the South had been guaranteed by the Constitution the right to hold slaves. Lincoln stood athwart only the *expansion* of slavery. And it was on the question of the expansion of slavery that the war was fought, since the irreconcilable issue was control of the West, which carried with it control of the nation.

Lincoln knew early and most northerners soon came to understand that if slavery were permitted in the western territories, settlement there of northern whites would be foreclosed. Northern whites would be loath to move there; control of the West would be won by the South. On that issue—the control of the West—the war was fought. Even after the war began, many northerners balked at calling slavery the issue. Members of an Illinois regiment proclaimed that they would prefer to stay in the fields until they were covered by moss than take any action that would help free the slaves.

When Lincoln issued the Emancipation Proclamation, which, we recall, freed slaves only in the states in rebellion, the legislature of the state from which he came, Illinois, drafted a memorial to the effect that it was the most dastardly act in the history of mankind. This was the mood of part of the North even at that late hour.

Of course, many Abolitionists, under the leadership of such men as William Lloyd Garrison, had long preached that slavery was immoral and un-Christian, and their agitation had undoubtedly helped bring on the war. But they considered slavery largely as an abstract institution. When slavery finally was eliminated as a result of the war, Frederick

Douglass—the leader of the Negro community to the extent that one can speak of a Negro community at that time—understood that the ex-slaves, with neither education nor property, would need considerable and prolonged help if they were to be integrated successfully into the larger society. At that crucial point, however, Garrison and his colleagues withdrew from the fray. With slavery abolished, they saw their work at an end. Most of them had little understanding of, or feeling for, the individual Negro.

To be sure, not all Americans had such little sympathy and understanding, but this was the dominant attitude even in Massachusetts, where Abigail Adams, the wife of our second president, found it necessary to nurse her sick old Negro servant personally because she could not get any white woman to help her.

Lincoln was a constitutionalist and a conservative. He believed the South had the right to perpetuate the institution of slavery, but he did not believe the Constitution gave the South the right to spread slavery to the new territories in the West. After the southern states started to secede, he repeatedly stated he would do nothing to interfere with the institution of slavery where it was established.

Although he tried to broaden the interpretation of the Declaration of Independence to include Negroes, Lincoln felt that as president of the United States he was not entitled to implement his personal views. He fought to maintain the integrity of the union. The expansion of slavery, not slavery itself, would, he believed, hopelessly corrupt our democracy; but if he could build a wall around the South, slavery would eventually die out.

Few northern leaders considered what might happen once the slaves were freed. Lincoln looked forward originally to a slow emancipation, to be completed only at the beginning of the next century. Thaddeus Stevens, who understood the preconditions for the social, economic, and political integration of the Negro, believed that a revolution in the South would be necessary before the Negro could sink roots as a freedman. Hence he initially opposed enfranchising the Negro, thinking that that ought to come second or third after economic security and educational gains.

For a short while after the Civil War, the North tried to help the Negro, not because northerners were interested in the Negro as a human being, but because they did not want to forfeit the gains of having won the war. The fact that the Freedmen's Bureau was originally to cease operations one year after the end of hostilities reveals how completely the North misunderstood the magnitude of the problem it faced. Even after the act establishing the bureau was amended, the bureau remained in operation for only four years. The victorious North, at least its

representatives in Congress, was unwilling to invest very much in helping the freed Negro, although individuals and missionary groups in the
North went South and started to teach Negro children and adults during
and after the war.

So much for intent. Now some comments about neglect: Although
the government never intended to do much for the Negro, most of the
benefits that did redound to the Negro were the result of fights among
white groups. During the Revolutionary War, for example, the British
had offered Negro slaves their freedom in return for fighting on their
side. In response, George Washington, who had originally refused to
take Negroes into the Colonial Army, reversed his position and accepted
them. Again, during the Civil War, Lincoln originally refused to take
Negroes into the Army. But when it became clear that failure to do so
would aid the Southern cause, he shifted tack and accepted them. Again
the Negroes benefited from the whites' fighting among themselves.

This recital of what the whites intended refers to the majority. There
was always a minority, most of them deeply religious, who were disturbed by the slave trade, by slavery, and by the inhumanity of the
nation's actions to the free Negro. But they were a small minority.

Booker T. Washington's famous speech at the 1895 Atlanta Exposi-
tion described the real plight of the southern Negro. Ninety percent of
all Negroes were still living in the South, existing precariously by the
grace of the southerners, who felt little good will toward them. Meanwhile,
the North had deserted the Negro. The South, now out of the main
stream of American life, had given way to the westward push of the
country from New York to San Francisco. Thirty million immigrants
were to come from Europe during these post–Civil War decades, pre-
empting opportunities that otherwise would have been available to the
Negro in the North or West. Had the North been interested in helping
the Negro after the Civil War, it would have provided opportunities for
their migration out of the South; it would have helped them obtain land
in the West. But the North was not interested. Indeed, it sought to keep
them in the South.

The fact that Northerners did not have to confront the situation
head on made it easier for the South to continue its oppressive ways.
There was no television, no radio, and little good reporting. The plight
of the Negro—even lynchings—wasn't news. President Theodore Roosevelt
reflected the North's attitude when he remarked that while he did not
condone lynching there were few alternative ways to protect white wom-
anhood in the South. As a matter of fact, it was not the North but the
white churchwomen of the South who finally put an end to lynching.

Another key fact in our history has been the controlling political
power of the North and West together. The South alone has never had

the votes to direct the nation. What has happened to the Negro, therefore, must reflect the attitudes and desires of the North and the West, for they have had the votes. But they were not interested. Until 1957 the Republican Middle West and West and the southern white Democrats had a silent agreement to keep the federal government out of race relations.

The national intent can also be read in the Supreme Court's decisions toward the end of the nineteenth century, which were intended to restrict the scope of the Thirteenth, Fourteenth, and Fifteenth Amendments. The country was weary of racial friction, and the Supreme Court sought to contribute to peace by handing the Negro back to the control and mercy of the southern states.

In the history of American democracy vis-à-vis the Negro, the end of slavery marked the end of stage one. World War I was a second turning point, for it accelerated the movement of Negroes out of the South and into northern industry. Four hundred thousand Negroes were drafted, and many of them saw service overseas. In their army service they saw a way of life they had never seen before. The postwar decade saw further mobility and progress, but the Great Depression wiped out many of these earlier gains.

World War II was the third, and in many ways most important, turning point. This time a postwar prosperity broadened and consolidated many of the wartime gains. Millions of Negroes were able to leave the South to come North, where they got jobs and lived reasonably well for the first time in their lives.

Another turning point was 1948. The Democratic platform in 1948 demonstrated for the first time in American history that the Negro had accumulated a significant degree of political power. With Truman's election, the Negro began to have some political leverage. During Truman's administration, desegregation in the armed services proceeded apace. Then Eisenhower, despite his conservatism, and encouraged by the Supreme Court in its tradition-breaking decisions, introduced the first civil rights bill since Reconstruction.

Because Negroes today have political power and growing economic power, they also have the power to affect their situation. Twenty million Negroes do not, of course, constitute a homogeneous group. Some southern rural Negroes are very poor and uneducated, as are many southern urban Negroes. But many other Negroes are neither poor nor uneducated. In Houston, Negroes buy at retail annually over $500 million; over $300 million in Atlanta; in New Orleans over $250 million. With that amount of purchasing power, Negroes can get banks to treat them civilly; they can get salespeople in department stores to want to sell to them. Recent data reveal that there are about a million nonwhites on the West Coast, most of them Negroes. The income distribution of the nonwhite group is exactly the same as that of the white population in the South. In Chicago, one-third of the Negro families have more income than half of the white families.

We see that a concept of 20 million poverty-stricken, uneducated, socially disorganized human beings is unfounded. There are many middle-class Negro families and even a few Negro millionaires. Serious problems remain, of course. Many Negroes are poor, but so are many white persons; in fact, there are many more poor white families than poor Negro families, although a higher proportion of all Negroes are poor.

In addition to the Negro's recently acquired political and economic power, another significant transformation has recently taken place. The Negro has decided to become directly involved in changing his relationships to the white community. The sit-ins heralded this transformation, which foreshadows the end of segregation, since those against whom discrimination has been practiced are no longer willing to be passive. A system of segregation can work only as long as those who are segregated are willing to tolerate it. When they decide to fight it, when they cause continuing disturbances, then the costs of maintaining the system outweigh the advantages of shoring it up. Picket lines put business in a turmoil; classes in school are disrupted; dissonance pervades the social system.

The Negro alone cannot change the fabric of the social structure, but his resistance and struggle to present inequities can encourage others to shift their position. This is the meaning back of the current civil rights struggle. The Negro stands a good chance of getting white America finally to grant him his constitutional rights.

To answer our third question, where do we go from here, we must first distinguish three centers: the rural South, the urban South, and the urban North. Fortunately, most Negroes have left the rural South, as have many white people. Nevertheless, a number of Negroes and white people have remained, and it is not a good place to be. Public services are inadequate, jobs are scarce, and income is low. The Negro there must still worry about his personal security. If he stands up for his rights, he may be permanently silenced. About one-quarter of the Negro population continues to live in the rural South. The urban South, where a slightly higher proportion of Negroes live, is a better environment, for urban communities need peace and tranquillity if they are to progress. Strong pressures therefore exist for granting an insistent minority its civil and political rights. The urban North, including the West—the home of almost half of the Negro population—faces the challenge of giving meaning to the political and civic freedom that the Negro possesses.

These are three different areas, three different sets of conditions, three different stages of adjustment. The rural South requires at a minimum some federal protection of potential Negro voters. If Negro voters in the southern cities learn to use their votes intelligently, they can influence state legislatures to protect Negro rights in rural communities. But rural Negroes need protection and help in acquiring and using their franchise.

With regard to the second area, we cannot talk about the urban South as an entity. There are big differences between the situation confronting the urban Negro in Florida and that facing him in Virginia. Nevertheless, here, too, a major goal for Negroes is to attain their full political and civil rights. In 1882, a Southern white journalist and novelist by the name of George Washington Cable, a friend of Mark Twain, wrote perspicaciously that at the rate the racial problem was being handled we would get to the moon before we reached a solution.

A second goal for the Negro in the urban South should be to get a better share of the tax dollar and a better share of the public services, particularly access to better schools and health services. Most important is the question of jobs. Here improvement will come slowly, however, because the South is a manpower-surplus area. The Negro is thus twice handicapped because there are not enough jobs even for white people.

In the urban North, the Negro, despite his considerable gains in employment, seems to be pursued by an evil fate, for many of his gains are now being liquidated by automation. His breakthrough in semi-skilled jobs came in the automobile industry, meat packing, steel, rubber, and other basic industries, where Negroes have recently been able to earn $2.50 to $3.00 an hour, which, with overtime, often brings weekly earnings up to $125 or better. But many of these jobs are just the ones that are being liquidated. In addition, jobs in the North are expanding relatively slowly, and the Negro is in a poor position to compete for many of them. More and more jobs are open only to educated individuals, which means that education is an important key to progress for the Negro in the North. But most Negroes have access primarily to inferior schools, a problem that is in turn tied up with their being for so long restricted to decaying neighborhoods.

These are the salient facts: It is hard for a minority to make significant gains without strong leadership; and one of the historical handicaps of the Negroes is that whenever they have developed a leadership, they have tended to lose it because of the tendency of many successful Negroes to separate themselves from their original communities. But this may be largely at an end. In the future, we can expect the Negro community to have the advantage of better leadership because of a rising racial consciousness and the fact that major political power can be wielded only by those who succeed in leading the Negro masses.

Second, the white sector of our society is clearly undergoing important changes in attitudes and behavior. Government has begun to act—not only the federal government but also state and local governments. Churches are becoming actively involved. For the first time the average citizen is forced to face up to the issue of freedom and equality for the Negro.

The ferment goes further. It includes Africa. The fact that large countries in Africa are now run exclusively by Negroes has an impact on both white and Negro in America.

Three steps must be taken now. The first is finally to grant the Negro the rights guaranteed him by the Thirteenth, Fourteenth, and Fifteenth Amendments. Second, we must begin to live in accordance with our democratic faith: We must not continue the discriminating attitudes, prejudices, and irrational behavior patterns that have for so long disturbed his life and ours.

Finally, we must realize that freedom is only the precondition for equality. There remain many poor Negroes and many poor white people in the United States who need jobs and income. A democracy that wants to make intelligent use of its strength—and we possess great strength—must clean up its own deficiencies before it can claim the right to lead the world.

CHAPTER 28

Career Choices of Middle-Class Negro Men

MOST YOUNG PEOPLE are concerned with acquiring a good education because of the leverage it will provide them in the competitive job world. Career concerns are closely linked to educational planning. This is particularly true of men, since they are expected to be active members of the labor force from the time they complete their schooling.

There are several specific linkages between educational and career planning. In school young people have an opportunity to test their interests and capacities. They acquire certain specific competences, which may lead them into particular occupations. They are able to develop and to refine the values and goals that will determine their eventual occupational choices. Finally, they are exposed to teachers and other adults who may influence their career preferences.

However, the occupational choice delineation of young people is not solely a function of their experiences within the educational environment. Other forces are important. There is, for instance, the question of models. Although teachers often are models, youngsters frequently find others outside of the classroom. The family and the neighborhood sometimes provide key career models, since young people are likely to be drawn toward particular careers if they are able to identify with people in those fields.

At present, young Negroes generally do not have a wealth of useful models. A considerable number of older Negroes are ministers or teachers, but few have achieved high distinction in those areas. Among the more successful Negroes are a limited number of physicians, lawyers, and government administrators. Negroes are poorly represented among businessmen, engineers, and scientists, and in many other occupations that have long offered substantial economic and social rewards to men in the white community.

Nevertheless, the important fact is not that so few have succeeded, but that some Negroes have been able to succeed despite overwhelming obstacles. Some may have been circumscribed by restrictions that bind them to the Negro community, but within those boundaries they are known and respected. Since they were born into the middle class, our subjects are more likely to be acquainted with these persons than are lower-class youth. They responded affirmatively to these models because the lack of social distance enabled them to identify with them.

On the other hand, young Negroes in college are beginning to realize that they are no longer limited to the few choices that were open to educated Negroes of an earlier generation. Therefore, they are attempting to find attractive fields for themselves, frequently without the assistance of established Negro models. One of the concerns of this chapter is to delineate the exent to which the occupational choices of Negro college youth are being modified in response to the reduction and elimination of racial discrimination in employment.

First, we shall review the careers that these students have selected. Next, we shall describe some of their career specifications. We shall then explore the gratifications they are seeking to realize from their work. By following these several spurs, we shall be in a better position to understand the dynamics of their occupational choices.

If we concentrate first on the choices of college seniors—as the oldest group, they are most likely to have realized their expressed preferences—we find that natural science is the selection of approximately a quarter of the students, followed by medicine, with engineering not far behind. This broad array of scientific fields is the first choice of about three out of every five seniors. The remaining preferences are distributed in descending order as follows: law, social sciences, business, humanities, and education. The most amazing finding, in light of Negro occupational history, is that only one college senior expects to specialize in education per se, although a few consider teaching specific subjects below the college level.

If we compare the tentative choices of the high school seniors and college sophomores with those of the college seniors, we find differences — but only within broad areas. Thus we have important evidence that these young people sense the revolution in opportunity that is under way and that they are responding accordingly.

One senior who is about to enter a management training program told us:

> At the end of the month, I'll begin working in Detroit at the Chrysler Corporation on a manager training program. For the first two years I'll be on rotation. That is, I will take accounting, data processing, and computer programming. At the end of two years I will be permanently placed in one of these fields, depending upon whether I am successful in dodging the draft.

Another senior limned his prospects as follows:

> I plan to work as a technician on an assembly line, some type of skilled factory line. Lockheed here has training courses. The company will send you to school in the summers and give you a job in the winter. I would like to do one specific job, so when I finish my senior year I would then become oriented in the job at Lockheed with preliminary training on the job. Then they would pay me to go to Tech or to Emory and . . . after you finish you can get the real important jobs like working as an engineer in this organization. . . . The field is so wide I can plan to work in a factory or else work in physics in the field of computer mechanics.

A northern college sophomore is weighing three general alternatives but with a considerable degree of practicality:

> I have three choices — actuarial work, which doesn't necessarily require a graduate degree, computer programming, and teaching. The last two do require a second degree. The first, actuarial work, requires extensive experience in order to get ahead, this is, in terms of making a big salary. My first choice is to go into the insurance field as an actuary. This doesn't mean that I'm against a graduate school, but that I prefer actuarial work over computer programming or teaching. If my grades are very good when I graduate in 1967, I will probably go to graduate school and do advanced work in math. If not, I'll go for an actuarial job and consider evening graduate school.

A young southern high school senior is aiming very high:

> I want to work for the federal government. . . . I am interested in government research and want to be a research lawyer and a staff worker in the National Labor Relations Board. My next choice is in the State Department handling foreign affairs. Then, later, when I

am older, I would like to go into politics, national politics, of course. I know you will laugh, but my final ambition is to become a member of the Supreme Court. First, I'll be a representative, a Senator for my state, then a member of the Cabinet, then Attorney General, and then become a member of the Supreme Court.

A key consideration in a study of occupational choice is to get some sense of how realistically a young person has approached the problem in terms of his own interests and abilities and of the opportunities available to him. The following excerpts reveal this.

A southern high school senior has strong pulls to medicine but also some strong aversions:

I will become a psychiatrist. First I decided to be a doctor, but I do not like organic functions. My father is a surgeon and I thought about my father's being called out at night, so I decided against that. I decided that I make friends easily so I am compatible. By being a psychiatrist I wouldn't have to operate on people, but I guess tampering with the mind can be as dangerous as cutting.

Recognizing both the need and the opportunity, a southern sophomore is fairly well set on what he wants to become:

I hope to go into social work or counseling of some sort. I believe it's an open field and on the basis of my experience in the civil rights movement, particularly in Americus, I know there are so many things which need to be done. So few people seem to be concerned about the basic social problems, especially about the problems of people in rural areas.

A northern sophomore looks forward to being in a more influential position:

I'm interested in the social sciences mostly because I have an interest in the racial problem and I can see myself effecting change through education, psychology, and sociology. At fifteen I noticed that I enjoyed working with people; and my family has always been interested in education, especially my father, mother, and oldest sister....I intend to take a master's in psychology with the goal of becoming school psychologist. I want to be in a position to influence an entire school system. I would work in any city with a large Negro population. As a later goal I would like to be a consultant to a school board or boards where my ideas might influence a whole school.

Another northern sophomore has had his eye on a career in the Air Force for a long time, and he is moving right along to realize his goal:

> I want to go into the AAF as a career. When I was nine or ten, I knew I wanted to go into the Air Force. I wanted to be a pilot. Right now I'm majoring in bio since I figured I'd get my best marks in it. You could even be an accounting major, as are some fellows in the ROTC now who plan to become pilots next year. I'll be twenty-three after I get my M.S. and I expect to get a captain's commission.

Some youngsters must cope with dual forces—what they like as well as what their parents like for them—such as another northern college sophomore:

> When I was nine, I spent five months in the hospital with rheumatoid arthritis. I fully recovered. I had a lot of opportunity to observe doctors. But before I was nine, I wanted to be a history teacher. I was fascinated by the past. I talked quite a lot about this at home, but my parents dissuaded me on the basis of its not being a lucrative field at that time. They encouraged me to enter medicine and I went along with it. Later I discovered that I didn't like biology—no, it wasn't a question of scholarship. I just didn't take to the subject matter and at that point I rejected medicine. I found myself thinking of history in terms of law—corporate law, international law, or the diplomatic service. I intend to go to law school but I haven't decided on a specialty. Each seems attractive right now.

A northern senior told how he juggled such alternatives as law, business, and economics, and decided among them:

> When I entered high school I knew I wanted to go to college so I began to consider the possibilities. I thought of being a lawyer. I felt that being a lawyer was a good possibility but the economics would be better in terms of opportunities. In high school I found out that there were more jobs in the business world in economics than any other field of liberal arts except education. Subsequently, I heard a guidance counselor state a similar point to a student. I forgot about law and saw economics as a semiscientific course of study employing formulas and it seemed more challenging than history or English.

Further evidence of the degree of realism with which these young people approach the question of their future work is demonstrated by practical considerations taken into account by older students who have recently made shifts in their plans.

A sophomore recently changed his goal from medicine to dentistry. He reported:

> This year I changed from wanting to be a doctor to wanting to be a dentist. For one thing, I don't have to specialize and it will not take quite as long to study dentistry as it would to study medicine.

A classmate decided that biological research is a less rocky road than medicine:

> I want to be a doctor, but I've been thinking that the professional training is too long and too expensive. I may work awhile and then go to graduate school. My major is biology. I may plan to go into biological research. My main reason for questioning medicine is the matter of time and money.

A senior related a more or less typical story of a gradual transition from a fantasy to a realistic career choice:

> When I was young, I wanted to be an astronomer. I read books about astronomy. Then I passed through the soldier phase, which I call my military phase. During high school, my aunts encouraged me to enter medicine, but this was totally out of the question. I didn't have the mental ability to step into medicine. It was too alien to my own ideas. I compromised with them so I entered physics, which was my first major. I changed because I didn't think I possessed the dedication to work in a laboratory. There was no contact with people. So now I'm in business administration.

A high school senior who still has time before him to make additional shifts is already far on the way to a definite choice:

> I had first thought of being an engineer back in the eighth grade. I like to build things and I liked math and sciences. I switched to accounting. I didn't do as well in my math as I wanted to, so I switched my major. I like math, and accounting is related. I am not enthused about accounting, but I am interested. I am taking it now; I like it; and I am doing well in it.

Some young men have approached the question of their occupational futures by realistically assessing the alternatives which they face with regard to graduate education. A Columbia sophomore said:

> I intend to enter law school on graduation. Yale is my first choice because the curriculum is easier, Columbia is my second, and Harvard is third but hazardous since the attrition is greatest—that is, a class of 500 dwindles to 350. NYU is my fourth choice. As far as financing is concerned, I anticipate fellowships, scholarships, and parental assistance. After law school I plan to take the Bar. After the Bar I plan to go to business school for six months and take intensive courses in banking.

Another Columbia senior is determined to acquire at least a Ph.D. and apparently will have no particular difficulties in doing so:

> The most important aspect of my future is to continue my education until I acquire at least a Ph.D. I have been offered a faculty

fellowship at $250 a month, a teaching fellowship at Michigan, and the Engineers Joint Council has offered me a practical traineeship for a minimal period of two to six months. I would be working for Shell Petroleum, and I will probably undertake the traineeship and, upon its completion, the faculty fellowship at Columbia.

A third classmate whose home is in the South is attempting to decide whether to attend medical school in the North or South:

My present plan is to go to medical school and study psychiatry. The immediate problem is whether I'll go to medical school in the North or the South. If North, I would choose NYU, Downstate, or Western Reserve. If South, Duke, North Carolina, or Bowman Gray. I'm torn right now.

Since so many of these youngsters are from families that are not able to guide them vocationally and since many did not receive much systematic guidance in school, it is striking that they were able to do so well in formulating satisfactory career plans for themselves.

It is illuminating to consider, if only briefly, whether the choices of these young people took into account their capacities, at least as they were reflected by the marks that they achieved in school. It is also relevant to consider more carefully the functions they hope to perform in their fields and the institutional framework within which they expect to work.

Since there were only six A and eight D students in the entire group, the important distinction is between the B and the C students. We find that three out of four of those majoring in the natural sciences are at least B students, as are three out of five who looked forward to studying medicine. The less able students are concentrated in the social sciences, business, and engineering. While it might be invidious to say that weaker students are more likely to make their way in the social sciences, it is safe to contend that only B students have much chance for success in science and medicine. To the extent that marks afford a clue, these young men are thinking quite sensibly about the fields in which they are likely to succeed.

Let us consider the type of work they see themselves doing in the future and the environment within which they expect to work. Somewhat more than a quarter of the entire group anticipate following professional careers in which they will be self-employed. About the same proportion look forward to holding down staff positions in business. A slightly smaller group hope to have careers in university teaching and research or in teaching at a lower level in the educational structure. The remainder expect to be owners or managers of business enterprises, or administrators or staff members in nonprofit institutions or in the government.

The striking facts that emerge from these specifications are that several youths anticipate that they will have positions in corporate management; that a significant minority look forward to reaching responsible staff posts in business; and finally, that a large number aspire to university careers.

These are all employment settings that have traditionally been closed to Negroes except where the institutions themselves were Negro-owned or -operated. That they are the goal of so many of these youths is an indication that recent moves toward integration of administrative, managerial, and professional staffs are breaking down barriers to the aspirations of Negroes.

However, a large number of students, primarily prospective doctors and lawyers, would like to be self-employed. This goal has become less popular among white students, who see the practice of medicine and law as increasingly institutionalized and who prefer security and freedom from pressure as employed professionals in preference to the responsibility and hazards of self-employment. For Negroes, however, the local doctor and lawyer have often been admired community leaders who function with a measure of personal independence that no organizational employment provides, particularly to members of their race. Thus there appears to be an understandable lag between the downgrading of the self-employed professional among whites and his continuing high esteem among Negroes.

Another dimension of the career choices of these Negro youths is the gratifications they seek to realize in their future work. About half of the group emphasize such factors as the nature of the career field itself, the challenge of the work or the interpersonal relations on the job—all of which relate to values that derive mutually from work and from one's own interests and values.

Next in importance are those gratifying aspects mentioned by almost two out of five students, which concern extrinsic factors such as income, prestige, conditions of work, and future opportunities. The remaining students, about one in six, state they have chosen a field in which they can be of service, either to people generally or to Negroes specifically.

The important conclusion to be drawn from this distribution is that a large number of young men—roughly three out of five—are choosing careers solely on the basis of personal satisfaction without reference to more objective factors. They believe that they can choose careers in terms of values that are important to them and that they are no longer under the same pressure as their parents or grandparents, who had to take whatever opportunities happened to be available without regard to personal preferences.

But this much expanded occupational horizon with its many new opportunities is not an unmixed blessing. Most young people find it difficult to undergo a process of weighing and discarding alternatives until they finally make a more or less permanent choice. Negro young-sters find it more difficult than their white classmates because so many of the opportunities now available to them were not previously open to their relatives, their friends, or their teachers. Consequently, they can receive little guidance from these sources.

This is what some of them told us about their parents' attitudes toward their plans. In some cases, their parents followed a hands-off policy, as in the case of a northern college sophomore:

> Becoming a pilot is mostly my baby. My parents couldn't care less and I don't really like people telling me what to do. I like to figure out things myself.

Two other northern college youths also reported that they had made their decisions without any encouragement from home. One said:

> I have decided on medicine. I received no encouragement or inspiration from home. I had to work out what I wanted to do in my own mind. I expect to finance medical school by taking a loan from a bank.

The other reported:

> My parents have played no part in my career plans. I didn't talk to them—I just told them what I wanted to do. I remember that when I was still a child I used to say I wanted to be a writer, but this idea was never encouraged.

The parents of others played a major role in their decisions. For instance, a southern senior heading for medicine said:

> My parents are all for my plans. We have a doctor in the family and they say, "We'll have a new doctor in the family at last." My father was in medical school. It was a very trying experience and he did not finish, but my uncle continued so that my parents are all for my becoming a doctor.

Another southern senior reported:

> My father always said, "You can win the Nobel prize." All the members of my family as well as the faculty at school encouraged me to go into science.

In some situations the parents push in one direction and the young men are influenced but not persuaded. A southern high school senior simply avoids discussion, or at least conflict:

I want to be a psychiatrist. My parents and I have had no
discussions in depth, but I don't want to argue with them. They think
I will change my mind and become a surgeon so I just skip it.

Evasion is not quite so easy for the Morehouse sophomore who said:

It is hard for me. I really need someone to talk to who understands my problems. My parents don't quite understand. I hate to do
anything that they do not wish me to do. I think they would like for
me to be a doctor and not a French professor as I would prefer.

One young man interpreted the source of conflict between himself
and his parents:

My family puts pressure on me to complete my work at Morehouse, which means continuing in chemistry from which I now want
to change. I believe the majority of Negro families who have had
little money put emphasis on getting in and getting out and earning.
There is very little support for a change of major.

Clearly many parents play a role in the choices which their sons
make. Some seek to stop their children from aspiring too high or from
pursuing fields in which they will encounter difficulties. Others, pleased
with their sons' prospective choices, are supportive, and others simply
consider it best not to interfere.

Although parents are often influential persons in a young man's
occupational decision making, others occasionally play a determining
role. A northern sophomore identified the key persons who influenced
his choice:

The critical people responsible for shaping my outlook are my
godfather, who is a professor of anthropology at Columbia and who
raised my horizons about history and law; my stepfather and mother,
who have always been interested in my achieving a career; and an
official at the Urban League. I knew her daughter, and in going to
her house, I met a lot of interesting people and mixed quite a lot with
varying social and cultural groups.

Sometimes a teacher was central:

In the eighth grade I had a history teacher who was an English
lady. She liked me and encouraged me to think about becoming a
history teacher. I decided then that I would become one.

Another reported:

In high school, one of the greatest teachers I have ever had, a
chemistry teacher, inspired me tremendously, and I decided then
that I wanted to be a chemist.

Still another had this to say:

> There was a Negro French teacher in high school and she inspired me to become a teacher. Since I was specializing in biology and was doing well, I made a decision that I would prepare to become a high school biology teacher.

Friends and acquaintances often play an important role:

> When I went to Boston with the glee club I stayed with a doctor who was just out of medical school and he gave me pointers. He was a recent graduate and made me more sure about becoming a doctor. You see, my uncle finished in 1940 and this young man in 1959. There was almost nineteen years difference and several changes had been made in this field which really helped me to decide.

Another heading for medicine said:

> There are many examples. There were doctors in the community. It was the way they carried themselves. A doctor in a small community is strangely set apart. People trust one man and go to him for help in solving their problems, problems that have nothing to do with medicine. They have an outstanding and strong influence in the community. And so this kind of man inspires respect in so many small communities.

Occasionally a young man referred to the influence of nationally known figures as evidence that certain fields had become open to Negroes and that Negroes could achieve eminence in established fields:

> There is a Bob Teague on NBC news who is a news reporter. I first saw him this summer at the California convention over TV. That was the first time I had seen a Negro on TV newscasting. It did show me some openings that would be available in that field.

Another said:

> As a young boy I developed an interest in the judiciary field, in law. People like Thurgood Marshall, Powell, and Edward Brooke, the attorney general in Massachusetts, have influenced me.

In addition to parents and other key persons, young people are frequently helped to clarify their occupational choices through formal or informal guidance and counseling. The young men in our group referred both to the guidance they received and the guidance they wanted but which was not forthcoming.

A Southern high-school senior reported about the guidance to which he had been exposed:

I want to be a CPA. That was my first choice. I have also thought of working in insurance, in the actuary department. A teacher of mine gave us booklets about being a CPA, but I have had no counseling about what is involved in being an actuary.

A northern high school senior learned about the educational prerequisites for aeronautical engineering from his school counselor:

When I first settled on aeronautical engineering, I spoke to the counselor here and he told me that I would not only have to continue my education by going to college, but that I would probably have to take graduate courses also. I plan to do that.

A northern high school senior reported:

When I was younger, before high school, I thought about being a lawyer or a writer, but my father said it was hard to get into the law field. My average in English is 75 to 80 and my English teacher said it would be better if I went into something else. I talked about it with my adviser and he agreed I should go into music since that was my love. That is when I decided to go into music.

Another young northerner had helpful teachers:

In junior high school I found that I liked ceramics in the industrial arts class. I want to go into ceramics engineering. The teachers here have encouraged me to go for a scholarship and I got one at Alfred.

On occasion, a school official can push so hard that the young person balks at his advice:

When I was a child a strange thing happened. I wanted to be a doctor but my principal in high school pushed me too hard. He obtained a six-year scholarship for me at Boston University. This was a six-year combined college and medical school. As good as their offer was I disliked being pushed and so I turned it down.

A northern college senior told us:

When I came to New York ten years ago, I didn't have the slightest idea of what to do in terms of a career. But in junior high school, high school, and college, I received sufficient information to help me to make up my mind.

Another Northerner, a college sophomore, also reported that his counselor had been helpful:

I would say that I got good guidance—I was even informed about scholarship opportunities available to Negroes.

Another offered a mixed report:

> At C_____ High School I was offered a scholarship to a Catholic
> university but no help in working out a career.

Against this generally positive assessment of the help received from
teachers and counselors in clarifying their educational and career plans
must be placed the considerable negative testimony offered by many.

A northern student now in college reported his experience and his
reactions to them:

> I think that representative college courses should be given in the
> senior year in high school so that students will know more about the
> challenge of college courses. I also think there should be more
> guidance in high school. I feel that part of my problem was not
> knowing what to expect.

A CCNY senior talked about his earlier experiences in the New York
City school system:

> There should be more guidance at the high school level. I was
> not advised to go to college. The guidance man just wanted to get me
> out of the school. The emphasis was that I now had a high school
> diploma and I could get a good job. While this didn't affect me, it
> could frustrate other Negro children. The prevalence of social
> problems, such as delinquency, interferes with the advisory function.
> No one ever mentioned scholarships to me. It was just assumed that I
> would not go to college.

A few young men explicitly stated that they believed that more
could be done with the use of psychometric instruments to help students
clarify their career objectives:

> I wish college could have offered an aptitude test to give us at
> least a general idea of our capabilities. I believe that the counseling
> system at Morehouse is very inadequate. There is no opportunity to
> find out about requirements or possibilities in various fields. The
> Placement Office provides booklets but little else. I have had no
> occupational guidance.

In some cases, the scores that a young man received on his aptitude
test caused him to alter his choice:

> I originally wanted to go into engineering when I was fourteen
> I liked math and science and thought this would be best applied
> in engineering. Several friends of the family were engineers and
> they influenced my choice.... In the ninth grade in high school I
> took aptitude tests. All grades were high except mechanical ability.
> I was told that the 56th percentile was not good enough for en-

gineering. So I changed to chemistry in which I had a 95 average in high school.

A southern college senior thinks that being Negro negatively affected the quality of his guidance:

> If I were white, I'd probably have had more help in making plans. My high school counselor concentrated on keeping students in school and urging them to go to college. Individual teachers stressed opportunities in teaching. I came to college looking for something else because I regard teaching as a last resort. My high school provided nothing except career days when job choices in general were discussed. I think the personnel department at college should offer students work opportunities related to career plans, more for experience than for money.

The young men in our study gave us a wide range of reactions to the extent and quality of guidance they received. A minority encountered no special difficulties in clarifying their occupational choice and in taking the right steps to pursue it. Another group received considerable positive support and encouragement from home, and they too were able to find their direction without too much trouble.

Still others were lucky enough to have friends or acquaintances who helped them to clarify their ideas about the future. But there were a great many—probably a majority of the entire group—who needed help from teachers and counselors. Some got help and, for the most part, it was constructive. But more reported an absence of information, testing, and counseling. They were left to resolve their own uncertainties without a helping hand either from their classroom instructors or from staff counselors.

Although better or more guidance may be a matter of some significance in the developmental experiences of all young people, the role of race in the decision-making process of most young Negroes can be determining. Minorities, faced with discrimination, often must forego utilizing their potential and education and settle for second or third best since the preferred positions in society are arbitrarily closed to them. This points to the importance of considering the principal obstacles in the process of occupational choice determination of these Negro youth.

Most of these young men referred to some obstacle that might interfere with the realization of their occupational goals, but few anticipated being blocked completely. They called attention to a miscellany of factors: limitations of money to finance an extended period of graduate or professional study, uncertainty as to whether they possess the intellectual capabilities or specific aptitudes required to perform at a high level of competence in a chosen field, and problems of personality that might make it difficult for them to persevere under the frustrations of a long and arduous course of studies. These were the principal types of obstacles which the young men think might upset their plans. Although the college seniors appear to be a little more aware of possible obstacles in their path — they were closer to the world of work — the overriding impression, despite notes of caution, is one of quiet confidence.

This is revealed in the following statements by three southern college men: A sophomore who hopes to be a dentist said: "I am pretty sure of my ability." A senior whose goal is to be a systems engineer remarked: "I will have a fairly easy time because I think I have the mental capacity to do this job." A sophomore who plans to be a doctor said: "It will be fairly easy. The work is difficult in this field, but no more difficult than anywhere else."

Dedication to their occupational goal was considered by two other southern college men to be a sound basis for optimism. A senior who wishes to be a doctor said: "It will not be too difficult. If you like what you are doing, it is not hard but worthwhile." A sophomore noted: "I've been interested in music all my life. I can't think of anything that would prevent my going on in music."

Some have considered the employment market and perceive it in favorable terms. A northern high school senior said: "I chose business administration because it is such a wide field." A southern college sophomore who plans to become an electrical engineer remarked: "Many industries are opening up for Negroes so it will be fairly easy to get into this field." A southern high school senior said: "I will make it, I believe. In time, by hard work I will make money. I will do things better because I am a Negro and have white competition. This competition will not stop me but will only make me work harder for the future."

Some students believe that their future depends very much on their own efforts. A northern sophomore who plans to be a CPA believes that "there are no obstacles other than myself."

A northern high school senior who is undecided about whether to follow law or pharmacy sees no obstacle "except making up my mind." A southern high school senior said: "I am ambitious and I feel I can be something if I want to be." A southern senior who expects to enter finance remarked: "I'll have an easy time. All that is necessary will be a good performance and favorable impressions. I'm a little conceited about myself."

One might almost see cockiness in the prospective psychologist who said that "nothing is keeping me back," and in the budding chemist who said: "I feel that my opportunities are unlimited right now. I feel I have the ability to do the work and don't foresee any discrimination which will affect me. I feel confident that I have the mental ability."

So much for the optimists. Some of the group, of course, see problems ahead. Several referred to financial problems. A southern sopho-more whose aim is to be a research chemist believes: "Financially it will be hard. I am an honor roll student but I need financial backing badly." A northern college senior said: "The financial aspect is the real obstacle. When I come out of the service, I will have to go to work in the best-paying job that is available and arrange to go to law school at night." A southern college senior whose goal is medicine reported: "It is difficult in the sense that I do need necessary funds. Otherwise, there is no problem as far as intellectual background is concerned."

Some had doubts about themselves, particularly about their desire and ability to stay with their studies. A northern senior who is planning to become a physician said: "I do feel apprehensive about the grind in terms of my ability to see it through." One of his classmates who wishes to be a history teacher reported: "I don't foresee any obstacles except my own feelings of indecision which I have to contend with sometimes." A southern college senior who hopes to be a lawyer feels: "I will be able to carry out my plans but it will not be easy. Any field you enter is hard at first. You must apply yourself." A classmate whose goal is aeronautical engineering realizes: "It requires hard work since the field is so new and broad. I am sure of myself and my ability, but to work at a job of this kind takes real dedication and I'm not quite sure I am dedicated to this extent."

From what these students, the confident ones and the doubtful, have revealed about themselves, we can see that they are little different from any other group of adolescents and young adults from middle-class backgrounds. They are neither unduly self-confident nor overly anxious about themselves and their futures.

We have left to the last their feelings about the element of race and whether they attribute much importance to it in shaping their choices or in their ability to implement them. The quotations presented here, most of them silent about race, suggest that many of our youngsters did not consider it very important in their decision making. Even when an occasional student mentioned the racial obstacle, he was likely to con-clude that, on balance, he would be able to surmount it without undue trouble.

A southern senior who anticipates a career in real estate believes: "The future will become more and more competitive as racial conditions change. There will be more opportunities but higher requirements. However, a Negro with ability and drive will have a pretty good chance." A northern college senior who plans to practice law in Atlanta said that the only obstacle he can see is "the hazard of a Negro living in the South and competing with white lawyers who command greater acceptance." A southern college senior, aspiring to be a doctor, thinks he will have to contend with "the preconceived notions about Negroes. The patients at the hospitals will probably draw back and think only that I am a Negro. But, studentlike, I hope to be able to conquer their dislike."

There are two ways of interpreting this underplaying of the racial factor in their expectations. One is to see it as evidence of their immaturity and naiveté in face of the continued difficulties experienced by Negroes in overcoming restrictive policies. The other is to see these Negro college men as eminently realistic insofar as their awareness of new opportunities for educated Negroes is concerned. They do not say they expect never to encounter discrimination, either in preparing for their careers or in pursuing them, but they do suggest that they expect to achieve their plans. That they are Negroes is no longer the crucial factor. Whether these young people are naive or realistic will be known only in the future. But it is likely that their relaxation about the racial element is sound, if only because of the growing demand for the skills of the well trained. Furthermore, it runs counter to Negro experience to err on the side of optimism.

Now that we have the wide range of considerations influencing these young men in their approach to career choice, we shall briefly summarize the key facts that have become clear. By and large the parents of these young Negroes, like the parents of middle-class white college students, play a part—but not the determining part—in the way their offspring approach their occupational choices. Although a few may insist that their sons prepare for specific occupations, most of them are willing to assume positions on the sidelines. They proffer advice when asked, they offer their criticisms in muted tones, and in general they are supportive.

The second important fact is that the conventional middle-class Negro vocational choices of elementary and secondary school teaching and the ministry have receded far into the background; in their place one finds such new fields as business management, science, and engineering. These young people have made their choices with considerable awareness of the new opportunities. In fact, only a very few give consideration to matters of race in weighing alternatives.

These young men will find it difficult to exploit fully the new opportunities, since there are few models in their immediate families or environs who can help them learn about styles of work and the best ways of getting prepared. In addition, the counseling they have received in school is frequently inadequate. Nevertheless, in one way or another, they are achieving that knowledge about the unknown that they need to get themselves pointed in the right direction.

For the most part their career goals are realistic. One young man may aspire to become a justice of the Supreme Court, and another hopes that he may some day be president of General Motors. But these are dreams, not serious plans. Most of the group are much more modest. They seek to enter fields within their competence and grasp.

The extent of their broadened opportunities is best revealed by the fact that when they consider their life work, they weigh not only such mundane matters as prospective income and opportunities for promotion, but also whether their careers will enable them to gain direct satisfaction from their work, irrespective of monetary rewards. Like many other educated people, they want meaningful and challenging work and they expect to find it.

CHAPTER 29

Tell Me about Your School

CONVENTIONAL WISDOM ABOUT GHETTO SCHOOLS

THE U.S. PUBLIC is duly exercised about the performance of public education in low-income areas of our big cities, and with considerable justification. They know that many youngsters drop out of school without acquiring the competences they need to be hired into any but the most unskilled job. Many who drop out are one, two, or even three years retarded in reading or arithmetic.

Another cause of widespread concern stems from the knowledge that many youngsters, while ostensibly on the school's rolls, are in fact spending most of their time on the city streets, often engaged in destructive behavior from vandalism to muggings. Neither truant officers nor others in the educational bureaucracy appear to be concerned about identifying the truants and they are certainly unsuccessful in assuring that they return to the classroom.

Trouble and crime in the streets is only one aspect of the nonengagement of students. There is also a great amount of trouble that occurs within the school—in the classrooms, the corridors, the lavatories, the lunchrooms, the study halls. At the extreme, teachers and others in authority are assaulted. The harassment of fellow students is so pervasive that nobody takes notice except the victim.

A no-win debate has long been underway over whether responsibility for these dysfunctional conditions rests with society, the educational leadership, principal and teachers, the community, the family, or the individual student. There are those who contend that if the public would spend as much or more on pupils in disadvantaged neighborhoods as on those attending schools in affluent suburbs, many if not all of the foregoing shortcomings could be eliminated. Others refuse to accept this interpretation because they point out that average expenditures per child in a low-income urban area (in the North and West) are considerably above the average for the nation as a whole.

Those who point to the educational bureaucracy as the source of the major difficulties call attention to subtle discrimination, teacher assignment systems that place the youngest and least experienced in the most difficult schools, and seniority systems that result in too few teachers and principals from minority groups. Each of these charges can be rebutted, surely in part, sometimes in whole. A few ghetto schools have been able to perform creditably in the face of these handicaps.

With respect to community control, two contrasting positions can be identified: those who claim that neighborhood schools fail to perform because of an absence of community control, and those who point to instances where conditions actually deteriorated after community boards were granted decision-making powers.

As one might expect, those with roots in the educational enterprise, particularly the classroom teacher and principal, are quick to point to the weaknesses in many of their pupils' families to explain why the school's efforts are often ineffectual. They point out that no school is able without assistance from the family to establish the discipline, motivation, study habits, and performance standards that are integral to effective learning. Many who teach in ghetto areas complain that all or most of these preconditions are absent in the case of their pupils. But others are loath to accept this explanation. They point out that in generations past many children whose families were poor and often disorganized coped with their lessons and obtained at least the basic education they needed to make a reasonable transition, when the time came, into the world of work.

There are observers who see the heart of the difficulty in the inherent shortcomings of the students themselves. Some believe that minority youth, particularly blacks, have greater difficulty than whites in conceptualization and analysis. Others call attention to the differences between the majority and minority populations with respect to motivational factors. The way they formulate the difference is this: Minority youth are more "present-oriented," more interested in immediate gratification, which translates into a lack of ability on their part to undergo the discipline and put forth the effort needed to profit from their schooling.

There is no point in trying to choose among these many explanations for the mediocre educational performance of many minority youth. Some of the explanations are complementary, some contradictory; the last mentioned is beyond the pale except for a few developmental psychologists who are convinced of the hereditary inferiority of the black population.

In the face of so many unproved and even unprovable hypotheses and conclusions, there is special merit in the reader's keeping his or her presumptions and prejudices under control as he or she follows what these youngsters have to say about their educational experiences. They may not possess an overview of what is right and what is wrong about the schooling to which they are being exposed, but it would be presumptuous for others to reach judgments about what should be done to make their schooling more responsive to their needs without paying close attention to what they report. . . .

INTERVIEWS

Eleven-Year-Olds

Barnes

Skills Well, I do math well, I read well, draw well and I do arts and crafts well. I like to make things out of wood and I like to make faces out of clay. I also like playing the flute because my teachers will let us keep the flute. I like to sing soft songs and English songs. I play baseball very well. I'm in the pee-wee league.

I got interested in them in school, the center and in the playground. One day my friends asked me if I wanted to play baseball and I said yes.

I would like to play the guitar, make cars, a lot of people like to ride in cars; play basketball because a lot of my friends always ask me to play and I don't know how to play.

School I like school because I like to work. I like to do math, reading, science, arts and crafts, and music. School is interesting. If I don't go to school, I won't be smart.

Some kids do bad things to the teacher like putting thumbtacks in the chair. My teacher wants to help, but the children resist. They feel that they should come to school and do what they want. The teacher makes a

list of the bad children to be given to Mr. R_____ [the assistant princi-
pal]. One time the bad kids made the teacher cry.

Yes, school is helpful, mainly because I'm learning how to read. In
Catholic school, all I did was fight every day. I wasn't learning. All the
children did was fight. They didn't want to learn. Now I'm learning a
great deal like math, arts and crafts.

Friends Some hate school. They are lazy and do not want to do the
work and they are bad. They don't want to listen to the teacher because
they say that the teachers are bad and they are bad to them. When they
do this, they prevent me from learning.

Homework Every day and on the weekends when we are bad.

Two to three pages of work in all my subjects [math, reading, and
science].

One hour [per night].

I get help from my older brother, he's thirteen, sometimes from my
father and mother.

Future I would like to be a doctor.

If you want to be a doctor you have to know all the subjects, if you
don't, you can't help the people get well.

Reading Stories, folk tales and fairy tales; comic books—I collect
them; Super Heroes, Hot Stuff and Archie.

What Else about School I like my teacher, sometimes she is strict, she
makes you do your work especially at lunch. There are some kids who
like to make trouble because they fight other children and tease them.
Sometimes when the teacher gets angry, the teacher punishes the whole
class. It's not fair because some kids like to learn, so half the class gets left
back. Parents should get involved with their children like my father does.
Girls play with boys a lot and don't want to do the work. Kids who want to
learn work together. My friend and I do homework together and test
each other.

Yes, my teacher wants us to learn. She cares about us. My teacher is
black. . . .

Additional Interview Material

Several of the young boys emphasize that the teachers "scream" at
them, something that they greatly dislike—the more so if they have not
been the cause of the trouble. Other terms that come through not only
occasionally, but repeatedly, are "mean" and "strict." Several of the
interviewees use the first to characterize both teacher and principal. With
respect to strictness, they are ambivalent. Some complain about their
teacher's being too strict, but others note that their teacher is not strict
enough.

One must be careful to balance these negatives with positives. Consider #28: "The principal is good; he helps us too, like the teachers." Of another, #31: " . . . if you want her [the teacher] to help you, she will help you only if you want to help yourself. If you don't want to help yourself, she won't help you." The same youngster said that his teacher "favors the girls in class, especially when answering questions." This is the only reference to favoritism that appeared in the interviews of the boys.

There were repeated references, as in #32, to disruption in the classroom: "I don't like what goes on. Usually there is a lot of fighting, talking and playing cards." Many who objected to the disturbance recommend that the unruly be "put out of school." An occasional student reveals a less extreme response, as in the case of #33: "Their mothers should come to school to talk with the teachers and should be given chances before they get suspended." Several, such as #34, said they could be learning more except for the disruption.

Among the strange insights offered was the following (#30): "When you go to the bathroom, the whole class goes with you. One of my teachers takes the girls, and the other takes the boys."

We asked questions about substitute teachers and discovered that the students were exposed to them relatively infrequently, mostly when their regular teacher was ill, which did not happen more than once a month.

After the interviewing had begun, we added several questions including how many hours a day they looked at television, whether they had a library card, whom they would consult about job information, and whether they knew any high school graduates who had obtained good jobs.

The replies fell in the following bounds: TV viewing time averaged about four hours daily; most students had a library card, but many got their reading material from the school library or from local stores; teachers, center directors, relatives were the persons they would consult about jobs; and few reported that they knew a high school graduate who had obtained a regular job. . . .

Amy

Skills Math, reading that's about it.

I like to draw. I can play the drums and sing. I can fix toys and play baseball, football, kickball, soccer, and tennis.

I learned to play the drums in church, and my brothers play baseball and football. I play with them. I got interested in soccer and tennis in summer school.

Drawing, I would like to be an artist.

School I like school because I like to learn but sometimes the teachers make us do things we don't want to do. Well, before we go on a trip the teacher will make everyone go to the bathroom even if we tell her we don't have to go.

The boys fight most of the time. They like to start trouble [pick fights] with the girls. The boys are nasty to the teacher. Sometimes she puts them in a corner, calls the assistant principal, or ignores them.

Yes, I'm learning how to write stories, how to sound out words, how to do different kinds of math, and how to play an instrument.

Friends I don't know, we don't talk about school.

Homework Yes, every day except half days.

Two hours a day.

My sister and grandmother.

Future I want to be an artist.

Yes, because on Friday we have art classes and we learn how to make things.

Reading I read *Fiesta, Air Pudding and Wind Sauce, How Mothers Are.* I like to read.

What Else about School The principal is nice. The teacher is mean. If the principal sees us doing wrong, she doesn't say anything, but if the teacher sees us she will punish us. Sometimes she pulls our hair or ear. . . .

Additional Interview Material

A ten-year-old (#4) says that she likes school because "sometimes my reading teacher lets me do extra reading and so does my math teacher." This same interviewee says that "I'd like to be a teacher because I like school and like teaching children."

An eleven-year-old (#6) reports that her art teacher got her "interested in drawing." Several of the respondents reported that they had acquired interests and skills from siblings, such as #8: "My sister taught me to make rugs last Christmas." This girl indicated that she wanted to be a nurse when she grew up, the most frequent choice among her peers, selected by about half of all the girls.

An unusual response to how her friends liked school was the reply of #9, who pointed out that they didn't care for school "because they say it is hard to get up in the morning and they just don't like it."

Interviewee #11 reported that she likes "music but I don't like the teacher because he screams at us if we make a mistake," a trait that was shared by the one principal who is mean (the other is nice): "The mean one screams at us for dumb reasons and he is strict."

One of the more traumatic experiences of school is to be accused unfairly and punished for something one didn't do: #13 — "I don't like school because my teachers blame things on me and then I can't go on trips. Sometimes they are right but sometimes they are wrong."

An eleven-year-old (#17) in West Harlem, replying to what goes on in the classroom, said: "Nothing much. The girls do their work. The boys are jumpy. They throw things at the girls when the girls do their work. When the teacher makes the girls monitors, the boys get jealous." The same youngster pointed up what was key to her school experience: "The teachers in my school are concerned about me. They like me and I like them."

The extent to which even interested and concerned teachers encounter difficulties is suggested by the comment of #19: "My teacher can't teach because the kids are talking all the time." On the other hand, #20 reports a different outcome: "People fight, the teacher screams at the kids but most of the kids do their work. . . . "

Fifteen-Year-Olds

Frank

Skills I'm good at reading, singing, hobbies, wood craft, and art.

I got interested in these things by coming to the center. I saw all the things the other kids were doing, so I became interested in them.

I would like to learn how to fix cars, airplanes, and in general, how machines and engines work.

School Sometimes I like school and sometimes I don't. First of all, Junior High School 1- was old. They showed us new pictures of the new school (P.S. 5-) and we were told that it was a better school, but in fact it was not. My school is a jail. If two classes cause trouble (fighting, name calling, food fights, etc.), everybody gets punished. If one person causes trouble like starting fights, ringing the fire alarms, the whole class gets punished. School treats us like children instead of adults.

When you teach a class everybody is suppose to pay attention, and when this doesn't happen, the teacher gets mad because she can't handle the class anymore. Everyone does whatever they want to do, this goes on all day. Kids talk to other kids, some fight, argue; people get mad at each other. The teachers are mad at us.

Friends They feel the same way I do. Sometimes school is fun, sometimes boring.

Homework We get very little homework. Once or twice a week. We mostly do our homework in school.

I spend about one hour on it, I do my homework first. They usually give us two hours worth, and usually it's a lot.

From my mother and father.

Future I would like to be an auto mechanic or a pilot.

No. My school doesn't have the equipment nor the teachers to teach us about cars and airplanes.

Reading Books, stories of famous movie stars, baseball players. . . .

What Else about School My school is very quick to change.

The teachers and principal, when visiting other schools, would try to make our school the same way.

If somebody acts up in class, the teachers scream at him, then there is an argument, then the kid gets sent to the principal for punishment, he's suspended from school, returns and does the same thing once again.

Jobs Yes, my counselor. Every Wednesday I see her.

She's been saying that I should want to go to school and I should improve my grades. Also, she's been discussing the kinds of high school I should go to but she doesn't discuss college.

Yes, because I like to have an education, a good life, a job so I could support a wife so I would not have to go on welfare.

Yes. I would like to go to college. . . .

Additional Interview Material

A considerable number, such as #21, reported that they knew no one who had finished school and who had succeeded in landing a good job. The same respondent said he would like to be a "black architect" when he grew up. This was a rare reference to the role of race in their lives. Respondent #24 said he "wanted to write about black people and about the ghetto and love."

One of the students, #22, who succeeded in gaining entrance to a selective high school, Brooklyn Tech, was sensitive to the close linkages between schooling and later work: "I feel that I have to go to school to get a good job. You have to have a profession in order to qualify for a good job." He was also the *only* respondent who said, "I'm going to college definitely."

The extent to which students who want to study resent their peers who make trouble in the classroom is suggested by the comment of #23, who said that the kids causing disturbances "should be put out of the class, or put away somewhere."

In answer to an inquiry as to whether summer school would be a good idea as early as the fourth grade, #24 said no "because they don't have that much trouble in learning. It's just in junior high school you start failing." The same student, in responding to what he would do if he were mayor to improve the educational system, said: "Provide a college fund or bonds for students who attend school and do well.

Although fathers are frequently absent from the home, the influence of other relatives can be seen, as in the following comment by #25: "Money is important but my grandfather said I'll get a good job with money if I get a good education, do good in school and earn a scholarship."

There was relatively little reference to sex and almost none to drugs. However, #26 talked about "some people checking out the girls." He went on to add: "If you want to learn, you learn. The teachers say, 'If you don't want to listen, don't listen; if you do, then listen.' Some of them think school is a drag; they don't like it. I know this guy who didn't go to school for two months." Small wonder that many students are negative: "The teachers think school is a jail; they don't let us out sometimes. They think we are criminals."

In #27, we see the influence of siblings on educational and career choices: "She [sister] says I should finish school and go to high school and college because that's the only way I'll be able to make it. She says I should think about being an engineer. You know my sister is in college and she says it's a good deal."

The tension between students and teachers is reflected in the following comment (#9): "Sometimes when the teachers get mad at the students and when they get sick they don't come in. Often they don't come in to school and if they're in school they just simply leave." Or the situation described by #11: "Some of the teachers might take advantage of the students, like if they hit you and you hit them back, they'll call the principal and have you suspended."

School may leave a great deal to be desired (#12): "I hate when people take your stuff—clothes, shoes, money—out of your locker. . . . But I feel that school is something I got to do because without it you can't do nothing like getting a good job. You have to get out there and get yours before they give you what you want."

Much the same sentiment is reflected by #14: "A lot of my friends ask me to play hooky, but I tell them that I have to get the education."

The difference in attitude between students and those in authority is suggested by another comment of #14: "The school has a lot of rules like don't bring no weapons to school. . . . "

Grace

Skills I love math and I'm good at it. I'm also good with horses.
I play basketball.
When I make a basket I feel I have accomplished something. When you help the team it's a good feeling. Math is fun. I like algebra and working with numbers. I've always liked horses. I love anything that has to do with horses.

I would like to play a guitar. I want to act, I love to do plays because you show people your talent.

School I think it's terrific. They're trying to teach us what we should know to make it in life.

My school is like a wild school. There are a lot of fights. When things calm down they get to the lessons. Everybody is quiet in their favorite classes like math, reading, social studies, and gym.

I'm nice to my teachers because if they have an interest in me they will want to help me more.

Friends Most of my friends are indifferent to school, but they go because they realize that they need a diploma to get a job. They go to school, the teacher marks them present and then they leave [play hooky]. They don't go to learn.

Homework No, I don't get homework very often except math. We get a work sheet and that's once in a blue moon.

About twice a month.

About twenty minutes—half an hour.

My mother helps me.

Future I really haven't thought about it. I'll probably teach kindergarten. I like to be with little people.

Reading I read biographies, mysteries, and books like *Roots*.

I learned how one race of people will use and take advantage of another. I learned about some of the things black people have gone through. I learned that if you concentrate you can solve a problem by using your brain.

What Else about School Some of the teachers try to teach and some don't care. A lot of teachers will tell you they get paid whether we learn or not. Some people don't care about themselves and some don't care about other people. They will do things regardless of whether it's right or wrong in order to be accepted.

Jobs Yes. They ask me how I feel about school. I tell them I love school. They ask me if I want to go to college, I tell them yes.

I plan to stay in until I finish because I'm interested in school. I like math, reading, the activities. It gives me a chance to learn. If I get my diploma then I will feel that I have made it in this neighborhood. . . .

Additional Interview Material

The young women appeared to be more positively oriented toward school.

In the view of #18, "my teachers are nice. For one thing they try to get everyone to come to school." And, the respondent continued, "I would encourage teachers who are afraid of students to be stricter and not just sit back and say I'll get paid whether they learn or not."

Interviewee #9 showed considerable understanding about the students who act up in class: "I would put them in special schools to help them with their problems. Some of them are neglected and just want attention." Others are unsympathetic and recommend suspension. Girls who get pregnant should be sent to "a special school because people tease them and call them stupid and talk about them." Interviewee #14 suggested that they stay out of school "because they might get into a fight and the baby would get hurt." But most recommended that they continue in school till close to their delivery.

One student (#20) wanted to take a strong line with those who disturbed the class: "Troublemakers should be sent to a separate school far away from their homes. They should spend the night there and if possible be taught manners."

In some cases parents and relatives exert considerable pressure on the youngster to stay in school and do well. Consider #2, who reported this is what her parents told her: "Stay in school, there's nothing out there on the street; you can't be anything on the street."

Several of the students agreed with #7 that "school sometimes is hectic because we have so many finals and tests." But another student (#8) reports that her friends like school "because their teacher lets them play." Another, #13, reports that those of her friends who don't like school "play hooky because it is boring."

A black student (#11), who attends a bilingual school is uptight because she reports that when "they have shows in the auditorium everything is in Spanish. Even during black history week the program is mostly in Spanish. Some of my teachers act as if they don't like black people and I don't like them."

WHAT THE STUDENTS TOLD US

If one juxtaposes the conventional wisdom about ghetto schools with the interview materials we have just presented, it becomes clear at once that many assumptions and beliefs about contemporary urban education require reassessment and correction. Without ascribing any significance to the ordering of the confrontations between the beliefs many adults hold and the views expressed by these young people, the following issues warrant reassessment.

The assumption that urban education is a wasteland, a place where the taxpayers' money is squandered by paying the salaries of teachers who don't teach and students who come to class to play and not to learn, is far wide of the mark. It is regrettably true that some teachers don't do much teaching, either because of excessive disruption in the classroom or because of their lack of interest or capacity to engage and interest those who are assigned to them. But if these eighty interviews about the educational situation in the largest black community in the United States are reasonably representative of large cities, the concept of an educational wasteland is an exaggeration.

What the interviews emphasize is that most teachers are interested in having their pupils learn and that most pupils (those who attend more or less regularly) are interested in acquiring both knowledge and a diploma. This does not mean that some teachers have not been defeated in their efforts to make a real impact on their students or that many students have not been turned off by their experiences in school. Both conditions prevail, and they are sufficiently pervasive to call for study and corrective action. But it would be an error to read the interviews as substantiating the pessimistic view that the negatives in the situation have come to dominate. That is not what our interviewees reported.

Consider the matter of whether the students read books. The pessimists hold that many or most ghetto students are so far behind the reading norms of students who attend schools outside of low-income areas that for all practical purposes they must be considered to be only quasi-literate. Such a judgment is probably extreme. It is improbable that both our younger and older interviewees would have reported that they borrow books regularly from the school library, from the neighborhood public library, or from stores in their locality unless reading for pleasure was a regular activity. Only a small number said they did not have a borrowing card from the public library, and only one student stated outright that she doesn't read much and seldom finishes a book because she prefers to be outside. . . .

Pessimists might counter with the claim that when one considers the amount of time these young people devote to reading and contrasts it with the hours they devote to watching television, one has clear evidence that reading plays only a minor role in their developmental experiences. Admittedly it was the exceptional respondent who told us that he or she preferred reading to watching TV, or that their parents rationed their TV watching during the school week. But it is not altogether clear how the greater investment in time in watching TV should be judged. True, the shows these young people mentioned as being among their favorites did not have a great deal of intellectual content, and it is likely that watching TV for three to four hours every evening was a poor investment of their time. But for low-income families TV is the principal recreational outlet — as it is also for many middle-class families. If a student pays close attention during the five hours he or she is in school and does one to two hours homework a night, one might conclude that several hours of TV watching should not be considered dysfunctional. . . .

Part of the conventional wisdom relates to the presumed weaknesses of low-income families, which many, both in and out of the educational system, believe responsible for the low performance of the student body in inner-city schools. We found the evidence of family weakness much less clear-cut. It is true that the reported absence of any reference to a father in the house suggests that many young people were growing up with only one parent. That surely is a source of weakness in emotional development, standard of living, role models, and much more.

One must quickly add, however, that a significant minority of the young people who indicated by indirection that their father was not a member of the household did refer to other family members as deeply involved in their development, in school and out of school. This was surely true of the mother who was the head of household; but references were made also to grandfathers and grandmothers, aunts and uncles, and especially older siblings. An elder sibling, even if a member of the opposite sex, can often be helpful to a young adolescent, especially if he or she has succeeded in breaking through barriers—for example, having gained admission to college. Moreover, their reports on how life is in such a new and strange environment, especially when the reports are positive, can help a younger person to set his or her sights a little higher by having proved through their own performance that passage into this new world is feasible.

In discussing these intergenerational relations of students and adults, one must emphasize the large number who hungered for and responded to teachers, guidance counselors, principals who were, as they put it, "interested in them." These young people yearned for caring adults who were able and willing to help them find their way in what is still a very hostile and discriminatory society for black people.

Although it is pure speculation, I am willing to assert that many of those who caused trouble in the classroom and who early became truants and lost interest in the educational venture were young people who failed to encounter any caring adults in or out of school. In many cases their families were under such great pressure that they lacked attention, support, and love at home and, forced back prematurely on their own resources, could not cope satisfactorily with the demands that school and society were making of them.

The girls and young women, for the most part, seemed to have somewhat less difficulty than their male counterparts in adjusting to the discipline of the classroom. Repeatedly, the girls reported that the boys started the fighting. In fact, one or two noted that the boys found it harder to sit still and pay attention to the teacher. Some of the boys accused their teachers of favoring the girls, an accusation that may have some justice if in fact the girls were more attuned and responsive to what was going on in the classroom.

The girls had a further advantage: Almost without exception, they had a role model at home. Their mothers apparently ruled them with a tighter hand and encouraged them from their early years in school to attend to their studies so that they could not only obtain their high

school diploma but also would be better positioned to go either into a
better job or to college. . . .

In answer to the questions that were related to their future, particularly those that explored their attitudes toward college and the world of
work, several notes come through. Interested teachers and guidance
counselors often urged the boys and girls to prepare themselves for the
tests they had to pass in order to gain admission to a preferred high
school or specialized curriculum. Regrettably, many were unable to
reach a passing grade and therefore had to settle for a run-of-the-mill
high school that offered less by way of curriculum, staff, linkages with the
job market such as cooperative education. . . .

After our interviewing began, we spliced a new question into our
inquiry that asked whether the student would be willing to attend summer school to improve his or her grades and broaden later options, even
as early as the fourth grade. With no exceptions, the answer to this
hypothetical question was in the affirmative. There is no way of telling
what these young people would in fact have done had such an opportunity been available to them. . . .

Although college surely was not absent from the plans of many of
these young people, the intensity of their commitment to the idea and
their ability to gain admission remained clouded. In only a rare instance
could one find sufficient resonance in the reply of the young adolescent
to be reasonably sure that he or she would in fact pierce the college
barrier. . . .

We asked whether they knew anybody who, by virtue of completing
high school, had secured a good job. A related question: Whom do they
seek out and talk with if they want to learn about jobs. It is disturbing to
report that a considerable number (a majority) of the older interviewees,
as well as the younger ones, were unable to identify a high school
graduate among their relatives, friends, or acquaintances who had found
the diploma as the way into a good job. Equally, if not more disturbing,
were the replies to the question whom they would consult to learn about
jobs and how one prepared for different types of jobs. A significant
number of the older interviewees again said they were unable to identify
such a source. Several mentioned their counselor or center director. . . .

But if their knowledge of labor market information and successful
job seekers was restricted, the overwhelming majority stated that graduation from high school, and preferably from college, was an essential
precondition for getting a job—especially one that paid reasonably well
and that held promise for the future. . . .

It is unnerving to find the striking gap between this pervasive belief
in the benefit of schooling and the lack of personal knowledge demonstrated by so many of the interviewees of individuals who, as a result of

completing their education had been able to make a satisfactory transition into the world of work. Either the doctrine of the value of an education for job and career success was false or something else was seriously awry. Doctrine and life experience were not in consonance.

In response to the question of what they were planning to do this summer (the interviews took place in May and June 1979), we were struck by two replies that characterized a large number of the total group. The first was that many stated that they would be going South, presumably to visit with relatives. If one has to speculate on what lies behind this visitation pattern, the probable answers lie first in the desire to maintain family ties—much more important among groups who have little money to spend on recreation or other optional expenditures. Second, the streets of New York, especially in low-income areas, are a dysfunctional environment for normal growth and development—the more so during the summer months, when school is out and the hot weather shortens tempers. Hence parents who are able to send their children South in the belief that the experience will be beneficial in terms of both what they gain and what they escape.

The other surprising response to the question of what they would do this summer was the considerable number who said that they would go to camp. Some who indicated they would go South added that they would divide the summer between visiting relatives and camp, but for the most part these were alternatives. . . .

There are two ways to see the entire group in perspective. Harsh realities dominate their lives: many families with only one parent; a level of income that at best enables most families to exist at a low standard of living; adults, when they are employed, working for the most part in unskilled occupations; housing and neighborhoods in disrepair; schools reflecting conditions in the students' families and the neighborhoods. The harshness of these realities can be readily appreciated if one contrasts a middle-class suburban community where two-parent families are the norm; where family income is sufficient to allow for considerable discretionary expenditures; where one or both parents is likely to be employed in a managerial or professional position; where the housing is solid and the neighborhood secure; and where the schools are the pride of the community.

This sharp contrast suggests that the young people from low-income areas in the inner city who, in addition, carry the heavy added burden of being black will be hard pressed indeed to find a suitable place for themselves once they stop their schooling—surely if they lack a high school diploma and even if they have acquired one. In fact, we can not be sure that those who remain in school until they acquire a college diploma will be assured entrance into a preferred job. Most of them may eventually succeed, but they will have to scramble.

The other perspective, a little less bleak, is to appreciate that although these young people are poorly positioned to compete for opportunities with the more favored sectors in U.S. society — white and middle-class — they are not so far off the reservation as to preclude many of them making a satisfactory adjustment, especially if offered a helping hand. Our interviewees had demonstrated that they were able to surmount the harshness of their environment, at least to the extent of trying to make use of the education available to them and recognizing that it was the foundation for their future. These young people were surely disadvantaged in competing for the better jobs and careers that a society has to offer, but they were not beyond the fringe. A few would make it even under present conditions, but a larger number would succeed if our society considered it important to expand their opportunities.

PART VII

Technology and the Changing Economy

ECONOMICS AND ECONOMISTS HAVE STRANGE CHARAC-
TERISTICS, but none is stranger than the fact that, with but a few
exceptions, the great contributors to economic thought have ignored the
subject of technology. Clearly it is not easy to delineate the role of
technology in economic development, since significant innovations and
their diffusion do not occur with any regularity. The random nature of
technological change, however, is not a justification for ignoring the
subject. Moreover, although main-line economists have neglected technology, there have always been an assortment of prophets and cranks
who have paid it special homage.

    Chapter 30 is an early 1960 piece that summarized the thinking
of a distinguished interdisciplinary group of scholars and specialists
who had explored the theme "Technology and Social Change." The
next two chapters on the service sector and on mechanization of work
were prepared as lead articles for issues of *Scientific American* in the
early 1980s and seek to illuminate some of the important changes under
way in the United States and other advanced economies, with atten-

tion to the role of technology in the shaping of these changes.

Chapter 33, my most recent piece, written in December 1983, addresses a perennially important theme: What is the impact of changes in technology on possible losses of jobs and skills held by certain groups of workers? I have attempted to weave together in this single piece the relationships between theory and history, together with a look at the policy implications that flow therefrom.

Chapter 34 calls attention to parallels and differences between the two sides of the Atlantic with regard to work and the values and behavior of workers.

CHAPTER 30

How to Think about Technology

A SEMINAR IS A CONTINUING DIALOGUE. . . . This chapter will extract from wide-ranging colloquies a group of themes that must be confronted directly and evaluated if the seminar is to move from the periphery toward the heart of its concern. . . . Our objective is to develop an agenda that will enable the seminar to select the questions it wants to probe in seeking to further its understanding of the complex interrelations between technology and social change.

KEY ASPECTS OF TECHNOLOGICAL CHANGE

Effective discussion depends on at least preliminary clarification, preferably the definition of key terms. The seminar faced considerable difficulty in sorting out and distinguishing sharply an array of related concepts, all of which are involved in considerations of technology and social change. We early recognized that technology cannot be considered effectively without considering science; and, in turn, trends in science depend in considerable measure on the education and training of scientists,

403

and the opportunities they have to pursue meaningful and constructive careers. We therefore gave considerable attention to the flow of funds available for research and development, and particularly to the significance of the fact that most of these funds are provided by the federal government in the furtherance of its defense and space missions.

In connection with our search for the sources of technological change, some attention was devoted to whether the United States might soon bump against a talent ceiling, because all those who have the intellectual potential to pursue scientific work are already in the field, or in other fields that require individuals with high orders of mental capacity. We noted that the day may be near when new social mechanisms will have to be developed to allocate the limited number of scientifically talented persons among competing national objectives.

Some consideration was paid to the recent vast increases in the number of scientific personnel and the relative infrequency with which significant scientific breakthroughs have nevertheless occurred. Many felt that a primarily quantitative approach might prove seriously misleading. There was even more concern about the fact that such a disproportionate number of scientists and engineers are engaged in military and space research and development activities, which are largely self-contained and do not readily spill over to stimulate the civilian economy.

In this connection, the excessive dependence of the aerospace companies on the federal government and the ways in which government contracting results in the wasteful utilization of scarce scientific and engineering talent came into focus. Concern was also expressed about the difficulties that large corporate enterprises grounded in the civilian economy experience in making effective use of their scientific work force. Some believed that the management of scientists and engineers offers no unique difficulties. If management manages effectively, it can manage research and development effectively. Others saw special difficulties growing out of the conflict between the inherently conservative stance of large corporations and the inherently dynamic orientation of scientists and engineers.

Some discussants felt that managers without special training in science and technology are not able to manage effectively employees whose work they cannot understand or appreciate. It was pointed out, however, that one way around this difficulty would be to select for positions of general management more and more persons with scientific training. Second, there is room for "translators"—individuals who know enough about both worlds to be effective interlocutors.

There was a general consensus that marked changes are under way in the search for and discovery of new knowledge and in its dissemination throughout the economy and society. No one assumed that this is solely a function of the government and other agencies in society spending ever larger sums for research and development and for education, but all agreed that major institutional changes are under way in government, in corporate enterprise, in universities—all of which are caught up in a radically different pattern from that which had prevailed even as recently as the 1930s.

Embedded in these preliminary explorations about technology are the following questions and themes that the seminar may want to pursue:

1. Is there any way of measuring the rate of change in scientific activity and its technological consequences? Are there limits that may soon affect the future rate of such activity?
2. What can be learned about the current utilization of scientists and engineers?
3. Is there a danger in the heavy concentration of scientific and engineering talent in the defense-space sector of the economy; and, if so, what policies and mechanisms might be employed to effect a partial redistribution of these resources?
4. Is there a management problem in corporate enterprise because many managers do not understand the theories and approaches that underlie the work of their technical staffs? If so, in what directions might solutions be sought?

THE RATE OF TECHNOLOGICAL CHANGE

A seminar entitled "Technology and Social Change" was bound to include many who would want to explore the widespread social, economic, and other disturbances and distortions assumed to be resulting from an acceleration of technological change and to seek solutions and remedies for them. But a group composed overwhelmingly of academicians and including a considerable number of economists would also include many who would question the premise that technological change is accelerating. Many academicians, because of the nature of their training, would ask for evidence in support of the thesis of acceleration. Economists would be certain to question such a contention, since they have been unable to uncover, despite detailed empirical studies, any solid evidence that the rate of productivity, or of economic growth, has been accelerating in the United States or in other advanced industrial societies. They would not say that the rate of growth in productivity or economic growth might not increase in the future. But acceleration— no! When confronted with such a claim, economists would remember, many from personal experience, the Technocrats of the early 1930s.

The seminar seesawed back and forth between extreme views on the rate of technological or economic change, with few middle positions. Some simply disqualified themselves from participating in the argument that started during the first meeting and continued unabated through the last.

A shredding out of the positions would include first the arguments for a contention of acceleration: the tremendous increases in resources, both money and personnel, that have been invested in research and development and that have been reflected in the corporate revolution; automation; the harnessing of atomic energy; advances in communications; the leap into space — and many other manifestations of a technology that is making large and rapid gains.

When pushed by the skeptics for evidence in terms of rates of economic growth, the proponents of the acceleration thesis retreated to the position that since the revolution is only recently under way, the future alone can provide the unequivocal evidence. They held that the revolution is too recent to be reflected adequately in historical series.

A second piece of circumstantial evidence advanced in support of the thesis of acceleration is the major breakthrough currently under way as a result of the computer revolution, which is clearly affecting how people think, how they act, and the types of goods and services they demand and use. Without the computer there would have been no jet plane, no exploration of space, and no prospect of the multiple breakthroughs in medicine and education that are already on the horizon.

This did not exhaust their armamentarium. The proponents of the acceleration thesis also called attention to the multiple pieces of evidence of economic tension and social conflict that are a direct consequence of the new technological changes. They pointed first to the evidence that unemployment is creeping upward, slowly but steadily, that it has in fact increased during each of the three last business cycles in the United States. They called attention to the forward march of automation, which is resulting in the dismissal of large numbers of semiskilled workers, many of whom, especially those in their late forties or fifties, have little or no prospect of ever again finding a satisfactory job. They noted in addition the economic difficulties again facing the poorly educated Negro who had found a toehold in the mass production industries of the North during and after World War II.

Still further evidence of acceleration was adduced: the fact that the scientist-technologist has had power thrust on him both in the business corporation and in the councils of government for the simple reason that he alone, among educated men, understands the new theories and their potential applications. Others in positions of power and influence have little option—at least in the short run—but to permit this while they seek to work out new mechanisms whereby they and the larger public can control their own future. The fact that a small esoteric group of intellectuals, steeped in the new mysteries, could take over the key decision-making posts in both industry and government is additional proof that changes in technology have gone far beyond any to which the Western world has been accustomed.

Thus evidence was marshaled. Any single piece might not stand close scrutiny, yet the sum could not be ignored.

Some members of the seminar, however, insisted on doing just that. They did not deny, for instance, that the nation was investing considerably more resources than previously in research and development, but they considered this to be largely beside the point. They felt the basic question was whether the additional resources were providing significant results or whether the yield was small. Economists have long been trained to think in terms of a point of diminishing returns from the application of additional resources. Many discussants felt that the heavy investments that had been made in research and development, particularly in the 1950s, had not paid off as expected, and that we might soon see a change with a leveling off or a decline in the rate of such investment.

Significant economic breakthroughs had occurred earlier in this century, when investments in industrial research had been almost negligible: The expansion in the electric-power and automobile industries were outstanding examples. Each decade has given evidence of continuity and change: For the most part, the improvements that were introduced into the major sectors of industry were minor and contributed only modestly to increases in productivity. But usually a few sectors experienced very rapid changes, such as we are now seeing in electronics. It is easy to select from the great number of industries the few that are undergoing very rapid change and to assume the entire economy reflects these few. This is easy, but it is an error.

An inspection of the data on research and development and of the state of industrial technology disclosed that the vaunted progress that supported the theory of acceleration was restricted to a few sectors of the economy, primarily those closely aligned with defense and space. The rest of U.S. industry was relatively backward with regard to both the level of investment in research and development and the physical state of its technology, much of which is outdated, especially when compared to the new plants in Europe and Japan.

In their repudiation of the acceleration thesis, the economists did not deny that the unemployment level is too high; but they pointed out that little over a decade ago—at the end of the 1940s—it had reached a higher level and had caused little comment. In the interim, however, our expectations and tolerances had changed. A good thing, perhaps, but not a change in technology.

As to the inroads of automation, the skeptics were even more skeptical. In some steel, automobile, meat-packing, rubber, and other plants, large new machines had been installed and output substantially enlarged, while employment remained steady or actually declined. This is hardly new or startling. It has long been the way of the economy. In fact, the basis of a continued rise in the standard of living is the ability of the economy to turn out more goods and more services while using less labor and capital. Since, over the last two decades, the economy had been transformed from one in which most workers were engaged in the production of goods to one in which the majority (more than three out of five) are engaged in the production of services, it does not appear likely that automation is an unlimited industrial threat. After all, it would be difficult, at least in the foreseeable future, for automatic machines to cook meals, cut hair, perform appendectomies, educate young and old, and take over the very large number of other tasks that currently can be performed only by talented or skilled or even unskilled persons.

The skeptics were equally unimpressed with the claim that the enthronement of the scientist-technologist in the centers of power is further proof of a technological revolution. The private manager and the public servant must in one way or another become sufficiently familiar with the competing claims for resources, for manpower and capital remain scarce. It is the duty of the manager in private and public life to weigh the relevance of conflicting claims. There is no way that this task can be transferred to the scientist, even if private entrepreneurs and the Congress were so inclined. Moreover, there is no evidence that those with power and responsibility plan to abdicate. Only technical decisions and expert guidance fall in the domain of the scientist specialist. The entrepreneur in search of profits, or a democracy in search of security, cannot walk away from the task of making decisions about how to use scarce resources.

This, then, was the confrontation between two divergent points of view about whether technological change has been accelerated. What questions remain and how can they best be resolved?

1. How can technological change be measured? Is there any way of gaining additional information about the potentialities of the computer revolution? Is there any way of comparing technological change over two time periods—for instance, 1900 to 1929, and 1940 to 1963?

2. Can automation be operationally defined and can any estimate be made of its progress to date and its future potentialities? Is

> the heavy emphasis of the U.S. economy on services a barrier to
> its rapid expansion?
> 3. In light of the very large-scale investments in research and
>   development in recent years, how can we explain that the rate of
>   technological change has not been more rapid? Is it likely that
>   the level of expenditures for research and development will
>   level off?

PRODUCTIVITY AND ECONOMIC GROWTH

As we have seen, the economists led the debate against the theory of
acceleration in technological change. Much of the work in their discipline in the last few years has been concerned with considerations of
productivity and economic growth. Growthmanship has become a political football as well as the academicians' plaything. Each year has seen the
able students in economics become ever more cautious about the ability
of the U.S. economy to increase significantly its annual rate of growth.
Among others, Denison has demonstrated the many and complicated
adjustments that are required to make small gains.

The question about whether changes of various sorts should be
measured in absolute or relative terms was touched on from time to time
but never thoroughly explored. A further aspect of the problem was
mentioned but escaped careful assessment. Some changes may cumulate
and others may not. The impact of changes on the economy and the
society will differ substantially depending on whether they are transient
or permanent, whether they have a restricted or a multiple effect. These
and other ramifications of the many facets of change still remain to be
explored.

It early became clear that the impact of technology on contemporary
society could be assessed only if some clear referents were identified and
a way found to measure them over time. For this reason, the seminar
repeatedly found the economists attempting to limit the terms of the
discussion to productivity and economic growth and shying away from
social change, where the categories are not specified and cannot be
measured.

Others in the seminar, of course, did not share the economists'
background and preconceptions. The fact that certain overall measures
of productivity did not show significant increases did not seem to these
noneconomists, or even to some of the economists, to minimize the
significance of technological changes. The fact that not one new job had
been added to manufacturing employment over a decade was significant

in its own terms—regardless of what was happening to productivity as a
whole.

It was acknowledged that the full potentialities of the new technology
might not be reflected in productivity data because of the continued
sluggishness of the economy during the last five years. It is well known
that productivity figures tend to increase as the economy approaches full
utilization of plant and equipment, and the last five years have been
years of substantial underutilization.

There are further limitations to measuring technological change
solely with reference to productivity trends. At least a third, and perhaps
as much as two-fifths, of our gross national product is currently accounted
for by the output of the nonprivate sectors—by government and nonprofit institutions. In the private sector the output of goods is constantly
diminishing, while that of services is increasing. The productivity data
as they relate to government and the service sectors are imperfect—
frequently worthless. Since these are the fastest growing sectors of the
economy, overall measures of productivity trends are seriously defective.
Moreover, it is always difficult to take full account of the changes in the
quality of manufactured goods. A 1963 Ford is quite different from a 1940
Ford. Here is still another limitation of the data.

The seminar found it difficult to distinguish among a series of
related but different economic measures: productivity, economic growth,
and economic welfare. Time and again, discussants inadvertently shifted
from one to the other. Economic growth has usually been accompanied
by increases in productivity, but it also involves the total number and
quality of resources available for investment. Productivity can increase
even though the national income, measured in terms of goods and
services produced, does not increase—if the number of people available
for work or the number of hours that they work should decline. Or the
gross national product can increase substantially over a decade, with
little or no increase in productivity, if the size and quality of the labor
force is substantially increasing or if the capital resources devoted to
producing the output are substantially enhanced.

Just as we found it difficult to develop estimates of productivity, so
we found it difficult to develop good estimates of national income—
particularly at a time when so many items that are being produced and
consumed fall outside the competitive market where the price mechanism could measure them.

Moreover, the big jump that many discussants made between technological change and economic growth could not be justified. It is not
impossible, surely not in the short run, for rapid technological changes
to lead to serious overcapacity in the durable goods sector of the economy,
with a consequent depressive action on the economy as a whole that

would slow, or even stop for a time, economic growth. In fact, the years after 1957 give considerable evidence of this type of linkage.

But there is also considerable validity to the proposition advanced by several members of the seminar that the U.S. economy is currently performing unsatisfactorily because of the slow rate of technological change. Since extraordinarily large numbers of young people are becoming available for work, the only prospect of their being employed would follow on substantial investment in new industries as well as the expansion of existing industries. One point, and only one, came clear: There is more than one path from technological change to economic growth. One could not subsume all cases under one generalization.

A further source of confusion that plagued the seminar from time to time grew out of the interchangeable use of the terms *economic growth* and *economic welfare*. The touchstone of economic progress is an increase in the amount and quality of the goods and services available *per head* of the population, not total output. There was general agreement that over the long run technological change had contributed greatly to both economic growth and economic welfare. Real income per capita in the United States has been rising over many decades, in fact centuries; and much of the credit for this was ascribed to advances in technology.

Some in the seminar believed the potentialities of modern technology are so great that, if institutional adjustments could be made, technology could now provide a satisfactory standard of living for everybody in the country and could also make a much greater contribution than hitherto to raising the standards of living of less prosperous nations. This position, simply stated, is that affluence has superseded scarcity. All we have to do to benefit from the changed circumstances is to unleash the full productive powers of the new technology.

No single position advanced in the seminar led to more acrimonious debate. The majority of the group believed this position was vastly overdrawn, and most of the economists considered it totally fallacious. They were impressed with the fact that many millions in the United States are living in poverty and that other families high in the income scale continue to show an appetite and desire for more goods and services. A 4 or even 5 percent annual rate of economic growth is not likely to meet all these domestic needs and desires for many years to come.

Another viewpoint maintained that as U.S. consumers become more affluent—as a consequence of increasing urbanization, among other factors— they need goods and services that cannot be readily supplied by the simple expansion of the private, profit-seeking economy. Many consumers want and need better interurban transportation, better recreational facilities, more and better access to health and educational services, and many other services that conventionally fall in the public domain. But with governments unable to increase their tax resources substantially, these needs remain unmet, with consequent losses in employment and welfare. Some discussants saw the effective resolution of these institutional issues as more important than the acceleration of technological change.

These, then, are some of the issues concerning productivity and economic growth and economic progress that require clarification:

1. To what extent do prevailing measures of productivity, economic growth, and economic welfare provide adequate criteria for assessing the impact of technological change on the economy? What other measures might be useful?

2. To what extent should attention be focused on absolute or relative rates of change? Can useful distinctions be made between changes that are cumulative and those that are not?

3. If the focus of inquiry is on the economic consequences of technological changes, should it be on specific industries, sectors, or on the economy as a whole? What types of questions could best be answered by what approaches?

4. Is it possible, or even desirable, to deal with the economic impact of technological change without simultaneously considering the other forces affecting productivity, growth, and progress? To what extent is it possible to identify and measure these other forces?

SOCIAL CHANGE

The considerable attention the seminar devoted to assessing the impact of technological change in terms of economic referents reflected the belief of many members that these referents are the only ones that can be delineated and measured. All else is shadowy and speculative. But the majority did not in fact adhere to this point of view. Indeed, it was denied by the title of the seminar, which explicitly included a concern with *social* change, which includes economic change but goes far beyond it.

Much of the methodological spinning reflected this cleavage between participants who wanted to limit the discussion to the economic consequences of technological change in the hope of pinpointing at least a few elements, and those who sought to roam farther afield even at the risk of getting lost and of pinning down nothing. It was this difference in orientation that led one discussant to remark at the last session that, difficult as it is to measure economic change growing out of technological advances, this is still easier than focusing on the much broader area of social change, which practically defies definition and measurement.

The composition of the seminar—which, in addition to economists, sociologists, political scientists, and other social scientists included participants from science, engineering, philosophy, history, architecture, government administration, and business—assured that the proponents of a broad construction would win out. Such a heterogeneous group, each of whose members by his presence demonstrated an interest and concern with the problem, could not be satisfied with a focus limited solely to the relationship of technology to economics. . . .

To follow a simple escalation approach, the seminar had occasion to note, although it did not probe, the way in which the new science and technology were likely to affect the education, training, work, and leisure of the average citizen. Stress was laid on the fact that our society would soon have no place left for the unskilled worker, and that even the skilled worker would have to undertake repeated training to keep his skills from obsolescing. Although there was general agreement that the general thrust of the technological advances was to place a premium on intellectual work and to threaten the employment prospects of those of limited education, a warning was introduced against exaggerating this trend. There is much work, particularly in the service fields, that apparently continues to require many people of modest skills—from serving meals to caring for the large numbers of the mentally ill and the aged.

A related suggestion was that since scientists cannot qualify to act as managers simply on the basis of their knowledge of science, and since managers cannot avoid making decisions that increasingly involve them in judgments about science and technology, one way out of the current dilemma is to broaden the educational base of both groups—all who attend college should acquire some knowledge of science, and all engineers and scientists should have some solid grounding in the humanities and the social sciences. It was further pointed out that even if these educational reforms are made, the leaders of the scientific community still have a responsibility to play a much larger role in interpreting the choices our nation faces and, in making this interpretation, to observe the greatest rectitude.

Considerable concern was expressed at many points in the discussion about the substantial changes that are being made in the structure and functioning of the major institution of the private economy—the corporation. In addition to the questions already mentioned as to whether industrial managers are capable of managing enterprises that are increasingly dependent on the advances of science and technology in its more esoteric manifestations, attention was directed to the loss of initiative that seems to characterize the large corporations that are heavily involved in government contracts, particularly in the aerospace industry. Much evidence was adduced to the effect that the officials in the Department of Defense, the National Aeronautics and Space Agency (NASA), the Atomic Energy Commission, pursue policies that surely restrict the scope for freedom and initiative of government contractors.

Many participants felt that important results would accrue from studying in some detail the impact and import of these new relations between government and business growing out of the significant scale of defense expenditures.

Several discussants asked whether the nation is deriving benefits in the civilian sector of the economy from the very large research and development expenditures that are being directed to defense and space. There was general agreement that the spillover is very modest and that it would be only a slight exaggeration to say the civilian sector is being starved for research funds and, even more important, for research personnel, who are overwhelmingly attracted to the more exciting work on the frontiers of defense and space. It was not clear, however, what mechanisms could be developed to insure that adequate personnel and funds would be devoted to urban renewal, housing, recreation, and the conventional areas of the private economy—particularly manufacturing— that had long held the key to economic progress.

The order of difficulty that our society faces in seeking to make the most of the potentialities inherent in science and technology was suggested by the discussion covering the need for a systems approach to take full advantage of these potentialities. It was suggested that our long-standing preference for the nurturing of competitive enterprises and our distaste for cooperative action among large corporations created a real block to the effective development of a "systems approach." We apparently can have more competition or more exploitation of technology, but it would be difficult—perhaps impossible—to have more of both simultaneously.

The antitrust laws are only one block. In housing—a basic area in which the nation continues to confront many urgent needs—an elaborate structure of small enterprises, strong unions, local ordinances, and restricted financing conspired to place major hurdles in the path of rapid technological development of the industry. Here is another conflict area between the institutional fabric and the potentialities of technology.

Failure to find solutions in these areas carries with it the heavy cost of slower economic growth and progress, but much more serious from the point of view of most members of the seminar are the challenges our society faces in any attempt to modify the institutions so that the new technology would not jeopardize but would strengthen our democratic principles and purposes. Many participants felt that if present trends in scientific and technological developments proceed unchecked, before long a relatively small elite will be in possession of most of the decision-making apparatus in business and in government, and the citizenry will no longer be able to participate in making the crucial choices that will shape their future.

This somber view was challenged by others who insisted that all that is transpiring to alter the shape of things is occurring within a political framework, for this is the nature of our society. There is no reason to fear that the democracy, which has proved itself repeatedly so resilient, will collapse under the challenge of the new technology.

It might not be easy for the average citizen to express himself with respect to these esoteric matters; it might not be easy for Congress to gain effective control over the decision-making apparatus with respect to science and technology. But there is no reason for despair. The citizen can understand the values posed by alternative scientifically precipitated policy issues, such as a test ban, even while remaining ignorant of the theories and methods by which they can be realized. At least, so it seems to those who are impressed but not overwhelmed by big science. All agreed, however, that the problems are complex and that they have not attracted the attention and the study they urgently require if sound solutions are to be developed.

Among the social changes the seminar identified as worthy of further study are the following:

1. What do the rapid advances in science and technology imply for education and training at every level?
2. To what extent is the dominance of the private corporation and the private economy being eroded by the large-scale participation of government in research, development, and procurement in many important sectors of the economy? What adjustments in mechanisms for improved planning, operations, and control are called for?
3. Can any meaningful generalizations be ventured about the impact of the new technology on the quality of the life of the individual citizen, his family, and the community? What adjustments, if any, are required so that he can benefit more broadly from the potentialities of the advances in science and technology?
4. What adjustments are called for in the political realm to insure that the citizenry will have the information and guidance necessary to exercise intelligent choices about the future shape of its society?

This chapter is a very abbreviated summary of the wide diversity of opinions that were expressed during the first meetings of the seminar. It was made selective in the hope that this would enable the participants

and others to see some of the more important themes that were identified
even if they were not fully explored. New knowledge and improved
judgments do not come easily or quickly, especially if the angle of
inquiry is broad and the subject matter complex. This chapter underscores more the confusion than the clarifications that were achieved, but
the recognition of the nature of disagreements and the specification of
issues embedded in them is a sound and tested way of making progress.
The seminar is now in a position to take the next steps ahead. . . .

CHAPTER 31

The Service Sector
of the U.S. Economy

A PROPOSITION that has gained popularity with the change of administration in Washington holds that the government should speed the "reindustrialization" of the U.S. economy. The economy, it is said, has lost momentum because of a failure to keep modernizing its basic industries. The same failure is said to have reduced the nation's competitiveness in exports. This proposition and its supporting rationale warrant close inspection and perhaps second thought.

Public discussion of the economy tends to focus on the short run: the next quarter, the next year, the next turn in the business cycle. Implicit is the assumption that the economy of today is basically the same as the economy of yesterday. Over the years, however, changes that go unperceived in the short run accumulate. A dynamic, growing economy inevitably undergoes structural transformation.

In 1929 the U.S. gross national product (GNP) was just over $100 billion. By 1980 it had grown twenty-four times, to $2,400 billion. Allowing for inflation, the growth (in constant dollars of purchasing power) was almost fivefold. Profound changes in the structure of the economy that

417

accompanied this growth are reflected in the distribution of the labor force and the gross national product. The data show that the provision of services has displaced the production of goods as the country's principal economic activity. Since much of this service activity is conducted by the government and by private nonprofit institutions, a vast not-for profit sector, encompassing government and nonprofit institutions, has emerged. Concurrently the growth of the economy has come to depend on human capital more than on physical capital. Finally, the growth of imports and exports as a percentage of GNP demonstrates that the economy has also become increasingly internationalized.

Hence in the perspective of a half century a fourfold transformation of the U.S. economy becomes apparent. We shall attempt here an assessment of these changes and their implications for national economic policy.

In defining services, we observe the convention of national accounting that allocates to services all output that does not come from the four goods-producing sectors: agriculture, mining, manufacturing, and construction. The service sector thus embraces distributive services such as wholesale and retail trade, communications, transportation, and public utilities; producer services such as accounting, legal counsel, marketing, banking, architecture, engineering, and management consulting; consumer services such as restaurants, hotels and resorts, laundry and dry-cleaning establishments; and nonprofit and government services such as education, health, the administration of justice, and national defense.

The U.S. economy in 1929 employed 45 percent of the working population in the production of goods; by 1977 that sector employed only 32 percent. Employment in the service sector therefore increased from 55 to 68 percent of the working population. Most of the shift came in the three decades after the end of World War II. Between 1948 and 1977 employment in goods production declined by 12 percentage points; the decline in manufacturing employment accounted for two-thirds—8 percentage points—of that decline. In 1948, when the nation was restocking its homes and garages after the long depression of the 1930s and the wartime restrictions on the output of consumer goods, manufacturing employed one worker out of three; by 1977 it employed fewer than one worker out of four. Over this period the service sector absorbed not only the percentages displaced from manufacturing but also those displaced from agriculture and mining.

The GNP figures in both current and constant dollars exhibit the same massive shift from goods to services. Current-dollar figures, although they grossly overstate the real rate of growth, have the advantage of reflecting more accurately the changes in relative prices and consumer preferences. Again, the major transformation came in the postwar years. In 1948 the goods-producing sector accounted for 46 percent of GNP and the service sector for 54 percent. In 1978 the figures were 34 percent and 66 percent. The major contributors to the total decrease of 12 percentage points in goods production were agriculture with 6 percentage points and manufacturing with nearly 5.

The disparity between the shares of the service sector in employment (68 percent) and in the GNP (56 percent) reflects differences between services and goods production in the type of labor employed and in the utilization of capital; it also reflects certain national accounting conventions. The share of government measured in terms of employment is much larger than it is in terms of GNP because of the large number of relatively low-paid wage earners (particularly women) on the public payroll and also because of the national-income accounting convention that measures the value of government output solely in terms of wages and salaries. On the other hand, producer services, with their many highly paid professional, technical, and managerial personnel, are more prominent in the economy as a share of the gross national product than as a share of employment.

Perhaps more dramatically than the relative comparisons, the absolute employment and dollar figures demonstrate the transformation of the structure of the economy over the three postwar decades. In 1948, 48.1 million people were employed, 20.9 million in goods production (15.5 million in manufacturing) and 27.2 million in services. The 1977 economy employed 79.5 million people, an increase of more than 30 million, 25.1 million in the goods sector (19.1 million in manufacturing) and 54.4 million—more than the total payroll of the 1948 economy—in services. Comparison here shows that manufacturing employed only 3.6 million more people (to account for a much bigger product, as will be seen below) and the expanded service sector employed 27.2 million more people, roughly 7.5 people for every additional worker employed in manufacturing.

In 1948 the gross national product had reached $259 billion, with the goods sector contributing $118.4 billion ($74.3 billion from manufacturing) and the service sector $140.6 billion. By 1977 the gross national product had increased to $1,900 billion, and the goods sector was contributing $649.8 billion ($456 billion from manufacturing) and the service sector, $1,250.2 billion. Of the $1,600 billion increase in GNP manufacturing generated $382 billion and services generated $1,100 billion, three times as much.

Accounting conventions here conceal an even more striking contribution to economic growth from the increasing number of people engaged in service occupations. The official figures indicate that manufacturing in 1978 contributed 24 percent of GNP and producer services 19 percent. The latter figure represents, however, only the contribution from independent accounting, architectural, advertising, investment banking, law, and management consulting firms. A more complete statement of the contribution from producer services would credit the input from people employed in the same kind of work on the direct payroll of goods-producing enterprises. Between 1948 and 1978 the number of nonproduction workers, including those in producer services, increased from 4.7 to 12.7 million. In manufacturing this element in the payroll increased from 2.7 to 5.7 million: 3 million of the total 3.6 million increase in manufacturing employment noted earlier. If a reasonable adjustment is made for the people engaged in producer-service functions, the remarkable result is that the value added by producer services now approximates the "value added by manufacture" in the U.S. economy.

This finding leads to our second thesis, which is that *human capital*, defined as the "skill, dexterity and knowledge" of the population, has become the critical input that determines the rate of growth of the economy and the well-being of the population. We contend that the competence of management and the skills of the work force, particularly of those engaged in producer services, determine the ability of enterprises to obtain and utilize effectively the other essential resources, such as physical capital, materials, and technology.

The concept of human capital is not new, but it has not generally been accorded priority in economic analysis or in business management. An insight into the dominance of human resources in the economy is provided by the finding that in 1947 the compensation of employees plus half of the returns (reflecting the input of labor) to farm and nonfarm proprietors amounted to 75 percent of the national income; in 1979 it had risen to 79 percent. The return to labor—labor of a new kind—now amounts to essentially four out of five dollars of national income.

The economist Edward F. Denison of the U.S. Department of Commerce has made a comprehensive study of the comparative contribution to the growth of the economy in this period of the several factors of production. Of the total growth between 1948 and 1973, he calculated, 15.4 percent could be credited to "more capital." The increase in the number and the education of the work force and the greater pool of knowledge available to the workers account for about two-thirds of the increased growth of the economy during this period. Even the remaining fraction of the growth still to be accounted for reflects the improved utilization of the human-resource factor by improved management and the shift of workers to more productive sectors.

The Denison calculations are buttressed by figures from other sources that show human capital formation proceeding at an impressive rate throughout the period under study. Taking education as a measure of improvement in human resources, the figures show that the median of the years of school completed by people in the civilian labor force stood at 10.6 in 1948. In 1978 the median was 12.6, a substantial gain within a generation and a half. The figures for secondary and higher education show still more impressive gains. As recently as 1957 fewer than half of the labor force had finished high school and only 9 percent had finished college. By 1978 three out of four workers had finished high school; a third had attended college, had obtained a college degree, or had attended graduate school.

Improvement in the educational preparation of the labor force is reflected in the upgrading of the occupations in which the workers are employed. Between 1959 and 1978 total employment increased by about 30 million. More than half of the increase—16 million new jobs—was in the higher-level professional, technical, managerial-administrative, sales, and crafts occupations. The white-collar work force rose from 42.7 percent of the total in 1959 to 50 percent in 1978. According to a 1975 survey by the Department of Labor, 42.1 percent of the white-collar employment in the service sector must be reckoned in the top white-collar occupational groups; in manufacturing the figure is 24.9 percent. The addition of craftsmen to these totals brings the respective percentages to 49.3 and 36.1. Considering the absolute number of jobs in the most rapidly growing producer and nonprofit service sectors, we find they employ more than double the high-level manpower employed in manufacturing. The upgrading of the labor force is also evidenced by the disappearance of 800,000 private-household jobs and a 2.5 million decline in farm employment.

The foregoing analysis does not deny that physical capital continues to play a prominent role in the country's economic growth. It does, however, support our thesis that human capital has come to play an increasingly dominant role. Simply put, it is the expansion of knowledge, skills, imagination, ideas, and insights of working people that creates the margins from which physical capital is accumulated, leading through productive investments to the further accumulation of capital.

We turn now to consideration of the not-for-profit sector, which includes private nonprofit institutions and all government, and of the contribution the growth of this sector has made, particularly over the past thirty years, to the growth of the entire economy. To begin with, it is to the not-for-profit sector that the country has looked for the enhancement of its human capital. From this sector there have come also the investment in infrastructure, specific demands for goods and services, and even outright subsidies that have given major impulsion to the growth of the private for-profit sector.

At first it is difficult to understand how the national political ethos, expounded by Republicans and Democrats alike, continues to maintain that five out of every six jobs are created by the private sector. That was true in 1929, when government expenditures were about 10 percent of the gross national product. It ceased to be true, however, in the depression years of the New Deal and in World War II, and it is surely not true today. The misconception arises in part from the classification of such nonprofit institutions as Columbia University, the Metropolitan Museum of Art and the Jet Propulsion Laboratory as private-sector enterprises and from categorizing the production of military aircraft by the Lockheed Corporation and nuclear submarines by the General Dynamics Corporation as private-enterprise activity. These classifications obscure the true situation.

To comprehend the actual dimensions of the government sector, one must count not only the people employed on the public payroll but also the people in the private sector who are employed because of government purchases from or grants to private-sector enterprises. Civilian employment on government payrolls increased from 11 million in 1962 to 16.5 million in 1978. Practically all these new jobs were created by state and local governments. In addition, during this same period purchases by government at all levels brought an increase in the direct employment in the private sector occasioned by such purchases from 6.3 to 8.2 million. Counting also employees in such government enterprises as the Tennessee Valley Authority, state liquor stores, and municipal power plants, the number of people employed by government increased from 18.4 to 26.2 million in those sixteen years. When the contribution of the private nonprofit sector is added to that of government, the not-for-profit sector accounts for more than a third of total employment and nearly a third of GNP.

The argument that such employment and expenditure are at cost to the "productive" side of the economy is belied by the historical record of the very period that has seen the rapid expansion of the not-for-profit sector. For the past several decades agriculture and the automotive industry were the movers and shakers of the economy, both at home and abroad. The role of federal government expenditures in research and development and in the operation of the agricultural extension service, which was in effect a technology-transfer enterprise, was crucial to the enormous gains of output per man-hour and per acre of the country's farms. Similarly, it was federal, state, and local outlays for highway building, greatly enhanced by the Eisenhower administration's interstate-highway legislation of 1956, that contributed to the prolonged prosperity of the automotive industry that has just recently foundered on fuel price increases and competition from imported automobiles.

Today the aircraft and the electronics industries continue to contribute significantly, along with agriculture, to the country's exports. The facts are clear: Huge government expenditures for defense and space, for research and development, and for the education of highly specialized personnel have underpinned and sustained the rapid progress of these industries. Hence although the private sector continues to dominate the U.S. economy, the government and the private nonprofit sector perform a large number of functions, as both investors and purchasers, that are critically important to the continued expansion of the private sector.

None of these functions is more important than the acknowledged responsibility and role of the not-for-profit sector in the nurturing and enhancement of the country's human capital. Between 1950 and 1979 total expenditures for education increased from $8.3 to $151.5 billion, of which all but $25 billion came from public treasuries. Expenditures for higher education alone increased nearly 30 times, from $1.7 to $48.9 billion, with the public sector covering two-thirds of the bill. In parallel with the growth of the educational enterprise, expenditures for research and development increased from $13.5 to $51.6 billion during the same period, with the federal government's share two-thirds of the total in 1960 and just under one-half in 1979. The resulting transformation and upgrading of the labor force contributed measurably to the increased wealth of the nation.

Another major contribution to human capital formation took the form of an expansion of the country's health care system, stimulated alike by expenditures by government and by nonprofit institutions such as Blue Cross. In 1950 expenditures for medical care were $12 billion, with consumers paying $4 of every $5. In 1980 these expenditures had climbed to $240 billion, with the government providing $2 out of every $5 and private and nonprofit insurance most of the rest.

The fourth dimension of the continuing transformation of the U.S. economy is the trend toward internationalization, which is reflected in the increased flow abroad of American trade, investments and grants and loans by the government. Between 1950 and 1979 total U.S. exports increased from $10.2 to $175.3 billion; exports and imports as a share of the gross national product rose from 6.8 to 15.4 percent. Taken by itself the trade account understates the real involvement of the United States in the world economy. In 1950 American private assets abroad totaled $19 billion. By 1978 they were $377 billion, twenty times the 1950 figure. In the single decade 1966–1976 the yearly sales of foreign affiliates of

American companies increased from $98 to about $515 billion.

Direct foreign investment in the United States meanwhile rose from $3.4 to $40.8 billion (twelve times). In the late 1940s the United States was earning annually about $1 billion net on overseas investments. In 1978 it earned $43 billion on overseas investments and paid out $22 billion to foreign governments and individuals, leaving a net balance of $21 billion. These "invisible exports"—preponderantly the yield from human capacity, particularly organizational and managerial capabilities—nearly offset the increased expenditure for petroleum imports that put the foreign-exchange account $7 billion in the red.

The increasing participation of the United States in the global economy has been accomplished largely by the nation's leadership role in international affairs since World War II and by the transformation of many large U.S. corporations into multinational enterprises interested in expansion and diversification. Corporations could frame and carry out such ambitions because they had the human capacity to plan, organize, and control global production, distribution, and financing systems. Critical to the success of their penetration abroad was a growing pool of specialized and experienced managerial and technical-professional people on their payrolls.

Therefore, four mutually reinforcing changes—the displacement of goods by services at the cutting edge of economic growth, the growth of the not-for-profit sector, the increasing importance of human capital, and the internationalization of the business system—have transformed the U.S. economy over the past thirty years. We now consider the linkages and interrelations among these developments. The discussion will examine how structural changes in the household, in the company and in government speeded the transformation.

Between 1950 and 1980 the participation of women in the labor force rose from about a third to slightly more than half. Three out of every five new workers were women. Most of them found their jobs in the expanding service sector. Most of them also were married women living with their husbands at home, and so their employment brought new affluence to the American household. Of the 47 million families (in 1977) consisting of at least husband and wife, the husband was the only worker in 12.7 million, but both spouses worked in 23.4 million. The median income of the former group was $15,400, of the latter $20,400.

If consumer spending is allocated to (1) basic necessities, (2) comfort and convenience, and (3) products and activities related to self-identity or way of life, the newly affluent households are spending less on the first two categories and more on the third, which includes leisure, travel, recreation, education, and so on. Between 1948 and 1978 consumers reduced their outlays for goods from 68.4 to 54.1 percent of their total outlays. Expenditures on services rose accordingly from 31.6 to 45.9 percent, reflecting primarily changes in taste associated with the continuance of education, higher income, and the need for support services (which are more in demand when the wife works), together with a relatively larger inflationary increase in the cost of services compared with goods.

The affluence of the years after World War II has substantially broadened and deepened the national market. In the 1930s President Roosevelt identified the South as the nation's primary economic problem. The region's agriculture was in decline; its industries were concentrated in low-wage manufacturing, and its poor whites and blacks were underemployed. By the mid-1950s, as a result of large-scale emigration of poor and unskilled people and of substantial expenditures by the federal government for regional development and defense that attracted a reverse migration of people with higher skills, the South had begun to boom.

The Southwest and the West similarly responded to federal outlays that placed the center of the new defense industries there and accelerated the population growth of those regions. Federal, state, and local investment in infrastructure underwrote the relocation of American households in suburbia, to the new "Sun Belt" and elsewhere in the country.

These changes in the national market brought the establishment of many new business enterprises in the South and the West, and many already established in the East and the Middle West expanded to beyond the Rockies. It is not surprising that for most of the postwar period the South and the West have had above-average rates of gain in employment and income, whereas in the Middle Atlantic and East North Central regions the rate of gain has been considerably lower.

At the end of World War II multiunit manufacturing companies employed only a third more workers and produced only a third more of the value added than single-unit companies. By 1972 the multiunit companies had three times as many employees as the single-unit ones and accounted for four times the value added. Responding to the growth of the national market, these large manufacturing companies had restructured their organization and had also changed their ways of doing business. They did these things primarily by establishing one form or another of decentralized operating structure and by building up decentralized groups of service functions—research and development, marketing, advertising, employee and government relations, legal, financial, accounting—to help them plan and control their multiunit enterprises.

Manufacturers of high-priced items such as automobiles, refrigerators, color television sets, and mobile homes recognized that they stood to

gain almost as much from extending credit (a service function) as from
the markup on their products. Between 1950 and 1978 the total amount of
consumer credit outstanding rose from $25.6 to $340.3 billion, or from
about 12 to 23 percent of disposable personal income.

Big companies could diversify into services as well as goods production,
decentralize their operations, and plan and control them on a national
scale because they could call on a wide variety of specialized knowledge
and talent in their growing cadres of managerial-administrative and
technical-professional personnel. Once an aggressive company had found
its way onto the national scene, its managers and professionals would
naturally look for new worlds to conquer. As early as the 1950s many
companies entered the rapidly recovering European market before the
Common Market erected barriers, and many others recognized that
during the second half of the century there would be a quickening of
economic activity in other areas: Asia, Australia, Latin America, and
even Africa. The experience these companies had acquired at home in
establishing close links with their customers and in tying the sale of
goods to financing and servicing gave them confidence that they could
surmount the special problems they would encounter in expanding
abroad. Their ventures abroad were also facilitated, directly or indirectly,
by foreign loans and grants extended by the federal government in the
amount of $234 billion between 1945 and 1978.

   Since services for consumers have to be provided where the consumers are, economists have long assumed that the economies of scale
characteristic of manufacturing could not be achieved in service enterprises. Services cannot be produced for inventory and cannot be shipped.
That, however, is not the entire story. Improvements in communications,
particularly in processing and transmitting numerical data, facilitated
the growth of large service companies in the postwar decades by linking together in single enterprises large numbers of small service establishments. Major banks were among the first to develop worldwide
systems of branches. Now multiunit hotel chains, automobile-rental
companies, and fast-food franchises have followed the example set by the
banks.

   The economics of these arrangements are based on the gains that the
large service company can achieve through integrated planning, financing,
accounting, marketing and similar functions. Even large producer-service
firms in law and accounting have increasingly expanded overseas through
the establishment of branches, partnerships, or franchises. This development helps to explain the surprising fact that legal services have recently
emerged as the largest export industry in New York City, outranking its
apparel industry.

Government contributed to this transformation as an investor in human and physical capital, as a purchaser of goods and services and as both a direct and an indirect employer. It also contributed through a variety of other activities: as a stimulator of foreign trade by granting loans to foreign purchasers and guaranteeing loans of American exporters; through its expanded regulatory activity, which had a substantial impact on the flow of private investment for such purposes as the construction of nuclear power plants; and through large income transfers, subsidies, and interest payments that flowed from one group of citizens to another, amounting in 1978 to $648 billion. These large transfers had uncertain but assuredly large effects on investment, consumption, and work.

In conclusion, let us consider the implications for policy that stem from the transformation of the economy. To begin with, the proposed reindustrialization of the country collides with the hard economic fact that traditionally structured manufacturing activity cannot be maintained intact while the service sector continues to expand. The loss of competitiveness in some companies and industries is inevitable in an increasingly open world economy characterized by changing technologies, enterprises, labor forces, and markets. Import quotas, tariff barriers, export subsidies, and the large-scale commitment of federal credit to shore up weak and failing enterprises would threaten the United States with the same consequences as had the British policy that subsidized labor and capital in dying industries and communities. Potentially profitable sectors of the economy would necessarily be deprived of resources they need to optimize their growth.

The United States cannot maintain its position among the industrial nations of the world unless it pursues policies that encourage the greater use of resources in which the country has gained a comparative advantage as a result of its generous investment in human capital, such as research and development, management and organization, the development of new products, and improved services ranging from financing to marketing. What is needed is not reindustrialization but revitalization of the U.S. economy.

Since people represent the principal input of an advanced economy, and since their contributions will vary according to their endowment, their developmental opportunities, and their motivation, the nation should pursue policies aimed at strengthening its human resources. The present scanting of public expenditure on education at every level of government constitutes a reversal of a public policy that has served the nation well over the past thirty years. Adverse demographic and financial circumstances are weakening the nation's major research universities, with the result that the pool of knowledge and the supply of future talent are likely to be diminished. The consequences for the continued growth of the economy may be serious.

The family has a strategic role in the process of human development. Many poor and disorganized families in this country, however, are not able to provide their children with the discipline and motivating experience they need, and the schools are not able to compensate for these shortcomings. As a result, many a young person reaches working age unable to get or hold a regular job. In spite of the large federal effort directed to training and employing disadvantaged adults and youths, which involved expenditures of $64 billion between 1962 and 1978, many of these people have been unable to cross the employment threshold; at best they continue to move in and out of marginal jobs. Only a few industrial companies and labor unions have recognized that they must help the government's effort to bring the excluded into the work arena. Unacceptable delays in achieving this priority are reflected in the riots, arson, and crimes against individuals and property that, in varying degree, beset every U.S. community with large numbers of disadvantaged people.

The obligation and opportunity to seek the enhancement of human capital do not rest alone with government and the schools, nor are they limited to the disadvantaged. The big public, private, and nonprofit organizations that loom large in the country's life can do more to improve the work environment in order to motivate their employees to develop their potential and use their skills for both their own satisfaction and the good of the enterprise. Participatory management, incentive rewards, flexible schedules, and opportunities for outside assignments are all appropriate working conditions for high-capacity personnel. As the U.S. economy comes to depend even more on trained manpower, this challenge becomes greater. It will be met only if large organizations learn to treat their human capital with the concern they have long devoted to their physical capital.

One of the unique characteristics of the U.S. economy is the important role of its private nonprofit institutions and the extent to which government accomplishes many of its missions by contracting with such institutions as well as with companies organized for profit. Although this pluralistic arrangement has served the nation well, the public is becoming aware of shortcomings. A pronounced shortcoming is the absence of reliable data that would enable legislators and the public to judge the effectiveness with which the nonprofit sector employs the large resources it commands.

Current estimates place the unreported income (from transactions kept off the books, from barter, from illicit arrangements and so on) at about 10 percent of the gross national product. Moreover, it is widely agreed that unreported economic activities are growing disproportionately fast. To the extent that these conditions exist, the American record of growth, productivity and well-being may be substantially understated.

Even if the economy is doing better than the reporting systems suggest, it faces many serious challenges, the solutions to which will not come easily. The shift from manufacturing to services is making it difficult for many poorly educated young people to find a regular job with career prospects. With the federal budget out of balance and defense expenditures going up, the federal government will be hard pressed to do more to increase investments that are critical for the nation's continuing economic growth.

Another challenge is that neither government with its monetary and fiscal policies nor the private sector with its wage and price policies has been able to control inflation or to find an answer to the accelerating costs of energy. Moreover, no mechanisms are in place or in sight that will help to keep wage payments in step with gains in productivity. Although the trend toward further internationalization of the world's economy is likely to be beneficial in the long run, many industries and many workers face a bleak future because of the dislocations that accompany the process.

The proposed reindustrialization of an economy dominated by services is an exercise in futility. Americans must unshackle themselves from the notion, dating back to Adam Smith, that goods alone constitute wealth whereas services are nonproductive and ephemeral. At the same time, they should act on Smith's understanding that the wealth of a nation depends on the skill, dexterity, and knowledge of its people.

CHAPTER 32

The Mechanization of Work

THE EASING OF HUMAN LABOR by technology, a process that began in prehistory, is entering a new stage. The acceleration in the pace of technological innovation inaugurated by the Industrial Revolution has until recently resulted mainly in the displacement of human muscle power from the tasks of production. The current revolution in computer technology is causing an equally momentous social change: the expansion of information gathering and information processing as computers extend the reach of the human brain. A recent issue of *Scientific American* was devoted to the latest stage of the historic process that has led from the most elementary force-transmitting machines to the most advanced information-handling ones.

The transformation of the U.S. labor force in the country's brief history tracks the progressive mechanization of work that attended the evolution of the agrarian republic into an industrial world power. In 1820 more than 70 percent of the labor force worked on the farm. By 1900 fewer than 40 percent were engaged in agriculture. Half a century ago, when the capitalist societies were sliding into the Great Depression, more than half of the U.S. labor force had shifted from the production of goods to the provision of services. It was then, as large-scale unemployment destabilized those societies, that national policy began to look at employment as much from concern to ensure the consumption of goods as from concern to secure their production.

Today employment in the services in the United States is approaching the same 70 percent that were bound to the soil a century and a half ago. Only 32 percent of the labor force are still engaged in the production of goods (mostly in manufacturing), and a mere 3 percent are employed in agriculture.

Although this transformation has been brought about largely by mechanization, it has been accompanied by social trends so pervasive that they must be included among the causes of the transformation as well as among its effects. For example, although women had begun to enter the labor force from the beginning of the Industrial Revolution, by 1980 they had come to make up 43 percent of it. The age of entry into the labor force has risen, reflecting the desire of Americans for more education and the higher level of training required by jobs in the increasingly sophisticated economy, as well as the release of human labor from the tasks of production. In 1940 the median number of years of school completed by the younger members of the population was 10.3; in 1980 it was 12.9.

A disquieting feature of these dynamic internal shifts in the labor force has been the persistence of high levels of unemployment among its less educated members. Such unemployment raises the question of how any society can function effectively over the long run without bringing all its adult members into its economic life, able not only to work but also to buy.

This chapter will of necessity deal with a limited number of themes: how the mechanization of work has been treated by economists, what its effect has been on the U.S. economy over the past few decades, and what its future effect is likely to be. Particular attention will be paid to the impact of mechanization on the shifting structure and character of the labor force and on the evolution of the work environment.

Adam Smith, in *An Inquiry into the Nature and Causes of the Wealth of Nations,* published in 1776, pointed to a basic dilemma: Efficiency in the generation of wealth is enhanced by the division of labor, and yet specialization that involves nothing more than routine, repetitive tasks diminishes the worker by depriving him of intellectual challenge and decision-making responsibility. Smith, preoccupied with issues of moral philosophy, expressed his concern that many workers, in a desperate effort to improve their economic circumstances, would drive themselves so hard that it would affect their health and even shorten their lives. Smith's book was written before the commercial success of James Watt's steam engine, and so Smith never had to confront the full force of modern industrialization. He nonetheless appreciated the close links between the work people do and the quality of their lives.

David Ricardo, who began his study of political economy after reading *The Wealth of Nations* in 1799, went on to establish the classical, or free-market, school of economics. In spite of his almost exclusive emphasis on the competitive marketplace, he cautioned that increased reliance on mechanization might not turn out to be an unqualified blessing. He could see that under certain conditions workers displaced by machines might not be able to get new jobs. What was good for the employer, he concluded, might be bad for the worker.

Karl Marx devoted some of the most telling chapters in *Das Kapital* to describing the adverse effects of mechanization on the minds and bodies of working men, women, and children in mid-nineteenth-century Britain. (Because women and children received lower wages, they were then replacing men in many branches of industry, from coal mines to textile mills.) According to Marx, the combination of machines, private property, and competition would soon result in the self-destruction of the capitalist system. The end would come, he said, when newer and more powerful machines would drive such a large proportion of the labor force out of work that producers would no longer have enough consumers to buy the goods their machines were turning out. With the advantage of hindsight, one can now see that Marx was better as a critic than as a prophet. He correctly perceived that the Industrial Revolution was harming millions of working people, but he did not allow for the substantial gains in well-being they and the generations of workers after them would enjoy because of the increased productivity resulting from mechanization.

Thorstein Veblen made technology the basis for his own penetrating analysis of modern capitalism, from his first major work, *The Theory of the Leisure Class*, published in 1899, to his last, *Absentee Ownership and Business Enterprise in Recent Times*, published in 1923. Veblen consistently maintained that the way work is organized to suit the requirements of machines determines how people think, act, and dream.

In general, however, most economists—free-market, Marxist, or otherwise—have failed to give technology its due. The classical theorists and their successors have built their systems and their reputations by explicating with ever greater subtlety how demand, supply, and price interact in competitive markets to establish or reestablish equilibrium. To pursue this static line of inquiry, they have had to ignore the influence of such dynamic factors as changes in demography, technology, and taste. Moreover, because they have a limited view of efficiency, they search for the margin where it pays an employer to install machines to replace workers, but seldom look into such factors as the quality of the

workplace and the home, both of which have come increasingly under
the influence of machines.

The shortcomings in the economists' approach to the mechanization
of work can help to explain many of the errors in perception and action
that have characterized the U.S. economy in the period since World War II.
A better understanding of the complex relations between mechanization
and the economic process can be gained by reviewing some of the more
important of these misperceptions and the inadequate policies they have
engendered.

In 1947 the U.S. instituted the Marshall Plan. If the countries of Western
Europe—both the victors and the vanquished—could agree to work
together, the United States promised to provide them with the capital
needed to speed the rebuilding of their devastated economies. Within a
few years the economies of Western Europe had turned around and were
growing rapidly.

The success of the Marshall Plan had much to do with the inauguration
of smaller-scale programs of economic assistance designed to accelerate
the industrialization of the less-developed countries. They too became
the beneficiaries of U.S. capital exports. Here, however, the record of
accomplishment turned out to be much less impressive. Little of the
so-called economic assistance went to economic development. Instead,
U.S. capital exports often went in the form of arms, and U.S. dollars
added to the personal wealth of those in power. Only in retrospect has it
been possible to understand the reasons for the difference in outcomes.
In Europe the war had destroyed factories, power plants, railroads, and
other facilities; but the knowledge required to run an industrial economy
had remained intact. This knowledge, accumulated over a century or
more, was drawn on to make good use of the new machines as soon as
they were installed. In most of the Third World there was no such pool of
experience, and as a result many of the imported machines were installed
only after considerable delay; frequently they were operated far below
capacity, and they were poorly maintained.

A second example of failure to bring mechanization into the center
of economic policy is provided by the U.S. automobile industry. Before
its recent troubles, that industry was looked on as the bellwether of the
U.S. economy, proof that the United States was the technological leader
among the developed nations. Year after year the industry's sales and
profits were large; and although working conditions in the assembly
plants were often unpleasant and arduous, the work force was well paid
and received excellent benefits. The misperception of what was happening in Detroit resulted from a widespread failure to recognize that the
industry's continuing high profitability rested primarily on styling,

advertising, and marketing, not on advances in engineering and in manufacturing technology.

In 1962 Congress, convinced that mechanization was resulting in the disemployment of many skilled workers who would never be reabsorbed into the labor force unless they could be helped to acquire new skills, passed the Manpower Development and Training Act. That act, together with its successor legislation, the Comprehensive Employment and Training Act (CETA), passed in 1973, led to the expenditure of more than $80 billion up to the beginning of the Reagan administration, mostly to help the poor and the near-poor. It is doubtful, however, that even 1 percent of the outlay was directed to the retraining and reemployment of workers who had lost their jobs through mechanization, because such workers could until recently make their own way into new jobs.

The most recent example of confusion about the mechanization of work arises from national economic policies ostensibly directed to "reindustrialization" (for example, tax cuts for accelerated depreciation of plant and equipment, a measure expected to start a new boom in investment). The United States is urged to pursue other policies, public and private, that will putatively enable it to regain its eroding leadership in the manufacture of a wide range of industrial and consumer products, from steel to automobiles and television sets. Much is made of the superiority of Japanese management and the dangerous decline in the productivity of U.S. industry. However the issue is formulated, the core elements are the same: The leadership of the United States in technology has slipped, and there is a serious dysfunction in the attitudes, behavior, and output of U.S. workers.

Actually, the available statistics suggest that on a per capita basis the United States is close to its long-term trend in gross domestic product (GDP): the output of all domestically produced goods and services. The unease centers on the recent sharp decline in productivity (measured as the ratio of total production to units of labor input). Any interpretation, however, is plagued by complications: The reported hours of work overstate the actual hours worked, exaggerating the measured declines in productivity; the U.S. economy has been shifting rapidly from goods to services, a shift that inadequately reflects the increases in output; the statistics also fail adequately to reflect changes in quality, investments in the public sector, and what is happening outside the market—notably in the so-called underground economy and in the household. If one were to understand and take proper account of these developments, the performance of the U.S. economy would probably be better—possibly much better—than the current statistics suggest. Americans may well be unduly worried over a phenomenon that reveals more about the limitations of economic analysis and statistical reporting than about the economy itself.

The fact remains that mechanization has continued to play a leading role in the transformation of the U.S. economy and other developed economies in the past half century, as it did in the preceding century and a half. New and better machines have contributed to reducing the average weekly hours of work in manufacturing from 44 in 1930 to fewer than 42 today. At the same time mechanization has contributed to major gains in the rewards for work: The average pay in manufacturing has risen from $1.60 per hour then to $3 now (in constant 1967 dollars). This excludes fringe benefits, which have grown on average to about 35 percent of base pay. Moreover, some economists have come to appreciate that the key to economic progress lies less with the accumulation of physical capital and more with the broadening and deepening of human capital, since it is human talent alone that is capable of inventing, adapting, and maintaining machines.

Part of the problem is that the majority of economists, with their strong bias in favor of the competitive market, have paid inadequate attention to the contribution of the public sector to accelerating the growth of human capital. Public support has taken different forms: the G.I. Bill of Rights of 1944; the expansion of public higher education; federal financing of research and development; and the large-scale proliferation of specialized training programs created as by-products of efforts to build up the country's military strength and to develop nuclear power, aircraft, computers, spacecraft, communications, and other large-scale technologies.

In the three decades between the election of President Eisenhower and the election of President Reagan, both per capita disposable income and family income, expressed in constant dollars, almost doubled. Trade unions have become a prominent feature of the industrial landscape (although their membership as a fraction of the total work force has declined since 1955), and a professional, college-trained cadre of managers has taken command of most U.S. corporations. It would be surprising indeed if, mechanization aside, the foregoing changes had not left their mark on how workers behave both on the job and off it.

Other factors must also be taken into account: the repeated involvement of the country in foreign wars, the growing threat of nuclear war, rapid changes in basic values and behavior involving aspects of life from sex to religion, increasing skepticism about and challenges to authority and legitimacy. Only those economists who believe everything in life is determined by the calculus of the marketplace would attempt to explain the difficulties in which the U.S. economy finds itself in 1982 as resulting from a collapse of the work ethic. The Luddites looked on the machine as the villain; the supply-siders blame the worker.

The second of the three themes I mentioned at the outset is the extent to which mechanization has helped to change the U.S. economy since World War II. Of the 41.6 million people employed in 1940 (excluding the self-employed and domestic servants), 54 percent were engaged in the production of goods: in agriculture, mining, construction, and manufacturing. Mechanization had earlier made steady advances in the grain-producing states of the Middle West, but it had only a minor place in the cotton culture of the Southeast. The South, in the view of President Roosevelt, was the nation's No. 1 economic problem. It conformed to the Marxian view that surplus labor would be concentrated on the farm, living at the margin of subsistence and awaiting an opportunity to relocate to urban centers when employers needed additional workers. As late as 1940 four out of five black citizens were still living in the South, the majority of them on farms they sharecropped.

World War II was the continental divide. Many blacks went into the armed services; others moved to the North and West, where employers faced growing labor shortages; still others moved into southern cities, many of which were being transformed by the infusion of military dollars. Other farming areas also sustained a large-scale exodus of surplus labor, setting the stage for the accelerated mechanization of agriculture. Paradoxical as it may seem, agriculture is now considerably more mechanized than manufacturing.

In the same four decades mechanization made rapid advances in bituminous coal mining as a result of two factors: the development of strip mining in the West and the decision of the United Mine Workers' Union, led by John L. Lewis, to favor higher wages over more jobs. In spite of the widespread belief that strong unions have inhibited mechanization in the construction industry, the evidence from the mechanization of excavation to the prefabrication of structures points to major advances in the application of sophisticated technologies. Although some construction unions have been strong enough to delay the introduction of new machines or to prevent the new machines from operating at full capacity, these delaying tactics have in certain instances stimulated the growth of nonunionized industry, where contractors were able to mechanize without interference.

At the height of the war boom the goods-producing sectors of the U.S. economy accounted for 69 percent of the employed labor force. In 1980 they accounted for 32 percent. The most striking shift in the goods-producing sectors was the decrease in the number, both absolute and relative, of agricultural workers. The second most prominent shift was the relative decline in manufacturing, where employment increased from 34 percent of all nonagricultural jobs in 1940 to 41 percent in 1943, but declined to 22 percent at present.

The decreasing employment in the goods-producing sectors of the economy was first matched and then exceeded by the increasing employment in the service sector. Between 1940 and 1980 employment in service occupations grew from 46 percent of total employment to 68 percent. Of all new jobs added to the economy from 1969 to 1976, 90 percent were in services.

What are the reasons for this shift? The answers differ depending on who is asked. Some economists deny that a significant shift has occurred; at most they will agree that there has been a slow, steady growth of service-sector jobs. Some acknowledge that a shift has occurred, but they ascribe it primarily to the explosive growth in health, education, and related services. They expect that the growth will level off and even decline now that the birth rate is down and the Reagan administration is pressing to reduce the level of government outlays. Others, including our own group at Columbia University, are convinced that there has been a tilt of demand toward more consumer services and that, even more important, changes have been made in the way goods are produced, calling for a vast expansion in "producer services." Thomas M. Stanback, Jr. and his colleagues at Columbia, in their recent book *Services/The New Economy,* note that the value added of producer services alone—financial, legal, accounting, marketing, management consulting, and communications—equals the value added of all manufacturing output.

A look at the changes in the occupational structure further illuminates the causes and consequences of the shifts identified here. Somewhat simplistic comparisons can be made among white-collar workers, blue-collar workers, and service-sector workers (narrowly defined as those who provide services primarily to consumers). In 1940 the proportions employed in these kinds of occupation were, respectively, 31 percent, 57 percent, and 12 percent; in 1980 they were 54 percent, 34 percent, and 12 percent. Bigger and better machines on the farm, in the mines, in the factory, and at construction sites call for fewer operatives. In modern oil refineries, chemical plants, and steel-fabricating mills there is a great deal of machinery but there are few workers, and many of the workers are engaged in white-collar jobs. The General Electric Company, which manufactures tens of thousands of different items from turbines to electric-light bulbs, has no more than 40 percent of its employees directly engaged in production; the rest work in what can best be classified as in-house producer services, from accounting to marketing.

If one looks at the qualitative changes that are suggested by the shift from blue-collar to white-collar employment, one finds a truly impressive growth in the two groupings in the standard categories of the Bureau of Labor Statistics that have the highest status and incomes: professional, scientific, and technical workers, and managerial and administrative workers. Between 1940 and 1980 the former group increased from 7.5 to 16 percent of the employed labor force, and the latter group declined from 20 to 13 percent. The last two figures conceal a major qualitative transformation, since they lump the owners and managers of small enterprises, whose numbers declined, and corporate and other high-level administrators, whose numbers rose.

Confirmation of the radical changes in the occupational structure can be found in the striking rise in the educational achievements of the younger members of the work force: those between twenty-five and twenty-nine years of age. One need not hold the philistine view of many human-capital theorists that educational preparation is determined solely by the estimates people make of their career and income prospects to see that the two factors are definitely correlated. The large increase in the proportion of those in the twenty-five to twenty-nine age group who have either an undergraduate degree or a higher degree is striking: from one in sixteen in 1940 to almost one in four in 1980.

There is a bias among economists going back to Adam Smith that only work resulting in a physical output is productive and that services, which are by their nature ephemeral, are unproductive. Smith, reacting to the excessive number of family retainers among the rich, misled himself and his followers about the nature of services. Economists finally realized, however, that an artist who gives pleasure to thousands or a surgeon who restores the health of hundreds must be considered productive. Nevertheless, the followers of Smith have been preoccupied with refining the manufacturing model. With few exceptions, the output of services has been downgraded or ignored.

This bias against service occupations was reinforced by a widespread belief that mechanization, the key to productivity and growth, has little or no role to play in the production of services. In fact, some contemporary economists have separated out the heavy, capital-intensive services—transportation, communications, and electric-power utilities—and treated them as either part of or closely related to conventional manufacturing.

A further bias has been at work. Many services are anchored in the public sector rather than the private sector; the leading examples are education; health; and such basic functions as police protection, fire protection, and sanitation. Economic theory based on the competitive marketplace has little to contribute to an understanding of such public services. Handicapped by tradition, economists have been slow to understand the shift of modern economies toward services and in particular toward services in the public sector, toward producer services, and toward mechanization in large service enterprises.

Most economists assumed that service companies would inevitably continue to be small, since service providers had to interact personally with consumers, as in the case of a restaurant, a dry-cleaning establishment, a physician, or an accountant. The model of the small, local consumer-service company, however, clearly does not fit the fast-food chains, the international banks with branches in 100 or more cities, the worldwide hotel chains, the national retailing chains, and many other national and international service enterprises that have been able to mechanize many of their critical functions from finance to personnel management.

As I have noted, the period since World War II has also been marked by a steady advance in the educational preparation and skill level of the work force, as exemplified by the increase in the number of white-collar workers and of professional, scientific, and technical workers. The question remains whether it is more difficult in the service sector than it is in the manufacturing sector to move from a less desirable job to a more desirable one. Stanback believes this has been the case. He points to the steelworker who began work in the yard and could move up many grades on the basis of seniority and on-the-job training. That is not the case, he observes, for the laboratory technician in a hospital or the paralegal worker in a law firm. In support of this argument, it has to be conceded that a college or professional degree is a prerequisite for competing for many of the best jobs in the service sector. On the other hand, talent appears to be as important as formal degrees in many occupations, such as advertising, design, and sports. In my view the issue remains open.

These last considerations are a bridge to the third theme I mentioned at the outset: the effects of mechanization on the work environment. To the extent that any generalization is justified, one can maintain that the conventional attitude of the American worker toward machines has been different from that of the European worker. For the most part American workers have had a positive attitude toward technological improvements, seeing them as making their work less onerous and as providing an opportunity for wage increases through increased productivity and for the enhancement of their job security through improvement of their company's competitive position.

In European countries, with their smaller markets, the job-displacement potential of the new machines has been more prominent in the thinking and action of the workers. Technological unemployment was viewed as a serious threat by the principal unions in the German Weimar Republic of the 1920s, and even the economic revival of West Germany after World War II did not dispel this fear. In the early 1960s the largest of the West German unions, the metalworkers, were host to a week-long international conference on mechanization and the involuntary unemployment it could cause. The issue is once again high on the agenda of the West German trade unions, particularly because of the disturbingly high level of unemployment in that country.

Marx railed against the dehumanization of work in which the machine set the pace, a theme that was resurrected in succeeding generations by John Ruskin, Edward Bellamy, and Emma Goldman and that was developed perhaps most imaginatively in Charlie Chaplin's motion picture *Modern Times*. One need not gloss over the physical and psychological strain of working on the assembly line to point out that at the peak probably no more than one in fifteen or twenty American workers earned a livelihood by such work. Robert Schrank, whose *Ten Thousand Working Days* is the most perceptive account of the diversity of working environments in the contemporary U.S. economy, makes a strong opposing case. Instead of the machine's dominating the lives of the workers, he writes, the immediate work group learns to organize its activities to enlarge its scope of freedom to do the things its members most enjoy: swap stories, fool around, play games, gamble, keep the foreman off their back, and otherwise interact with one another—investing little of themselves in carrying out their assignment.

Three decades ago, in the book *Occupational Choice*, my coauthors and I distinguished three returns from work: intrinsic (direct work satisfaction), extrinsic (wages and benefits), and concomitant (interpersonal relations on the job and in the work environment). Advocates of improving the quality of work life see major opportunities to enhance the intrinsic and concomitant returns that workers are able to get from their work. In my opinion they exaggerate. The scope for decision making by workers on the factory floor or in the large office is severely limited. An extreme division of labor results, as Smith perceived, in routine, repetitive tasks from which decision-making functions have been extracted.

Although American trade unions may have been too confrontational in their attitudes, their underlying conviction is that, beyond pressuring management to make the work environment safer, cleaner, and more attractive, there is not much management can do to improve the intrinsic rewards from work. Accordingly, unions have pressed and will continue to press for improvements in extrinsic rewards: job security, equity in selection for promotions, participation by the unions in discipline and discharge, better wages and fringe benefits, and more free time.

As my colleagues Ivar Berg, Marcia Freedman, and Michael Freeman have documented in their book *Managers and Work Reform*, much of the agitation of the U.S. economy is a function of the expectations workers have about their jobs; there is a real danger that many are overeducated for the work to which they are assigned. Furthermore, much of the dissatisfaction of workers stems not from their limited scope to participate in decisions that affect their work but from their frustration with managers who fail to perform effectively.

Much of the preceding discussion of the workplace, worker motivation, and the quality of work life has been in terms of the modern factory. Since the labor force is now overwhelmingly employed in the service sector, however, it seems desirable to call attention to a few future developments in the relation of mechanization to the work environment there.

Because of the critical importance of quality in the service sector, the control of work and workers confronts management with a new and difficult challenge. Service-sector work has more dimensions and complexities than factory work, particularly considering the much higher proportion of professional, scientific, and technical people employed in service industries. It is the hallmark of such personnel that their training has conditioned them to decide what work to do, how to do it, and even when to do it. The members of a university faculty, although they are members of a department, a school, and a larger institution, consider themselves as self-directed, autonomous individuals to whom the chairman, the dean, and the president can address requests but not give orders. Increasingly this academic model is spreading to industry and government, to the research laboratories, to corporate staffs, and to government agencies. There is growing tension between the traditional hierarchical structure of organizations and the implicit (and increasingly explicit) demands of professionals for greater autonomy in their work. How these demands will be reconciled with traditional modes of management remains to be seen, and the process of reconciliation may prove as difficult as it is important.

At the other end of the occupational scale, it appears that the increase in the number of service-sector jobs has been correlated with the decrease in the fraction of the work force that is unionized. Many observers believe trade unions will be further weakened as the growth of the service sector continues. This may in fact happen, but several countervailing factors must be considered. Many service jobs pay low wages and provide limited benefits. More women, concentrated in low-paying service jobs, are becoming regularly attached to the work force. The computer revolution seems ready to make major inroads into the office, a development that holds a threat to the job security of many white-collar workers. The continuing erosion of the real earnings of workers by inflation makes these employees receptive to union organization. It is easy to write off the trade union movement, particularly since it has had a conspicuous lack of success so far in restructuring itself to meet the challenges of a changing economy. Even if the unions finally succeed in making sizable gains in the service sector, they will face not only the conventional challenges of achieving higher wages and better fringe benefits for their members, but also the challenge of contributing to a more stimulating workplace.

Veblen once explained the success of Germany in overtaking Britain as an industrial power in terms of the advantages of being second (or third). The latecomer did not have to carry the burden of obsolescent machinery or business practices. Many analysts in the United States in 1982 think Japan and the leading nations of the Third World have the same advantages Germany once had. The analogy is suggestive, but it is faulty. For some years various manufacturing activities have been moving to low-wage countries not only out of Western Europe and the United States but also out of Japan.

There is widespread concern about the periodic imbalances of U.S. trade in commodities with the rest of the world. In 1980 the deficit in such trade amounted to slightly more than $25 billion. That is not the whole story, however. Fees and royalties on direct U.S. investments abroad amounted to almost $6.7 billion, and net earnings on foreign investments, excluding these fees, came to $32.8 billion, resulting in a net surplus of more than $13 billion in goods and services (adjusting for the small net deficit in travel receipts). Goods and services do not lead totally independent existences; and, as I have noted, services have come to play a much more important role in the production of goods. The challenge to the U.S. economy is not reindustrialization but, rather, *revitalization,* in which mechanization has an important role to play with respect to both goods and services.

It is moot whether any new specific policies are required to speed revitalization beyond a recognition that the U.S. economy is moving ever more strongly into services and that the country's legislators and administrators should deal equitably between the different sectors in the creation and implementation of trade, tax, and employment policies. The Reagan administration, through the Office of the Special Representative for Trade Negotiations, has demonstrated a growing concern with international trade involving services. In the private sector a recently established consortium of major service companies is further evidence of attention and action.

A conclusion that government should not venture into the formulation of industrial policy does not imply that the state has no role to play in the strengthening of the industrial infrastructure. It is important to remember that government has played a major role in leading U.S. industries: in agriculture, aeronautics, nuclear power, electronics, computers, communications, genetic engineering, and other emerging technologies. If the present administration has its way, the support of universities, the education and training of specialists, and the underwriting of research and development will not be carried forward at an appropriate scale or with the adequate lead times. The machines that are invented, improved, and put into operation throughout the economy depend on a steady accretion in the pool of knowledge and on the availability of enough technicians. If the country had to wait for the big corporations to train their own technical personnel from the ground up, it could wait a long time. Even if they wanted to do it, they could not. The ideologues may swoon over the beatitudes of the competitive market, which clearly has much to commend it; but the U.S. economy, for better or worse, is a pluralistic system in which government, nonprofit institutions, and privately owned companies have complementary relations. No one of them, left to its own devices, can prosper in a technologically sophisticated world.

It would be a distortion to end this introduction to a series of articles on the mechanization of work without considering its problematical consequences. I shall therefore take up some of the consequences of mechanization for women and for the undereducated.

With respect to women, mechanization unquestionably paved the way for many of them to escape the confines of the home as a result of labor-saving devices, which eased the chores of housekeeping and, equally important, reduced the role of physical strength as a qualifying characteristic for many jobs. The positive role of mechanization in the liberation of women had little or no influence, however, on such untoward trends as the ominous rise in the number of households headed by women, the disturbingly large number of youngsters being brought up solely by their mothers, and the large fraction of those families who live at or below the poverty level. These trends can be disregarded only by a society that is indifferent to human deprivation and unconcerned about its own future.

Before the introduction of sophisticated machinery as well as afterward, all economies have faced difficulties in providing jobs for everyone who needs work. In spite of the good record of the U.S. economy with respect to the creation of jobs in recent decades, Arthur F. Burns, the former chairman of the board of governors of the Federal Reserve System (and the current U.S. ambassador to West Germany), recommended in 1975, in the face of the continuing difficulties that many young people were having in finding and keeping jobs, that the federal government become "the employer of last resort" at wages 10 percent below the legal minimum wage. Some believe the shift of the economy toward services is currently making it more difficult for the undereducated to find a niche. An increasingly white-collar economy has no place for functional illiterates.

I have one concluding observation about the relation between mechanization and work. There is a widespread belief in the U.S. and Western Europe that young people have a smaller commitment to work and a career than their parents and grandparents had and that the source of the change lies in the collapse of the "work ethic." The question of why the work ethic collapsed is seldom raised, although sophisticated analysts suggest it is linked to economic affluence and the shift of concern from the family to the self.

I would suggest that the success of modern technology, which has put each of the superpowers in a position to destroy the other (and much of the rest of the world), presents a basic challenge, not only with respect to work but also with respect to all human values. It remains to be seen whether or not the potential of modern technology will turn out to be a blessing. Many young people are betting against such an outcome, and others are waiting before committing their modest stake.

CHAPTER 33

Technology and Jobs: What Lies Ahead

PERSPECTIVE

I HAVE BEEN ASKED TO WRITE about the policy implications that will result from the technological upheavals of the 1980s and the 1990s. This subject ought to be high on the agenda of the developed nations on both sides of the Atlantic, since they are beset by chronically high levels of unemployment. Technological upheavals added to levels of national unemployment of 8, 10, 13, and in some instances even higher percentages, could result in increasing tensions in economic and political environments of these nations, which might reach a magnitude equal to, or even greater than, the decade that preceded the outbreak of World War II.

Economists respect the doctrine of comparative advantage; in my eighth decade, I am in a position to assess the probability of technological upheavals from the vantage point of a direct knowledge of developments on both sides of the Atlantic since shortly after the end of World War I. A record of personal experiences does not guarantee that the resulting analyses and evaluations will have greater validity than those derived from quantitative data and econometric analyses, but they can provide a check on the numbers game.

During my first visit to Berlin in the spring of 1922, our well-to-do uncle from South Africa took my sister and me for a trip in an automobile around a private racetrack on the outskirts of the city. In the late 1950s, after I and other members of the board of directors of the American Friends of the Hebrew University had visited Albert Einstein at Princeton, I attempted to explain to my six-year-old son a little about Einstein and his theory; during the telling I referred to a "trolley car." Jeremy appeared to follow my simplistic illustration of "relativity," but then he asked, "What's a trolley car?" . . .

When I studied at Heidelberg in 1928–1929, I attended Professor Emil Lederer's seminar on labor, which had as its theme the "rationalizing" of German industry. When I started to teach at the Graduate School of Business at Columbia in 1935, a group known as the technocrats had their offices in the adjacent building. They were preaching the doctrine that the depressed state of the U.S. labor market, with unemployment in the 15 percent range, was the direct consequence of rapid technological changes. They prophesied that continuing advances in technology would further increase the number of persons without jobs.

The advance of the U.S. economy during and after World War II, with corresponding large increases in employment, erased all interest in, and concern with, the writings of the technocrats. But by the late 1950s, the theme reemerged when a group known as The Triple Revolution, composed of assorted economists (Kenneth Boulding and several publicists) warned that the computer and other technological advances threatened to make more and more workers permanently surplus. In 1963–1964, the Columbia University Seminar on Technology and Social Change focused on this issue; as the prepared papers and the summary discussions disclose, many of the participants, but by no means all, shared the concerns of The Triple Revolution (see *Technology and Social Change*, edited by Eli Ginzberg, Columbia University Press, 1964).

The passage of the Manpower Development and Training Act by the Congress in 1962 was predicated on the belief that skilled workers who were losing their jobs as a result of automation would not be reemployable unless they were retrained. In 1964, when the recovery from the preceding years of a suboptimal economy was finally under way, Congress authorized the creation of a National Commission on Technology, Automation, and Economic Progress, which reported in 1966 that "there is no evidence that there will be in the decade ahead an acceleration in technological change more rapid than the growth of demand can offset, given adequate public policies."

We should note that at about the time the German economy was getting into full stride, the Metal Workers Union held its second international conference on "Rationalization, Automation and Technical Progress" at Oberhausen, at which I presented a paper focused on the U.S. experience.[1]

Now, in the early 1980s, the theme has once again come to the fore. A growing number of trade unionists, academicians, and publicists are concerned about what the future holds as the developed world stands on the threshold of the fifth generation of computers. The complexity that surrounds the subject is described by a recent extended review in the *New York Review of Books* (October 27, 1983) written by Joseph Weizenbaum of MIT, of *The Fifth Generation* by Edward A. Feigenbaum and Pamela McCorduck. The reviewer, questioning the claims made by the authors for Artificial Intelligence, calls attention to a forecast made by H. A. Simon and A. Newell in 1958 that thinking machines were already in existence and that it would not be long before they would become operational. Now, a quarter of a century later, the Japanese are making the same claim!

These selected personal references can help to remind us that at least in each generation, some doomsayers foresee that the future impact of technological changes on employment may contain sufficient threats to arouse the concern of those who place heavy weight on labor markets being able to provide jobs for all, or for almost all, who want to work. For reasons that we will address shortly, those who periodically worry about the possible adverse effects of technology on jobs are not reassured by optimists who believe that there is no basis for concern, who point to the long and unequivocal record of simultaneous progress of technology and the expansion of employment and economic growth.

THE SEVERAL CAUSES OF CURRENT HIGH UNEMPLOYMENT

During the last decade the developed economies have been buffeted by a great many adverse factors, including a loss of momentum from the long post–World War II reconstruction boom; the international oil crisis and the consequent distortions of prices, costs, and capital flows; accelerating inflation; disenchantment with Keynesian demand policies; the relocation of many manufacturing plants to low-wage countries; and voter resistance to the continued growth of the public sector. Other unsettling and disturbing events include, most recently, the concern generated by the vulnerability of the international financial structure because of the excessive indebtedness of many Third World countries.

It may be useful to schematize this potpourri of recent unfavorable economic developments along a relatively few axes in order to get a better fix on our central issue of technology and jobs.

First, there has been a serious *cyclical* decline in the U.S. economy between 1979 and the beginning of 1983. This decline was of sufficient length and duration that it had a serious dampening effect on the economies of most of our trading partners and on many of the Third World countries that depend heavily on exporting to the developed nations in order to cover their essential imports and to achieve some reasonable rate of growth.

At the time of this prolonged and deep recession, most of the developed nations were facing a series of challenges that can best be subsumed under the heading of *structural* changes. In the developed nations, many sectors of manufacturing, on which previous economic growth had been predicated, were no longer competitive because of an underinvestment in new or appropriate technology (as was the case in the U.S. steel industry); because of the much lower wage rates in the Far East (electronics); or for a host of associated reasons, most of them related to a failure of many industries to sense the changing directions of consumer demand (U.S. and U.K. automotive industries). The adjustments of developed economies to structural shifts have always been difficult, particularly when their economies are also undergoing a cyclical downswing.

A third major contributor to the weakened economic and employment conditions that characterize most of the developed nations can be subsumed under the heading of *macroeconomic policy.* For the quarter century after the establishment of the Marshall Plan and the concomitant U.S. steps to assist Japan, the major economies pursued a neo-Keynesian policy in which government expenditures played a large role in helping to keep their economies operating at close to their optimum.

The inflation that accelerated after the first oil crisis in 1973 resulted in a new set of conditions and constraints such that all the developed nations—some, such as Germany, sooner, and others, such as the United States, later—decided they had to alter their macroeconomic policies to give the highest priority to containing inflation, even at the cost of increases in unemployment and the losses in output that a restrictive monetary and fiscal policy entails.

This brief account of the combined influence of cyclical, structural, and macroeconomic changes on the performance of the developed economies during the past decade, and the probability of their continuing influence in the period immediately ahead, should be a useful reminder that new technology is by no means the only factor, nor necessarily the most potent one, that accounts for shortfalls in the ability of the labor market to provide an adequate number of jobs for all who want and need to work.

The foregoing helps to explain why the Bureau of Labor Statistics of the U.S. Department of Labor is convinced, on the basis of its ongoing studies, that technology has been a relatively minor factor (in the 25 percent range) in accounting for shifts in the number and composition of the labor force from one decade to the next, and why the bureau does not see any major threats from technology in the decade ahead.

TECHNOLOGY AND JOBS: SOME BASIC CONSIDERATIONS

So far this analysis has drawn attention to two striking phenomena—the periodic, rather than continuing, concern with the potential negative effects of technology on employment, and the difficulties of distinguishing clearly between the impact of technology and the host of other factors that together determine the level of employment.

The difficulties mentioned earlier point to the desirability of setting forth, if in condensed form, a limited number of propositions about technology and jobs that command broad agreement among a large number of scholars, although no single scholar would subscribe to all of them.

- Technology, narrowly conceived, is often defined as improvements introduced into existing processes and products, including the introduction of entirely new products and ways of producing them. Technology, broadly defined, would take account also of the organizational concomitants and societal shifts that flow from new technological innovations, such as the move to the suburbs that followed the widescale introduction of the automobile.
- A minority of economists believe that technological inventions come in long waves (Kondratief); a larger number see them as randomly bunched (Schumpeter). Those who have paid the greatest attention to the timing of inventions, their introduction, and widespread diffusion, however, have not been able to discern regular temporal patterns because of the difficulties of distinguishing among discovery, introduction, and diffusion, among other reasons.
- The major industrial nations spend about 3 percent of their GNP on research and development, with a heavy bias, in the case of the superpowers, on military technology. The World War II breakthroughs of radar and the atomic bomb underscored the

importance of targeted efforts, with the result that all the developed
nations have vastly increased their outlays for research and development in recent decades. In the United States, R&D as a
percentage of GNP has risen about sixfold, from 0.5–1 percent in
1950 to around 3 percent today.

- The nub of the difficulty in assessing the impact of technology on
  jobs is that the outcome can vary according to the specifics. In a
  mature industry, new technology may be labor-displacing because
  reduced costs and prices will not be reflected in increased sales
  and employment. Without new technology, however, the job losses
  could be greater because of large-scale losses to more efficient
  producers. In the United States, however, most technological improvements have led to a growth of the market and a growth of
  jobs, which explains why, at least until recently, U.S. labor has
  had a positive stance toward technological change.

- The nub of the difficulty in assessing the impact on jobs derives
  from the fact that the long-term effects of technological changes
  that introduce new products and their secondary consequences
  (automobile—suburbanization) can be assessed only in retrospect.
  The displacement effects are more immediately visible.

- The role of time compounds the difficulties not only for assessing
  delayed benefits but also for taking account of delayed costs.
  Every developed economy can provide evidence of large human,
  economic, and social costs that result from technological changes.
  Two illustrations from the United States: After the textile industry moved South in the 1930s in order to accommodate the new
  machines, the mill towns of Massachusetts went into decline,
  with consequences that are still visible a half century later. And
  the horrendous unemployment and social problems of the disadvantaged black populations in northern cities are directly linked
  to the technological revolution in agriculture during the past
  half century. In balancing the books, however, we must note that
  most displaced blacks gained from being forced to relocate.

- A related issue can be formulated in the economist's language as
  the *dislocation* effect. Technological changes can have quite different effects on various industrial, occupational, and income groups,
  as well as on different communities, regions, and countries. For
  example, the firms producing robots will expand employment,
  while many that install them will cut the size of their work force.

- The most egregious problems arise when technological change
  forces a large plant shutdown in a community in which a high
  proportion of the work force is employed by a single firm and
  there are no other labor markets within commuting distance.

Under these conditions the plight of the disemployed and their families tends to undermine the livelihood of the rest of the community and also leads to the erosion and destruction of public infrastructure. (See my *Grass on the Slag Heaps: The Story of the Welsh Miners* [New York: Harper, 1942].)

The foregoing brief account of the range of impacts of technology on jobs should help to inform the uninformed that the two extreme positions— that technology destroys jobs and its counterpart, that technology creates jobs—are both overly simplistic, and that the nub of the analytic and policy challenge is to assess the conditions under which new technology is introduced. Only then can the employment effects be weighed.

OMENS AND UPHEAVALS

There are only sixteen years until the end of the century, and the editors have asked me to consider this period in assessing the impact of emerging technologies on employment. My own work life has been slightly more than three times sixteen years so far, and therefore I have a longer perspective within which to explore the interactions among technology and jobs. When I began to teach at Columbia in the mid-1930s, my office had a telephone, a typewriter, an adding machine, and a mimeograph machine. Today the telephone works faster; my secretaries use a word processor (an improvement but not a revolution); my staff uses computers, but I continue to do most of my computations in my head; and a photocopier has replaced the mimeograph, with the result that it is often more difficult, not less, to retrieve the piece I want from among the great accumulation of paper.

Clearly, these limited technological gains do not tell the entire story. I will mention three others: The airplane has enabled me to lead a double life, as a professor in New York City and as a consultant to the federal government in Washington and abroad; there have been advances in medicine that I have not had occasion to use, although my wife has been a major beneficiary; and I have benefited from a host of conveniences and recreational items, from credit cards to TV, all of which have added something—but not a great deal—to the quality of my life.

Two major technological breakthroughs, nuclear power aside, the jet airplane and the computer, in a half century should be a powerful reminder that the next sixteen years, which will take us to the year 2000, are not likely to see major technological upheavals although this reassurance should not be interpreted as implying the absence of difficulties in the employment arena, including some engendered by progress on the technological front.

Let us consider briefly but critically the areas of potential upheavals that have come to the public's consciousness. The leading candidate, by far, is the microprocessor, generically defined, which encompasses a number of discrete threats such as robotics, the office of the future, and the computer-telecommunications linkage—to mention only these three.

The expansion of robots and their steady improvement is well under way. Although the experts differ substantially in their estimates of the number that will be in place by the year 2000, even the lowest forecasts point to substantial penetration by that date.

A recent publication by the AFL–CIO Committee on the Evolution of Work—*The Future of Work*, August 1983—presents data from the Robot Institute of America that indicate that there were about 4,200 robots in use in the United States in 1981. The committee reported that one expert predicts that "eventually robots will replace about three million workers in the metal working industries." The term "eventually" provides the expert a wide escape hatch. The Upjohn Institute for Employment Research has two estimates for 1990 based respectively on a slow and a fast growth economy: 50,000 and 100,000. If the low forecast turns out to be right, it means a twelvefold gain in nine years; if the higher percentage is closer to the mark, the rate of increase will be about twenty-fourfold. Some time ago the newspapers carried a quotation from a Carnegie-Mellon professor to the effect that by the turn of the century, U.S. manufacturing would employ no more than 5 million workers, which would represent a reduction of about three-quarters from the present total. In striking contrast is the projection of the U.S. Bureau of Labor Statistics, which looks forward to an increase of over 2 million in the number of manufacturing employees between 1979 and 1990, from 21.4 to 23.5 million.

Several points in elucidation: Robots, in terms of the current and near-term developments, are high-cost units and are most cost-effective when used in high-volume, standard-output production. But the market is increasingly moving in the direction of batch outputs with small runs. It is likely that some time in the future robots will also fit this newer environment, but that development appears to be some years off. A reasonable assumption is that several hundred thousand, possibly half a million, jobs in U.S. manufacturing may be at risk during the next decade; but this prospective large loss will be reduced by the numbers of workers who will be employed in manufacturing, selling, operating, and servicing the new robots. A further consideration, often overlooked, is the possible recapturing of work that had earlier been lost to low-wage countries by virtue of the efficiency gains that can be achieved through the use of robots. There is scattered information that some jobs have already been recaptured.

The AFL–CIO report cited earlier calls specific attention to the computer revolution that has been under way since the early 1960s and the continuing rapid rate of its progress, which so far gives no evidence of slowing down. The cost per function of processing information continues to drop, and the number of components that can be built into a single chip continues to increase. In my view, the report argues correctly that even if, as anticipated, high-tech jobs expand quite rapidly—computer occupations are projected to increase by 40 percent, from 1.5 to 2.1 million, between 1980 and 1990—in total they will account for less than 2 percent of the labor force in 1990. On the other hand, the report indicates that there is considerable anxiety about the impact of the new technology on existing jobs, particularly office and clerical work.

The outlook, however, once again, as in the earlier case of manufacturing, is far from clear. The U.S. Bureau of Labor Statistics estimates that clerical workers will continue to be the fastest-growing group, increasing their share of total employment from 18.1 to 22.5 percent over the decade of the 1980s. One thing is certain: The rapid growth of computers over the last two decades did not have adverse employment effects. Whether adverse effects will develop in the remaining decade and a half of this century is difficult to assess, but the following considerations should be noted.

The word processor is in place, but it is often overlooked that secretaries spend, on average, no more than 20 to 25 percent of their time in typing. Much of their time is devoted to setting up appointments, retrieving materials from files, arranging travel plans, answering inquiries and seeking specialized information, and keeping a brief record of what transpires during the course of a day. As discs become the new files, as distributed computing becomes more widespread, as telephones and other communication devices are linked to computers, the office of the future will surely be different from the office today.

Probably the office of the future, broadly defined as encompassing not only clerks, typists, and secretaries but also the large numbers of junior and middle managers—who yesterday and even today spend much or all of their time entering items in records, analyzing the records, and then recommending or taking action based on the figures—will see its work radically restructured and often simplified once the emerging links between the computer and the new telecommunications technology are effectively forged. Although R&D efforts are proceeding at an accelerating rate to tie the two powerful technologies more effectively together, which will further reduce the costs of data transmission and will have other consequences that cannot yet be anticipated, the development of this new basic infrastructure will require more than successes in the laboratory.

Much data transmission involves crossing national frontiers, which makes sovereign states critical participants in future developments. Even within the boundaries of a single nation, significant hurdles remain, such as the establishment of standards, the wiring of buildings, the establishment of networks, and the control of access to such networks. The history of the railroad and the telephone suggests that the establishment of new infrastructure arrangements is not likely to be accomplished within a few years, especially in the face of the high capital requirements and considerations of national security.

Recently, attention has been directed to the person-machine interface. Advocates of the new technology realized only belatedly that its widespread adoption depends in no small measure on the ease or difficulty that the work force, managerial and other, experience in working with the new machines. With the advent of the personal computer, more and more young people in the United States and other developed countries will be exposed to the new technology at home and in school; hence they will be attuned to it as they enter the work force a decade or two down the road. But what about the large numbers who are already at work and past the point where they find it easy to change their ways of thinking and behaving? The only reasonable conclusion is that the effective penetration of a radically new technology is always geared to generational flows: The established managers and workers must leave the scene and the new generation must be in control for a new technology to be enthusiastically embraced.

A senior official of a major computer company known for his deep interest in its technological aspects recently sought to demonstrate to me the many new functions that his most advanced office equipment could perform. After several false starts he gave up and called on his secretary, who experienced no difficulty in getting the machines to "do their thing." She was comfortable with them; the senior executive belonged to a generation that had not grown up with them.

In my view, however, it would be a mistake to minimize the upheavals that may still develop before the end of this century as a result of the computer revolution, despite its controlled rate of diffusion, which results from the fact that, except for a small but growing minority, the existing work force are not comfortable with the new technology, fear it, and have neither the inclination nor the incentives to master it. Some of the difficulties and dangers—I find *upheaval* too strong a term—are grounded in reality; others represent my best hunches of what lies ahead in the remaining decade and a half of the twentieth century.

By way of background, it is important to recall that all advanced economies are moving at different rates out of *goods production,* defined as agriculture, mining, construction, and manufacturing, into the remaining sector of the economy, broadly categorized as *services.* In the United States the approximate proportion of services to total output is, in GNP terms, just below 70 percent; in terms of total employment, a few percentage points higher. Since the major impact of twentieth-century technology, especially since the end of World War II, has been to shrink the absolute—and, even more, the relative—numbers of persons employed in the goods-producing sector, most employment expansion has taken place in services. The question we must ask, even if we must wait for a definitive answer, is whether the next stage of the computer revolution will have a major retarding impact on job generation in services. As noted earlier, the U.S. Bureau of Labor Statistics does not so believe, but the bureau has not always been right.

Even if large-scale labor displacement in services is avoided, significant difficulties may arise. Some of them are currently underway, and more loom on the horizon. To note several of the more important threats:

• The banks and financial institutions, large-scale users of computers, have raised their hiring requirements for entry-level clerical and other office positions on the ground that career employees must have a sufficiently broad educational base to make it relatively easy to retrain them as the technology changes, as it certainly will, in the years ahead. This change in hiring standards is exacerbating the unemployment of high school dropouts in urban centers. A recent analysis prepared by the New York Regional Office of the U.S. Bureau of Labor Statistics called attention to the following serious imbalance: Fewer than half of all minority youth in the city complete high school, but they will be considered for employment in only 17 percent of the occupations with the greatest number of job openings.

• Another adverse trend is the continuing transfer of many back-office jobs from the large urban centers, with their high commercial rents and limited pool of suitable new workers, to smaller communities, particularly to communities in low-wage areas with relatively large pools of female high school graduates. Citibank has recently moved some of these back-office operations to South Dakota, and others to Tampa, Florida. The major improvements in the computer-communications network are speeding such developments, with corresponding adverse effects on poorly educated urban young people in search of jobs.

• Recent investigations that are still under way suggest that there may be a major restructuring of the insurance industry. As computerization advances, the relationships among sales personnel, local and district agencies, and middle managers at headquarters are being altered as at least one level of supervision becomes redundant. The salesperson who is able to access the computer directly can obtain the necessary information almost instantaneously and thus can make the customer a firm bid. The implications of this radical organizational restructuring is underscored by Andrew Tobias's estimate in *The Invisible Bankers* (Simon and Schuster, 1982) that the potential exists for a reduction of the current work force in the insurance industry from 2 to 1 million. Clearly, the insurance industry is a prototype. There are a great many other middle managers in other industries whose jobs may be at risk when the information they have controlled for so long, on the basis of which they make decisions, becomes directly accessible to their superiors and subordinates.

• My colleagues, Professor Thomas Stanback, Jr. and Dr. Thierry Noyelle, as a result of their earlier studies, *Services: The New Economy* (Allanheld, Osmun, 1981), and reinforced by their current investigations of the impact of the computer on selected industries and occupational groups, are convinced that the new technology is contributing to a less even distribution of income, whereby more professionals will earn high incomes, more unskilled workers will be caught in low-wage jobs, and the numbers of those in the middle will be reduced. We know that the internal labor market in manufacturing enabled a great many workers to start at the bottom and to work their way up several rungs of the occupational and income ladders to earn both good wages and benefits, far above the average for workers in the service sector. At this early stage in the evolution of the new technology, it is hard to determine whether there will be a substitute for the internal labor market in the service sector. One possible development will be a combination of return to school for additional skill acquisition and shifts among jobs in the same or different industries, which will provide the employees with additional skills. Such a development would fit the traditional U.S. pattern that characterized the heyday of manufacturing. In a dynamic economy some workers are always at risk from technological progress and market shifts, but these losses will be contained if the job market is expanding.

Policy Directions

Since 1973 the developed nations have been experiencing a level of unemployment that is much too high for societal cohesion and personal well-being. As former Chancellor Helmut Schmidt recently remarked at Vail, Colorado, the level of unemployment in Germany is at 1931 levels. He reminded his audience that the still higher level of 1933 provided the opening for Hitler.

We have not been able to identify a prospective substantial worsening in the already bad employment situation as a result of the disemployment effects of technological upheavals, surely not within the remaining sixteen years of this century. Nevertheless, we can point to a number of instances where technological changes could add substantially to the adjustment problems workers currently face.

We must also call attention to additional sources of difficulty confronting developed nations—the still unabsorbed surplus population in agriculture; miners who face relocation and reabsorption; the continuing transfer of manufacturing jobs to the LDCs; and the more modest expansion of service employment, particularly public-sector jobs.

There is one counterpoint to this downbeat assessment. It is possible that the economic expansion that is clearly under way (as of November 1983) will gain strength and be sustained over a sufficiently long period to bring the excessively high level of unemployed persons in the developed nations down to a more tolerable and less explosive level. This optimistic forecast, however, must be leavened by the many structural adjustments that remain to be accomplished; the fragility of the international financial system; the unbalanced federal budget in the United States, which presages continuing high interest rates or renewed inflation; and the vulnerable economic position of many Third World countries.

If the world's economy is definitely on the mend, it probably makes sense for the developed nations to avoid major policy initiatives directed at the labor market at this time. If, however, as I suspect, the recovery will be modest and short-lived—if inaction in the face of long-term double-digit unemployment is an invitation to societal disaster—then it is none too early to chart new directions. As a modest contribution to such an effort, I present my own position on jobs and job-related issues.

Employment Policy

The time is long past when developed nations should accept as the price of economic progress the recurrence of widespread and persistent unemployment, even when it is mitigated by various social-welfare measures that assure that the unemployed will not starve. Keynesian macro policy, which served very well for about a quarter of a century, cannot be expected to repeat its stellar performance; nevertheless, governments of the developed nations cannot avoid responsibility for providing jobs for all who are able and want to work—surely, for all who need to work. Since there is little or no prospect that the private sector on its own can provide and maintain employment at a satisfactory level, it is the clear responsibility of national governments to respond to this challenge. They should offer public-sector jobs for all who want to work at or close to the minimum wage, a suggestion that Ambassador Arthur F. Burns advanced during his chairmanship of the Federal Reserve Board. Developed nations have no option but to improve the workings of the pluralistic economy; a high priority is assuming responsibility for providing employment opportunities for all who are able and willing and who need to work.

Research and Development Policy

It is important to emphasize, particularly in an analysis that focuses on the potential adverse effects of technology on jobs, that over the long run a dynamic economy requires accretions to its knowledge pool to speed technological innovations and their diffusion. The human input into the U.S. economy now accounts for over 80 percent of the total. Since economists have good reason to believe there will always be a shortfall in investment in instances such as basic research where private investors cannot capture the full returns, national governments must continue to make adequate investments in R&D. Nothing could be more injurious to the long-term welfare of a developed economy than a large-scale cutback in such investments on the ground that the new technology might have a deleterious influence on the employment of some part of the work force. To fall behind in the technological race would place not a few, but most jobs of a lagging economy in jeopardy.

Trade Policy

As most developed nations, including our own, experience continuing high levels of unemployment, they are increasingly resorting to trade restrictions. This trend threatens a repetition of the 1930s, when the world pursued a beggar-thy-neighbor policy, with disastrous results for all. The problem is that much more acute because the major international lending authorities are pressuring the Third World countries that have horrendous debts to reduce their imports, which of course are the exports of other countries. It is highly questionable that the employment problems of the developed nations can be significantly repaired without a major restructuring of the world's debt, a subject the political leadership of all nations prefer to temporize with rather than to confront and solve.

Industrial Policy

The financial and economic policies of all the developed nations are influenced by the direct and continuing intervention of their governments—some more, as in the United States, France, and Japan—some less, as in Germany. Currently, most of the intellectuals associated with the Democratic party in the United States are looking with favor on industrial policy as the preferred way to cope with the structural problems facing the United States economy. I am afraid, however, that general industrial policy can do little to help to shrink noncompetitive industries or to expand new sectors with potential for rapid take-off. My own preference is to stay within the ad hoc efforts that today make up U.S. industrial policy, from dairy supports to large-scale underwriting of R&D for military communications systems.

Regional Policy

Since shortly after the end of World War I, the United Kingdom has been a consistent advocate of regional policy. Most European countries, however, have also resorted to regional policies from time to time; the single largest investment was made by Italy in its efforts to energize its southern region. My tentative judgment of these efforts is that they devour sizable amounts of public capital, with little to show for the outlay other than a short-term salvage of jobs, which eventually disappear because government cannot afford to maintain them. Meanwhile the national savings invested in the job salvage operations are lost, and the alternative use of the capital to speed an expanding sector of the economy has been preempted. Admittedly politicians, aware of the large numbers of potential and actual unemployed persons in declining areas, face a political challenge that they cannot duck. In my view, most regional policies have been the least effective of the options.

Retraining Policy

As the long-term chairman of advisory committees and commissions on employment policy of the U.S. government, I was involved in the oversight of about $100 billion of public expenditures for training and retraining between 1962 and 1982. Although most of this sizable sum went to help needy persons, new skill acquisition by experienced workers was modest; most of the money went to subsidize work and earnings for the unemployed (Eli Ginzberg, ed., *Employing the Unemployed* [New York: Basic Books, 1980]). Sweden and Germany have had more success with retraining, but even in these countries reemployment of the unemployed has depended more on the renewed buoyancy of the labor market than on the acquisition of new skills by the unemployed. A series of articles in *The Washington Post* in early November 1983, about a major retraining effort in the Los Angeles area of former automotive workers for computer occupations, provided little optimism.

Transitional School-Training-Work Programs

These are needed to help the significant numbers of young people who reach working age without having acquired functional literacy to do so in order to have access to the wide range of service jobs that are coming to dominate advanced economies. No young person should be left to flounder without skills, work, or direction. If the economies of the advanced nations continue to operate at suboptimal levels of employment for years to come, as was postulated earlier, the outlook for poorly prepared young people (aged sixteen to twenty-two) will be particularly bleak unless special remedial programs are available to help them. Failure of public policy to respond to the needs of unprepared and unqualified young people would increase significantly the risk to society from political extremists.

Social Policy

Implicit in my first recommendation anent employment policy is a strong preference for work relief over home relief. Furthermore, I question the soundness of European efforts to use early retirement as a way of reducing unemployment. I much prefer the Swedish approach, which permits a commingling of pensions and part-time work for persons in their sixties. Second, the German use of unemployment funds as a method of avoiding layoffs in periods of cyclical recession has proved itself. One difficult arena for governments is how to use housing policy to help workers move out of declining industries and locations to other, more prosperous locations. If regional policy to maintain faltering jobs or to encourage the location of new firms in distressed areas has little to commend it, as noted earlier, government-financed schemes to enable workers, if they relocate, not to lose all their equity in their homes might turn out on balance to be the least costly form of public support to assure a higher level of labor mobility.

Collective Bargaining between Employers and Trade Unions

Wassily Leontief, Nobel laureate in economics, is convinced that the German and other trade union movements are on the right track as they gear up to demand a reduction in the standard hours of work as a major balancing device in an unbalanced labor market. The AFL–CIO report quoted earlier generally supports this strategy. Most economists question whether the demand for shorter hours is sensible and whether, if it is successfully negotiated, it would greatly alleviate the problem. Employers should be pressured to agree to a range of flexible hour assignments (e.g., forty, thirty-two, or twenty-five hours per week) that would accommodate a large number of workers with differing needs and preferences and would help to expand the total number of jobs. In addition to adjustments in hours, employers and trade unions should be encouraged to pursue many cooperative undertakings to moderate the adverse impacts of a rapidly changing technology. Included in such efforts should be maximum reliance on attrition rather than discharges to accomplish labor savings; provision of in-service retraining to help the existing work force cope with the new technology; and availability of intra- and, on occasion, intercompany job transfers where appropriate.

CONCLUDING OBSERVATIONS

In a book written to honor a German banker[2] with close ties to the trade union movement, it is fitting to extract a few markers from his long and productive life that have bearing on the themes this chapter has addressed:

- Technology has long been viewed as a threat to employment, but there is no evidence in this century that these fears are justified. The reverse is true: Technology has played a major role in expanding jobs and incomes.
- If technology can be cleared of this charge of contributing to large-scale unemployment, the failure to address the other causes and to take corrective action cannot be viewed as acceptable public policy. As Schmidt recalled only recently, massive unemployment gave Hitler his chance. Unemployment is again at unconscionably high levels. If it is left unattended, major dangers loom ahead.
- The market, despite its many achievements, cannot be relied on

to correct the shortfall in jobs. Only the intervention of the public sector holds promise of amelioration. The loss of faith of the majority in developed nations in collective undertakings is ominous and must be reversed. . . .

CHAPTER 34

Work and Workers: Transatlantic Comparisons

THE U.S. SCENE

THE STARTING POINT for this interpretative analysis is a set of three doctrines that have wide currency in the United States at the beginning of the 1980s. The first holds that there has been a serious erosion of the work ethic. The second postulates that a severe decline in productivity has occurred, the causes of which are embedded in the loss of discipline in the work place, largely a reflection of the growing power of trade unions. The third warns about the imminent collapse of Western democratic societies because of their responsiveness to the claims of the populace for more and more social services, which is undermining the competitiveness of their economies.

Before taking a closer look at what is happening on the other side of the Atlantic that might illuminate this conventional wisdom, a brief review of recent U.S. developments may sharpen the focus. In these introductory considerations we will raise challenges rather than search for balanced answers.

A few facts about the erosion of the work ethic:

1. During the several decades since the end of World War II there has been a steady rise in the employment-population (E–P) ratio, which reflects the percentage of the total population over sixteen that is in the labor force, holding down or looking for a job. In the case of the female population the ratio has increased from roughly one-third to over one-half. Even in the case of young people reaching working age, whose numbers increased from around 2 to 4 million per year, the E–P ratio recently reached an all-time high.

2. Although there has been some decline in the hours employees work over the course of the year as a result of longer vacations and more paid holidays, the basic work week has not been altered except at the fringes: It was 40 hours in manufacturing in 1950, and it is roughly the same today; about 35 hours for office work then and now. The officially reported figures for moonlighting—that is, the proportion of the work force that holds more than one job—has not shown any secular decline, but rather a small increase. A significant minority of workers in industries in which overtime is the pattern work more than the standard number of hours and for the most part are eager to do so. True, younger workers are pressing employers to make overtime voluntary. They don't want intrusions into their life off the job unless they are consulted.

3. In all analyses of work and workers, it is an error to focus solely on what transpires in the regular economy. Many important shifts are underway in the manner in which people apportion time and energy between household and job. Consider the explosion in "do-it-yourself," from painting the house to paneling the den. More telling are the long hours of work reported by wives who hold down full-time jobs and who at the same time continue to carry most of the responsibility for running their homes and raising their children. Their behavior surely does not support the argument that the work ethic is weakening.

4. While no reliable data are available, current statistics seriously underestimate the total work that the U.S. population performs because of the sizable and almost certainly growing importance of the "unreported economy." An estimate of 10 percent of the GNP is increasingly used as a first approximation of the size of this unreported sector.

Admittedly the foregoing makes no reference to such countervailing trends as the increasing number of individuals who are able to live without working—those on welfare, unemployment insurance, social security, and private pensions. But except for those on welfare the nonworker has contributed to the system that now helps to support him or her. Some receive more from the system than they put in, some less.

The gross data provide little support for a decline in the work ethic. Of course, protagonists can argue that the gross data are beside the point: What they mean by the erosion of the work ethic is not that workers have stopped punching in at 8 a.m. and out at 4 p.m., but that they have stopped doing a day's work for a day's pay. But the protagonists have never come up with data to substantiate their contentions.

What about the second proposition, the decline in productivity that is seen as a result of a loss of discipline in the workplace, among other reasons because of the growing power of trade unions? A few questions:

1. How good are the measures of productivity? The answer is, not very. National income accounting in such important sectors as government, banking, and other large service areas uses labor inputs as a proxy for output. But the gross data do point to a marked deceleration of productivity across the economy since the late 1960s. However, if perspective is lengthened one finds that recent developments are more or less on trend, and what really requires explanation are the increases above trend that occurred in the twenty years after World War II. The reason lies ready at hand: absence of international competition that the U.S. economy enjoyed following World War II.

2. If the conventional wisdom about the decline in productivity is suspect, one must be doubly cautious in assessing the correlative claim that a loss of discipline in the workplace because of the growing power of the trade unions is the explanation. As to the power of unions, the truth is that in recent years the proportion of workers belonging to unions has been declining, not increasing, despite the fact that through legislation and administrative action many workers previously excluded have been brought within the purview of the National Labor Relations Act.

3. Union membership aside, the question of workplace discipline is worth inspecting. Again, the gross data in terms of work stoppages and loss of work time through strikes lend no support. They show no upward drift, but rather an erratic pattern. In the early 1960s and again in the mid-1970s, my colleagues and I made two efforts to get beneath the surface to see whether we could discern any significant long-term trends that would support generalizations about discipline in the workplace. In both

instances the evidence was mixed but served to point in the direction that, union or no union, a management that knew what it was about maintained discipline, and one that was flaccid was likely to be in trouble.

The work-satisfaction data tend to support this reading. They show no clear-cut trend in the direction of growing worker dissatisfaction.

This brings us to the third proposition, that the welfare state in the United States and in Europe is threatening the long-term survival of advanced democracies. The neoconservatives support this claim by calling attention to several ominous developments:

1. Voters, through the ballot box, are forcing governments to provide increasing benefits whose costs so far outpace tax revenues that the printing presses take over, the prelude to disaster.
2. Special-interest groups from farmers to workers facing plant closures have learned how to intimidate politicians into protecting them so that the market can no longer perform its allocative functions, thereby slowing or stopping economic growth.
3. The public's expectations are out of control, with the result that in their efforts to protect the environment, the worker, the old and the young, minorities, and many others who are vulnerable, modern democracies are spending too much, investing too little, and thereby jeopardizing their future.

By way of reclaimer, the following are some cautionary observations about accepting this dire assessment.

Inflation has been a mounting threat to the long-term viability of the U.S. economy, but it has nonetheless finally been confronted by the federal government as of early 1981.

Special-interest groups have a potent influence on legislators, but no persuasive argument has ever been advanced that the United States would have been better off had assistance been denied Penn Central, Lockheed, and most recently Chrysler. One of the overriding responsibilities of democratic governments is to cushion the damage the market occasionally inflicts on dedicated workers and competent employers. The real challenge to government is to undertake only those interventions that have a prospect of long-term success.

The issue of excessive expectations is complicated. Any society worth its salt should strive to respond to challenges it has failed to meet adequately in the past, from reducing and eliminating discrimination to protecting its natural and cultural heritage. Admittedly, if the public overestimates the rate at which the economy will continue to grow and underestimates the cost of desirable new programs, it can run into trouble.

That is what happened when the expensive Great Society programs were followed by the costly new environmentalism. But as the recent pressures for tax discipline have come to the fore, both in the states and in Washington, evidence suggests that a democratic society is capable of learning from its errors.

TRANSATLANTIC PERSPECTIVES

The three prongs of the conventional wisdom about work and workers that have just been examined from the U.S. vantage point provide a perspective for looking at the comparable experiences of our friends and allies in Western Europe. There is always something, sometimes a great deal, to be learned by escaping from a narrow parochialism.

The observations offered here on the European scene reflect a half century of activity on my part as resident, visitor, consultant, and researcher. I will comment in turn on the three central themes: the work ethic; productivity and discipline; expectations and the welfare state.

With respect to the work ethic, I have been impressed by the following:

> The relatively slow decline in the conventional hours of work in most advanced European economies, alongside of quite liberal vacations. Paris empties out in August. The Swedes warn one not to get sick in June or July; most physicians are away. In the Netherlands the welfare grant covers a two weeks' vacation for the recipient. Many European unions continue to press for retirement as early as sixty, largely because of their unease about employment opportunities for the younger age groups.

> The German trade unions, worried about rationalization and automation, are pressing for a reduction in the conventional hours of work to thirty-five, not because they place such a high value on leisure but rather because they fear that in the absence of such a reduction there will not be enough work to go around.

> The Western European countries, some more and some less, with the Netherlands at the end of the queue, have witnessed the increasing participation of women in the labor force. But since the slowdown in economic growth in the mid-1970s, most of these countries have taken latent or overt actions to impede, if not stop, the flow of women, particularly married women, into the labor force. Again, however, such action does not reflect a weakening in the work ethic, but rather an anxiety of the male leadership in government and in the trade unions about a shortfall in employment opportunities for regularly attached male workers.

In Sweden, some years ago, there were no young native males employed on Volvo's assembly line. Inquiry disclosed that in the face of a booming economy it was harder and harder for management to recruit natives for manufacturing jobs, particularly for work on the assembly line. In France and Germany guest workers had been imported in large numbers and directed to jobs that the natives shunned, such as street cleaning; other unskilled types of employment; and some dirty, heavy blue-collar work. Although the French government has belatedly sought to upgrade some of these laboring jobs via wage adjustments and fringe benefits in the hope of reducing the nation's reliance on guest workers, it remains to be seen whether this positive approach will work. If Michael Piore is right, and I suspect that he is, there will always be jobs at the bottom of a nation's structure that are rejected by natives but prove attractive to foreigners who come from a more impoverished environment.

Two years ago my wife and I arrived at Heathrow Airport, London, on the evening of the second day of a three-day holiday, and waited a long time for a taxi. Inquiry disclosed that at the current high marginal tax rates many drivers opted for leisure over working on holidays. This explanation was offered to describe the behavior not only of taxi drivers but of the great mass of British workers.

During the course of that visit, I learned that off-the-books employment at every level from unskilled work to the highest professional activity was increasingly common in the United Kingdom, which tends to confirm a recent analysis in *The Economist* suggesting that national income (and hours worked) may be underreported by 7 percent or so.

These perspectives lead one to doubt that the work ethic is eroding. True, natives may avoid low-paying, unpleasant work; they may prefer leisure to overtime when most of their extra earnings go to the government in higher taxes; but they apparently seek additional work when they can pocket the wages without incurring a tax liability.

The second theme deals with the triad of productivity, work discipline, and trade unions. Here the challenge is more complex because of both the variability among the several countries and my limited knowledge of details. But the following may prove suggestive:

In Sweden, where social democracy in terms of welfare benefits provided by the state has proceeded farther than in any other Western European country, management control over the workplace has remained strong. U.S. automobile workers report that certain lines operate at a higher speed in Stockholm than in Detroit.

This is only part of the story, however. The other part relates to the severe financial penalties that Swedish employers face if they discharge older workers; the high wage settlements they have been forced to accept; and most recently (1980) the collapse of the long-established system of national bargaining, which held to a minimum hours lost through strikes and lockouts. High labor productivity, good discipline, and labor cost increases that jeopardize a country's balance of payments are not necessarily mutually exclusive.

The German situation differs markedly from that of its neighbors to the north, west, and south. One hears little about a decline in labor productivity and a weakening of discipline in the workplace. In fact, the powerful trade union movement is constantly on the lookout that high investment leading to increasing productivity does not result in displacing workers faster than they can be reabsorbed. Moreover, the unions have been willing to participate with employers and government authorities in keeping the wage bargain within bounds.

What one does hear from conservatively inclined observers of the German scene are the handicaps under which management labors as a result of the political evolution that has placed worker representatives on key management boards. But the continuing strength of German industry suggests that these fears must be exaggerated or their effects long delayed.

In the United Kingdom the situation is strikingly different. Here many trade union members at the shop level are engaged in ongoing warfare with their managements, a struggle that has been led by communist or fellow-traveler shop stewards. I have a different interpretation, however.

Britain remains, in my opinion, the most elitist of the so-called democratic countries, as reflected in the wide gap between top and middle management and the still wider gap between management and the work force. Almost forty years ago I warned in *Grass on the Slag Heaps: The Story of the Welsh Miners* that the shabby way in which the nation under Baldwin treated the unemployed and underemployed was a certain invitation to labor strife once the balance of power shifted, as it did after World War II. The evil that men do lives after them, as the poet said. The workers in the shop may feel a little less hostile when the prime minister is a member of the Labour party, but not sufficiently to lower their fists, especially against most managements that have little desire or ability to reach long-term accommodations with them. The remarkable fact is not the decline of Great Britain as an industrial power but the fact that she cannot yet be written off, although her revival remains problematic in the face of this unresolved class struggle.

The French situation bears some resemblance to that of both Germany and Great Britain. On the one hand, France became a significant industrial power after World War II, an accomplishment resulting from effective collaboration between the bureaucrats and the captains of industry, with labor acquiescing. While the French trade unions are less powerful than the British, a smoldering class conflict persists in France. The glorious revolution of 1789 has not yet been completed. The distribution of income is more uneven in France than in any other developed European country. The large Communist party may not be growing, but neither is it declining.

Italy, the last of the arrivals among the advanced industrial countries, is at once the simplest and the most confused. Since the bloody summer of 1968, the trade unions have become a dominant force. They do not always get their way; but without their support, or at least their acquiescence, no management can manage. In public-sector enterprises in which unions confront government-appointed managers, efficiency is generally very low since the unions have the muscle to prevent dismissals of surplus workers and reassignments aimed at improved utilization of the work force. But in typical Italian fashion the economy has demonstrated its continuing vitality and resiliency by the rapid growth of the unrecorded sector, which one cabinet minister estimated a few years ago constitutes at least 20 percent and possibly more.

What about the third theme, the charge that the welfare state has overreached itself and in the process undermined its economy and jeopardized its democracy. The charge can't be dismissed out of hand.

Although economists disagree on details, they see a close link between the severe inflation that has come to characterize most developed societies and the ambitious goals the welfare state has been pursuing. When resources fall short of expectations, the printing press is called into service.

Sweden, the Netherlands, France, Italy, and the United Kingdom all suffer from destructive inflationary pressures, which are rooted in government control over half or more of the GNP. However, recent evidence suggests that the public has begun to have second thoughts. There have been significant changes—altered political leadership in Sweden and the United Kingdom, a new economic policy in France, and a partial shift to the right in Italy—all of which suggest that the overreaching of the welfare state, long disguised but now on the surface, has forced voters to make some hard choices.

The expansion of the unrecorded economies in each of these countries, with many employers and employees finding ways to beat the high tax and regulatory systems, is also forcing a reassessment of expectations.

But let us be clear; the expectations that led to the rapid growth of the welfare state had much to commend them. They sought to narrow the gap between those lower and higher in the socioeconomic-political status system by opening higher education to many people previously excluded, protecting workers from hitherto ignored risks, providing minimum support for older persons, improving access to health care, addressing the special needs of special groups from unmarried mothers to handicapped children. In all these developed countries the advance of the welfare state represented an intensified effort to shift the distribution of political power from a small elite to the masses, and to extend the reach of the democratic ethos from the political arena into the workplace.

Large-scale enterprises can achieve and maintain a high level of efficiency only in the presence of labor peace. Hence the expansion of social services and the redistribution of political power were not sideshows but potent contributors to the high-level performance of these modern economies. In the case of Great Britain, where conflict dominated the workplace, the economic results were dismal.

The neoconservatives who rail against the welfare state and who predict that the pursuit of equity will retard economic growth and reduce democratic freedoms have missed the point. Unless the mass of the working population believes the socioeconomic structures are being modified to give them a fair shake, they will prevent the economy from functioning at anything approaching its true potential. Although the welfare state may have moved too far too fast, it was essential that it move.

SOME UNPRETENTIOUS CONCLUSIONS

Having completed our selective review of three critical dimensions of work and workers, where do we come out?

The contention that the work ethic is being rapidly eroded both in the United States and Western Europe has not been substantiated. True, certain groups of workers may opt for nonwork over work because the gains they can achieve from not working exceed those that they can realize from taking a job, increasing their hours of work, or remaining in the labor force. Further, as real per capita and national income have increased, the alternatives to work from extended schooling through early retirement have expanded. Despite this, however, more married women are at work than ever before.

We found little supporting evidence that productivity is falling because of lack of discipline in the workplace, encouraged and supported by the growing power of trade unions. In the United States unions are losing, not gaining power as far as numbers are concerned; discipline in the workplace has more to do with the competence of management than with the behavior of trade unions; and reported slowdowns in productivity have been effected by a host of factors, some linked to workers' behavior but others reflecting failures to report activities in the unrecorded economy. One need not deny that the changing climate of industrial relations has any influence on productivity to avoid ascribing undue influence to it.

Finally, we found that the rapid growth of the welfare state reflected the broad-based search for equity. To conclude that expectations advanced more rapidly than resources is not the same as contending, as some have done, that the welfare state was an error and should be dismantled. Unless the developed nations continue to respond to the aspirations of the masses for a more equitable distribution of income, status, and power, they will lack the cooperation required to operate their complex economies efficiently.

History is a grab bag that debaters dip into to support their contentions. The ominous trends with respect to the weakening of the work ethic, the slowing of productivity, and the expansion of the welfare state are contrasted with an idealized version of the past, when workers labored from sunup to sundown, when the employer's word was law, when government was frugal. Conservatives who look back to the good old days, as well as reformers who yearn for the improved society that is still to come, are impatient with the complexities of the human condition. But societies are complex, and they are subject to continuing change in which every action or reaction opens still further opportunities for initiatives and responses. Only an analysis that is sensitive to this dynamism can contribute constructively to policy.

Human Resources Management in Large Organizations

THE CENTRAL THEME OF PART VIII has absorbed a lot of my interest and energy in recent years as my collaborator George J. Vojta and I have explored the subject and presented our findings in Beyond Human Scale: The Large Corporation at Risk. My interest, which dates back to my first encounter with the large corporation in 1933–1934, was reinforced by my full-time work in the War Department during World War II and later consulting assignments for the Department of Defense, the Army, and the Air Force.

The four selections that make up Part VIII require only short explanations. The first is from *The Human Economy.*

Chapter 36 dates from the mid-1950s, when I had a unique opportunity to lead a round-table discussion among business and public leaders for eight sessions directed at answering the question "What Makes an Executive?"

Chapter 37 is based on my Pentagon swan song. In 1971 I forwarded to the Defense Science Board the final report of my task force on manpower research. In 1972 and 1973 I gave two lectures to the Industrial

College of the Armed Forces, of whose faculty I am an honorary member. Chapter 37 represents my 1973 presentation.

I do not recall what prompted my writing the short piece on the "Inevitability of Manpower Waste in Large Organizations" for the *Columbia Journal of International Business* (Chapter 38); but if proof were needed that my new book with Vojta was the result of a long period of preparation, here is the evidence.

CHAPTER 35

The Employing Organization

...NO ORGANIZATION, no matter how large, how profitable, or how powerful, can move solely on the basis of its own momentum without considering the forces in the macroenvironment that impinge on it and to which it must remain alert and responsive. For the purpose of the present analysis, however, the interactions between the large organization and the economy and society within which it operates will be treated only in passing; primary attention will be directed to the internal forces that shape the organization's manpower strategy.

This approach has been adopted for several reasons. First, the discipline of economics has only recently recognized the large corporation as the principal unit that organizes activity in developed societies, and it is finding it difficult to modify its tools and theories to encompass the dynamics of these large aggregations of resources and power. Consequently, the gap between theory and reality remains wide. Second, the extant theories do not address the congruence and conflict among the different sectors of the work force of a large organization and the consequences thereof for efficiency, profitability, and work satisfaction. Finally, even the best managed organizations have only recently realized the importance of developing a manpower strategy and adapting it to changing opportunities and threats.

The concern here with the manpower strategy of large organizations is a direct outgrowth of the basic theme, . . . namely, the preeminent importance of the manpower factor, which can be understood only within an institutional context. This chapter will outline the opportunities and constraints that large organizations confront in assuring that they have the manpower resources they require now and in the future—at every level, from janitors to the chief executive officer—to discharge their several functions effectively. We start with the extant large organization, which, on the basis of experience, has subdivided its functions into a number of job assignments that call for workers with specific characteristics and skills. The nub of the organization's manpower strategy is to fill these positions with suitable applicants and assure that the organization contains in its work force individuals with the requisite skills and experience to fill openings in the higher ranks in the future.

Although there are clear differences among large organizations such as General Electric, the U.S. Navy, and Massachusetts General Hospital, there are also important structural and operational parallels, especially relating to manpower, which permit us to treat all large organizations under the same rubric. Some of the important parallels follow.

Every large organization has both a decision-making center and a number of operating units, which, in turn, have varying degrees of freedom to determine their own goals and particularly how best to accomplish them. There never has been and never can be a large organization in which all decisions, small as well as large, are made at the center. These two loci of decision making—top central and lower divisional—are integral to the structure of every large organization; and, more important, they establish the basic tension in all large organizations that surrounds the allocation of scarce resources, particularly manpower resources: The center seeks to restrict allocations, while the operating divisions press for more.

A second aspect of large organizations is their reliance on career personnel, especially for middle and top management. Each large organization has a distinctive history, preferred ways of operating, and an admixture of formal and informal policies that determine the manner in which its people act and react. The effectiveness of every large organization depends on whether the middle and top management share a common understanding about how work is to be carried out and decisions reached. This implies mutual understanding and trust, which can be achieved only among people who have been exposed to the same environment over a long period of time.

In a dynamic economy in which there are expanding opportunities, especially for persons with energy and talent, a large organization can attract and retain able persons only by offering them a combination of inducements in the form of attractive work, adequate compensation, promotional opportunities, security, and deferred benefits—a total compensation package that on balance is equal or superior to what persons with similar skills could command elsewhere. Since the working life of an executive may encompass thirty-five to forty years, the fortunes of the organization and the economy are likely to undergo several major shifts during a person's working life. Consequently, every large organization must balance its commitments to its career managers with the need for continuing flexibility to respond to new conditions.

The allocation of resources, the critical importance of career personnel, and the conflicts between commitments to them and changes in the internal and external environment establish the parameters that determine how the manpower strategy of all large organizations must be designed and implemented.

Before addressing the components out of which a corporate manpower structure is built, we will review briefly certain structural and functional characteristics of large organizations to which a manpower strategy must be responsive. The strength of a large organization rests in the first instance on the fact that its existence is not constrained by the span of one person's life. The Catholic Church can point to an unbroken history of almost two millennia. Many industrial and commercial corporations in Western Europe boast, in their advertising, that they were established in the eighteenth century or earlier.

Although survival is the leitmotif of large organizations, growth via specialization and diversification is not far behind. In fact, survival and growth are ineluctably linked. In a world in which organizations, like nations, must struggle to survive, an organization can assure its future only by adding to its strength. To do so, it must diversify and expand.

Organizational survival and growth are linked to the quality of leadership, including its provision for succession. The principal advantage that a large organization has over a family enterprise is its freedom to go farther afield in seeking talent. In selecting its potential leadership, it is not constrained by ties of blood or marriage.

The critical importance of a talented leadership derives from the vulnerabilities of every large organization to inertia, factionalism, and incompetence. The strength of a large organization derives from its proven capacity to survive and function, but it cannot rest on its record. To find the proper balance between policies that should be continued and strengthened and innovations that must be introduced is a critical challenge to every leadership.

The leadership must also ensure that its activities continue to provide useful goods or services, the test of which is the willingness of government to allocate funds to support its activities or the willingness of consumers to buy its output at a price that provides a profit. In addition, the leadership must create and maintain an effective manpower system. Thus another continuing challenge to the organization's leadership is to find the balance between responsiveness to its clientele and providing conditions for its work force that elicit acceptable performance.

These, then, are the five principal elements generic to all large organizations: the need to survive, the need to grow, the need for talent, the need to balance continuity and innovation, and the need to be responsive to both their clientele and their work force.

The social sciences have not yet developed a useful model for the study of large organizations; they are even farther away from a model for the systematic analysis of their manpower resources. Conventional economic theory, which considers the corporation as an income-maximizing entrepreneurial unit, provides little guidance for ordering the realities of corporate life, which involve conflicts over goals, resource allocations, and investment decisions—the issues that continually engage competing groups. Therefore, this chapter . . . should be read as an effort to identify and structure the key elements in an early theory of manpower strategy in large organizations.

A first step in understanding the shaping of an organization's manpower policy is to consider the implications that flow from the goals that have just been identified. Since survival is the first objective of every large organization, and since large organizations depend on the willingness of thousands of people to work cooperatively in pursuit of their disparate goals, senior executives must avoid actions that could weaken or undermine the basis of cooperation. However, the leadership cannot pursue policies of placating the work force if the consequences of doing so are likely to jeopardize the organization's economic survival. Many profitable small companies that were absorbed by conglomerates were liquidated shortly thereafter because of the dismissal of their people at the top and the ensuing confusion and discontent among those who remained. The post–World War II experience of Great Britain points to the opposite danger. Both private and public management were so concerned about maintaining industrial peace that, in attempting to placate their work force, they incurred such high labor costs that they eroded their financial base.

Every large organization is composed of large or small units that see the organization's future from their own vantage. A critical task of top management is to prevent one of the parties from shoving the organization too far in one or another direction. For example, prior to World War II, the U.S. War Department was niggardly in making resources available to the Air Corps. During the war, however, when the importance of air power was belatedly recognized, the General Staff sought to meet almost every request of the Air Corps. Again, in science-based companies it is never easy, especially in years of poor profits, for top management to allocate sufficient funds to the research department in the face of arguments presented by other departments that with increased resources they can provide a quicker payoff. The "old school tie" on which Great Britain relied to such a marked degree for its leadership cadre in the heyday of the empire was a source of pronounced strength. A high proportion of those in leadership positions were related to or school chums of everyone else, which greatly facilitated the decision-making process. This inbreeding, however, even though it was diluted by a few talented outsiders, simply did not provide Great Britain with a sufficient pool to meet its total leadership requirements.

The leadership of every large organization must constantly assess new external challenges and opportunities. The more an organization is rooted in tradition, as is the Catholic Church, the more caution its leaders exercise in responding to changes; but an excessively conservative policy carries its own costs—witness the problems that faced Pope John XXIII when he sought to close the gap that had developed between the leadership of the Church and the laity. The corporate world provides a contrasting illustration of companies that are so committed to growth for its own sake that they pay little heed to maintaining continuity of structure, policies, and managerial personnel. A large organization that seeks to change more quickly than do the people who work for it may run into trouble, because most people can absorb only a limited amount of change within a limited time period.

We see then that top management must shape its manpower strategy in such a manner that it facilitates the organization's drawing strength from continuity while retaining flexibility to respond to the new. A management that is insensitive to the legitimate claims and expectations of its personnel is as likely to undermine the organization as one that, in an effort to avoid the costs of conflict, is so supine that it jeopardizes its economic future.

These brief considerations have sought to highlight the interface in every large organization between its basic goals and its manpower policy options. While top management always has some, and often a considerable, degree of freedom in shaping its manpower policies, it operates within two fundamental constraints: Those introduced by external factors over which it has little or no direct control, and those embedded in the enterprise's past—its collective experience, which is both a source of strength and an important constraint on its rapid transformation.

A better understanding of the elements that constitute an organization's manpower strategy will be derived from a brief consideration of the differences between a true strategy and the conventional view that employers obtain the skills they need in the labor market. First, we must note that the large employer goes to the market to recruit workers for entering jobs. With few exceptions, however, that is the beginning and end of his direct recourse to the market.

A second difference is embedded in the mere acceptance of a job offer by the applicant and his interest in making a long-term organizational affiliation. To the extent that the latter is his concern (and it usually is), he will place less importance on the initial salary offer and more on the developmental opportunities that may be open to him and the prospects of his profiting from them. Recruiters of college graduates in the United States have repeatedly noted that these young people, at the beginning of their work life, raise questions about the company's pension system, the benefits of which often become available only after thirty years of employment.

The employer, on the other hand, realizes that the contribution of the employee after his initial assignments will depend in no small measure on the opportunities available to him to broaden his knowledge, skills, and competences. These opportunities, in turn, depend in large measure on the assignments, on-the-job training, and formal instruction that the organization provides.

The newly hired employee who seeks a long-term affiliation early understands that his progress up the job ladder will be a result not only of the assessments of his performance made by his supervisors but also of the judgments of his peers and subordinates. He will consequently pay attention to such matters as organizational style and behavior, since his successful accommodation to these will have as great an influence on his future as his technical proficiency.

Basic to the market theory of employment is the belief that people are recompensed at a rate that reflects their productivity. However, the manpower systems of large organizations are predicated on a hierarchical structure of positions which conventionally carry specified salaries. While trends in the market exercise some influence on an organization's manpower strategy, market trends do not determine the specifics of a large employer's manpower policy.

The schema we will use to analyze an organization's manpower strategy focuses on three major dimensions: assignment, including the antecedent steps in the process—hiring, orientation, and indoctrination; evaluation and promotion, including rewards and benefits; and educational and training experiences that are linked to assignments and promotions to the higher ranks. Since considerable variability exists among large organizations within the same sector and even more among those in different sectors, a quasi-schematic approach will have to be followed in describing the dominant practices and procedures characteristic of large organizations in an advanced economy such as the United States.

Except in periods of severe financial stringency, every large organization annually adds young trainees to assure itself future middle and top management. Its requirements may vary substantially over time, depending on the rate of its losses through resignations, retirements, and deaths, and, further, on its present and prospective rate of expansion. At times, some large organizations may be unable to increase their trainee pools because of limitations in the existing educational-training structures, which provide the new supply. But in general this is not likely to be a major problem, since they can usually tap alternative sources. For instance, although the Armed Forces may prefer to have more graduates of the service academies in a period of rapid buildup, they can increase the flow of officer personnel by drawing on the reserves or expanding officer candidate schools, and by direct commissioning.

There is considerable variability in the amount of effort large organizations devote to actively recruiting executive personnel, both at the entrance level and for higher positions. To take the last point first: As we have noted, most managerial positions routinely are filled by insiders. However, from time to time an organization may decide to fill certain key positions from the outside. For example, the top positions in the federal government turn over almost completely with each change of administration. In addition, many corporate and nonprofit organizations frequently look beyond their own staffs to find a chief executive, a senior operating official, or a key staff specialist. On rare occasions a large enterprise may bring in a new senior team, as happened in the immediate post–World War II period, when the Ford Motor Company reorganized and established a management consisting primarily of key executives who had previously worked for General Motors.

The dominant pattern of obtaining trainees in the United States, surely among large corporations and increasingly among large government agencies and nonprofit organizations, is to send representatives to college campuses to recruit young people as executive trainees or junior specialists. After making a first selection, the recruiting organizations invite the more interested and attractive candidates to visit their headquarters or a branch for further screening in the form of interviews, testing, or other exercises and exposures. Thereafter, offers of employment are made to the most promising candidates.

In hiring specialists—that is, young men and women who have been trained in accounting, chemistry, information systems, economics, marketing, or other fields of specialization—recruiters place considerable weight on the applicant's academic record, his work history and extracurricular activities, and the recommendations of his teachers. Although considerable information about the applicants is collected and sifted and additional efforts are devoted to intensive individual interviews, the inherent limitations of even the most thorough screening efforts must be pointed out. There is no firm basis for judging how a young person who has not held a regular job will react to a specific company and particularly to a specific unit within that company. The high turnover rate of newly hired college graduates—between 30 and 50 percent leave during the first three to five years of their employment—speaks to the limitations of the selection procedure. Observation of the process of college recruitment suggests that large organizations might do almost as well and possibly better if they were to ask the registrars of the institutions where they recruit to list the graduates by their general and specific grade averages and then, after eliminating the lowest fifth or sixth on grounds of possible intellectual or emotional limitations, make offers to the rest on a first-come basis. In light of the considerable sums spent every year on college recruiting, large organizations with high recruiting costs might well consider a controlled experiment.

Although it is difficult to generalize about the recruitment-selection process, a few tentative conclusions can be advanced. Every person with the authority to hire tends to consider himself an expert, surely about his own needs and, if he serves in a staff role, about the needs of those for whom he recruits. The usual pattern is that young men and, recently, young women who appear to fit the organizational prototype tend to be selected. The attempted matching of newcomers to insiders implies that a preference is given to individuals who will "fit in." In the seminary, all novitiates are kept under close supervision, and those whose faith begins to weaken are separated before they are ordained. In the service academies, the cadets ostracize the deviant in the hope that he will resign. The search for congeniality is universal, and since organizational performance and personal satisfaction depend on easy and relaxed relations among the members, this emphasis is understandable. But no matter how much effort is made to find young people who will fit in, the success rate is not likely to be high because both the choosers and the chosen are making decisions largely in the dark.

The manpower policies of most large organizations are predicated on the assumption that productivity, morale, and loyalty will be enhanced if the organization has the opportunity to indoctrinate its new members. The church and the military long ago established a tight control over the indoctrinational systems through which all newcomers must pass. Medicine, the most closely knit of the professions, has fashioned an extended educational-training process, a principal aim of which is to shape the young physician in the image of the established professional.

Many large corporations spend considerable time, effort, and other resources in orienting and indoctrinating their newly hired executive trainees in their philosophy and policies. An occasional company may rotate a new employee through various assignments, including a spell of formal education and training, for a period of up to two or three years. But this extended orientation has a disadvantage because most recent graduates have been passive for many years—listening to lectures, conducting experiments under direction, or writing assigned themes— and they look forward to putting their knowledge and skills to work. Consequently, they are unhappy if they are sent from one division to another for three to six months at a time; the arrangement has more in common with their experiences in college or graduate school than with their idea of a real job where they have an assignment which they must complete within a stipulated period of time. The high rate of early resignations among trainees confirms the shortcomings of this approach. The units that are obliged to make room for trainees question the effectiveness of an orientation process that requires them to find assignments for the trainees, even if they are make-work from which they receive little useful output. Finally, top management has increasingly realized that morale building is a long-term process that cannot be condensed into special efforts concentrated during the initial period of an employee's career.

Many corporations now believe a more constructive approach would be to establish and keep open lines of communication with all key groups, including young executives. They believe that if they clearly state their aims, the plans and programs that are being readied for implementation, and the likely changes that will follow from these new initiatives, the young executives will be likely to support and identify with their corporation's goals. However, although little corporate identification is likely to occur without effective communications, communications must not be confused with successful indoctrination and persuasion. New members of an organization, especially those whose education has stressed a skeptical approach, will pay more attention to actions than to words. No matter how clearly top management communicates the criteria on which it evaluates performance for the purposes of promotion, young executives will wait to see whether the actions and results conform to the promises. Only if they do will top management have made its point. If a gap develops between what is communicated and what actually occurs, morale is weakened. Lyndon Johnson's loss of credibility with the American people as a result of his repeated optimistic assessments of the course of the war in Vietnam is only an extreme case of attempted morale building that backfired because there was no basis in fact.

A man's initial assignment is crucial, since it determines the first work he does and his pay and perquisites and also foreshadows the probable next stage in his career. As we have seen, large organizations are subdivided into operating units that have varying degrees of autonomy, including control over their manpower resources. While top management can assign and reassign individuals among its divisions, it seldom does this without consultation and negotiation with the divisions involved. Top management cannot hold a divisional manager responsible for meeting his production quota or his profit goal if it can unilaterally remove key persons from his control and press him to accept a replacement who is unacceptable to him. Even during a war, the chief of staff may find it difficult to obtain the release of a key officer from a theater commander.

The underlying sources of tension in the arena of assignment can be readily identified. The individual with the potential for advancement can add to his skills and experience only if he is reassigned after he has extracted what he can from his current assignment. However, if he performs capably, his superior will not be inclined to release him. The third party of interest is the personnel staff that has responsibility for assuring that the organization will have an adequate pool of qualified persons ready to assume senior positions when they become vacant. The development of such a pool requires broadening the experience of individuals with potential, which in turn requires their periodic reassignment.

The larger and more complex the organization, the more difficult is the assignment process. No one at higher headquarters can know personally more than a small proportion of the total managerial and technical group. Moreover, the assessment of an individual's competences and skills that is stored in a computer is frequently misleading. Some social scientists believe the computerization of the personnel function can improve the use of human resources, but even when many details are logged into a computer, obstacles remain. Hard decisions are required about what factors should be entered and at what frequency, how the stored information is to be tapped, and what additional inputs beyond the computerized record are needed for selecting individuals for new and important assignments. Without a strong centralized personnel system, most individuals remain the hostage of the division to which they are assigned, at least until they themselves take the initiative to relocate, until their supervisors relocate them, or until the central staff decides to act.

Such a restricted personnel attachment process lies at the heart of every large organization. People identify with the division, sometimes with a small unit within the division, where their work is centered, their friends and associates are located, and their career prospects lie. This can be demonstrated by reference to such diverse organizations as the Catholic Church, where members relate first and foremost to their order or diocese; the military, where a man is first a "submariner" and only thereafter a member of the U.S. Navy; the university, where a professor considers himself a historian and a member of the history department rather than an employee of Harvard or Stanford; the government, where federal civil servants see themselves as employees of the Social Security Administration or the National Institutes of Health rather than as employees of the Department of Health, Education and Welfare; and industry, where the executive introduces himself as working for Cadillac or Chevrolet, not for General Motors.

Assignment is one of three legs of the personnel stool. The second is evaluation and promotion; the third, education and training. In every large organization, there are many people in the lower ranks and successively fewer toward the top. Thus the process of promotion is crucial to both the individual and the organization. In many large organizations, promotion up the first two or even three rungs of the ladder may be quasi-automatic: In the military, initial promotions depend on time spent in grade; at many universities, the earning of a doctorate leads automatically to promotion to the rank of assistant professor.

But when automatic criteria can no longer be used and several individuals are left behind for every one who is advanced, the organization must resort to some form of acceptable evaluation system to support its decisions. The conventional approach is that a person's superior grades him or her on various aspects of performance, and the next higher supervisor reviews these evaluations and confirms or modifies them.

However, the personnel literature is replete with evidence that no matter what type of evaluation system is used, there is a strong tendency for supervisors to make favorable evaluations. Many more people are rated as excellent or very good than as fair or unsatisfactory. This *halo effect* reflects the difficulty of maintaining confidentiality in a large organization where many people have access to the records. Supervisors anticipate that their ratings will soon become known to those whom they have evaluated, and in many organizations provision is made for formal feedback. Although the supervisor may have ample evidence to back up a poor rating, he is reluctant to enter it on a man's record because of the tensions it will create, unless he plans to reassign or discharge him. Large organizations make their peace with employees with borderline competence. Consequently, as long as the superior does not feel his own position will be endangered by a poorly performing employee, he is likely to avoid taking action that could lead to the discharge of the worker.

Relatively few persons in the managerial ranks are discharged for inefficiency. Even if some who leave "voluntarily" are eased on their way by friendly advice that they had better look elsewhere, the total number of managers who are eased out is small.

Evaluation procedures are almost as limited in selecting people for promotion as they are for identifying those who should be discharged. The halo effect singles out as suitable for promotion a number usually in excess of the opportunities available. Moreover, most openings are in units of the organization that have specialized requirements. Although top management may favor or even encourage lateral movements among production, marketing, and various staff assignments, the supervisor responsible for filling a specific opening may be less inclined to gamble: He wants the new man to carry his new responsibilities as quickly as possible. This helps to explain the adage that the successful applicant is often the person in the right place at the right time. Most openings are filled by persons in a lower echelon of the same division. As they move toward the top, they are likely to become linked with others higher up who then consider them their protégés. These alliances work both ways. As the sponsors move higher, they help to pull their followers along. On occasion, however, when two senior groups become locked in conflict, the key members of the losing team may have to leave.

The foregoing emphasis on allegiances, alliances, and conflicts helps illuminate the extent to which the critical promotional process is governed less by objective evaluations of competence and potential and more by the coincidences of experience, exposure, and political considerations. Both the men who lead large organizations and the scholars who study them tend to downplay or ignore this reality, possibly because to acknowledge it would undermine the belief in fair and open competition in which the best man wins.

The third strand of the personnel process, education and training, is linked to both assignment and promotion. Executives, like other workers, learn by doing: they need to have different assignments to broaden their understanding of the complexities of the organization and to increase their skills in coping with them. A middle manager is more likely to be appointed to a senior position if he has had an opportunity to acquire broad experience. In the Armed Forces, the career development system aims at the early identification of officers with the potential to move toward the top, followed by the provision of successive assignments that will broaden and deepen their exposures and experiences. Only in this way will they be prepared for a top position. Every large organization must develop a group of experienced personnel from which to select its top management. But for various reasons, including rapid growth, unexpected losses of key personnel, and belated evidence that some of the aspirants will not be able to perform successfully in top positions, senior management may suddenly find that it has no eligible candidates within its own ranks, and it must look outside to fill key assignments. Some companies, of which General Motors is the prototype, believe in multi-backup for each executive in the upper ranks. But this approach has limitations because it is difficult to keep able men in a holding pattern for long. Even if they can be bribed by high salaries and other perquisites to stay with the organization, their abilities and skills will obsolesce if they do not have sufficiently challenging assignments.

Although learning is built into the assignment process, most large organizations, especially since the end of World War II, have resorted increasingly to various types of continuing education and training of a more formal nature, an approach that has long been followed by the church, the military, universities, and the professions. Despite the considerable resources that corporations invest in executive management training programs, little is known about their effectiveness. Most companies, however, continue to underwrite these programs, even in years of poor profits. If those who attend these formal courses are promoted soon thereafter, a favorable ambiance is created about these educational efforts. But when men who have been introduced to new ways of thinking and analyzing their problems are returned to their former assignments with little or no opportunity to put their new knowledge to use, they are likely to become frustrated.

Many large organizations believe that they will achieve enhanced productivity and morale by making more educational and training opportunities available to their managerial staffs, who, in turn, soon consider these opportunities a fringe benefit. The organizations may be right in this judgment, but it would require more feedback and analysis to be certain that the outcome is positive. To encourage managers to attend courses and seminars or otherwise participate in learning situations may be counterproductive if the goals are not clearly delineated and the rewards are problematic.

To attract and retain competent management, a large organization must provide competitive opportunities and rewards. There tends to be a rough comparability in the hiring salaries for the same types of position among large organizations in different sectors of the economy—that is, business, government, and the universities. But the reward systems among different organizations become increasingly differentiated at the middle and higher levels of management. The rate of advancement, salary levels, working conditions, and fringe benefits differ substantially among organizations and sectors; consequently, only rough comparisons can be made. If a person has many options by virtue of native ability, education, and experience, he or she can afford to respond to different inducements, depending on his or her values and goals. Those who desire status and money are likely to shift jobs and careers for relatively small income differentials within the same company, between companies, and even among sectors of the economy. Others, more committed to a particular pattern of work or perhaps more concerned about long-term security, will forgo an opportunity to increase their immediate earnings, even by a substantial amount, if it requires that they change the nature of their work or accept the risk of lessened job security.

Different organizations seek to design reward and benefit packages that are responsive to their special needs. For many decades the federal government paid relatively low salaries but sought to make long-term service attractive through reasonable assurance against job loss, liberal fringe benefits, and good retirement income. On the other hand, certain large department stores offer the opposite: little job security but quick promotions and high salaries for the successful merchandiser. In fact, success in retailing involves a commitment on the part of the young, and even older, executives to work long hours, including nights and Saturdays.

In prestigious universities, the principal attraction has always been the relative freedom of the faculty member to be master of his own time. His formal teaching responsibilities may require less than 100 hours a year, and his responsibilities to his university, including committee work and consulting with students, may be discharged within a total of 300 hours. But the very individuals who devote so few hours to their formal duties are likely to be constantly engaged in reading, lecturing, experimenting, and writing, which makes them among the hardest-working members of society. But they work for themselves, for scholarship, and for science—not for their dean or president. And that makes a difference.

In a pecuniary economy, large business organizations rely primarily on monetary incentives to attract and hold competent people. The federal government and nonprofit institutions now realize that the salaries they offer must be competitive with those offered by industry if they are to find, attract, and retain competent people. Since the mid-1960s, the pay scale of the U.S. Civil Service has been adjusted annually so that it remains abreast of changes in the private sector. Moreover, it is no longer exceptional for the head of a large hospital, museum, or foundation to earn between $75,000 and $100,000, which is additional evidence of the importance attached to high salaries in attracting capable managers. Marked variability continues, however, in the earnings of the chief executives of major U.S. corporations. The modal range in the mid-1970s is about $250,000 to $300,000, but many receive only half that amount, while a few earn three times the average. There is no simple explanation for this wide disparity, but company and industry traditions hold part of the answer.

Because of the much larger numbers of middle managers, even highly profitable companies keep a close eye on competitive salaries.

They are less concerned about the generous salaries earned by the relatively few at the top than about the distortion of the entire salary scale that results from the fact that high salaries for the senior group will exercise an upward pull on the scale for middle management.

Increasingly, the salaries executives receive are related to the positions they hold rather than to the specific contributions they make. Although executives in sales may be rewarded in direct relation to their performance, this is not, nor can it be, the general pattern, because so much of the work in a complex organization reflects the joint efforts of a group. In such an environment it is difficult to identify the high producer.

Another trend in organizational compensation is to provide perquisites in addition to salaries for executives. They include liberal expense accounts, company limousines, and travel at company expense to attend meetings in exotic places (to which wives are also invited). Since most of these benefits are tax-free, large companies have increasingly resorted to these fringes; they are highly valued by the recipients, and their cost to the organization is relatively small. As with many aspects of personnel policy in large organizations, relatively little is known about the extent to which liberal salaries and benefits contribute to important goals, because these goals are often not specified with sufficient clarity to make a meaningful analysis possible. A safe assumption is that the prevailing patterns are determined largely by an admixture of company tradition and market trends.

To assure a steady supply of managerial personnel who can be advanced to higher levels of responsibility, most large organizations have relied increasingly on compensation systems which tie important benefits to long service. The objective has been to make it costly, in the form of lost benefits, for a manager to leave once he has spent a decade with a company. Many company retirement and pension plans require relatively long service—from fifteen to twenty-five years—before the individual becomes eligible for benefits. The outstanding exception has been the Teachers Insurance and Annuity Association, which, through the assistance of the Carnegie Corporation, has made all professorial retirement benefits portable.

In recent years, the logic of tying benefits to long years of service has come under increasing criticism; moreover, considerations of equity have also come to the fore. To take the last first: A plethora of evidence has been presented to various congressional committees concerned with pension reform that many long-term workers have been cheated of their retirement benefits because, through no fault of their own (business recession, company bankruptcy, illness, plant closure, fraudulent action by the employer), they have not worked the specified number of years. For this reason, new legislation has been passed that establishes tighter public control over pension systems and provides for earlier vesting.

But the issues go deeper. The logic of deferred benefits aimed at locking executives into a company has been challenged by both experience and theory. Many large organizations have discovered that some of their older managers find it increasingly difficult to meet their responsibilities effectively and, worse, stand in the way of younger people who are ready and waiting to be promoted. As a consequence, many large organizations are moving to adjust their personnel policies to facilitate the early retirement of managers whose energies have waned. This process has been accelerated by the realization that it is deadening to an organization to have high-salaried executives merely waiting until they reach the age of retirement.

The broad outlines of the manpower strategies pursued by large organizations in the United States, especially the corporation can now be set forth. A barrier now separates the mass of blue-collar employees from those with managerial responsibility. Manufacturing foremen still are drawn from the rank and file, as is an occasional plant superintendent. But for the most part, the future executive comes from a different pool and is treated differently. In order to find new employees, most large employers tap into the pool of recent college and university graduates. Although company recruiters seek to identify young men and women with the qualifications and potentials for becoming effective managers, the high rate of early turnover of junior executives underscores the tenuous assumptions and fragile procedures that characterize the selection process.

We have found that the critical assignment function is hobbled by the difficulty most large organizations have in assembling and keeping up to date relevant information about their managerial personnel and, equally important, by the tensions between divisional units with direct control over some personnel and the central staff's concern with long-range career development.

Shortfalls also exist in current approaches to evaluation techniques and promotional procedures, educational efforts, and compensation. In each case, the large organization seldom knows enough about the complex elements involved in the process. It does not have adequate instruments to differentiate reliably among those in competition for promotion. There are no reliable follow-up studies of managers who have participated in executive development programs which would enable the corporation to reach sound conclusions about the costs and benefits of these efforts. A review of established policies and practices with respect to salaries, fringe benefits, and pensions also indicates that current approaches are vulnerable on both conceptual and procedural grounds.

The weaknesses in the manpower strategies of large organizations which have been identified suggest alternative explanations. The least radical holds that these weaknesses reflect first the relatively recent date at which top management began to appreciate the importance of developing a manpower strategy, and it suggests that these weaknesses will be addressed if not remedied in the years ahead. A second interpretation focuses on the obfuscations that result from the presumably scientific nature of the theories and techniques employed in the personnel arena and that help to insulate established practices from criticism by outsiders. A third interpretation predicates that since all large organizations are by nature complex political organisms, their manpower strategies cannot be put on a scientific basis. This interpretation implies that critical personnel decisions, however they are rationalized, inevitably follow the ebb and flow of power among competing organizational cliques.

Belated recognition of the critical importance of the manpower factor, poor conceptualization, questionable personnel practices, and the neglect of the political element in large organizations are not mutually exclusive explanations. The present state of the manpower strategy of large organizations probably reflects them all. The more important question is: What will happen in the future?

Ad hoc approaches to manpower are likely to be subjected increasingly to critical scrutiny, since top management now recognizes the complex arrangements required to assure an effective corps of able and competent managers. Recognition of the importance of manpower resources and the complexity of managing them presages the investment of additional time, effort, and leadership to improve an organization's manpower strategy.

Recognition of the need for a manpower strategy is an essential first step. The second step is more difficult: It is the challenge to top management to fashion a strategy and assure that it is sensitive to the changing environment within which the organization operates. Each organization must develop its own strategy, which must include a responsiveness to its idiosyncratic experiences. A generalized manpower strategy for all large organizations, even those operating in the same sector of the economy, is no more possible than is a common strategy of financial or facility planning for all profit-seeking enterprises. If large organizations share broad experiences and are exposed to similar environmental stimuli, their manpower strategies will include common elements. Nevertheless, each strategy will also be characterized by elements that are unique to each organization's experiences and circumstances.

Although attention from top management and improved staff efforts can go part of the way to strengthening the manpower systems of large organizations, a final challenge remains. The goals of the leadership of an organization are not necessarily congruent with the aspirations of those lower in the hierarchy. Many in the ranks of middle management eventually realize that they will never reach the top, and their subsequent goals and actions reflect this. . . . No manpower strategy can avoid the necessity of reconciling the goals of the organization with those of the managers and workers who are affiliated with it.

CHAPTER 36

The Executive and
the Organization

TO INITIATE THE ROUND TABLE'S DISCUSSIONS, the members
had been asked if they believed there were many similarities between
superior performance in business and outstanding success in such other
fields as the army, the church, and government. . . .

There was always present the underlying and basic question of
whether executive potential was a general quality common to the top
leadership of different types of organizations, or whether it was a more
delimited quality which could only be understood within the context of a
specific environment. . . . The case was reported of a man who had retired
from the U.S. Army as a colonel. However, it was sheer fate that he had
not ended his career with two, three, or even four stars. Early in the war,
this colonel had been chief of staff to a lieutenant general who was slated
to take command in the Far East. Just as the planning had been more or
less completed, the lieutenant general had trouble with Washington and
was not given the assignment. Stilwell got it and moved in with his own
staff. The new group needed one man who was in on the prior planning,
and they took this colonel. However, he was never able to really join the

new group. If his old boss had gotten the assignment, as had been planned, he would probably have soon moved up to brigadier and then major general, with a chance to compete for the top positions in the theatre. . . .

Many large corporations seek a synthetic leader; they want a chief executive who can, within himself, give expression to the interests of the major groups within the organization. They do not want too strong a personality with individual ideas. They prefer someone who can maintain a balance among the interest groups that already exist. . . .

The basic question was raised: How does an organization or a particular industry attract the raw material for future leadership? The retailing field is very concerned about its failure to attract a sufficient number of good people to insure a proper selection of future leaders. . . . The department store president had this to say:

> One reason we do not attract enough men of the right caliber is that most persons have the feeling they are not going to develop rapidly enough. Retailing, particularly the department store, has been looked upon as an unstable industry. However, it is by no means certain this is the whole answer, or that we deserve such a reputation. We are trying to get at the basic reason and correct it.

The danger of generalizing about the top leadership of different types of organizations was pointed out. One member recalled a conversation he had with General Eisenhower shortly after the general had accepted the presidency of Columbia University. Their discussion had emphasized that, whereas the man who was appointed deputy chief of staff or assistant chief of staff in the Army was a key individual likely to be picked later for the top job, it would be an error to assume that the deans at a university are necessarily the strongest people in the organization. On the whole, the most productive scholars and scientists do not become deans. Often the deans represent those among the professors who prefer administration to scholarship. . . .

A partial approach to an answer was suggested by one member who stated that "when you have a crisis like a war I believe you develop better leadership because many people then have an unusual opportunity. Ordinarily we fail to challenge people sufficiently. They are put in a mold early in the educational process and frequently never get out of it."

Another member agreed. "I think there is lots of evidence that the average twenty-one-year-old who became an officer during the war grew and developed at a rate that was out of all proportion to what would have happened to him had he remained in civilian life." . . .

The psychiatrist doubted whether so much stress should be given to the unique situation. He felt that the situation could not call forth qualities that did not exist. He further believed that, if these qualities did exist, there would be enough stimulation in the normal course of events to evoke them even without a major crisis such as war. He did not deny that existing qualities, hitherto unperceived, might be evoked by a crisis.

The extent to which an unusually able and aggressive person seeks opportunities to advance was illustrated by a member who told a story about one of the country's most successful advertising men. One of his first jobs was in a New York City bank. On the morning that he was being introduced to his job, he asked his guide to tell him a little about the men holding down the vice-presidential jobs. The guide told him one man had been brought in from Kansas City, another from Tulsa, the third from Seattle, the fourth from Butte. They had either been presidents or vice-presidents of banks in these cities. The young man resigned on the spot. He said that was no place in which to start working, since the top jobs were reserved for people from the outside. The speaker added that conditions had changed in that bank. It no longer brought in men of forty or forty-five as vice-presidents. It would take too long to integrate them and make them effective members of the team.

SENIORITY, RETIREMENT, AND EXECUTIVE DEVELOPMENT

Later, the same member emphasized that "you have to have movement in an organization. If you have turnover every ten years, or preferably faster, a fellow sees this and knows he does not have to wait until someone dies to advance. Then he will be interested in the job. When we talk about retirement, we make the mistake of always talking about the person who will retire, but seldom about all those underneath who will have more important work to do. One of the great thrills is when the boss goes away for awhile and you take over part of his job. Today, we frequently think men of thirty-five are pretty young; but when we were thirty-five, we thought we were hot stuff. These boys want to get ahead, and I see no real difference between these boys today and ourselves at the same age."

Another member substantiated the correctness of using the ten-year figure for effective turnover. He related that he had analyzed the average period of service of his company's top executives—trustees and directors— since 1890. He had found they had served on the average only between eight and ten years. "You must allow, therefore, for turnover within a ten-year period. The age factor and the turnover factor are the guts of how effectively you can develop responsibility."

One member asked what happens when a man is doing a very good job but his superiors do not want to risk upsetting things by moving him up, so they try to make up for it by giving him more money.

"It is up to the individual to get himself out of a situation like that," a member declared, "and he will if he has something on the ball." One member stated that a man moves to the top because of aggressiveness, competence, and confidence in himself. When such a man reaches the top, he said, he tends to avoid choosing as immediate subordinates men who are counterparts of himself.

> President Roosevelt was a very mediocre user of his staff, though he was a man of surpassing brilliance. The staff was only valuable as it handled his decisions on the way down. He did not use it on the way up. Roosevelt was not interested in their ideas. He was satisfied with his own. When a man has such enormous confidence, he is not interested in having next to him a man with similar confidence, whose judgment must sometimes differ from his.

Another member asked: "Do the qualities just outlined as being necessary for a man to reach the top in business also apply to the Church and the Army, which are more rigid organizations, and where the influence of seniority is much greater?" As far as the Army was concerned, the former secretary of the Army noted: "Seniority is certainly dominant in a man's career. You would not find a forty-year-old chief of staff."

Asked whether the Army should have such a young chief of staff, he answered:

> For so large an institution as the Army, I would have to say no. To have at least one man of forty near or at the top would be beneficial but you cannot have this without disrupting the system, and slowly but surely this system generates competence at the top, at least in a stimulating period such as the 1940s or 1950s. I admit this was not true in the 1920s and 1930s, when a chief of staff sometimes got to the top for no other reason than he was good at obeying orders.

Another member stated:

> I think the same factors apply in the Church, which goes by seniority. Much is done by seniority, no matter what a man's capabilities are, and the good men do not necessarily get to the top. You very seldom find a young man in a high position, because of the way in which the hierarchy operates. I know of many excellent men going to rot when they ought to be in key positions.

Asked what such men accomplish if they eventually get a chance, he replied: "The man's enthusiasm has waned, whereas if he had started earlier he would have done a magnificent job. I believe the seniority system stops the most competent."

The psychiatrist indicated how medicine tries to deal with the seniority problem: "In a large hospital, you can stay at a particular level only for a stipulated number of years. If you do not get beyond this level, you are retired. In former years, one could remain at the lower level, that of adjunct, until sixty or sixty-five. This blocked the possibility of new appointments."

A member asked about politics in hospitals. The psychiatrist remarked that this arbitrary system was introduced in order to reduce the role of politics, which, however, continues to play a part in initial appointments:

> You can be a very good adjunct, but if you reach, let us say forty-eight, and have not been promoted to the next higher grade, that of associate, you are out. This opens the route for men in their late thirties or early forties to demonstrate their ability and to go the whole way. The center of politics is choosing the man in his late thirties for the post of adjunct, which is the beginning of the ladder.

The former secretary of the Army pointed out there is a close parallel in the Army. All officers are retired at sixty. People wonder why the Van Fleets are retired at the peak of their mental and physical achievement so that colonels can get to be generals. "When I was secretary, I required that in each grade 5 percent be promoted on competence irrespective of seniority. This was an enormous stimulant to the younger men. We kept seniority, but rewarded competence."

Opportunities for Maximum Development

... The discussion of seniority led to a more general discussion of the relations between openings at the top and the number of men with potential down the line. One member stated, "We try to make our company attractive to younger men so they will want to come to us, and I think our executive rating system is definitely one of our major attractions."

Another member pointed out that it is important to consider executive potential not only from the viewpoint of the individual company, but more particularly from a broad national basis. In a company with 60,000 employees, relatively few can become executives. Very few executives can get to the top because there are not enough jobs. The member asked what industry might do to avoid wasting this potential.

Contrasting what he believed to be the situation in business with that in government, he pointed out:

> In government everyone's working for the same boss. There are shifts from one department to another when some avenues of advance-

ment close. What happens in business and the church when the top
positions are occupied? How does one take care of people who have
the potential to rise? I think it is a great waste from a national
viewpoint if many men who might do better elsewhere are held down
because there is no place at the top in their company. And as every
year goes by, it gets more difficult for them to transfer. What can
business do to avoid this waste?

A member replied: I don't think there is any waste. There are
many places where reasonably high talent can perform. Their names
may never reach the public, but they are earning forty to fifty
thousand dollars a year and are making a real contribution. They
may be managing a unit that does three hundred and fifty million
dollars worth of business a year. I believe it is fair to say they are
reasonably well satisfied.

The argument continued: "If sixty men are able enough to be one of
the top six executives of a company but can't get there because the six top
jobs are filled, isn't there a waste from a broad national viewpoint if these
men are kept in a production job?"

"No company suffers from having too much talent. Nor do I think
that the men suffer. Take General Motors. They have all high-class men
at the top, and the men are not frustrated. Despite their lesser titles there
is a place for these talented people."

"I'm not thinking of titles. I'm thinking of pay and also intangible
things, like the personal satisfaction that comes from being at the top. So
far as the individual is concerned, I would think he would feel that his
qualifications entitled him to more pay, more power, and a lot of other
rewards, not just an additional or different title. While I admit that the
company might be helped if all of its 60,000 men were top-notch people,
does the individual feel that his own talents are being underutilized?"

A third member remarked:

> The other day we gathered all our supervisors together, from the
> lowest grade all the way up, about 1,500 out of the 15,000 employees. I
> made a short presentation and then invited free discussion. Their
> problems were exactly the same as those we are talking about here.
> They were worried about what to do with the person who showed
> progress and the person who did not. They thought they were mak-
> ing a real contribution at the level at which they were working, and
> in my opinion they were. . . .

Later in the discussion, a member suggested that

> life in a large corporation is pretty much like politics. A fellow
> gets along pretty much on what kind of an organization he has been
> able to gather around him. I spoke to one of our senior men in the

gas field who has been rotated through many jobs for quite a few years. I asked him if he had learned much. He said he hadn't learned anything that he couldn't have learned out of a book, but that he got to know a hell of a lot of people, and if he has a question now he knows where to go to get it answered. As far as I am concerned the lone wolf with no friends will get nowhere, either in business or in politics. . . .

I do not think there is the same competition for good men in industry as in government. In government the way is open to a greater extent than in business, where the president of the company is anxious to hoard all the good men he can, as we have just heard. I suppose this is also true of a cabinet member or head of a department, but not to the same degree. I admit, though, that a man must be willing to take risks—leave civil service protection and strike out for himself. I think it is done more often in government than in business, and I again raise the question whether there is anything that business can do to avoid hoarding top executive potential.

A member asked what happens to institutions that do not operate on a profit basis, such as universities and hospitals:

> Business is able to pay very attractive salaries and set up other attractive conditions. What happens to institutions that are unable to match business? Only recently, General Bradley indicated his deep concern that the incentives for career officers in the armed services were now so poor that the military will be left with low quality manpower unless we do something about it.

A member with academic background indicated that he thought the universities were at the present time in a very dangerous competitive position: "They are unable to hold many excellent people because of their very low salary scales. It takes a most unusual person to decide to stay in academic life these days, especially if he has skills that enable him to shift easily to business."

A participant noted that the management philosophy of an organization, or of a department within an organization, can influence its ability to get people to work for it and can then help it to do a much better job of developing them:

> A department with a certain management philosophy will draw people who are more alert, more aggressive, more willing to take risks. This department will furnish a larger proportion of top management people than would be warranted by size alone. We see this everywhere. In fact, we have a good illustration in the military. Take the Corps of Engineers. A census of the Army's General Staff disclosed that 55 percent were from the Corps of Engineers.

The Transfer of Executive Effectiveness

The chairman reminded the group that the basic question was whether the qualities of leadership were the same in all fields, or whether specific institutions required leaders with specific characteristics: "What about Charles Luckman, who moved into Lever Brothers with a fine record, stayed at the top for only a short while and, after moving out again, is now doing very well?"

This illustration did not impress one of the members, who argued: "I still think the qualities are the same everywhere. I admit that there is a difference in the case of a company that deals primarily with a scientific article. Under those conditions, a scientist might be the best man to have at the top. But if you are dealing with people, I think the essential characteristics are the same."

The member with a long record of public service declared: "I have seen businessmen who tried to become politicians and I do not think the necessary qualities are the same in both places." Another member mentioned James Farley's success in business. But the speaker who argued there were differences in the demands made by different fields of activity insisted, "Successful businessmen usually do not make good politicians. . . . "

Two positions were developing. The first saw the essential core of leadership in a person's ability to pick associates and weld them into a team, to establish and project morale through an organization. If this approach is valid, then the key qualities are within the individual and are largely independent of his experiences in the particular organization in which he is operating. The other position emphasized that the kind of leadership a person exercises depends very greatly on the institution.

"There are tremendous differences," a participant maintained, "between being the head of a large company, a cardinal of the Church, or president of the United States. The way in which these men behave depends on the training, experience, and adjustments they have made along the line. No person coming in from the outside would be likely to do a very good job in any of these positions if his experience had been entirely different."

One member stressed that "You don't have to go outside of business fields to note the influence that a period of twenty years has. I feel that anyone with twenty years of experience in a big corporation would have a very difficult time running a small business. But I agree with the speaker who argued that the initial potential qualities may have been the same. After twenty years, however, one can no longer consider them transferable." . . .

The original proponent that leadership qualities were really the same regardless of the organization came back with this illustration:

> I remember moving into the barrel business when all I knew about barrels was that they were something you built bonfires with, and later into the frozen food business when all I knew was that if food was frozen it was spoiled. I had no previous experience in either line. I may say immodestly that I did not fail in either. I do not think that you need specific training. It's different, of course, if one is going to head a technical business based on advanced scientific knowledge. But if your job is really to pick the men to do the job, then the same qualities are required in almost any top leadership post. . . .

An illustration was noted of the way a specific situation can result in the discarding of a leader. Early in the invasion of North Africa, a man who had risen to the rank of lieutenant general in the U.S. Army, and therefore had been under constant assessment for a period of many years, had to be relieved of his post. The commanding general learned that he had set up his headquarters on a protected hillside sixty or seventy miles back of the front. Apparently, up to this point in his career there had been no opportunity to test this individual's courage. When the test came, he was found wanting. Despite his other strong qualities, he had to be relieved.

COMPANY SIZE AND EFFECTIVE PERFORMANCE

At the final meeting of the group, one member reflected on the entire range of the discussions:

> No pattern of development has really appeared. There were many different ideas about what could or should be done. But the thing that I got out of the discussions was that the size and scope of one's operations definitely affects what one should do in a training program. For instance, General Electric has gone much further than smaller companies. I would rather pick a pattern for my own kind of company than conclude there is any general overall recommendation which would fit all different types of businesses.
>
> I think that when you talk about recommending executive development programs, your program has to be aimed at what you want and what your needs are. They are different in different organizations. If General Foods tried to carry out a program like General Electric's, they would be wasting time and wasting people. You have to take into consideration what you need, what you are training men for, and how many men you now have who are already trained. Initially, men must have broad training. I am not talking about the basic training they get in college, but rather what the company does later on. . . .

The member who stressed the role of the individual replied:

> But if you say management's job is getting results from the work
> of other people, there is little difference between the president of
> your company and the president of ours. Anyone who has any kind of
> managerial job is essentially confronted with the same job—to get re-
> sults through the efforts of others. If you concentrate on that and on
> giving the individual what is best for him, and individuals do not really
> change much with time or with situations, there need be no serious
> difference between a very small business and a giant corporation. . . .

SUMMARY

When the Round Table discussed whether different types of organizations require different types of executives or whether a good executive
can perform effectively in any type of organization, it recognized that it
would probably not be able to offer definitive answers because of the
complexity of the subject. Several members recalled incidents in which
well-qualified individuals missed deserved promotions because of chance
events—for example, a sudden change in the top leadership and the fact
that the new man promoted his own associates. . . .

By the time the group ended its discussion, two positions had emerged.
One was that since all executives operate by handling people, the type of
organization in which they find themselves makes little difference. The
other position stressed the extent to which the size and scope of an
organization calls for specific qualities in its executives. All the participants agreed, however, that this crucial subject would require much
research before it could be adequately answered.

CHAPTER 37

Heretical Thoughts on Defense Manpower Management

...EVERYBODY TENDS TO BELIEVE THAT HIS OWN ORGANI-
ZATION is unique, and in many respects, of course, every organization
is unique. But organizations also have many things in common, and the
military especially has many of the characteristics and problems of other
large organizations.

About a year ago we did a study for Assistant Secretary of Defense
Foster on manpower research in the Pentagon. I entitled the final report
"Manpower Research and Management in Large Organizations: A Study
of the Department of Defense," trying to emphasize that the way to think
about the defense establishment was to determine to what extent the
problems that it faced and the solutions that it went after were generic
problems, problems common to all large organizations.

The military is about to lose the draft—all the services, not only the
Army. Even though the Navy and the Air Force do not rely on the draft
directly, the practical effect of the draft has been to force many pseudo-
volunteers into the Navy and the Air Force. So the fact that the draft is
now coming to an end, at least for an interim period, means that the

Department of Defense (DOD) as a whole will have to compete with other manpower users.

My approach will be as follows: first, some general observations about the armed forces and the general labor market. Then I will analyze some of the preconceptions concerning manpower that I have observed in the people who run the defense establishment. Finally, I have some suggestions to put forward, drawn primarily from my own experience, of how DOD might do a better job in handling its manpower problems.

CAN THE MILITARY COMPETE?

The services will have to be concerned, in the coming competition for manpower, about the attitudes and values of the young people whom they must sell on the attractions of military life. Not all young people are on college campuses, but many are.

In preparation I looked at a report that Yankelovich, one of the big pollsters, did for John D. Rockefeller III on campus values. It has been published in paperback and is well worth reading. Young people in colleges and universities, it points out, believe that of all the major institutions in U.S. society—the Supreme Court, big business, schools, and so on—the military is most in need of restructuring. These young people will be in leadership positions beginning about ten years from now, and they think that the military, more than any other institution, has to change. That's point number 1.

Second: this survey also reveals that, as of last summer (1972), young people on campuses believe that the most serious problem facing the United States is still the war in Vietnam. What's more, they expect more Vietnams after this one is finished. The overwhelming view among this sector of our youth is that as a nation we have not learned enough from our experience in Vietnam to avoid the same kinds of mistakes in the future.

The third attitude that seems significant to me is their response to the question: Under what conditions is it worthwhile to fight? Not even a third believe it makes any sense to fight for something labeled *national interests* or *national honor.* And as for resisting communist aggression, only a few—some 18 percent—see any reason for resorting to force.

This is not completely new or surprising. The pollsters have been asking these youngsters the same questions for years, and the trend lines have all pointed in the same direction.

On the positive side, there is no question that the recent military pay increases, especially in the enlisted ranks, have made military service competitive among young people, perhaps for the first time in our history. Moreover, as the war in Vietnam winds down, the military will have more interesting assignments to offer young people, and this too will help make military service more attractive. I think many young people would prefer to spend two years in West Germany or Athens or Honolulu than in Schenectady, Detroit, or Pittsburgh.

I would also list in the favorable category some of the internal reforms in the military in recent years, especially the reform of military justice. I think much remains to be done on this front, but there is a growing feeling that a man is more likely now than earlier to get a fair shake if he gets into trouble in the military.

The military, as I stated earlier, is a very large organization, but its relative size is declining. One trend is that the manpower costs of the Department of Defense are going through the roof, even as the number of people go down. Fifty-six percent of this year's total budget of DOD is represented by manpower — pay and allowances, training costs, retirement costs, Reserve costs. The estimates are that that will go to 60 percent within the next few years. Only eight years ago, just before the buildup in Vietnam, DOD manpower costs were only 43 percent of the total budget. There has been a 13 percentage point rise in manpower costs, along with an actual decline of 300,000 people in the armed services. Since fiscal 1968 the manpower budget of the Department of Defense has gone up $15 billion; $7 billion can be ascribed to inflation, but the remaining $8 billion represents real increases in pay and benefits.

With the armed services now being reduced to a little over 2 million, together they still represent a very big organization, the biggest in the country. But they are only about one and a half times the size of the next largest, which is AT&T. That's important. The military used to be in a ball park all their own; now they are only one of several mammoth organizations. In terms of manpower we are talking about maybe 2.5 percent of the total labor force, or less if DOD drops to a 2 million total.

So, on the one hand, in a dollar-cost sense, military manpower is an increasing drain on the military budget. On the other hand, it is a dwindling factor in the country's total manpower budget. . . .

My last broad point is that the military is involved in every aspect of the human problems of this country by virtue of the large numbers in its ranks. It is involved in the country's race problems, drug problems, youth problems, liberated-women problems, and all other human-resources problems. Some are only beginning to make their presence felt, and some have not hit yet. But they will. Sooner or later, all the problems that face the country will be reflected in the military establishment.

To sum up these introductory comments, I would say, first, that the manpower dimension of the total defense effort is getting bigger, surely in monetary terms; it will soon account for three-fifths of the total budget. Second, in an establishment of 2 million-plus the Department of Defense has all of the management problems of any large organization. Third, unless manpower management is strengthened, there will continue to be a large waste in dollars and people.

BIASES AND FOLKLORE

Over the past thirty years, in the course of my continuing relations with the military, I have observed some persistent and pervasive preconceptions among those responsible for manpower policy. These attitudes are not by any means limited to the military. Most big employers share them—but that does not mean they are any more relevant or correct.

A good organization, we are told, depends on selecting good people; the key to good organization is good personnel. That's a familiar proposition. It sounds like an endorsement of motherhood. That does not make it wrong?

The first thing wrong with it is that every large organization must, of necessity, accept an *average* cut of the population and not look to a special cut. It must expect its personnel to reflect the larger society. If you were organizing a laboratory, you could be selective. But if your organization is the largest one in the country, or even the third or fifth largest, you can't expect to rely on differential selection. Obviously even the nation's largest organizations, including the DOD, do not have to be a mirror image of the manpower pool, but they must hew close to it.

AT&T is just waking up to this fact. The Bell System is urban-based. Most large cities have undergone fundamental population changes: White people have moved out; blacks and other minorities have moved into the city centers. The Bell System has no alternative but to live with these changes and adjust its personnel policies accordingly, but it has been slow to recognize this new reality.

There is no way, in my opinion at least, for large organizations to escape from the basic constraints of the manpower pool. Parenthetically, the Israelis manage to call up about 94 to 96 percent of each age group for military service. This leads one to question our selectivity. The Israelis seem to have a pretty good army, using 96 percent of their able-bodied population.

Also, selectivity can backfire. Overselectivity can be as bad as underselectivity, if the people you select do not fit into your organization or are not happy in it. In short, you can be too selective—which means faulty selection based on the wrong criteria. If overqualified people are selected, the separation rate will rise. I do not believe, for example, that there has been enough study and analysis in the military of the reasons behind the premature resignations of academy graduates. The high resignation rate is a signal that something is wrong in the system, fundamentally wrong.

A colleague of mine, Ivar Berg, wrote a book called *Education and Jobs* that carries the subtitle *The Great Training Robbery*.[1] The burden of his analysis is that many large employers do not realize, because they do not study their own records, that they are suffering excessive turnover and other problems because they have overselected their personnel. What all this adds up to is that selection is important but no cure-all. The critical question is: What people are good for your organization?

A second preconception has to do with the military education and training system. The armed services are engaged in education and training in a big way. The Air Force spends on the order of $5 billion a year on training.

The question I would raise is: What kind of training is required, and how much of it ought to be provided within the military? I believe the extent to which the military should run its own training deserves much more study than it has yet been given.

There are great advantages to the military in running a big training program: It swells the total personnel base and provides additional jobs up and down the line. But from a national point of view this may not provide an optimal solution. Obviously, even now the military does not do all of its own training. It takes in professional people, sometimes paying for part or even all of their civilian training.

It might make more sense to center the basic skill training in the civilian community. I do not say it *would*, but that it *might*. There has never been a serious study of the implications of so radical a change. The idea implicit in this proposal would be that the military would provide specialized training only for task-specific jobs. Basic electronics and other basic skills would be learned in the civilian world.

Another point is that the military, like the rest of the society but even more so, is probably skewed too much in favor of school training, and too little toward on-the-job training. The former runs up costs, failure rates, and other negatives. We need a better balance between institutional and on-the-job training. In any case, the large schooling operations in the military are too inflexible. People can not move through at their own speed. Improvements are constantly being made, but in my opinion they are not nearly enough.

When I talk about military training, I mean, of course, nonmilitary technical skills. I'm not talking about techniques of night patrolling or infiltration or special actions. It's the technical support skills used in civilian society, on which specifically useful skills must be superimposed. What needs to be studied is the preferred pattern for a national training policy in which the military clearly has a role to play but not necessarily as dominant a role as at present.

THE RAMIFICATIONS OF UTILIZATION

It is my observation that the Department of Defense, in formulating a manpower policy, is preoccupied—understandably so—with military personnel on active duty. It tends to overlook the other manpower resources at its disposal, which are not insignificant, or it deals with them separately. There are a million civilian personnel in the Department of Defense; there is a reserve structure of a million; there are indigenous personnel overseas. What I am saying is that the Department of Defense does not have a total manpower strategy that looks at all these resources and seeks to optimize their use in a coordinated way. DOD has an overwhelming preoccupation with the career military.

This is understandable, but in the long run it just won't do. A million civilians add up to lots of money and also lots of talent. The Reserves are far from insignificant, even though they take less money. One has to think more about the manpower pool in its totality.

Nor has enough consideration been given, for example, to the possibilities of greater reliance on contracting out for services. There are complicated trade-offs here. Admittedly, the military needs some minimum of transport under its own control, ready for an emergency. But more generally the question of the relation of the military to the civilian economy—what it staffs for and what it buys—warrants more study.

. . . It might be useful to tell this to Congress, something I have done on occasion. It is unrealistic to expect an organization voluntarily to cut itself down to size. Its members, after all, have a vested interest in the existing structure and size, and that's true from the privates at the bottom to the generals at the top. No organization ever opts for reduction. It's only the people who control the funds who are likely to do so.

The next point relates to the tendency of the military to plead what might be called defense necessity to excuse poor utilization of manpower. Whenever evidence appears showing misuse of personnel, the conventional explanation is the emergency in Vietnam or some similar justification. I don't doubt that the explanation of special needs is often valid. The military is, after all, created to deal with emergencies. But I think this is a lazy man's explanation. I don't believe one should sweep under the carpet ineffective utilization practices   by claiming military urgency. That's too pat.

Back in World War II, I was involved in medical logistics. We used to get whining letters from medical officers stationed on islands of the Pacific far behind the advancing front, who felt they were out of things and not being properly used. I used to write back, asking, in effect, "What do you want MacArthur to do, take more casualties so you can be busy?" They had been left behind by a rapidly moving situation.

But they had a point. With medical officers in scarce supply, how long should they remain stranded on those islands? Some of them stayed there for many months, even years, and headquarters simply forgot that they were there. There was no real effort to sop up these scarce resources and redeploy them. That's the kind of question that comes up over and over in personnel utilization. My own view is that there are just too many easy excuses for poor utilization based on the plea of military necessity.

There is also a tendency in large organizations, military and civilian, to depend too much on the system—the computer, the SOP, routine forms, and so on. One pushes buttons and assumes that everything will happen automatically and efficiently.

Most systems aren't that good. We need to ask people, especially in the more important parts of the organization, what they would like to do, what kind of assignment they would like to have. You can't satisfy everybody's preference, but you can make fewer mistakes. It is my observation that all large organizations are disinclined to make the effort to inform themselves about people's preferences and to take them into account. Some people like cold climates, some people like hot climes. Some people like to live in crowded areas with lots of interaction; some people like to hunt and fish. These things are not likely to show up on punch cards.

Many assignments would be a lot better, and we would get a lot more good work out of people, if we'd just ask them what they want and try, within reason, to satisfy their preferences. But this goes against the grain, because personnel officers, as a tribe, believe they know best, and that the system was created for them rather than to serve the people in the organization.

A good way to get a handle on the utilization problem is to talk to those who leave, the good people who don't stay. They are the ones whose views and attitudes should be studied for clues to the utilization problem. I'll wager you will find, if you can get them to talk honestly, that their major complaint is the absence of meaningful work assignments. That's the key factor. People who have meaningful work and are making a living do not leave an organization. It is when they have been repeatedly misused and underused that they get fed up and decide to leave. . . .

MANPOWER AND ORGANIZATION

There is, of course, a close interface between manpower and organizational reform. I would say, quite bluntly, that the military will have to make some big changes in the way it is structured in order to manage its manpower better.

Secretary Foster told our committee, at our farewell luncheon after we had submitted our report, that he was distressed by the fact that the defense establishment was being eaten alive by the manpower requirements for maintaining inferior equipment. Equipment that the contractor had said would operate effectively for months or years broke down within thirty days. Foster's estimate was that 1.5 million people were tied up in maintaining equipment.

This is one of the areas where, it seems to me, serious reform is needed. In my view the planning and development of weapons systems have never adequately taken account of the manpower dimensions. I first stumbled on that problem during the Korean War, when I discovered that new signal equipment in the field was not being used because nobody had been trained to use it properly. It was too complicated. People were using the old World War II machines, which they knew how to handle.

Our society is obsessed with technology, and the military reflects this obsession. Even after our experience in Vietnam, which has shown up many of the limitations of advanced technology, we still don't understand enough about the proper mixes between equipment and people.

Another area where manpower management and organizational reform come together is the grade structure. It's one aspect of the problem of the officer-enlisted man relationship. . . .

Last May I was in Western Europe for the Ford Foundation, looking at some industrial problems centered around work satisfaction.[2] The principal complaint we heard in the Netherlands, Sweden, Norway, France, and Italy was excessive middle management—too many people sitting on top of those who did the work. My own observation is that this is a serious problem in the military. John Gardner once said that middle management in large organizations is like the Van Allen belt; nothing can get through in either direction.

A third area where imaginative change is needed relates to military retirement systems. Why are there only two options: early-out at one end and twenty- or thirty-year tours of duty at the other? Why not a sliding scale of options? The men you want to keep and who can be promoted quickly will stay anyway. The men you don't have room for should go. The great mass will be in the middle, staying for varying periods of time.

One needs a range of options to accommodate these differences.

For years I have been preaching to the large corporations: Make more and more of your pensions portable; have more fringe benefits that are optional both ways—that is, for management to encourage people to leave or stay; loosen up the organization so that it doesn't get stuck with people who are only waiting out their time.

SOME MODEST SOLUTIONS

Of course, I have no magic solutions to all these problems. But I will outline the directions in which progress may lie.

First, one must grasp the full implications that 56 percent of the Defense Department budget is manpower. What this means is that one must stop treating manpower and materiel as distinct and move to a planning structure that deals with them jointly.

The ultimate resource for the performance of defense missions is dollars. Manpower and materiel are intermediate resources, both of which reflect dollars. Dollars are the limitation on the performance of Defense missions. What we need, I would argue, is better planning to get more bang for the total dollar. That's the first and basic point.

Next, in managing manpower, I would say it's time to shift the emphasis from improving the reward system, which is now increasingly competitive with other large organizations for most age groups, to utilization problems and output. You simply must do a better job on utilization. That means you must identify malutilization practices and see what you can do about them, instead of trying to get more money from Congress— because I'm afraid that source is drying up.

More efficient utilization would mean, among other things, fewer officers, especially in an organization built on the principle that officers do nothing but manage the people who actually do the work. There are exceptions, of course: In the Air Force, pilots are officers. Excessive numbers of officers comprise the swollen middle management.

For ten years I was a consultant for one of the largest chemical companies in the world, during which time I studied its research and development operation in depth. A project proposal used to go up through about seven levels to get approved and seven levels back. So there were fourteen initials on each piece of paper. I told them it was no wonder they got only a 10 percent return on their research dollar; they spent all their time moving papers. In every large organization I know, DOD included, collapsing the middle-management structure is long overdue. This struck me forcibly when we did our recent study on manpower research for the Department of Defense: We ran into the double-layering of military chiefs and civilian chiefs in the personnel laboratories and all the way down the organization.

If the mission of the organization isn't clear, its manpower utilization is likely to be inefficient. It took the United States a long time to decide that the two-and-a-half-wars' mission for DOD was perhaps a bit excessive, and that one and one-half wars would be enough. But one critical question is whether the mission of two and a half or one and a half wars was arrived at by objective analysis of the threat that might materialize, or by estimating the national resources prospectively available? I don't pretend to expertise in this area, but it does seem to me that pursuing three alternative nuclear delivery systems at the same time might warrant reassessment.

Then there is the competition among component parts of the establishment. Surely there are ways to organize the establishment and order the appropriation system so that the services will have some elbow room for determining their needs and performing their unique missions, but will also have to coordinate their operations more effectively than they now do. I would argue that, in general, the control of the military services is less effective today than it was thirty years ago. We used to have two services; now we have four, plus the thick layer on top. In my day, Secretary of War Stimson had three civilian assistants, and about five military people reporting directly to him. That was the structure of the Army plus the Army Air Corps at the top. It is not clear that the system has improved much over the past thirty years.

A critical challenge is how to get more attention and talent brought to bear on manpower management. The best way I can think of is to make officer evaluations hinge on manpower utilization much more than is now the case. Years ago Secretary of the Army Pace did make some changes in the officer evaluation forms. Several of us convinced him that if he allotted 10 percent of the evaluation to manpower utilization, officers would pay more attention to managing the manpower allocated to them.

One thing that bothers me, however, is that authority in personnel matters in this mammoth organization has been so constricted that it's hard to evaluate anybody's utilization of his manpower, because he has little discretionary authority to utilize it as he thinks best. He is bound by so many different rules and regulations that for all practical purposes he is only a transmitter and implementer of rules and regulations. Here, again, I'm afraid it is another aspect of the swollen middle-management problem that I've identified earlier.

Manpower research: Not much more money is needed here, but the quality of the research can be improved if the selection of researchers and the problems they work on are more carefully considered. The research staffs need an infusion of new blood and they need more constructive interest from command.

I am pleased that the Air Force has scheduled a first joint conference on personnel management with industry next May. An exchange of information with other large organizations on personnel management problems is likely to be helpful. I think the relative isolation of the military from the rest of the society is an error. Problems of manpower selection, manpower research, and manpower management are common to all large organizations; and shared experiences should be helpful to all.

My final word of advice stems from the problem I identified earlier: Good people don't have enough challenging things to do. That is a tragedy; it's costing the country a lot of money, and it's really a stupid way to run a big organization. If the best people leave, the outlook is grim.

These are unsettled times, as I noted at the outset. I believe that basic questioning of values and goals will go on for a long time, including the values and goals of the military. I recently met a former government official who told me that he had been offered a position as assistant secretary of defense. When he told his family that evening of the offer, his two young sons aged twelve and fourteen said, "You take that job, we leave home."

DOD is not likely to solve all its manpower problems in the near future but it should be able to make progress in solving some of them.

DISCUSSION

Question: Would you expand your comments on the shortcomings of the military-justice system, with which, incidentally, I happen to disagree.

Dr. Ginzberg: Well, I'm not an expert in this arena, but as I see it, the basic difference between the military and the civil systems of justice is that in the latter one is judged by one's peers, and in the former by one's superiors. In the military, the judicial system is really part of management. I question the necessity of this. As a people, we believe in due process; that means not only the rule of law, but judgments being reached by persons who have no personal stake in the case at issue. When the system of justice is intertwined with the command and management system, I question whether justice can be objective. I'll leave it at that.

Question: About three years ago the Air Force detailed an officer to do a survey of Negro NCOs and their children, under your supervision. Could you tell us something of the findings?

Dr. Ginzberg: Yes. The purpose in studying this particular group was to determine whether the black youngsters growing up in the military have different career aspirations and goals from those in civilian life. The study has just been completed. It is called "The Children of Air Force Sergeants: The Impact of Desegregation on their Career Plans." It will be out shortly. What we found was that black youngsters growing up in the Air Force did have more contacts with whites than do blacks in civilian life, but that on the whole their career aspirations were not that different. There were some incidental findings that were interesting—for example, that the wives of black Air Force NCOs worked more frequently than the wives of whites. Also, black NCOs were not promoted as often as whites with equivalent service and education.

The most interesting single finding, from my point of view, was that black youngsters who were attending college were more interested in segregated education than we had expected. Although only a minority of the group surveyed favored school segregation, the rate of prointegration sentiment rose with increasing educational attainment. This reflects, of course, a strong feeling about the importance of building racial solidarity among many young blacks.

Question: Competition is supposed to be one of the foundation stones of our society, and yet you indicated that it's unhealthy for the services to compete instead of cooperating. What would you suggest as an alternative?

Dr. Ginzberg: Well, I think we need X amount of competition and Y amount of centralizing and coordination. In our manpower research recommendations, we recognized that each of the services had unique personnel problems that would justify their doing some studies on their own. But we also saw a lot of common areas—recruiting, induction, and so on. Surely many of the basic problems of utilization are the same.

So we suggested that the new increments to the research monies should go to the Department of Defense, to plan studies of servicewide application, and let the three services compete for that money. One or another service or a civilian competitor would carry out the study. This, we thought, would give us the best of both worlds. We found a lot of important problems were not being studied because no one service considered them of high priority. So we said: Give the money to the Department of Defense and let the individual services compete against each other and against civilian firms for the study contract.

I think the choice is not one between competition and no competition.

It's rather a question of whether competition has reached an excessive point and of more central planning.

Question: Early in your presentation you referred to the end of the draft as an "interim" measure. Do you believe the all-volunteer force is unlikely to work out?

Dr. Ginzberg: Well, I'm a cautious fellow. I still believe we are going to need defense forces for an indefinite period, but I don't know at what levels. I have no doubt it will be feasible, with the new pay scales, to go off the draft in July 1973. But I don't know when the next crisis will come, and I'm not sure we can continue to recruit the numbers we may need in the future.

So I was just hedging a little, because I really don't know what the requirements will be. If the world stays peaceful, then I think we will have no draft for an indefinite time.

Question: Would you elaborate on your recommendations concerning training? If I understand you correctly, you favor more OJT (on-job training) and less in the classroom. Would this not reduce the contribution the services are now making to national education through their varied educational programs for both veterans and people in the service?

Dr. Ginzberg: I made two points on education and training. First, it might be more efficient if more of the basic and technical training for military service were done in the civilian community. This might be done through an enlisted-reserve training program, under which, say, an electronics technician or a medical technician would get basic technical training in a civilian institution before coming on active duty, and thus be able to devote more of his duty tour to work assignment. Also, I believe the basic technical training would be better.

The second point is that more of the training done within the military system should be on-job training. In general, I would say that the closer the training is brought to the job, the better.

Question: From a national standpoint, is it wise to push for more efficient utilization of manpower when the country is burdened with massive unemployment and underemployment, with a $2 billion program in make-work projects for public-service employment?

Dr. Ginzberg: That's an interesting question and I've worried about it. Parenthetically, if you think this is a problem in our country, imagine the situation in a country like India where there are literally tens of millions of people looking for work. Yet when I go there as a consultant I suggest that they should improve their utilization practices.

My only answer is that we should not undermine our institutions and degrade the level of work performance simply because we have another problem that is not being dealt with effectively. I think we ought to be doing much better than we are in creating employment opportunities, but the existence of a vast pool of unemployed is no excuse for inefficient utilization in the military and other organizations.

Take a poor country suffering from overpopulation. You might argue that newborn babies should be allowed to die, since we have too many people and can't afford to feed all of them. In point of fact, in many countries many of them *are* allowed to die, but we don't regard that as a very efficient way for a society to operate.

CHAPTER 38

The Inevitability of Manpower Waste in Large Organizations

WHAT IS THERE TO ADD to Parkinson's brilliant insights about the ways in which large organizations expand their staffs and then create work to justify the expansion? Only this: Swollen work forces are but one dimension of manpower waste in large organizations.

Although a management that seeks a profit may handle manpower problems differently from one that is free of this pressure, size may be more significant than any other determinant of organizational behavior. Thus large organizations are not limited to profit-making enterprises but may also include nonprofit agencies and government bureaucracies.

No economist will dispute that size frequently contributes to efficiency and economy, but the seamy side of the relationship tends to be ignored. There are several ways in which organizational size contributes to manpower waste. Some general propositions may be usefully examined.

Large organizations are inevitably political in the sense that employees can get ahead only by forming mutual offensive or defensive pacts. All who seek to gain and hold power must devote a large proportion of their time and energies to its pursuit, rather than to accomplishing specific assignments.

One reason boards of directors seek to avoid frequent turnover at the top is to prevent the turmoil that usually accompanies change. Because of the cliquish nature of most top management structures, change at the top has two almost certain consequences. First, many of those who were on the losing side will be bypassed when promotions are made or will be encouraged to accept early retirement if they can avoid being fired. Thus valuable talent is frequently lost. One ludicrous example dates back to the early months of the Eisenhower administration, when new appointees decided that senior civil servants were not trustworthy. In many departments, the secretary and his principal assistants refused to confer with experienced and knowledgeable staff.

The other unfortunate consequence of managerial cliques is that they tend to restrict the selection of key personnel—from the top man down. For example, because Italians occupied the center of power in the College of Cardinals for several hundred years and were determined to stay in control, many able non-Italians were bypassed for key assignments. The same principle operated in the selection of the Army's Chief of Staff after World War II: Only men who had served under Eisenhower were chosen. In the Air Force, only officers identified with the Strategic Air Command have risen to the top.

Often a strong contestant for the top job is unable to secure it for himself but is able to prevent his principal rival from obtaining it. The result is that a compromise candidate is selected, often someone who lacks the strength and ability to lead. As a consequence, the organization fails to make effective use of its resources and fails to respond to its opportunities. When those who are further down the ladder perceive a weakness at the top, many decide to take it easy and wait to see how things develop.

Large organizations try to keep errors hidden or, if mistakes are recognized, from being remedied. During the Great Depression of the 1930s, it became clear to acute observers at Columbia University that its president, Nicholas Murray Butler, was slipping. With a frozen budget, the university was on the downgrade. One dean suggested retirement for all administrative officers over the age of sixty-five, which would have taken both Butler and himself out of the scene. Butler flatly refused, and the trustees, who were his allies, supported him. The dean, on the other hand, abided by his pledge, with the result that the university lost one of its best administrators through early retirement! Moreover, the absence of mandatory retirement resulted in almost no new blood being added to the top ranks during the entire decade. It also took a long time to remove

Sewell Avery from Montgomery Ward, and for President Johnson to get rid of a secretary of defense who, for over three years, had repeatedly been found wrong about Vietnam.

Another characteristic of large organizations is that they recruit people in their own image and then indoctrinate them in acceptable ways of acting. There are several consequences of this practice. There may be an unbalanced assortment of talents and skills, since certain kinds of people learn not to apply for positions or are rejected, and some of those who are accepted leave after a few years. When this happens, those who remain are likely to be understimulated and, lacking strong leadership, do not perform at their best. Some years ago, Captain Nimitz of the U.S. Navy resigned from the service on the ground that he could not accept assignments that made no demand on his skills and experience.

HARD TO CHANGE

Another consequence of the fact that large organizations are difficult to alter as long as they are successful, or appear to be successful, is the tendency for the in-group—cardinals, generals, professors, corporate executives, senior civil servants—to develop personal objectives and goals rather than to pursue the larger purposes of the organization. There is no shortage of tales about generals who sacrifice men to advance themselves; about churchmen who are more concerned with money than with God; about corporate executives who have personally profited from deals involving their companies. Such improper actions by those at the top carry a heavy toll in the form of lowered morale on all levels of the organization.

Another pronounced characteristic of large organizations is that, with the passage of time, they accumulate "deadwood." Regardless of how sharp a recruitment policy is, it is questionable whether it can be more than moderately successful because a certain number of those who are hired will turn out to be ineffective. Although it would make sense to let ineffective people go, the tendency is to be softhearted and to hold onto them even if, as at IBM, they are moved out of the mainstream or demoted. Most organizations keep a large number of ineffective people until they are retired; in the process, the organization suffers a double loss: These people fail to produce, and they get in the way of others. Among the most interesting reforms that the Catholic Church recently introduced was a method of persuading older prelates to retire. The practice of retiring a man who has been passed over twice for promotion in the armed services is one that has not yet been broadly imitated. And it would be hard to find a more counterproductive arrangement than academic tenure.

The older economists, such as Alfred Marshall, postulated that the only resource that is not indefinitely reproducible is management. The dominant view today is that decentralization has broken down this barrier. Large organizations, it is said, can be subdivided into many small organizations, each with an effective management. This view may be in error. Broad policy can be made only at the top. Although middle management can be given more discretion than formerly, it must still be held on a tight rein.

The manager of a General Motors plant cannot negotiate with the United Auto Workers any more than a field commander can decide whether or not to invade. All key decisions must be made at the top, which means that delay, inadequate information, and overwork on the part of the top executives are built into the process. The two-way communications channel, up and down, is likely to be clogged by many gatekeepers who see advantages to filtering the information flow. One is reminded of the tollgate keepers on the Rhine in the fourteenth century, who made a living by levying charges on all goods that passed in either direction. The perversions that result from decentralization can be seen in the loss of about $450 million by General Dynamics a few years ago, when the management of Convair decided to go its own way. Another example is the faulty intelligence from Vietnam that was made available to President Johnson during his term in office.

CONTROL

Because of their nature, most large organizations cannot be controlled effectively. As a consequence, a great number of people, up and down the line, are poorly led and poorly directed. It frequently takes too long for those at the top to become aware of serious weakness and to take steps to remedy it. In the meantime, valuable manpower and other resources are wasted.

Although the health of an organization depends on the selection of effective management, evaluating performance is difficult. In a few arenas, the marketplace can provide a reading. The performance of salesmen can be measured. The output of academicians can be assessed in the arena of scholarship. But how is one to judge among the tens, hundreds, and even thousands of lower and intermediate managers who make up the staff of a large corporation, especially if, as is increasingly common, they perform their work as members of a group?

Most people are judged by supervisors with whom they are often in subtle competition, as well as by their supervisors' supervisors. The readings that are made, and on which personnel decisions are usually based, have more to do with how well a person impresses those higher up than with demonstrated or potential capability. Large organizations may boast about their hardheadedness and concern for efficiency, but they operate largely in response to convention and personality.

Can any generalizations be made about organizations from these remarks about their political and bureaucratic nature; their constricted personnel policies governing selection, evaluation, promotion and retention; and the difficulties of operating on a decentralized principle?

The old economists had a simple view of manpower utilization: People would work harder if they could see the advantages that would accrue to them. Owners would be more concerned with efficiency and profitability than would a hired management. After an organization had reached a certain size, resources of capital and personnel could no longer be effectively controlled because competence at the top was limited and could not be readily reproduced.

What have we learned since then? It is difficult for men in a large organization to follow a road other than that of adjustment to the conventional ways in which work is conducted. If they deviate from the norm, others will bring them to heel or, if necessary, force them to leave. Large organizations require adaptability. They demand that newcomers learn not to rock the boat. New employees must work as those before have become accustomed to work.

Second, large organizations are geared to do tomorrow what they were successful in doing yesterday. This means they place a premium on new people who learn the methods and techniques that have been tried and found effective. Although large organizations are willing to and, to some degree, must innovate, they can afford to do so only after they have checked and rechecked to see that new procedures and methods will work and can be adapted to the old. Routine and momentum are among their greatest assets. Each worker is encouraged to avoid errors that could jeopardize the proven system. There is relatively little payoff for the individual who wants to innovate because often innovation means changing the very things that have formed the foundation of the organization's success and security.

The most important conclusion is that in very large organizations the people at the top can no longer exercise effective control. One is reminded of President Kennedy's quip after reviewing a new proposal: He said he favored it but was not sure how the government of the United States would respond. In very large organizations, employees recognize that the few at the top do not control them. Many respond by going their own way, seeking their own ends, often fighting each other, and only sometimes cooperating. The final score is not known to the participants until the game is long over.

The early economists had insights into the conditions contributing to manpower waste. So did Parkinson. What should be added is this: Large organizations are concerned only indirectly with the efficient use of manpower resources. They have higher-priority goals. By misusing their manpower, however, particularly when selecting people for the top, they eventually pay a high price.

In other words, when large organizations go their own way, manpower waste is inevitable because manpower considerations are only incidental to their purpose. If they waste the capacities and potentials of many of those whom they hire and pay, they may admit that it is regrettable. But that is the way it has been for a long time, and that is the way it will continue to be for a long time.

PART IX

Metropolitanism: Focus on New York

THE DATES OF EACH of the six selections help to underscore an important point. Concern with metropolitanism and the city of New York represents the latest shift of my intellectual interest, barring only my contemporary concern with newcomers to the United States. All but the first piece (Chapter 39) were written in the 1970s.

I am a pure New Yorker, in fact a pure West Sider. I was born and have lived all my life within approximately one mile of Columbia University. Moreover, I am a booster of the Big Apple. Even when New York City was on the ropes, literally hours away from bankruptcy in 1975, I never believed that the city would go over the precipice. I always believed that with time it would recover from many, if not all, of the wounds that prolonged mismanagement had inflicted on it.

I have also found from my travels abroad that one gains perspective on the problems at home. Chapter 41, in which New York City and Paris are compared, gives concrete expression to this approach.

In the mid-1970s the Rockefeller Brothers Fund, through Mrs. Marilyn Levy, a staff associate, encouraged the Conservation Project to focus on the problems of New York City. Chapter 43 presents the "Executive Summary" of a study of corporate headquarters that I carried out in association with Professor Matthew Drennan of New York University.

The final chapter in Part IX, Chapter 44 on "The Japanese Presence" can be read as an extension of the preceding that emphasizes the critical role of producer services in an increasingly internationalized world economy.

CHAPTER 39

Manpower Strategy for the Metropolis

... THE QUARTER OF A CENTURY since World War II has unleashed many new forces and has reinforced earlier trends that have altered the structure and functioning of the nation's major metropolises. From the present analysis, which has been focused on the manpower dimensions of this revolution, the important findings are:

1. A continuing and rapid erosion of the comparative advantages of many of the nation's largest cities, and simultaneous accelerated growth of smaller cities. Since a slower rate of growth, stability, or decline of the economy makes adjustments between the labor force and the job market more difficult, the mismatching of people and jobs has been accentuated in the slower-growing major metropolises.

2. The flight to the outlying regions of white middle-class families from all metropolitan areas, together with the relocation of many enterprises, from manufacturing to retailing, has further contributed to this mismatching. As many of the established urban groups became suburbanites, migrants from the South and from Puerto Rico moved into the central cities in search of jobs and a new life. Since municipal

authorities were unable or unwilling to enforce the building codes, the numbers who squeezed into the vacated space exceeded the numbers who had left, with the result that buildings and neighborhoods deteriorated. This in turn exerted pressure on the remaining white families to follow the move to the suburbs. In this major reshuffling of populations, the major cities of the North and West were filled with in-migrants who were poorly prepared for the complexities of urban life. One consequence was the substantial increase in welfare and related costs that had to be met by municipal government; because of the consequent high taxes, the city became a less attractive place for many business enterprises.

3. This was not, of course, the first time in the development of the United States that cities received large numbers of immigrants and in-migrants who were handicapped in adjusting to urban life and work. There were, however, some important differences between the recent and the older streams. A high proportion of the recent newcomers are Negroes, who were subjected to much more severe discrimination in jobs, housing, and all other aspects of living than were the immigrants of an earlier day. Moreover, the city, which until World War I had had a great many jobs for unskilled workers, now was hospitable primarily only to professional, technical, and other types of white-collar workers. The out-migration of many enterprises in manufacturing and trade had reduced the number of blue-collar jobs in the central city. Hence it became much more difficult in recent years to match the new in-migrants with the available jobs.

4. The experience of Western Europe since the end of World War II teaches that among the principal reasons that New York and other U.S. cities have had such difficulties in absorbing the new in-migrants into profitable employment has been the generally slack level of demand for labor during most of the last quarter of a century. Except during the early 1940s, and again at the height of the Korean War, the level of unemployment and underemployment has been markedly higher in the United States than in Western Europe. Those who have the least to offer employers are those most likely to be in the peripheral labor force — minority groups, women, and old persons.

5. Much effort and money has been directed during the past years to programs aimed at removing or alleviating the handicaps of the poorly endowed and poorly trained in the hope and expectation of improving their prospects for employment. There are narrow limits within which such a policy can operate, however. If the total demand for labor remains slack, then improving the qualifications of one part of the supply will simply result in their advancing in the queue. Another group will become the last hired, first fired. Moreover, since there are limited prospects for advancement for many who are regularly employed, it is

difficult for the less qualified to get and hold a job, particularly a good job.

6. The shift from manufacturing to service jobs in metropolitan employment has resulted in the availability of a large number of low-paying, dead-end, and intermittent work opportunities for the poorly educated and trained. One of the challenges facing the metropolis is to improve its overall job structure so that only a small minority must hold these jobs. Since many young Negroes who enter the labor market have little opportunity to get a job other than one that pays little, has little status, and offers few if any prospects for advancement, this unquestionably adds to the alienation of these young people and to their frustration and hostility.

7. The difficulties of absorbing poorly educated and poorly trained young people and adults into the urban economy have been accentuated, as we have seen, by the flight of many enterprises to outlying areas in search of more suitable land, lower taxes, and better access to transportation networks. The impact of various technological developments—particularly those associated with the automobile and the truck—has been to speed decentralization. One possibility is a new turn in technology that may lead to a reversal of this trend when important advantages may once again accrue to those who decide to locate, remain, or expand their operations within the city proper. Although the balance between the powerful forces that still pull enterprises to the periphery and the new forces that may start to pull them to the center is hard to determine, the fact that technology may contribute anew to centralization is an important finding for those who must plan for tomorrow.

8. Since the core city is ineluctably linked to the suburbs and since the economic well-being of one is closely linked to the prosperity of the other, it is essential that transportation networks be improved so that the present difficulties in bringing people and jobs together are reduced. In this connection attention must be directed to reverse transportation movements—that is, to enabling ghetto populations to travel to the suburbs easily and cheaply so that they will have greater access to the blue-collar and service jobs that are available there. The rate of expansion on the peripheries of cities will be slowed unless the available labor force within the city can be tapped.

9. Most of the findings recapitulated here have dealt with the problems connected with successfully absorbing the poorly educated in an increasingly sophisticated urban economy in which many of the fastest growing areas require primarily only professional, technical, and other types of white-collar workers. The vitality of cities depends in considerable measure on solving the problems of the hard-to-employ and in assuring that new and expanding enterprises have ready access to large

numbers of trained persons to fill the ever larger proportion of managerial and technical positions. Since this supply is crucial for the continued
growth and prosperity of the urban economy, the size and strength of the
educational and training facilities within the metropolitan area are of
paramount significance. The city that has many junior colleges, colleges,
technical institutes, universities, and other facilities to produce a large
number of educated and trained personnel in a wide range of fields will
have a distinct advantage over other cities which have fewer educational
facilities.

The contribution of higher education to the urban economy must be
assessed not only from the viewpoint of the number of regularly enrolled
students pursuing an undergraduate or graduate degree, but also in
terms of its contribution to the large numbers in the community who
must pursue their studies on a part-time basis because they must work,
keep house, or fulfill some other commitment.

10. People work in the city, others live in it, some come for recreational
purposes, others to study, some to seek medical treatment. Whether
those who come to the city stay for a short time or remain permanently,
whether they opt to work there and whether they also make their homes
there depends in considerable measure on the quality of the urban
environment relative to the realistic alternatives. We know that a great
many families have decided they will not live in the city even if they
work there. We know further that although many are attracted to the city,
others are repelled by the dirt, the noise, the congestion, and the lack of
personal safety. The metropolis cannot offer all the advantages of cosmopolitan living and at the same time provide the amenities that attach to
small-town life. Some of the consequences of density—the essence of
metropolitanism—are inevitable. But it does not follow that the urban
environment need deteriorate to a point where people are frightened to
walk the streets, where the public schools are shunned by parents with
college-bound children, or where transportation is an ordeal.

There is no point in trying to solve a large number of specific
manpower problems, ranging from jobs for the hard-to-employ to an
adequate flow of talent and competence, and including additional challenges such as the effective use of educated women, the reduction of
peripherality in employment, and the provision of meaningful career
opportunities to young workers, or to concentrate on answers to these
admittedly high-priority problems, if we continue to neglect the overriding issue of how the city can maintain its attractiveness to the many
groups of able and energetic people who are the keystone to its vitality
and prosperity. The fact that a high proportion of these people are
unwilling to live in the city is warning that, if the urban environment
continues to deteriorate, they may refuse to work there. This threat must

be recognized, met, and turned back. A successful manpower strategy for the metropolis must be tested by using the simple criterion that able people can see their future as urbanites. Every program and policy must be weighed on this scale.

POLICIES AND PROGRAMS

... We will present some of the important suggestions for public and private action at the metropolitan level.

First, we will note briefly the range of actions that fall within the domain of the federal government. While we must not overlook the scope for constructive action that lies within the competence of a local population, we must not assume that major cities can, on their own, solve their economic and manpower problems. They cannot. ...

If the labor market is slack, as it has been throughout so many of the postwar years, it is inevitable that considerable numbers of persons within the labor force and on the periphery, such as young people, married women, and older persons, will be unemployed, underemployed, or will not even look for a job although they want and need one.

It is generally agreed in this post-Keynesian world that the maintenance of a generally high level of unemployment is the clear responsibility of the federal government. It is less clear, however, whether the federal government can reduce the unemployment rates, as currently calculated, below the 4 percent level through reliance on general fiscal and monetary policy without generating serious inflationary pressures. If the country can at present provide more jobs only at the cost of rising prices, the federal government must explore alternatives that may accomplish the first without the second. Congress is slowly edging up to serious consideration of a major job creation program to help absorb many of the unemployed or underemployed, particularly in ghetto areas. ...

Since 1962 the federal government, particularly through the Manpower Development and Training Act and the programs of the Office of Economic Opportunity, has made sizable sums available to improve the capabilities of the hard-to-employ in the hope and expectation that through literacy and skill-training their employability would be enhanced. Many who were trained obtained jobs for which they otherwise would not have qualified. But a training approach can be successful only if the number of potential jobs equals the number of potential job seekers, and only if training opportunities are available for all who want and need them.

We have noted that there has been a shortfall of jobs in the economy.

Now we must add that there has been a substantial shortfall of good training slots. A rough calculation of the gap between the need for and availability of training opportunities in New York City indicates a ratio of 6 to 1. Moreover, the administrative relations among the federal government, the state, and the localities have been so cumbersome that the potential effectiveness of the federal dollars has been greatly reduced. If training can contribute significantly to raising the level of manpower utilization in the nation's major cities—and it unquestionably can—better policy, more funds, and greater involvement of community leadership are required.

An unique dimension of the large concentrations of hard-to-employ in the ghetto areas of the cities of the North and West is that so many Negroes and Puerto Ricans are among the in-migrants who have relocated from farms, towns, and small cities. The failure of the federal government to mount significant programs to help prepare these migrants prior to or after their relocation has meant that their difficulties in sinking roots in their new metropolitan environment have been unmitigated, and their new neighbors in turn have found it difficult to adjust to them. The large-scale movement of people across state lines calls for federal assistance even if state and local governments must also be involved in the process.

The federal government has long been involved in highways and housing and recently in interurban transportation. The record suggests, however, that the federal government is only belatedly becoming aware of the importance of using its great powers to encourage planning for the entire metropolitan area in such fashion that the needs and interests of minority groups are not disregarded or sacrificed for the benefit of other stronger members of the community. To rebuild the central city at the expense of uprooting the poor, to use federal funds so that discrimination in housing in the suburbs is reinforced, to build highways that destroy the enterprises that provide jobs for the unskilled and semiskilled— these elements of federal policy in the past have made the minority poor pay for whatever urban progress we have seen. Recently, the terms of federal grants for metropolitan planning and action have included criteria which show more sensitivity for the economic and social needs of low-income and minority groups. But the scale of federal funds remains much too small. The urban environment continues to deteriorate at a rate faster than remedial action is instituted.

Recently, the federal government has begun to take an active interest in mass interurban transportation, which is at the heart of metropolitan planning. Congress has made some small appropriations, but here too we are still losing ground.

Although much more federal assistance will have to be forthcoming on both the housing and transportation fronts, the states and localities can do, and are doing, a great deal to help themselves. This is also true about other aspects of the urban environment such as air and water pollution. Federal involvement in these areas must grow, but the other units of government also have an important role to play.

We have seen that the cities of tomorrow require a much larger federal involvement to create and maintain a viable, physical, social, and economic environment. The following paragraphs will set forth the lines of action that can and must be taken by local leadership, both public and private, if the large metropolis is to remain a viable community. Again within the context of this analysis, emphasis will be on how the city's manpower resources can be more effectively trained and more productively employed.

1. Only 60 percent of the age-relevant population in New York City graduate from high school. When we add to the 40 percent who drop out the considerable group who have learned little although they have acquired a high school diploma, it is clear that the city's schools are not adequately preparing young people for the world of work. This is not to say that there is no future for the high school dropout, but that such high dropout rates are prima facie cause for concern in an overwhelmingly service economy in which communication and quantitative skills loom increasingly important. High on the city's agenda is to make the necessary changes in the shortest possible time to enable the education system to do its job. New York's economy and society will deteriorate a generation hence if the schools continue to pour into the labor market so many young people who are unprepared to find meaningful jobs that will enable them to advance and achieve security.

2. Although concern with those still in the school system is important, the large numbers of younger people who have passed through it and are now struggling to make a place for themselves in the economy and society must not be disregarded. There are a great many, with varying degrees of educational achievement, who as they mature realize that they have need for more education and training. While New York has a tremendous array of public and private educational and training facilities, there are still unmet needs for free and low-cost adult educational and training opportunities for the high school and college dropout. A major challenge to community leadership is to identify these deficiencies and act to remedy them forthwith.

3. The fact that so many youths have left high school without acquiring a diploma and the certainty that this pattern will continue for many years to come—although we hope that the proportion will decline—makes it essential that municipal government restudy its hiring requirements to determine the relevance of its standards and to lower them when indicated.

Once its own house is in order in this regard, it should encourage private and nonprofit employers to do likewise. The maintenance of artificially high standards has been demonstrated to be a serious cost not only to the potential worker but also to the employer.

4. Since the dynamic sectors of the city have an unmet need for people with high orders of ability and competence, the large pool of educated women represents an important potential asset. To tap it effectively, however, will require adjustments along a great many fronts: in colleges and universities, to facilitate the entry and reentry of women into degree and nondegree programs; in the provision, under public, nonprofit, and private auspices, of competent guidance and placement services; by employers, in scheduling; in the expansion of child-care facilities; and in opening company training and promotion opportunities to able women.

5. Over 70 percent of all jobs in New York City are in the service sector of the economy. Many of these jobs pay poorly and worse; they are not part of a job hierarchy; a person entering at the bottom can look forward only to the same low-level job or to leaving. Effective manpower utilization requires that people be afforded an opportunity to learn while they work and to be promoted as they acquire competence. Hence it is incumbent on all employers—private, nonprofit, and government—to restudy their job ladders and to provide for orderly progression. In this connection, unions can and should advise employers of the desires and needs of workers for in-service and extramural training opportunities.

6. Almost 6 percent of all jobs in New York are in the health services industry, and it is likely that this proportion will grow under the forced draft of Medicare and Medicaid as well as the willingness of consumers to spend more of their income on health care. The health field has provided employment opportunities for the poorly educated and trained as well as for those in the top professional ranks. Despite the rapid growth of employment in the health field, many manpower shortages exist and more are anticipated. The ability of New York to maintain its leadership position in this industry will depend in part on its willingness and determination to improve its training and utilization practices. The high density of medical installations within the city provides an excellent opportunity for rationalizing and improving the training that is now carried on largely under the auspices of individual hospitals. The City University and the community colleges have begun to move into the field, but much more can be done to bring all the involved educational institutions into a more integrated plan, to determine by agreement the fields of specialization for the several colleges and universities, and to improve the relations between them and the service institutions, which must continue to provide opportunities for clinical and laboratory

experience. Employment can be increased through cooperation among the Hospital Association, the several trade unions, and the professional associations. Here is a splintered market that can be greatly strengthened through cooperative arrangements which will redound to the advantage of the workers, the employers, and the public. Part of any effort at rationalization should be a hard look at present standards for certification and, equally important, a determination of how ways can be made to enable people to advance up the skill hierarchy as they acquire greater competence on the job or through additional education.

7. The cutting edge of modern industry is the research and development laboratory; therefore, the city with ready access to large numbers of educated and trained persons has an advantage. The large higher educational structure of New York City and environs, together with its significant number of nonprofit foundations and research laboratories, is a major asset. The many corporate headquarters and industrial laboratories in the area represent another source of strength. Yet the full exploitation of these assets requires more planning and coordination than has as yet been accomplished, when all the initiative has been left to the individual enterprise to tap into the rich human resources pool. There is no agency, government or other, that is concerned with a closer correlation between the emergent needs of enterprise and the best ways of meeting them from among the strong scientific and research resources of New York. For instance, no one agency is concerned with attracting to the city more federal research and development grants, or with determining the steps that must be taken by the community in anticipation of expanding one or another of its research functions. There is no leadership clearly responsible for assuring that the research potential of the city is effectively husbanded and utilized.

Although there are councils and committees that provide for some interchange between the public and private institutions of higher learning, both within the city proper and in the metropolitan area, a strong planning and research effort aimed at correlating the growth and specialization of the two types of institutions cannot be mounted at present because of inadequate structure and staffing.

8. Two major factors have contributed to weakening the city's ability to provide jobs for all its people, particularly those with little education or skill. One is the absence of effective transportation links between the places the poor reside and the jobs they could fill. More attention must be directed by municipal authorities to improving transportation from the core city to the periphery so that the ghetto populations have greater opportunity to find work. This involves reliable transportation and low cost. A person who must spend inordinate amounts of time getting to and from a job, or must allocate to traveling a disproportionate amount of

earnings, will not even begin to search for employment far from home.

To improve the linkages between minority groups in the inner city and jobs on the periphery, responsible government agencies must be informed about where employment is expanding, where employers are most pressed for additional workers, and how the available transportation network might be supplemented (usually by an additional bus line) in order to bring potential employees to the jobs. Equally important is the establishment of a reasonable fare, which might require a partial subsidy. In instances of acute labor shortages, it might be possible for the city to interest a group of employers to contribute to the subsidy. Without special and continuing efforts on the part of the municipal officials to move into the breach, the nonfit between stranded workers and available jobs is likely to persist.

Municipal officialdom must also develop sophistication in the assembling, zoning, and leasing or selling of land within its borders. No resource is more scarce within a city; no resource requires more careful handling to make its maximum contribution to the continued vitality of the urban economy. A dynamic city needs a balanced population for the expansion of high-wage employment and for the growth of strategically important social overhead structures—from universities to hospitals. To achieve this end, the proper planning and control of its land is the most critical challenge facing the municipal authorities. As with every facet of planning, the responsible officials can make major contributions by innovations. Planning for better land use would involve the collection of discrete parcels into larger units for special purposes; the exploitation of air rights; fill-ins along the water front; and above all the stimulation of public-private cooperation for large-scale, industrial, residential, and service developments. Neither government nor private enterprise alone is likely to be able to raise the sums required to transform deteriorated areas into vital neighborhoods, but together they can do a great deal.

9. The pull of the city is strong because it offers an exciting life. The density of population has facilitated the specialization of functions that has underpinned economic growth and development, and it has also provided the base for a wide range of activities that depend on the proximity of large numbers who share goals and objectives. But density brings costs as well as gains; and lately the costs have risen to a point where many who want to work and live in large cities have had second thoughts. Among the worst drawbacks have been dirty air, dirty streets, slow traffic; crimes of violence; group antagonisms; poor public services; and other dangers, difficulties, and annoyances that have convinced increasing numbers of Americans that the city is a bad environment for children and a questionable environment for themselves.

To say that more policemen should patrol the streets is easy, but how can this be done without increasing taxes? If taxes go up, will it not encourage the exodus of various enterprises, with the result that the tax base will shrink and compound the difficulties of raising revenue for essential services? To take another example: If the proportion of children from racial and ethnic minorities increases to where the public schools are predominantly nonwhite, the removal of the remaining white children is likely to be accelerated. If that occurs, white middle-class families with children will not want to remain in a city where their own children will constitute a minority.

There is no single group that alone can reverse these trends. The protection of sound neighborhoods and the rehabilitation of deteriorated neighborhoods requires the cooperation of all who live and work in the city. Employers, trade unions, churches, large voluntary organizations — all who have a stake in the viability and vitality of the city — must be able and willing to participate in the fashioning of policies and programs that can contribute to the well-being of the metropolis.

Implicit in such cooperation is the willingness of all key groups to work toward the speedy dissolution of the rigid demarcations that still prevail in all U.S. cities between the Negro minority and the white majority. No city can look forward to the future with equanimity if present patterns of segregation and discrimination are maintained. They represent a cancer that can undermine even the strongest city. The strength of a metropolis is grounded on the free and willing cooperation of all who live therein. If a significant minority is denied the opportunity to participate fully in the life of the city, it will sooner or later undermine the health of the entire metropolis. Those who are concerned about the city of tomorrow must make possible the participation of the excluded minority today.

These considerations do not relate only to the city proper. The city can no longer be left to struggle alone with the multiple problems of the minority poor while the white middle- and upper-income classes retreat to the suburbs after work, to live unconcerned and undisturbed by the unsolved problems of the metropolis. Those who earn their livelihood in the city must help solve these problems, else their own livelihood is in jeopardy. The artificial separation of city and suburb must be broken down. The person who works in the city during the day and sleeps in suburbia is a citizen of the metropolitan area.

10. We do not now have the political instrumentalities to reunite city and suburb. Only a beginning has been made, through the establishment of regional planning bodies and through interstate compacts involving basic services such as water, sewage, transportation. We do not even have in the city proper the instrumentalities to assure effective cooperation between the private, nonprofit, and government sectors. This is an essen-

tial first step, since all the strengths of the metropolis must be harnessed if its survival and prosperity are to be assured. We need new and effective mechanisms to relate the central city to its satellite communities so that the actions of one can be assessed in terms of the consequences on the other.

New and improved relations must be established between the city and the metropolitan region and state government. Similarly, many problems can be resolved only as adjoining states develop new and effective ways of jointly assessing and solving problems that confront their separate areas.

Recently the federal government has begun to develop new mechanisms for assisting the metropolises where so many of the nation's acute problems are centered. The metropolises certainly need the assistance of the federal government, but many problems remain to be resolved, particularly how the new federal-municipal relations can be articulated within the traditional system.

Manpower strategy for the metropolis can be successful only if two developments take place. First, every city must develop a research potential so that it can assess emerging economic trends and weigh the policy alternatives among which it must choose. Second, a successful manpower strategy requires the establishment and elaboration of more effective mechanisms for policy assessment and determination at every level — city, metropolitan area, state, region, nation — and, equally important, effective coordination among these several instrumentalities.

We can no longer take for granted the economic well-being of metropolitan America. Since three-quarters of the total population will soon live within these metropolitan areas, the future of the country depends on our ability to meet and solve the key problems confronting the cities. Research and organization are essential ingredients of a successful strategy.

A successful strategy for the metropolis requires that all who live therein play a part in fashioning it, and that all who will be affected by it have an opportunity to profit from it. The strength of a metropolis is that the whole can utilize the contribution of each member and that each member in turn can draw strength from the whole.

CHAPTER 40

In Praise of Cities

TWO PROFESSORS AT MIT named Forrester and Meadows have been developing apocalyptic views of urban society. They have been simulating futures that forecast that cities are doomed. I will try to prove that if cities are doomed, the world is doomed—and obviously, if the world is doomed, humanity is doomed. I should also note that I don't believe in futurology. Let me give you an example of why.

When my father-in-law was graduated from Harvard Law School in 1912, he talked with Dean Pound about two offers he had received, one from Chicago and one from New York. Dean Pound said, "Oh, take the Chicago offer. New York is finished; it is not going anywhere. You go to Chicago; that is the up-and-coming city." So, with his usual skepticism, my father-in-law came to New York, did quite well, and was still running his firm in New York City when he died in 1977.

Consider another case. If anyone foresaw in 1960 that during the next ten years the United States would become mired in a nasty war in Vietnam, that the cities would explode in violence, that students would revolt, that the women's liberation movement would emerge, he was a seer.

My point is that I don't believe we can see clearly ahead for even ten years, much less a hundred and ten. Even Orwell did not foresee the possibility of a nuclear holocaust.

Nevertheless, when the secretary of the Housing and Urban Development Department says that the U.S. government does not have the power to reverse real estate deterioration in large cities, when crime costs perhaps $100 billion a year, when murders no longer attract attention, when the population drift from city centers to the periphery continues, one does get the impression that prophets who preach that the cities are doomed may be correct.

Is this in fact the case? First, let us look at some of the evidence concerning cities in general. This may give us a better perspective on New York.

Let's begin with a contemporary comparative view. During the last two decades I have traveled extensively throughout the world. In each of the five continents I am acquainted with, cities are growing rapidly—not declining. But this is not a peculiarly modern phenomenon; it has been taking place throughout history. Since antiquity people have been fleeing the countryside for the cities, and they continue to do so.

Of course, there is no scientific proof that what has been will continue to be; but despite all the gruesome views about cities declining, the world's evidence seems to go the other way.

Second, I would like to call attention to the findings in a book titled *The Metropolitan Economy*, which was written in 1970 by two associates of mine, Thomas Stanback and Richard Knight, and published by Columbia University Press. In this work, Stanback and Knight studied all the Standard Metropolitan Statistical Areas (SMSAs) in the United States and carefully analyzed what had been happening throughout the country. They found the most rapid urban growth rates not in very large cities such as New York or Los Angeles, but in cities ranging in population from 750,000 to 2 million. This also is a growth phenomenon.

Third, let us consider the work of Professor Gottman of Oxford. In his study of large U.S. metropolitan centers some years ago, he saw the population of the United States draining into three colossal strips—one along the Atlantic coast from Portland to Miami, the second along the west coast from San Francisco to San Diego, and the third along the Gulf coast. These are all city phenomena. Years ago Gottman came up with the interesting finding that more land was being put back into forests than had been taken out. That is, we were in a reverse cycle resulting from the population concentrations that are taking place. It would be interesting to consider the contributions of such factors as birth control, abortions, and higher educational levels to the future quality of our cities. They may assure that the poor do not multiply indefinitely. Until now, one of the severe problems confronting all cities has been the tendency of immigrants, usually poor and less educated, to reproduce rapidly.

Some figures on New York City welfare clients indicate that when government-subsidized abortions were introduced, there were sizable reductions in the number of children born to welfare families. I have no doubt that long-term factors such as increased income levels and increased higher educational levels are also at work; but abortion, the poor person's most effective birth control technique, is a qualitative contribution to speeding this process and assuring that we will not be inundated by poor people.

Fear of an uncontrolled birth rate among welfare clients has begun to show in our figures. As a result of their nervousness about the ethnic redistribution of populations, the white middle class has been fleeing to the suburbs. In turn, land values in the suburbs keep rising, the amount of inexpensive space in the suburbs keeps diminishing, and one must go farther and farther away from the city for space.

Many of the city's problems extend to the suburbs. We have not really looked at the counterpart figures, but I am convinced that the homicide rate per capita in the suburbs must approach that of New York City. In any case, I think large numbers of urbanites are beginning to stay and fight rather than to run. We are beginning to see this in the determination of ethnic groups to maintain their neighborhoods. To the extent that this happens, a further change in the urban population would be less likely. For economic and social reasons, the instability of the urban population may slow substantially.

Let me make some generalized observations about economic phenomena that relate to the future of cities, especially to U.S. cities in general and to New York City in particular. The first is that the U.S. economy is increasingly a service economy. Two-thirds of all jobs are service jobs; big cities—especially the diversified ones such as New York—are overwhelmingly service economies.

Second, the economies of the Western world are becoming increasingly national and international—and New York is the most international city in the world, the center of all cities. Tokyo, Stockholm, Rio de Janeiro, all are more closely related to New York than to any other place. The more the cities and the trade of the world become interlinked, the more important become the key communication centers, of which New York is the leader.

Next, the modern economies of the world are increasingly made up of large corporations and large trade unions. If the dynamism of national and international economies is increasingly linked with large organizations, then it is the large cities that are the headquarters of these organizations that are most closely related to the dominant economic forms.

Moreover, ours is an increasingly pluralistic economy in the sense that the private sector, the nonprofit sector, and the government sector are closely linked. New York is the only great city of the world that is not a capital; but it is only an hour away from Washington by air, and this close interface with government is important. For example, I have been an active consultant of the federal government for decades; I spend almost as much time in Washington as in New York. This is possible only because of the short distances involved.

A recent advertisement in *The New York Times* by the New York Telephone Company emphasized that New York will be around for a long time because it has the greatest collection of people. We are increasingly a talent economy, as indicated in my book *The Human Economy.* We are no longer an economy based primarily on extractive industry or involved primarily in manufacturing. These have been rapidly declining sectors for years. Now we are primarily a talent economy. The whole thrust of the service sector means that the economy depends increasingly on the skills and capabilities of people—and large cities obviously have the greatest aggregations of people with talent.

Even the fastest-growing suburbs such as Rockland and Suffolk have a labor force that is very much smaller and thinner than that which remains in New York.

As ours becomes an increasingly national and international economy, communications of every form, shape, and kind—from newspapers to books to radio to television, computers, and telecommunications—become critical. These vehicles must be bound together, and this again takes place best in an urban area. Major communications enterprises do not locate in exurbia.

To the extent that we are dealing with increasingly large aggregations, the aggregation of financial resources becomes important. Houston has been making a major effort to become a financial center, but it can in no way match New York City as a market and, in fact, is dependent on it. For that matter, there is no other money market in the world that can provide the financing New York can.

Finally, as we become more affluent—at least in the Western world, or the Western world plus Japan—we tend to become more interested in style. People who live close to the limits of subsistence must be concerned with subsistence; but as one becomes more affluent, the niceties and the variations become important—and the city is the center of trends and styles.

You can be sure that the bright young people around the country are not going to live in the suburbs—not for a while, at least. They may eventually be forced to live in suburbs, but at least the more active young workers want to have some exposure to large cities. The city offers them the excitement of being in touch with what they consider the future will be.

What about the countertrends? How powerful are they? What do cities have to worry about?

The first countertrend is the existence of the automobile and other communications devices. As a result of these, it is said, it is as easy to locate in the suburbs and elsewhere as in the central city. This is not the case, however. In our book—*New York Is Very Much Alive*—Professor Stanback has a chapter entitled "Suburbanization," which points up the extent to which the suburbs depend on the vitality of the city for their survival.

Moreover, urban liabilities are also present in the suburbs: At quitting time White Plains is as bad as Wall Street. It is impossible to move; people are going in all directions; everyone is in a gridlock. So, although it is true that the automobile has given us a considerable degree of mobility, the fact that there is such low density on the peripheries of the cities means that one can waste a great amount of time and energy.

Second, Americans like to own their homes—there is no question about this. At the same time, the notion that we will continue indefinitely to build individual homes for everyone seems to be disappearing: The costs of land and construction are simply prohibitive. Thus one of the big pulls to the suburbs—namely, that here one could own one's home—becomes increasingly problematic. Instead, more and more multistory dwelling units are being built in the suburbs.

There are those who have been prophesying for some time that breakthroughs in telecommunications will foreshadow the end of large cities for people will be able to interact with each other from near or great distances for very little cost. They will not have to agglomerate in one spot to interact. This may yet happen but not today or tomorrow.

The next point deals with the escape from urban pathology. Some pathology already exists in the suburbs, of course. This is partly an artifact of the way the police act when they pick up wild kids in the suburbs. They bring them home and tell the parents, "You'd better keep an eye on them; we caught them with drugs, we caught them with alcohol, etc." In the city, if there are no parents at home, the police may book them.

Then there is the question of whether, and to what extent, the headquarters of the various divisions of large corporations—and this is very important for New York—interface with each other. For example, is it in General Foods' best interest that the marketing division, the financing division, and the production division interface so that headquarters can move en bloc to White Plains? Or is each better off interfacing with the market and competition? DuPont is headquartered in Wilmington,

Delaware, a small city between nowhere and nowhere—that is, between Philadelphia and Baltimore. Since it was for so long such a self-contained heavy chemical company, its location did not handicap it. But its effective headquarters for textiles has long been New York; and now that it is putting more emphasis on consumer products, its location is increasingly dysfunctional.

I have long believed that one of the causes of the weakening of U.S. Steel has been its split headquarters operation, with the plants reporting to Pittsburgh and the financial decisions being made in New York City. The company really needed a closer integration of the two, but the bankers did not relish the idea of being in Pittsburgh.

New York and the other older cities do have a serious problem. Their infrastructure is aging, and they face colossal capital requirements. For example, the subway is in poor shape; sewers are wearing out; schools are old and need equipment replacement. New York has been suffering from undermaintenance for a long time and the remedy carries a high price.

The next thing we hear about is the attractiveness of the suburbs. We are told that the key decision makers—male executives—don't like the city, don't like to travel, and prefer suburban life. One of the consequences of the women's movement may be of advantage to the cities for if women, especially the better educated women, are to have real opportunities, they must be city-based or have easy access to the city. Women cannot easily operate a home in the country and work in the city; therefore, those executive husbands who like to live in the suburbs will have some new counterpulls. These are starting to come from their wives who are working in the city, and I suspect this may become increasingly important with the passage of time.

The declining birth rate ought to help the cities. If families are small, the cost of education decreases. Regrettably, the public schools are in a state of disrepair; I don't know how long it will take to turn them around. For families with only one or two children rather than four, private school, though not cheap, is at least within the limits of possibility for certain elite groups. Therefore, the city becomes a little bit less forbidding.

Although there are forces operating against the central city, let us remember the crucial fact that as the periphery becomes more crowded there is a spillover effect that actually helps the urban core—the periphery does not support itself. I think a rebalancing of forces is occurring.

I expect the suburbs and exurbia to grow, but I don't think the core is nearly as weak as it seemed during the 1950s, 1960s, 1970s. We may have gotten excited about many problems that, though very real and difficult, were not necessarily *city* problems. Rather, they may be national problems that happened to hit the cities especially hard.

Let us look at certain critical functions in the United States and their location. Take higher education, a major enterprise. We used to locate it in the hinterlands—consider Cornell and the big state universities. Today, no one wants to expand the big state universities in rural areas; instead we see the development of major branches of state universities in the large cities where the population is.

Major medical centers are another example. The future of medicine depends on the concentration of specialized talent in the medical specialties in a limited number of central cities, because a medical center needs a concentration of patients and staff. There can not be a neurosurgical unit without neuroradiologists, neuroanesthesiologists, and neurologists. So again we have an urban phenomenon.

Next, we are putting more money into the arts. What does this mean? By and large, the investment will go into large cities—their orchestras, theaters, and so forth. It is simply not possible to scatter large sums of money among many little groups in many little places.

Now we come to the matter of our becoming an increasingly consumption-oriented economy. Disposable income is growing, and one of the things people like to do with marginal dollars is to get some excitement from them. A few get their marginal excitement from trout streams and from beaches. But a good part of the excitement, especially if you live in a town of 10,000 or even 100,000, is not in the trout fishing, which you can do regularly—but in coming to the city. So I would say that consumption patterns pull people into large cities in considerable numbers.

I have emphasized talent as the key dynamic of the modern economy. In this respect, the range of talent offered by a large city is unmatched. This is the unique quality—and essence—of a large city. Take sports, an activity with important economic implications. You can not run big, modern commercialized sports without mass numbers of both talent and spectators. Where are the big developments? Again, they are in the big cities. And this is not unrelated to the subject of style, which we mentioned earlier.

What, then, is the shape of things to come?

The first proposition is that metropolitan areas, with cities as the urban center, are likely to continue to grow, with population draining into them from other areas.

There are no trends as yet that would seem to counter the continuing drainage of population into the metropolitan centers. At the same time, it seems inevitable that the larger increment of this growing urban population will locate on the periphery of the urban core. In turn, however, as suburbia and exurbia grow, this should contribute to the dynamism of the inner city. Exurbia and suburbia are not independent self-maintaining places. There is an interplay between these various segments of megalopoli.

Our second proposition: As options become narrowed between "out there" and "in here," many people will opt back to the central city— simply because despite its many negative features, it has many positive ones as well. I believe the negatives have been connected primarily with the redistribution of minority and low-income populations over the last twenty years. Our fantastic internal migrations seem to be quieting down; the minorities will become a quasi-majority; they will be assimilated into the life patterns of the city.

The excitement incident to this readjustment of the past twenty to thirty years will, I think, be reduced considerably. There are no longer that many people left to move—the big movement has taken place. Relatively, there are fewer blacks left in the rural parts of the United States than there are whites; in twenty years blacks have become a more urbanized population than whites. This, in fact, is the great impact of World War II and postwar changes.

The third proposition is that although people may continue to drift out of the central city, we may begin to see a considerable drift back as families get smaller and pass the critical years of family raising. People don't want big houses in the country after their children have left. We must, however, have houses and apartments in New York City that people can afford. I don't know exactly how we will build these; but I suggest that there are a thousand and one good reasons to live in the city, at least after a certain critical point in family rearing.

Obviously one of the things that has happened to many cities is that they have not had effective leadership during the past thirty years. The troublesome forces played themselves out without any attempt being made to mobilize the counterforces. It is unbelievable that in New York—the largest, most dynamic city in the history of the world— the business community, the government community, and the non-profit institutions were not able to mount an effective countercampaign until just now. These matters require a large amount of joint action. It is essential to establish organizational coalitions that will operate together.

In my neighborhood on the Upper West Side, when Alexander's wanted to build a department store, because a few people objected that they didn't like the kinds of jobs that Alexander's was going to provide, the store was not built. What kind of city permits a handful of vocal negatives to win out over a large number of silent positives?

It is simply a matter of political incompetence and lack of organization, plus timidity and fear. Obviously, New York is going to be in trouble if we go through a whole series of such episodes. We need more consensus-building groups.

Years ago, when I visited the Chamber of Commerce in Houston, they were figuring out ahead of time what the next great big dynamic push was going to be, after the last dynamic push had begun to level off. They had a planning operation that recognized that any force that was going to push the city ahead could not remain at the same angle of the projectile. They were working ahead of time to figure out the next dynamic.

We have a long way to go in New York City. We have had mayors who were so busy attending to other matters that essentials were long neglected. We really need some new efforts, but they need to be more serious than moves aimed at decentralizing a few functions.

Since the city is so hard pressed to provide a decent level of essential services, we are witnessing a major move in the direction of private services—from private guards who patrol the streets to commercial buses that bring people to work from outlying areas.

Years ago I wrote that there is nothing wrong with the U.S. economy that a more effective government structure would not cure. The same is true for large cities. The city can not resolve all its problems by itself; it needs a strong state. The state is one of the few instruments that can effectuate a new deal between the suburbs and the city, one of the few instruments that can do something about transportation and other key functions that must be attended to. We are not going to go for regional government that fast, but we can get some regional activities going if we have a reasonable liaison between the federal government, the states, and the cities. I think that is the link to strengthen.

There is no final escape for suburbanites from the problems they have been trying to get away from. That is the great hidden weapon of the city. Nations also believed that they could escape by isolation. We lived through an isolationist period in the United States, when we did not want to get entangled with foreign countries. There was no escape, however.

There is no escape now in the United States from resolving the black problem. It has been with us for over 350 years. We have neglected it; we have mistreated millions of people. The nation simply has to solve it. There is no escape. We cannot run away to the countryside; that is nonsense. There are a series of national problems that people do not want to deal with; but there is no escape, and the suburbs are beginning to learn that. For the first time, county administrators are finding that they have problems, that they need to come into alignments with New York City mayors. Otherwise, they cannot get consideration in Albany.

I believe we are beginning to fashion new political alliances, especially with the inner suburbs, which are not growing at all. They have real problems, for they have no place to go: They are locked in. I think we have a good chance of making the whole metropolitan area a more reasonable place because that is where most of the people are going to be.

If we do that, the inner city is still the best place to be because it costs less to get around, there are more people to interact with, and most of the capital equipment is located there—office buildings and infrastructure. My logic as an economist tells me that when you have the control over the choice land, the choice people, the best specialization, large metropolitan communities ought to flourish.

CHAPTER 41

New York: A View From the Seine

PARIS IS A GREAT CITY because the kings of France and their elected successors were able to spend huge public sums to build public monuments—from Notre Dame to the Invalides—within a contained, small space. The structures were built with an eye both to the immediate setting—Place de La Concorde, l'Etoile, etc.—and to the necessity for a larger balance between buildings and people, which the Parisians designate as the need for "green spaces"—the smaller and larger parks. When one realizes that the Hotel de Ville was rebuilt to reproduce what had stood on that spot before it was demolished by the Commune, one can appreciate the weight of the past in shaping the contours of the future. The slow progress in determining what should be erected to occupy the place of Les Halles, vacated a decade or so ago, is further evidence of the difficulties of finding solutions in which respect for the past often comes before the needs of the present and the future, in which ambience is as important as if not more important than as functionalism.

Although planners in New York City are placing increasing importance on the preservation of landmarks, there is little likelihood that, even if they succeed in gaining broad-scale support for their efforts, the preservation of the old will stand in the way of creation of the new. There

are relatively few buildings, monuments, settings of such historic or
aesthetic value to command public support for their protection against
sensible plans for modernization and redevelopment.

Although New York was once the nation's capital, it did not retain
that position for long. Paris has long been, is, and will long remain not
only the capital of France but also its dominant urban center. There are a
great many consequences of this reality, but none more important than
the long-term difference between the attitudes of the national governments of France and the United States for the present and future welfare
of their major city. To put the matter bluntly: France could not contemplate the bankruptcy of Paris. What happens to Paris is linked too closely
to the prestige of France. Although the mayor of Paris has recently been
engaged in a heated argument with the national government about who
should pay for the additional police required to provide security in the
city, the national government has long allocated large resources for the
city and its environs. While arguments continue in the United States
about the exchange relations between New York City and the federal
government in terms of taxes paid and benefits received, no one has yet
contended that New York City is specially favored by the federal government. The most extreme formulation suggests that the transfer system is
less unfair to New York than many have believed.

There are certain demographic differences between the two great
cities that warrant attention. Paris proper has a population of around 2
million. The population of the Paris region—the inner and the outer
rings—amounts to 8 million, bringing the combined total to around 10
million, or 20 percent of the national total. The comparable figures for
New York are 7.5 million in the city proper, another 5 million in the
inner ring, and an additional 5 million in the outer ring, adding up to 18
million or about 8 percent of the national total, a much smaller proportion than that of the Paris region.

Another critical difference relates to the scale of population mobility
including the in- and out-migration of foreign elements, citizens from
overseas areas as well as relatively large numbers of foreign workers.
Persons of color, North Africans and blacks alike, represent a high
population of the estimated 350,000 recent in-migrants to Paris. Though
substantial, this "foreign" element represents a relatively small part of
the total population in the Paris region, less than 4 percent compared
with a much higher and different concentration in New York City. In
Paris, three out of four residents live outside the city proper as a result of
the limited housing for the poor inside the city and national policy
aimed at dispersing them to the inner ring.

A related phenomenon is the heavy concentration of jobs in Paris
proper, circa 2 million for a resident population of 2.3 million. Every day

approximately 1 million workers from the inner and outer rings travel to Paris to work, sometimes spending up to two hours from home to workplace. The New York picture reveals a quite different pattern: Most of the newcomers are housed within the city proper, which is also where they work. The total number of commuters is no more than 600,000, or about one-fifth of total central-city employment, compared to one-half in Paris.

Looking at Paris, one cannot fail to note that New York City faces exacerbated difficulties as a consequence of lesser involvement of the national government in its well-being, the challenge it faces of absorbing much larger numbers of ethnic and racial minorities, and the fact that most of the newcomers live in the central city. Its one relative strength is the fact that it is less inhibited by the past than Paris, which provides it more freedom to direct its future.

IMPORTANT SIMILARITIES

These substantial differences, however, are only part of the story. There are considerable similarities on the surface and, particularly, beneath it. Both Paris and New York have lost population and jobs, although the shrinkage of jobs has been much more severe in New York than in Paris. Moreover, planners in both cities substantially miscalculated the rate of development of their respective regions and have been forced to cut back their estimates to a point at which the projections no longer closely resemble the figures they advanced as late as one decade ago. In both instances, demographic, economic, and social changes conspired to undermine the expectations of a rapid growth of population and jobs. The continuing rapid decline, more recently the prospective stabilization of the population, pulled one prop from under the expansionary estimates. The softening of the national, regional, and local economies pulled a second prop. The national decisions in France to force decentralization and diffusion away from Paris, and the counterpart market forces in the United States that have favored the Sunbelt, have eroded still another of the forces expected to stimulate growth. Finally, in both places, the middle class's preference for a primary or secondary home outside the urban area has slowed the inflow and speeded the outflow of the population from the cities proper.

Each of the two agglomerations retains great power and potential. But the intermediate prospects for both are little more than stabilization or, at most, modest growth. For the time being, the accelerated trend toward urbanization and ever larger metropolitan complexes appears to have been broken.

Both Paris and New York are, increasingly, service centers; manufacturing is declining in absolute terms and surely in relative terms as a producer of income and as an employer. To the extent that Parisians believe a quiet city must maintain some reasonable balance among groups of residents and groups of workers in a spread from the richer to the poorer, they are concerned about the same problem that New York faces. If manufacturing continues to erode, the poor will increasingly have difficulty in securing the types of work within the city that they are capable of performing and that can yield them a reasonable income. Paris, like New York, has begun to identify some areas at the center's periphery that might be suitable for small- and medium-sized manufacturing and is exploring how these areas might be prepared for new manufacturers. But in both cities suitable space is limited, and the problems of transporting people as well as raw and finished materials will be large. I surmise that only high value-added manufacturing (pharmaceuticals, advanced electronics, luxury products) will find the city congenial. It remains to be seen to what extent these more sophisticated products will provide useful employment for the newcomers and their poorly prepared children.

In both cities the children of the poor tend to be poorly prepared for work, primarily because academically oriented schools offer a curriculum that does not match their potential and interests and also because it is difficult to implement vocational training due to cost and design considerations.

In both cities, major improvements have taken place to facilitate the large-scale movement of workers from suburb to city—in Paris via the extension of the Metro, in the New York region via the improvement of the commuter railroads. If the old New York–New Haven line linking the high-income areas of Darien, Stamford, and Greenwich with the corporate headquarters complex in New York City had not been substantially improved in recent years, the out-migration of corporate headquarters might have cascaded to a point from which New York could never have recovered.

In both cities the leadership and, increasingly, the voters are concerned about upgrading the quality of the urban environment. Although both publics remain consumption-oriented—that is, they are interested in having more money to spend on private consumption—they are coming to realize that much of the satisfaction they can obtain depends on public amenities, from the quality of the air to the preservation of the natural environment. France's efforts to clean up the Seine and improve the neglected network of canals should serve as a reminder to New Yorkers of their unbelievable long-term neglect of the waterfront, which should be better maintained for public use and enjoyment. In the face of public resistance to higher taxes, it will take considerable ingenuity on the part of both public and private sectors to find the resources for the capital improvements and operating expenses needed to turn the desire for improved amenities into concrete action.

This discussion of amenities provides the backdrop for another parallel between the two great cities—the deepening conflicts over whom the city is to serve. The fact that half the housing in Paris dates from World War II and that the level of rents for comparable apartments is higher in Paris than in New York suggests that the private construction industry has received a great deal of government support—in the form of freedom to act as well as financial subsidies—to bring about so substantial and sustained a boom. Although there has been some public housing in the city proper, most of the effort has been directed at upgrading the quality of low-income housing, much of which lacks inside toilets and other amenities. Still, a considerable number of dwellings, even after recent efforts, fall far below acceptable U.S. standards.

New Yorkers are all too familiar with the lack of interest and concern of the richer suburban areas with the city's problems, despite the fact that up to 70 percent of the suburban income is city-generated. Our French counterparts spoke of the substantial tensions between Parisians and the people of the inner and outer rings. The litany of difficulties includes the desire of Parisians to maintain their very low real estate tax rates by not concerning themselves with establishing and maintaining amenities for their work force, many of whom live in the inner ring; the conviction of the suburban communities that they have no economic stake in improving transportation into the city (although 1 million commute daily); and the hostility of many smaller communities in the outer ring toward more affluent Parisians who have a second home in the outer ring but who make no positive contribution to the maintenance of long-term ambience, and whose presence in increasing numbers is undermining it. The details of the conflicts differ, but the lack of harmony between city and suburb is as deep in metropolitan Paris as in metropolitan New York. The resolution of such conflicts, too, is equally elusive.

One more important parallel is easier to sketch than to explain. If the lessons from comparative analysis are to be utilized, one should ask to what extent the large-scale investments that local or national governments undertake to shape the future of a metropolitan area via social infrastructure—new towns, transportation, suburbanized housing, regulation, and still other devices—achieve their goals in the face of uncontrollable elements. New York has been in the unfortunate situation for many years of having only a small capital budget to refurbish and expand its infrastructure. As the fiasco of the Second Avenue subway suggests, however, there is nothing easy about using public funds wisely, even when they are available. The recent history of Paris provides the following insights: Much private investment failed to go into the new towns, landing mainly in the interstices between the new areas and the city; new housing does not make a community—many of the foreign workers forced or encouraged to find housing in the inner rings have not become integrated into the community, the youngsters do poorly in schools, and the sense of alienation runs deep. When the Algerians return to their villages on holiday, their children are viewed as outsiders, a close parallel to what happens when New York–born Puerto Ricans return to the island, where they are nicknamed "Neo-Ricans."

As "world cities," Paris and New York are open to international influences that extend all the way from the flows of tourists to changes in the capital markets and the communications industries. Both cities are forced, at least in some measure, to find substitutes for the jobs and income they are losing not only in response to changes within their national economies but also in response to developments overseas, sometimes as far away as Southeast Asia or Latin America. It may be that once the great cities have lost most of their manufacturing—which has happened in Paris and New York—the next challenge they will face is whether they can protect and expand their commercial agglomeration. Both New York and Paris face some risks from the electronics revolution, which could speed the exit from the city center of a great amount of clerical and administrative work that does not require continued personal interaction with middle and top management.

Clearly there are a great many similarities in form and often in content between Paris and New York. To summarize: In both metropolitan areas population and employment are stabilizing or declining; their economies are increasingly service-oriented; protection of the environment has moved to the top of the public agenda; severe tensions exist between city and suburb; and both cities, despite their international importance, are vulnerable to forces they cannot control and cannot easily address.

REFLECTIONS ON THE PLANNING PROCESS

The American participants at the conference emphasized various efforts to respond to the unresolved social problems of urbanization in the New York area. They called attention to reconstruction efforts in Bedford-Stuyvesant, to neighborhood stabilization approaches aimed at preventing the flight of property owners before the onrush of poor and minority newcomers, to securing trade-offs with private builders through the incremental zoning efforts of the City Planning Commission, to assuring the location of attractive public spaces inside and outside of the new skyscrapers, and to establishing local community boards by such ambitious political reform as charter revision.

John Keith, head of the Regional Plan Association, provided an overview of the physical characteristics of the entire region under the sobriquet "spread city and spread region" and stressed the importance of rebuilding the inner city, not only in New York but in Newark, Jersey City, and Hoboken. With the exceptions of this overview and my analysis of the urban manpower condition, which focused on the larger macro and manpower programs, the French attendees were in something of a quandary, as evidenced by one of their questions: How many Bedford-Stuyvesants will the public sector, even with private assistance, be able to launch and carry through? No direct answer was forthcoming, but most of the Americans called attention repeatedly to the necessity of involving local groups in the formulation and implementation of urban policies directed toward facilitating the integration of the poor and racial minorities into the mainstream of urban life.

The French listened to us sympathetically, unsettled as they were by some of the unfavorable results of their more ambitious efforts at "planification," which included the establishment of five new cities as well as the new commercial center of La Defense some miles beyond l'Etoile. . . . But they failed to understand how our responses could possibly be adequate, given the scale of the social difficulties to which they were addressed. Time and again they stressed the importance of state action in the purchase of land and in the specification of its future use. Moreover, they had only recently come to the end of a very large and sustained capital investment boom that had included huge sums for public infrastructure, from transportation to housing. How New York could ever hope to make an impact on its serious problems of unemployment, underemployment, and poverty of its minority groups—ameliorated to some extent by time and the market—remained unexplained to them except by the casual remarks of Edward Costikyan that the federal government was making almost $750 million per year available to the city for manpower and community development programs and that the city's total budget for education approximates $3 billion. If these large sums could be effectively deployed and redeployed, both people and neighborhoods could be rehabilitated and their integration into the mainstream speeded.

The U.S. contingent called attention to the critical role of private realtors in the shaping and reshaping of the city and to the ever sharper conflicts between profit-seeking enterprises and community groups about new developments that threatened to alter the existing physical or social relations. Such conflicts, though not unknown within Paris proper, had surfaced only infrequently because large-scale redevelopment had never even been contemplated. The limited amount of land available for new construction is so limited as to reduce, if not eliminate, such conflicts.

Several recent developments have contributed to increasing the level of political tension in matters of urbanization in France. Only recently, the national government agreed that Paris could have its own mayor, who henceforth would speak for the city as a whole, not a particular district within the city. That the mayor is locked in combat with the president and represents a depressed region in the Parliament suggests the depth of the conflicts of interest that exist and that are not likely to be quickly resolved.

Then there is the matter of the Communist-dominated new towns in the inner ring, whose leaders surely see the world through different lenses from those of the spokesmen for the Parisian bourgeoisie. The actions of the national government with respect to the region as well as those of the city and the inner and outer rings are very much dominated by this interweaving of national, regional, and local politics and economies.

Politics, however, is not quite the same as participation, surely not local participation. Until now, Paris and its region have been shaped by large decisions of the national government, which have included a formal policy of decentralization. This commitment provided many of the resources required for the building of the five new cities, which never would have come into existence without these funds.

It is not clear what lay behind the accelerating trend of the national government to place increasing responsibility for decision making on Paris and on the surrounding communities. I suspect it is linked to a strong desire to shift financial responsibility for the Paris-region infrastructure from other regions—as reflected in the national budget—to the local tax base.

The same weakness in structure and power for mounting regional activities exists in Paris and New York. Much of the politician's time and effort in Paris is directed not to working out common solutions to common problems—from improved interurban transportation to the appropriate balance of amenities between central city and the outskirts—but to never-ending arguments over who should pay for what, which result in many desirable actions being delayed indefinitely.

The best way to summarize the changing planning-political process in the two metropolises is to quote the comment of a French participant that while the day of the technician (planner) is coming to an end, that of the politician is coming to the fore.

SOME FINAL OBSERVATIONS

One need not look closely at Paris to appreciate that New York City and its region continue to face major hurdles in human and economic development if the existing urban concentration is to remain vital. There is both disquietude and comfort to be drawn from such a perspective. If the Paris region has difficulty in absorbing a relatively small number of foreigners, the magnitude of the task facing New York becomes that much clearer. The French have not thrown in the sponge, but they are looking to strengthen the attractiveness of manual work—better working conditions, better pay, and better benefits—with the hope and expectation that they will become less dependent on foreign workers without whom at present most of the region's unpleasant work would not be done. If Michael Piore is right, this effort is likely to fail, since he has argued persuasively that in every country native residents shy away from accepting the "worst jobs." But as we know from the experience of the New York City Sanitation Department, bad jobs can be transformed into good jobs—at a price. So the French may find a practical, if not total, solution to their present heavy reliance on foreign workers, whom the French are unable to absorb into their social fabric.

The French, as noted earlier, are looking to policies and programs that will encourage the return migration of foreigners to their homelands—an unlikely outcome, particularly for their children who, born on French soil, are citizens. New Yorkers, on the contrary, must recognize—if they think about the problem at all—that blacks and Puerto Ricans will not leave. They have no place to go. The most that can be anticipated is a relative shrinkage of these minority groups within the total population as newcomers cease to migrate, the local poor enter a much lower reproduction level, and more whites return to the city. Even this outcome is problematic, some might say highly problematic. In short, New Yorkers have clear-cut alternatives. Either they develop policies that will speed the successful integration of minority groups into the life and work of the city, or the city has no real future. Unlike the French, New Yorkers need to waste no additional time pursuing phantom solutions.

It is necessary to improve the decision-making mechanisms in the city proper and, in fact, at the national level, where actions affect the urban area and its people so heavily. Paris has decided that there is a limit to the reliance that should be placed on planners. True, one must try to see into the future as clearly as possible before committing very large public (and private) funds for infrastructure and other types of investment. But the best of planners cannot succeed; they can only reduce the margin of error. The French have come to recognize a further limitation to excessive reliance on planners. The people affected by their decisions have been ignored, and even in an imperfect democracy the continued neglect of the community in urban development and redevelopment spells trouble.

What about New York, where planning is so weak, where local community boards have demonstrated a growing capacity to delay almost every worthwhile project until it no longer can attract investors, public or private? As Edward Costikyan pointed out at the Paris Conference, the City Planning Board has been slow to recognize that now that the local boards are in place, the Planning Board's primary responsibility is to speak for the city as a whole, not as an advocate of local groups.

Moreover, both Paris and New York are seriously deficient in implementing effective *regional* decision-making bodies. Much of the required structure is not in place; worse, the political understanding and consciousness required to make regional bodies effective are lacking. It would appear that for all of New York's shortcomings, it is less deficient than Paris in such mechanisms.

A related observation is the growing restiveness of the national government in France about continuing its heavy involvement in the life and work of the city just at a time when the federal government in the United States has begun to formulate an urban policy. In Paris, the political leadership fears the result of the tensions reflecting the division of the country into two parts: the Paris region (Paris and the Ile de France) and the rest of the country. As budgetary demands multiply and additional resources are difficult to marshal, the national government is seeking to force Paris and the region to assume more responsibility for their own future. In addition, the national government continues its policy to force dispersion of people and industry out of the Paris region whenever the opportunity arises, a policy that has begun to evoke concern of some critical observers that the unique agglomeration will be weakened without any real gain for the rest of the country.

The current stage of U.S. urban policy can be described as a "hope and a lick." The same administration that has made a commitment to the cities is also advocating a stepped-up tax write-off on new investments that cannot fail to attract people and jobs out of older cities.

One final point: Every society is composed of groups which share interests and goals with other groups. At the same time, however, there are conflicts, often severe, in the ideology, objectives, and mechanisms to which these groups are attached. The future well-being of every society depends on the relative strength of the forces for consensus versus those that are divisive. Nothing is more divisive in France than the continuing conflicts between the bourgeoisie, which seeks to protect its property, and the working population, which seeks status in a society in which status depends on the possession of capital (including human capital). The tensions among the national government, Paris, and the region cannot be understood solely by this gross generalization; but it provides more weight than any single alternative hypothesis. What is more, it suggests that the development of greater consensus in the face of these deeply rooted differences over property will not come early, if at all.

The New York situation is somewhat different. The key to its problem at national, regional, and local levels is more closely rooted in matters of race, although race of course is closely linked to such basic economic issues as opportunity and income.

It is hard to predict whether Americans will face up sooner or later, or after it is too late, to reducing and removing the canker of race that is the principal source of urban infection, and that, if not treated effectively, will jeopardize the future of the nation. The conference on Paris and New York took place in May 1978 against the backdrop of the massacre in Zaire, an event with the most serious racial implications, which was not discussed but was never far from the consciousness of the participants. If consensus leads to intensified action, the two great cities have a secure future. But no city, great or small, can survive if one part of the populace decides it has more to gain from conflict than from participation.

CHAPTER 42

New York City:
Next Turn of the Wheel

THE FORTIETH ANNIVERSARY of the New York City Planning Commission occurs in the same year as the fortieth anniversary of the Conservation of Human Resources Project at Columbia University, which I have directed since its inception. Our initial research was focused on studying the long-term unemployed in the city (*The Unemployed,* Harper, 1943) just before the mobilization for World War II turned the economy around. In fact, I have experienced no fewer than five turns of the wheel during my adult years in the city. The first four are:

- The New Era (the 1920s). This period ended with the stock market crash of 1929. These years saw the early stages of out-migration from the city, the early weakening of manufacturing, the strengthening of business services, and the development of many favorable and unfavorable trends cheek by jowl.
- The Great Depression (1930–1940). Prior to the New Deal (1933), this era saw people scavenging in refuse cans for food and men

standing on street corners selling apples at five cents a piece to earn their next meal.

- The World War II period and the years up to the 1970s. This was a period of major changes, including the 4 million swap in population. Two million middle-class whites moved to the suburbs, while in-migration and high birth rates resulted in the addition of 2 million blacks and Puerto Ricans. These years also saw the great commercial building boom, the continuing decline of manufacturing, the further growth of the service economy.

- The Seventies (1970–1978). The first five years of this decade saw the rapid weakening of the economic and financial foundations that culminated in the crisis of 1975, and the slow upward trek since then. Alongside the loss of 600,000 jobs—and probably 400,000 people—these years also saw one new source of strength— the increased inflow of foreign money and people.

Within my adult years, then, I have seen no fewer than four major turns of the wheel—five, if, as I believe, we are now on the threshold of a new upward turn in the city's fortunes. Although there is always room for differences of opinion about what the facts disclose and what the trends may reveal, this reference to the past should be a warning to one and all—that a great metropolitan conurbation has great resilience. It is an error to underestimate its recuperative powers.

This is how I see the next turn of the wheel, which, in my view, has already begun.

POPULATION ADJUSTMENTS

I would expect the city to move toward a lower population level, somewhere between 6.8 and 7.2 million, down some 10 percent or more from the long-term peak of 8 million. If this occurs, it will prove easier for a new balance to be achieved between job seekers and jobs. The city will not need to return to the 3.8 million job level to provide employment opportunities for all who seek work. The passage of time implies that the children of the newcomers who came in the 1950s and 1960s should find the city less difficult to negotiate: It is their city. In a recent study, *The Corporate Headquarters Complex in New York City*, we found that 160,000 blacks were employed in this cutting edge of the city's economy— admittedly, mostly on the lower and middle rungs, but still employed in a sector where opportunities for advancement were greatest.

Two more points about recent and prospective population trends:

The major streams of poor people from the South and Puerto Rico have ceased, and the city is in fact losing some. On the other hand, immigrants from Asia are increasing. New York now boasts the largest Chinese community in the United States. It has also been receiving large numbers of Indians, Pakistanians, Koreans, and other Asians, many of whom have skills and entrepreneurial talents. They are taking over many of the retail stores from Jewish and other older ethnic group owners.

MAGNET FOR FOREIGN TALENT AND CAPITAL

Ever since Hitler, and even before, the city has been a haven for middle- and upper-income groups of professionals, capitalists, and other persons with money and talent who desired or were forced to leave their homelands. My associates and I recently completed a study on *The Economic Impact of the Japanese Business Community in New York*, which revealed that the Japanese accounted for close to 60,000 jobs and $800 million of annual income. Between 1970 and 1976 foreign deposits in the banks of New York City increased from $10 billion to over $40 billion. The names on the stores on Fifth Avenue north of 50th Street reveal the extent to which Italian retailers have been attracted by the luxury trade in the city. With political instability in Europe, the Middle East, Latin America, and South Africa, New York City should be able to look forward to receiving a steady stream of rich and capable foreigners for many years to come.

THE WORLD CITY

In-migrants and immigrants are only the tip of the iceberg. The expansion of the U.S. and world economies should provide a continuing stimulus to the city's economy. Despite its recent troubles, New York remains the dominant city in the United States, far in advance of Chicago, Los Angeles, and Houston. It is not likely to be seriously challenged by any of them in the years ahead, considering Chicago's climate, Houston's congestion, and Los Angeles' spread—not to stress New York's many assets as the center of finance and the arts. The same is true in terms of its competitive advantage over other world cities: New York has relatively little to fear from London, Paris, Moscow, Tokyo. Consider London, the center of a lagging United Kingdom economy; Paris, with a population of less than 2 million; Moscow's combination of climate and communism; and Tokyo's location and language. New York has every prospect of remaining *the* world city.

THE TRANSFORMATION FROM MANUFACTURING TO SERVICES

While New York has seen the erosion of about 600,000 manufacturing jobs—almost one out of every six jobs—there are two upbeat observations to be made about this doleful development. It is likely that most of the manufacturing jobs, which were vulnerable in the sense that their output could be produced more cheaply elsewhere, have already been lost. What remains for the most part are manufacturing jobs required to meet the very large local and regional market (printing, food, and clothing, for example) and jobs where New York has a comparative advantage because of style. Further, with about four out of every five jobs located outside of manufacturing and construction—that is, in services, broadly defined—the city's economy is better positioned towards the future with its great strength in high value-added business services, from banking to management consulting. That is the direction of the nation's and the world's economy, and New York is already out in front.

CHANGING LIFE–STYLES: CITY AND SUBURBS

There is no question that the recent troubles of the city were in large measure the direct consequence of the suburbanization process, which resulted in the heavy loss of the middle-class population with subsequent decline in urban amenities as reflected in street crime, the decline of the schools, and many other dysfunctional concomitants. No one should assume, particularly in light of the cessation of new construction for middle-class families, that this outflow will soon turn around; but there are some favorable trends. The city has always attracted young people of talent. What is new is the much-enlarged group of career women whose prospects of advancement are best if they are city-based. Since many of these women marry career-oriented men (two able law graduates started life this year with an annual income of $56,000), they can readily cope with the high rents in the city. If they eventually decide to have a child, or even two, they should still be able to remain in the city, making use of private schools. The renewal of selected neighborhoods in the southern part of Manhattan and the near sections of Brooklyn speaks to these new urban settlers. They are almost certain to increase in the years ahead. The gentrification of the city is definitely under way.

TRANSFER INCOME

While the city has suffered from the large increase of unemployed and poor people over the last decades, it has not been generally appreciated that these people also attract funds from higher levels of government that contribute to the local economy — not enough perhaps but still significant. At the end of the 1960s transfer income to individuals in the city amounted to under $4 billion or slightly more than 10 percent of total income; in 1976 the figure was $9.4 billion and accounted for 17.6 percent of total income.

LIABILITIES INTO ASSETS

People in other sections of the country are uneasy, if not hostile, to New York City because they see it as a center filled with immigrants, minorities, foreigners, radicals, offbeat types. Their view that New Yorkers are less tied to the dominant American value structure is correct, but this tilting of the city is not all bad. The regional director of the Bureau of Labor Statistics, Herbert Bienstock, recently estimated that there are about 600,000 jobs in the city where knowledge of a second language is an asset. The continued growth of economic relations with Latin America makes the point: Knowledge by many New Yorkers of Spanish is clearly an asset; and the same goes for knowledge of Chinese, Russian, Japanese, German, and other tongues and cultures.

There is also a negative side, however. Many young people going through the local schools are failing to master the essentials: Lack of knowledge of written English is a serious handicap, as is an inability to handle numbers. The new chancellor of the Board of Education, Frank Macchiarola, is alert to these serious shortcomings and is determined to reduce them. With close to half a billion dollars of CETA funds flowing into the city from Washington, we ought to be able to put many more through successful second-chance programs.

THE FOREIGN DIMENSION

Reference was made earlier to the inflow of capital and competence from abroad and of the expanded economic relations with overseas. But such ties are growing in both directions. Consider the following: About three out of four foreign companies planning to establish a headquarters in the

United States prefer the New York area, and most of them locate in the city. Tourism has become the city's second-largest earner, and there is no reason to believe that it is near peaking—that is, unless we only build new hotels where the room charge is $80 per night and up! Still another favorable trend is the de facto devaluation of the dollar against many of the major currencies. It always takes time for the trade effects of foreign-exchange shifts to work their way through the system. To illustrate: North Carolina textile manufacturers who do their selling and shipping through New York City report that they are now competitive in the world's markets with Hong Kong.

CREATIVE POTENTIAL: THE WORLD'S MEDICAL CENTER

Shortly after World War II the leadership in Houston decided that one way its plans for growth could be speeded was to attract an outstanding medical leader and to build a major industry around him. They persuaded Dr. Michael DeBakey to relocate from New Orleans to Houston, and over the succeeding decades he did in fact contribute greatly to making Houston the leading medical center in the South. New York City has seven medical schools, outstanding teaching hospitals, by far the largest array of clinicians in this or any other city. The question that suggests itself is: What would it take in the form of improved linkages among the medical institutions and special transportation and living accommodations for prospective patients to realize the full potential of these medical assets, especially in attracting and treating well-to-do foreigners? The newspapers report horror stories about how bad conditions are in municipal hospitals and they point to excess beds, Medicaid mills, and much else on the seamy side. But if truth be told, New York has unique strengths and the potential for delivering more first-class medical care.

PUBLIC–PRIVATE INTERFACE

Great cities need great benefactors—kings, legislators, multimillionaires. New York has had the good fortune to gain greatly from the beneficence and determination of the Rockefeller family, not once but four times— Rockefeller Center, the United Nations complex, Chase Manhattan Plaza, and the late Governor Nelson Rockefeller's World Trade Center. But the larger the city, the greater its challenges, the more complicated the task of building and renewal. We have reached the point where public-private sector cooperation is essential to plan and implement major changes. That is the moral of Lincoln Center, and that will be the story of the transformations still to come. The key to future innovation and growth lies in strengthening the interface of the private and public sectors, not only for large public projects but also for the creation and maintenance of a conducive environment for economic and social progress.

A decade ago effective relations between the two sectors were largely nonexistent. Politicians and corporate executives went their respective ways, assuming that if each did his thing all would be well. The crisis of 1975 exploded that myth. Default was prevented only because the politicians, the bankers, and the trade unions—with an assist from Albany and Washington—learned to work together. The major challenge at the end of the 1970s is that they stay together beyond finding a permanent solution to the financial crisis, and cooperate broadly on all facets of economic development, from speeding the Convention Center to lobbying for sensible tax and expenditure policy. An inviting challenge would be the development of the city's waterfront, a much-neglected asset. Mayor Edward I. Koch has already announced that the revitalization of the waterfront is a high priority of his administration.

The Next Turn of the Wheel

It is always dangerous to tempt fate by forecasting what lies ahead, but there are several signs that suggest that the next turn of the wheel has begun. A year ago the leaders of the real estate industry did not expect a revival to occur before the early 1980s, but in fact 1978 saw the turn. New York City's employment outlook, though still cloudy, may be turning. Costs in the city are rising less rapidly than in other major cities. Race relations are a step or two ahead of other metropolitan areas. The arts are flourishing. Talented young people—the source of future economic well-being—continue to flock to New York.

Of course, many negatives remain: Poor schools, high relief rolls, dirty streets, excessive crime, shortage of middle-class housing, arson in the ghetto, the erosion of city services, and many other dysfunctional aspects are there for all to see.

Cities operate in open economies. Their future is greatly affected not only by what they themselves do—or fail to do—but by actions at state and federal levels. The tight budget that President Carter has announced for fiscal 1980 and beyond underscores that the city's problem will not be substantially reduced, much less solved by actions in Washington.

What about Albany? No one who followed the containment of the financial crisis of 1975 and the successive efforts can question the constructive role that Governor Hugh L. Carey played. But it is fair to say that to date Albany has done less than one might have expected, or hoped for, in providing additional financial aid. True, the state had first to get its own house in order. Now that it has done so, there is reason for hard-pressed New York City to look for a helping hand.

Mayor Koch has indicated that he plans to remove from the city's budget several costly programs such as higher education and mental health in the hope and expectation that the state will pick them up. Governor Carey has signaled his intention to seek a new allocation formula for state aid to education that could provide important additional assistance to the city. There are many other ways the state can help, both directly and indirectly—not least by encouraging its intermediaries, such as the Port Authority, to play a more active role in the economic development of the region, which now appears to be in the cards.

But important as the federal and state governments have been and will continue to be, New Yorkers know in their heart of hearts that it is up to them to solve as many of their own problems as possible. Only then will external aid assure that the wheel keeps turning in the right direction.

CHAPTER 43

Corporate Headquarters Complex

THIS EXECUTIVE SUMMARY presents the principal findings and policy directions of a year long study of the Corporate Headquarters Complex in New York City carried out by the Conservation of Human Resources Project, Columbia University, under a grant from the Rockefeller Brothers Fund with the active participation of an advisory committee of corporate leaders and professionals. The focus is on the corporate headquarters and on the corporate service firms (financial, legal, accounting and other) that are concentrated in Manhattan's central business district. Account is also taken of firms providing ancillary services to these corporate enterprises such as printing firms, hotels, restaurants, and entertainment establishments.

Since the fiscal crisis of 1975 many studies have addressed aspects of New York City's economy, but they have concentrated on the steep decline in manufacturing and the high tax burdens on businesses and individuals resulting from the heavy expenditures of municipal and state government. In contrast, the present inquiry is focused on the corporate headquarters complex to determine whether the forces that brought about the unparalleled agglomeration of managerial, financial, and professional power that made New York first among the great com-

mercial centers of the world are persisting or whether counterforces have
begun to undermine this complex.

This inquiry into the future of the agglomeration process—the
clustering together of firms that gain from easy face to face interactions
with each other on which the corporate headquarters complex rests—
analyzed the information contained in various local, state, and federal
governmental reports in an effort to learn more about the agglomeration
process. Further, a sample of twenty-seven corporations was developed,
including companies whose headquarters remained in New York City,
moved to the suburbs, or relocated to more distant places, with an aim of
interviewing senior executives so that we could better understand their
decision making when they confronted the issue of remaining in the city
or relocating. In addition, these executives were asked to fill out a
detailed questionnaire containing factual information that threw additional light on the background and consequences of their locational
decisions.

The members of the advisory committee made their extensive experience available to the staff and several developed special data, based on
their own operations, that threw additional light on the corporate headquarters complex in New York. Finally, as the chairman of the advisory
committee has already noted, the staff was able to make liberal use of the
new data and analyses contained in their colleague Robert Cohen's
forthcoming book on *The Corporation and the City.*

FINDINGS

The findings relate to four important areas: (1) the scale, scope, and
significance of the corporate headquarters complex for the economy of
New York City; (2) the increasing mobility of corporate headquarters;
(3) the continued concentration of corporate service firms in the city;
(4) the growing interest of foreigners in locating overseas branches of
their banks and corporate headquarters in New York.

Corporate Headquarters Complex

1. This complex accounts for over one-fifth of all wage and sala-
    ried workers (586,000 workers) and a considerably higher propor-
    tion, over one-fourth, of total payroll ($8.7 billion). As such, it
    represents the largest aggregation of economic activity in the
    city, considerably larger in terms of jobs and income than

manufacturing, municipal government, or nonprofit enterprises.

2. Corporate headquarters employment is the smallest of the three components of the complex, accounting for 135,000 jobs. The largest element is the corporate service firms, which provide 314,000 jobs. Employment in firms producing ancillary services is estimated at 137,000.

3. Employment in corporate service firms is around 2.5 times larger than in corporate headquarters. What is more, whereas employment in corporate headquarters is much lower now than in the early 1960s, the opposite is true with respect to corporate service firms.

4. The concept of *corporate headquarters* hides almost as much as it discloses. It may refer to a company with 3,000 employees in the central business district that includes top management, operating divisions, and supporting administrative and office personnel. On the other hand, it can include no more than fifty persons, consisting of the chief executive officer, the financial vice-president, and secretarial and clerical staff. To complicate matters further, when a corporation relocates its headquarters out of the city, it may leave behind a smaller or larger segment of its former headquarters, such as the financial, international, legal, or marketing division or divisions.

The Increasing Mobility of Corporate Headquarters:

5. There has been much understandable concern about the economic loss entailed when large corporations relocate their headquarters out of New York City. Of the 128 corporations on the *Fortune* 500 list with headquarters in the city in 1965, only 62 were still in New York a decade later. But the facts are not all that ominous: 28 corporations were added to the list, 6 by moving in and 22 by reclassification due to growth or mergers. Of the 66 corporations that were lost, 7 no longer qualified and 21 were merged. The hard data are that New York lost 38 headquarters, 25 to the suburbs and 13 to more distant locations.

6. New York City has not been alone in the loss of corporate headquarters. In the two decades between the mid-1950s and the mid-1970s, the number of *Fortune* 500 headquarters located in the principal metropolitan areas declined not only in New York but in most other centers including Chicago, Philadelphia, Detroit, Pittsburgh, and St. Louis. In 1957 the ten largest metropolitan areas in the Northeast and North Central states accounted for

302 headquarters; by 1974 the total had shrunk to 237, a decline
of about one-fifth. The New York metropolitan area suffered a
somewhat greater loss, approximately one-fourth. This national
trend points up that large corporations have increased mobility
with respect to the location of their headquarters and that an
increasing number no longer feel compelled to remain in one of
the nation's large metropolitan areas.

7. Among the key factors encouraging corporate headquarters
   mobility are the following:
   a. Improved and less costly air transportation. Between 1950
      and 1975 air fares declined 2.4 percent per annum in con-
      stant dollars.
   b. Improved and less costly telephone communications. Between
      1960 and 1975 long distance telephone rates between New
      York and Chicago and San Francisco declined respectively 5
      and 7 percent per annum in constant dollars.
   c. Both improved highway transportation and the growing
      number of married women in the labor force made it pos-
      sible for corporations relocating in outlying areas to secure
      adequate support personnel.

8. The deterioration of New York City's competitive position as a
   headquarters city came as a result of the following developments:
   a. New York State's progressive income tax imposes an extra
      burden, unmatched in other states, on key executives who
      have substantial influence over where the corporation's head-
      quarters is located.
   b. A growing discrepancy between New York City and the
      Sunbelt cities in the costs of living for key personnel. In 1976
      the budget for a higher living standard for a family of four
      was $29,700 in New York City compared to $21,500 in Atlanta
      and Houston.
   c. Space costs at the end of the 1960s, which on an index of 100
      for New York found Greenwich at 67, San Francisco 69,
      Atlanta 33, and Houston 37. A substantial narrowing of this
      gap occurred in the 1970s, with San Francisco at 100 and
      Houston at 78 in 1976.
   d. Wage rates for secretaries and clerks in New York tend to be
      higher than in other metropolitan centers. Moreover, the
      increase in these wages between 1965 and 1975 was somewhat
      greater in New York than in other areas. Further, New York
      personnel appear to have a shorter work week.

9. On the basis of our interviews with the chief executive officers
   or their surrogates the following summarizes the principal rea-

sons for a corporation's moving its headquarters out of New York City:

   a.   The precipitating factor in most cases was the termination of a lease or pressure to consolidate elements of a headquarters that were scattered in multiple locations throughout the city.

   b.   The increasing difficulty that corporations faced in reassigning middle management to headquarters because of the growing negatives in the New York City environment ranging from high personal taxes to the lack of personal safety.

   c.   The long, costly, and until recently poor commuting both on the New York, New Haven & Hartford and the Long Island Railroads. Relocation to the suburbs could bring the headquarters closer to the homes of senior executives.

   d.   The growing belief that continued location in the city was no longer essential to accomplish corporate goals and that many benefits could be achieved by relocating a headquarters to a suburban location including lower personal income taxes for managerial personnel, lower space cost, greater efficiency through consolidation, less time spent in commuting, and overall a reduced hassle.

   e.   Finally, some of the principal economic benefits that New York City provided would not be jeopardized by the move out to the suburbs. The corporation could still keep its link with its corporate service firms in the city, have ready access to nearby airports, and continue to make use of the city's cultural and entertainment resources.

10. Corporations whose headquarters continue to be New York–based include those that did not face explicitly the problem of relocation, those that considered relocation but decided to remain in the city, and a few that moved in. These are the principal advantages they see from a New York City location:

   a.   Avoiding the internal disruption of a major relocation that could result in a loss of momentum if large numbers of supporting staff had to be recruited and trained to man the new site.

   b.   Having their managerial personnel continue to operate in an urban setting where the pace is fast and exhilarating and where the exchange of critical information is facilitated.

   c.   The ability to bring together on short notice senior corporate personnel and key members of the corporate service firms whenever such meetings are required.

11. Various statistical tests failed to reveal any clear-cut differences

in the performance of the movers versus the nonmovers except for one finding: The corporations that remained in New York had a more rapid increase in their overseas sales. It should be emphasized, however, that some of the consequences arising out of relocation may be delayed. The most important issue that remains moot is the quality of future management of corporations whose executives lack the stimulating environment of a large metropolis.

The Concentration of Corporate Services

12. As noted earlier, corporate service firms continued to expand and more than compensated for the decline in corporate headquarters employment that occurred during the past two decades. The three most important subgroups among corporate service firms are banking, legal services, and accounting. The importance of each is underscored by the following:

   a. In banking, the 10 largest commercial banks in the nation accounted, at the end of 1976, for 45 percent of the deposits in the top 200 banks. Six of these top 10 are New York banks, which account for $173 billion or 27 percent of the deposits of these 200 largest banks. When it comes to foreign deposits in U.S. banks, which totaled $161 billion at the end of 1976, the New York City banks are even more important: They held $86 billion, or more than half the total of these foreign deposits.

   b. In terms of the large law firms (over eighty-one members) that provide a wide range of specialized corporate services, New York has one-third of the nation's total, 16 out of 48; while Chicago has 7; and Philadelphia and Washington each have 5. If these data for the mid-1970s are compared with those for the mid-1950s, one finds little change other than an increase of large law firms in Washington from two to five. During this same period New York also maintained a leadership role as a center of firms specializing in international law, the number of such firms in the city increasing from 54 to 131, the number of members from around 600 to about 2,250. The other principal centers of firms specializing in international law are Washington, Chicago, Houston, and Los Angeles. The New York law firms serve far more *Fortune* 500 headquarters, both in and out of the city, than do the big law firms located in any other city. Further, they serve almost all of the *Fortune* 500 firms' investment banks.

c. In accounting, six of the big eight firms have their main office in New York City. The New York–based firms have as clients 356 of the *Fortune* 500 list and 29 of the nation's 47 largest banks. Chicago is in second place, far behind New York, with 79 *Fortune* 500 corporations and 6 banks. The international offices of all eight major accounting firms are located in New York City.

13. The continued concentration of corporate service firms in New York rests on the strength of the agglomeration process, which, with minor exceptions noted later, keeps these firms cheek by jowl in the central business district of Manhattan:

a. The banks are constrained by state law from moving freely to new locations.

b. The investment banking houses, with one or two exceptions, have not made any serious effort to relocate, a reflection of their need to have frequent, almost continuing face-to-face contacts with one another.

c. A considerable number of the large New York law firms have moved to open branches abroad (Paris and London) and to a lesser extent in Washington to take care of key clients or to take advantage of an exceptional demand for their specialized skills. But to date there has been almost no relocation to suburban settings.

d. The major accounting firms have moved to establish a national network of branch offices, as the result of which they increasingly handle some part of the work for corporations that have relocated their headquarters from a nearby suburban branch.

e. Overwhelmingly, marketing, advertising, public relations, management consulting, and other corporate service firms continue to serve their corporate clients that have relocated to the suburbs from their New York City offices. Occasionally one or another of their corporate service firms has been willing to open a branch office to serve a major corporate client in the suburbs.

f. There is little likelihood that there will be a sufficient concentration of corporate headquarters in any suburban location in the near future that would lead to a substantial relocation of corporate service firms such as commercial banks, investment banks, and large law firms.

g. The fact that corporate service firms serve many clients outside the New York area further tends to keep them concentrated in the central business district of Manhattan.

14. In sharp contrast to the difficulties that various corporate head-quarters reported in reassigning middle management to New York City, no significant evidence was uncovered that talented professionals interested in successful careers in banking, corporate law, accounting, or management consulting were declining positions in New York City. Admittedly they sought initial salaries and subsequent increments that took into account the higher cost of living in the city. But the corporate service firms have been able to continue to attract the talent they need.

15. The interviews throw additional light on the continuing linkage between corporate headquarters that have relocated and their corporate service firms. Many corporate executives assumed that most of the inconvenience resulting from their relocation would be borne by the bankers, lawyers, accountants, and other specialized personnel on whom they rely for technical assistance. But there was some evidence in our interviews that these corporate executives underestimated the time costs to themselves in keeping in constant touch with these specialists and the additional dollar costs added to their bills by professionals whose charges reflect their total time devoted to a client.

16. Although corporate moveouts, even to a nearby suburb, represent a loss to the city's economy in terms of jobs, purchasing power, rent, and taxes, a critical issue is whether the corporation continues to use the corporate service firms located in the city. Our interviews reveal that the corporations that moved to the suburbs continued to use the same banking, legal, accounting, marketing, advertising, and other service firms that they had used when they were located in the central business district. Their continued reliance on these corporate service firms helps explain the continued preeminence of the city as a corporate headquarters complex.

17. Relatively low cost, fast, and frequent air travel has contributed to the growth of the corporate services sector by enabling service companies, particularly those with highly specialized skills, to serve industrial corporations and others in major metropolitan areas throughout the country. There has been widespread exporting of these skills from a New York base.

The International Dimension

18. The last two decades have seen a substantial increase in economic relations between the United States and foreign countries

with respect to financial transactions, trade, and investments in plant. Much of this expansion has been through firms located in New York. In the mid-1970s the foreign sales of the *Fortune* 500 firms in the top fifty Standard Metropolitan Statistical Areas totaled $213 billion. Corporations located in the New York area accounted for $99 billion, or 46 percent of that total. Detroit was second with $21.5 billion followed by Pittsburgh, San Francisco, and Chicago, each with between $15 and $11 billion.

19. The more striking development, however, has been the growth of foreign economic activity in New York City, reflecting in particular the location here of banks, branch headquarters, and increased activity in the real estate market, as evidenced by the following:

   a. An analysis in the early 1970s of over 1,700 foreign firms operating in the United States disclosed that 60 percent were headquartered in New York City and another 15 percent in the suburban area. If the location of Canadian firms is disregarded, the concentration in New York City ranged between 98 percent for Italian firms to 68 percent for firms from the Netherlands.

   b. Between 1970 and 1976 the number of foreign banks in New York City increased from 47 to 84 and their assets increased from $10.6 billion to $40.3 billion or almost four-fold.

   c. Between the beginning of 1975 and 1977, foreign concerns leased 466,000 square feet of office space in New York City with an aggregate rental value of $88 million. From September 1975 to April 1977 there were ten major purchases by foreigners of New York City properties.

20. New York's attraction to foreign businessmen rests on several important assets including:

   a. Superior air transportation. In 1975 there were 6 million enplaned international passengers, 2.9 million of them from the New York area, or over 39 percent of the nation's total. In the first week of May 1977 there were out of New York seventy-three direct flights to London, thirty-eight to Paris, and twenty-eight to Tokyo; from Los Angeles the comparable numbers were twenty-one, ten, and thirty-eight; and from Houston, none.

   b. By international standards reasonable living costs. In 1976 the cost of selected goods and services in New York was one-third lower than in Tokyo, about 10 percent lower than in Stockholm and Geneva, and about the same as in Paris and Brussels.

    c. The availability of a large bilingual and multilingual labor force that facilitates staffing.

    d. The rich intellectual, cultural, and entertainment resources available in the city.

    e. The cosmopolitan nature of the resident population and its tolerance for people from foreign lands.

POLICY DIRECTIONS

The future of a great metropolis such as New York City is not subject to direct control by any one or even multiple groups, no matter how great their economic or political power. Changes in technology, markets, international affairs, national policy, and life-styles will determine the future of the city. But if most of the shaping forces are not subject to direct control, some can be channeled so that their impact is positive rather than injurious.

The following sets forth the policy directions growing out of the in-depth inquiry into agglomeration that hold promise of contributing to the continual growth and vitality of the corporate headquarters complex in New York City:

1. With the corporate headquarters complex in New York greatly dependent on the city's primacy as a money center, the leaders of the financial community, together with the local political leadership, should be constantly alert to actions in New York, Albany, and Washington that could strengthen the predominance of the city as the leading financial center of the world. The recent debacle over the bond transfer tax illustrates the need for continuing vigilance and cooperation. With the decline of London as an international money center and the increasing importance of the Middle East as a source of investment funds, the leadership of the financial community should explore how changes in the federal and state laws and administrative practices could make New York more attractive to foreign investors.

2. Since corporate location decisions are greatly influenced by problems involving space utilization, the continued vitality of the corporate headquarters complex in New York requires a strong commercial construction industry. If the city is to maintain its position as the leading corporate headquarters complex, new commercial office buildings must be erected at costs and

rents that are reasonably competitive with alternative locations. The last years have seen substantial narrowing in the gap between the cost of prime space in New York and other competitive locations. The leaders of the construction industry, the construction unions, and local government should seek ways of cooperating to assure that the city's new office buildings are completed at a rental cost that will encourage corporate headquarters and corporate service firms to remain and expand in the city and that will help attract others here.

3. A major spur to corporate relocation to the suburbs has been the desire of middle and upper management to rear their families in a favorable environment. The new trends to later marriages, fewer births, and the increased career interests of educated women provide the city with an opportunity to attract and retain professional couples both of whom hold good jobs and are career-oriented. To do so, leaders of the real estate industry and city officials should intensify actions aimed at neighborhood conversion and neighborhood rehabilitation to provide such couples with a wider range of desirable living accommodations.

4. A major source of the city's strength has been its attraction to individuals who place a premium on a wide range of cultural activities including theater, restaurants, and concerts. Since this cultural-entertainment complex not only provides important ancillary services to the corporate sector but also much needed employment to many recent in-migrants, continuing efforts involving business and labor leaders and government officials should be directed to maintaining and strengthening this important sector. An expansion of the hotel industry should be high on the agenda.

5. Another favorable opportunity that the city should seek to exploit is the potential for further increases in foreign banks, foreign headquarters, foreign investors, and foreign visitors. Most foreigners find New York City attractive. The foreign business community should be an important target for the forthcoming public-private effort directed at placing before businessmen the multiple strengths of New York City in the hope of encouraging them to locate activities there.

6. Special attention must be paid by business and government leaders to maintaining the excellent air transportation that has done so much to keep New York the focal center of domestic and international economic activity. The maintenance and improvement of interurban and intraurban transportation can likewise contribute to strengthening the agglomeration process.

7. In years past the estrangement between business and political
   leaders contributed to the exodus of corporate headquarters
   because many chief executives concluded that local government
   was at best uninterested and at worst hostile. Recent cooperative
   actions aimed at achieving and maintaining the fiscal viability
   of the city is a major step in the right direction. So too are efforts
   to put a lid on business and personal income taxes and where
   possible to reduce those which weaken the competitive position
   of New York City.

The agglomeration process that has catapulted New York City into a
position of leadership in the corporate and financial world is constantly
affected by new forces being generated in the regional, national, and
world economy. This inquiry has sought to illuminate dimensions of
agglomeration that have not previously been adequately explored. As a
result of our research we believe that the directions for policy sketched
earlier provide the people of New York with the opportunity to take
actions that will help assure the future well-being of the city's economy
and thereby add to the security of their jobs and income.

CHAPTER 44

The Japanese Presence

THE IMAGE OF A SHRINKING GLOBE is by now firmly embedded in the minds of most citizens of modern nations. We receive instantaneous television broadcasts from around the globe, talk on the telephone via satellite to remote parts of the world, and can travel via supersonic jet to practically any place on earth in less than a day. Technology has made it possible for people, goods, and ideas to move easily and quickly across oceans and national boundaries.

These technological advances have had profound economic implications. One such impact has been a rapid growth in trade among nations. Since the post–World War II period, when the value of all exports from the nations of the world was $57.5 billion (1948), the volume of world trade has increased rapidly to reach $154.5 billion in 1963, $578.7 billion in 1973, and a current level of approximately $1 trillion annually.

The United States has been an active participant in this rapidly expanding flow of goods around the globe. In the twenty years immediately following World War II, exports from the United States grew from $9.8 billion to $27.5 billion; in the next ten years there was a nearly fourfold increase to $107.6 billion in 1975. During 1977 the U.S. Department of Commerce estimated that the United States exported nearly $119 billion in goods and services to nations around the world.

Of course world trade is a two-way street, and Americans import as well as export goods. Consequently, the net effect of the expansion of trade on the United States economy, and particularly on domestic employment, has been a subject of debate among both the interested parties and economists. On one side are those who argue "from the basic tenets of the principle of comparative advantage which claims that if trading countries specialize in the products in which each has a comparative advantage or the greatest relative efficiency, trade will benefit all partners through increasing the potential production possibilities of each country which in turn will raise employment levels due to increased output and GNP." In contrast, others have argued that because the United States' comparative advantage lies in capital-intensive rather than labor-intensive industries, trade will have the net effect of reducing domestic employment. Numerous empirical studies have been conducted to estimate the net effects of trade; but because of a lack of agreement on time periods to be considered, assumptions applied, and mathematical estimating procedures, the results vary widely, from net gains from trade of 28,900 jobs to net losses of 176,600 annually.

Although the debate over the net effects of foreign trade in the total economy is likely to rage on in the coming years, there is much wider agreement on the fact that trade can have strong adverse or favorable effects on particular industries and particular localities. There is little debate over the fact that U.S. textile, apparel, automobile, and other industries have lost jobs because of the substitution of imported goods for their products. Similarly, few would question the positive employment effects of trade on selected industries such as transportation. For example, the American Association of Port Authorities has estimated that over 1.1 million jobs are dependent on international trade and water transportation.

The purpose of this chapter is not to resolve or even contribute to the debate over the impact of international trade on the U.S. economy. Rather, we have the more modest purpose of analyzing the impact of business organizations from one particular country—Japan—on one particular metropolitan area in which they have chosen to locate—New York—specifically focusing on the positive economic effects of the presence of Japanese-owned firms in New York City.

NEW YORK'S JAPANESE BUSINESS COMMUNITY

The emergence of a economically significant Japanese business community in the New York area seems to have occurred in the mid-1960s.

Although there had been a few Japanese firms with offices in New York even before World War II, it was not until the late 1950s and early 1960s that the volume of trade between the United States and Japan became great enough to warrant the establishment of New York offices for a larger number of firms. Whereas imports from Japan to the United States totaled only $432 million in 1955 and represented less than 4 percent of all U.S. imports, the volume of Japanese imports grew by over 250 percent in the next five years and made up nearly 8 percent of U.S. imports in 1960. In the next five years the value of Japanese imports more than doubled, and by 1965 the nearly $21.4 billion in goods from Japan equaled over 11 percent of all U.S. imports.

Although the value of Japanese imports continued to grow at a lively pace all through the late 1960s and early 1970s, by 1965 the trade was great enough to have led to the establishment of a significant Japanese business community in the New York area. In that year there were 319 Japanese corporations located in New York, with 1,866 Japanese business-men assigned to these firms. While in the next ten years another 137 corporations established offices in New York and the size of the Japanese business population more than doubled, the industrial character of the community had been already well established by the mid-1960s.

Japanese corporations did not come to the United States, and more particularly to New York, to establish plants for the manufac-turing of their goods. Rather, they came to market the goods they produced in Japan and, later, in less-developed countries. Thus the Japanese firms that established offices in New York were manufacturers who produced goods for sale in U.S. markets and the trading companies that assisted Japanese manufacturers in selling their goods abroad. Of the 365 Japanese corporations in New York in 1968, fully 282 were either trading companies or manufacturers. These firms accounted for over 80 percent of the 2,450 Japanese businessmen then in New York, with trading companies assigning 1,030 people and manufacturers assigning 968.

Because trading companies play such a large role in New York's Japanese business community—and, more generally, in Japan's world of trade—it is important to understand the character of these institutions. Not since the days of the British and Dutch trading companies that helped found the American colonies have there been commercial enter-prises active in the Western world that rival the contemporary large Japanese trading companies.

There are over 5,000 trading companies in Japan. The vast majority are small firms, which handle only a specialized range of merchandise. But there are about thirty general trading companies that handle a range of goods from peanuts to guided missiles. Among these general trading companies the nine largest, known as the Big Nine, dominate the scene. These giant firms account for over 57 percent of all of Japan's imports and exports. Each of the Big Nine firms has established offices in the New York area, as have some 78 smaller trading firms.

These large trading companies have a network of offices around the globe. For example, Mitsui and Co., Ltd., Japan's second-largest trading company, has, in addition to its forty-six Japanese offices, sixty-three offices overseas and twenty-five subsidiaries, each in a different country. Its United States subsidiary, Mitsui and Co., Inc., is headquartered in New York but has fifteen offices in cities around the United States.

With their worldwide network of offices, the large Japanese trading companies can play a significant role in world trade. First, they help manufacturers in the United States and other foreign nations to import goods to Japan. Second, not only do they handle Japanese imports and exports, they also service foreign producers throughout the world by shipping and marketing goods among countries outside of Japan. Their established connections in developed and less developed nations help manufacturers make the arrangements necessary to enter new markets with their products. Again using Mitsui as an example, approximately 9 percent of its sales in 1976 were accounted for by such "offshore" trade, compared to 39 percent involving exports from and imports to Japan (the remainder were domestic sales within Japan).

The character of Japanese manufacturing firms operating abroad is also worth noting. In a study of Japanese multinational firms, Yoshi Tsurumi has argued that the nature of these firms in the United States underwent a shift around 1970. Up to that time Japanese manufacturing firms with offices in the United States were relatively small and were engaged primarily in the sale of Japanese products for industrial use. In the more recent period a shift has taken place toward larger firms with a greater emphasis on consumer goods. Following the success of SONY, other Japanese consumer-goods manufacturers have sought to enter the U.S. market by selling under their own brand names and establishing their own service networks. Entering the market in this fashion generally requires the manufacturer to establish his own office in the United States rather than relying on a trading company.

This change appears to have affected the character of New York's Japanese business community. The share of Japanese businessmen employed by trading companies dropped, while the share employed by manufacturers increased after 1970. This shift has other implications for the local economy as well, since the marketing of consumer goods by Japanese firms required their use of American advertising and other business services.

Another point should be made about both the Japanese trading companies and manufacturers located in New York. After a period of rapid growth, the number of such firms peaked in 1975; and the number of firms and employees declined between 1975 and 1976. This fact is probably related to the overall pattern of trade between the U.S. and Japan. In 1975 U.S. imports from Japan fell to $11.4 billion from the previous year's volume of $12.4 billion. In 1976 and 1977 imports returned to their earlier growth pattern, and this should be reflected in subsequent growth in the number of manufacturers' and trading companies' employees in New York.

In addition to trading companies and manufacturers, the third significant component of the Japanese business community in New York City is financial corporations—primarily banks, but also securities dealers and insurance companies. For most of the last decade these firms have accounted for almost 10 percent of the Japanese business community, with their share rising to 15 percent in recent years as the manufacturing and trading companies have declined. By 1976 there were fifty-four Japanese financial corporations in New York, employing 534 Japanese, with banks accounting for nineteen of the corporations and 390 of the Japanese workers and the remainder divided among security dealers and insurance firms.

Japanese banks initially entered the United States in both New York and California to service manufacturers and trading companies by financing their international trade. Although early operations were primarily as agencies—making loans, not receiving deposits—New York State law was liberalized in 1961 to permit foreign branch offices to provide a full range of banking services, and recently there has been a noticeable shift toward branch or subsidiary operations. The Japanese banks in New York have become involved in a range of activities beyond booking loans to Japanese trading companies and manufacturers.

In the period since 1969 New York has grown rapidly as a world financial center, and Japanese banks have participated in this growth. As the Eurodollar market has grown, and as New York has become a center for Eurodollar trading, many foreign banks, including Japanese banks, have opened and expanded offices in New York. This second function of Japanese banks, besides servicing Japanese trade activity, helps explain the rapid growth of the Japanese banking community in New York during the early 1970s and its continued growth in 1975 and 1976, at a time when trade activity was lagging.

The remaining component of the Japanese business community in New York is a variety of transportation, service, and other firms that have set up offices in the United States. Included in this group are such transportation firms as Japan Air Lines, which has its Western Hemisphere headquarters in New York; various shippers, freight carriers, and tourist organizations; communications firms, including Japanese business journals, newspapers, and telecommunications operations, and a wide assortment of other business service firms. Together these organizations account for about 10 percent of the area's Japanese business community.

Finally, no discussion of the Japanese business community in New York would be complete without some mention of the Japanese restaurants which have opened to serve both Japanese businessmen and New Yorkers. No accurate figures are available, but knowledgeable estimates are that about 100 to 120 Japanese restaurants are operating in the greater New York area, with total sales of about $20 million and total employment of about 800.

JAPANESE FAMILIES

Together the various corporations comprising the Japanese business community in New York have brought to the area 3,657 Japanese citizens to live and work. But these men and, far less frequently, women generally do not come alone. By 1976 the Japanese employees of Japanese firms had brought to New York with them almost 8000 dependents. Thus the total size of the Japanese community associated with the Japanese business presence in New York was over 11,000 people.

The fact that most of the Japanese who came to New York to work are family men is reflected in the data from the survey questionnaires returned by a sample of Japanese firms. Approximately 88 percent are married, and 82 percent of the married men report having one or more children. The vast majority (70 percent) have only one or two children; only 12 percent report three or more children.

Like many American families, the Japanese employees seem to prefer suburban living. Just over half of these households live in New York's suburban counties, with another 40 percent living in the suburban boroughs of New York City. Only 9 percent of these Japanese employees live in Manhattan.

These families provide a significant stimulus for their local merchants as well as for the metropolitan economy as a whole. It is estimated that in 1976 the average annual salary for all (both Japanese and local) employees of Japanese firms was approximately $24,100. Since a Japanese employee is likely to be supporting his family in the metropolitan area, most of his earnings will be spent locally. This points to an estimated total expenditure of over $88 million in the local economy by Japanese businessmen and their families living in the New York area.

EMPLOYMENT OF LOCAL RESIDENTS

The Japanese firms which open offices in New York do not, of course, operate exclusively with staff from Japan. They generally hire additional personnel from the local labor market and thus provide employment opportunities to New York area residents. In fact the 436 Japanese corporations in the New York area employed 7,726 local residents in 1976. Thus for every person brought from Japan to work in New York, there are 2.1 jobs created for local residents.

The greatest number of local residents are employed in the offices of manufacturers. These firms employ 4,452 local residents, with a ratio of 3.1 local jobs for each Japanese employee. While trading companies employ another 1,934 local residents, this represents only 1.5 local jobs for each Japanese employee. Financial institutions employ 1,300 local residents, with an estimated 2.6 local jobs for each Japanese employee. The remaining service firms employ relatively few local residents and are staffed almost exclusively by Japanese nationals.

The nearly 11,400 jobs linked directly to the Japanese business community carry with them a sizable payroll. Based on questionnaires returned by 117 Japanese firms representing 4,338 employees, we estimate the payrolls of Japanese corporations in New York to total $274.3 million. Average annual wages tend to be highest among manufacturers ($26,700) and trading companies ($25,600), and lowest among financial institutions ($16,000). Further analysis suggests that within the financial sector the banks have the lowest annual average wage ($14,200), while other financial corporations have relatively high average wages.

More important than the variation in average wages among types of Japanese firms is the basic fact that these corporations collectively have a relatively high average wage — $24,100 — and thus their economic impact on the local economy is greater than their employment levels alone suggest. Over $250 million is fed into the local metropolitan economy by the payrolls of Japanese firms, and perhaps two-thirds of that amount is paid to local residents.

TAXES

When Japanese firms establish themselves to do business in the United States, they generally become subject to the tax laws of the federal government as well as the state and local governments of the areas in which they locate. As a result there is a significant gain in American tax revenues.

In estimating the taxes paid by the Japanese business community, it is important to define carefully the taxes to be considered. For example there are significant personal income taxes paid by the employees of Japanese corporations. It was estimated earlier that approximately $274 million is paid in salaries and wages by Japanese firms. Thus it is reasonable to estimate that perhaps $55 million of this money is paid in income taxes. Similarly, it has been estimated that about $12 million was paid by employers in social security and related payroll taxes. To this could be added an almost equal amount in payroll deductions to cover employees' shares of social insurance contributions. However, in order to avoid the double counting that such estimates reflect, the discussion of taxes has been limited to taxes paid directly by corporations as a result of their New York operations. This figure is estimated to be nearly $95 million. While this discussion focuses on this $95 million, it is worth noting that by the most generous definitions Japanese businessmen do generate perhaps $170 million in taxes for American governments.

Of the nearly $95 million in taxes paid directly by Japanese firms, the largest share, nearly $77 million, is paid to the federal government, primarily in the form of corporate income tax. The next largest share, totaling $10 million, is paid to the city of New York through its various business taxes and, in the case of firms owning their own buildings, through local property taxes. Moreover, it should be noted that these figures do *not* include local property and occupancy taxes paid by property owners renting to Japanese firms; Japanese firms use a substantial amount of commercial space, and their rentals include a sum which is eventually paid as local taxes. New York State received about $5.8 million directly in taxes from Japanese firms. State and local governments in New Jersey receive an additional $1.9 million from firms in the metropolitan area.

Trading companies account for the major part of all taxes paid, primarily because of the large amount of federal taxes they pay. Included in this sum are payments of import duties reported by the New York offices of the trading companies. The federal tax payments would be even larger if all import duties, including those paid directly by the home office in Japan, were included. Banks, despite the fact that they comprise only a small share of the Japanese business community, account for the largest portion of taxes paid to New York City. This is due to both local taxes levied on banking operations and the greater propensity of banks to own property in the area and thus pay local property taxes.

Boost to the Local Real Estate Market

To open an office in the New York area necessarily requires that a Japanese firm rent or purchase commercial space in the region. And when more than 400 corporations seek to maintain offices in New York, the cumulative effect is a substantial boost to the local real estate market. In fact, Japanese corporations occupy nearly 4.8 million square feet of commercial space in the New York area.

Two important points should be made about the nature of the commercial space occupied by Japanese firms. First, the vast majority of it is office space. Over 3.7 million of the nearly 4.8 million square feet (or 78 percent) is office space, with the remainder being warehouse, storage, and other commercial space. This reflects the largely headquarters character of the operations Japanese firms have established in New York. Second, the bulk of the space is located in New York City. Nearly 87 percent of the office space and over 50 percent of the other commercial space is located in the city rather than in suburban areas of the region.

Among the four major sectors of the Japanese business community, the use of office space reflects their level of employment. Manufacturers, who have the largest number of employees, also occupy the largest share of office space, with trading companies being the second-largest user. The financial corporations and other firms each occupy somewhat less than one-half million square feet of space.

The large volume of space used by Japanese firms requires substantial expenditures for occupancy costs. An estimated $33.9 million are spent by Japanese firms annually in the local real estate market. Because office space is more expensive than other commercial space, the share of the occupancy costs accounted for by offices is even greater than the volume of space would suggest. About $30.9 million or over 91 percent of total occupancy costs are accounted for by office space. For similar reasons expenditures for space are heavily concentrated in New York City. About $37.4 million or nearly 93 percent of total occupancy costs are for space in New York City.

Purchases of Specialized Business Services

The fact that a larger number of Japanese corporations have chosen to locate their American headquarters in New York is no accident. These firms, like their American and other foreign counterparts, choose their headquarters locations on the basis of a number of factors, but one of the leading considerations is the availability of the specialized business services that headquarters operations generally require. Included in this category of "advanced corporate services" are many legal, accounting, management consulting, financial, and other specialized services readily available in New York City.

In making use of these specialized services, which are at the root of New York's comparative advantage, Japanese corporations spend considerable sums, which go directly to local businesses. Estimates from the questionnaire responses and other sources suggest that Japanese firms spend over $99 million on payments to New York City–based firms providing specialized business services. The single largest expenditure within this category, over $44 million, is for advertising agencies. Legal services also require large expenditures, nearly $7.5 million, while accounting firms and management consultants require smaller amounts. In addition to these enumerated business services, the Japanese firms reported an estimated $33 million more was spent for a variety of other specialized business services. For example, many firms have telex installations and other expensive communications equipment which they rent or purchase from local communications firms; Japan Air Lines uses local firms for some of its meals and for cleaning; trading companies make use of customs brokers on a large scale; all types of firms use temporary manpower services.

Manufacturers accounted for the major share of business service expenditures, spending far more than trading companies, banks, or other types of firms. The large expenditure by these firms for advertising reflects the shift, noted earlier, toward greater sales of Japanese consumer goods under their own brand names within the U.S. This effort generally requires the use of an American advertising agency, and Japanese manufacturers have been quick to notice the advantages of using American, and generally New York–based, advertising firms to help sell their products in this country.

The introduction of miniature transistorized television sets by Sony in the early 1960s provides a classic example of the critical link between Japanese manufacturers and American advertising agencies. In order to market these tiny television sets at a time when Americans seemed to want bigger and bigger screens, SONY relied upon the firm of Doyle Dane Bernbach, who were also helping to market small foreign cars—Volkswagens. The agency's successful campaign firmly established SONY in the minds of Americans as producers of unique, quality products and the link between SONY and Doyle Dane Bernbach has lasted through to the present campaign to market SONY's Betamax color television recorders.

STIMULUS TO CAPITAL MARKETS

In addition to the panoply of specialized business services, another attraction of New York City for the headquarters of Japanese manufacturers and trading companies is the concentration of financial institutions. Moreover, a significant component of the Japanese business community is Japanese banks themselves. In return the presence of these firms and banks appears to provide a significant stimulus to the local financial institutions.

Estimates from the questionnaire responses suggest that Japanese firms, excluding banks, pay over $169 million in interest and banking fees. It was not possible from the questionnaire responses to determine how much of this amount was paid to domestic versus Japanese banks (although all the payments are made within New York City). It is likely that Japanese firms rely on Japanese banks with offices in New York for much of their borrowing needs, but some share of this business may also flow directly to domestic banks.

In addition, the questionnaire responses indicated that Japanese banks themselves paid over $52.8 million in interest and fees to other banks in New York. This suggests that a substantial part of the financing used by Japanese banks may be raised from other banks, and thus the Japanese banks are providing a net increment to the business of domestic institutions.

The complementary, rather than exclusively competitive, manner in which domestic and foreign banks can operate has been noted in other contexts. A paper for the House Committee on Banking, Currency and Housing makes the following points:

- Loans by the Japanese agencies in New York and California have financed the bulk of U.S.–Japan trade over the last decade. These activities are directly or indirectly financed in turn by U.S. banks since the Japanese government limits the amount of funds which the parent bank can supply to their U.S. agencies and they therefore depend on the domestic or Eurodollar interbank markets for funds.
- The U.S. agencies of Japanese banks also make heavy use of the U.S. acceptance market to finance Japanese trade with third countries. In January 1975 there were $18.6 billion acceptances outstanding of which $9.7 billion—more than half—were drawn to finance trade between countries other than the United States and largely involved Japanese exports and imports.
- The U.S. branches and agencies of foreign banks are part of the

mechanism which generates growth in the Eurodollar market. They can borrow dollars in New York for the parent bank's London or Nassau branch while the parent's foreign network supplies Eurodollar funds to be loaned in the New York interbank market and for direct lending to U.S. corporations.

In sum, the presence of Japanese banks in New York City has helped expand the reach of domestic financial institutions and opened up for them new wholesale, if not retail, credit markets. With the help of the Japanese banking community, New York is increasingly becoming the center of the world's capital market.

EMPLOYMENT AT THE PORT

The impacts of trade with Japan on the New York area economy are not limited to the direct employment generated by the expenditures of Japanese corporations. Goods imported to the United States from Japan must be moved through ports and shipped across the country, and the handling of these goods generates a number of jobs. Since about one-sixth of all Japanese imports are handled through the Port of New York and New Jersey, many of these jobs are filled by New York area residents.

In 1976, the most recent year for which figures are available, over 769,000 tons of goods valued at nearly $2.5 billion dollars were imported from Japan to the United States through New York's port. The bulk of these goods were transported by ocean vessel, but over $460 million worth of goods arrived by air.

These imports from Japan represent a significant share of the total volume and value of goods flowing through the local port. Japanese imports accounted for nearly 11 percent of all such imports when measured by dollar values, though less than 2 percent by tonnage. However, for goods arriving by air, Japanese imports accounted for nearly 9 percent of both total tonnage and total value.

It is difficult to equate these measures of imports directly with expenditures and employment, but a conservative estimate suggests that approximately $2.1 million in expenditures by the Port Authority is linked to trade with Japan. And the Port Authority itself represents only a small share of all the activity and employment dependent on handling goods from overseas. Private organizations employing longshoremen, truckers, and others also depend on foreign trade. The Port Authority has estimated that 55,559 people are employed at its three major airports and 10,030 are employed at its Marine Terminals. If 2 percent of these jobs are tied to trade with Japan, this suggests that over 1,300 people are employed because of goods traded with Japan that flow through the Port of New York.

AID TO AMERICAN MANUFACTURERS

While much of the discussion of the economic impacts of the Japanese business community has necessarily focused on Japanese *imports* to the United States, it should also be noted that Japanese corporations are increasingly playing a role in *exports* from the United States. As noted earlier, the large Japanese trading companies are unique commercial institutions. Their worldwide network of offices permits them to buy and sell goods that others with less extensive ties to makers around the world would have far more trouble trading.

American manufacturers are taking increasing advantage of the expertise and special advantages of Japanese trading companies to help market their goods overseas. Among the trading companies surveyed for this study, eleven furnished replies that indicated that their sales resulting from *exports* from the United States were greater than their sales from *imports* to the United States. Data from all 22 trading companies that responded to appropriate questions indicate that over $6.5 billion in goods were exported from the United States by Japanese trading companies with American headquarters in New York.

JAPANESE VISITORS TO NEW YORK CITY

The rapid growth in business relations between the United States and Japan has been accompanied by a growing number of persons from Japan visiting the United States and particularly New York City. As Japanese firms deal more with the United States, they also have more reason to visit U.S. cities or to meet with their own representatives stationed here and/or with their U.S. counterparts. Growing business relations between the two countries has also led to greater numbers of Japanese visiting the United States as tourists for both cultural and recreational purposes.

These trends are evident in the figures the U.S. Travel Service provides on foreign visitors to the United States. Since 1965, when Japanese travel to the United States began to grow rapidly, the number of visitors has increased more than seventeenfold, from 44,385 to 772,386 annually.

However, in 1975 there was a slight decline in the volume of such travel, and growth in 1976 was very modest (3.5 percent) compared to the rapid increases of earlier years.

The rapid growth in the number of Japanese visitors to the United States in recent years had led to a little known fact: Japan is now the largest source of foreign visitors to the U.S., excluding the neighboring countries of Canada and Mexico. In 1968 the number of visitors from Japan exceeded that from France for the first time; in 1970 it exceeded that from Germany; and since 1972 Japan has been the largest source of overseas visitors to the U.S.

Of course not all persons coming from Japan to the U.S. visit New York City. Many are destined only for Hawaii, where they vacation, but many others do head for New York, or at least include New York on their itinerary, which may cover several American cities, or include New York as a stopover on the way to Europe. Precise figures are not available for the number of Japanese visiting New York, but the Japanese National Tourist Organization has recently begun estimating this figure, and their estimate for the period from October 1975 to September 1976 is 162,000 Japanese visitors to New York City. This represents about one-fifth of all Japanese visitors to the U.S., reflecting the large number of Japanese tourists who restrict their visits to Hawaii or the West Coast.

The 162,000 Japanese who visit New York City provide a major gain for the local economy. Precise figures on typical visits are not available, but some reasonable estimates can be made. If the typical visit lasts five days, then on an average day 2,220 hotel beds, or about 1,750 hotel rooms, are filled with Japanese visitors. Since the average room rate in 1976 was $32.17, these visitors represent approximately $20.5 million in income for the local hotel industry.

Visitors do not spend money on hotels alone. Surveys for the New York City Convention and Visitors Bureau suggest that hotel expenses represent about two-fifths of the typical visitors' total expenditures of over $51 million annually. Included in this total are over $9.5 million in restaurant expenditures, $8.6 million in retail store sales, and several million dollars additional for beverages, theaters, local transportation, and other items.

IMPACTS AND EXTERNALITIES

These direct impacts on local employment and income are of even greater significance than the figures suggest because of what economists refer to as the "multiplier effect." Money entering an economy will be spent by those who first receive it and thus will stimulate additional employment in local industries such as supermarkets and retail stores, personal services, housing, and others. Research in urban economics suggests that the multiplier for employment in metropolitan areas ranges between 4 and 5 and that a reasonable estimate is 4.6. This suggests that the estimated 12,500 jobs directly related to the presence of Japanese firms in the New York area ultimately support a total of 57,500 local jobs.

To place these figures in perspective, it may be useful to compare the economic impact of the Japanese business community to the economic impacts of other sectors of the local economy which have been subject to similar studies. In a study of "The Impact of the Broadway Theaters on the Economy of New York City," Mathtech found that in 1975 the theaters themselves contributed about $43 million to the economy of New York City and that theatergoers themselves spent another $62.1 million on restaurants, taxis, and related items. This $105 million attributed to the theater industry is less than one-seventh the amount contributed to the local economy by Japanese corporations.

In another study, Alan Parter has assessed "The Economic Impact of the Diplomatic Community on the New York Metropolitan Area." Parter concluded that the entire diplomatic community in New York, including the United Nations and its specialized agencies; the missions to the United Nations; consulates; various commercial efforts such as catering, banking, and others related to the United Nations; media; and non-governmental organizations all combined provided 13,501 jobs, of which 4,327 were held by U.S. citizens. Thus the employment generated by the Japanese business community for *local residents is nearly three times greater* than that provided by the entire diplomatic community.

With respect to the city's economy, no attempt has been made here to assess the extent to which the expansion of Japanese enterprises, from banking firms to restaurants, might be at the partial expense of local enterprises. Clearly, to some extent, the growth of the former may have resulted in the slower growth or even decline of the latter. But that is only one of several secondary consequences.

Large metropolitan centers, particularly a center such as New York City, seek to stay in the lead by maintaining old and developing new foci of specialization such as in national and international banking. The establishment therefore of a strong Japanese banking element in the city has the effect of adding to the city's specialization as a money market, thereby strengthening its short- and long-term economic prospects.

The secondary consequences for New York's future as a center of world trade extend even further. The local presence of Japanese banks and the major trading companies may provide American importers and exporters with broadened opportunities to extend their sources of supply and to enlarge the markets in which they sell because the Japanese are able to provide U.S. firms with services not previously available to them. Again, one must take note of the fact that to some extent the flow of work from U.S. business to Japanese firms may be at the expense of U.S. banks and trading companies and hence do not represent a net gain in employment and income to the city. On the other hand, the improvement of services in terms of cost or quality by Japanese firms to U.S. exporters and importers in the city must be seen as a net gain to the productivity of the American economy and to the further specialization of the city's economy.

The presence of a substantial Japanese business element in New York City, it should be noted, has roots that extend beyond the U.S. economy. Several of the larger enterprises reported that they oversee from New York their entire North American (mainly U.S. and Canada) operations, and occasionally their South American activities as well. In fact, one large enterprise reported that it was modifying its long-term personnel system so that after an initial period of training and employment in Tokyo managers would henceforth rotate between New York headquarters and South American operations. The volume of business being conducted in the Western Hemisphere justified this further specialization. Clearly if more and more Japanese and other foreign firms decide to oversee their Western Hemisphere operations from New York City, and if their level of business continues to increase in both South and North America, that augurs well for the increased vitality of the city's economy.

In assessing the economies of great cities in terms of what Jean Gottman has defined as quarternary services—the advanced transfer of information—the presence of a critical mass is of great importance. It is fortunate that circumstances early on led the leaders of Japanese business to favor New York over other U.S. cities for their headquarters operations. The fact that New York is now home away from home for close to 4,000 Japanese businessmen and has developed a growing business and social infrastructure for them will serve as a further magnet. The Japanese community has its several trade organizations; increasingly close linkages with corporate service firms; a growing cultural and social infrastructure involving hotels, restaurants, and suburban residential neighborhoods; private clubs; and still other institutions and supports.

Informed opinion holds that young Japanese managers and the members of their families welcome assignment to New York City and that they frequently regret when the time comes that they become available for reassignment. The range of cultural activities in New York, the wide diversity of people and cultures, the substantial freedom afforded women, the wide array of consumer goods, and the relatively modest price level in comparison to Tokyo all reinforce the attractiveness of New York as a work assignment.

For many generations, Japan and the United States were each, for different reasons, among the most self-contained economies and societies. Each looked inward for its strength and transformational dynamics. But this is no longer the case. Increasingly, Japan and the United States, together with the advanced industrial nations of Western Europe, are becoming an interdependent whole. This growing interdependence offers the greatest prospect for continuing economic development. New York City is the center of the crossways where Europe, the United States, and Japan have an opportunity to meet and transact a great amount of mutually beneficial business, which in turn will redound to the well-being of the inhabitants of the world's leading commercial entrepôt.

PART X

Programs and Policy

THE OLDER AMONG US have seen the most momentous upheaval in the U.S. economy, World War II and its far-reaching consequences and realignments, a quarter century of rapid economic growth, the rise of the welfare state, the unsettlements brought about by inflation and the oil crises, and much more that led to tidal waves that permanently altered the shorelines. Chapter 45 tries to put one segment of these stupendous events in perspective. Chapter 46 is a more narrowly focused exercise in which I review the evolution of national manpower policy, the arena of my specialization.

The remaining four chapters, 47 through 50, take up sequentially still narrower but nonetheless relevant themes within the manpower arena, where the federal government, especially since the early 1960s, has sought to exert leverage. In these efforts I have had two roles, as researcher and as an active adviser to the legislative and executive branches of the federal government.

Despite a substantial flow of funds and the commitment of a large number of able and concerned persons, the record of what was accomplished leaves much to be desired. That is my reading of what happened in the areas of manpower training, youth unemployment, the inner cities, and federal job creation.

There is another reading, however: A democracy that responds to the central problems it confronts will always have another opportunity to do better.

CHAPTER 45

Social Programs
and Economic Realities

...LET ME BEGIN by positioning myself. I don't follow Hegel, who argued that there was nothing to be learned from history, but neither do I agree with Santayana, who contended that, unless we learn from history, we must repeat all our earlier mistakes. I am in between. I plan to review some major programmatic initiatives that were undertaken during the last forty to fifty years and seek to interpret them, knowing full well that my interpretation won't help to chart directions for the future. At most it may alert us to some pitfalls. If we can cut all possible future errors in half, we'll be ahead. Specifically, I plan to inspect five major social programs on which we lavished much concern and resources; to analyze why they worked up to a point and why they didn't work beyond that point; and to extract a few lessons from this review for public policy. The five program areas are:

- Employment
- Income transfers and welfare
- Education and training

602 UNDERSTANDING HUMAN RESOURCES

- Housing
- Health

Let's begin with employment. I became an adult early in the Great Depression; I graduated from college in 1931 and received my Ph.D. in 1933. In early 1933 the unemployment rate was surely not less than 25 percent; it was probably more, if we take account of the large numbers who were underemployed. When people talk today about a soft economy, I am reminded that they have a different reference point from mine. Unemployment never dropped below 10 percent during Mr. Roosevelt's first and second terms. Unemployment of crisis proportions did not yield until we entered World War II. Whether you like the Marxist interpretation or not, it was the war that pulled us out of the Depression. We had fared considerably better with Mr. Roosevelt than with Herbert Hoover, but it was the war that pulled us out of our deep depression.

We passed the Employment Act in 1946, a modest piece of legislation that directed the federal government to use all its powers to prevent the recurrence of a major depression such as the country had suffered in the 1930s, and to use its powers to restore the economy if it went into a decline. Many have forgotten that the act was a success. From that day to this, however poorly we may have handled other matters, we have never had a depression with serious, prolonged unemployment. Of course, some individuals were victimized by long spells of unemployment, but they constitute a small minority. By contrast, in 1939 I was able to locate hundreds, even thousands, of men in New York City who had not worked for five or seven years. We have not experienced unemployment like that since World War II.

A second point: Starting in the 1940s and continuing into the 1950s, we saw the trek of many underemployed poor people off the farms of the South. Cincinnati must have been the new home for many of these southern migrants. Considering the size and nature of the migration, I don't think we should be surprised that we have major urban problems centering on minorities.

In talking with my black students, I have learned that it is difficult, often impossible, for them to understand that, however bad the present condition of many urban minority families, their earlier situation in the pre–World War II South was worse, often considerably worse. This is a point worth considering, even though it must not be used to excuse inaction today.

A third impact of World War II on employment relates to the new role of married women in the job market. My first government assignment was in the Executive Office of the president. Five days after Pearl Harbor I recommended that we start to register college-trained women.

At that time there were still around 10 million unemployed men in the country. My colleagues thought I had lost my mind. But I warned that if it was going to be a long, hard war, as I expected it to be, we would need to use all capable women before the war was won. Although the registration of women was not undertaken, my hunch turned out to be right. The war years saw a revolution in the role of married women in the labor force. Today, more than half of all married women and almost three out of five women above the age of sixteen are in the labor force. The most amazing statistic is that more than two out of five women with children under three years of age are at work. I'm not saying that this is good or bad; I am only reporting that in my lifetime the country has witnessed a major revolution in the relationship of women to work. The Swedish data suggest that before long the participation rates for women will differ only slightly from those of men.

A fourth development in the employment arena involves the lowering of the barriers of segregation and discrimination in the labor market. Let me use a personal example. The Graduate School of Business at Columbia was founded in 1916. When I left for war service, I had been on the faculty for seven years. My friends said, "You are crazy to hang around. They'll never give you tenure." There was no Jewish professor with tenure in the School of Business in 1942. My dean had tried several years earlier to get a tenured appointment for Nathan Isaacs, then in Cincinnati, but he had failed. After a quarter of a century, the faculty still had not appointed its first Jew. My college class of 1931 had only a handful of Jews, Irish, and Italians and one or two blacks. Although discrimination—religious, ethnic, sex, or race—has surely not disappeared from the labor market, the barriers have been lowered by an order of magnitude. Not good enough, but still they are much lower.

A final point about employment: Few people are interested in work unless it yields a reasonable income that enables them to enjoy a reasonable standard of living. Between 1940 and 1970 the productivity of the U.S. economy rose rapidly. The real income per hour of labor was about 150 percent greater at the end than at the beginning of the period. Recently the gains have been much smaller but that's another story, not for this presentation.

Re employment, the key points are these: We have avoided large-scale prolonged unemployment; married women have entered the work force in large numbers; discrimination is much reduced; the returns per hour of work are greater. A respectable, many would say an impressive, record.

The second programmatic area we will consider involves income transfers and welfare. The January 1982 issue of *Scientific American* has a long article I wrote on the Social Security system. One of our great achievements has been to put a system in place that enables most of the elderly to receive sufficient income from all sources so that no more than 3 to 4 percent live in poverty. Although a considerable number are not much above the poverty line—and that leaves room for further improvement—it does not diminish what has been accomplished.

Hard as it is to believe, in 1932 the American Federation of Labor opposed national legislation on unemployment insurance. In its view, the national government had no business in the collective bargaining arena. At present the unemployed can receive twenty-six weeks of benefits, and in some instances they can receive up to thirty-nine weeks. As recently as 1975 we had coverage up to sixty-five weeks. The National Commission for Manpower Policy, of which I was the chairman, recommended to the Congress that it cut back the maximum length of coverage to thirty-nine weeks. Most victims of cyclical unemployment usually find jobs within thirty-nine weeks—not everybody, but most. The nation did pretty well; during the New Deal we had established a system to provide basic income to persons who suffered short-term unemployment. They were assisted to maintain their customary standard of living.

Now to welfare, which is really a bad term. It refers to Aid to Families with Dependent Children (AFDC). When originally put on the statute books in the late 1930s, its goal was to enable women with young children who had lost their husbands, or whose husbands could no longer support them because of illness or disability, to keep their families together. Previously, many such families were broken up and the children were sent to orphan asylums or foster homes. The objective of AFDC was to let the mother and the children stay together, clearly a humane and desirable objective.

In 1956 we improved the Social Security system by providing benefits for persons judged to be permanently disabled. The aim was to prevent their being forced onto welfare. Instead, by paying an additional tax all workers would be insured and, if they became permanently disabled, would be entitled to benefits.

In the 1930s we didn't deliberate at length when we set sixty-five as the age at which beneficiaries could claim their Social Security benefits. In the early 1960s we compounded our problems by moving rather hastily to amend the Social Security Act so that men at age sixty-two could draw 80 percent of their benefits. Putting the matter of age of entitlement aside, I would argue that we did well in starting our Social Security system and unemployment insurance, in providing for AFDC, in adding benefits for the permanently disabled.

The third programmatic area relates to education and training. I want to begin with the GI Bill passed at the end of World War II. It was a remarkable piece of legislation because it gave a large number of persons with low incomes, who earlier had access to only limited schooling, a second chance. Usually one gets a second chance only after he gets to Heaven. But to those who survived World War II, the country offered a chance to refashion their life. My colleagues, almost to a man, were convinced that the ex-GIs would be a poor lot of students. In fact, they turned out to be the most exciting of all cohorts to teach: They were mature and they took their schooling seriously.

The federal government was not alone in this; the states also got into the act. Ohio was among the leaders. Many states came to realize that higher education had to be expanded. Community colleges multiplied, as did state colleges; and state universities opened branches in urban centers. Many, possibly most, large state universities had initially been located in small towns out of the reach of the low-income urban masses. This was a not-too-subtle way of controlling admissions. But the push to equity after World War II forced most states to bring higher education to the commuting student. New York City and Cincinnati were among the few cities that earlier had supported an urban college or university. Some measure of the post–World War II expansion is suggested by the following. In 1931, one in twenty of my age group graduated from college. At the peak of the Vietnam War, about nine in every twenty white males were attending college, and about one out of four graduated. Clearly the United States did open up opportunities for youngsters to acquire a higher education.

State and local governments also increased substantially their tax dollar flow into elementary and secondary education. In New York City current outlays for education through high school amount to around $40,000 per student. Some say this is not enough, but I contend that it is a substantial public investment. Certainly many youngsters don't learn enough. That's a problem we must look into, but we can't argue that we have not supported public education. That is simply not true.

Because the Russians scared us with Sputnik in 1957, Congress passed the National Defense Education Act (NDEA). Dwight Eisenhower, the president I knew best, didn't want to sign that bill because he didn't believe that the federal government should get into the financing of education, but his hand was forced by the tie-in with national security.

NDEA was a watershed. Prior to 1958 many low-income youngsters were unable to finance going to college. After NDEA, finances were a minor hurdle. The proof of this change is in the 1952 report of the National Manpower Council, of which I was director of research and of which Charles Taft was a charter member. *A Policy for Scientific and Professional Manpower* (Columbia, 1952) focused on the need to lower and remove the financial barriers to higher education, which loomed high at

that time. The record was noteworthy: Financial barriers to higher education had been removed, and considerably enlarged resources were available for elementary and secondary education.

I am in a good position to report on the federal efforts in the training
arena since I served for nineteen years, from 1962 to 1981, as chairman of
the successive advisory bodies. My estimate is that the federal government spent about $84 billion through Department of Labor programs on
what are designated as "manpower programs," which were later dubbed
"employment and training programs." In all honesty, I don't think that
we did a good job in increasing the skill and competency levels of the
hard-to-employ. They obtained current income through these programs
but we failed in most cases to help them get into the regular job market.
It was a serious effort, but it had only limited success. The story is set out
in a book I edited, *Employing the Unemployed* (Basic Books, 1980).

On the housing front: We started in the late 1930s to establish public
housing units. Although the president and other liberals were interested
in improving housing for the poor, the program would not have gotten
off the ground but for the depression in the construction industry. The
builders pressured the government to help them revive their industry,
and in the process the poor were helped. Many public programs owe
their origin to such an alliance between business interests and the poor.

To sharpen this point: I was a friend of Aneurin Bevan, the minister
of health and later the foreign secretary of Great Britain. In the mid-
1950s we had dinner together in London. Nye—as he was called—was
more excited than usual. He shouted at me that he was sick and tired
of having to adjust His Majesty's foreign policy to accommodate the
interests of U.S. farmers. Our farmers had apparently put pressure on
Washington, which in turn pressed Whitehall to do something it didn't
want to do.

I remember that my father-in-law, Robert Szold, and his associates,
who were leaders in cooperative housing, were convinced that if people
were able to live in a good environment—a good physical environment—
most social problems would vanish. But we now know that the theory
does not work.

One long-term result of World War II, at least in New York City, has
been rent control. It is still in effect, and I happen to be a beneficiary. But
as an economist I can state unequivocally that rent control four decades
after a war is an error. It has protected many who didn't need protection
and has seriously distorted the market.

At the end of World War II, we initiated a more constructive effort
by providing large mortgages for veterans at low rates of interest. In the
process we helped inadvertently to undermine many cities by increasing

the rush to the suburbs, but we also raised the housing standards of many young families.

But even that program has had its dysfunctional aspects. The federal income tax statutes, by permitting taxpayers to deduct interest payments and taxes on the houses they own and live in, provide a benefit of $25 billion or so per year to many middle- and upper-income families. President Reagan and his allies are railing against entitlement programs for the poor and the near poor, but they remain conspicuously silent on the subject of the benefits that accrue to the middle- and upper-income groups, a subject that Mr. Peterson, the head of Lehman Brothers, recently elaborated on in *The New York Times Sunday Magazine.*

One more point about housing: In St. Louis the effect of concentrating the lowest-income families in a large public housing complex created so much social pathology that nothing short of dynamiting the buildings offered a way out. Such is the distance sometimes between a social goal and its unanticipated consequences.

The fifth arena is health, to which I am currently devoting much of my research effort. Mr. Roosevelt made a decision in 1935 that national health insurance (NHI) would be left out of the social security system. Some said that he did so because the father-in-law of one of his sons, the famous neurosurgeon, Dr. Harvey Cushing of Harvard, wanted to become the president of the AMA, and NHI would ruin his chances of winning. I think that Mr. Roosevelt made the right judgment and it had nothing to do with Dr. Cushing. NHI would have jeopardized the passage of the Social Security bill, and that was a risk that FDR did not want to take. Moreover, the concept of NHI had been around for a long time. Teddy Roosevelt had first introduced it in the Bull Moose Campaign in 1912. Any matter that had been around since 1912 was not that pressing in 1930 nor, for that matter, in 1982!

World War II introduced many servicemen to a higher level of medical care than that they had previously known as civilians. At the end of the war, partly for this reason and partly because of significant advances in therapeutic medicine, Congress decided to broaden the access of the citizenry to a higher level of medical care by financing the construction of hospitals in small communities. Senator Robert Taft was a strong supporter of the Hill-Burton Act.

Another legacy from World War II was the nation's new awareness of the importance of biomedical research, which led to the large-scale expansion of the National Institutes of Health, which in turn enabled the United States to assume the leadership role at the cutting edge of medical knowledge.

In 1965 we passed legislation that established Medicare and Medicaid. It was clear that elderly people needed financial help to pay for their hospitalizations, which were becoming increasingly expensive. The poor surely needed help to gain access to medical care. We may have failed to see how Medicare and Medicaid would inflate health care costs, but basically the new legislation accomplished what it set out to do.

The early and mid-1960s also saw Congress act to expand the physician supply, convinced that the promise of more care for the elderly and the poor could be achieved only if more physicians were trained. I was not persuaded by this argument, since I believed that access to the health care system was not the same as increasing the number of physicians. And I surely didn't believe in the hypothesis that more physicians meant better health. In World War II, we had withdrawn 40 percent of the national physician manpower supply to serve in the armed forces, but the health of the American people improved. When cross-examined on this point by a skeptical congressional committee in 1950, I pointed out that the mystery was not difficult to unravel: During the war many unemployed got jobs; family income went up; people ate better; they felt engaged in the struggle against Nazism.

Now for the score card. In my view, employment policy worked remarkably well: Unemployment never returned to depression levels; job creation was substantial; discrimination was reduced.

With regard to income-transfer programs, they helped the poor and the unemployed and significantly improved the economic position of the elderly.

With respect to education, we substantially eliminated the financial barriers to higher education, a feat no other country in the world has accomplished. We also added substantial resources to the system.

On housing, we did a great deal for the middle class. As Anthony Downs has stressed, we probably spend too much money on housing. It is difficult to tell other people how to spend their money, but he believes that the nation, by tax breaks and other devices, has encouraged too much money to flow into housing. Nevertheless, housing for the poor has improved.

In health, we accomplished two major goals. We opened up the system to almost everybody and the system provides a reasonably good level of care.

So much for the positive side. What are the negatives? It is appalling that we have not succeeded in expanding employment opportunities for minority youth. Children who have no responsibility for having been born, no responsibility for having been born into broken families, no responsibility for attending schools whose teachers fail to teach, reach working age and can't find work. It is not that they do not want to work, as many in and out of Washington believe, but they cannot get jobs because of two shortcomings. There are not enough jobs available, and they don't have the competences or skills that employers require. We are playing with a delayed time bomb. If we continue to ignore this challenge, we will be accumulating an ever larger pool of adults without a stake in our society, clearly a potentially dangerous situation.

Second, we paid too little attention to the ratchet effect between wage increases and price increases. General Motors was willing over many years to acquiesce to many of the demands of the United Auto Workers. It was able to settle with the UAW since it could turn around and raise its prices. In the process, GM lost much of its market to foreign competitors.

The income-transfer record also has serious blemishes. We started with the idea that we wanted to keep a family unit intact and provided government support to mothers to keep their children. Unfortunately, in recent years AFDC has become a means of support for young women who have children but who have never had husbands. Many of them are in their teens when they become mothers and some are forced to drop out of school. We do little other than provide money for these young mothers. They need help in getting back to school, acquiring diplomas, getting jobs. Instead, welfare helps to hold them prisoners.

On the educational front, our failures consist of too many youngsters who come into the labor market functionally illiterate, and a low rate of success in our remedial training programs.

In housing, we erred by extending rent control. We also gave too much to the middle class in the form of tax benefits. And much public housing, especially in large cities, was poorly conceived and poorly executed.

In the health area, if we didn't have to worry about the bill, we could be satisfied with the record. But costs accelerated steeply. In 1950 we spent somewhere between $12 billion and $13 billion of 1950 dollars for the entire health care system. In the calendar year 1981, we spent $276 billion. More and more people believe we must slow our rate of spending for health care. I agree.

What lessons can be extracted from this exciting half century of social programming? Unlike President Reagan, I believe that the federal government has a major role to play in initiating and expanding social programs that will help to improve the lot of citizens who require assistance. Admittedly the federal and state government are imperfect instruments. Many programs will at best result in a mixed record. But in my view, despite its imperfections, the federal government is a major instrument for social progress. We must be careful when we use it and how we use it, but we cannot afford not to use it.

The reason is simple: A democratic society must be concerned with equity, especially the pursuit of equity. No matter how unequal the society may be, it must strive toward equity. Its rate of progress will depend on how successful it is in developing a consensus. Good ideas lead to good actions only if a majority of the citizenry can be persuaded to act. Consensus comes more easily when the nation has come through a searing experience such as the Great Depression, which gave FDR his opportunity. Kennedy's assassination opened the path for President Johnson, who was far ahead of the country but who, for a time, was able to pull the electorate with him.

We often fail to realize that government can do a great deal for the public weal without spending lots of money; in fact, it can often act without spending any money. Consider the Supreme Court's decision on school desegregation in 1954. That decision provided the spark to encourage blacks to organize and to take to the streets. This in turn helped to bring about the Civil Rights Act of 1964, which was abetted by the employer community which helped to turn the act into a reality. Many leaders had come to the conclusion that the color of a person's skin should no longer be a criterion for employment.

Another important lesson is that the performance of the economy will have a major impact on the welfare and well-being of the citizenry. For a long time we believed that the president and the Congress could determine the effectiveness with which the economy performs. I doubt it. They can surely make bad worse, but I doubt whether they can make bad better. It is worth stressing again that between 1940 and 1970 the real wages of an hour's work increased by about 150 percent. A critical question to which no one has the answer is whether we will be able to have such high real growth in the 1980s. Most economists doubt it.

Another lesson relates to the unexpected results from anticipated actions. Many of the plans of men and governments go awry, at times more than at other times. Clearly that is what happened with AFDC.

It is easy to develop excessive expectations, which can lead to serious trouble. For instance, during the 1960s the Democratic economists in Washington used to talk about "fine tuning the economy." Week after week I would say to my students: "I don't know what they're talking about and I suspect they don't know what they're talking about. They have no instruments with which to fine tune anything. They just say they are fine tuning." But the economy continued to work well. I still expected that one day it would go into a decline. Month after month passed, and I was proved wrong. The economy got better and better. This continued for one hundred and seven months—the longest expansionary cycle in the history of the United States. But in the 108th month, the economy started to slip. Proof was at hand that the economists could not fine tune the economy.

Another mistaken expectation is that the U.S. should aim at a single level of health care. In a society such as ours with gross inequalities in income and capital, this is not possible. A wealthy patient can afford to have round-the-clock nurses even if he or she is not seriously ill, but a society surely cannot provide that for everybody, not even for those who could profit from such care. Excessive expectations are dangerous, especially as more and more people take them seriously.

Another lesson is the importance of leadership, the essence of which is timing. The great presidents were astute, particularly with regard to their timing. I remind you that Mr. Lincoln never referred to freeing the slaves until late in the Civil War; he stressed that he was fighting to preserve the Union, which was quite a different matter.

Roosevelt illustrated the same principle. He had no clear view about where he was headed after 1933, but he sensed that the public wanted him to try to improve the economy and would support him as long as he kept trying and conditions got a little better. And they did. But in 1937, with his plan to pack the Supreme Court, FDR lost his touch and lost his support. Only the war saved him.

Eisenhower is another case in point. People, especially the academics and the literati, considered him weak. But Ike understood that the American people were tired from two wars and from the heavy hand of government. Except for the European alliance, NATO, which he was determined to protect, he pursued a largely passive role and in so doing turned out to be much smarter than his critics.

Lyndon Johnson, as noted earlier, was out in front of the public, an almost unheard stance for a politician. But LBJ wanted to accomplish a great deal—to improve the lot of the blacks, to get federal dollars into public education, to improve the health care system, to eliminate poverty. He was in a great hurry, and that hurry, together with Vietnam, was his undoing.

The present incumbent in the White House has made a mistake in interpreting his election, which he won with 53 percent of a small total vote. By no stretch of the imagination can such a margin be called a national mandate to alter fundamental social and economic policies. True, many taxpayers wanted relief, and some were entitled to have their taxes lowered. And regulation had gotten out of hand. But the president is engaged in a much more radical effort, which I believe is doomed because it has no support in logic or experience. Small wonder that Wall Street is bearish.

A country that is divided usually pulls itself together around issues of national security, which serve as social cement. But Vietnam proved the opposite. We are still paying a high price for our involvement in Vietnam because this was a war that Congress had not authorized. It was also one of the most unfair wars in this nation's history. The poor and the near poor were drafted while the rich and well-to-do enrolled at

Columbia, Harvard, and Princeton; at state universities and the University of Cincinnati. It was a disgrace, and we are paying for it to this day. To make matters worse, so many untruths and lies about that war came out of the White House and the Pentagon over the five or six years that the public lost faith in its leaders.

Another point relates to the difference between the dynamics of politics and the dynamics of the market. The dynamics of politics is the next election, and that's never more than a few months away. To complicate matters, in politics it is hard to sort out what is theater and what is reality. Both politicians and voters have difficulty in distinguishing verbal solutions from real solutions. At voting time, words rather than reality often control. But reality has a way of catching up. Mr. Hoover promised a chicken in every pot, but during the Great Depression many Americans were hungry.

The final lesson points up that in a democracy the mass of the population must agree before action is taken; and the poor, who are in the minority, suffer from that fact. Although everybody is suffering from inflation and many are unemployed, and although many others may be afraid of losing their jobs and even their homes, the majority of the population is still pretty well off. Until the majority are in bad shape, as happened during the Great Depression, or until most people come to a new understanding of old problems, such as happened with Civil Rights in the 1960s, we have no option but to live with the system as it operates which, as Churchill reminded us, is not very good, but it's the best of all the systems that we know. That's a hard lesson for the poor and for the hot-tempered reformers to appreciate, but it is a truth worth pondering.

Five concluding comments. First: A nation without vision will perish. Every nation must renew itself, and it can do so only by returning to the best of its traditions. Nations, like individuals, have a mixed past, good and seamy. The challenge they face is to seek renewal from their springs of strength.

Second: Leaders have the responsibility to persuade the populace that a society that does not accommodate to the needs of the poor, the marginal, the sick, the old, the weak, the ostracized, is a society at risk. Every leader must try to strengthen the social fabric.

Third: Every society needs multiple institutions of which the family is key. Then it needs intermediate institutions: corporations, trade unions, colleges, hospitals. Finally, it needs a governmental structure that can help to dovetail the multiple layers so that each can function better.

Fourth: Beware of those who have simple answers to complex problems, such as the ideologist who preaches about the beauties of the free market or socialism or the work ethic. A world that has known

Stalin and Hitler should be immunized against slogans.

Finally, I suggest that we can do no better than to stumble along, seeking to learn more as we go, applying what we learn to the policy arena; to remain on the lookout for what works and what doesn't and make appropriate adjustments as exerience teaches us; to remember that we are mortals, not divine, and that error will also be with us, but that justice and love can make this a better world.

CHAPTER 46

Manpower Policy: Retrospect and Prospect

THERE IS MORE THAN ONE WAY to address the theme of manpower policy during the past half century within the context of the Joint Economic Committee's concern with economic stabilization over the business cycle. We could take advantage of the long time span since the Great Depression and, at the beginning of 1980, identify a series of themes, some recurrent, some unique, that emerged during these five decades and that warrant attention and evaluation for their possible contribution to the armamentarium of cyclical policy instruments. Alternatively, we could opt for a chronological approach and pay attention to the specific macro conditions that prevailed at different stages of the economy's evolution and that called forth different manpower responses. A third approach, an attempt to merge the thematic and the chronological, is the one I will follow.

One of the most powerful doctrines in economics is the theory of comparative advantage, which implies that gains follow specialization; and it is anomalous that economists frequently fail to benefit from their own theories. As a long-time participant-observer of the manpower scene,

I see every reason to take advantage of direct experience. Unlike the more scientifically oriented of my colleagues, I do not believe that economists or any other social scientists can escape from their values, preconceptions, and prejudices; I believe that the same holds for those in the natural sciences, although the theories of the latter can usually be subjected to more rigorous objective tests.

My decision to start with a chronological approach is reinforced by a conviction that societies, like individuals and intermediary institutions, repeatedly confront an uncertain future to which they must respond, if only by deciding to do nothing different from what they have been doing—which, of course, itself is a response. Hence, to understand the evolution of manpower policy in the United States, it is not only desirable but necessary to probe the different challenges on the employment front to which manpower policies sought to respond.

Let me recall the different reactions of my two mentors, Wesley C. Mitchell and John Maurice Clark, to the Great Depression of the early 1930s. It was Mitchell's view that the federal government should intervene as little as possible in 1932 and 1933, since he was convinced that the long-delayed recuperative forces of the market would soon turn the economy around. J. M. Clark was an activist; he had a view of the economy that Keynes later elaborated and popularized: Once the downward threshold had been pierced, income and employment could keep declining until the economy ground to a halt. If two of the nation's—in fact, the world's—leading economists could assess the evidence so differently and offer such different advice, there is clearly much to be gained from a retrospective on manpower policy that remains sensitive to the changing macro context. To assist the reader in following the details of the story, we will establish some gross demarcations: the first covers the sixteen years of the "Depression, War, and Reconversion"; the next, the Truman-Eisenhower era which can be designated as "The Years of Domestic Tranquillity"; third, the last two decades can be entitled "Activism and Uncertainty," encompassing the administrations of Kennedy, Johnson, Nixon, Ford, and Carter.

CHRONOLOGY

Depression, War, and Reconversion

A historical account of manpower policy in the United States that would include more than its cyclical manifestations would have to start at the beginning of the Republic, when a slave was defined for purposes of representation in Congress, followed by the proximate termination of the slave trade, open immigration, and the use of the military in the conquest and settlement of the West.

Moreover, if the focus of the present effort were to move beyond federal policy and include private-sector efforts, we would have to include the attempts of leading corporations in the 1920s to reduce seasonal and, to a lesser extent, cyclical fluctuations. But in the present context the Great Depression is clearly the start of the story.

For the larger part of the 1930s the nation was afflicted with the most devastating depression in its history: The unemployment rate reached a peak of at least 25 percent; many workers were forced onto part-time schedules; manufacturing wages dropped to 5 cents an hour. Unemployed persons sold apples on the streets, foraged in refuse cans for food, stood in line for a bowl of hot soup provided by a philanthropic organization.

The overwhelming electoral victory of Franklin Delano Roosevelt over Herbert Hoover was an unequivocal signal from the American people that they had lost faith in the market to provide jobs and income for all who were able and willing to work. Consequently, President Roosevelt acted early and strongly to provide, through the newly established Civilian Works Administration, later the Works Progress Administration (WPA), both jobs and income for millions of the unemployed.

Even in retrospect it appears that the new administration had little option. It is possible that the new leaders might have legislated a dole without work, but the experimental mood and mode of the New Deal did not favor such a choice. The work ethic was deeply embedded in the American way of life. There was no reason to flout it once it had been decided to rely on a spending policy to turn the economy around.

Moreover, the passage of the Social Security Act in 1935 indicated that the federal government, on its own and in cooperation with the states and the private sector, would establish income supports for persons who had lost conventional sources of earnings as a result of unemployment, old age, or death of the principal wage earner.

Cyclical and secular goals can never be sharply differentiated. The Aid-to-Families-With-Dependent-Children provisions were adopted to help reduce the inflow of women into the labor force. Old Age and Survivors Insurance (OASI) was also expected to reduce the numbers seeking jobs. Unemployment Insurance (UI) gave the short-term unemployed some income when they were laid off or discharged.

With all these new federal supports in place, the national economy was shored up against a new severe decline. Nevertheless, doubts were soon raised about the effectiveness of public employment, not only through WPA but also the Civilian Conservation Corps (CCC) and the

National Youth Administration (NYA), as a lasting solution to the nation's severe unemployment. With the 1937 setback and the slow recovery that followed, the doubts increased. Many saw no early escape from the high, if falling, levels of chronic unemployment that had characterized the entire decade. In 1938 over 10 million workers were unemployed and fewer than 29 million were on the payrolls of nonagricultural establishments.

The nation's mobilization for war in 1940 and 1941, followed by its becoming an active belligerent on December 7, 1941, led to a strikingly rapid change in the labor market. The expansion of the defense industry and the armed forces proceeded at such a rapid pace that the more than 10 million unemployed in 1938 shrank to 2.7 million in 1942 and to 1 million in 1943, while the total number of employees in nonagricultural establishments expanded by almost 10 million between 1938 and 1942.

From the standpoint of manpower policy, we should note that the federal government made a decision to rely as far as possible on the "free labor market" to obtain the workers it needed to man the new wartime factories and offices. The government established some facilitating machinery, such as the War Manpower Commission and its regional offices, which sought to match job seekers and employers; the president, reacting to the pressure of black leaders, moved to reduce discrimination in war employment; the propaganda machines urged women to enter the labor market as a matter of patriotic duty, and they responded in large numbers.

Only rarely were the powers of the Selective Service System used to force workers to accept or remain at designated civilian jobs. In 1944 the undersecretary of war, Robert Patterson, asked Congress to legislate the regulation and control of the civilian labor market. Although some shortages engendered by a strike or other malfunctioning of the labor market interfered with military output, Congress and the nation, satisfied with how well the voluntary system was working, refused to respond to Patterson's request for draconian controls.

As the war finally drew to a close, there was concern about the recurrence of a major depression and large-scale unemployment as a result of the demobilization of military and naval establishments, which comprised more than 11 million persons, and the necessity to convert the economy from war to civilian output. The passage of the GI Bill contributed to reducing the number of veterans immediately searching for jobs; but except for this one piece of legislation, the diffuse concerns about a postwar depression did not lead to action, at least federal action. Nevertheless, the Committee for Economic Development under the leadership of Paul Hoffman undertook a major educational campaign to encourage businessmen to move as expeditiously and strongly as possible once the war wound down to reconvert their factories to meet what he correctly estimated would be an explosion of civilian demands on the economy.

In 1945 and again in 1946, Congress debated the desirability of a Full Employment Act, which eventually was passed into law as the Employment Act of 1946. The story of this legislation has been chronicled. An oversimplified view might see the Employment Act as the institutionalization of the lessons of the New Deal. This legislation stipulated that never again should the federal government stand by and fail to act if the economy went into a tailspin. In the Employment Act, Congress declared that it was the obligation of the federal government to use all its powers to facilitate the economy's operating at a high level of employment, output, and income and, in the event of a decline, to use its powers to help restore the economy to a high level of performance.

The Years of Domestic Tranquillity

The economic recession that so many economists expected to follow the Armistice fortunately did not materialize, but during the second half of the 1940s the unemployment rate reached a monthly peak of over 7 percent. President Truman, however, beset by difficulties abroad and feuding with the Congress on many issues, did not launch any manpower initiatives other than some steps to desegregate the armed forces after his surprise election in 1948. The lackluster performance of the economy and the soft employment picture remained characteristic until after the outbreak of hostilities in Korea.

President Eisenhower did not believe presidents had to be activists; he was certain that, after the traumatic experiences of the Great Depression, World War II, and Korea, the American people looked forward to the federal government's keeping a low profile. Advised by an ultraconservative secretary of the Treasury, George M. Humphrey, and a sophisticated academic economist, Arthur F. Burns, the president interpreted the Employment Act of 1946 to mean that in the event of a cyclical downturn, the federal government could incur a budget deficit for one year.

His conservative stance notwithstanding, President Eisenhower signed an important piece of manpower legislation in 1958, the National Defense Education Act, which Congress passed in response to the launching of Sputnik and which legislated the expansion of the nation's supply of scientists and engineers. Although the president did not really approve of the federal government's financing higher education, he could not veto a measure that Congress defined as a priority closely linked to the nation's defense. But he vetoed, not once but twice, Senator Douglas's bill aimed at having the federal government assist distressed areas to improve their economies and increase their employment.

Activism and Uncertainty

During his campaign for the presidency, John F. Kennedy talked about "getting the country moving again," but in accordance with the dictates of politics and his own underlying conservatism he did not specify just how he planned to accomplish this goal if he emerged the victor. In 1961 the Area Redevelopment Act (ARA), a modification of Senator Douglas's twice vetoed effort to help distressed areas, was passed and was signed by the new president. With this legislation the federal government reentered the manpower arena in a modest and unobtrusive fashion. The ARA authorized the use of federal funds for the short-term training (up to ninety days) of the labor force to encourage employers to relocate in areas of high unemployment. For the first time since the 1930s, the federal government became directly involved in funding manpower training with an aim of expanding employment. Although it was a modest effort with small funds spread over a great many locations, it did represent a departure in policy: It was an acknowledgement that the market alone might not assure jobs to all who wanted them and were able to work.

Despite the president's campaign promise to "get the country moving again," the unemployment rate during the early months of 1962 rose above the 7 percent level, and the recovery from the third recession in a relatively few years found the country at a new high level of unemployment. Largely under the congressional leadership of Senator Joseph Clark and Representative Elmer J. Holland of Pennsylvania, an extensive record had been developed in 1960 and 1961 through hearings, research, and expert testimony about the "manpower problem"; this record laid the basis for a more direct and focused effort to cope with the distressingly high levels of unemployment. Much of the responsibility for rising unemployment was ascribed by manpower advocates to automation, which in turn suggested the remedy: retraining the workers who had lost their jobs as a result of technological advances.

The Council of Economic Advisers (CEA) under Walter Heller was unimpressed by both the analysis and the remedy. In its view the trouble stemmed from a deficiency in overall demand; the solution lay in macrostimulation. But the manpower protagonists found support among the Federal Reserve Board, in the U.S. Department of Labor, and above all in both houses of the Congress and in both political parties.

The Manpower Development and Training Act (MDTA) was passed with large bipartisan majorities in March 1962 as a federal-state training program with an appropriation of $81 million. Not long thereafter, the CEA's education of the president began to bear fruit, and he became willing to pursue an expansionary macro policy, which coincided with the turnaround of market forces.

By the time Congress looked at MDTA in the late spring of 1963, it was clear that the CEA had won out over the structuralists: Weak demand, not automation, had been the cause of high unemployment; the recovery had led to the reemployment of most skilled workers who had earlier lost their jobs. But the structuralists were also right: MDTA revealed the existence of a large number of marginal workers who needed training— workers who were poorly educated, without skills, with little work experience. The 1963 amendments to MDTA opened the program to these disadvantaged persons.

Additional federal innovations were made in the following year via the manpower provisions of the Economic Opportunity Act, which established the Job Corps (residential training centers) for seriously disadvantaged youth and the Neighborhood Youth Corps in which youngsters from low-income families would enroll in a work experience program that would provide them with a modest weekly wage. This latter program, it was hoped, would keep the cities cool during the long hot summer.

When the economy continued to expand after 1965—less because of the success of the fine-tuning of economists than because of Vietnam and the growing inflation—both the administration and Congress shied away from new legislative initiatives in the manpower arena. The group most in need of help were inner-city blacks, and in 1968 President Johnson sought the help of the National Association of Businessmen; he asked them to lend a hand by recruiting and hiring large numbers of minorities. But the effort was aborted by the recession that got under way late in 1969.

The first Nixon administration saw the emergence of a new dimension of manpower policy, federal job creation, which had been dormant since the New Deal. In December 1970 President Nixon vetoed the new manpower act because it contained a provision for direct job creation. Six months later, faced with the release of large numbers of Vietnam veterans into a soft labor market and a Democratic Congress committed to federal job creation, the president signed the Emergency Employment Act—a $2.2 billion, two-year job creation effort. It should be noted parenthetically that the AFL–CIO was a principal lobbyist for the job creation approach.

In the succeeding two and a half years the administration of manpower programs clearly called for decentralization and decategorization, but this essential reform was held up because the Nixon administration did not want to accept a permanent job creation title in the design of the Comprehensive Employment and Training Act (CETA). A compromise was finally worked out, which limited the new job creation title to a relatively small number of slots, 200,000, to serve the structurally unemployed.

President Ford took office in August 1974; in September he reviewed the state of the economy with 100 leading authorities and received an optimistic assessment, but shortly thereafter the economy turned down, headed for its worst post–World War II recession.

The Democratic leadership in the Congress, dissatisfied with the administration's cautious proposals, decided to take the lead to cushion the impact of prospective large increases in unemployment and large losses in consumer purchasing power. It moved along three interrelated fronts by creating about 200,000 additional public-service jobs, this time for the cyclically unemployed; extending the UI system to provide support for up to sixty-five weeks; and providing unemployment assistance for considerable numbers of workers who had previously not been covered by the UI system. Since even at its peak, public-service employment (PSE) provided work and income for no more than 1 out of every 25 of the unemployed, unemployment insurance and unemployment assistance carried most of the responsibility for supporting those who had lost their jobs. But the Congress had established the principle of using PSE as an explicit countercyclical tool.

The response to the recession of 1974–1975 had drawbacks. There were two distinct PSE programs on the books, one aimed at helping the structurally unemployed, the other, larger effort directed to the cyclically unemployed. In 1976, under the leadership of the Senate, Congress moved to increase the targeting of PSE in favor of the structurally unemployed, a position it reaffirmed and strengthened in the reauthorization of CETA that it passed in 1978.

But we must go back and look more closely at the early days of the Carter administration, which came into office in January 1977. Within the first few months, the new administration placed heavy bets on manpower policy, most importantly by allocating half of its $20 billion stimulus package for the expansion of manpower programs (mostly PSE) and using its influence to obtain a comprehensive Youth Act from the Congress. The administration promised to expand PSE from a level of under 300,000 to 725,000 within twelve months, a promise it kept and even exceeded.

Doubt and confusion accompanied the successful expansion of PSE. The budget advisors found the program very costly; the CEA expressed doubts about whether these large-scale federal expenditures were leading to a net increase in jobs or only to a substitution of federal for state and local dollars; many members of Congress were concerned about the fiscal and administrative integrity of CETA. The unchecked enthusiasm for manpower policy did not survive the first year of the new administration. The prolongation of recovery, not only into 1978 but also into 1979, with the concomitant decline in the unemployment rate to below 6 percent also helped to erode support for the costly manpower programs, especially in a period of accelerating inflation.

The budget for fiscal 1980 reflected the relative strengths of the opposing sides; the critics were able to obtain some reductions in the scale of the PSE program, but they were not able to gut it. The budget for fiscal 1981, submitted at what appeared to be the onset of the long-delayed recession, contains the preceding year's compromise, but with the important addition of the president's signaling his concern for the horrendously high and unyielding unemployment rates among disadvantaged teenagers by requesting additional budgetary authority that, over two years, would result in $2 billion additional funding.

A THEMATIC RECAPITULATION

Now that we have presented the chronology of federal manpower policies and programs, we are in a better position to focus on the principal themes that have informed this almost half century of federal effort, involving fifteen administrations from the first term of FDR to the fourth year of the incumbency of Jimmy Carter.

The themes that offer the most understanding are those that address the ends Congress sought to accomplish with its several interventions, although most legislation of course is responsive to multiple, not single goals. We will consider then the groups in the body politic that Congress singled out as beneficiaries of the new programs and the specific programs Congress passed to accomplish its multiple objectives. An assessment of these different manpower programs and policies will help inform the prospective section at the end of this analysis.

It is relatively easy to identify at least fifteen specific objectives that Congress hoped to achieve through manpower programming. Here in brief is a short summary of each of the objectives:

- To provide jobs for the chronically unemployed, was the major goal of the New Deal efforts, when so many regularly attached members of the labor force suffered long spells of unemployment, and the more recent focus on the structurally unemployed — that is, on those who, despite the generally upbeat nature of the post–World War II employment situation, experienced substantial difficulties in getting and holding regular jobs.

- To assure, through the job creation programs of the 1930s as well as those of the 1970s, that the unemployed who were placed in federally supported jobs contributed to useful social output. The history of WPA is replete with illustrations of such useful output from construction projects to the production of original and attractive art. Dr. Richard Nathan's studies of the work performed by persons on PSE in the late 1970s also point to useful output.

- In light of our ethos that it is better for a person to earn his way than to receive a handout, members of Congress have sought to protect the self-respect of the unemployed by providing them with opportunities to work on useful projects, preferably where their skills can be utilized, but in any case to work.

- To bring the economy closer to full employment or at least to reduce the gap between performance and potential were surely high among the congressional objectives during the New Deal, the response to the recession of 1974–1975, and the Carter stimulus package of 1977.

- Although there were specific regional stimulation objectives in the ARA legislation of 1961, it was not until 1973, when Congress legislated the decentralization of manpower programming under CETA, that specific localities, of which South Carolina is an outstanding example, had increased scope to stimulate local economic development through the judicious harnessing of the federal training funds to assure new employers of a ready work force.

- The fact that training programs could be approved under MDTA only after a finding had been made by local officials and representatives of employers and labor that there would be jobs for the workers to be trained, suggests that the goal of the training effort in the 1960s was closely linked to meeting the requirements of communities for specific orders of skill.

- At the time of the wind-down of hostilities in Vietnam, President Nixon was willing to sign, if reluctantly, the Emergency Employment Act of 1971 on the ground that it would help ease the demobilization effort at a time of a soft civilian labor market.

- Basic to the philosophy underlying both MDTA and CETA was the belief that persons first entering the labor market and those who had obtained jobs but were still at the bottom of the ladder could be helped by entering a training program through which they could add to their human capital and could look forward to securing better jobs with more income and better career prospects.

- Closely related was the belief when MDTA was first passed in

1962 that unless retraining opportunities were provided by the federal government to workers who had lost their jobs in a number of industries where automation had made rapid progress, such as coal mining and steel, there was a real danger that many skilled workers would never make it back into the regular labor market, surely not into good jobs.

- Both during the New Deal and after 1964 when the federal government explicitly focused on the problems of youth, one important objective was to provide students in high school with some earning opportunities so that they would be encouraged to remain in school and secure a diploma, which, it was assumed, would later ease their transition into employment.

- The Neighborhood Youth Corps (NYC) of 1964 had a related objective that had not been included in the New Deal/NYA work-study program. The intervening years had witnessed the substantial relocation of the black population from southern farms to the inner cities of the North. With racial tensions rising rapidly—Watts followed within one year of the passage of NYC—Congress hoped that the $600 to $700 or so that a high school student could earn during the summer would prevent the cities from exploding.

- The Civilian Conservation Corps of the New Deal made it attractive for large numbers of out-of-school youth with little prospect of securing jobs to spend a year or so on environmental projects, many of which were aimed at beautifying our national parks and making them more accessible to tourists.

- The Job Corps—a creation of the Great Society—had a related but distinguishable objective. Here the emphasis was on rehabilitating the most seriously disadvantaged of urban youth, those from low-income homes, who were school dropouts, most of whom belonged to minorities, in residential centers where they would be afforded the opportunity for educational remediation, skill training, personal counseling, and assistance in career development.

- Since the unemployment rate among white married men was low or very low during most of the 1960s and 1970s, MDTA and, even more, CETA focused attention increasingly on blacks and to a lesser degree the Hispanic communities, which were afflicted with differentially high levels of unemployment. A striking response was the provision in the Emergency Employment Act of 1971 to facilitate the upward mobility of minorities into the regular civil service by affording them opportunities to acquire job experience and training while holding PSE jobs.

- Finally, and most important, these many varieties of manpower programs, together with the ever broader unemployment insurance system, aimed to provide income to those at the lower end of the distribution, and particularly to those whose unemployment cut off their normal source of earnings.

A few strands run through this synopsis of rich and variegated federal manpower programing. There are, first, the two extremes of public manpower policy: One mandates income transfers to the unemployed so that, despite their loss of jobs, they will obtain the income they need to protect their basic standard of living, even if many of the extras in their usual consumption might be jeopardized, especially if they remain out of work for a long period of time.

At the other extreme, the federal government seeks to compensate for the employment shortfall in the regular economy by creating public service jobs. The earnings from such jobs have tended to provide a level of income considerably higher than transfers under UI; and, with liberal state or local supplementation, some of the unemployed lost little.

In between these two contrasting modes there are a variety of training efforts directed to helping to prepare the unemployed for the job market or to increase the skills of those who have been poorly prepared. Here too there is a considerable range between efforts that are heavily income-transfer-oriented, such as the Summer Youth Program and most other so-called work experience programs for adults, and true training programs such as training for practical nurses or automotive mechanics, which provide enrollees with ten to twelve months of serious skill instruction with the aim of assuring their permanent advancement up the skill and income hierarchy.

One other set of observations is suggested by the chronology. In the manpower programs and policies since 1962, there has been a distinct shift in the targeted groups. Except for the early years of MDTA and the 1974 countercyclical PSE program, white adult males with more or less regular attachment to the labor force have not been singled out. Instead, the programs have increasingly sought to enroll disadvantaged white and minority adult males with poor or no labor market experience and youths with similar characteristics, in which low family income has been an important selection criterion. Although many disadvantaged women, both white and black, have participated in these programs, they were seldom singled out for special attention by either the Congress or the prime sponsors.

Except for the Job Corps and a limited number of other experiments, the manpower programs served poorly the seriously disadvantaged, those released from institutions, and older persons. Since congressional funding fell far short of the sums required to assist those with lesser handicaps for employment, the manpower officialdom decided to concentrate on those more likely to make the transition into regular jobs.

RELATED MANPOWER PROGRAMS

So far we have considered the manpower policy arena as consisting of the specific programs under the jurisdiction of the U.S. Department of Labor, together with the federal-state unemployment insurance system and the special legislation for unemployment assistance benefits passed in 1974. But, as with all boundary demarcations, the lines could be drawn somewhat narrower (without UI) or broader. The following paragraphs provide a brief consideration of the nature and goals of a group of related federal efforts that have had as one of their principal objectives facilitating the employment or reemployment of persons able to work.

The oldest of these efforts, dating back to the Public Works Administration in the New Deal, involves federal funding for public works in periods of high unemployment, where one major objective is the direct and indirect increase in employment. For many reasons—including the relatively high cost per worker employed, the difficulty of hiring large numbers of unskilled workers, the long start-up time, the out-of-sync relationship with the recovery phase of the business cycle—Congress has been chary about using the public works approach as a countercyclical tool, but not so chary as to neglect it completely. Several times in the post–World War II era sizable public works activities were nonetheless launched for countercyclical purposes. The assessment made by the Brookings Institution of the earlier efforts reached a negative conclusion of their utility as a countercyclical tool. The study concluded that there may be a way to improve early planning, to stress "soft" public works, to insist on the hiring of the structurally unemployed, but it is questionable how far, even under the most favorable of circumstances, public works can be used as a major instrument for countercyclical employment policy.

In 1967 and again in 1971 Congress decided that special efforts had to be directed to finding jobs for the rapidly growing numbers of employable persons on the welfare rolls; it therefore legislated Work Incentive Programs, WIN I and II. These two programs required women on AFDC with no child under six at home and otherwise employable to make themselves available for training or placement. Those who were placed were permitted to retain some earnings above their welfare allowance to compensate them for job-related expenses and to encourage them to remain employed. Through these programs, several hundred thousand women are removed from the welfare rolls each year but because of limited skills, low earnings, and recurrent family problems, a significant proportion rejoin the welfare rolls. The Carter administration at the beginning of 1980 is seeking to launch a substantial demonstration program that will provide a job for the principal wage earner in every family with children on welfare. The results will be monitored to determine whether a more carefully crafted effort will in fact prove successful in moving large numbers of employable persons from welfare into permanent jobs.

In 1976 and in 1978 Congress passed special tax legislation aimed at stimulating increases in employment. The first provided relatively modest benefits for employers if they could demonstrate that they had expanded the total numbers on their payroll from the preceding year. The latter act was a targeted tax credit which provided larger financial advantages over two years to employers who could demonstrate that they had newly hired structurally unemployed persons.

Since there is no easy or direct way to assess the employment creating efforts of these two approaches, much less to sort out costs and benefits, there are substantial differences of opinion among the experts about their employment-creating potential. The issue is further complicated by the U.S. Treasury's dragging its feet in popularizing such tax reduction schemes. Even the skeptics admit that the use of the tax approach could, under a supportive bureaucracy, operate with some speed and success in stimulating employment gains in soft labor markets; there is less agreement about the potential costs of such an approach. The Treasury has argued with some justification that most employers would gain a tax advantage for hiring persons whom they would have added in any case, and this elicits the response from proponents that the same could hold true for the special benefits that are provided for accelerated capital investments.

The last related federal program with clear manpower objectives is the Equal Employment Opportunity structure, which was given a legislative basis in the Civil Rights Act of 1964 and which has been elaborated and refined since then via legislation, administration, and judicial interpretation. The aim of affirmative action programs is to decrease and remove the discriminatory barriers against minorities and women—as well as against older persons and the handicapped—so that they can share more equitably in jobs, careers, and income. Unless affirmative action programs succeed in altering employer personnel practices, there is relatively little that federal training programs alone can accomplish for minorities. In fact to the extent that affirmative action programs are successful—and they have been in varying degrees—to that extent manpower programs are likely to prove more effective.

This brief consideration of manpower programs rooted in public works, welfare, tax, or affirmative action helps to underscore the multi-dimensional and multifaceted aspects of employment in an advanced economy even if one's perspective is restricted to federal policy alone. If we broaden our perspective to include the major determinants of employment in the private sector of the economy and in the transformations that characterize the larger society, we will multiply these facets many times.

THE TRANSFORMATION OF THE U.S. LABOR MARKET: THE LONGER VIEW

With the advantage of hindsight, we can distinguish the following major transformations that have occurred during the past half century and can briefly indicate the major forces that contributed to these developments:

- The accelerated movement of persons off the farm, including a high proportion of all blacks, encouraged by the Agricultural Adjustment Act of the New Deal and subsequent federal farm support policies; the strong demand for unskilled labor during World War II; the broadening experiences of the millions who served in the military forces; the continuing rapid expansion of nonfarm employment in the post–World War II era. The economy accommodated well to these changes. However, many minority group workers who relocated in urban centers suffered high unemployment. Prior to moving they suffered from high underemployment on southern farms.
- The rapid growth, both absolute and relative, of the numbers of women who hold jobs. Among the principal factors contributing to this transformation have been the response to the patriotic appeal for married women to enter or reenter the economy during World War II; rising levels of education; smaller families after 1957; a shift of the economy toward services; metropolitanization; and, more recently, the women's revolution reflected in changing aspirations, career preparation and life-styles.
- The generally strong demand for labor (but not strong enough to provide jobs for the rapidly growing numbers who wanted to work) during the four decades from 1940 to 1980, which kept the country free of any serious or sustained decline in employment. In the quarter century between 1950 and 1975, the United States experienced a 50 percent gain in total employment and, in the four years since the turning point in the recession of 1974–1975,

the economy has added another 12 million jobs, or a gain of roughly 14 percent.

- The rapid growth of the labor force particularly since 1960 reflected a doubling of the numbers of young people reaching working age—from 2 to 4 million annually—reinforced by the steep increases in the numbers of women in the labor force, with further additions from immigrants, both legal and illegal.
- The two previously mentioned developments resulted in the fact that despite its rapid growth in total employment, the U.S. economy has been characterized by an unsatisfactory level of unemployment throughout most of the last four decades except for the three wartime periods, when the labor market varied between tight and very tight.
- In the depressed 1930s, as an effort to hold young people out of the labor market, and in the post–World War II era, educational expenditures were increased rapidly, with the result that more and more young people acquired their high school diplomas and a significant proportion went on to acquire an associate, college, or higher degree. Thus a better-educated labor force contributed to the flexibility of the U.S. economy in coping more effectively with the opportunities it confronted in the post–World War II era, and which were reflected until recently in high productivity and rapid growth.

A fuller account of the important transformations in the employment scene would have to go beyond the factors noted—migration from farm to urban centers, increase in women workers, continuing high level demand for labor, rapid growth of the labor force, high levels of unemployment, and rising educational achievement. Attention would have to be paid to trade unions, trends in technology, the growth of income transfers, early retirement, and the many other developments that have had important impacts, direct and indirect, on the employment scene. But the critical point of an enlarged perspective is that manpower policies and programs have had only a modest impact relative to the far-reaching effects of the underlying forces propelling the economy and the society.

PROSPECT

The principal advantage of a retrospective view is that it is possible to discriminate between the more important causes and consequences and those of less importance that have helped to shape the course of events. Without the advantages of time and distance, it frequently is impossible to separate the important from the unimportant. But we must be careful in extracting the lessons of the past; we must not apply them indiscriminately to the future, which will always differ from the past. Within these parameters we will attempt to set out our understanding of the potential and limits of manpower policy against a concern for economic stabilization. We will set out the guiding principles with only a modicum of supporting analysis. As a rhetorical device the perspectives that follow are divided into two groups: lessons and problems.

Lessons

It is not practical to seek to distinguish too sharply between cyclical and structural causes of unemployment and to develop specific remedies for each. A loose labor market, such as existed in the later 1930s, and to a lesser degree in the later 1940s, 1950s, and mid-1970s, illustrates how cyclical and structural components run into each other and confuse and compound policies and programs that seek to distinguish sharply among the unemployed as to the causes of their unemployment. This is not to say that in the face of limited federal dollars it is not desirable or feasible to distinguish among unemployed persons in terms of their need for and ability to make use of special manpower assistance, but in a national economy with substantial differences among local economies there are limits to making a rigid separation between cyclical and structural unemployment. The confusion in the early days of MDTA and the difficulties in operating CETA with two Titles II and VI after 1974 speak to this point.

How far can manpower programs go to absorb the unemployed? Clearly quite far if they are financed at the level of the New Deal, when they provided employment at peak for around 3 million workers in comparison to less than 30 million employed on nonfarm jobs. On the other hand, not very far when we look at the more recent record: The 425,000 increase in PSE jobs between March 1977 and March 1978 must be considered in the perspective of a nonagricultural work force of around 85 million. Without further elaboration at this point, we can postulate that manpower policies should be viewed not as a substitute for but as an addition to macro policy, which must retain primary responsibility for enabling the economy to operate at a continuing high level of employment.

Manpower policy has demonstrated its capacity to assist particular groups of unemployed or underemployed persons to improve their employability prospects and thereby to help them to obtain regular jobs or better jobs with more earnings and security. This was most clearly the case when, as under MDTA, disadvantaged adults and youths had an opportunity to enter serious training at the conclusion of which they were able to find jobs at double the legal minimum wage. The same favorable result can be deduced for some young people who entered the Job Corps and, through this second-chance opportunity, were able to remedy their educational deficiencies, obtain preskill training, and upon completion enter desirable apprenticeships.

In a culture such as ours, which continues to place a high value on work, there is clearly a place for manpower policies and programs which through income maintenance, training programs, or public-service employment aim to make a contribution to future employability of the unemployed. One proviso: This logic does not cover the regularly attached worker who is laid off and who is likely to be recalled, even in a severe recession, before his twenty-six or thirty-nine weeks of unemployment insurance runs out. Nevertheless, the logic probably holds for most of this group who have been continuously unemployed for thirty-nine weeks, at which point they should surely be encouraged to enter a retraining program, search for a job in a distant community with the help of a relocation allowance, or accept a PSE position as the price of necessary continuing income assistance.

Although the evidence from the new Youth Entitlement program will not be available until 1981 or later, the record of the New Deal's NYA and the Great Society's NYC leaves serious questions about whether the opportunity for high school students to earn while they learn is sufficient inducement to keep potential dropouts in school, or to induce significant numbers of dropouts to return to school to acquire their diplomas. There is a rationale for encouraging students to remain in school if they can profit from instruction until they earn their diplomas, but if the school provides a dysfunctional learning and socializing environment, as many do, the use of manpower programming to keep young people on the rolls can be self-defeating. Many of these young people really need a more constructive environment, such as a well-designed and operated cooperative educational program.

It is easier to see a role for manpower programming to assist young people who are out of school but who are having difficulty in developing an effective attachment to the labor market. To permit them to flounder, to move from one short-term unskilled job to another with long intervals of unemployment in between, may result in their reaching their mid-twenties without a regular attachment to the labor market. This bodes ill for their long-term opportunities to work and support themselves and their dependents. Better by far to help them remedy their educational deficiencies, acquire work experience and skill, and facilitate their transition into regular jobs.

The same logic applies to persons who are released from institutions — reformatories, drug rehabilitation units, prisons, mental institutions. Almost all these individuals will find it difficult to get regular jobs on their own. Their prior institutionalization makes most employers wary about hiring them, particularly since the job seekers frequently have little skill or experience.

Although periodic efforts to link work and welfare more closely, such as WIN, have had only modest success since the New Deal, the about-to-be-launched experiments to provide jobs in the private or public sector for the principal wage earner in each family on welfare with children (over age six) speak to the continuing concern of administrations and the Congress that employable persons not receive public assistance without working. The difficulties that have not been surmounted to date involve finding solutions that rely less on compulsion and more on incentives; how to operate a two-tier public employment sector without the lower-paying jobs threatening the wage and working standards of regular civil service employees; assuring that an enlarged number of PSE jobs for unemployed persons does not lead to the artificial creation of new households for the purpose of qualifying for one of these positions; assuring that those who obtain a government work assignment will sooner or later move into the regular economy. This simple list of these difficulties helps explain why progress in linking work and welfare has so far proved so difficult. But that is no reason to give up: The challenge remains. Clearly manpower programming should be able to assist in the reduction of employables who receive welfare or other forms of income transfer.

We have identified seven important lessons from the nation's uses of manpower policy, which should help in the period ahead in improving the employability and employment of vulnerable groups in the population and in easing the transitions of such groups from nonwork to work settings.

The lessons we have extracted do not provide a blueprint for the future but they point to directions where manpower policy can prove constructive.

Problems

To exploit fully the past for the light it can throw on the future requires that attention also be directed to a set of issues where the findings are equivocal and the recommendations for future policy no more than suggestive.

Many economists, including some who are ideologically friendly to government's assuming a redistributive goal, believe that in an economy with less than full employment, manpower programs directed at improving the employability and employment of disadvantaged groups can do little more than alter the positions of persons in the queue. In their view, if one person gains another must lose. The theoretical constructs which they use to demonstrate this inevitable outcome are powerful but not necessarily fully convincing. Improvements in the quality of the labor force, particularly increasing the numbers able to meet employers' routine hiring standards, may have a marginal effect on the numbers hired. In any case, even the skeptics are usually willing to admit that manpower programs may have a beneficial outcome in terms of equity since they expand opportunities for the disadvantaged even when they do not enlarge the total numbers who are employed.

A closely related issue, only recently joined in debates among economists, is the potential of selective manpower policies—that is, expenditures targeted at locations and groups that experience differentially high unemployment. The advocates contend that selective measures can contribute to employment increases without substantially worsening the current inflationary pressures. While the theoretical analysis is sophisticated, this approach must still prove itself. If it could, the potential for manpower policy in an inflationary era could be promising indeed.

The economy is steadily shifting away from goods production to output of services; as many as 2 out of every 3 workers are employed in a service industry today. Since service employment is more heavily concentrated among small and medium employers, upward mobility is harder to pursue since it frequently involves changing employers. Since many entrance jobs in the service sector pay little, the lack of clarity about how to get a better job at better pay in the future may be a deterrent to certain young people who confront such jobs. This formulation is no more than an hypothesis to explain some aspects of the youth labor market. But the critical role of jobs and income mobility in influencing workers' behavior surely justifies a more careful study of the growing importance of service jobs in the U.S. economy.

The experience of the economy in the 1960s and 1970s points up new interrelationships among rapid job creation, the rapid growth of the labor force, and the slow downward response of the unemployment rate. If it is true, as it appears from this recent experience, that a ratchet effect has been operating whereby new jobs attract new members into the labor force, the size of the overhang is critically important in any national effort to move toward a full employment economy. Estimates made in the late 1970s suggest that there may be as many as two potential workers for every counted unemployed worker. Whether this calculation is sound and how long the ratio will hold requires study.

A related phenomenon involves the likely consequences of having raised the compulsory retirement age from sixty-five to seventy in a period of continuing inflation. Half of all workers have been retiring prior to the age of sixty-five; if they now decide to remain until they are seventy, the implications for the labor market, in terms of both competition for jobs and opportunities for advancement, warrant attention. In some sectors such as higher education, the implications can be serious if the new legislation blocks opportunities for new hires and tenure appointments.

We need to know much more about the interactions between changes in the domestic labor market and the flow of newcomers, legal and illegal, to the United States. If some of the more extreme estimates of illegal newcomers are correct, and if the potential stream of immigrants is as large as some believe, manpower policy must reckon with these present and future flows at least until they have been brought under more effective control if this should become the declared and enforceable policy of the United States.

These six problematic areas, which are illustrative rather than inclusive, have been identified for the sole purpose of warning against simplistic views concerning the potential of manpower policy in the years ahead. In light of the limited extant knowledge of the determinants of employment external to our economy and society that will affect the future supply of labor, we must see manpower policy as no more but also no less than what it is—an evolving tool to improve the realization of the nation's employment goals.

CHAPTER 47

Federal Training Programs

ANALYSTS WHO HAVE LOOKED CAREFULLY at one or another aspect of the nation's manpower policy and programs during the past two decades have reached some broad judgments about their value to the individuals involved and to the nation at large. They have identified both positive and negative conclusions about the different training programs.

Those who looked at the distributional effects on personal income of these manpower efforts concluded that long-term effects were usually nonexistent or trivial. However, they concluded that those who participated in these programs were better off than they would otherwise have been.

Analysts who have addressed the interface between manpower and macroeconomic policy concluded that there is a role for selective-employment programs that can expand the number of jobs for the hard-to-employ. Such jobs generally pay low wages and therefore have less inflationary potential than jobs stimulated through the use of macro measures. But these analysts see little or no possibility of reaching the goal of full employment in the near future.

Most analysts have noted that weaknesses in the data base interfered with reaching clear-cut judgments. We know too little about every aspect of these programs—who entered; how long they stayed; what auxiliary services, such as occupational counseling, they received while they were in the program; whether they were assisted after they completed their programs; when they obtained jobs; how long those who obtained jobs held them; and how much they were paid.

If better data had been available, however, that alone could not have assured that assessments would be valid. Consider the following difficulties in reaching valid judgments: The programs were in constant flux, partly as a result of changes introduced because of experience (Job Corps); shifts in eligibility requirements modified, often radically, the kinds of persons accepted for training or employment; variations in the management, content, operations, and linkages to employers in the same program at different locations made each program more or less unique.

A second source of complexity reflects differences in the external environment. In a tight labor market, such as existed in the late 1960s, it may be possible to persuade employers to provide large-scale on-the-job training programs, but this kind of cooperation cannot be elicited in a loose labor market. A large public-service employment program will have better prospects of succeeding in a city that is under severe fiscal pressure and where its civil service workers have a relatively weak organization than in a city in which one or both of these conditions are absent.

Finally the political ambience and the public's mood are important factors in determining outcomes. It is easier to launch a new program or expand an existing one when legislators are enthusiastic and the public is supportive, as in early 1977 when Congress more than doubled the scale of the PSE program and passed the new Youth Act, than when enthusiasm has been dampened, as happened two years later.

These realities that constrain social intervention in a democracy are the justification for the broad assessment that will be ventured herein. That assessment is informed by the judgments of specialists, but it is not bounded by them. I have relied in large measure on my ongoing research in the manpower arena, reinforced by the unique opportunity I have had since the onset of the federal programs to serve as the chairman of successive advisory bodies to the president, the Congress, and the secretary of labor.

CRITERIA FOR EVALUATING PROGRAMS

Since we have considered the difficulties of assessing federal manpower programs, it may be helpful to also consider how criteria, parameters, and target groups are likely to affect the outcomes. With respect to the criteria for evaluation, we can differentiate the effects on the individuals who participate, on others affected by the program, on the economy, and on broader considerations of social welfare. A few words about each. If we focus on the individual participant, we will want to consider whether the person in training or in a public-service job is better off in terms of income and other benefits than he or she would be otherwise. Since most manpower programs have been voluntary—the principal exception being WIN—there is a presumption that enrollees see advantages in participating. The allowances or wages paid them while in a program usually add an increment, sometimes a relatively large increment, to family income.

However, the answer to whether the individual gains from participating in a program is elsewhere: The key question is whether, as a result of participating, the individual will have more employment and more income in the future. The answer, then, is in the postprogram effects, and here a related question is whether the gains will be for a relatively short period, a year or two, or for a longer period.

Although the immediate and later impacts on the participant are important, they are only the beginning of a comprehensive effort at assessment. If one assumes, as most economists do, that the demand for labor at any point in time is determined by macroeconomic policy, then government efforts to improve the competitive position of one group of workers are likely to be at the expense of another group that will be pushed further back in the hiring queue. A concrete illustration of such substitution can be seen in municipalities discharging civil service workers for budgetary reasons at the same time that they are adding PSE workers who will perform some, if not all, of the tasks of those who were let go.

It is even more difficult to assess the impact on the economy of manpower programs. For instance, some economists believe that the demand for labor is not independent of the quality of the available supply. Consequently, they argue, building skills and competences in persons on the periphery of the labor force can make a difference in the total numbers who obtain employment. But even these economists find it difficult to determine when the balance tips from positive to negative outcomes in undertaking additional public investments to raise the skill level with an eye to expanding employment.

The current view, as indicated above, is that selective-employment programs aimed at expanding employment opportunities for the hard-to-employ are less inflationary than is macroeconomic policy. But even if we accept this conclusion, it does not provide much policy guidance as to the scale and design of these programs.

Much the same uncertainty exists in the case of policies aimed at reversing the decline of urban neighborhoods, cities, and regions by encouraging the employment of underused manpower resources. Unemployment and underemployment are serious wastes. The potential contribution of unemployed workers is permanently lost. But since large public resources are required to turn a declining area around, and since, even with such investments, the reversal may not occur, the outcome will be negative. The jobs that could have been created in other areas with these resources exceed the numbers that were in fact added.

To complicate the question we should consider further the difficulties of assessing, prospectively or even retrospectively, the trade-offs in a period of high inflation, such as at present, between short-term stimulation of the economy through a large effort at job creation and the impact of such a policy on the inflationary environment and on long-range employment.

Finally, we shall briefly consider the difficulties of assessing the social-welfare costs and benefits arising from different manpower programs. Some analysts believe that any public program that transfers income from the affluent to the poor justifies itself, and most evaluations suggest that the short-run distribution effects of manpower programs meet this test.

These illustrations are a reminder of the limitations of the available data as well as of accepted theory to definitively assess the impact of alternative manpower policies on the performance of the economy.

Opinion-survey data point up that the American people continue to place a high value on work. Hence they prefer that the unemployed work rather than live off government income transfers. But the critical issue is how fast can useful jobs be created and for what proportion of all potential job seekers? If job increases, private or public, call forth additional numbers of job seekers so that new entrants or reentrants obtain most of the newly created jobs, it may prove difficult, and in the short run impossible, to drive the unemployment rate down to a socially acceptable level without precipitating runaway inflation.

The American people have been energetically tackling the reduction and removal of discrimination against racial minorities and females in the labor market. To the extent that manpower programs are targeted on these groups, they should be assessed for their contribution to realizing this important societal objective.

Adults who do not have jobs use their time to seek some income, to keep busy, to find a role. We know that many young people who are out of school and without jobs engage in different kinds of antisocial and illegal activities from muggings to selling dope. We have no way of knowing what proportion of such youngsters, as well as older adults who follow a life of delinquency and crime, would prefer the alternative of a regular job if one were available. In any case, a democratic society will want to include the possible benefits of reduced antisocial behavior when it assesses the balance sheets of training and manpower programs.

These considerations of the criteria for assessing manpower programs—the participants, other individuals, the economy, and the society—underscore the limitations of evaluations, even with improved data. The extant theories are inadequate to encompass and analyze the interacting variables in a changing world.

ADDITIONAL PROBLEMS

If the problem presented by these criteria could be handled effectively, two additional sets of difficulties would remain. They relate respectively to the types of assistance required by different groups and to the responsiveness in programmatic design elicited by changing conditions in the economy and society.

Different Client Groups

First, as we focus on groups with high claims for assistance, we can distinguish the following four categories of clients—young people, regularly attached members of the work force, the structurally employed (including in particular minority groups), and adult female entrants or reentrants into the labor market. One need do no more than list these four categories to appreciate that they have specific needs that cannot be met by one specific type of training or employment program.

The following observations are directed to distinguishing the needs of these several groups and the preferred responses to them.

If we postulate that most young people, as a result of their developmental experiences and with the help of their family, can make the transition from school to work without difficulty, we should focus on the cumulative deficits of those young people who cannot obtain steady work because they lack socialization and competence. Years of being buffeted in the labor market may reduce some of these handicaps, but failure on their part to find and hold regular jobs will add new and telling deficits that future employers will weigh heavily in their hiring decisions.

To reduce significantly the number of disadvantaged youth entering the labor market would require improved developmental experiences through remedial education and skill acquisition and, above all, assistance in finding regular jobs.

With regard to the regularly attached members of the labor force, we can note the following conditions that warrant interventions: lack of opportunities for unskilled and semiskilled workers to obtain additional knowledge, training, and knowhow in order to improve their job prospects. Although many large employers provide such opportunities, many others do not, and this is the rationale for federally supported upgrading opportunities.

The U.S. economy continues to be buffeted by recessions that lead to large-scale layoffs and discharging of individuals who in better times would be firmly attached to their jobs and progressing in their careers. Since most of these individuals will be called back to work by their employers before their unemployment compensation runs out, a reasonable response to their plight is to insure that the unemployment-insurance system operates at effective benefit levels and duration, and to insure that some combination of income transfer and manpower assistance is available for those who exhaust their benefits or who have no prospect of being recalled to their jobs. Whether and to what extent public-service employment should be used to moderate cyclical unemployment is considered later.

Structurally unemployed adults are those who have never made a firm attachment to the labor force because of their developmental deficits, including inadequate educational preparation and lack of skills training, or whose attachment has been broken because of plant closure, area decline, or personal disabilities (including aging). The younger among the structurally unemployed are likely to need both training and job placement, including in many instances help in relocation from areas in decline. For older unemployed persons, especially those in declining areas, long-term public-service employment may be the preferred solution until they reach retirement age. Here is one arena where the prospects of selective-employment policies should be explored.

During the post–World War II decades there has been a large and sustained influx of adult women into the labor force, an influx that continues. The overwhelming majority of these women have been able to find jobs in the burgeoning service economy, primarily in clerical or sales positions. Their general education, maturity, and discipline are traits that employers seek. In recent years the attention of students of this phenomenon has begun to focus on one group of mature women who find it difficult to enter or reenter the labor market—those who have been homemakers for a decade or two and who suddenly must find jobs to support themselves and often their dependents. There are no reliable data about how many such displaced homemakers are seeking jobs, how many need help, or the types of help that would be most useful to them. The numbers are sufficiently large, however, to warrant government intervention.

The categories of present and potential claimants for manpower services have been kept deliberately short here to illustrate the range of problems they confront and the different types of assistance they require. If we were to add Native Americans, migrant workers, veterans, the physically and emotionally handicapped, ex-offenders and ex-addicts, as well as the other groups that have been identified in the current legislation as worthy of special consideration, the complexities of meeting the discrete needs of so many different categories of claimants would appear horrendous.

Designing Manpower Programs for Changing Conditions

The other complication in assessing manpower programs flows directly from the changes characteristic of our dynamic economy and society, which can weaken or undermine sound efforts at intervention to enhance the employability and employment of persons who need assistance.

We called attention earlier to the differing responses of employers to on-the-job training in periods of tight and loose labor markets. However, the cyclical and structural changes in the economy impact every facet of manpower policy and programming, from expanding or contracting the numbers in search of assistance to the resources available and their effective deployment. Since the 1980s may differ from the growth trends of the two earlier decades, manpower policymakers may be faced with the new challenge of an environment of slow growth.

Although opinions differ about how effectively the nation is dealing with its double-digit inflation, there is a consensus that until the present rate is cut substantially, the public agenda must continue to give priority to the issue. This preoccupation cannot fail to affect all economic and social policies and will certainly leave its mark on manpower programming in the years ahead.

National policy reflects responses to challenges on the international and domestic fronts as well as to changing national expectations. Although the Full Employment and Balanced Growth Act, which was passed in 1978, consisted of little more than a listing of objectives, the act included for the first time a national commitment to full employment, and it defined the commitment in terms of an acceptable unemployment level of 3 percent for adults and further stipulated that a level of 4 percent total, including youth, be achieved for 1983. The goal will not be achievable by 1983, but it will influence economic and employment policy as long as it remains on the statute books. There are many different interest groups that will remind Congress and the administration of this commitment and press them to take whatever steps appear possible to turn promise into reality.

The implementation of manpower programs has not been static in the past and the full-employment goal speaks to more changes in the future. In their first decade, federal manpower programs were *federal* in the sense that the federal government was responsible for the entire effort and the nongovernmental sector had a minor role. Since 1974 the principal actors have been state and local governments, with the federal role restricted largely to that of financier. However, the federal government continues to be responsible for a few specialized programs such as the Job Corps.

Recently there has been a new turn of the wheel; the administration, the Congress, and many other leaders of opinion are now looking forward to an enlarged role for the private sector. If the private sector becomes actively involved in the design and operation of manpower programs at the local level, the modest results achieved in the past may not be predictive of future outcomes.

There are two further references to possible changes. First, the administration has proposed that 400,000 PSE positions be reserved for the principal wage earner in families on welfare as the fulcrum for the reform of the welfare system. At this point we do not know whether the bill will be passed; but if it is, it will almost certainly leave its mark on the manpower system.

Second, there is a steadily increasing concern, in and out of Congress, with the large flow of undocumented workers into the United States, whose presence, it is now realized, has a significant effect on the supply of unskilled workers, wages, and working conditions in selected labor markets. This presence must affect the opportunities open to the many hard-to-employ young people and adults who are the primary targets for manpower assistance. Any radical change in immigration policy would also influence future manpower programs.

Further complications that must be borne in mind stem from the weaknesses of the management-information system, the absence of control groups in most evaluations, and the wide differences in need, as earlier suggested, between different client groups, all of which have an impact on the ability of Congress and the administration to design and improve manpower programs. It is further important to recall that good evaluations that point up the limited success of various programs do not solve the problem but only point to the need for improved programming.

Judgments about Manpower Policy and Programs

The thrust of these diverse considerations affecting the assessment of manpower policy and programs has been to underscore its continuing evolution. Even carefully developed analyses, based on firm data, will not permit more than a balanced judgment of past efforts in projecting policy into the future. We know that considerations germane to the environment within which the program initially operated and was evaluated cannot be uncritically projected.

The fact that objective inquiry is limited in all matters affecting public policy carries two implications: the necessity for the public to make judgments even when the facts are few and the theory weak, and the correlative necessity of placing considerable weight on the judgments of informed persons. The need for judgment grows out of the imperative of a democratic society to weigh its options and to take action whenever it appears likely that a specific intervention will contribute to increasing equity and/or efficiency. If the public is unwilling to approve action until the case for intervention has been proved, action will be indefinitely delayed. Translated, this means that the status quo, with all its shortcomings, remains entrenched.

Guided by these considerations, I consider it necessary to set forth as tersely as I can my judgments about the potential of manpower policy and programming based on the last eighteen years of American experience. I will follow this with a series of problematic formulations, which will remain unanswered until we move from conception to pilot model to full implementation.

With respect to the potential of manpower policy and programming, my views, as of the fall of 1979, are as follows:

- An advanced economy such as that of the United States must continue to experiment with manpower policies and programs for the reason that it cannot rely solely on the self-corrective forces of the market to assure optimal employment opportunities. Neither can it make use of fiscal and monetary policy alone to reduce the unemployment rates for specific groups to an acceptable level without generating unacceptable levels of inflation. Reworded, this means that there is latitude—how extensive remains to be discovered—for manpower policy and programs to play a constructive role in contributing to the employability and employment of selected groups in the population.
- The destructive effects of gross inequalities in opportunities and rewards reach across generational lines. The children of the

poor, the unskilled, and the undereducated are likely to enter adulthood ill prepared to cope with the responsibilities of work and citizenship. While our society spends sizable sums on education and a variety of other measures contributing to the development of poor children, these efforts still leave many offspring of poor families so badly positioned that without special assistance they will remain on the periphery of society and the economy. It is not easy for manpower programs that deal with eighteen-year-olds to compensate for the cumulative deficits that a young person has sustained up to that age. But as the Job Corps experience underscores, a multifaceted effort directed at remedial education, skill acquisition, and job placement can make a real difference. Many young people need a second chance, not only on grounds of equity but also for the benefits that will accrue to society.

- The most favorable method for assisting low-skilled persons to improve their long-term occupational status and income is to provide them with training that leads to a desirable job, such as a year's course in practical nursing or in auto mechanics, where the demand for specific skills remains relatively high. Once they have acquired these new skills, they are likely to enjoy more or less permanent employment at wages double, or more than double, their previous earnings.

- Short training courses of approximately four to six months' duration have much to commend them when they are undertaken after the person has been hired or when arrangements have been worked out ahead of time with employers to hire all those who satisfactorily complete the course. In a tight labor market, such as existed in the late 1960s, the prospective placements may be sufficiently assured that they do not require pretraining agreements. There is a disturbingly large body of evidence, however, that points to the failure of job placement following training, which serves to estrange still further the frustrated trainee who, having made a special effort at self-improvement, discovers that employers are still not interested in hiring him.

- A society with a large number of adults in need of jobs and income that the regular economy fails to provide, even under conditions of rapidly expanding employment such as existed during most of the 1970s, has every reason to experiment with public-service employment. It is clearly preferable for unemployed persons to be engaged in useful work than to deteriorate through idleness. Although as yet we lack effective mechanisms for preventing such workers from occasionally jeopardizing the jobs of regularly employed civil service workers, from restraining an upward pull on the wages of unskilled workers in the private economy, or for facilitating movement into regular employment after the PSE job has come to an end, these problems do not diminish the importance of public-service employment in an economy characterized by job shortfalls. Further efforts must be concerned with relating PSE wages to conditions in the market-place rather than to the income needs of the assignees, with building in a training component to enhance the eventual transition to a regular job, and with linking the entire PSE effort more closely to the hiring practices of private- and public-sector employers.

- A beginning has been made in connection with the Youth Act to raise the contribution of the educational system to the occupational skills and goals of the student body and, more broadly, to improve linkage among the schools, employers, labor, and the manpower authorities. One must ascribe to manpower policy much of the credit for strengthening the educational system so that it is capable of making a larger contribution to the millions of high school students who each year complete their studies with or without acquisition of a diploma. Since the cumulative expenditures of the educational system for twelve years of instructional costs are three to four times as large as a year's remedial course in a Job Corps center, the importance of improving the productivity of the regular educational system is underscored. Given the fact that there is little prospect for young people to make a satisfactory transition from school to work unless they have acquired the basic competence that an educational system should provide them, one can assume that the manpower-stimulated reform of the school system will continue even if progress will be slow and halting. Similar systemwide impacts can be seen in the prospective role of job creation in welfare reform; in the reassessment of the limits of extended unemployment compensation benefits, with congressionally expressed preferences for recourse to manpower services after thirty-nine weeks in place of continued income transfers; and in prospective experimentation to use the unemployment-insurance system to compensate for a short time in order to reduce layoffs and discharges in periods of recession. It is fair to say that the potential effect of manpower policy on these related human-resources systems has only recently been recognized, and judgment must be suspended until more evidence has been accumulated.

- Once a democratic society becomes cognizant of gross inequities and inefficiencies, with respect to the long-term neglect of minorities and the poor, as it did in the 1960s, it does not have the luxury of turning its back on its newly acquired knowledge and insight. Response is imperative. Had manpower programs been judged to have been less effective than the evaluations have found, the national effort to provide the disadvantaged with second-chance opportunities, and such other benefits as sizable income transfers, would nevertheless have to be seen as positive. This is not to say that a large proportion of the poor and minorities who participated in manpower programs (and one must remember that most did not have an opportunity to participate) succeeded in gaining a regular attachment to the labor force. But political tensions and social unrest would have been much greater had the federal government not demonstrated a concern and had it failed to act. Manpower programs may have fallen far short of what was needed, but they surely were preferable to a policy of indifference and neglect.

• The evolution of the manpower infrastructure has facilitated the launching of a variety of demonstrations focused on a number of groups on the periphery of society whose income and employment needs were overlooked in earlier years. Prominent among these are ex-offenders who in the past have been released from prison with little more than pocket money, a practice that virtually assured a high frequency of recidivism. Former drug addicts and released mental patients are two other large groups for whom manpower services have been designed in the hope that with training and a job many might eventually become regularly employed and lead normal lives.

PROGRAM ACCOMPLISHMENTS AND POTENTIAL

One can contend that the opportunities for experimentation with these hard-to-place groups have not been pursued with vigor and imagination; nevertheless, without a federal manpower effort in place and slow but steady gains in its capabilities to respond to a diversity of challenges, even such experimentation as occurred would not have been undertaken. The full exploitation of structured demonstrations and experiments to contribute to knowledge and policy lies in the future, but the potential exists.

The foregoing delineations of the potential of manpower policy and programs have been formulated conservatively in order not to exaggerate what has been accomplished and to avoid excessive expectations for the future. But by using a wide lens, the potential was found to be substantial. The interventions that were undertaken have enabled some hard-to-employ persons to become regularly attached to the world of work with significant gains in income; have provided jobs and income for large numbers of poor, near-poor, and unemployed persons through public-service employment; have taken early steps to improve the transition of young people from school to work, and in the process have challenged the schools to reappraise their orientation and performance in order to contribute more effectively to the employability of disadvantaged young people; and have initiated demonstrations and experiments aimed at (1) modifying important income transfer systems such as welfare and unemployment compensation and (2) addressing the employment problems of the most disadvantaged groups in our society, whose lack of opportunities to work had not previously engaged the public's attention.

These significant potentials exist. But the critical questions that remain are how fast and how far they can be more fully realized. The following brief consideration of the problematic elements in the future use of manpower policy speaks to these questions.

- Although there is a renewed attempt to involve the private sector in various aspects of manpower policy and programming aimed at accelerating the training and employment of the structurally unemployed, it is premature to assess the success of this effort. The record leaves much to be desired: Only once in the past—and then reinforced by strong presidential leadership and a conducive labor market—did the private sector respond enthusiastically, and that was a decade ago. It is questionable whether even the sizable tax benefits provided by the Targeted Jobs Tax Credit Program (TJTC) and federal funding for the new Private Industry Councils (PICs) will entice more than limited employer response. If the president should lean heavily on the business leadership to play a leading role, stronger response can be anticipated. But effective business participation will require organization at the local level involving small- and medium-scale enterprises that do most of the hiring. This will surely prove difficult, perhaps impossible. However, unless the private sector participates, enabling enrollees in government-sponsored training programs and in PSE jobs to make the transition into regular jobs, the federal manpower programs will remain little more than stopgaps in the search of the hard-to-employ for work and income.
- There is an emerging consensus, even among left-of-center

economists, that so long as the nation is suffering from double-digit inflation, it would be unwise or downright foolhardy (a judgment depending on one's theoretical predilections) to drive the economy close to full utilization for fear of adding to the inflationary pressures. Given this major barrier to early or rapid movement toward the statutory goal of full employment, the question remains as to how venturesome the administration and the Congress will be in experimenting with selective-employment policies that hold promise of adding the unskilled to the nation's payroll without significant adverse effects on wage rates and inflation. At this moment such efforts are supported largely by theory; guidance is needed from experience as well. If Congress experiments along this axis, what will the experience reveal? If selective-employment policies can fulfill their promise, then manpower policy may, in the 1980s, really come into its own. We must recognize that unless we experiment with selective manpower policies on a controlled but expanding scale, millions of poor people will be doomed to a life of intermittent employment.

- One of the most difficult and perplexing aspects of structural unemployment has been the concentration of large pockets of peripheral workers in the cores of our major cities, in smaller communities that have suffered an erosion of their economic base, and in declining rural areas. Among low-income minorities, youth and adults alike, mobility is not likely to provide an escape mechanism from unemployment and poverty. There is no reason for a black youngster in Philadelphia to assume that he will be better off if he relocates in Houston or for a New York City youth of Puerto Rican extraction to be attracted to Denver. Accordingly, efforts to moderate the excessively high level of unemployment must focus largely on the areas where the structurally unemployed now reside. Although it is not practical in terms of public policy for the federal government to attempt to reverse the economic decline of every city, it may be able, with the assistance of state and local governments and the private sector, to contribute to the economic revival of many to the extent that their excessive unemployment is absorbed. We are in an early stage of improving the coordination of funding for federal manpower programs, with the funding for housing and economic infrastructure made available by the Housing and Urban Development Administration (HUD) and Economic Development Administration (EDA). To the degree that they succeed, these federal efforts will stimulate additional funding by other levels of government and the private sector. But the open issues are: How extensively will these different funding sources be coordinated? How well will the funds be invested in viable economic development projects? How much will they stimulate employment, particularly for the structurally unemployed? To list these questions is to underscore the complexity of what lies ahead.

- It is often overlooked that the U.S. economy has performed well in new job creation; the problem is that most of the new jobs are filled by persons other than the structurally unemployed. Recently, Congress has moved to target the federal manpower programs on the most needy. With total funding always insufficient for the numbers who can profit from manpower services, the logic of targeting on the most needy is appealing on grounds of equity and social welfare, if not always on economic efficiency. In addition, the reluctance of employers to hire the hard-to-employ must be anticipated. They may calculate that the tax incentives, subsidies, or grants made available by the federal government will not overcome the additional costs of hiring only members of targeted groups. If this occurs, it may prove necessary for the federal government to increase the incentives, loosen the targeting criteria, and establish qualifying standards for eligible individuals, which might reassure employers that the unemployed could perform a day's work. A more radical proposal would be to make the financing of government contracts conditional upon the willingness of successful bidders to hire a given proportion of their workforce, say one out of three, from the rolls of eligibles certified by the employment service. More time must pass before a judgment can be reached about the present targeting regulations, and an even longer time will be needed to experiment with one or more of the above alternatives. But no manpower effort can fail to address and attempt to solve the issue of how to improve the outcomes for members of groups most in need of assistance.

- Ours is a society that looks to earnings from regular employment to provide most adults with the income required to support themselves and their dependents. During the last decades, however, our society has recognized the desirability of government's providing income to selected groups who are unable to work because of serious disabilities or competing responsibilities. Recently the availability of large income-transfer funds has been found to have an adverse effect on the work potential of many individuals who may gain little if any advantage, and on occasion may actually suffer losses, by accepting a job. While such dysfunctional effects of income-transfer systems can be reduced, they cannot be eliminated once one recognizes that the level of subsistence allowances from the welfare system may equal and even exceed earnings from low-paying jobs. A related problem in the work-income arena is posed by the increasing amount of income that people earn from off-the-books, illicit and illegal sources. The total of these streams may approximate $200 million annually, a sum that would translate into the equivalent of earnings for one out of every six jobs. Faced with these alternative ways of earning money, many young people, as well as adults, opt for a life of risk, excitement, and more dollars per hour of work, in preference to regular employment at an unskilled job with low wages and poor working conditions. The presence of these options — income transfers and illegal earnings — sets limits to the interim, and even long-term, goals that manpower programs can hope to achieve. There are a considerable number of individuals — the question is how many — who in the face of these irregular opportunities will probably eschew the assistance that manpower programs provide. They will play it their way, not society's way.

Even this abbreviated consideration of the limits that lie in the path of manpower policy and programs should suffice to dampen excessive optimism. It is unquestionably true that manpower policy has considerable potential to contribute to expanding the opportunities for many persons to improve their employability and obtain regular employment. But it is also true that the road ahead is uncertain. The constraints growing out of the continuing inflation, the wariness of the private sector, the difficulties of coordinating economic development with manpower policy, employer concerns about tight targeting, and the limits to a job policy introduced into the system by alternative sources of income are individually powerful, collectively even more so. But even in total they do not cancel out the potential; rather they point to the difficulties that must be overcome in order to realize it.

Politics and Manpower Policy

While the interaction between potential and problematics will influence the future evolution of manpower policy and programs, the determining factor will be politics. Without undertaking an extended consideration of the political parameters and how they are likely to impact manpower policy in the years ahead, considerable illumination can be gained from a cursory review of the stances of the principal constituencies.

Most low-income persons belonging to minority groups have not benefited nearly as much as they need to from manpower programs. However, many CBOs have been established and expanded with the support of manpower funding and many among their leadership have made occupational and career advances as a result of manpower programs. Accordingly, one can assume that the spokesmen for minority groups will continue to be strong advocates of larger manpower programs, particularly if they are focused on the structurally unemployed.

Although the trade unions have been supportive of manpower programs since their inception, their interest increased substantially once public-service employment was added to the range of available services. In a loose labor market that is likely to persist for some years to come, one can postulate that labor will remain a strong supporter of manpower programs and manpower policy, since they offer assistance in moving toward the goal of full employment.

The third major constituency consists of the chief elected officials of medium-sized and large cities and counties, especially those that continue to operate close to their allowed taxable ceilings. The funding of manpower programs, particularly PSE, has been of major assistance to hard-pressed urban centers struggling to continue to provide basic and desirable services to their electorates. It is reasonable to expect that most mayors and county executives will remain strong supporters of manpower programs in the years ahead.

When it comes to the business community, both the leadership of the large corporations and representatives of small- and medium-sized enterprises, the outlook is uncertain. If the targeted tax credits and the work of the PICs find favor among large numbers of businessmen, one can look forward to support from a substantial segment of the private sector. However, if the present and prospective manpower programs impress only a small minority, the best that can be anticipated is neutrality, the worst, outright opposition.

This suggests that the future of manpower policy and programming will depend in considerable measure on how the average working-class and middle-class white voter reads the record and assesses the future. With the programs heavily targeted on low-income minority groups, the white voter may decide there is nothing in them for him except higher taxes and may signal his legislative representatives to vote against such programs. In that event, the future of manpower programs is not encouraging. On the other hand, the political leadership may conclude, as did Vice-President Lyndon Johnson in 1962, that many, particularly blacks and other minority groups on the periphery of American life, will never be able to support themselves and their dependents unless assisted in obtaining training and employment.

The real choice the American people face is not greater or lesser support for manpower programs in the future, but rather the basic decision as to whether or not they desire to affirm the nation's long-term commitment to a society built on work. In the event that they affirm this commitment, they have no option but to support the further elaboration of manpower policy and programming, which is a necessary if not sufficient condition for achieving this primary national goal.

CHAPTER 48

A Policy for Disadvantaged Youth

A NATIONAL COMMITMENT TO DISADVANTAGED YOUTH

ALTHOUGH UNEMPLOYMENT RATES for youth are very high, most youth make the transition from school to work without serious problems. In fact, among white youth, the proportion successfully entering the labor market over the past decade has increased. Among minority youth, on the other hand, there has been a marked decline in the proportion both seeking and finding work. The consequences of not attending to this situation are serious and include crime, alienation, and reduced social mobility as well as lower incomes and lost output.

Past efforts to deal with the labor market problems of disadvantaged youth have tended to stress the provision of jobs and have not fully come to grips with the cumulative deficits produced by growing up in a low-income minority family and community. Enhancing the employment prospects of these youth can be achieved only if schools, community-based organizations, training institutions, and the job market are more effectively involved in joint efforts to overcome the legacy of poverty and racial discrimination.

655

Given the seriousness of the problem and the nature of the deficits that must be overcome, the National Commission for Employment Policy believes that:

- The president and the Congress should identify the employability and employment problems of disadvantaged youth as a domestic issue of critical importance to the future well-being and security of the nation and pledge that the federal government and the nation will devote the resources and efforts necessary to its amelioration.

- Although the federal government should take the lead role, state and local governments, business, labor, education, and community-based organizations must undertake substantial responsibility for improving the employment prospects of disadvantaged youth. The local leaders of all these organizations should make a new commitment to work together on ameliorating the problem, and local employers should be fully involved in helping to plan and implement these efforts.

- Federal resources should be targeted on youth most in need. While there is no simple way to identify this group, those youth most at risk come from low-income families, are members of a minority group, or live in areas with high concentrations of low-income families.

- The major objective of federal education, training, and employment programs for youth should be to improve the long-term employability of these youth—that is, their basic education, work habits, ability to absorb new skills on the job, and other competencies that will permit successful integration into the regular work force.

ELEMENTS OF A YOUTH POLICY

The reasons that disadvantaged youth have problems in the labor market are many, and these reasons interact. Based on the commission staff's analysis, the most important causes of their joblessness appear to be the inability of the economy to absorb all those who want to work combined with educational handicaps and discrimination which put disadvantaged, and especially minority, youth at the end of the hiring queue, regardless of the state of the economy. The lack of sufficient job opportunities for these youth, or of opportunities for upward mobility consistent with their aspirations, has produced a situation in which many of our youth no longer strive for excellence in the classroom or the workplace. Employers, for their part, have turned to other sources of labor, leaving subsidized work experience programs in the public sector as the dominant source of employment for minority youth. Although these programs provide income and job opportunities that would not otherwise exist, they appear to have few long-term benefits and a limited ability to integrate youth into the regular labor market.

Based on these findings, the commission believes that any new set of policies should be based on the following set of principles:

- Youth unemployment should be viewed principally as a structural problem and long-term solutions sought. Nevertheless, there is no question that sustained high levels of employment are an important precondition for substantially improving the labor market prospects of disadvantaged youth.

- Remedying the educational deficiencies of disadvantaged youth must be high on the nation's agenda. Without basic literacy skills, youth are unable to take advantage of further education or training and will be permanently consigned to the bottom of the economic and social ladder.

- Our nation should renew its commitment to eliminate racial discrimination and cultural stereotyping in the labor market. In particular, all our institutions must be involved in creating a new environment of trust and confidence between those who come from different backgrounds so that access to good jobs and treatment on the job are based on performance alone.

- Youth themselves must be more fully involved in improving their own employability and must make greater efforts to meet the performance standards set by our educational and employing institutions. To encourage disadvantaged youth to do so, these performance standards must be clearly articulated and greater rewards for success in meeting them provided at each stage of the employability development process.

- Employment and training programs should be carefully targeted to provide second chance opportunities to those youth, who for reasons of family background, poor schooling, or race, are likely to be permanently handicapped in the labor market. These programs should be restructured, where necessary, so as to have a cumulative impact on the long-term employability of participants.

- There must be a new emphasis on moving those disadvantaged youth who are ready into unsubsidized private and public sector jobs. While sheltered experiences may be appropriate at various stages in their development, the ultimate goal should be to create opportunities for them in the regular labor market. The federal government should consider using a variety of expenditure, tax, and regulatory powers to achieve this objective.

In the sections that follow, the commission provides a number of more specific recommendations that it feels would further these objectives.

ADEQUATE JOB OPPORTUNITIES

The commission believes that the employment problems of disadvantaged youth will be severe no matter what the state of the economy and most of its recommendations are directed to needed structural changes for the longer-term. Nevertheless, it is concerned about the possible impact of a recession on the employment prospects of youth. The evidence is clear that youth employment, and especially minority youth employment, is even more sensitive to the business cycle than adult employment. Moreover, in periods of economic slack, other measures will simply reallocate existing opportunities and will be strongly resisted for this reason. Thus the commission recommends that:

> (1) In the event that the unemployment rate rises substantially, that is to 7 percent or higher, and more particularly if it stays at such a high level for a sustained period, Congress should expand funding for priority national goals such as energy conservation. In so doing it should stipulate that private firms which obtain contracts to further these goals must hire a percentage of disadvantaged youth and adults who are designated by the Job Service or by CETA prime sponsors as being ready to work.

NEW DIRECTIONS FOR EDUCATIONAL POLICIES

Mastery of basic reading, writing, and computational skills is a prerequisite for other kinds of training, including on-the-job training, with the result that these skills are almost universally demanded by employers. High school dropouts, who are disproportionately black and Hispanic, face a significantly higher probability of becoming unemployed than do high school graduates. Even among those who graduate from high school, especially from inner-city schools, the acquisition of basic skills is likely to be deficient. Any serious strategy for improving the labor market prospects of disadvantaged youth must put major emphasis on closing the basic skills gap. If this gap is not closed, the employment prospects of these youth will worsen as unskilled jobs in industry or agriculture continue to decline as a proportion of total job opportunities.

The federal government has made a strong commitment toward providing funds for low-income students who wish to go on to college or other postsecondary training. An equally strong commitment must be made to provide funds for remedial programs to serve low-income youth who are not college-bound but who lack the basic skills.

The schools have been, and should continue to be, the primary institution for providing these basic skills. However, it is critical that a partnership with employers and employment and training programs be forged so that disadvantaged youth will have more learning opportunities outside of the regular classroom and greater motivation to acquire the basic skills. Accordingly, the commission makes the following recommendations:

(2) The president and the Congress should support new funding for compensatory education in the secondary schools. These funds should be used to improve the basic skills of young people from disadvantaged backgrounds, through well-funded, intensive programs involving special tutorial efforts, extra after-school sessions, alternative schooling opportunities, compensatory education linked to occupational training, and in-service training for teachers. The effectiveness of Title I of the Elementary and Secondary Education Act in the elementary schools must not be jeopardized by a reduction in funding at this level. What is needed is a comparable program at the junior and senior high levels (a) to sustain the positive effects achieved at the elementary level and (b) to provide a second chance for those not adequately served at the elementary level.

(3) To encourage a partnership with other local institutions, a portion of the new compensatory education funds recommended in (2) should be set-aside for allocation on the basis of close consultation between the schools and CETA. This would be comparable to the 22 percent set-aside under the Youth Employment and Training Program which should continue to be allocated on the basis of such consultation. The new set-aside would encourage additional joint efforts on behalf of CETA-eligible youth and might lead to the development of more alternative schooling opportunities.

(4) The secretary of education should be provided with special funding to collect, integrate and disseminate information about exemplary programs, such as the adopt-a-school programs in Oakland, Baltimore, and Dallas. While schools must retain flexibility to deal with local conditions, what has been learned about effective ways of motivating and assisting disadvantaged youth to acquire the basic skills should be mobilized to promote wider sharing and adoption of the successful models.

BROADENING OPPORTUNITIES FOR
MINORITY AND FEMALE YOUTH

The policy of the Equal Employment Opportunity Commission (EEOC) to identify patterns of systemic discrimination against minorities and women and to encourage employers to voluntarily pursue remedial actions that will bring them into compliance with Title VII of the Civil Rights Act of 1964 provides a significant opportunity to increase the number and proportion of minority and female youth who can be placed into regular jobs. The EEOC is in a position to identify by prime sponsor area those employers whose work forces are not representative of the local labor force.

Accordingly, the commission recommends that:

> (5) The EEOC should encourage companies with overall low minority and/or female utilization to improve their utilization by hiring job-ready youth from inner-city schools or those trained through CETA programs.

Improving the employability of disadvantaged young women, the vast majority of whom are going to have family support responsibilities at some point in their lives, requires opening up to them a wider range of occupational choices than those that most working women currently have. All youth-oriented labor market policies have a potential impact — for better or worse — on future patterns of occupational segregation which currently confine women, and especially minority women, to the lowest paid jobs.

Within the group of disadvantaged young women, teenage mothers have special needs. They not only need income support but also require money for child care services while completing their schooling or training in order to obtain the requisite skills that will enable them to earn an income equal to or above that available to them as welfare recipients.

It is with these needs in mind that the commission recommends that:

> (6) Education, vocational education, and CETA programs should be implemented in ways that will broaden the occupational opportunities of young women from disadvantaged backgrounds.
>
> (7) Teenage mothers should be treated as a high priority group in both WIN and CETA and their child care and income needs should be fully met, with no diminution of support under AFDC when they participate in an education or training program.

Linking Performance to Rewards

Too often, both in our schools and our employment and training programs, performance standards have not been established or maintained. The result is that graduation from high school or completion of a CETA program has had less value in helping young people obtain jobs than would be the case if employers had confidence in these credentials and were willing to commit jobs based on them. This lack of standards is one reason that disadvantaged youth themselves have had little incentive to succeed. They need to be convinced that if they take steps to improve their competencies these efforts will be appropriately rewarded in the labor market. Unless they are motivated to improve their own educational competencies or employability, the chances that such programs can be successful are slim. Therefore, the commission recommends that:

> (8) Schools and prime sponsors should be encouraged or required to establish local performance standards and disadvantaged youth who achieve the standards should be rewarded with entrance into a more generously stipended program or with a job opportunity. Those who fail to meet the standards should be given second chance opportunities, whenever possible.
> (9) Prime sponsors should encourage the Private Industry Councils to obtain specifications from employers about the criteria they use in hiring young people, and, to the greatest extent possible, secure commitments from them that young people who meet their requirements will have a job opening when they leave school or a training program.

New Directions for Youth Employment and Training Programs

The Youth Employment and Demonstration Projects Act of 1977 was designed to promote a reassessment and redirection of youth employment programs. Through a variety of new program initiatives and a large-scale research and demonstration effort, much has been learned about what works best for whom, and the relationships between schools, employment and training programs, and the private sector have been explored and fostered.

While the results of these efforts are not complete, the Commission believes enough information is available to recommend that:

(10) The Administration should request, and Congress should
enact, a consolidated youth title under the Comprehensive Employment and Training Act, the principal goal of which should be to
improve the employability of economically disadvantaged youth
aged 16 through 21.

The Commission has been reluctant to support separate programs
for separate groups under CETA. However, the severity of the employment problems for disadvantaged youth and the importance of establishing
collaboration with the school system in serving this age group convinces
us that a separate title is needed at this time.

The Youth Title should provide for a new comprehensive program
which would replace the Youth Employment and Training Program
(YETP), the Youth Community Conservation and Improvement Program (YCCIP), and the Summer Youth Employment Program (SYEP).
The present level of funding for these programs must be at least maintained
if the desired results of consolidation are to be realized.

Because of severe deprivation, disadvantaged young people need
access to a wide range of services including remedial education, skill
training, work experience, and knowledge of how to look for and get a
job. For this reason, the commission rejects prescribing approaches under
the new youth title. However, for youth in need of comprehensive
remediation, programs must be of sufficient quality and duration to
make a contribution to the youth's employability. Therefore, the commission recommends that:

(11) The Department of Labor should encourage CETA prime
sponsors to invest substantial funds in remedial programs for the
most disadvantaged, even if this increases costs per individual and
results in a smaller number being served.

One of the most successful employment and training programs is the
Job Corps, which provides comprehensive services in residential centers
to the most seriously disadvantaged youth. Because of its demonstrated
record of success in recent years, the commission recommends that:

(12) The Job Corps should be maintained as a separate program,
and once current enrollment limits are reached, the program should
be further expanded.

Youth from economically disadvantaged backgrounds are more likely
than other youth to be in need of employment and employability development assistance. It is especially important to reach this group—half of
whom are nonwhite or Hispanic—at an early age. Accordingly, the
commission recommends that:

(13) The Congress should designate the eligible population under the new consolidated youth title as all youth from families in which income was at or below 70 percent of the Bureau of Labor Statistics lower living standard.

This recommendation reconfirms the position taken by the commission in its *Third Annual Report* that a single set of basic eligibility requirements be used throughout CETA and that youth programs be income-conditioned under the same definitions of income that prevail in other parts of CETA.

To this the commission would add one variation. The commission's Youth Task Force heard testimony at its field hearings that a strict income limit may unnecessarily penalize youth from families with incomes slightly above the limit, youth from working poor families and others who are greatly in need of help to succeed in the labor market. Therefore, the commission recommends that:

(14) Prime sponsors should be permitted to utilize up to 20% of their funds under the youth title to assist youth who do not meet the income requirement but nevertheless face substantial barriers to employment.

Whether the purposes of a youth title can be achieved and youth most in need served depends on the way in which funds are allocated. If there is poor articulation between the distribution of the population most in need and the distribution of available funds, the employment problems of disadvantaged youth will persist. Moreover, the commission believes that intensive targeting on areas where there are concentrations of low-income families is needed. Finally, sufficient funds should be reserved to the secretary of labor to provide incentives for innovation, coordination, and exemplary performance.

Accordingly, the commission recommends that:

(15) The majority of the funds for the consolidated youth title should be distributed by formula to local prime sponsors. However, a sizable portion should be set aside for supplemental grants to areas with high concentrations of low-income families and another portion should be reserved to the secretary of labor to reward superior performance or to fund innovative programs, particularly those of an interdepartmental nature.

Under the Youth Employment and Demonstrations Projects Act, the secretary of labor was granted a significant amount of money for research and demonstration. In its *Third Annual Report,* the commission noted that it recognized the value of such programs, but stated that once these programs have operated long enough to be assessed, the successful ones should be folded into general allocations to the prime sponsors. Now that this large scale effort has been undertaken, the commission recommends that research and demonstration money under the youth title be reduced. There are, however, two projects the commission would like the Secretary to pursue under recommendation (15) above. In collaboration with the secretaries of Education, Commerce, Housing and Urban Development, Health and Human Services, and the administrator of the Community Services Administration, the secretary of labor should support efforts aimed at utilizing funds from various agencies on joint programs and services to improve employability preparation for young people, and to enhance community economic development, particularly in the nation's cities and counties with the largest concentrations of disadvantaged youth. Efforts should be taken to disseminate the findings from the more successful efforts and to modify departmentally funded programs to reflect the new findings. Second, although all prime sponsors should be expected to achieve their prescribed performance goals, the secretary should establish an incentive program to reward prime sponsors who do an exceptionally good job at meeting their performance standards.

Crucial to the effective operation of youth employment programs is adequate planning and implementation time, a stable funding and programming environment, and dedicated, experienced staff. To accomplish these objectives and promote more effective cooperation among local educational, training and employer communities, the commission recommends that:

> (16) Congress should provide for forward funding, a five-year authorization, and additional emphasis on staff development under the new youth title.

It should be noted that the major federal education programs already have these components.

MOVING DISADVANTAGED YOUTH INTO REGULAR JOBS

Federal employment and training programs have failed in the past to adequately involve the private sector in the employability development process. The Youth Employment and Demonstration Projects Act contained several new experiments to encourage the private sector to participate more actively in training and employing young people with labor market handicaps, including up to 100 percent subsidy of their wages. In addition, the Private Industry Councils created under Title VII of CETA have been encouraged to undertake a number of activities to improve the employability of youth. Private Industry Councils, by virtue of their independence and the community standing and experience of their members, are in a unique position to contribute to improving the employability development of youth by insuring that it is related to the skills employers seek and by opening up opportunities for training and later employment in the private sector. Finally, the Targeted Jobs Tax Credit, passed as part of the Revenue Act of 1978, provides incentives for employers to hire disadvantaged youth between the ages of eighteen and twenty-four.

The commission has earlier supported all of these initiatives for integrating youth more effectively into the private sector, and believes that such efforts should be carefully monitored and wherever possible expanded. In particular, the current prohibition against private sector work experience under CETA is depriving youth of opportunities to learn more readily transferable skills, to be exposed to a wider variety of work settings, and to acquire valuable contacts and references for future employment. In addition, such experiences could help to break down the resistance of many employers to hiring youth from disadvantaged minority communities. Accordingly, the commission recommends that:

> (17) Short-term subsidized work experiences in the private sector should be permitted under CETA with safeguards to insure that employers do not misuse the program and that the youth are provided with a carefully structured and supervised learning experience or training opportunity.

Although the foregoing efforts to integrate youth into the regular job market are important, they by no means exhaust the leverage of the federal government since the latter accounts, directly or indirectly through its grants to other levels of government and to private contractors, for a substantial proportion of all employment.

With a civilian work force of 2.8 million and a uniformed military force of 2.1 million, the federal government is the nation's largest employer. Since it believes that the federal government should take the lead in providing opportunities for disadvantaged youth, the commission recommends that:

> (18) The president, with advice from the Office of Personnel Management, should consider making youth, who have successfully completed a CETA program involving experience in a federal agency, eligible for conversion to entry level positions in the career service on a noncompetitive basis.
>
> (19) The president should direct the secretary of defense to review the experience of Project 100,000 during the late 1960s, which was successful in recruiting and providing special training for 246,000 young men who did not meet the regular qualifications.

Federal grants-in-aid to state and local governments are now in the range of $80 billion per year. While a substantial portion of the grant-in-aid funds are used to provide services or benefits to individuals, such as grants for Medicaid and income security payments, many of the grants sustain or generate employment. Some movement toward targeting a portion of the employment generated by grant funds has taken place in the recent past. Mandatory approaches were proposed in the Labor Intensive Public Works Act of 1978, and voluntary approaches in the National Public Works and Economic Development Act of 1979. Serious consideration is also being given to the possible use of administrative requirements and incentives to accomplish employment objectives.

The commission believes these efforts should be extended and recommends that:

> (20) When the various pieces of legislation that authorize grants-in-aid are being considered for adoption or renewal, the administration and the Congress should consider writing in provisions that would encourage or require that the grant recipients employ a specified percentage of disadvantaged youth who are referred to them as job ready by either the Job Service or the CETA prime sponsor.

During fiscal 1978 the government spent some $95.6 billion through contracts for supplies and equipment, research and development, and construction and other services. About 35 million workers are covered by federal contract compliance regulations under Executive Order 11246. Although the contract procurement mechanism has long been considered a potentially fruitful area for pursuing a targeted employment objective, relatively little is known about the range of employment that is generated through the procurement process. The commission believes that, as a result of the establishment of a Federal Procurement Data Center under OMB's Office of Federal Procurement Policy, it is now possible to begin to collect data that will help to illuminate the question of whether procurement policy should be used to pursue targeted employment goals. Thus the commission recommends that:

> (21) The president should direct the Office of Management and Budget, with the assistance of other appropriate agencies, to determine whether and how the procurement process might be modified so that there would be new incentives for employers to hire structurally unemployed adults and disadvantaged youth.

MONITORING PROGRESS

It will not be possible to eliminate the employment problems of disadvantaged youth quickly or cheaply, and the commission believes the nation will need to make a sustained commitment over many years if real progress is to occur. This progress must be monitored and changes in programs implemented as more knowledge becomes available. For these reasons, the commission recommends that:

> (22) Congress should review annually the extent to which the gross discrepancies in the employment to population ratios and the unemployment rates for minority youth relative to white youth and adults are narrowed as a result of implementing the foregoing recommendations. In the absence of substantial and continuing progress in narrowing the gaps, the administration and the Congress should seek to fashion revised and new programs which hold greater potential to ameliorate the present intolerable situation where our society has no regular job opportunities for many young people who come of working age.

CHAPTER 49

Urban Priorities

June 20, 1980

The Honorable Ronald V. Dellums
Chairman
House Committee on the District of Columbia
1310 Longworth House Office Building
Washington, D.C. 20515

Dear Representative Dellums:

As I explained to your staff when they invited me to testify before the House Committee on the District of Columbia which you chair, I stay put on Martha's Vineyard during the summer to study and write so that I may have something to contribute during the rest of the year. But I did promise to send a letter in lieu of appearing in person. Here is my best effort to address the issues outlined in your Mailgram of June 10th addressed to urbanologists. I have taken the liberty of reformulating some of your questions in order to enable me to provide you with sharper and more incisive replies in terms of materials that I control.

I. *What has happened to cities since the Kerner Commission Report?*

    a. The central thrust of the Kerner Commission (K.C.) Report was to warn about the division of the U.S. into two races in which hostility and fear rather than cooperation and assimilation would dominate. The heavy concentration of blacks in most central cities characterized by poor education, poor jobs, poor housing, poor environment is a sharp reminder that the K.C. was not far off the mark. On the other hand it was unduly pessimistic. A substantial number of blacks born into and raised under disadvantageous conditions are making it through the school system, up to and including college, and are obtaining jobs that enable them, surely if they have a spouse who works, to earn a satisfactory living.

    b. The most unsettling evidence of the adverse circumstances in which many young blacks are being reared is the steep climb in female headed households, many of which are below or at the poverty level; and the correspondingly large numbers of teenage unmarried blacks who have children. These young women frequently face family responsibilities before they have completed high school or before they have acquired any skills that would enable them to find a suitable job. Once they have a child to care for they become less able to be self-supporting and many of them settle into a life on welfare.

    c. In the years since the K.C. the employment experience of young blacks has been particularly adverse reflecting among other forces the demographic bulge, their limited employability skills, discrimination in the job market, alienation and still other adverse factors. I am enclosing a report of mine from the May issue (1980) of *Scientific American* in which I review this onerous development at length.

    d. Under separate cover I am mailing a recent report, *Tell Me about Your School,* that two of my students and I prepared on education in the ghetto (New York City) as seen through the eyes of black youngsters. It is a sad story because so many of those youngsters are eager to learn but the schools fail them.

    e. Also under separate cover I am mailing a book that I recently edited and to which I contributed—*Employing the Unemployed.* The chapter by Dr. Bernard Anderson bears directly on matter of your concern.

    f. I do not have any special knowledge of trends in housing but on the basis of what I have been observing along the East

Coast and particularly in New York, I am impressed with the following:

— Most ghettos seem to have been thinning out, often as a result of arson.
— Middle- and upper-income blacks have apparently been able to move into neighborhoods that were previously closed to them.
— The suburbs have opened up, but only slightly.
— The deterioration of the housing stock, especially where welfare clients are concentrated, continues apace.
— Gentrification will place pressure on many poor urban blacks to relocate. The question is where?

g. I also have no special knowledge of police-community relations, but as a participant observer in New York City as elsewhere, I am impressed by the following:

— The uneven progress that has been made to increase the proportion of minority personnel on the police forces of the nation.
— The importance of leadership in the City, of the police, and in the community to establish and maintain reasonable relations between minorities and the police.
— The explosiveness that is visible even in a relatively calm community such as New York when the police injure or kill a minority person in what appears to be unjustified response on their part.
— In the face of multiple adverse pressures in the ghetto communities it is not surprising to me that the local population periodically out of frustration reacts violently toward law enforcement authorities who represent the "establishment." The only long-term insurance against such outbreaks would be a marked improvement in the condition of life for people living in the ghetto.

II. *How Do Federal Programs Aid or Hinder Solutions to Local Problems?*

a. The racial problem compounded by the stigmata of poverty, etc. represent an inheritance of over 350 years. No city can on its own significantly alter in the short run the cumulative effect of such long exploitation and deprivation. The federal government can help through making resources available but it too cannot easily wipe out such cumulative pathology.

b. The critical factors that would make a significant difference in my opinion are:

— Public commitment to change: This is weak on both the

federal and most local levels. Without strong and sustained community commitment progress is likely to be two steps ahead and one back.

— Suitable jobs: In my view no group can help to raise itself, and unless it does outsiders can help only a little, unless its members have access to suitable jobs. A high proportion of black males and teenagers have not had adequate employability opportunities. I see much of the weakness of the black family as a direct reflection of this inability of many blacks to find work and be self-supporting.

— Effective schools: It is impossible in an increasingly sophisticated economy requiring knowledge and skills for young people to make their way into the economy unless they have the opportunity to acquire employability skills at home and in school. Currently most ghetto schools are failing a large proportion of their students and there does not appear to be any substantial improvement in sight.

c. If the foregoing identification of the principal assists that minorities require is more or less on beam one must conclude that the federal government has made at best a modest contribution to providing the conditions required for speeding amelioration. On the plus side I would place the substantially high level of job creation during most of the period since the K.C. I would also give a good mark to Affirmative Action. Title I and II of the Education Act have been helpful. But the combined force of these several actions has been much too weak to overcome the long period of serious deprivation.

d. And part of the value of the foregoing has been reduced by the large number of federal policies that have favored the Sunbelt adding to the troubles of blacks in northern cities; the favorable tax treatment of house owners which have continued to draw white people out of the cities; the limited success of public housing; the many negatives of the welfare system.

e. In terms of effective use of federal funds to help the poor, including the minority poor, I would give a good mark to the Food Stamp program not as a long-term strategy for mobility but as a contribution to making life a little less bleak for those caught in poverty.

f. I regret to say that as far as MDTA and CETA are concerned which I have monitored carefully since MDTA was passed in

1962, their major contributions have been as income transfers not as vehicles for helping minorities into permanent jobs.

III. *Urgent Urban Problems*

a. In light of my replies in the foregoing Section II, I would place major stress on an educational improvement-job expansion effort. The President's youth bill is a step in the right direction, but we need to elicit much greater participation of local leadership in bringing about significant modifications in the educational system and linking young people more effectively to the world of work.

b. More federal funding without local leadership would have a very low payoff. The PICS established under Title VII of CETA offer some hope but the critical question is whether and to what extent the white and black leadership groups will really see that they meet their challenge.

c. I see no prospect in the face of slow growth and continuing high-level inflation for the federal government to appropriate very large sums that would make a radical difference in the near term on conditions in the ghetto. Unless local leaders see the explosiveness of permitting the present situation to continue—that is to take the analysis of the K.C. seriously—they are likely not to rise to the challenge. A much better organized and led minority could put pressure on the white leadership, but I don't see much new strength from that side.

IV. *Priorities and Progress*

a. The burden of my previous replies has been to point up the large gap between the problem and possible solution. If nothing dramatic changes, I do not expect any significant change in the thought and action of the key parties—federal and local, black and whites.

b. Unless the U.S. continues to have a sustained high level of employment the prospects for minorities will worsen. Hence I would urge the federal government to do what it can to keep the economy operating at a sustainable high level of employment. This is an absolute necessity, if bad is not to become worse.

c. The total amount of federal funding for manpower and manpower-related activities is considerable. I would keep these funds targeted as best possible on the disadvantaged and I would try to use the federal dollar to improve the employability of young people, in and out of school.

    d. I would hope that future presidents of the U.S. would be able to explain to the public more effectively than past presidents the close links between improving if not immediately solving the problems of minorities at home with our capacity to continue to lead the free world. If we lose the battle at home we will surely lose it abroad. But presidents can do little by themselves. They need the strong and continuing support of the populace.

V. *Supplemental Observations*

    a. I must note for the record that while my reply has been couched in terms of blacks, I am aware of the fact that probably before the end of the century Hispanics will represent our largest minority.

    b. While Hispanics currently suffer many of the same disabilities as blacks (and in the case of education the findings are even more unfavorable) their overall status is more encouraging, in fact because they are more heavily concentrated in the Southeast and West, booming areas.

    c. While there are differences of opinion among urbanologists as to whether urban concentrations will weaken, stabilize or strengthen, I consider it a fair bet that with high energy costs many cities, but by no means all will make a comeback. That is already happening. However, such a revival may not yield many immediate benefits to minorities and may, as noted above, complicate their housing difficulties.

    d. I consider it essential that all women have the opportunity to secure an abortion if they so desire and that this is of critical importance for teenage blacks so many of whom become pregnant.

Sincerely,

Eli Ginzberg

CHAPTER 50

Public Job Creation

INTRODUCTION

WHEN THE NATIONAL COUNCIL FOR FULL EMPLOYMENT asked me to prepare this paper, I immediately said yes because I have been distressed that the subject of public job creation has dropped far down on the agenda for public action. Since I have spent my entire professional life studying problems of employment, and since I chaired both the National Manpower Advisory Committee and the National Commission for Employment Policy from 1962 to 1981, I was happy to comply.

Moreover, the term *public job creation* implies a great variety of different interventions, and I believe that if there is no consensus among the U.S. public about the correct goals for a program, the program will be stillborn or have a short life. Let's remember that Emergency Employment Act of 1971 was phased out after two years and that the Public Service Employment (PSE) program, expanded from 350,000 to 750,000 jobs by President Carter in 1977, fell into disfavor within two years even with the Democrats in control of the Congress and was liquidated by President Reagan in 1981.

Since I believe that understanding is prerequisite for consensus, I plan to discuss sequentially the following:

- The characteristics of the U.S. labor market that have a bearing on the need for and the structuring of public job creation.
- The lessons we have learned from the multiple efforts at public job creation since the establishment of the Manpower Development and Training Act in 1962.
- The directions that a long-term public job creation effort should pursue.

THE U.S. LABOR MARKET: THE LONG VIEW

1. The labor market has been characterized by a general tightness only once during the past half century, during World War II (1943–1944), when the reported unemployment rate was approximately 1.5 percent. At that time some people were hired who were incapable of doing a day's work and whose removal added to total output. There were other times when communities, occupational groups, and industries suffered spot shortages, but they were just that—spot, not general, shortages of workers—and these shortages were generally overcome within a relatively few weeks or months, seldom longer.

2. The Works Progress Administration, the National Youth Administration, and the Public Works Administration—the building blocks of the New Deal's public job creation effort—were major undertakings that provided opportunities for millions of adults and youths to work for income rather than live on the dole. Their labor contributed much of lasting value, from building LaGuardia Airport to beautifying our national parks. Nevertheless, during the eight years from 1933 to 1941 the national unemployment rate never dropped below 10 percent. Public job creation was better than the dole. Useful work was performed, but it was only modestly successful in reducing the chronically high level of unemployment.

3. Despite our present concern with the high level of unemployment and the likelihood that the level will remain high at least until the second half of this decade, we must not overlook the substantial potential of the U.S. economy for job creation. Even during the uneven 1970s, 19 million new jobs were created. This is an accomplishment that should be neither minimized nor jeopardized. The private economy has demonstrated a high job-creating potential—not once, but repeatedly.

4. When large federal deficits are "monetarized" by the Federal

Reserve Board, as occurred after 1965, the stage is set for a price-wage spiral that can take off long before "full employment" is achieved. Easy money, oligopolistic industries, and free collective bargaining create a conducive environment for inflation. If we want to run the economy at near full employment, one or more of the elements of the equation must be altered.

5. Conservative economists and politicians reviewing the post-1965 experience have moved the criterion of full employment from 3 percent to at least 6.5 percent unemployment. They contend that the U.S. economy cannot operate in a period of expansion with fewer than 6 to 7 million unemployed persons without a new period of accelerating inflation. I have one response. Theories and rationalizations of the status quo should not be used as a guide for public policy.

6. Despite the fact that all of our presidents from Kennedy to Reagan have stated that ours is a market economy, it is important to emphasize that one of about every three jobs is in the government sector or is paid for by government or nonprofit funds. This suggests that the criterion of public action on the job front may not be as incompatible with a strong economy as many believe.

7. There are multiple causes of the present high level of unemployment and no public jobs program can hope to be responsive to all of them. We must distinguish among:

- Unemployment resulting from a tight money policy aimed at reducing inflationary pressures.
- Unemployment resulting from a cyclical decline in business.
- Unemployment reflecting structural (plant closing) adjustments in the economy.
- Unemployment reflecting a nonfit between workers' competences and skills and employers' requirements.

As noted later, I do not believe that public job creation is the intervention of choice for all of the types of unemployment, although it has a role to play with respect to each.

What We Have Learned about Public Job Creation

1. Although a few senators (Prouty, Javits) pushed for public job creation in the mid-1960s, they were unable to elicit broad support. The trade unions became interested in such an effort during the recession of 1970, but Nixon vetoed the manpower bill (December 1970) because it contained such a provision. Six months later he signed a $2.5 billion two-

year emergency employment act (EEA) mostly because of his concern with the large numbers of Vietnam veterans who needed jobs.

2. One of the objectives of the EEA was to move disadvantaged persons (particularly minorities) into regular civil service jobs at state and local levels. The funds were allocated with the proviso that after a specified time on EEA jobs, competent workers would get permanent jobs. In well-organized programs, this happened, and the public job creation effort had a beneficial *long-term* outcome.

3. In response to the severe recession of 1974–1975, Congress increased the number of PSE jobs under the new CETA legislation (Title VI) and made them available without an income test for workers who had been unemployed for more than seven days. But this confused this part of the program with Title II jobs, which were directed to the disadvantaged. In 1976, under the leadership of the Senate, Congress beat a retreat and put more severe criteria in place for persons to qualify for PSE jobs.

4. Unlike EEA, the PSE Titles II and VI paid little attention to training workers or to their transition into regular jobs.

5. In early 1977 Carter made an unusual decision to use an expanded PSE program as a mechanism to stimulate the economy. The target was raised from 350,000 to 750,000 PSE jobs within the year, and would be funded by an outlay of about $5.5 billion a year. As a second departure, many of the new job slots were to be provided through community-based organizations (CBOs). Both actions, the accelerated expansion and the new role for CBOs, made it more difficult for the federal government to set standards and evaluate performance. As a consequence, disillusionment with PSE set in both among the public and in Congress.

6. The National Commission for Employment Policy (NCEP) had serious questions about the use of PSE as a countercyclical device except for individuals who remained unemployed for more than twenty-six or thirty-nine weeks. Likewise, the commission had serious questions about public works (regular or soft) for job creation on the grounds of cost, timing, and the small numbers of unemployed who obtained jobs. It recognized, however, the importance of useful social output and believed that the public would be more supportive if it could see the utility of government outlays for direct job creation.

7. In 1976 Senator Bellmon was able to secure an amendment to the CETA legislation that required the NCEP to study the issue of whether federal funds were being substituted for state and local funds in job creation. The study was carried out by Professor Richard Nathan (Brookings Institution and Princeton University). Nathan concluded that some state and local funds were being replaced by federal funds somewhere in the range of 33 percent and less in the case of jobs created through CBOs. However, the lower substitution rate appeared to be

linked to work that the public considered to have less value.

8. During the late 1970s Congress also resorted to tax credits for job creation in general and later targeted on the disadvantaged. The record is equivocal. The U.S. Treasury was not in favor of an approach which resulted in billions of lost tax revenues. Many employers were loath to permit the IRS to look over their shoulders; the AFL–CIO was worried that employers would fire one group and hire another group of workers to obtain the tax advantages, and the credits were not large enough to encourage most employers to hire the severely disadvantaged. The NCEP never became enthusiastic about the concept of tax credits for public job creation.

9. In cooperation with other federal agencies, the U.S. Department of Labor made funds available to the Manpower Demonstration Research Corporation (MDRC) to carry out a major pilot demonstration using "supported work" to move seriously disadvantaged persons—mothers on welfare, ex-addicts, ex-offenders—into regular jobs. The results with the AFDC mothers were a resounding success and proved that a controlled work experience could serve as a bridge into regular jobs, at least for this group.

10. Although many unemployed persons are poor, many of the poor are not necessarily unemployed. While a PSE job provided work and income to the disadvantaged participant, it frequently made no contribution to his or her long-term employability because of the absence of both a training component and a mechanism for helping to move these persons into regular jobs. To make matters worse, Congress entitled about 16 million persons for assistance under CETA but never provided more than 750,000 jobs and a total of 2 million training slots, work experience slots, and jobs.

DIRECTIONS FOR A PUBLIC JOB PROGRAM

The following elements must be included in the design of a public job creation program that aims to be more than one additional device for getting money into the hands of the unemployed and low-income persons:

1. Even in good years, the United States labor market is unlikely to provide jobs for all who are able and willing to work. Accordingly, the U.S. public must either renounce its basic tenet that individuals should support themselves or must start putting in place a system of "assured jobs" that will enable certain groups of individuals (discussed later) to get public jobs when there are no private jobs available.

2. As President Franklin D. Roosevelt suggested, such public jobs

should pay more than welfare but less than regular jobs to keep the program from ballooning. At minimum wages and allowing for proper supervision, materials, and so on, the per annum cost of a public job with a built-in training component will approximate $13,000. That means that a program to create 1 million public jobs will cost about $13 billion *gross.* The net cost to the Treasury may be closer to $9 billion if we allow for the value of the output.

3. Arthur Okun (see *Jobs for Americans,* edited by Eli Ginzberg, Prentice Hall, 1976) reminded us that spending in either the public or the private sector will create jobs. With a $200 billion deficit the federal budget is clearly expansionary, far beyond anything any Democratic leader had previously advocated. One could argue that by reducing the DoD budget and spending more on direct job creation, the employment effect could be enhanced, but it is unclear whether Congress will consider such a shift. It is more likely simply to reduce DoD's budget in order to reduce the total federal deficit.

4. Since there are more than 10 million unemployed workers today, and since it will cost at least $9 billion to create 1 million public service jobs, it is essential that protagonists of a public job program decide what purposes it is to serve, who is to be served, and how. My preferences are to focus the program initially on:

- Cyclically unemployed workers who have been out of work for 39 or more weeks.
- Displaced workers in high-unemployment areas who are over fifty-five years of age, are unlikely to be reemployed locally, and need an opportunity to work until they reach age sixty-two and can qualify for Social Security benefits.
- Persons on welfare who need a work-training experience in order to get a regular job.
- Displaced homemakers who meet the income test and who, like persons on welfare, need a work training experience to get a regular job.
- Young people between the ages of sixteen and twenty-four who lack competences and skills and who require a work-training experience, without which they are likely to remain only marginally attached to the labor market throughout their entire adult lives.

5. A focused public job creation program such as the foregoing requires that

- State and local governments demonstrate a desire and a capacity to design useful public jobs.

- Employers and trade unions participate in the design and oversight of these programs.
- Remedial education and skill acquisition be built into the program.
- Monitoring be undertaken to assure the transition of persons off public jobs into regular employment.
- As federal, state, and local governments develop greater know-how and competence in designing and operating public job creation programs, additional groups of persons seeking work be entitled to apply. *The long-term goal should be that any person able and willing to work who cannot find a regular job should be eligible for a public job.*

CONCLUDING OBSERVATIONS

1. It is unconscionable that an affluent democracy such as ours continues to insist that people support themselves and their dependents and fails to provide jobs for those who need and want to work.
2. The administration acknowledges that there is little or no prospect of unemployment declining to tolerable levels for many years. It is essential that the American people understand the urgent necessity to put into place a public job program that can be expanded as we gain experience.
3. The first step is to secure public and congressional understanding of the urgent need to launch such an effort and to focus it on targeted groups of severely disadvantaged persons such as outlined earlier.
4. A self-respecting society cannot afford to ignore the horrendous personal and social as well as economic costs that result when many individuals are unable to participate in the economy because they cannot get jobs and support themselves. We do not know all there is to know about how to operate a successful public job program, but we know enough to start.

Afterword:
Gleanings and Challenges

IN THIS AFTERWORD I will set forth without elaboration or proof what I have learned about human resources during a half century of research, even though some of my formulations will not be acceptable to many of my peers. In the social sciences no proposition is inviolable, no matter how overwhelming the evidence, how careful the analysis, how temperate the evaluation. Having acknowledged the uncertain and fugitive nature of the "truth" in social research, I will leave all caveats behind and present my formulations about human resources.

• The family remains the primary developmental institution. One does not need to be a staunch adherent of Freudian psychology to recognize that the experiences young children undergo during their first five years of life are likely to have a determining influence on their intellectual and emotional development, including the establishment of basic patterns of behavior and response. Children who are understimulated at home are likely to have learning problems, and children who are deprived of love are likely to develop emotional disturbances that will later interfere with the efficient use of their energy. The existence of rare exceptions to this formulation does not detract from its validity.

• The second critical shaping institution in the human developmental sequence is the school. In advanced economies, twelve or more years of formal schooling are prerequisite for obtaining a regular job and a desirable career. The learning that takes place within the educational system is graded and dovetailed. The student must master the basics before mastering concepts and ideas. Only those who have completed a sixteen-year cycle, through college, are admitted to graduate or advanced professional study. If the educational system malfunctions, its student body will not acquire basic literacy and numeracy. Many among these failures will become adult misfits.

• No one can be forced to learn, at least not in a democratic society that has outlawed the use of corporal punishment and other compulsive devices such as ridicule, restrictions of freedom, and social disapproval. Whether children and young people attend to their studies depends, aside from the quality of their teachers, in large measure on the encouragement they receive at home, their self-images, community support, and peer pressures. Children from low-income families, particularly members of minority groups, often live in such oppressive family and community environments that they early decide not to try to learn in school since they believe the society is prejudiced against them and they will never have an opportunity to better their positions.

• Much learning takes place outside the formal school system, at the dinner table, in Sunday school and in church, on the street, at museums and theater, in camp, by travel, through reading, and even by watching television. These advantages, of course, are available primarily to children whose parents have disposable income. They will have the largest and most varied experiences. Although the son or daughter of an impoverished family who loves to read will have access to much of the world's treasures, a great many among the poor never learn to read for pleasure and for self-improvement.

• Employing institutions, large and small, in the private or public sector usually have a choice among applicants for jobs. In reaching a hiring decision, they place heavy weight on who has referred the applicant as well as on the applicant's educational credentials and other evidence of training and competence, including such highly subjective judgments as whether he or she will fit easily into the work environment. Again, the prospects a person encounters at the beginning or later in his or her job search and career development are broadly determined by earlier experiences. In this way the strengths and weaknesses of parents are passed on to their children.

• Important as are these family-based factors and their correlates, such as neighborhood, residence, social relations, and schooling, they do not operate alone in broadening or constricting the opportunity matrix.

In a modern advanced economy, the macroeconomic and political environments often play a determining role in creating and maintaining a condition of peace, war, or revolution; of high or low levels of employment; of liberal or niggardly support for the disadvantaged. Wars and revolutions almost always result in a substantial reshuffling of life chances; some persons at the top lose their lives and fortunes, and some at the bottom have the opportunity to advance rapidly and far. In less tumultuous times, the trend of the labor market and the economy can also expand or narrow opportunities for many individuals. Finally, note must also be taken of the generosity or niggardliness with which a society is able and/or willing to assist families who are experiencing difficulties in obtaining employment and income.

• Important as these macro forces are in the development and utilization of a nation's human resources, they do not dominate the day-to-day scene, which is largely under the control of the employing institution. The ways in which large, medium, or small enterprises are structured, and the ways in which they assign, supervise, control, and reward the members of their work forces, are the determining influences on how well people are able to use and expand their skills and potentials. Since the employer has goals and objectives that differ from those of the persons he or she employs, a constant tension exists between his or her aims and the aims of the work force. Those institutions that are most adept in reducing and reconciling these conflicting goals are likely to be most successful; but, no matter how well structured and managed these institutions are, significant conflicts cannot be eradicated—they can only be modified. A person who runs his own business knows he will be the sole beneficiary of his efforts. Those who work for others—the overwhelming majority of all workers, and especially those who work for large corporations, also represent a high proportion of all workers—are forced to follow rules and regulations that are highly dysfunctional when it comes to utilizing their own skills or adding to them.

• The perennial shortage of jobs even in a rapid growth economy—particularly of desirable jobs that pay well and lead to more attractive positions—helps to explain why different groups in positions of leverage over these more attractive opportunities have tried, with high orders of success, to restrict them to members of their own sex, race, ethnic group, or religion. Access to these jobs carries high returns, and the in-groups seek to restrict these opportunities to individuals for whom they have affinity. But this type of discriminatory labor market behavior is increasingly recognized in democratic countries as being in fundamental conflict with other doctrines that have been growing in strength—optimizing the nation's human resources for defense and economic objectives, and fulfilling the ideological commitment of equality of opportunity for all members of the polity. Although there is no easy or certain way for a democracy to reduce and remove long existing discriminatory barriers against various groups, in the United States particularly against women and racial minorities, since the onset of World War II, the past two generations have seen outstanding progress on both fronts. Nevertheless, many additional changes are required before discrimination in the labor market, and in the larger society, will have been effectively eliminated.

• Although Adam Smith warned about the immobility of labor, most of his followers have used a labor market model that assumes that people, like capital, will flow quickly to wherever the returns are higher. We have learned during these last several decades, however, that large and persistent differences in the population-to-employment ratio and the unemployment rate can persist between central cities, with their large concentrations of poor minorities, and the suburbs, with their much larger proportion of middle-class whites. Moreover, wide differences have continued to persist between areas undergoing rapid economic growth and those in decline. The issue this finding raises is whether a modern society should attempt to speed the processes of labor market adjustment and the probability that it will be able to intervene effectively if it decides to venture the attempt. There is no simple answer. What is clear is that if the society decides not to intervene, many vulnerable workers may be forced into a marginal relationship to the labor market for the whole of their working careers, since the market adjustment process may require a generation or two.

• Another major type of dislocation in the labor market can arise through the introduction of a radical new technology that can weaken and destroy the jobs, skills, and income of particular groups of workers. It is possible that the same new technology will create a large number of new and good jobs that will improve the prospects of many more workers than it has harmed. A responsible society, however, must face the question of whether it should seek to affect the balance of losses and gains among different groups of workers. Moreover, as in other instances, a determination to intervene is not enough: The question is whether the instruments at its control—retraining, early retirement, special income support, temporary tariff protection—can be used effectively to achieve a better outcome, or whether resort to them will lead to only a few positive outcomes.

• During the course of this century, but particularly since the New Deal, significant changes have been taking place in the age at which people leave their regular jobs and remove themselves entirely from the labor force. The trend toward early retirement has been pronounced, with the principal explanations embedded in the higher incomes available to older persons and a corresponding shift in their attitudes toward work and leisure. The weight of the evidence suggests that until now most people who retire early, as well as the predominant number of those who do so by the time they reach age sixty-five, are pleased with the decisions they have made. If the average life span continues to increase, however, so that most men who reach sixty-five will live into their early eighties and women into their later mid-eighties the current patterns of retirement at or before sixty-five would warrant reassessment. In fact, the recent amendments to the Social Security Act point in that direction.

The foregoing gleanings about human resources add up to the following: The development and utilization of the potentials and competences of a people depend on a range of interacting institutions, including the family unit; the educational system; employing organizations; economic and political trends; and the potentials for change stemming from advances in technology, real income, and mortality. The labor market is not a single market and certainly not an efficient one; it operates with many imperfections that can be moderated and removed only over long time spans. There is every reason to believe that the human-resources potential of a modern advanced economy is being more effectively developed and used than in any preexisting society. Nevertheless, the margins for further improvement are substantial and depend on how quickly and efficiently advanced societies deepen their understanding of the human-resources factor and act on the new knowledge they are able to accumulate. The following is a highly selected catena of the areas where new and improved knowledge about human resources is needed.

• The sizable gains in real income during this century have not added to family stability, even allowing for remarriage of divorced persons. The incontrovertible fact is that in the United States a disturbingly high proportion of children live for some time with only one parent before they reach their eighteenth year. Since one-parent families tend to have less income and suffer from other disabilities, the question must be raised to what extent changes in the labor market are linked to this dysfunctional trend and, further, what societal interventions might help to moderate and remove it.

• A closely related question is: With more and more instances of both parents working in families with children under eighteen, what is known about the preferences of parents for a different distribution of time on and off the job with corresponding changes in their combined earnings and career opportunities? We can identify a number of changes that are under way, from the equalization of opportunities of each spouse to pursue his or her career goals, to the manner in which they spell each other in alternating higher education and earning income, to a new sharing of responsibilities in the home including the care of children. But the crucial open questions are what changes should employers be encouraged to introduce and what parallel changes in public and community policies, from tax revision to provision of day care centers, might contribute to a better social well-being for parents, for their children, and for the larger society.

• The single largest disability that afflicts the children born and bred in poverty, other than those that stem directly from inadequate family income, is the ineffectiveness of the schools they attend. But there are a number of ghetto schools that perform effectively; there are teachers and counselors who are better attuned to the needs of these pupils; there are arrangements that link such schools to local employers; there are government training programs (such as the Job Corps) that have a demonstrated record of success. Our society is not helpless when it wants to respond. It could do a better job if it knew more about how to counter the erosion of spirit and energy that result from lowered self-esteem and alienation; how to gear classroom instruction more closely to the life experiences of children reared in poverty; how study and work can best be combined for adolescents so that each helps to reinforce the other. The most serious lack is not inadequate knowledge but inadequate political will and commitment toward the children of the poor.

• Despite the large-scale investment of resources in the theory and practice of management that has characterized the U.S. economy, especially since the end of World War II, relatively little attention has been paid to the interactions between the tendency to organizational growth and the development and utilization of the nation's human resources. Nevertheless, there is a slow but growing recognition that there are flaws on this front: Witness the large number of corporate spinoffs that have occurred in the early 1980s and the recent experiments that some large corporations have instituted to encourage entrepreneurial activities among their managers. But the interplay between structure and the performance of human resources in large organizations calls for more attention and study. Some knowledgeable persons believe that a large organization that uses half the competences and potential of its work force has a successful record. Most do not even approximate a 50 percent utilization.

Within the context of the present agenda of identifying major areas where new knowledge and new action are needed, the highest priority must go to the reform of the employing organization. The employer determines the environment and sets the conditions under which his or her employees must carry out their assignments. A dysfunctional environment and unfavorable conditions take their toll every day, five days a week, for forty-eight to fifty-two weeks a year. Better understanding of the conditions that might stimulate workers to make greater use of their energies and skills would yield substantial returns to all concerned—the employer, employees, and the economy.

• For a quarter of a century (1945–1970), the advanced economies believed they had found the answer to the worst scourge of modern industrialism—high unemployment. Since 1970, however, legislators have been so intimidated by the evils of inflation that they have retreated into a position of nonaction when it comes to the stimulation of employment. It is worse than cynical—it is downright dishonest when advanced democracies preach that the individual has primary responsibility for himself and his or her dependents, but do not provide adequate job opportunities for all who want and need to work. When the simplistic neo-Keynesian approach was found wanting, the advanced economies confronted a dilemma. They did not have in their armamentarium an effective set of public job creation policies, and they were unwilling to experiment with developing new and efficacious intervention devices. Without social experimentation, new and better solutions will not be forthcoming. Once again, political will and the accumulation of knowledge must advance together.

It would be easy to identify a number of additional frontiers where new knowledge about human resources would yield potentially high returns. But a sufficient number of major arenas involving the family, the educational system, the employer organizations, and the public sector have been delineated to warrant the conclusion that if we address the critical issues in each of these domains, add to our fund of knowledge, and use the knowledge to introduce new and improved policies, the level of human resources development and utilization will be significantly improved with corresponding gains in the well-being of individuals and our society.

Notes

FOREWORD

1. Eli Ginzberg, "The Decline of Antiquity," *The Social Studies 26*, no. 2 (February 1935).
2. Eli Ginzberg, "The Economics of British Neutrality During the American Civil War," *Agricultural History 10*, no. 4 (October 1936).

CHAPTER 8

1. Eli Ginzberg, "Toward a Theory of Occupational Choice: A Restatement," *Vocational Guidance Quarterly 20*, no. 3 (1972).
2. Eli Ginzberg, Comment in *Feedback* re Donald Super, *The Personnel and Guidance Journal 57* (1979).
3. Dale L. Hiestand, *Changing Careers after 35* (New York: Columbia University Press, 1971).
4. D. W. Morse and S. H. Gray, *Early Retirement: Boon or Bane?* (Montclair, N.J.: Allanheld, Osmun, 1980).

5. D. W. Morse, A. B. Dutka, and S. H. Gray, *Life after Early Retirement: The Experiences of Nonsupervisory Personnel* (Montclair, N.J.: Allanheld, Osmun, 1983).
6. R. P. O'Hara and D. V. Tiedeman, "Vocational Self-Concept in Adolescence," *Journal of Counseling Psychology 6* (1959); R. J. Tierney and A. Herman, "Self-Estimate Ability in Adolescence," *Journal of Counseling Psychology 20,* no. 4 (1973); G. I. Kelso, "The Relation of School Grade to Ages and Stages in Vocational Development," *Journal of Vocational Behavior 10* (1977); L. S. Gottfredson, "Circumscription and Compromise: A Developmental Theory of Occupational Aspirations," *Journal of Counseling Psychology Monograph 20,* no. 6 (1981).

CHAPTER 33

1. Gunter Friederichs, *Automation: Risko und Chance* (Frankfurt: Europaische Verlasanstalt, 1965).
2. Eli Ginzberg, "Technology and Jobs: What Lies Ahead," in *Walter Hesselbach: In Honor of His 70th Birthday* (Bonn: Friederich Ebert Stiftung, 1985).

CHAPTER 37

1. Ivar Berg, *Education and Jobs: The Great Training Robbery* (New York: Praeger, 1970).
2. Eli Ginzberg, "The Humanizing of Europe's Assembly Line," *World,* September 26, 1972.

Sources

SOME OF THE CHAPTERS in this book have been retitled or substantially edited since original publication. The following listing refers to the chapter number in this volume, the source number in the bibliography, and the chapter number in the original publication, and indicates change in title (tc) and/or content.

Chapter 1   86-2
Chapter 2   81-7-tc
Chapter 3   86-4-tc
Chapter 4   82-9-tc
Chapter 5   1-8
Chapter 6   38-2
Chapter 7   4-4-tc
Chapter 8   *The Theory and Practice of Career Development,* Duane Brown
             and Linda Brooks, eds. (San Francisco: Jossey-Bass, 1984).
Chapter 9   22-11
Chapter 10   30-16-tc
Chapter 11   2–Book 2
Chapter 12   5-7-tc
Chapter 13   12-5-tc

Chapter 14   13-11-tc

Chapter 15   16

Chapter 16   15-10-tc

Chapter 17   16-tc

Chapter 18   71

Chapter 19   *Women Returning to Work,* Alice M. Yohalem, ed. (Montclair, N.J.: Allanheld, Osmun & Co. Inc., 1980), Foreword, Chapter 1.

Chapter 20   Summary of Proceedings, Conference on Facilitating the Reentry of Women to the Labor Force, Paris, November 28–30, 1979.

Chapter 21   "Strategic Factors in the Adjustment of Older People," Fourth International Gerontological Congress, Merano, Italy, July 1957.

Chapter 22   *Policy Issues in Work and Retirement,* Herbert Parnes, ed. (Kalamazoo: Upjohn Institute, 1983), Chapter 2.

Chapter 23   *Work Decisions in the 1980s,* with Daniel Q. Mills, John D. Owen, Harold L. Sheppard, and Michael L. Wachter (Boston: Auburn House Publishing Company, 1982), Chapter 3, based on D. W. Morse and S. H. Gray, *Early Retirement: Boon or Bane?* (Montclair, N.J.: Allanheld Osmun, 1980).

Chapter 24   "The Social Security System," *Scientific American 246,* no. 1 (January 1982).

Chapter 25   "The Elderly: An International Policy Perspective," *Milbank Memorial Fund Quarterly/Health and Society 61,* no. 3 (Summer 1983).

Chapter 26   8-6-tc

Chapter 27   21-1

Chapter 28   26-5-tc

Chapter 29   71

Chapter 30   23-6-tc

Chapter 31   "The Service Sector of the U.S. Economy," Eli Ginzberg with George J. Vojta, *Scientific American 244,* no. 3 (March 1981).

Chapter 32   "The Mechanization of Work," *Scientific American 247,* no. 3 (September 1982).

Chapter 33   "Technology and Jobs: What Lies Ahead," in *Walter Hesselbach: In Honor of His 70th Birthday* (Bonn: Friederich Ebert Stiftung, 1985).

Chapter 34   *Making Organizations Humane and Productive,* "Work and Workers: Some Transatlantic Comparisons," H. Meltzer, ed. (New York: Wiley, 1981).

Chapter 35   38-11

Chapter 36   7-7

Bibliography

I. Human Resources

Books

1.   Eli Ginzberg. *Grass on the Slag Heaps: The Story of the Welsh Miners.* New York: Harper and Brothers Publishers, 1942.
2.   Eli Ginzberg, Ethel L. Ginsburg, Dorothy L. Lynn, L. Mildred Vickers, and Sol W. Ginsburg, M.D. *The Unemployed: I. Interpretation; II. Case Studies.* New York: Harper and Brothers Publishers, 1943.
3.   Eli Ginzberg, assisted by Joseph Carwell. *The Labor Leader: An Exploratory Study.* New York: Macmillan Company, 1948.
4.   Eli Ginzberg, Sol W. Ginsburg, M.D., Sidney Axelrad, and John L. Herma. *Occupational Choice: An Approach to a General Theory.* New York: Columbia University Press, 1951.
5.   Eli Ginzberg and Douglas W. Bray. *The Uneducated.* New York: Columbia University Press, 1953.
6.   Eli Ginzberg, Sol W. Ginsburg, M.D., and John L. Herma. *Psychiatry and Military Manpower Policy — A Reappraisal of the Experience of*

World War II. New York: Kings Crown Press, Columbia, 1953.

7. Eli Ginzberg, chairman. *What Makes An Executive? Report of a Round Table on Executive Potential and Performance.* New York: Columbia University Press, 1955.

8. Eli Ginzberg, with the assistance of James K. Anderson, Douglas W. Bray, and Robert W. Smuts. *The Negro Potential.* New York: Columbia University Press, 1956.

9. Eli Ginzberg and Ewing W. Reilley, assisted by Douglas W. Bray and John L. Herma. *Effecting Change in Large Organizations.* New York: Columbia University Press, 1957.

10. Eli Ginzberg. *Human Resources: The Wealth of a Nation.* New York: Simon and Schuster Publishers, 1958.

11. Eli Ginzberg, James K. Anderson, Sol W. Ginsburg, M.D., and John L. Herma. *The Ineffective Soldier: Lessons for Management and the Nation,* Vol. I. *The Lost Divisions.* New York: Columbia University Press, 1959.

12. Eli Ginzberg, John B. Miner, James K. Anderson, Sol W. Ginsburg, M.D., and John L. Herma. *The Ineffective Soldier: Lessons for Management and the Nation,* Vol. II. *Breakdown and Recovery.* New York: Columbia University Press, 1959.

13. Eli Ginzberg, James K. Anderson, Sol W. Ginsburg, M.D., John L. Herma, Douglas W. Bray, William Jordan, and Major Francis J. Ryan. *The Ineffective Soldier: Lessons for Management and the Nation,* Vol. III. *Patterns of Performance.* New York: Columbia University Press, 1959.

14. Eli Ginzberg, Dale L. Hiestand, and Beatrice G. Reubens. *The Pluralistic Economy.* New York: McGraw-Hill Book Company, 1965.

15. Eli Ginzberg, Ivar E. Berg, Carol A. Brown, John L. Herma, Alice M. Yohalem, and Sherry Gorelick. *Life Styles of Educated Women.* New York: Columbia University Press, 1966.

16. Eli Ginzberg and Alice Yohalem. *Educated American Women: Self-Portraits.* New York: Columbia University Press, 1966.

17. Eli Ginzberg, James K. Anderson, and John L. Herma. *The Optimistic Tradition and American Youth.* New York: Columbia University Press, 1962.

18. Eli Ginzberg and Hyman Berman. *The American Worker in the Twentieth Century: A History Through Autobiographies.* New York: Free Press, 1963.

19. Eli Ginzberg and Ivar E. Berg, with John L. Herma and James K. Anderson. *Democratic Values and the Rights of Management.* New York: Columbia University Press, 1963.

20. Eli Ginzberg and Alfred S. Eichner. *The Troublesome Presence: American Democracy and the Negro.* New York: Free Press, 1964.

21. Eli Ginzberg, ed. *The Negro Challenge to the Business Community.* New York: McGraw-Hill Book Company, 1964.

22. Eli Ginzberg and John L. Herma, with Ivar E. Berg, Carol A. Brown, Alice M. Yohalem, James K. Anderson, and Lois Lipper. *Talent and Performance.* New York: Columbia University Press, 1964.

23. Eli Ginzberg, ed. *Technology and Social Change.* New York: Columbia University Press, 1964.

24. Eli Ginzberg. *The Development of Human Resources.* New York: McGraw-Hill Book Company, 1966.

25. Eli Ginzberg and Herbert A. Smith. *Manpower Strategy for Developing Countries.* New York: Columbia University Press, 1967.

26. Eli Ginzberg, with Vincent Bryan, Grace T. Hamilton, John L. Herma, and Alice Yohalem. *The Middle-Class Negro in the White Man's World.* New York: Columbia University Press, 1967.

27. Eli Ginzberg and the Conservation of Human Resources Staff. *Manpower Strategy for the Metropolis.* New York: Columbia University Press, 1968.

28. Eli Ginzberg. *Manpower Agenda for America.* New York: McGraw-Hill Book Company, 1968.

29. Eli Ginzberg, ed. *Business Leadership and the Negro Crisis.* New York: McGraw-Hill Book Company, 1968.

30. Eli Ginzberg. *Career Guidance: Who Needs it, Who Provides It, Who Can Improve It.* New York: McGraw-Hill Book Company, 1971.

31. Eli Ginzberg. *Manpower for Development: Perspectives on Five Continents.* New York: Praeger Publishers, 1971.

32. Eli Ginzberg and the Conservation of Human Resources Staff. *New York Is Very Much Alive: A Manpower View.* New York: McGraw-Hill Book Company, 1973.

33. Eli Ginzberg and Alice Yohalem, eds. *Corporate Lib: Women's Challenge to Management.* Baltimore: Johns Hopkins Press, 1973.

34. Eli Ginzberg, ed. *The Future of the Metropolis: People, Jobs, Income.* Salt Lake City: Olympus Publishing Company, 1974.

35. Eli Ginzberg, Jerome Schnee, James W. Kuhn, and Boris Yavitz. *The Economic Impact of Large Public Programs: The NASA Story.* Salt Lake City: Olympus Publishing Company, 1976.

36. Eli Ginzberg. *The Manpower Connection: Education and Work.* Cambridge, Mass.: Harvard University Press, 1975.

37. Eli Ginzberg, ed. *Jobs for Americans.* Englewood Cliffs, N.J.: Prentice-Hall, 1976.

38. Eli Ginzberg. *The Human Economy.* New York: McGraw-Hill Book Company, 1976.

39. Eli Ginzberg. *Good Jobs, Bad Jobs, No Jobs.* Cambridge, Mass.: Harvard University Press, 1979.

40. Eli Ginzberg, ed. *Employing the Unemployed.* New York: Basic Books, 1980.
41. Eli Ginzberg. *The School/Work Nexus: Transition of Youth from School to Work.* Bloomington, Ind.: Phi Delta Kappa Educational Foundation, 1980.
42. Eli Ginzberg and George Vojta. Beyond Human Scale: The Large Corporation at Risk, Basic Books, 1985.

Monographs and Reports

43. *Work Load Studies for Personnel Strength Control* (Eli Ginzberg). Armed Service Forces, 1943.
44. *Reports: Manpower in Israel.* Eli Ginzberg, Department of State, Washington, D.C., and Government of Israel. Jerusalem, Israel, 1953, 1956, 1961, 1964, 1967, 1971.
45. *Manpower for Government: A Decade's Forecast.* Eli Ginzberg and James K. Anderson. Chicago: Public Personnel Association, 1958.
46. Eli Ginzberg, ed. *The Nation's Children,* Vol. I. *The Family and Social Change;* Vol. II. *Development and Education;* Vol. III. *Problems and Prospects.* New York: Columbia University Press, 1960.
47. Eli Ginzberg, ed., with Foreword by John W. Gardner. *Values and Ideals of American Youth.* New York: Columbia University Press, 1961.
48. *Manpower for Aviation: Final Report to the Aviation Human Resources Study Board.* Federal Aviation Agency. Eli Ginzberg, Dale L. Hiestand, and Samuel B. Richmond. New York: Conservation of Human Resources, Columbia University, 1964.
49. *The Social Order and Delinquency.* Eli Ginzberg, Ivar E. Berg, Marcia K. Freedman, and John L. Herma. The Report of the President's Commission on Crime in the District of Columbia, Appendix Volume, 1966.
50. *A Manpower Strategy for Ethiopia.* Eli Ginzberg and Herbert A. Smith, U.S. Agency for International Development. Addis Ababa, 1966.
51. *Manpower for Library Services.* Eli Ginzberg and Carol A. Brown. New York: Conservation of Human Resources, Columbia University, 1967.
52. *Perspectives and Policies on Employment Problems of Youth and Juvenile Delinquency.* Task Force on Individual Acts of Violence, National Commission on the Causes and Prevention of Violence, Washington, D.C. New York: Conservation of Human Resources, Columbia University, 1968.

53.   *Federal Manpower Programs, An Evaluation.* National Manpower
      Advisory Committee (Eli Ginzberg, chairman). U.S. Department
      of Labor, 1968.

54.   *People and Progress in East Asia.* Eli Ginzberg. New York: Columbia
      University, 1968.

55.   *Mobility in the Negro Community.* Eli Ginzberg and Dale L. Hiestand.
      U.S. Commission on Civil Rights, Clearing House Publication,
      no. 11, 1968.

56.   *One-Fifth of the World: Manpower Reports on Iran and South Asia.* Eli
      Ginzberg. New York: Conservation of Human Resources, Colum-
      bia University, 1969.

57.   *Manpower Research and Management in Large Organizations: A Report
      of the Task Force on Manpower Research.* Defense Science Board (Eli
      Ginzberg, chairman). U.S. Department of Defense, 1971.

58.   *Perspectives on Indian Manpower, Employment and Income.* Eli Ginz-
      berg, Ford Foundation, New Delhi, and Conservation of Human
      Resources, Columbia University, 1971.

59.   *Private and Public Manpower Policies to Stimulate Productivity.* Prepared
      for the U.S. National Commission on Productivity. Eli Ginzberg,
      with James W. Kuhn and Beatrice G. Reubens, 1971.

60.   *The Job Crisis for Black Youth.* The Twentieth Century Task Force
      on Employment Problems of Black Youth (Eli Ginzberg, chairman).
      New York: Praeger Publishers, 1971.

61.   "The Manpower Reach of Federal Policies." Eli Ginzberg, Chapter
      1, *Manpower Report of the President.* U.S. Department of Labor, 1972.

62.   *Manpower Policies and Programming: An Evaluation.* Eli Ginzberg. A
      working paper prepared for the National Manpower Advisory
      Committee, 1972.

63.   *Manpower Advice for Government: Letters of the National Manpower
      Advisory Committee.* U.S. Department of Labor, 1972.

64.   "New York's Future: A Manpower View." Eli Ginzberg with Charles
      Brecher. *City Almanac,* October 1972.

65.   *The Great Society: Lessons for the Future.* Eli Ginzberg and Robert
      M. Solow, eds. New York: Basic Books, 1974.

66.   *Federal Manpower Policy in Transition, Letters of the National Man-
      power Advisory Committee* (Eli Ginzberg, chairman). U.S. Depart-
      ment of Labor, 1974.

67.   *An Economic Development Agenda for New York City.* New York:
      Conservation of Human Resources, Columbia University, 1975.

68.   *The Corporate Headquarters Complex in New York City.* In coopera-
      tion with an Advisory Committee of Corporate Headquarters
      Executives and Professionals. New York: Conservation of Human
      Resources, Columbia University, 1977.

69.   *The Economic Impact of the Japanese Business Community in New York.* New York: Japan Society, Inc., 1978.
70.   National Commission for Manpower Policy, The First Five Years 1974–1979: A Report by Eli Ginzberg, chairman.
71.   *Tell Me about Your School.* Report #35. Washington, D.C.: National Commission for Employment Policy, 1979.
72.   Keynote Address, *Women in the Work Force: A Conference on the Economic and Social Impact of Working Women in the 1980s.* Sponsored by American Telephone and Telegraph and Ladies Home Journal, New York City, January 1980.

National Manpower Council Publications (Columbia University Press)

In the period 1952–1959, Eli Ginzberg served as director of research and as director of staff studies and contributed to the first seven publications of the Council.

73.   *Student Deferment and National Manpower Policy,* 1952.
74.   *A Policy for Scientific and Professional Manpower,* 1953.
75.   *Proceedings of a Conference on the Utilization of Scientific and Professional Manpower,* 1954.
76.   *A Policy for Skilled Manpower,* 1954.
77.   *Improving the Work Skills of the Nation,* 1955.
78.   *Womanpower,* 1957.
79.   *Work in the Lives of Married Women,* 1958.
       Education and Manpower, Henry David, ed., 1960.
       Government and Manpower, 1964.
       Public Policies and Manpower Resources, 1964.

II. OTHER BOOKS

General

80.   *Studies in the Economics of the Bible.* Philadelphia: Jewish Publication Society, 1932.
81.   *The House of Adam Smith.* New York: Columbia University Press, 1934.
82.   *The Illusion of Economic Stability.* New York: Harper and Brothers Publishers, 1939.

83. *Report to American Jews: On Overseas Relief, Palestine and Refugees in the U.S.* New York: Harper and Brothers Publishers, 1942.

84. *Agenda for American Jews.* New York: Kings Crown Press, Columbia University, 1950.

85. *Keeper of the Law: Louis Ginzberg.* Philadelphia: Jewish Publication Society, 1966.

86. *The House of Adam Smith Revisited.* Philadelphia: Temple University, School of Business Administration, 1977.

87. *American Jews: The Building of a Voluntary Community* (in Hebrew). Tel Aviv: Schocken, 1979.

Medical and Health

88. The Committee on the Function of Nursing. Eli Ginzberg, chairman. *A Program for the Nursing Profession.* New York: Macmillan Company, 1948.

89. Eli Ginzberg. *A Pattern for Hospital Care.* New York: Columbia University Press, 1949.

90. Eli Ginzberg and Peter Rogatz, M.D. *Planning for Better Hospital Care.* New York: Kings Crown Press, Columbia University, 1961.

91. Eli Ginzberg with Miriam Ostow. *Men, Money, and Medicine.* New York: Columbia University Press, 1969.

92. Eli Ginzberg and the Conservation of Human Resources Staff. *Urban Health Services: The Case of New York.* New York: Columbia University Press, 1971.

93. Eli Ginzberg and Alice Yohalem, eds. *The University Medical Center and the Metropolis.* New York: Josiah Macy, Jr. Foundation, 1974.

94. Eli Ginzberg. *The Limits of Health Reform.* New York: Basic Books, 1977.

95. Eli Ginzberg, ed. *Regionalization and Health Policy.* Washington, D.C.: U.S. Government Printing Office, 1977.

96. Eli Ginzberg. *Health Manpower and Health Policy.* Montclair, N.J.: Allanheld, Osmun, 1978.

97. Eli Ginzberg, Warren Balinsky and Miriam Ostow. *Home Health Care: Its Role in the Changing Health Services Market.* Totowa, N.J.: Allanheld Osmun, 1984.

98. Eli Ginzberg and Miriam Ostow, eds. *The Coming Physician Surplus: In Search of a Public Policy.* Totowa, N.J.: Allanheld Osmun, 1984.

Appendix: $ Equivalency Table

(Taking the November 1983 $ as the standard dollars earned in each of the following years should be multiplied by the equivalency factor to estimate the purchasing power in consumer goods for the year in question.)

Year	Equivalency Factor
1925	5.7
1930	6.0
1935	7.2
1940	7.1
1945	5.6
1950	4.2
1955	3.7
1960	3.4
1965	3.2
1970	2.6
1975	1.9
1980	1.2
1983 (November)	1.0

Index